Recent Research in Psychology

Gerhard Stemmler

Differential Psychophysiology: Persons in Situations

Springer-Verlag
Berlin Heidelberg New York London Paris
Tokyo Hong Kong Barcelona Budapest

Author
Gerhard Stemmler
Albert-Ludwigs-Universität, Psychologisches Institut
Belfortstr. 20, W-7800 Freiburg i. Brsg., FRG

ISBN 3-540-54800-9 Springer-Verlag Berlin Heidelberg New York
ISBN 0-387-54800-9 Springer-Verlag New York Berlin Heidelberg

Printed in Germany

Typesetting: Camera ready by author
Printing and binding: Druckhaus Beltz, Hemsbach/Bergstr.
26/3140-543210 – Printed on acid-free paper

To Judith and Nelly

Foreword

Those interested in the relationships between psychological and physiological functions will again and again be impressed by the fact that great individual differences and large situational variability are manifested in psychophysiological data. *Psychophysiology* from a *differential perspective* has been an enduring theme throughout the history of personality and temperament research. However, the present book is the first to bear the word *differential* in its title. Actually, this monography is not only concerned with psychophysiological personality research, but with a much broader program of systematic investigation.

Multivariate research methodology permits one to operationalize physiological response profiles, both with regard to lasting differences between persons and the discrimination of situations. In order to determine functional relationships between person characteristics and situational demands, that is, to determine the processes of stimulus-response mediation, one first needs to systemize these various sources of variance in assessment models and subsequently partition the observed covariance. A series of the author's own investigations in the Hamburg and Freiburg laboratories shows just how fruitful this research approach can be.

What is fundamentally new in the author's psychophysiological research is the combination of the multivariate approach with a pharmacological autonomic blockade strategy. This makes possible the generation of a model of cardiovascular activation components, which provides an alignment of empirical data and theoretically anticipated structures. The three main system components of vegetative regulation, which can be distinguished by partial dual blockades of autonomic receptors, allow both an advanced descriptive and an explanatory characterization of activation processes. This approach functions as a construct validation (a) for the interpretation of individual cardiovascular and other autonomic parameters and (b) - in a theoretical respect - for the more precise formulation and testing of hypotheses on psychophysiological concepts, for example, emotionality or anger reactions.

This book is a compelling and comprehensive research report presenting crucial results employing this new approach and providing a heuristic for future studies. The monograph also is an excellent textbook of psychophysiological methodology, dealing with various aspects of scientific theory and research logic. Dr. Stemmler has developed and formalized a differential psychophysiology which will likely be a standard for comparison in this area for many years.

Jochen Fahrenberg

Acknowledgements

Although the delivery of this book is in my sole responsibility, many persons joined me in the labor. Without their help the result would have looked different.

Experiments 1 to 3 were conducted at the Forschungsgruppe Klinische Psychophysiologie at the Psychiatric Clinic of the Hamburg University Hospital. I am indebted to Dr. B. Andresen, E. Irrgang, G. Sternkopf, and E. Thom for their assistance and support. Dr. W. Spehr was the medical coordinator and experimenter in Experiment 2, as was PD Dr. Dr. R. Dittmann in Experiment 3. I am indebted to both of these highly competent clinical researchers, and it was a great pleasure to collaborate with them.

Experiment 4 was conducted at the Forschungsgruppe Psychophysiologie at the Psychology Department of Freiburg University. I wish to thank I. Burgdorf, V. Höppner, W. Müller, and A. Sondhauss for their assistance and support. I am indebted to Prof. Dr. M. Myrtek for lively discussions about many topics of the present treatise. I owe special thanks to Dipl. Math. Friedrich Foerster, who adapted the biosignal analysis programs for the needs of Experiment 4 and who invested his inspiration and effort into the estimation of cardiovascular activation component parameters, especially the development of the multistage linear estimation algorithm described in Chapter 5.3.2. Dr. P. Grossman amicably shared his expertise in cardiovascular psychophysiology with me and influenced the final formulation of the Model of Cardiovascular Activation Components. I greatly appreciate the work of these two colleagues, as well as the efforts of my students M. Henschen, E. Meinhardt, H. Schäfer, and H. Schmid.

Much of what is written in this book bears the stamp of Prof. Dr. J. Fahrenberg's scientific influence, which has been of great importance in my academic life. Only through his continued support and encouragement could my thinking about psychophysiology and differential psychology cristallize in this book.

My wife Judith sustained me effectively not only in proof-reading the entire book, especially with regard to the English, but also in maintaining our curtailed family life so well.

Contents

Part A: Concepts, Models, and Methods

1 Psychophysiology

1.1 Definitions and Mind-Body Positions

To begin a book with a definition of the key terms of its title is a commendable practice in many scientific works. However, a definition of "psychophysiology" and of "person" as well as "situation", *as understood in this treatise,* amounts to articulating its thesis, which is not practicable in a one-sentence definition. Actually, this and the following chapters are devoted to attempts at clarifying what I understand under these terms. Evidently, they are embedded in a rich history of philosophical, meta-scientific, and psychological discourses, of which the mind-body enigma and the question of how we acquire knowledge (epistemology) remind us. Therefore, rather than beginning with definitions, in these introductory chapters of this book I will give an abbreviated and necessarily limited account of previous definitions, philosophical positions, and principal assessment procedures, which in sum provide an explication of the underlying assumptions of this treatise.

Essentially, psychophysiology is concerned with the relationship between constructs, processes, and events that are described in *psychological* terms, and constructs, processes, and events that are described in *physiological* terms. Stern (1964) emphasizes in his definition of "psychophysiology" that the independent variable is psychological and the dependent variable is physiological.

This emphasis on dependent and independent variables seems to offer a convenient way of operationally distinguishing psychophysiology from physiological psychology. Physiological psychology, according to Stern, deals with the manipulation of physiological variables and the ensuing observation of psychological effects. However, Stern's definition has been criticized:

- for not being consistent with current research issues in psychophysiology (Fahrenberg, 1988), because psychological data are often observed as a consequence of experimental manipulations that are primarily describable in physiological terms (e.g., experimental pharmacological interventions) and because the correlational approach to psychophysiological processes (e.g., the concomitant psychological and physiological changes of a phobic reaction over the course of a therapy) does not fit into the experimental cause-effect scheme;
- for being focused on what investigators in psychophysiology purportedly *do* instead of what they are *interested* in (Furedy, 1983). According to Furedy, psychophysiologists are interested in psychological processes of the organism as a whole: "Psychophysiology is the study of psychological processes in the intact organism as a whole by means of unobtrusively measured physiological processes" (p. 13). Investigations that try to elucidate the physiological mechanisms that underly psychophysiological measures would more properly belong to physiology or to physiological psychology and be secondary to the psychophysiologist's primarily psychological orientation. Furedy acknowledges the position of other psychophysiologists who, like the late Paul A. Obrist, maintain that it is more useful to focus on physiological mechanisms than on attempting to index behavioral processes through physiological measures. This issue will be further pursued in Chapter 1.3.

Schwartz (1978) presents a thoughtful discussion of three different approaches to a definition of psychophysiology, which - although offered in the context of clinical psychophysiology - is of general interest. The first approach to a definition, according to Schwartz, is centered on the methods and procedures used in psychophysiology. Besides simple enumerative efforts which would be overtly ambiguous for definitional purposes, a potentially more interesting aspect of methods and procedures already appeared in Furedy's definition, that is, the *unobtrusiveness* of measurements of physiological processes.

The reason why measurements should be unobtrusive is evident from the goal of psychophysiology, that is, elucidating psychological-physiological relationships: Inflicting apprehension or even pain through obtrusive measurements - especially through those that are invasive - would clearly alter the psychophysiological state of the organism and change the object under study. However, a moment's reflection reveals that the distinction between obtrusiveness and unobtrusiveness is more a matter of degree than of dichotomy. For example, placing electrodes on the surface of the skin to measure endogeneous potentials may also cause apprehension and therefore constitute an obtrusive measurement; in the same sense, a video camera that is directed toward the face of an experimental subject in order to permit a later rating of his or her affective facial expression can provoke evaluation anxiety and thus is an obtrusive measurement. Obtrusiveness is a matter of degree because nearly all measurements (for exceptions, see Webb, Campbell, Schwartz, & Sechrest, 1966) are reactive. In sum, neither an enumeration of methods and procedures nor some putative unobtrusiveness of measurements, although being a steady source of concerns for psychophysiologists, can lead to a definition of psychophysiology.

The second approach to a definition of psychophysiology Schwartz (1978) names tries to delineate psychophysiology through underlying mechanisms. The discipline that makes inferences about neural functioning through observable behavior or through physiological assessments is called neurology in the medical sciences and neuropsychology in the behavioral sciences. From a systems point of view, any one

> simple action occurring over time (such as the movement of the eye) [should be viewed] as *simultaneously* being a behavior, a physiological change, and a peripheral expression of a complex pattern of neurophysiological changes in the central nervous system. (Schwartz, 1978, p. 68; italics by the author.)

Compared to neurology, physiology, and to the behavioral sciences, psychophysiology, with its usage of psychological terms to describe antecedents, consequents, or correlates of the physiological components of behavior, should then be understood as interested solely in a different level of analysis of the same organism but not in a separate activity. According to this view, "psychological processes are an *emergent* property of patterns of neural functioning" (Schwartz, 1978, p. 71; italics added).

The third approach to a definition of psychophysiology is more an extension of the previous emphasis on mechanisms and system levels: It stresses that "physiology is an integral component of the desired biobehavioral outcome" (Schwartz, 1978, p. 74). This outcome-related notion of psychophysiology can be incorporated into an information processing approach to psychophysiology and behavior, in which physiological activity is seen as a means to invoke and sustain a particular behavior. This behavior will affect the environment such as to reduce the error detected by some internal comparator through the comparison of sensory input and the desired state of the organism (see Pavloski, 1989). More than any other does this approach point to the function of physiological activity and thereby it brings into focus the notion of the fit between specific physiological patterns and the particular situation responded to.

These two approaches to psychophysiology, one via a systems analytic view that focuses on mechanisms and the other via a functional view that adds to the mechanistic view the role of physiological processes in the situational context of behavior, constitute a description of broad research areas rather than preliminaries to a definition. The focus on mechanisms and structure of physiological and neural systems has been a prominent line of inquiry in psychophysiology, often pursued under the heading of "activation theory" (see Chapters 4, 5, and 9), as has been the focus on functions. The functional focus asks for the effects of varying situational antecedents of behavior on physiological processes, for the effects of physiological activation on behavioral outcomes as in operant autonomic conditioning, or for the self-regulation of behavior as in biofeedback research, to name just a few applied areas. Psychophysiological contributions to emotion theory (see Chapter 12) and to personality theory (see Chapter 11) can also be viewed from a functional perspective if the search for psychophysiological *correlates* of emotions and of personality is supplemented by the question concerning the functional role of physiological activation for behavioral regulation during particular emotions and of persons in their situational context.

The difference between the two research programs can be further characterized by a brief examination of the role of the concept of "situation" within these approaches. Mechanisms cannot be fully explored if the actual range of psychophysiological responses is not evoked, systematized, and understood in terms of molecular and molar systems at the same or at different levels of the organism's organization. The elicitation of a broad range of psychophysiological responses can be effected through an array of environmental stimuli, through pharmacological agents or through neural, for example, brain, stimulation. Within mechanism-oriented research it is not so much the subjective meaning attached to the stimulus by the subject, nor its judged relevance for behavioral control, that is of primary concern, but more so the capability of the stimulus to evoke distinct psychophysiological profiles. Functions, on the other hand, cannot be fully explored, if not subjective evaluations, goals, or plans (Miller, Galanter, & Pribram, 1961) are taken into account (I would not, however, ascribe solely to cognitive variables the steering function in behavior regulation but one that can vary in degree from complete absence, as in automatic and reflexive behavior, to dominant influence, as in volitional or problem-solving behavior). In the process of behavior regulation, it therefore becomes important for the organism to assess stimuli, their meaning, and change over time actively. According to the functional view, rather than being passively exposed to stimuli, man is involved in a transactional process where his or her behavior acts on the environment and the environment through the active process of perception acts back on behavior.

One important question that any attempt at a definition of "psychophysiology" faces concerns the mind-body problem. What is the relation of mind and body, of psyche and soma? Are they categorically distinct and completely independent (as an extremely dualistic position would assert) or are they in some sense one (as a radical monistic position would posit)? The extreme dualistic position raises the question how mind and body can influence one another. At least four more moderate dualistic and five monistic positions as solutions to this question have been proposed in the mind-body discussion (after Bunge & Ardila, 1987):

Psychophysical dualism. *Autonomism*, the most extreme dualistic position, asserts that mental and neural events are mutually unrelated. This doctrine would render research into the mind-body problem useless. *Parallelism* claims that every mental event is accompanied by a synchronous neural event. A somewhat weaker form of parallelism posits that not all, but perhaps most, brain states have mental "correlates". This view is a safe one to adopt, because it accounts for all possible data. Exactly for this reason, however, it is scientifically of dubious value because it cannot be (easily) refuted (Popper, 1963), if one acknowledges that there are no mental states without a living brain. *Epiphenomenalism* states that neural events cause mental ones, but that mental events do not in turn effect neural ones. This view implies two fundamentally different laws: Those of physics connecting the events in the physical world in a causal manner and those of psychophysiological correspondence. Because of the unidirectionality of the physical causing the mental, the latter could be just as well disregarded and solely the physical world studied. Why bother with elucidating the laws of correspondence? Hence, epiphenomenalism cannot conclusively object to an eliminative materialism. *Animism* gives the mental the primary role: Mental events cause neural or physical events, but there is no opposite direction of causation assumed. *Interactionism* asserts that the mental and the physical interact, that is, one can cause or can be caused by the other.

Psychophysical monism. *Idealism* (spiritualism, panpsychism, or phenomenalism) posits that all is mental. Neutral *monism* (double aspect view) views the mental and the physical as different manifestations of an unknowable neutral substance. Neurophysiological terms and the corresponding phenomenal terms differ widely in their sense (intension), and hence in the methodologies they imply, but they have identical referents (extension). *Eliminative materialism* is the monistic counterpart of idealism: Nothing is mental. This position would predict that with the advancement of science, psychological terms will gradually disappear from language, and their descriptive and explanatory function will be resumed by neuropsychological terms. *Reductive or physicalist materialism* says that mental events are just physico-chemical events occurring in the brain, whence physics and chemistry should suffice to account for them. *Emergentist materialism* (psychoneural monism) asserts that mental events are specific neural events that occur in special subsystems of the brain and that cannot be explained solely (i.e., reduced to) by physics or chemistry. The mental and the physical have their own concepts, hypotheses, and methods, and they should be studied therefore separately, both by psychology and neurology/physiology.

After this only sketchy enumeration of ten mind-body positions (for a detailed presentation see, e.g., Bieri, 1981; Bunge, 1980; Metzinger, 1985; Popper & Eccles, 1977) one may wonder whether philosophical discourse or logic alone can clarify the mind-body problem. The ongoing discussion, beginning in documented history with the ancient Greek and Chinese philosophers and continuing without loss of fervor into the present, suggests that the mind-body problem, understood as an ontological problem, is not likely to be answered in the near future. Instead it might prove more useful to consider the *function* or role of positions concerning the mind-body problem in the conduct of research (the pragmatic aspect) and in scientific research paradigms (in the Kuhnian sense; Kuhn, 1962; the paradigmatic aspect).

The pragmatic aspect refers primarily to the methodology of research. The methodological consequence of adopting the position of eliminative or reductive materialism is that the entire psychological domain can be dismissed with. Likewise, research under the doctrine of idealism need not be concerned with neural and physiological events. Epiphenomenalism regards psychological data as dependent variables and neural or physiological data as independent ones, whereas animism entails just the opposite view. The other mind-body positions acknowledge that, for the time being or in principle, the neural and physiological realm on the one hand and the psychological realm on the other hand have to be treated with their respective methodologies. Fahrenberg (1979) argues forcefully in favor of such a pragmatic position. He presents a mind-body view, *the model of complementarity* of categorial structures, which leaves the ontological question deliberately unanswered and tries to combine "the customary empirical-phenomenal dualism of ways of description (observation methods, aspects, attributes, languages) with the idea of the unity (correspondence, identity) of the underlying life processes" (p. 157; transl. by G.S.). This model of complementarity is similar to both neutral monism and emergentist materialism. The similarities pertain to the explicit statements of the necessity for an adequate description of psychophysical processes, of a combined neural-physiological-behavioral, and of a categorially different phenomenal-psychological frame of reference. But the complementarity view exceeds other positions in the precision and explicitness of the demands for an adequate psychophysiological methodology.

The actual conduct of research is often not the consequence of an explicitly formulated position with regard to the mind-body problem but rather of a passive adoption of a mind-body position and its allied methodology that characterizes the "paradigm" to which an investigator contributes with his or her "puzzle"-solving activity (Kuhn, 1962).[1] The functions of a particular mind-body position include:

- The stated mind-body position serves as a justification of the research program; this position cannot be tested and refuted, because it belongs to the core assumptions of the research paradigm;
- the stated mind-body position has a heuristic value in that it gives research a certain direction; this position is like a promise to the investigator who hopes it will come true;
- the stated mind-body position is an aid for correctly formulating empirical hypotheses; conversely, a research program might render a particular mind-body position improbable and contradictory with respect to available empirical facts.

---

[1] Porges, Ackles, and Truax (1983) give a systematic account of implicit mind-body assumptions in the context of general psychophysiological research questions.

This short discussion of possible functions of mind-body positions within research paradigms might leave the reader somewhat uneasy. Is the mind-body problem a metaphysical riddle, is a mind-body position nothing but a highly organized and internally consistent belief system? This seems to be a scientifically unsound point of departure. Or is the mind-body problem actually an empirical (neuropsychological, psychophysiological) rather than a philosophical problem, is a mind-body position nothing but a hypothesis reflecting the current empirical knowledge? This would define the mind-body problem largely as one of psychology and/or of the neurosciences. The role of philosophy would be reduced to a pathfinder for logical consistency, whereas psychology or the neurosciences would prescribe the language in which the mind-body positions and the empirical hypotheses be formulated (indeed, the philosophical language of almost all of the discourses on the mind-body problem is not suited to construct an empirical test).

Brain research (e.g., the effects of a commissurectomy or of electrical brain stimulation) and psychology (e.g., the effects of the hallucinogen LSD) have already furnished strong evidence against the autonomy of mental events and with it against autonomism, animism, and interactionism (see Metzinger, 1985). Psychophysiology could add many of its results, for example, on activation processes, interoception, or behavior therapy outcome, in order to demonstrate a substantial amount of independence between psychological and physiological descriptions. This clearly argues against any sort of eliminative materialism.

Two consequences of the foregoing discussion may be drawn. First, the mind-body problem is becoming more and more an empirical rather than a philosophical challenge. In the current protoexperimental stage (with regard to tests of the mind-body positions), psychophysiology can contribute to the mind-body problem by accumulating an empirical body of knowledge from which conditions of testability, candidate experimental procedures, or methodological specifications can be inferred. Second, if mind-body positions should be empirically validated or refuted, research cannot start with a position that ignores either the mental or the neural/physiological event, because positions that ignore one of the branches of the psychophysical domain could not be evaluated. Therefore Fahrenberg (1979) demands an "epistemically neutral" methodology which allows for the specificities of categorial structures and methods of the mental as well as the neural/physiological. This view is directed at increasing our knowledge of mind-body relations through empirical knowledge, that is, it has a positive heuristic function.

Psychology not only can contribute to elucidating the function of the mind-body problem for research, psychology could also address the question *why* the immediate experience of the mental and the physical as two separate kinds of events for most people is so evident. Schwartz (1978) explains the widely held belief in a dualistic mind-body position with his "brain self-regulation paradox".[2] The brain self-regulation paradox refers to the fact that the activity of the brain during perception or during the generation of action is not sensed by itself but in the periphery (even if the peripheral part of the body has been removed, as in the phantom limb phenomenon). We do not experience what systems are doing the controlling, but rather what peripheral endorgans are being controlled.

This placement of subjective sensory and motor experience at the periphery, according to Schwartz, might well have evolutionary significance, insofar as it helps to construct an experience of reality in three-dimensional space. Likewise, the experience of mental events, such as imagery, is also not felt somewhere in the brain, although it is actually created by the brain. Thus, although both physical (sensory and motor) and mental experiences are, according to Schwartz, emergent properties of neural patterning that cannot be directly experienced (this hypothesis is a monist view), the brain normally has the capacity to discriminate between sensory or motor experiences and solely mental ones (this discrimination is the alleged basis of the dualist view). In sum, the "classic mind/body dichotomy, according to this hypothesis, reflects a functional property of the nervous system that has adaptive, survival characteristics" (p. 70).

1.2 Place in Psychology

When psychology in the middle of the last century embarked as a science of its own, the influences from philosophy and physiology were clearly present in the academic and research careers of psychology's founders. Wilhelm Wundt has received the lion's share of the credit as a founder of modern psychology because he explicitly called himself a psychologist, formally established a new and independent domain of science, tried to integrate diverse streams into an organized discipline, and because many of the pioneers of experimental psychology joined him (Hearst, 1979). Wundt was an assistant at Helmholtz's new physiological institute, where, at the end of this period of his career, he published the *Fundamentals of Physiological Psychology* (completed in 1874). For Wundt, physiological psychology and experimental psychology were virtually synonymous because psychology as a science should employ those methods and approaches that a physiologist would use. The difference between the two fields was supposed to lie in their points of view: Physiology observed its subjects from the outside, psychology from the inside.

Although much of Wundt's research in his Leipzig laboratory involved reaction-time measures and standard psychophysical determinations,

---

[2] Interestingly, philosophers too appreciate if mind-body positions are more or less congruent with everyday intuitions (Metzinger, 1985).

introspection was the distinctively psychological technique by which conscious experience was to be analyzed into its elements. One of Wundt's most influential followers, Edward B. Tichtener, elaborated exclusively on the structure of the mind through the method of controlled introspection. According to Titchener, anything that did not appear in conscious experience was not really a part of psychology. Thus, he considered behavior to be part of biology rather than psychology. Psychology was to be a "pure" science, biology or physiology were judged to be irrelevant to a proper study of the structure of the mind. However, the "structuralist's" view of psychology was overtly narrow and it was almost completely dependent on the reliability of the reports of exceptionally well-trained introspectionists.

In the second decade of the twentieth century the difficulties of a use of introspective data as the sole source of information in psychology were becoming more and more apparent. Furthermore, the structuralists' approach to psychology was accused of only labelling but not explaining mental life. One movement in the psychology of the first quarter of this century, functionalism, stressed the functions and purposes of consciousness, the processes of learning, motivation, sensation, and perception for the adaptation of organisms to their environments. This focus on functions was in sharp contrast to structuralism. William James has been called a direct precursor of the functionalist view (Hearst, 1979) with his treatment of psychology as a biological science. James Angell, Harvey Carr, Stanley Hall, James McKeen Cattell, Edward Thorndike, and Robert Woodworth have been most frequently associated with functionalism. But even though this movement was prescribed to greater methodological objectivity, the willingness of its participants to employ introspective reports (of untrained subjects) and measures of behavior as sources of information in psychology was criticized for its continued adherence to mentalistic, subjective approaches and terms.

Of course, these criticisms were put forward by the founder of another very influential movement in the first quarter of this century, by John B. Watson. Behaviorism was Watson's answer that should render psychology into a "purely objective experimental branch of natural science" (Watson, 1913, p. 158). According to Watson, the introspectionist definitions (in terms of "nonmaterial stuff") of invisible mental faculties like images, emotion or will by both structuralists and functionalists was an obstacle for the scientific pursuit of psychology. Instead, psychology should redefine mental terms according to the principles of natural science, that is, with reference to peripheral, objectively defined actions, such as the production of words or the movements of skeletal and smooth muscles or secretions of glands. "Consciousness" was redefined as the objectively observable behavior of a person describing the internal and external world. "Emotion" ceased to be referred to as an affective quality and was defined instead as a visceral response. "Thinking" was not a mysterious process initiated and controlled in the brain, but consisted of specific covert behaviors - tiny movements of speech muscles which could be made visible only through a suitable recording equipment - in response to specific stimuli. Thus,

Watson posited (rather than investigated himself; see McGuigan, 1978, for an account of psychophysiologically studied covert behavior during cognitive processes) that covert behavior, which is only accessible by physiological assessments, follows the same laws governing more molar, overt forms of behavior.

According to the early behaviorists, behavioral responses should be predictable solely from knowledge of the stimulus conditions a person is exposed to. However, such a single-stage S-R model was soon doubted to be able to encompass all the phenomena that psychology should study and explain. One response to the dissatisfaction with Watson's behaviorism was to reject the behavioristic framework altogether, another response were "neobehavioristic" refinements that introduced multiple hypothetical constructs intervening between the stimulus and the response (e.g., the "fractional anticipatory goal response" of Hull, 1943, or the "mediating reaction" of Osgood, 1953), that is, multi-stage S-O-R (stimulus-organism-response) models.

The notion of covert responses and the metaphor of multi-stage models can be incorporated within current system-theoretical views of interdependent stages in a hierarchical organization of the organism. The system-theoretical point of view combines the study of single stages within the organization of the organism (e.g., the physiology of the heart) with the study of the relation between different stages (e.g., bulbar mechanisms regulating cardiac functions) with the aim of describing and understanding the whole system and predicting its behavior. This point of view is particularly interesting for the science of psychology if it is linked with the mind-body notion of an emergentist materialism (which posits that mental processes are brain processes, but that they have properties emergent from those of the brain): Psychological and physiological processes can then be studied with the understanding that both are levels or stages within an organismic system, where psychological states, events, and processes are brain states, events, and processes that are located at high levels of the organismic system, that is, they are capable of entraining and modifying the states of lower level stages by way of volition. The role of psychophysiology within psychology, according to a system-theoretical view of the organism and an emergentist materialistic position, is to shed light on the mechanisms governing the modification of lower level through high level stages and, conversely, of high level through lower level stages, and to study individual differences of these mechanisms, their modifiability, and their ontogenetic development.

This characterization of the place of psychophysiology within psychology could imply that psychophysiology is primarily a methods- and instruments-oriented discipline which accomplishes measurements on various organismic levels *in the service of* different substantive domains of psychology. Indeed, psychophysiological techniques (instruments, experimentation, methods) have been employed within many content areas of psychology, for example, clinical psychology (Lader, 1975a; Turpin, 1989), differential psychology (Gale & Eysenck, in press; Fahrenberg, 1967, 1977; Strelau & Eysenck, 1987), social psychology (Cacioppo & Petty, 1983; Wagner & Manstead, 1989), cognitive psychology (Jennings & Coles, in press; McGuigan, 1978), and health psychology (Dienstbier, 1989; Feuerstein, Labbe, & Kuczmierczyk, 1986). On the other hand, within a broader perspective psychophysiology could gradually develop into a truly integrative discipline which studies diverse psychological areas of interest, like emotion, attitudes, cognition, or personality, not in isolation but with reference to one another. Currently, psychophysiologists tend to apply psychophysiological methods to selected areas of application (this constitutes a "quasi-paradigmatic research program" after Herrmann, 1979) rather than establishing a psychophysiological theory which could be applied to different substantive areas of psychology (this constitutes a "psychological domain program" after Herrmann). However, many researchers applying psychophysiological techniques see themselves primarily as psychophysiologists, with their own scientific societies and journals. The growing awareness that the time has come for genuine psychophysiological theorizing is reflected in the open forum on "theories in psychophysiology" in the newly founded *Journal of Psychophysiology* (Levey & Martin, 1987, 1989).

Steps towards more comprehensive psychophysiological theorizing include both the bottom-up research strategy (i.e., the attempts to link lower levels in the system hierarchy to higher ones) and the top-down strategy (i.e., the attempt to find explanations of psychological concepts in terms of physiological ones). An example of the bottom-up research strategy is the multi-component analysis of psychophysiological reactivity (Fahrenberg, 1987a), one for the top-down approach is research on event-related brain potentials as markers for cognitive events (Coles, 1989; Johnson, 1986; Rösler, 1983).

A metatheory of "biopsychology" which includes, according to Birbaumer and Schmidt (1990), psychophysiology, physiological psychology, and neuropsychology, has been presented by Bunge (Bunge, 1980):

> Biopsychology is the scientific study of behavioral and mental processes as biological processes... The driving assumption of biopsychology is that the behavior of animals endowed with a nervous system is controlled by the latter, and that their mental or subjective life, if any, is a collection of neural processes. (Bunge & Ardila, 1987, p. 139.)

This is the emergentist identity hypothesis referred to repeatedly before. The major advantage of this position is that it permits an explanation of behavior and subjective experience in the manner of the natural sciences:

- By studying behavioral and mental phenomena one may make free use of some of the concepts and methods of biology, and one may go from description to explanation;
- the identity of mental processes with neurophysiological processes facilitates the construction of mathematical models, in particular the analysis of the state space of the organismic system, where every possible state of the system is represented as a point, and where a system change from one state to another entails a change in the location of that point (see Chapters 7 and 9);
- the degree of testability of psychological hypotheses and theories is enhanced.

1.3 Explanations in Psychology and Psychophysiology

A straightforward consequence of positions in the mind-body problem can be seen in the kinds of explanations proposed to account for human behavior. As with the question about mind-body relations, the nature of psychological explanations has also been a matter of considerable controversy among psychologists and among philosophers of science (e.g., Borger & Cioffi, 1970; Cummins, 1983; Fodor, 1968; T. Mischel, 1976; Nagel, 1961). At the core of this controversy is the issue whether human behavior should be explained alone with recourse to "causal" laws, thus following standard physicalist explanations, or alone with respect to "mental" suppositions such as purposes, volition (free will), and intentions as steering forces behind human actions, or with reference to both kinds of explanations.

This controversy is particularly relevant to psychophysiology as a field of inquiry directly at the interface of events, processes, and concepts that are described both in terms of psychology and physiology. The distinction between physicalist and psychological explanations has already surfaced behind the two approaches to a definition of psychophysiology, the mechanistic (what are the mechanisms by which behavior is initiated and maintained; i.e., a "how" question) and the functional definition (what is the goal and outcome of behavior; i.e., a "why" question). In this section, I will (1) give a necessarily brief historical account on the nature of psychological explanations (based primarily on T. Mischel, 1976) and consequences for research on psychological-physical relationships, and (2) introduce the notion of "levels of explanation" which is of particular relevance for psychophysiology.

1.3.1 Explaining the physical by the psychological: The right program for psychology?

The contributions of Descartes, Hobbes, Hume, and Kant demarcate historical positions in the discussion of psychological explanations of human behavior. These positions have left their marks in modern psychology. In the train of the scientific revolution of Galilean physics (which replaced the Aristotelean question about the causes of natural processes with the question about how things happen), theorists soon attempted to construct mechanical explanations for the behavior of living organisms. In particular, Descartes (1955/1641) held that all animal behavior could be explained by the operation of various bodily mechanisms. Some forms of human behavior, too, could be plausibly construed as reactions caused by physical stimuli which activate various bodily mechanisms. However, according to Descartes, physical mechanisms could not fully explain all of human behaviors, in particular not intelligent actions which are chosen by people for achieving goals or for following rules or norms. In posing the ontological question: *What sort of thing is man*?, and answering in the dualistic sense that man, in addition to a body, must also have a nonmaterial mind, Descartes offered a possibility for distinctly psychological explanations (dependent on the existence of a nonmaterial mind) apart from purely mechanical explanations.

Hobbes (1955/1641), on the other hand, concluded that man was to be conceived of solely as a material system. The explanation of behavior had to follow therefore the same form as mechanistic explanations in physics. Voluntary actions were, according to Hobbes, actually initiated by external stimuli which propagated internal motions and, in the end, movements toward or away from the stimulus object. From this perspective, psychological explanations of actions in terms of purpose or intention are nothing but prescientific myths and should be avoided because no psychological states or processes enter into the causal explanation of behavior.

The Cartesian conception of man endowed with consciousness to which he or she has privileged access continued to be the mainstream opinion during the eighteenth and nineteenth centuries. In particular, both "empiricists" (Hume, Locke) and "rationalists" (Leibniz, Wolff) held this view but differed from one another primarily with regard to whether mind is initially a "tabula rasa" or contains "innate ideas". The empiricists construed the workings of the mind to follow physical laws: Hume (1886/1739) and his successors saw psychological explanations as quasi-mechanical ones. That is, ideas became the analogue of material particles, and the principles of association the analogue of the principles of mechanics. It is important to note that this "association psychology", while adopting the Cartesian picture of the mind, eliminated all notions of agency or activity of the soul. Mental life was seen much from the point of view of a privileged but passive spectator; although supposed to exist and function according to mechanical laws, the mind failed to impose direction upon behavior. Mind ceased to have a role in explaining behavior. From this notion of a "passive" mind it was not far to the early behavioristic theory about the association of stimuli and responses.

According to Kant (1966/1781), there are two different points of view about human behavior which are simultaneously valid. One of these perspectives is that of theoretical sciences like physics: The explanation of actions as physical phenomena must be found in other material things in the brain and nervous system. The second perspective is that of the agent who has purpose, volition, and intention, and who tries to act accordingly. In particular, rational beings form conceptions about the meaning of situations and behaviors, and by way of such conceptions have the power to act. Thus, Kant's claim that human beings are agents is not a Cartesian claim about the role played by inner states as determiners of overt behavior, but is a claim about man's forming conceptions of things. The crucial point is that the same behavior may be explained psychologically or physically, not because these explanations refer to the operations of ontologically different substances, but because of the attempt to answer different sorts of questions. Thus, psychology does not differ from physics because it is concerned with minds rather than bodies, but because it is concerned with how man acquires conceptions of his or her engagement in the world, and with how these conceptions enter into behavior.

The next paragraphs describe the positions of some influential psychologists and philosophers (Wundt, Brentano, Watson, Tolman, and Skinner) with respect to the nature of psychological explanations. As mentioned in the previous chapter, Wundt sought to establish psychology as an experimental science, much in opposition to Kant's view that psychology could never attain the status of a science (like physics). Wundt, Titchener, and other introspectionists made the subject's point of view central to psychology, much in line with the Cartesian conception of the mind as a center of consciousness which is accessible only through introspection. Wundt did not, however, adopt Descartes' notion of mental substances independent of the body; instead, he conferred to the position of psychophysical parallelism, according to which physical processes always run parallel to the psychological processes of which we are conscious. The doctrine of psychophysical parallelism provided the rationale for an experimental approach to psychology, because the manipulation through experimental procedures of the physical state of the subject also controlled the occurrence of the parallel mental process. Psychological explanations referred to elements of the mental apparatus which were only privately accessible. The lack of objectivity in psychological explanations, as they were conceived by the structuralists, finally led to the dismissal of introspectionism: Psychological explanations in Wundt's sense could not free themselves from the air of being pseudo-explanations.

Brentano (1874) distinguished mental from physical phenomena by way of the relations that mental phenomena can enter: Mental acts are always directed towards some content, they are intended or meant by someone. The object of a mental act is "intentionally inexistent"; the object is that which is intended by the mental act, it is not describable in physical terms. Similarly, a bodily action can only be understood in relation to the agent's intentions - what he aimed at doing - , whereas bodily reactions are describable in physical terms. Brentano's criterion of "intentional inexistence" can serve to distinguish between mental and physical phenomena, however not with the purpose of differentiating two different entities (the Cartesian stance) but with the intent of providing different ways of describing phenomena (the Kantian stance). The difference between psychological and physical explanations thus amounts to the fact that whereas physical data are explained without reference to intentions on the part of the phenomena studied, psychological data are explained, according to Brentano and later adherents of intentionalistic psychology, with reference to the agent's interpretations of his or her actions. In conclusion, Wundt's hope of making psychology a science "parallel" to the natural sciences, was severely questioned by Brentano's analysis (and consequently denied by Kant).

In the present context concerning the nature of psychological explanations, behaviorism can be seen as an attempt to get rid of a psychology from the agent's point of view and the intentionalistic interpretation of data. With the introspectionist's failure to found a science of psychology that parallels the natural sciences, many psychologists came to the conclusion that "objectively" ascertainable behavior should be psychology's concern. Watson's characterization of behavior as whatever "movements" occur in response to stimuli (covert physiological responses or overtly visible body movements) blurred the distinction between psychological and physiological phenomena: As noted previously, it had been the hope to redefine psychological phenomena in physiological and behavioral terms enabling a natural sciences approach to psychology. But neither has such an ambitious program been actually carried out under Watsonian methodological behaviorism (although psychophysiological research in the last fifty years has repeatedly tested whether terms such as personality, emotion or cognition can be redefined in physiological terms - with varying success; see Chapters 11 and 12), nor has complex human behavior been investigated to any considerable extent.

Tolman, in contrast to Watson, acknowledged that physiologically and physically defined molecular behavior had to be supplemented with molar definitions of behavior (Tolman, 1932). Molar behavior involves the observable actions of someone in relation to gross objective features of the environment; this relation is constituted through purpose and cognition. Thus, purposes and cognitions can be defined, according to Tolman, by an outside observer who does not know the agent's private or intentionalistic view. On the basis of a neorealist epistemology (cf. Smith, 1986), with this concept of deriving mental phenomena from behavior, Tolman attempted to translate "mentalese" (common-sense mentalistic language) into an extensionalistic "physical thing" language. Such an approach may work within the confines of highly controlled experimental conditions, like Tolman's mazes, where the experimenter as the observer of a rat's behavior has certain expectancies through ample experience with the behaviors of many other animals under same and varied stimulus conditions. However, such an approach cannot take account of behavior outside highly restricted conditions because the ascription of purposes or intentions to someone's behavior depends essentially on knowledge of his or her beliefs which caused or motivated the actual purposes.

Through his operant conditioning paradigm, Skinner's radical behaviorism overcomes the obstacles the methodological and purposive behaviorism met in eliminating the agent's private point of view from psychological explanations. Operants are responses of the organism that are defined in terms of the effect they produce. The particular pattern of overt or covert movements is not of concern; evidently, the same effect (e.g., pressing a bar) can be achieved by way of quite different movement patterns. Consequently, operant conditioning deals with molar behavior acts, while the basic goal of behaviorism is maintained because operants are defined from an external point of view, irrespective of any privately held intentions on the part of the observed subject. Since operants are controlled by the consequences they produce, Skinner can treat individual purposes and intentions in the same way evolutionary theory treated phylogenetic purposes: An organismic feature developed not for the sake of future survival but as a result of consequences for survival which in the past followed certain biological changes. Similarly, intention is brought within the framework of natural science:

> Instead of saying that a man behaves because of the consequences which *are* to follow his behavior, we simply say that he behaves because of the consequences which *have* followed similar behavior in the past. (Skinner, 1953, p. 97; author's italics.)

Intention is thus an introspective observation of a condition produced by prior reinforcements. Intentions and other mental states cannot initiate or direct behavior, they are caused by other physical conditions. Because mentalistic concepts can be "translated" into behavioral contingencies, they can be bypassed in the scientific analysis of the causes of behavior: Inner states have the same cause as the behavior they are supposed to explain (Skinner, 1974, 1989). The "meaning" of situations and behaviors is a matter of causal history, rather than intentionality. Skinner maintains that the causal history of behavioral contingencies is not stored by the organism, however it changes its neurophysiological system. Whether or not these physiological changes will be discovered some day by physiological investigations, the behavioral psychologist can continue to fill the physiological gap between past environmental contingencies and present behavioral acts. Evidently, Skinner's program for a science of human behavior is a coherent attempt to provide psychological explanations without causal reference to mentalistic terms. However, its success in the application to complex human behavior is more a promissory note because a particular behavioral act could have been caused potentially by innumerable past contingencies, which are difficult if not impossible to reconstruct.

To sum up so far, the nature of psychological, in contrast to physical-materialistic, explanations has been and continues to be the subject of vehement controversies. The brief historical account presented above may have demonstrated that ontological and epistemological decisions on the part of philosophers and psychologists have had an extraordinary influence on the conception of explanations in psychology. All of the positions presented - from Cartesian ontological dualism over the associationist "physicalization" of the mental, Kant's two perspectives of describing the same behavioral act, Brentano's intentionalistic stance, the introspectionist attempt at an access to consciousness, and finally to the behavioristic refusal of mental faculties that exert their causal effects on behavior - all positions struggle with inadequacies that were already inherent in theoretical conceptions (e.g., the lack of intersubjective objectivity in introspectionism) and then became apparent during the course of research (e.g., methodological and purposive behaviorism).

What can be learned from the controversies about the nature of psychological explanations? First, the use of psychological terms referring to mental states and processes cannot easily be dispensed with. Whether given a causal or an epiphenomenal noncausal role in the explanation of behavior, psychological terms are an important component of psychological theorizing not least because they are the expressions that human beings actually use when (whether rightly or wrongly) explaining their behaviors.

Second, psychological research, as opposed to guesses about the true nature of a mental substance, should and actually does proceed by the interplay of the description of a specified area of phenomena and the construction of local theories within those areas. In order to avoid the dangers of reification, psychological terms might be most profitably construed as hypothetical constructs. From a biopsychological point of view, these constructs demarcate neurophysiological areas still insufficiently known. From a radical behavioristic point of view, they designate the incompletely known past behavioral contingencies. From a cognitive psychological point of view, they designate (mostly unconscious) processes and results of the selection, transformation, and use of information extracted from external and internal stimuli.

Third, if psychological terms are given the status of hypothetical constructs, it is necessary to ask how these constructs can be validated (see Chapter 1.4 on constructs and their validation). Briefly, construct validation approaches can take an inductive or a deductive route (Ozer, 1986) depending on whether or not a well-developed theory exists. The inductive program emphasizes the examination of the relations within and between sets of behavioral acts, physiological responses, and verbal reports of inner states. Constructs then serve as inductive summaries of the observed relationships (Cronbach & Meehl, 1955). The deductive program emphasizes instead the test of specific predictions derived from a theory: Does this particular behavioral act, this physiological response, and this verbal report have the meaning predicted by the theory? In the deductive program, constructs are theoretical statements that are not reducible to observational or empirical statements.

The differentiation between the inductive and the deductive research program within the construct validation approach illuminates an important aspect within the controversy about the nature of psychological explanations. The question of how behavior should be explained has, in the philosophical and psychological-metatheoretical proposals mentioned above, been answered in terms of ideal models of mental-physical relationships. The question of how behavior should be explained by psychological constructs therefore essentially asks for the deduction of hypotheses from a general law using the ideal model as a schema of the "real-world" phenomena the law supposedly deals with.

There are at least two problems with this approach. (1) These deductions necessarily run into insurmountable difficulties when they start from psychological predicates, because what is deducible (by the laws of logic) must have already been inherent in the predicate. This is obviously not the case with behavioral and physiological explananda. (2) Many of the stated ideal models are much too vague as to serve as general laws embracing psychological predicates as theoretical statements interconnected with other theoretical and empirical statements. This vagueness becomes apparent when one attempts to deduce specific behavioral or physiological predictions from psychological predicates.

Both the problems encountered in deduction and the vagueness of the imposed "laws" often exclude (with the possible exception of cases where Skinnerian theory applies) the possibility of an explanation of behavioral phenomena through psychological constructs following a deductive construct validation approach. However, the inductive research program poses the question differently to start with: Given behavioral, physiological, and verbal responses, what do these observable responses imply about a particular psychological construct? What are the laws that could subsume the former under the latter? Although inductive reasoning is no more than informed guesswork it offers a heuristically useful research program that is progressive since it builds upon "lower-level laws" in the behavioral domain (e.g., the laws of conditioning), the physiological domain (e.g., receptor physiology, physiology of the central and autonomic nervous system, etc.), the cognitive domain (e.g., memory processes, learning, language), and the social domain (e.g., social interaction, cultural specifics).

In sum, from the biopsychological perspective, which is adopted here as a metatheoretical position for psychophysiology, psychological descriptors of behavior and of inner states are viewed as emergent properties of brain processes that in the program of current research are profitably used as hypothetical constructs. These constructs should be subjected to a thorough inductive validation strategy which incorporates lower-level laws about component processes. In short, we should not seek to explain behavioral, physiological, or self-report data in psychological terms (which is the common-sense approach), but conversely disclose psychological phenomena and the brain processes which give rise to them, by deriving empirical generalizations and law-like structures from knowledge expressible in other than psychological terms.

A brief look at how explanations work may substantiate this claim. Standard accounts on the philosophy of science (e.g., Stegmüller, 1969) or of psychology in particular (e.g., Groeben & Westmeyer, 1975) distinguish between explanations of facts (empirical explanations) and of laws (theoretical explanations). Empirical explanations of a factual explanandum are derived from an explanans that consists of a law and an antecedent condition; theoretical explanations of a law are derived (often in the form of a reduction) solely with reference to another law. If the law stated in the explanans is deterministic, the explanation obtained is called "deductive-nomological". If the law is probabilistic, the explanation is "statistical"; in the case of an empirical explanation it is a "statistical analysis", and in the case of a theoretical one a "deductive-statistical" explanation.

Deductive-nomological explanations have been formalized by Hempel and Oppenheim (1948). Of relevance for the (above questioned) admissability of psychological explanations for physical phenomena is an inspection of the "conditions of adequacy" which must be met if deductive-nomological explanations should be valid. Among these conditions are that the law stated in the explanans has to be true (strong version) or at least well-approved (weak version). But instead of having true or well-approved deterministic laws about psychological-physical relationships to start with, we have ideal models or more or less well-informed guesses about those relationships, unless we use the potential of the inductive construct validation program in order to sharpen our guesses on a broad descriptive basis and to construct laws inductively. For example, the proposal to assess physiological activation processes in terms of temporally unfolding configurations, that is, by repeatedly measured profiles of physiological responses instead of single physiological variables, has been put forward after empirical research questioned the generality of single physiological variables for indexing activation processes (Fahrenberg, 1986, 1987, 1988). Likewise, the use of repeatedly registered physiological profiles is much needed for "inferring psychological significance from physiological signals", as is argued in a lucid exposition of problems in the mapping of the psychological on the physiological domain (Cacioppo & Tassinary, 1990a).

Consequently, deductive-nomological explanations of physical through psychological phenomena have their place in the course of a research program that has already accumulated a broad descriptive basis. However, given the uncertainty and indefiniteness of inductive reasoning (Chalmers, 1986), deductive-nomological explanations based on inductively attained at explanantia remain tentative and valid only within the hypothetical system within which the explanantia are thought to be valid.

In sum, the stance taken here is that psychological phenomena cannot causally explain physical phenomena on any a priori basis, but that in the course of a research program hypotheses about psychological-physical relationships are inductively formed and tested deductive-nomologically. As such, delineating an inductive-hypothetico-deductive research program is not very original (see Cattell, 1966a). However, in light of the almost unanimously quoted task that the science of psychology supposedly has (i.e., to explain behavior, physiological processes or verbal reports with reference to psychological phenomena) this research program should shed light especially upon the characterization of psychophysiology, if the implied notion of a causal influence from the psychological upon the physical domain were turned upside down, and the task of *psychology defined as illuminating the psychological through the physical domain.*

Even if psychological explanations are not Humean causal explanations and behavior therefore cannot be logically explained with reference to the agent's intentions, it is equally true that no a priori arguments can show that an empirical, as opposed to a logical, reduction might not be carried through. This leads to the question of how psychophysiology could help in closing the empirical gap.

1.3.2 Levels of explanation

It has been argued above that a system theory view may provide a conceptual framework for theory and research in psychophysiology. This framework's usefulness for psychophysiology becomes apparent when one considers important questions dealt with in physiology and psychophysiology, for example, what is the structure and function of the cardiovascular system; how do central and autonomic nervous systems interact; how do high-level systems like those brain functions that are involved in the initiation and organization of behavior provide the necessary coordination and integration for the unitary organism; what are the effects of stimuli, events, actions, thoughts, etc., on the different levels of the organism; how does an organism adapt to its environment. Questions such as these conceivably are directed to a system which is hierarchically composed of levels of subsystems. A system is a set of interacting units with relationships among them. Such relationships depend both on the structure of the system and the processes occurring within it. The structure of a system is the arrangement of its subsystems and components in space at a given moment of time; more specifically, the structure of a system is the "pattern of interrelationships belonging to a set, in a space of stated coordinates" (Foa & Turner, 1970, p. 204). Structure is not invariant over time. Processes within a system refer to all changes "over time of the matter-energy and information of the system" (Royce & Buss, 1976, p. 2).

The concept of system levels can accommodate the issue of emergent properties as those system properties which are both more than the sum of the characteristics of the units and not observable at lower levels. Of particular relevance for the task of psychophysiology is the system-theoretical tenet held by Royce's system theory account of individuality, that the closer a system level

> is to the apex of a within-system hierarchy, the greater its potential influence will be on that class of behavior and the greater its role will be as a personality integrator ... the closer a higher level system is to the apex of a hierarchy of systems, the greater its role will be as a system integrator of personality. (Powell & Royce, 1981, p. 821.)

A prominent task for psychophysiology is therefore the assessment of higher levels of physiological subsystems that are integrators of relevant within-system hierarchies and which support certain classes of behavior (see Chapters 4 and 9). Such higher-level activities might correspond much closer to a molar psychophysiological perspective than can be brought about by most of the lower-level physiological activities (often a recorded endorgan activity) which constitute rather a molecular psychophysiological perspective.

The notion of "levels" is sometimes used in a metaphorical sense when levels refer to different "universes of discourse" (Kline, 1961), where "such a universe consists of events describable within a single frame of reference, of the same order, and of such regularity of occurrence as to appear relatable to each other" (Kline, 1961, p. 1004). The universe of discourse is usually fixed by the questions we are asking, for example, a physiological, neurological, pharmacological, or psychological question, and it should be answered within that universe of discourse (Kline, 1961). What follows from this rule for our current discussion of psychophysiological explanations is that answers given within a certain universe of discourse cannot be employed as answers in another universe.

Although this seems to be another obvious rule because it would merely constitute an inference by analogy, it is easily forgotten and not adhered to. For example, if physiological assessments show bodily activation, this does not necessarily imply that the person "is activated", which would require also his or her feeling of activation. Conversely, the psychological meaning of "stress" may be only vaguely related to any physiological counterpart. Finally, this error of applying answers determined or proposed within one level or universe of discourse to another one (if the levels included in the argument are not reducible onto one another) is not restricted to the psychophysiological domain. For example, Broadbent (1985) commented in an article entitled "A question of levels: Comment on McClelland and Rumelhart" that the distributed model proposed by McClelland and Rumelhart is highly valid on the physiological but not on the computational level of discourse.

On the other hand, answers to "how" questions that are provided on different levels or universes of discourse may complement one another and produce a more coherent picture of what is being answered or explained (recall the principle of complementarity in Chapter 1.1 and Kant's view on physical and psychological explanations in Chapter 1.3.1). For example, personality theory attempts to explain human behavior by at least three different approaches that have been treated by their adherents as intrinsically incompatible: (1) in terms of a set of personality traits that a person possesses (dispositional approach), (2) with reference to the specific meanings and experiences of a person (cognitive, phenomenological, and psychodynamic approaches), and (3) in evolutionary terms as biological dispositions that exist because they functioned to enhance the person's reproductive success (biological and evolutionary approach). However, as Wakefield argues,

> much of this conflict over explanatory approaches is misplaced, because a complete personological account of any behavior must involve attention to all of the aforementioned explanatory approaches, woven into one integrated and multilayered explanation. Thus, the ideological tensions between the different approaches represent a failure by the field to achieve a metalevel understanding of the mutual dependence of the approaches in the overall personological enterprise. (Wakefield, 1989, p. 333-334.)

1.4 Constructs

It has been claimed in the previous section that psychological phenomena should not be reified, for example, by taking a verbal descriptor of mental events or processes for the phenomenon itself, but to treat them as hypothetical constructs. Of course the same reasoning applies to physiological events and processes that cannot be assessed directly, for example, central or autonomous nervous system activity, not to mention specific brain processes giving rise - according to the biopsychological perspective - to mental processes.

As theoretical statements, hypothetical constructs are the building blocks of theories. They have, however, no clear boundaries of meaning, or stated differently, the set of observable referents (i.e., empirical statements) is open and not completely specifiable (in distinction to intervening variables which are simply unknown bridges between specific empirical statements; MacCorquodale & Meehl, 1948). What is the formal relationship between theoretical and empirical statements?

Logical positivism held that a theory is characterized as a linguistic structure having a kind of hierarchical nature (for a detailed statement and evaluation of this positivistic view, cf. Suppe, 1977). At the top of the structure is a purely formal set of axioms. The axioms themselves are taken to be an "uninterpreted system" that provides implicit definitions of the high-level theoretical concepts. Just below the axioms are the various theorems that are derivable from the axioms by logical reasoning alone. At the base lie the statements expressing pure observations. From these, the empirical concepts and low-level laws of science are constructed by means of empirical definitions. With the appropriate selection of correspondence rules, the empirical and the theoretical levels can be joined together. The whole system gains empirical meaning from the data base upwards to the theoretical statements. In this scheme, a considerable burden is placed on the correspondence rules since they provide the link between purely theoretical and purely empirical components of the structure.

The fundamental principles of logical positivism that all theoretical statements are analytic, verifiable by observations, or meaningless, helped to ban any metaphysical stance from science, but they were not tenable (Popper, 1959). Under the heading of "theory-laden constructivism", Royce (1976; p. 5) subsumed different strains of the current philosophical Zeitgeist. His major claims form a clear contrast to logical positivism:

- "... all observations are theory-laden; that is, an observation is made within an overall conceptual framework". Although this assertion originally referred to the constructive aspects of sensory and perceptual processes and hence to the properties of the constructing nervous system, in contrast to the "real thing out there", this assertion can be extended to transforms of observations. For example, if we want to register the response of the heart rate to some stimulus, we would proceed to observe the heart rate both before and after the stimulus and enter, as our "primary observation data", perhaps their difference into our ensuing calculations; or, we might form the percentage increase or decrease. Although decisions (or habits) such as these will often be arrived at without suspecting theory to intervene it can be shown (see Chapter 4.3) that theoretical assumptions are actually involved.
- "... the basic concepts of a theory are constructed by the investigator". This entails that the choice of particular hypothetical constructs is guided by the investigator's interests. It also entails that there is much room in choosing how the constructs are arrived at: (a) strictly deductively from a set of axioms, (b) inductively from a body of empirical knowledge, or (c) purely speculatively.

The first kind of theory construction yields truly explanatory theories (probably not present in psychology), the second kind of theory construction yields descriptive theories with an average level of theoretical power within a circumscribed domain, whereas the third kind of theory construction remains empty speculation without a solid empirical foundation. Such weak theorizing may evolve into more explicit theories if empirically based hypothetical constructs can be identified, if highly reliable empirical laws can be generated, if viable taxonomies can be developed, and if empirical generalizations can be achieved.

The remaining of Royce's claims will be only briefly noted as they do not add much to what has already been said:

- "... scientific findings are, in some sense, man-made inventions or constructions";
- "We choose between competing theories primarily on theoretical grounds, only secondarily on empirical grounds ...";
- "The role of observation is not that of arbiter between competing theories ..."; and
- "The primary role of empirical observation is to provide the empirical correlator of one or other theory-laden construct; that is, observation provides the substantive content of the conceptual abstractions of the theoretician."

The difference between the logical positivist and the constructivist views on constructs as well as their implications for psychological measurement has been further elucidated by Messick (1981). He presents three epistemological perspectives:

- The realist view states that behavior is a manifestation of real "traits". For example, in his theory of personality Cattell (1957) proposes that source traits literally cause the configuration of surface consistencies of behavior (which are modulated also by situational influences). Thus, behaviors are signs of personality structure. In the realist position of Skinner (1974), behaviors are elicited and maintained by environmental conditions, especially reinforcement conditions. Related behaviors form a response class because they enter the same functional relationships with antecedent, concurrent, and consequent stimulus conditions. Thus, behaviors are samples of response classes. The assessment model underlying the realist view of constructs, then, is especially compatible to an operationist approach to measurement, in which "the concept is synonymous with the corresponding set of operations" (Bridgman, 1927, p. 5; see also Bechthold, 1959; Bunge & Ardila, 1987, p. 125-130). Although logical positivists quickly recognized Bridgman's operationism as a view closely allied to their own,[3] operationism concerned itself with the empirical

[3] In fact, Herbert Feigl, who was a student of Moritz Schlick, the founder of the Vienna circle, and who was an influential philosopher of science during and after the heydays of logical positivism, also studied with Bridgman.

sense of concepts rather than with the logical positivistic attempt at constructing theoretical relations between concepts understood as theoretical statements.

- The constructivist view of constructs (a) as inductive summaries of observations that (b) have surplus meaning beyond the observations actually at hand, because (c) they are embedded in a nomological network of theoretical statements, does not give constructs a reality status outside the theoretical system. The main emphasis of this logical positivistic view (also shared by Cronbach & Meehl, 1955, see the post-positivistic critical review thirty years later by Cronbach, 1986, 1988) was the development of strong theory and valid predictions of previously unobserved empirical relationships from the theoretical implications of the nomological network.
- The constructive-realist (or critical realist) view assumes that the entities labelled "constructs" have an existence outside the mind. However, these entities cannot be perceived directly but must be viewed through constructions of the mind. By attributing reality to causal entities while requiring a logical construction of observed relationships, this view provides an heuristic perspective to the biopsychological perspective: First, the differentiation between observations, constructs, and underlying causal entities reflects the actual biopsychological distinction between the registered (behavioral, physiological, and verbal) responses, the inductive summaries of these observations in terms of constructs, such as "activation", "arousal", "stress", or "emotion", and the brain processes giving rise to the phenomena observed. Second, the differentiation between observation, construct, and the actual causal entity has methodological consequences for the identification of sources of error in building and validating constructs. Not only could the allocation of observable variables to constructs be erroneous (through a specification error, i.e., a variable does not belong to the construct assumed or through the error of surplus meaning, i.e., a variable belongs to more than one construct but is interpreted to refer to just one; cf. Cattell, 1966c) but also the alleged unity of concepts (e.g., of the stress concept, Mason et al., 1976; or of the activation concept, Lacey, 1967) or their alleged disparateness (e.g., the anxiety concept and the repression - sensitization concept) with regard to the causal entity. Whereas the study of the relationships between variables and constructs and the possible errors of allocation has been the (psychometric) domain of convergent and discriminant construct validation strategies (Campbell & Fiske, 1959), the relationship between causal entities and variables or constructs has, within the biopsychological approach, been advanced through centrally acting pharmacological agents (e.g., Gray, 1982, regarding anxiety) and neurophysiological methods (such as brain stimulation or ablation; e.g., LeDoux, 1987, with reference to emotion).

To sum up thus far, a "theory-laden constructivism" (sensu Royce) coupled with a "critical realist" epistemological position (sensu Messick) provides a frame of reference for the notion of hypothetical constructs that is particularly useful for the research program of psychophysiology. This program should follow an inductive-hypothetico-deductive line of inquiry comprising the construction of constructs (the inductive route), their validation both via psychometric and neurophysiological approaches, and the development of coherent local theories with the deduction of new empirical predictions.

The meaning and validity of constructs need further characterization. To start with, the meaning of a construct is not the same as its validity. Whereas the latter refers to the empirical demonstration of the hypothesized relationships between observable variables, the former depends solely on the variables actually observed. For example, the concomitant increase in heart rate and skin conductance levels during a white noise stimulation has been predicted because of two hypotheses: first, noise increases the level of the construct of activation, and second, heart rate and skin conductance are indicators of activation. If the prediction actually holds, then the construct of activation has been validated in this instance. The meaning of activation derives from the two variables measured; the meaning would differ, however, had the electroencephalogram been registered.

As words, so do constructs also have two different types of meaning. One is its sense contained in the network of cognitive structures representing the symbolic dimensions of the word; it is its intensional meaning (Frege, 1892). The other type of meaning comprises the events in the world to which the word refers; it is, according to Frege, its extensional meaning. For the logical positivists, constructs were meaningless unless they had referents in the real world. But even if a referential meaning is lacking, the sense meaning of the construct will always remain. However, empirical science strives for an evaluation of the truth value of propositions. Such an evaluation can be achieved only with regard to some empirical event; or, expressed in terms of meaning, the truth value of a proposition in empirical science applies to the referential meaning.

This distinction between types of meaning at first glance does not seem to be more than a plea for empirical tests of hypotheses, but there is more to it: Constructs can assume different (extensional) meanings and truth values as a function of the sources of empirical information (Kagan, 1988). Sources of empirical information not only include the particular variables measured (also not without a certain measurement theory) but also the environmental context in which the measurement was obtained. Thus, with a change in any or all of these sources of empirical information, there is a chance that the construct has changed, too, because the referential meaning is no longer the same. Examples are the discrepancies between interpretations based upon self-reports or physiological data with respect to emotions (see Chapter 12), or the low generalizability of individual differences in physiological response from the laboratory to the field experiment (Fahrenberg et al., 1986). If the empirical findings do not allow other conclusions, the assumption of the generality of constructs across very different assessment contexts will be questionable (Bridgman, 1945).

Two consequences might be drawn in this situation: (1) Larger constructs could be subdivided into separate smaller ones (Fiske, 1983), each corresponding to another kind of referent or method to obtain data; (2) the theory is enriched by specifications under which assessment contexts to expect different kinds of relationships among the referents (Hogan & Nicholson, 1988; the changes in the biological personality theory of Eysenck are an outstanding example for this approach, see Chapter 11). However, upon closer inspection both kinds of consequences amount to quite similar solutions, because the former approach calls for a specification of the theoretical relationships among the smaller constructs which finally amounts to the same kind of elaborations produced by the latter approach. In sum, inconsistencies between theory-derived and actually obtained empirical relationships are a signal to reconsider the theory, if misconceptions and misuses of the assessment theory and the assessment context are to be reasonably excluded.

In conclusion, constructs and the attempts at validating them are central to the scientific endeavor of psychology and, equally so, of psychophysiology. Constructs are the inductive summaries of the empirical knowledge and at the same time the building blocks of theories. They are necessarily open concepts, open with respect to their referents or indicators, other related constructs, and the underlying real entity, if such can be reasonably stipulated. Thus, the investigation and elaboration of the nomological network in which a construct is embedded is carried out and advanced by the process of construct validation.

1.5 Assessment Models

Assessment is related to "theoretical" and "empirical" issues: It is related, on the one hand, to a substantive theory, particular constructs highlighted by the research question, and a theory of the measurement device and, on the other hand, to the conditions under which the assessment is done, the psychometric properties of the measurement device, and the treatment of the data obtained. In this final section of the first chapter, the conceptually oriented stance pursued in the preceding sections will be continued in order to complete the characterization of psychophysiology from a metatheoretical point of view. The empirical and, to a lesser extent, the theoretical issues have been broadly dealt with in the psychophysiological literature; therefore it may suffice to refer the reader to a selection of references that cover issues ranging from measurement techniques, data treatment, the social setting, to questions of interpretation (Averill & Opton, 1968; Cacioppo, Petty, & Marshall-Goodell, 1985; Cacioppo & Tassinary, 1990b; Carver & Matthews, 1989; Coles, Donchin, & Porges, 1986; Fahrenberg, 1983; Gale & Baker, 1981; Gale & Edwards, 1983; Greenfield & Sternbach, 1972; Haynes, 1978; Kallman & Feuerstein, 1977; Krantz & Ratliff-Crain, 1989; Martin, 1973a, 1973b; Martin & Venables, 1980; Ney & Gale,

1988; Ray & Kimmel, 1979; Ray, Cole, & Raczynski, 1983; Schandry, 1989; Stemmler & Fahrenberg, 1989; Stern, Ray, & Davis, 1980; Strube, 1989; Williamson, Waters, & Hawkins, 1986).

It has already been emphasized that the tentative construction of constructs (guided by theoretical ideas and inductive summaries of empirical relationships) and their validation are central endeavors of psychology as an empirical science. Assessment is intricately related to theory both in the construction and validation stages of constructs. In the following, for both of these stages the relationship between assessment strategies and different theoretical conceptions of a construct are described.

1.5.1 Assessment in the construction stage of constructs

The construction stage begins with a guess about the nature of the construct. Even if this is a still relatively vague idea, it nevertheless incorporates three theoretical statements: (1) about the "locus" of the construct, stating "where" the construct is to be found, (2) about the "homogeneity constraints" within the input-construct-output system, that is, homogeneity of members within either the input variables (situations, stimuli or conditions), the "possessors" of the construct (subjects), or the output variables (response variables, indicators), and (3) about the "unit of assessment", that is, the part of the input-construct -output system that is being assessed. Similar to Cattell's covariation chart (Cattell, 1946), the three constituent parts of the system can be assigned to each of the three theoretical statements, yielding six (plus three, see below) assessment models (see Table 1). The meanings of the three terms, "locus" of the construct, "homogeneity constraints", and "unit of assessment" will become clearer in the following description of the assessment models.

Assessment Model 1. Here it is assumed that the construct can be identified through variations in the salience of the construct that exists (in various degrees) in different individuals. For example, traditional trait psychology sought to identify personality traits through presumed individual differences in that trait. In psychophysiology, Wenger (1966) defined the construct of "autonomic balance" across individuals. Thus, the "locus" of the construct expresses an investigator's assumption (based on prior evidence, convention, or guesswork) of where to find differently large instantiations of the construct. In the first assessment model, then, differently large instantiations of the construct are assumed to occur among different subjects. The investigator will therefore sample his or her observations from a specified population of subjects. Between-subjects variance of a particular variable is therefore an estimate of the variation in the salience of the construct within the population (if a random sample was

Table 1. Assessment Models for the Construction Stage of Constructs

Assessment Model	Locus of Construct	Homogeneity Constraints	Unit of Assessment	Technique[a]	Variance Analyzed
1	Subjects	Variables	Condition	R	BS
2	Conditions	Variables	Subject	P	BC
3	Conditions	Subjects	Variable	S	BC
4	Variables	Subjects	Condition	Q	BV
5	Variables	Conditions	Subject	O	BV
6	Subjects	Conditions	Variable	T	BS
7	Subjects x Conditions	Variables	SxC		
8	Conditions x Variables	Subjects	CxV		
9	Variables x Subjects	Conditions	VxS		

Note. BS = Between-subjects. BC = Between-conditions. BV = Between-variables. SxC = Subjects x Conditions interaction. CxV = Conditions x Variables interaction. VxS = Variables x Subjects interaction.
[a]Techniques of analysis identified in Cattell's covariation chart.

drawn), as reflected in that variable.[4] It should be evident by now that "locus" of the construct is not meant in the sense of a physical place.

In this first assessment model, the "homogeneity constraints" refer to the variables observed. One of the primary aims of the concept construction stage is to identify variables that can serve as indicators of the constructs under study. The probability that a specified construct gives rise to the observed between-subjects variance and covariance increases with the number of variables. With just a few or only one variable, errors of misallocation to the construct in question can easily occur because variables are often influenced by more than just one construct, but also by unsystematic (error) or irrelevant sources of variance. In the first assessment model, an irrelevant source of variance is the one arising from subject x condition interactions (which can be present in each one condition although not demonstrable within just one). It is therefore desirable to observe for each construct several putative indicators; if found to be homogeneous, they may belong to the population of indicators for that construct. Whether or not it is the construct in question cannot be decided on purely empirical grounds; one needs a priori knowledge to judge.

The unit of assessment is, in this assessment model, the condition in which the observations are obtained. It is called the "unit" of assessment because all conclusions drawn from that stage of analysis apply only to that unit; without further theoretical assumptions, conclusions are not generalizable beyond it. This point is all too often forgotten. For example, if subjects' autonomic balance

---

[4] The between-subjects covariance of two variables indicates their similarity of variation in the salience of the construct.

is registered during resting conditions, any results refer to resting states and not to conditions or occasions in general.

It should be noted that there is a slight contradiction when the "locus of the construct" and the "assessment unit" statements are viewed together: If the "locus" is defined as between-subjects, this general statement excludes the existence (or relevance for the construct in question) of subject x condition interactions. If such interactions are left out of consideration, then theoretically the same between-subjects variance and covariance should be observed in any one condition. As a consequence, one should be able to generalize from one particular condition, that is, unit of assessment, to all the others.

But the unit of assessment had just been introduced as a limit on generalizability. This contradiction can be resolved if a distinction between the relational structure of theoretical statements and their empirical validity is made. Whereas the theoretical analysis by virtue of logic is correct in that conclusions can be generalized to all possible units of assessment, an empirical investigation in the concept construction stage can draw conclusions only conditional to the correctness of the assumptions underlying the investigation, in particular the assumption about the locus of the construct. If the assumption about the locus is correct, then generalizability of conclusions indeed holds beyond the specific unit of measurement. If, however, the assumption is false, then the investigation's results cannot be generalized to other units of assessment beyond the one actually chosen. As a safeguard against incorrect conclusions in case of erroneous assumptions, it is good advice to restrict one's conclusions to the particular unit of assessment chosen for the investigation.

It may finally be noted that the first assessment model corresponds to the R-technique of correlation and factor analysis. In R-technique factor analysis, between-subjects variance and covariance of variables (observed in a particular condition) is factored to yield linear combinations of variables (i.e., factors) in variable-space. Actually, the construct identification stage has much in common with Cattell's program of identifying source traits through factor analysis. Factors are the estimates of constructs; variables that are homogeneous with respect to one factor (i.e., have high loadings on it), are the construct's indicators; subjects are the axes of the space where variables and factors are located, that is, subjects are in a literal, geometrical sense the locus of the construct.

Now that the general scheme of assessment models has been described in some depth for the first model, the following ones can be characterized more briefly.

Assessment Model 2. The locus of the construct is between conditions, homogeneity constraints are again imposed on variables, and the unit of assessment is a particular subject. The locus of the construct indicates that different conditions lead to variations in the salience of the construct. In contrast to the traitist point of view expressed in the first assessment model, the second model is clearly process-oriented. In psychophysiology, the construct of activation comes close to this conception, since activation changes to a large extent in anticipation of and in accordance with the demands on cognitive, motivational, emotional, and somato-motor systems. Interestingly, this basic assumption about the construct of activation has only slowly been realized and only recently offered as an explanation for the "covariation problem" (i.e., the generally low between-subjects correlations among physiological variables; cf. Fahrenberg et al., 1979; Myrtek, 1984; Venables, 1984). However, at least part of the astounding covariation problem can be traced back to the questionable use of a trait-oriented, instead of a process-oriented assessment model. Within personality psychology, both the concept of states and an extreme view about the stimulus dependency of behavior (situationism) would fall within the scope of this assessment model.

In sum, between-conditions variance and covariance of variables (observed within a single subject or after forming a group average) are analyzed with the aim of identifying those variables that indicate a construct's fluctuations. If the variance-covariance matrix is factored (P-technique), the resulting factors are linear combinations of variables within a space defined by condition-axes.

Assessment Model 3. The locus of the construct is again between conditions: A construct, if assessed with this model, is defined as a process. Homogeneity constraints apply to subjects, that is, it is hypothesized that there are groups of subjects sharing a similar process-construct. The unit of assessment is a particular variable which is assumed to be a valid indicator of the construct. This assessment model is not suited to provide information about putative indicators but to identify homogeneous subject groups. For example, if it is hypothesized that the period of biological pacemakers (construct), as manifested in the temporal pattern of release (locus of construct) of a particular neurotransmitter in the human brain (unit of assessment) differs among individuals, this assessment model could be of use in identifying subject groups with different pacemaker rhythms (cf. Weiner, 1989, for an evaluation of the importance of biological oscillators in psychosomatic medicine). In personality psychology, this assessment model applies to the view that the behavior of some of the people is consistent only some of the time (alluding to Bem & Allen's, 1974, article "On predicting some of the people some of the time: The search for cross-situational consistencies in behavior"). This model would help to determine those individuals that share the same particular sort of behavioral consistency in an array of conditions.

In terms of factor analysis, this assessment model corresponds to the S-technique, where conditions are the axes of the space within which factors formed by linear combinations of subject vectors are located.

Assessment Model 4. Here, variables are the locus of the construct. This seems at first rather odd, since variables are usually counted as indicators of constructs and not as their locus. However if it is realized that a very large (if not infinite) but empirically never completely known profile of variables may be characteristic of a condition (this assessment model) or a subject (the following model), then the actually observed sample of variables is still an indicator (statistically: an estimator) of the population of variables. Homogeneity constraints are again imposed on subjects, that is, homogeneous classes of subjects are hypothesized to exist and to be discovered. The unit of assessment is a particular condition. A psychophysiological example for this model is easily found in "Individual Response Specificity" (see Chapters 3.1 and 6.2). This principle states that individuals have a characteristic response profile across very different conditions of measurement. Q-technique in factor analysis is the parallel technique, where linear combinations of subject vectors in a space spanned by variables are sought.

Assessment Model 5. Variables are again the locus of the construct. In distinction to the previous model, conditions are the mode in which homogeneity constraints are sought. The unit of assessment is a particular subject. An example from psychophysiology for this assessment model is "Situational Response Specificity" (see Chapters 3.1 and 6.2). This form of specificity states that conditions elicit a characteristic response profile across a sample of subjects. This model corresponds to the O-technique of factor analysis, where linear combinations of situation vectors form factors in a space spanned by variables.

Assessment Model 6. As did the first, this model has subjects as the locus of the construct. Homogeneity constraints are imposed on conditions, and a particular variable is the unit of assessment. Thus, in this model, it is postulated (1) that the constructs in question vary in their salience between subjects and (2) that different conditions are "coordinated" by a construct in a way that makes them equivalent in terms of the particular variable observed. For instance, Allport's definition of traits fits the perspective of this assessment model better than the perspective of the first model. For Allport (1961), a trait is defined as a "neuropsychic structure having the capacity to render many stimuli functionally equivalent, and to initiate and guide equivalent (meaningfully consistent) forms of adaptive and expressive behavior" (p. 347). That is, individual differences give rise to common traits and they function to form equivalence classes of conditions, not in terms of the physical but in terms of the psychological characteristics of conditions. This assessment model corresponds to the T-technique of factor analysis, where linear combinations of condition vectors are sought within a space spanned by subjects.

Assessment Model 7. If it is hypothesized that the constructs under study can be defined by neither between-subjects nor between-conditions variations alone but by some form of mutual dependence, then the appropriate locus of the construct must consist of or include the combination of subjects and conditions. A mutual dependence of subjects and conditions can be stated when subjects respond differently to given conditions. The current assessment model reflects the theoretical statement that only the interaction (subjects x conditions) variance accounts for different instantiations of the construct. Homogeneity constraints concern the variables, that is, it is hypothesized that there are clusters of variables that converge on the construct and may serve as indicators. Note that the notion of the unit of assessment is no longer applicable here, because the locus of the construct subsumes both the subjects and the conditions modes. If, however, it were not reasonable or feasible to draw random samples from a subject or a condition population, then the constraints imposed on the sampling from each mode (e.g., using conditions usually classified in behavioral medicine as "mental stress tests", such as mental arithmetic or the Stroop Color Word test) can be said to constitute the unit of assessment beyond which generalizations of results might be questionable.

An application of this assessment model is appropriate whenever the nature of a construct is postulated to be interactive in subjects and conditions, as in interactive notions of personality (see Chapter 2.2).

Assessment Model 8. This assessment model states that the locus of the construct is to be defined across the combination of conditions and variables. Homogeneity constraints are imposed upon subjects. The model is applicable when it is hypothesized that given the same situations some subjects are characterized by a certain ensemble of situation-specific response profiles, and other subjects by different ones.

Assessment Model 9. The remaining assessment model hypothesizes that the locus of the construct is defined by the mutual dependence of variables and subjects. Homogeneity constraints are imposed upon conditions. This assessment model is appropriate if it is postulated that conditions or groups of conditions are characterized by an ensemble of subject-specific response profiles.

Further assessment models can be constructed through combinations from among the nine basic ones. For example, if it is held that a construct is both trait- and process-related, that is, subjects' processes operate on different levels, then a combination of the first and the second assessment model would be called for. Consequently, the analysis of the subjects x conditions x variables data set would be performed on between-subjects plus between-conditions variance. Similarly, if the locus of the construct is assumed to be both subjects and subjects x conditions interaction, then the analysis of between-subjects plus subjects x conditions interaction variance (both of which comprise the within-conditions variance) would be mandatory. If the locus of the construct is hypothesized to be both conditions and subjects x conditions interaction, then the analysis of between-conditions plus subjects x conditions interaction variance (both of which comprise the within-subjects variance) would be called for. Finally, if the locus of the construct is thought to be in subjects, conditions, and their interaction, then the sum of all three variances (which is the total variance minus error variance) would be analyzed. However, even if the locus of the construct is defined to cover more than one mode, a separate analysis of each single mode might precede the overall analysis.

In conclusion, the construction stage of constructs depends to a large extent on theoretical assumptions which guide the protocol of observation, the variance analyzed, and the permissable conclusions. This view of the construction stage contrasts remarkably to the caricature saying that it is simply "data-driven" and without guiding theoretical concepts. Such a distorted view reveals a grotesque misunderstanding of empirical science: it takes one step within this construction program (that of searching for convergences and regularities within the data obtained, the inductive step) for the program itself. But quite to the contrary, theory and a priori assumptions actually determine which data are gathered, where convergences and regularities are expected to be found, and how these findings can be used to advance theory.

1.5.2 Assessment in the validation stage of constructs

The validation stage of constructs follows the construction stage. If the attempted validation is not successful, the construction stage has to be reentered with modified theoretical statements. If the validation is successful, the nomological network of the theory in question could be expanded.

In principle, the same assessment models apply in the validation as in the construction stage of constructs. Also the same kinds of theoretical statements have to be made,

- about the mode(s) (subjects, conditions, variables) where the locus of the construct is constituted,
- about the elements of the mode homogeneity constraints are imposed upon,
- about the mode which defines the unit of assessment, and
- about the convergence of the putative homogeneous elements of the selected mode within the construct in question and not within another one (Krause, 1972).

The difference between the construction and the validation stages is the formulation and test of hypotheses in the latter, which on the one hand aim at showing differences between constructs in terms of the observed elements of the mode with homogeneity constraints and on the other hand convergences of these same elements with respect to each one of the constructs. The multitrait-multimethod (MTMM) matrix, proposed by Campbell and Fiske (1959) as a scheme for construct validation, is a general layout for performing these tests. Although Campbell and Fiske's original proposal described a correlational approach, the scheme is based on an additive linear model that is equally well applicable to analysis-of-variance-hypotheses concerning differences between means (a demonstration follows below).

The rather abstract formulations in the last paragraph now will be reformulated using the terminology of Campbell and Fiske's well-known elaboration of Assessment Model 1. They described the case where personality "traits" (i.e., constructs) were measured by different "methods" (i.e., by elements of the "methods" mode homogeneity constraints are imposed upon; e.g., questionnaire scales, ratings by significant others, and behavior observations are the elements of the "methods" mode). The following theoretical statements are the basis of this construct validation example:

- Subjects are the locus of the construct,
- homogeneity contraints are imposed upon the variables measured,
- the unit of assessment is the condition during which the observation or testing took place (in this example it is obviously not one and the same condition), and
- the different methods applied within each one construct converge on the construct aimed at and not on another one (i.e., the questionnaire scale, the ratings, and the observations intending to indicate, e.g., the trait of extraversion, if they converge or correlate highly will actually indicate extraversion and not neuroticism).

The hypotheses to be tested are: (1) do the methods within each trait converge?, and (2) do the methods discriminate between different traits?

Campbell and Fiske (1959) had proposed to compare correlation coefficients within the monotrait-heteromethod diagonal to evaluate convergent validity and discriminant validity by comparing the monotrait to the heterotrait triangles within the correlation matrix. Current approaches to the analysis of MTMM-matrices make use of structural equation modelling in an attempt to cope with a number of shortcomings inherent in Campbell and Fiske's (1959) procedure for comparing correlation coefficients (cf. Schmitt & Stults, 1986; Widaman, 1985). In some cases, however, the hypotheses of convergent and discriminant validity can also be tested by a comparison of means. If, for example, different contexts of emotion induction (during real-life or imagery) are hypothesized to converge on anger and fear in terms of physiological response profiles (i.e., context profiles should be identical within emotions), then the physiological profiles of contexts within each emotion are assumed to be identical. Similarly, under the hypothesis of discriminant validity, context profiles should be different between emotions (see Chapter 12).

In order to arrive at a progressive theory development, the construct construction and validation stages have to be thoroughly related to one another. This mutual relationship is the leading idea behind the research program presented in this book. Construct construction stages are presented in Chapter 9 on situational variation for an analysis of "activation". These attempts of construct construction are then applied to the characterization of situations, personality, and emotions in Chapters 10 to 12. If these stages of construct construction and validation are not related to one another, the assessment of constructs remains ad hoc and is doomed to failure.

An example of such a failure has emanated from the "Three-Systems-Model of fear and emotion" (originally proposed by Lang, 1968, 1971, 1978 and later supported in the writings of Rachman; e.g., Rachman, 1978). The "triple response system theory", as this model is also termed (e.g., Strosahl & Linehan,

1986), holds that fear is a construct with only loosely coupled indicators sampled from verbal, somato-motor-behavioral and physiological (autonomic, cortical, neuromuscular) methods of measurement. The often reported low correlations between the three methods (see the "covariation problem" alluded to in the context of Assessment Model 2) suggested such a heterogeneity of indicators. This heterogeneity runs counter to the intention of the construct construction and validation efforts that impose homogeneity and not heterogeneity constraints on the indicators (Assessment Models 1 and 2).

In a penetrating analysis of the "definitional focus" of fear under the Three-Systems-Model, Hugdahl (1981), has found an inherent circularity in this model "insofar as, in the end, neither stimuli, nor responses can be ultimately relied on when defining emotional concepts" (p. 78). Stimuli cannot be relied upon because people perceive them differently; responses cannot be relied upon because the model gives no prior validity to one of the methods. Thus either (1) the notion of a unitary emotion construct has to be abandoned and replaced by the assumption of many different small-scale construct-method units (e.g., somatic fear, cognitive fear, etc.), or (2) the assumption of a unitary emotion construct is retained and supplemented by additional theoretical statements which could explain the low degree of correlation among the putative indicators (e.g., individual response specificity), or (3) the assessment model and with it important theoretical assumptions have to be changed.

It thus appears that the Three-Systems-Model is still on a very low theoretical level by just giving a label to the recurrent observations of low between-subjects correlations between fear indicators and that it fails to offer an explanation for these low correlations (Evens, 1986). Strosahl and Linehan write:

> We believe that the triple response system theory may undersimplify or substantially misrepresent the complex relationships underpinning intraorganismic organization. [...] we should not hesitate to change theories simply because it is methodologically inconvenient to do so, particularly when research data argue for theoretical expansion. (Strosahl and Linehan, 1986, p. 21.)

Kozak and Miller (1982) present the critique of the Three-Systems-Model in a nutshell, "In short, we have been told where to look, but not what to seek, nor how to tell if we have found it" (p. 349). To rephrase this point, the assessment of constructs is "data-driven" in that we have to look and seek, but at the same time it is "theory-driven" in that we have to know where to look, what to seek, and how to tell if we have found the construct.

2 Situation and Person

2.1 Epistemology and Definitions of "The Situation"

How do we come to know? One of the classical answers to this question, empiricism, says that we know to the extent we correctly perceive. This position implies that sensory experience is the only source of human knowledge. Rationalism posits that knowledge comes from the logical consistency of thought, whereas sensory experience cannot provide knowledge. Realism assumes that there is an external world that is independent of our conceiving mind. Idealism, however, accepts only an inner reality.

These four epistemologies present the cornerstones for a discussion of "the situation". Is the "situation out there in the external world" something real that can be perceived with our senses? Empirical realism, also called naive realism, would answer in the affirmative. Does the "situation out there in the external world" really exist, although it can be perceived only through a mental reconstruction and not through sensory experience? This position is held by rational realism, or critical constructivism as it was termed earlier. Finally, is "the situation" nothing but a mental construction without a real counterpart in the external world, "known" from the action of our senses, as in empirical idealism?

Both naive realism and idealism are often found to be inadequate positions in psychology. On the one hand, perceptual processes have been shown to analyze and transform sensory information such that distortions occur, for example, of the photographic retinal image during higher visual processing stages as can be seen in constancy effects (Marr, 1982). On the other hand, human action deals invariably with "real things out there" even if the action and its results cannot be experienced other than through the eyes of the mind. Under this perspective it is therefore legitimate to speak of "the development of personal theories of reality" (Epstein & Erskine, 1983) or of a construct system enabling one to anticipate future events (Kelly, 1955).

Different epistemological positions entail quite different research strategies when studying the determinants of behavior. Whereas naive realism implies that the objective situation is capable of acting as a determinant of behavior, idealism would assert that idiosyncratic experiences do act in this way. In the former case, situations could act as independent variables; in the latter case, situations could clearly not be conceived of as independent variables but rather as multiply determined by individual beliefs, expectancies, and intentions, and are thus as much a product of person variables as they are a possible determinant of behavior (see, e.g., Craik, 1981). Critical constructivism holds elements from both positions: On the one hand, it is acknowledged that there is an objective stimulus, on the other hand, it is conceded that individuals perceive through constructions of their minds. Thus it follows from critical constructivism (1) that differences among situations can be studied by treating them as independent variables and additionally (2) that individual differences in mental constructions can be assessed by exploring correlates of the within-conditions variability among subjects in one or more response variables.

The distinction between external and internal, distal and proximal (Brunswik, 1956), objective and perceived (Pervin, 1978), physical and psychological (Wakenhut, 1978), or alpha-press and beta-press (Murray, 1938) stimuli, situations, or environments has been a prominent one in the literature (Gibson, 1960; Pervin, 1978). In addition, definitions have been attempted in terms of reactions to the respective situation, such as self-reports about inner experiences or behavioral responses (Frederiksen, 1972; Magnusson & Ekehammar, 1975).

The definition of stimuli, situations, or environments (see below for a differentiation between these notions) in objective physicalistic terms has been put forward by behaviorists and situationists (cf. Bowers, 1973), leading to attempts at a taxonomy of situations. For example, Sells (1963) defined situations in terms of objectively measured characteristics (e.g., terrain, natural resources, social organization, novelty, role expectation, etc.). Barker (1968) introduced the notion of the "behavior setting", a concept similar to that of situation.

Behavior settings have defined boundaries and physical properties that lead them to be associated with ongoing patterns of interindividual behaviors ("synomorphy"). Although behavior settings are believed to have characteristic influences upon the behaviors of persons in general, Barker acknowledges too that behavior settings are perceived differently by various individuals leading to individualistic behaviors. Constitutive attributes of behavior settings are (1) their structure, that is, the existence of synomorphies, or, structural equivalences between the setting and the behaviors of persons within the setting, (2) their internal dynamic, that is, the interdependence of different synomorphies, and (3) their external dynamic, that is, the degree of independence of synomorphies between different behavior settings.

Moos (1973; after Endler, 1981) describes six major methods that can be used to characterize environments, (1) ecological dimensions, (2) behavior settings involving both behavioral and ecological properties, (3) parameters of organizational structure, (4) behavioral and personal parameters of the environmental inhabitants, (5) organizational psychosocial and climate variables, and (6) variables relating to reinforcement or functional analyses of environments.

Rotter (1981) also favors an objective definition of the situation, which should be obtained by the "common sense terms of the social group, subculture, or culture" (Rotter, 1981, p. 172). Rotter emphasizes that the "objective situation" as independently defined of the person establishes the referent for what we are talking about when treating the situation as a psychological and meaningful situation. In social-learning theory, the psychological situation is defined

> as a complex set of interacting cues acting upon an individual for any specific time period. These cues determine for the individual the expectancies for behavior-reinforcement sequences and also for reinforcement-reinforcement sequences. (Rotter, 1981, p. 170, original emphasis of last sentence omitted.)

Herrmann (1982) similarly refers to the agreement of reliable observers as an objective definition of a particular situation.

Two different approaches to an objective characterization of situations have been included in the last few paragraphs: the delineation of attributes of the physico-biological situation by technical assessments (for details, cf. Craik, 1981, Walsh & Betz, 1985) and the consensual impressions by raters of situations as an instance of observational assessment (cf. Craik, 1981, Walsh & Betz, 1985). Block and Block (1981) contrast these approaches in their delineation of three different levels of situational analysis. These analytical levels should reflect successive stages of how the experiencing individual interacts with the situation. The first level concerns the *physico-biological situation*,

> the infinitely detailable, perceptually unfiltered and uninterpreted, sensory available intakes by the individual. The physico-biological situation has something of an autochtonous structure - it is not entirely inchoate - as a function of evolution-ingrained perceptual and action schemata that the ages have by now wired into the human nervous system. (Block & Block, 1981, p. 86.)

The second level is called the *canonical situation*, the consensually defined, constructed, or accepted situation, similar to Murray's (1938) "alpha press".

> It is the psychological demand-quality or structure of the situation as specified by widely established categories of objects, concepts and relations, rules, standards, and normatively provided expectations ... the raw, boundless, and even overwhelming physico-biological world is conditioned to become much less, but also much more, than it was, namely, a world structured to exclude certain possibilities and to emphasize others. (Block & Block, 1981, p. 87.)

The authors emphasize that "because of our common humanity, the perceptual and cognitive ontogeny of individuals proves to be surprisingly and strongly similar" (p. 87).

The third level of situational analysis is the *functional situation* which has been referred to above as the psychological or subjective situation. Murray (1938) called it the "beta press" and Lewin (1936) the "life space". The functional situation is the specific representation within an individual which is a result of the individual's perception, his or her personality structure and the immediately present motivational and cognitive state. It is the functional situation to which the individual responds. Interactional personality psychology has emphasized this definition of the situation (Bowers, 1973; Endler, 1981; Endler & Magnusson, 1976; Magnusson & Allen, 1983) taking the risk of blurring the distinction between "the person" and "the situation", or, as Raush (1979) mentions,

> if the *subjective environment* is the person's perceptions and cognitions, the conceptual border separating *person* from *situation* fades to obscurity. (Raush, 1979, p. 100, author's emphases.)

Block and Block (1981) similarly argue for a definition of the situation independent of the person, that is, in terms of the canonical instead of the functional situation:

> ... the characteristics of the normatively described, consensually received canonical situation must be defined independently of any one person. Otherwise we are mired in an oft-remarked, science-preventing tautology: On the one hand, we can know the *functional* situation of the individual only afterward, through observing the individual's subsequent behavior; on the other hand, we are presumably trying to study, before the fact of behavior, the effects of the situation on the individual's response. Thus, we understand the situation from the behavior and the behavior from the situation! (Block & Block, 1981, p. 88, authors' emphasis.)

We are in danger of a similar circularity if the situation is defined in terms of the behaviors associated with the situation (Frederiksen, 1972; Magnusson & Ekehammer, 1975). This approach is similar to Barker's described above, where behavior settings are characterized by the global interindividual structural equivalences between the setting and the behaviors of persons. Such a conceptualization of situations in terms of the behaviors that are common to the persons within the situation will be termed the *modal situation*. It avoids the risk of circularity because individual differences in behaviors within any one situation are independent of different modal situations (technically speaking, subjects x conditions variance is independent of between-conditions variance).

A definition of the situation on the basis of *individual* behaviors obviously carries information about the functional situation but also about other psychological factors that enter into the selection of the actual response. For example, although the functional situation may be highly significant for me, there may be reasons not to act as if this were the case. This stimulus for actual response selection and organization will be called the *effective situation*. A model of stimulus-response mediation which treats the physico-biological, canonical, functional, effective and modal situations as different constructs, each with their own operationalizations will be presented in Chapter 3.1. By way of summary, the five notions of "the situation" are depicted in Table 2.

Stimulus, situation, and environment have been used above without further detailing their defining characteristics. Attempts at defining these concepts have been put forward by Magnusson and Allen (1983) and by Pervin (1978). Although these authors utilize different terms, stimulus, situation, and environment are thought to denote different levels within the complex system of factors establishing an individual's total environment. Magnusson and Allen (1983) define

- the *situation* as that part of the total environment that is accessible to sensory perception on a certain occasion,
- the *micro-level of the environment* as that part of the total environment the individual is in contact with (e.g., in the family, at school, at work), and
- the *macro-level of the environment* as that part of the total environment that influences or determines the character and functioning of the micro-environment (e.g., laws, culture, language, housing).

Each of the three levels of environments has certain characteristics (both structure- and content-related) and functions (as a source of active stimulation and as providing a general context for ongoing behavior). Pervin (1978) makes a similar point in distinguishing between stimulus, situation, and environment primarily on the basis of the scale of analysis - ranging from the concern with molecular variables in the case of stimuli to molar variables in the case of environments. We speak of a stimulus when we are interested in a specific object of a person's attention (the focal stimulus according to Cattell, 1966b). A situation is characterized by our interest in the individual's engagement with a number of objects and actions over a certain time span. A situation is defined by the organization of three components: (1) who is involved, (2) where the action takes place, and (3) which kind of action occurs. In the case of environments, we are concerned with the particular situations a person encounters in his or her daily living and the relationships among them.

It is apparent that Pervin emphasizes the interest of the investigator for delineating the three concepts. Thus, one and the same "variable" may be considered a stimulus, a part of a situation, or a part of an environment. For example, noise can be a focal stimulus if we are interested alone in its effects on a person. Noise can be a situational variable if we are concerned with noise in its relationships with other aspects of the situation. Finally, noise may be considered to be part of the environment if it is a relevant component of many or all situations.

Table 2. Five Notions of "The Situation"

Situation	Characteristic
Physico-biological	Attributes of the physical world
Canonical	Consensual construction of the world
Functional	Individual evaluation of the world
Effective	Individual response organization
Modal	Interindividual correspondence of responses

These definitions allow putting the usage of the terms "situation" and "context" more precisely as they are employed later on in this book. Inasmuch as the empirical studies to be reported deal with laboratory rather than field experiments, the micro-level of the environment in these experiments is the laboratory including the experimenters and the technical staff. The situation is characterized by the collection of stimuli presented to the subject by the experimenter, its time span is clearly limited by the experimental protocol. "Situation" is used equivalently to "task" or "condition". The term "context" is used to designate a level between the micro-level of the environment and the situation. The context comprises (1) the situations already gone through during the experimental session, the time elapsed, and so on, (2) the general rules (e.g., "sit quietly") and specific instructions which invoke the setting during a particular situation (e.g., "listen carefully to what I say" or "close your eyes"), and (3) the background stimuli (Cattell, 1966b) during a situation (e.g., dimmed lights). The important aspect to note is the independent experimental formation and combination of "situation" and "context".

2.2 Determinants of Behavior: Notions in Personality Psychology

Personality psychology, more than other fields of psychology, has been concerned with the determinants of behavior in the "triple typology" (Bem, 1983) of persons, behaviors, and situations. Thus, in the extant literature on personality we can hope to find theoretical accounts and empirical evaluations of person and/or situation characteristics as determinants of behavior. Space precludes presenting more than a brief sketch. I will begin with a brief overview of groups of theories in terms of the triple typology.

The task of constructing theories of personality includes the specification of equivalence classes that certain persons will behave in certain ways in certain situations. Personality theories can be loosely arranged in groups with respect to the kinds of specifications they adopt. Bem (1983) suggests the following arrangement in groups of theories.

First, "*nomothetic individual-differences approaches to personality: certain persons/ certain behaviors/ all situations*" (p. 567). This is the traditional individual-differences approach to personality as employed by psychodynamic, personological, and trait or type theories. These theories specify equivalence classes of persons behaving in a characteristic way. However, there is no delimiting or specifying class of situations for which such person-behavior correspondences should be valid. The lack of restrictions on the part of the situation mode has provoked recurring criticism of these theoretical orientations (e.g., Mischel, 1968; Peterson, 1968), emphasizing the obvious lack of cross-situational consistency of behavior. Refinements on these positions include the moderator-variable strategy (which specifies moderator variables such as self-monitoring, Snyder, 1983, or the metatrait of consistency, Bem & Allen, 1974; Baumeister, 1988), which constructs more finely differentiated equivalence classes of persons.

The trait model assumes that traits are the prime determinants of behavior and serve as a basis for apparent response-response (between-subjects correlational) consistencies of behavior. Thus, the type of law sought is primarily of the R-R variety (Endler & Magnusson, 1976).

Traits can be defined with respect to two aspects, their ontological status and the type of consistency (cf. Herrmann, 1972; Hirschberg, 1978; Zuroff, 1986). As to the ontological status, traits can be viewed

- as real, causal entities that correspond to as yet unknown neurophysiological structures (Allport, 1937; also advocated by the biopsychological approach explained in Chapter 1),
- as descriptive summary statements of a person's past behavior without invoking a status of causality and reality (see Buss & Craig's, 1983, act frequency approach), and
- as a dispositional concept or a construct that describes a tendency to perform a certain class of behaviors without implying the actual occurrence of that behavior in every situation (dispositions do not provide causal explanations and they are not real entities).

As to the type of consistency over situations that traits require for their definition, the somewhat caricatured picture of trait theories stated above (i.e., equivalence classes of persons correspond to those of behaviors in *all* situations) needs to be qualified. Consistency in contrast to specificity of behavior in a theory can be demanded to be absolute or relative (Magnusson, 1976) and broad or narrow (Zuroff, 1986). Whereas absolute consistency means identical behaviors across different situations (a position no one explicitly advocates for healthy individuals, but which may be descriptive in pathological cases, e.g., severe mental retardation, cf. Mischel, 1984), relative consistency means a constant rank order of subjects with respect to a specific behavior across a variety of situations (stastistically speaking, the underlying model is additive in person and situation parameters). The broad versus narrow aspect of consistency refers to the extension of the class of situations that elicit behaviors associated with a certain trait. The smaller the class of situations having this property of trait excitation, the farther apart from the cliché of trait theory and the more related to interactional personality theory is the resulting position.

Allport (1961), for example, held that

> [t]here must be some demonstrable relationship between separate acts before [a trait's] existence can be inferred. Yet the occurrence of dissociated, specific and even contradictory acts is not necessarily fatal to the inference. (Allport, 1961, p. 363.)

A special case of trait consistency on the broad versus narrow aspect has been advocated by Epstein (Epstein, 1979, 1980, 1983, 1984), who defines a trait as a person's average level of response over a given range of situations. Buss and Craik's (1983) act frequency analysis of traits presents still another position on the type of consistency to be expected of a trait. They define a disposition (trait) according to how frequently acts prototypical of that disposition occur in a fixed period of time. It should be noted, however, that instead of situational consistency they advocate temporal consistency independent of the particular evoking situations.

Another aspect of current theorizing under the trait model that is related to interactional positions is the supposition of cognitive mediators, such as a person's implicit theory of reality (Epstein & O'Brien, 1985) or "stored information (knowledge and past experiences)", which "serves as a frame of reference for the interpretation of situational information" (Magnusson, 1976, p. 264). This view suggests shifting the consistency issue of traits from consistency in terms of actual behaviors to consistency in terms of cognitive mediating processes (Wakefield, 1989). Consequently it can be hypothesized that

> [t]he way in which an individual's mediating process functions in selection, interpretation and treating of situational information is stable and consistent. (Magnusson, 1976, p. 265.)

Similarly, Mischel (e.g., Mischel, 1984) emphasizes the meanings the individual finds in the situation and the purposes the individual brings to the situation. Although not regarded a trait psychologist, Mischel (1984) recently has argued that the personologist should seek narrow classes of situations for which "local" or "specific" consistencies exist:

> Instead of seeking high levels of consistency from situation to situation for many behaviors in a wide range of contexts or looking for broad averages, one might try to identify unique 'bundles' or sets of temporally stable prototypic behaviors, key features, that characterize the person even over long periods of time but not necessarily across most or all relevant situations. (Mischel, 1984, p. 362.)

In retrospect it becomes evident that the concept of trait with its emphasis on stable person characteristics (in a narrower or broader sense with respect to the classes of situations related to each trait) for most current writers in the personality field seems indispensable (Amelang & Borkenau, 1986; Buss, 1989; Kenrick & Funder, 1988; Zuroff, 1986). However, "traits themselves require further explanation; they are, after all, only promissory notes (for causal explanations)" (Briggs, 1985, p. 17). Promissory, too, is the alleged role of cognitive mediators of behavior; while being of immediate appeal, the empirical evaluation of this proposal is still in its beginning and probably will face difficult methodological problems (e.g., stemming from the solely subjective self-report data about cognitions in contrast to the potential multimodal perspective on behavior, i.e. by oneself, by others, and through physiological recordings).

Bem's second group of triple typologies, that is, equivalence classes of persons, behaviors, and situations, is called *"idiographic/morphogenic approaches to personality: this person/certain behaviors/all situations"* (Bem, 1983, p. 567). If the moderator variable approach employed for a definition of still smaller classes of persons is carried through to the extreme, there remains but one person in a class. As a result, there are possibly different equivalence classes of behaviors for different persons. This feature characterizes the idiographic approach to personality, which claims that persons should be described on their own selection of descriptors, and contrasts with the nomothetic approach assuming a common set of descriptors for all persons. From the idiographic perspective, the lack of trait consistency in a sample of persons with respect to certain behaviors can be explained by the unwarranted use of common descriptors for the group of persons under study.

There is another sense to the term "idiographic" made clear by Allport (1962) and termed "morphogenic". The distinction nomothetic-morphogenic is concerned with the way persons are characterized in relation to other persons. Whereas the nomothetic assessment characterizes persons with respect to their relative standing in comparison to other persons on the common set of descriptors, the morphogenic assessment characterizes a person with respect to his or her profile or configuration of responses by comparing ipsatively the different responses within the profile. An example of morphogenic assessment (while maintaining a common descriptor basis) is the MMPI questionnaire, on the basis of which an individual can be classified according to the configuration in that subset of scales showing elevated scores.

The distinction between nomothetic and both idiographic and morphogenic approaches illuminates another aspect of the consistency issue. Whereas the typical nomothetic approach to personality assessment begins with a set of trait terms, then finds the salience of persons in various situations with respect to them, and finally notes the degree of inconsistency in the person's behaviors, the combined idiographic and morphogenic approach has a quite different stance toward consistency. In this combined approach to personality, which is probably also the lay person's way of characterizing others, one first reviews a person's behavior and then tries to identify that subset of descriptors which is purportedly characteristic of it.

The crucial point is the identification of the proper descriptors. We often assume the behavior of a person to be consistent after we have found the proper trait descriptors, and inconsistent if we have not found one. For example, if a child is consistently observed to lie and cheat at all opportunities that present themselves, we are likely to find the trait descriptor honesty-dishonesty for that child. If, however, a child is observed to lie only when being accused of bad behaviors, we would not say that the child is inconsistently dishonest but search for another descriptor, for example, fear of punishment. Thus, under the idiographic and morphogenic view, inconsistency is often in the eye of the beholder (or more precisely, it is a concept-formation task not properly solved) rather than in the person himself or herself.

Bem's third group of triple typologies is called *"process approaches to personality: all persons/certain behaviors/certain situations"* (Bem, 1983, p.

570). Here equivalence classes of behaviors and situations are postulated that should be valid for all persons. In personality psychology, this is the position of situationism which states that behavior is a function of the situation. This is basically a stimulus-response (S-R) approach, most notably exemplified in experimental work and its typical analysis-of-variance treatment of the data, where almost always the specificity of obtained responses with regard to certain experimental conditions is hypothesized. Social learning theory (Bandura, 1969; Mischel, 1976; Rotter, 1975) is one example of S-R laws, although the reciprocal relation of the person and the situation has been emphasized (Bandura, 1989; for a critique of reciprocal determinism, see Phillips & Orton, 1983). Another example is Skinnerian radical behaviorism which has sought to derive principles of behavior from an empirical analysis of the reinforcing stimulus and the reinforcement contingencies that shape behavior (Skinner, 1960).

Whereas this approach is nomothetic because it sorts all persons with the same history of reinforcing stimuli into the same equivalence class of situation-behavior pairs, it is at the same time idiographic because probably no two persons have one and the same history of reinforcing stimuli. Thus, S-R processes are formalized nomothetically, but the situation term S is treated idiographically. Consistency of individual behavior is not to be expected because behavior is situation-specific.

A comparison of the traitist and situationist power of prediction has been hampered by the different kinds of statistics usually calculated within these two approaches. While the trait approach utilizes correlations (of the R-technique type) to determine effect sizes in terms of shared variance of a personality trait and a particular behavior, the situation approach calculates a test statistic (t- or F-value) in order to gauge the difference between two (or more) situation means. It remained for Funder and Ozer (1983) to show that when compared directly in terms of effect sizes, the traitist and the situationist powers of predicting behavior in a number of often cited empirical studies were essentially similar (amounting to a linear effect of about 0.40).

It should be noted that the S-R approach treats the situation (in the sense of the physico-biological situation) as an independent variable (as demonstrated in the experimental method). Adopting, however, instead of a naive realist a constructivist point of view, the situation (in the sense of the functional situation) is as well a dependent variable, depending upon the person's cognitive and motivational system. But if the situation is a function of the person then it is impossible to separate the situation from the person (Bowers, 1973). This leads to interactional accounts of behavior.

Bem's last group of triple typologies is *"the interactional approach to personality: certain persons/certain behaviors/certain situations"* (Bem, 1983, p. 572). This is the most general perspective because it includes traitist and situationist explanations of behavior determinants. The central tenet of interactionism, however, is that behavior is determined to a nonnegligible part by the individual impact of situations on a person's behavior, that is, by the functional situation. How can the effects of functional situations be determined?

Firstly, the presence of differential effects of the functional situation on the behaviors of a group of persons (exposed to the same set of situations) is reflected in the person x situation interaction source of variance which gave this approach to personality its name. It should be noted that the effects on behavior of different functional situations can be derived only under three conditions, which have been termed, slightly derogatorily, "mechanistic interaction" (Olweus, 1977):

- more than one situation is presented to a group of persons (this enables a separation of person x situation from person variance),
- the experimenter has selected the set of situations under the provision that they are different, either with respect to physical or biological attributes (physico-biological situation) or with respect to a consensual definition of independent raters or by his or her own judgment (canonical situation), and
- the experiment is replicated (this enables a separation of person x situation from error variance).

Second, the effects on behavior of the functional situation can be studied by correlating indices of the psychological situation with behavior. Such indices can be obtained through ratings on a given set of dimensions or through a multidimensional scaling approach where psychological stimulus dimensions are derived from the stimulus comparisons performed by the subjects. Magnusson and Ekehammar (1975, 1978) have presented studies following this second approach to gauging the effects of the functional situation.

However, with the functional situation, the interactional approach does not only provide an alternative determinant of behavior which is as much dependent on the physico-biological situation as it is on the person. This approach is also presented by its major proponents as a theory of behavior: It goes beyond mechanistic interaction in postulating "dynamic interactions" or "transactions" according to which (1) certain persons seek or avoid certain situations and (2) certain persons will actually modify situations or engage in reciprocal transactions with them (Olweus, 1977). Consequently, the type of laws sought in the interactionist approach is of the S-R-S-R ... type. Such laws describe the "reciprocal causation" of situations and behaviors ("... not only do events affect the behavior of organisms, but the organism is also an active agent influencing environmental events"; Endler & Magnusson, 1976, p. 969) and have to be studied with process analysis instead of analysis-of-variance techniques that "are not appropriate techniques to study dynamic interaction" (Edwards & Endler, 1983, p. 226).

According to Ekehammar (1974), one major reason for the reemergence of the interactional perspective in the 1970's after similar proposals in the 1920's (Kantor, 1924) and 1930's (Lewin, 1935; Murray, 1938) has been that appropriate statistical techniques were not available previously. However, the discussion about appropriate techniques has not been settled yet (cf. Kahle, 1979).

In sum, the main assumptions of an interactional theory of behavior (Endler & Magnusson, 1976) are:

- Actual behavior is a function of a continuous process or multidirectional interaction between the person and the situation;
- the person is an intentional active agent in this process;
- cognitive factors are the essential determinants of behavior;
- the psychological meaning of the situation (i.e., the functional situation) is the important situational aspect in determining behavior.

The interactional just as the trait approach postulates consistency of behavior, albeit of a different kind which Magnusson (1976) termed "coherence". In accordance with the interactional emphasis on the dynamics of behavior, coherence assumes that a person's *pattern* of stable and changing behavior across a wide variety of situations is consistent and characteristic for the individual.

The hotly debated controversy about which of the positions described above would constitute the most reasonable approach to study personality has given way to a more balanced view acknowledging the theoretical relevance and heuristic utility of all of the approaches (McFall & McDonel, 1986). As has been noted in the section describing the trait approach, dispositional constructs are more and more employed in addition to, and not only in contrast to, situational or interactional explanations. Thus it seems safe to conclude (Kenrick & Funder, 1988) that

- traits influence behavior only in particular situations,
- a person's traits can lead to a change of a situation,
- persons with different traits are likely to choose different situations,
- traits can change with chronic exposure to certain situations, and
- traits are more easily expressed in some situations than in others.

A more balanced view such as this would not likely have emerged had the various approaches to personality not addressed different questions and contributed a unique share in the explanation of behavior.

A consideration of the assessment models underlying the different conceptions of consistency in the approaches to personality discussed above underscores that, indeed, they pursue different questions:

The *nomothetic individual-differences trait approach* follows Assessment Model 1. It assumes that the locus of the construct "personality" is between subjects. Relative consistency refers to the generalizability of construct identification (i.e., subject rank order) across different units of measurement, that is, situations (recall the discussion on generalizability in Chapter 1.5).

The *idiographic/morphogenic approach* follows Assessment Model 4 where the locus of the construct is between variables making it possible to characterize each person by his or her own profile of behavioral variables. In psychophysiology, this assessment model has been used to study "individual-specific responses". Consistency refers again to the generalizability of construct identification (i.e., the particular variable profile) across different units of assessment, that is, situations.

The *situationist process approach* follows Assessment Model 2. Situations are the locus of the construct that is invoked to explain regularities in behavior. Although it has not been discussed in the literature, this situationist approach too involves a consistency postulate: The construct should be generalizable across different subjects, which are the units of assessment in this assessment model; therefore, it can also be termed *"nomothetic" situation approach*.

Similar to the mutually exclusive conceptions of the trait and the idiographic models (with the former postulating a common descriptor basis in terms of behavior variables for all persons and the latter a unique descriptor basis for each person), there also exists an "idiographic" counterpart to the "nomothetic" situationist approach just described. Interestingly, this *"idiographic" situation approach* has not been explicitly dealt with in the personality literature. Assessment Model 5 defines such an "idiographic" situation approach by placing the locus of the construct between variables: each situation may be characterized by its specific profile of matching behavioral variables. As mentioned in Chapter 1.5, psychophysiology has studied this assessment model under the term "situation-specific responses". Consistency refers to the generalizability of the construct identification (i.e., equivalences of situations to classes of behaviors) across different persons.

The *interactionist approach* to personality follows Assessment Model 7 which specifies that the locus of the construct "personality" is to be found in the combination of subjects and conditions. As has been noted in Chapter 1.5, generalizability of construct identification is not easily integrated into this assessment model, because it is exactly a person's pattern of stable and *changing* behavior, that is, the individual's situational adaptability and inconstancy that is characteristic for coherence. But what is the criterion for judging whether a person's behavior is coherent or not? In the same way as a rigid, nonadaptive and "stable" behavior can be said to be indicative of maladjustment and psychopathology (Mischel, 1984), so can also a highly unstable behavior be a bizarre sign of maladjustment. It remains to be demonstrated that "coherence" is more than a fashionable verbal label and that it can serve as a criterion for the interactional position with the same rigor and power as the criterion of consistency in the trait approach. A prime criterion for coherence is the stability of "the pattern of stable and changing behavior" within a person. But given the emphasis of the interactional approach on the functional situation and the related conviction that there will never be two identical (functional) situations (recall the Buddhist wisdom that you will never take your bath twice in the same river), the stability of behavioral patterns will be difficult or impossible to study. For the same reason, observing the pattern of behavior in another sample of the "same" situations and obtaining the degree of pattern similarity with the first sample runs into the same problem. However, a necessary although not sufficient condition for coherence can be tested: the degree of dissimilarity of different persons' behavior patterns across situations.

Finally, the two remaining Assessment Models 3 and 6 cover cases that have been briefly mentioned in the section about the traitist approach. Both are concerned with the same generalizability problem: Does the construct identification hold across different behavioral variables? Assessment Model 3 defines the locus of the construct between situations with equivalence classes of subjects being related to each one construct. This model is the basis for the *moderator variable approach* which characteristically leads to subgroups of persons showing a particular trait consistently in particular situations (Bem & Allen, 1974). Assessment Model 6 states that the locus of the construct is between subjects with equivalence classes of situations being related to each one construct (trait). *Allport's* (1937, 1961) *position* has been noted (see Chapter 1.5) to be related to this assessment model. According to Allport, individual differences give rise to common traits which function to form equivalence classes of situations.

In conclusion, a review in the context of the underlying constructs and assessment models of the different conceptions of consistency shows that they refer to different questions. Several of these questions can coexist, others are contradictory. *Contradictory questions* are those referring to assessment models with the same units of assessment, that is, the pure trait (Model 1) versus the idiographic (Model 4) approach, the "nomothetic" situationist (Model 2) versus the "idiographic" situationist (Model 5) approach, and the moderator (Model 3) versus Allport's (Model 6) approach. *Coexisting questions* are those that refer to assessment models with the same homogeneity constraints, that is,

- the trait, the situationist, and the interactionist approach (Models 1, 2, and 7),
- the moderator, the idiographic, and the conditions x variables interaction approach (Models 3, 4, and 8), and
- the "idiographic" situationist, Allport's, and the variable x subjects interaction approach (Models 5, 6, and 9).

The three terms within each set of assessment models each correspond to a parameter in the structural equation of a two-factorial analysis of variance, that is, two main effects and the interaction effect, all three of which are potential contributors to the variance of the dependent variable. To quote Bowers (1977):

> ... consistency and specificity are not exclusive features of personality and behavior but find their respective places in an emerging pattern of person-environment interchanges. (Bowers, 1977, p. 74.)

The coexistence of seemingly contradictory concepts is thought to be possible because specificity and consistency refer to different levels of organismic organization:

> ... the consistency of *personality* is often juxtaposed with and discredited by references to the situational specificity of *behavior*. (Bowers, 1977, p. 74; italics by the author.)

This view implies that there is no single answer to the question, "What determines behavior; traits, situations, or their interaction?". Instead of seeking all-purpose answers to a global question, it might be more fruitful to acknowledge that three different constructs, each with its own assessment model, are involved. The different constructs represent different points of view, each having its own research question, criterion of utility, and way of construing human behavior. But it is also true that these points of view are related to one another because they refer to the same explanandum, human behavior. Furthermore, it has been suggested above that there are three sets of such triplets of constructs, each referring to different research perspectives (the homogeneity constraints in the assessment models), which aim at finding groups of variables, groups of persons, and groups of situations that constitute homogeneous indicators of the construct in question.

The discussion of different notions in personality psychology about the determinants of behavior has in this chapter evolved from reproducing these notions and their seeming disparateness to their integration into the conceptual framework of assessment models. This integration has the merit of providing conceptual tools by which the different notions can be analyzed, compared, and meaningfully related to one another. It can be concluded that the adoption of the assessment model framework into personality psychology may provide a conceptual integration of a highly controversial field. This result encourages using the assessment model framework also for the task at hand: the study of differential psychophysiology.

3 Stimulus-Response Mediation in Psychophysiology

3.1 A Model of Stimulus-Response Mediation in Psychophysiology

In the preceding chapter I have discussed various notions of the "situation" and of determinants of behavior as discussed in personality psychology. The task of this chapter will be to apply the previous discussion to the psychophysiological domain and to offer a working model of stimulus-response mediation from which the main concepts to be used later on in this book can be inferred.

The activity of the autonomic nervous system is part of the efferent processes preparing the organism for and subserving its behavior. With reference to Pribram and McGuiness (1975), but extending their notion to include both central as well as peripheral (somatic, autonomic, and hormonal) systems, the totality of efferent processes will be called *activation*.[5] Therefore, subsequent to the general discussion of determinants of behavior in the preceding chapter, activation can be said to reflect both stimulus and person characteristics, in particular

- effects of certain stimulus properties, for example, stimulus intensity (i.e., effects of the physico-biological situation),
- effects of a stimulus analysis including its meaning and significance for the person at a particular time (i.e., effects of the functional situation), and
- effects of motivational and cognitive person variables, such as drives, specific kinds of motivation, plans, goals, outcome expectancies and their subjective value, and the individual competencies (Mischel, 1973), which combine with the physico-biological and the functional situation to bring forth the effective stimulus.

---

[5] Activation processes can also influence afferent processes, but these processes are not of concern here.

It is hypothesized that the effective stimulus leads to the selection of a response program which differentially activates the efferent response channels (qualitative aspect) and allocates a certain amount of "energy" to each response channel (intensity aspect). This specific allocation of "energy" will be called the effective stimulus of a particular response channel. In sum, the effective stimulus shapes the specific profile of physiological responses, the indicators of activation.

These three kinds of influences have long been distinguished in theoretical accounts on activation. Fiske and Maddi (1961), for example, termed the momentary contribution to the activation level of an organism the *impact* of a stimulus. According to these authors, three factors contribute to the impact of a stimulus (which can be an external or internal event).

- the intensity of a stimulus, that is, the physical energy delivered by it (a property of the physico-biological situation)
- the meaningfulness of a stimulus (the functional situation), which is closely related to Hebb's cue function (Hebb, 1955), and
- variation (another aspect of the functional situation) with regard to both the extent of stimulus change and the preceding stimulus sequence (i.e., its unexpectedness). Both aspects of variation are closely related to Sokolov's neuronal model which attempts to explain the physiological orienting response (Sokolov, 1960) and Berlyne's collative properties of stimulus patterns, such as novelty, surprisingness, complexity, ambiguity, vagueness, and puzzlingness (Berlyne, 1968).

The patterning of physiological responses has long been described in psychophysiology (see Chapter 4) although such response patterns have often been referred to as indicators for all kinds of psychological constructs (e.g., emotion, attention, orienting, personality characteristics), but these response patterns have to a much lesser extent been understood as behavior (see Chapter 3.2 for a brief discussion of B.T. Engel's recent "Essay on the circulation as behavior"). To view activation as behavior implies that the specific response profiles observed are a consequence of some sort of response selection.

The primary task of this chapter is to cast the three influences on activation in a model. This formalization shows much more clearly than text alone the key methodological concepts necessary for a differential psychophysiology: The five notions of a situation (i.e., the physico-biological, the canonical, the functional, the effective, and the modal situation), person characteristics, as well as *individual*, *situational*, and *motivational response specificity* (which includes *situational individual* and *individual situational response specificity*, see below).

To begin with, activation has been described as being influenced by (at least) three factors: the physico-biological situation (SP), the functional situation (SF), and motivational and cognitive person variables (PV). More specifically, these three influences have an important effect upon the effective stimulus (SE) which actually triggers the efferent activation processes.

First, it is well known that some properties of a stimulus *j*, in particular its physically describable intensity, can have a direct influence on activation (e.g.,

Davis, Buchwald, & Frankmann, 1955; Turpin, 1986) without any apparent intervening stimulus evaluation or determination of subjective stimulus significance, as is most clearly demonstrated in the withdrawal reflexes immediately following painfully intense stimuli. However, stimulus properties have to be sensed at the receptor sites and transmitted to (unspecific and specific sensory) brain areas before a response of the central nervous system can be elicited. Of course the sensitivity of sensory systems, f, differs between persons and with it the effect of a situation j's (S_j) stimulus properties on the individual central nervous system. Thus, the physico-biological situation can be described as

$$SP_{ij} = f_i(S_j)\,. \tag{1}$$

In terms of information-processing theory, these "direct" effects of stimulus properties on the efferent systems follow the mode of "automatic processing" (Shiffrin & Schneider, 1977). Automatic processing relies upon relatively permanent innate (reflexive) or automatized connections between SP and SE acquired through practice.

Second, the functional situation, SF, by definition is independent of physical stimulus properties. For example, a low-intensive stimulus might be highly significant for one but not necessarily for another person. It should be noted that averaging the functional situation across persons yields the canonical situation,

$$SC_j = SF_{.j}\,, \tag{2}$$

where a point denotes the arithmetic mean across the cases represented by the substituted index. In terms of information-processing theory, these kinds of influences on the efferent systems stem from "controlled processing" (Shiffrin & Schneider, 1977). The controlled processing mode is elicited when some pre-attentive processes (Kahneman, 1973; Öhman, 1979) "conclude" that neither it is known from previous experience how to cope with the demands of the momentary situation (there is no available automatized response in working memory) nor it is safe to ignore them.

Third, motivational and cognitive person variables are characteristics of persons (recall the notion of traits in recent accounts of trait psychology as more or less stable cognitive features) and thus carry only the person index i, PV_i.

Figure 1 gives an overview of the stimulus-response mediation model. The formal presentation of this model begins with a characterization of the effective stimulus $SE_{ij(i)m}$ for the response channel m:

$$SE_{ij(i)m} = g_{ij(i)m}[SP_{ij}, SF_{ij}, PV_i]. \tag{3}$$

The function $g_{ij(i)m}$ represents the allocation of "energy" to the response channel m on the basis of the individually effective integration of situation properties SP, their evaluation SF, and person variables PV. Note the index $j(i)$ attached in addition to the person index i and the response channel index m both to SE and the function g. The index $j(i)$ expresses the expectancy that given idiosyncratic stimulus evaluations and individually shaped person variables, one and the same

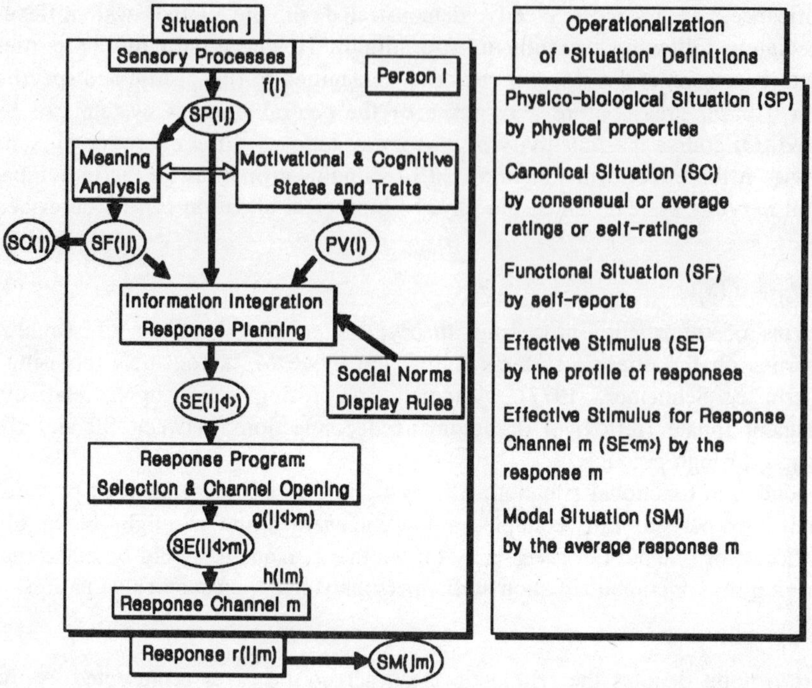

Figure 1. A model of situation-response mediation with particular emphasis on different definitions of "the situation" and ways of operationalization. PV = Person variables.

situation *j* within different individuals may lead to an activation of quite different response programs. A simple example for this notion is the response to a conditioned stimulus in classical conditioning: Someone who has not been exposed to the conditioning procedure will respond decisively differently to the same stimulus compared to a person who has been conditioned.

The observed physiological response *r* of channel *m* is proposed to be a function of the effective stimulus and the individual "transfer function" h_{im} which accounts for the anatomical and physiological individuality of response channel characteristics (Stemmler, 1987a),

$$r_{ijm} = h_{im}(SE_{ij(i)m}) \,. \tag{4}$$

It is interesting to introduce the transition from the purely idiographic notion of the effective stimulus in Equations 3 and 4 to a nomothetic one. Denoting the person average of the effective stimuli under situation *j* as $SE_{.j(.)m}$ and the deviation of the individual from that average effective stimulus as $SE_{i(j*i)m}$, the relationship

$$SE_{ij(i)m} = SE_{.j(.)m} + SE_{i(j*i)m} \tag{5}$$

holds. Note that the average of the individual deviations is zero,

$$SE_{.(j*.)k} = 0 . \tag{6}$$

Interestingly, Equation 5 translates into two well-known psychophysiological principles.

First, the average effective stimulus under situation j (the first expression on the right of Equation 5) is closely related to the concept of *situational response specificity* which postulates that different situations first evoke specific response programs, then specific effective stimuli for response channels, and finally specific observed response profiles. The average effective stimulus under situation j is thus the building block for the definition of situational response specificity. It should also be noted that the average effective stimulus under situation j "elicits" the average response which was defined above as the modal situation,

$$SM_{jm} = r_{.jm} . \tag{7}$$

Second, the deviation of individual i's effective stimulus under situation j from the average (the second expression on the right of Equation 5) is the building block of *individual situational response specificity* which postulates that there are stable individual deviations from the average response.

Substituting these interpretative terms into Equation 5 yields

$$SE_{ij(i)m} = SSR(SE)_j + ISSR(SE)_{ij} , \tag{8}$$

where SSR(SE) stands for "situational response specificity at the level of SE" and ISSR(SE) for "individual situational response specificity at the level of SE".

Whereas Equation 5 explained the individual effective stimulus in terms of situation j's average effective stimulus (across persons), the following Equation 9 explains the individual effective stimulus in terms of person i's average effective stimulus (across situations), $SE_{i.(i)m}$. This individual average is the building block of *individual response specificity at the level of SE.*

$$SE_{ij(i)m} = SE_{i.(i)m} + SE_{i(j\#i)m} , \tag{9}$$

where the second term on the right side expresses the deviation of person i's effective stimulus under situation j from his or her average effective stimulus. It should be noted that the situation average of these deviations is zero,

$$SE_{i(.\#i)m} = 0 . \tag{10}$$

If these deviations are stable for repeated exposures to situation j, the terms $SE_{i(j\#i)m}$ constitute the building blocks of *situational individual response specificity*. Substituting the interpretive terms into Equation 9 gives

$$SE_{ij(i)m} = ISR(SE)_i + SISR(SE)_{ij} , \tag{11}$$

where ISR(SE) stands for "individual response specificity at the level of SE", and SISR(SE) for "situational individual response specificity at the level of SE". Combining Equations 5 and 9 gives

$$SE_{ij(i)m} = SE_{.j(.)m} + SE_{i(j*i)m} = SE_{i.(i)m} + SE_{i(j\#i)m} \,, \tag{12}$$

which upon substitution of interpretive terms yields

$$SE_{ij(i)m} = SSR(SE)_j + ISSR(SE)_{ij} = ISR(SE)_i + SISR(SE)_{ij} \,. \tag{13}$$

The importance of Equations 8 and 11 is that they elucidate the dual perspective from which the individual effective stimulus under situation j can be conceptualized; on the one hand, from a nomological perspective taking the effective stimulus under situation j averaged across persons (i.e., the SSR(SE)) as the point of reference, and on the other hand, from an idiographic perspective using the individual effective stimulus of person i averaged across situations (i.e., the ISR(SE)) as the point of reference. Parenthetically, the relationships given in Equations 8 and 11 lead to different assessment models. Equation 8 implies a combination of Assessment Models 1 and 7 and Equation 11 a combination of Assessment Models 2 and 7. In addition, Equation 13 points to the coexistence of these perspectives, as had already been noted at the end of Chapter 2.2 (where it was stated that Assessment Models 1, 2, and 7 coexist).

To sum up, given a model of stimulus-response mediation formulated on the level of the individual person, different aspects of the effective stimulus, which "energizes" a response channel, can be distinguished. Four of these aspects have been identified to be the building blocks of situational, individual, individual situational, and situational individual specificity in terms of the effective stimulus. Such specificities are the empirical basis of the construct construction stage. It has also been shown (see Equation 13) that the four kinds of specificity are systematically related. The introduction of the *specificity concept at the level of the effective stimulus SE* suggests a distinction from the usually obtained *specificity effects at the level of the observed responses r* (see Chapter 6.2 for a further discussion of this topic).

3.2 Notions of Stimulus-Response Mediation in Psychophysiology

3.2.1 Comparison of the proposed with other stimulus response models

In this section I shall further comment upon the situation-response mediation model by comparing it with other such models.

Comparison with nonmediational stimulus-response (S-R) models. A nonmediational S-R model would posit that the state of the organism or any independent agency within the organism does not alter or interfere with the (primarily mechanistically conceived) throughput of stimuli to the response produced. O'Connor (1981) has listed the following five objections against a nonmediational S-R model:

- The lack of stimulus constancy. One stimulus will in some but not in other contexts elicit the same response; a different stimulus can sometimes evoke the same response.
- Responses may occur in the absence of a stimulus. For example, conditioned responses are often self-activated by learned expectancies.
- Variation of responses are seen over repeated trials of the same experimental condition.
- There is response fractionation of physiological response systems, that is, there must be some contribution of the organism leading to the selection of a particular response program. Note that if this contribution is postulated to be passive, as in the case of a conditioned stimulus-response program linkage, response fractionation would not constitute an argument against nonmediational S-R models.
- Individual differences in response would also argue against a nonmediational S-R model if, similar to the previous point, these individual differences are not explainable by "passive mechanisms", such as response channel constants and sensitivities.

The stimulus-response mediation model proposed (see Figure 1) has no difficulty in accounting for the problems of a nonmediational model: With the inclusion of the functional situation (based on meaning analysis or individual stimulus-response contingencies) and motivational and cognitive person variables, as well as the inclusion of an instance for response planning and program selection, such problems do not arise.

Comparison with passive mediational S-R models. A passive mediational S-R model accepts mediational constructs such as "need", "drive" or "arousal" but assigns them no independent function other than a very general physiologically based interference with S-R throughput. This conception leaves the primacy of the external stimulus and its function as a cause of the response (the effect) maintained. O'Connor (1981) raises two objections against this passive mediation model:

- The supposition of passive mediators can become tautological because there is no indication of their operation other than the alleged effects they have on the response.
- Passive mediation models do not offer any solution for the inconstancy effects in psychophysiological recordings noted above, and if they do, then at the expense of "a great many post hoc suppositions which destroy the very parsimonious merit of the construct and reflect its empirical unsoundness as a single predictor" (O'Connor, 1981, p. 122).

However, these objections are also open to criticism. The first objection can be refuted with recourse to the status of passive mediators as constructs. It is true that with just one response variable a construct cannot be validated and the noted danger of a circular argument is justified. But with more, and often fractionated, responses the techniques of construct validation can be invoked without the risk of tautological reasoning. The second objection is actually not directed against the passive mediation model but against some of its uses: The post hoc supposition of functional relationships between a mediator and a stimulus or a response effect (e.g., the inverted-U function between "arousal" and task performance) clearly is scientifically unsound if done post hoc. Conceiving of, for example, arousal as a unitary entity and hence a single predictor does also not follow from the passive mediation model but is a decision on the part of the investigator. However, in contrast to an active mediation model, a passive mediation model does not explain "qualitative" differences in responses to one and the same situation such as when someone deliberately alters the display rules of facial expressions. The stimulus-response mediation model in Figure 1 clearly allows for a non-passive mediation primarily because the effective stimulus for the effector systems is conceived of as the endproduct of sensory processes, meaning analyses, and motivational and cognitive person variables. The effective stimulus is thus distinctly different from the situation impinging upon the organism.

Comparison with trait, situationist, and interactionist models. These models emanate from the discussion in personality psychology (see Chapter 2.2). The "pure" trait model corresponds to a view postulating an exclusive or a predominant influence of person variables on the effector systems (the PV-pathway in Figure 1). The "pure" situationist model has already been commented upon in the earlier description of nonmediational models; it corresponds to ascribing the sole importance for the effector systems' activation to the physico-biological situation (the SP-pathway in Figure 1). The "relaxed" trait model takes both sources of influence into account. The interactionist model adds to these the functional stimulus (the SP-pathway in Figure 1); differences between persons with respect to the functional stimulus contribute to the person x situation interaction of observed responses. Thus, the stimulus-response mediation model of Figure 1 incorporates these behavior mediation models of personality psychology.

Some comments are in order with regard to the person x situation interaction notion. This notion has been criticized on various grounds (see below). It will be argued that these criticisms are likely to misrepresent the notion of "interaction". In order to advance my arguments against these criticisms, I have to point out the distinction between a functional model such as the one proposed in Equations 2 or 3 and a statistical model such as the one in Equation 7. The functional model specifies various system stages that are hypothesized to be important in the generation of the observed response but that often are not directly accessible to measurement. The statistical model partitions the observed response variance into components due to the parameters of the structural equation which represent sources of variance but not necessarily specific system stages. For example, on the basis of the stimulus-response mediation model of Figure 1, it has been shown above (see Equation 13) that the person x situation interaction term arises from two sources, (1) from idiosyncratic contributions to the effective stimulus (the SISR terms) to be traced back to the individual functional situation not shared by other persons and (2) from individual response channel sensitivities. Other mediation models might, of course, specify different likely contributors to an interaction term found in the observed responses.

The notion of person x situation interaction, when equated with the analysis of variance interaction term, has often been criticized for being "mechanistic". The distinction between a "mechanistic" person x situation interaction (i.e., arising from the experimentally controlled exposition to situations) and a "transactionally" interpreted interaction (i.e., arising from persons' actively selecting the situations they are exposed to), as put forward by Olweus (1977), is a distinction between two functional models. The functional model implicit in the transactional interpretation seems to include a latent variable responsible for the initiation of behaviors in accordance with individual goals and life plans that might direct the probability of exposure to freely selectable situations. (Such a latent variable is incorporated in Figure 1 as the set of motivational and cognitive person variables.) In terms of mediation models utilized above, the "mechanistic functional model" is a passive mediation model whereas the "transactional functional model" is an active one. But as a "mechanistic" so does also a "transactional" functional model lead to the observation of an interaction effect if only all of the situations actually selected by persons could enter into the statistical design.[6]

Another criticism of the notion of person x situation interaction has been advanced by Clarke and Hoyle (1988). These authors make the point that behavior should not be explained by reference to both situational and psychological factors (which leads to the notion of an interaction between persons and situations), but that situation-behavior relations should be explained by reference to psychological processes. The merit of this criticism is that it urges investigators in the personality field to specify a functional model of person-behavior relations (Figure 1 is an example). Actually, Clarke and Hoyle's proposal leads to a redefinition of how research in this field should be performed: Psychological factors should take the role of independent variables and situation-behavior relations that of dependent ones. (O'Connor, 1981, in his proposal of an "intentional paradigm" arrives at the same conclusion.) But again, if persons' psychological factors lead to different situation-behavior relations, then within a statistical model a nonnegligible person x situation interaction effect in terms of the observed behaviors will be obtained.

---

[6] In such a statistical design, situations are nested within persons. As usual, person x situation interactions can only be derived under replications.

Bandura (1978) criticized the notion of person x situation interaction as reflecting a unidirectional causation. He proposed instead a social-learning view of interaction, the principle of "reciprocal determinism", where "behavior, internal personal factors, and environmental influences all operate as interlocking determinants of each other" (p. 346). Phillips and Orton (1983) have conclusively argued that the principle of reciprocal determinism does not invoke a new type of causality different from the unidirectional one. What Bandura actually was pointing at was the often encountered neglect to take the *history* of interactions between a person and the environment into consideration. Introducing the time perspective lets one recognize that previous behaviors and their effects may have altered motivational and cognitive person variables (in particular, Bandura's self-regulatory processes), which at a later time entails different selections of situations, and so forth. But adding the time perspective does not alter the primary conception of individual-specific psychologically and physiologically describable components within the organismic system which leads to the observation of person x situation interactions.

3.2.2 Stimulus-response mediation in selected psychophysiological research programs

There is abundant evidence in psychophysiology that physiological responses are modifiable or, in some instances, even determined by subjective evaluations, the individual history of response contingencies, and motivational and cognitive person variables. This evidence underscores the importance of considering both the functional situation and person variables as effective contributors to the patterning of physiological responses. Evidently, it justifies the program of *psycho-physiology*, although it is to a large extent an open question whether the psychological should explain the physiological or, conversely, the physiological the psychological realm. It might be recalled from Chapter 1.3.1 that the stance taken here is to favor the latter strategy because psychological explanations cannot be causal with respect to physiological and behavioral explananda rendering a biopsychological program a preferable and viable alternative. The biopsychological program treats psychological phenomena as neurophysiological, albeit unknown, processes and hence as constructs.

The importance of considering the functional situation and person variables when interpreting physiological responses will be illustrated with reference to some selected research programs that had a considerable impact upon psychophysiology. For example, John Lacey (1962), when discussing psychophysiological approaches to the evaluation of psychotherapeutic process and outcome, concluded on the basis of his extended research on psychophysiological response patterning that the subjectively perceived situation and a general, intersubjectively valid characterization of a situation (e.g., its "threat-content") both contribute to the individual autonomic response. The following quotation also expresses Lacey's conclusion not to regard autonomic responses to be simple indicators of the one or the other factor:

> We cannot use the autonomic response in specific situations as an indicator of *the* 'threat-content' or 'arousal value' of that specific stimulus, because we are not yet in a position to measure the 'threat-content' of the total situation, and the interaction between patient and examiner. The autonomic response reflects all these aspects; so far we are not able to disentangle the effects. If we attempt to set up situations with 'maximal threat-value,' to test the limit of adaptation of the organism, we would have to know how the subject perceived the situation, and this would require purely psychological and phenomenological observation. In this sense, autonomic responses cannot be used as a convenient and objective *substitute* for other purely psychological observations. (Lacey, 1962, p. 176, author's emphases.)

If the effective stimulus for the efferent systems is influenced by several sources which are difficult to disentangle in the individual person and which, in addition, could be nearly independent across persons, both the interpretation of individual autonomic responses in one particular situation and an individual differences approach to the solution of this problem are likely to face major obstacles (more on this in Chapter 4.3).

In contrast to Lacey's approach emphasizing profiles of physiological responses, much work has been devoted to the study of the "significance" of stimuli as demonstrated in single physiological variables. For example, electrodermal recovery time has been repeatedly shown to "provide unique information regarding behavioral significance of a stimulus" (Janes, 1982, p. 129). Electromyograms have been proposed to reflect "the extent and affectivity of ongoing information processing" (Cacioppo & Petty, 1981, p. 453). Tonic heart rate has been analyzed with regard to its "motivational significance" arising from such factors as action instigation, anticipation, initiation of responses, and the presence of incentives (Elliott, 1969). Fowles (1980) later argued that these and other factors, such as active coping (Obrist, 1976), "could all be seen as reflecting the influence of a central appetitive motivational state" (Fowles, Fisher, & Tranel, 1982, p. 506; see also Jennings, 1986). The person variable of engagement-involvement has been emphasized as a moderator of physiological responses:

> All told we believe the level of newly or recently activated and intensely committed engagement-involvement behavior was central in demonstrating relationships between transactional behavior and the level of cardiovascular or psychoendocrine responses. (Singer, 1974, p. 9.)

Mason (1971) objected to Selye's notion of a general adaptive or non-specific endocrine response to many different noxious stimuli and instead proposed that this response reflected a specific, psychological factor common to the various unpleasant situations. Weiner (1989), in his recent essay on "The dynamics of the organism: Implications of recent biological thought for psychosomatic theory and research", also concludes that "students of animal (...) and human behavior agree that the responses to an environmental signal or contingency depends [sic!] on its interpretation" (p. 620). Weiner quotes Levins and Lewontin:

> As Levins and Lewontin ({1985}, p. 42) point out, the most advantageous response to a signal does not depend on ... [its] ... physical form but on its value as a predictor or correlate.' Different environments or contexts '... require different responses.' Conversely, different environments may require the same behavioral response. (Weiner, 1989, p. 620.)

The literature on event-related brain potentials (ERPs) also is replete with discussions about the identification of psychological factors that might be translated into certain parameters of the ERP, such as the amplitude of the P300 wave or the contingent negative variation. Donchin (1979) sketches this research program much in line with my previous outline (see Chapter 1.2) of biopsychology and its underlying emergentist identity hypothesis of mind-body relations:

> They [neural elements] happen to have a property of being simultaneously activated at certain critical points in the information-processing activity of the cortex. We try to map the receptive field of this cell population, in what might be called 'cognitive space.' This, of course, is a rather nebulous concept and not as well defined as visual space. Cognitive space consists *inter alia* of the decisions, expectations, plans, strategies, associations and memories that we can manipulate in the experimental psychology laboratory. We engage in systematic exploration of this space while observing the behavior of the ERP component. (Donchin, 1979, p. 36; author's italics.)

Similarly, Rösler (1983a) makes the case that a strictly behavioristic approach (i.e., one that disregards factors other than the physico-biological situation, in particular factors of the functional situation) is not sufficient but that instead a cognitive theory of endogeneous ERPs is needed. Johnson (1986) proposes a "triarchic model of P300 amplitude" which specifies three dimensions that influence P300 amplitude:

- The first dimension is information transmission, that is, the extent to which the full amount of stimulus information is transmitted to the subject. Loss of information is attributed to two variables, (1) loss due to equivocation which "describes the amount of information loss that occurs during the presentation of a stimulus as a result of the subject's a posteriori uncertainty about having correctly perceived an event" (Johnson, 1986, p. 374) and (2) loss due to inattention of the subject, produced, for example, by the experimental instructions to "attend" vs. "ignore" a stimulus.
- The second dimension is subjective probability, that is, the unexpectedness of the stimulus, or the amount of uncertainty reduced by it. Two experimental variables have been found to produce variations in subjective probability, (1) the a priori probability of a stimulus, and (2) sequential expectancies developed over a number of trials. Within the triarchic model, this dimension is one of two branches (the second will be described next) emanating from the information transmission processing stage. The subjective probability processing stage is part of an automatic processing mode. This is the first branch of information processing to influence P300 amplitude.
- The third dimension is stimulus meaning, that is, the significance of an event. Experimental variables of this dimension include task and stimulus

complexity, stimulus value, task demand and difficulty, intentional engagement, or resource allocation. Stimulus meaning is a processing stage within the second branch between the information transmission stage and the generation of P300 amplitude. This branch belongs to the controlled processing mode.

A model of information processing such as Johnson's triarchic model of P300 provokes the question of how it might be related to the stimulus-response (S-R) mediation model proposed in the previous section. Interestingly, although these models have been developed from independent sources of evidence, there is a striking similarity between them. First, the triarchic model overlaps with the S-R mediation model in the part prior to the "response program selection and channel opening" stage (ignoring, however, the person-variable branch; see Figure 1). This limitation of the triarchic model seems justified when it is recalled that the S-R mediation model is primarily concerned with somatic and autonomic response variables, whereas the triarchic model's dependent response variable is a specific parameter of brain activity, which is much closer to the various hypothetical brain processing stages than the autonomic response variables. Second, within this common part the models exhibit the same features: The information transmission stage in the triarchic model corresponds to the function f_i in the S-R mediation model; the subjective probability stage of the automatic processing mode corresponds to the physico-biological situation SP; lastly, the stimulus meaning stage of the controlled processing mode corresponds to the functional situation SF. Given the proposed determinants of P300 amplitude, it might be tentatively regarded as an operationalization of the "information integration" stage in the S-R mediation model.

Another research program that considers the functional, besides the physico-biological, situation important when interpreting physiological responses is the research on the orienting response (OR). Sokolov proposed, in a sequence of contributions (Sokolov, 1960; Sokolov, 1963; Sokolov, 1966), a number of different models of OR elicitation. First, Sokolov postulated a neuronal match-mismatch model. This model states that the physical properties of stimuli are neuronally encoded and that incoming stimuli are compared with the neuronal trace of the previous stimulus; in case of a mismatch an OR would be elicited. However, empirical data suggested that a mismatch between *actual* and *expected* stimulus, or novelty, and not between their physical properties is a critical feature of OR elicitation. Eventually, Sokolov formulated an entropy model where the information carried by a stimulus reduces the uncertainty concerning the actual event. Thus, it was no longer a physical stimulus property but a cognitive stimulus evaluation on the part of the individual subject that came to play the role of the OR elicitor. However, other authors (see Bernstein, 1979; Maltzman, 1979; Velden, 1978) postulated a motivational factor such as the importance, relevance, or significance of a stimulus as the critical feature. Clearly, this motivational factor relates to the functional situation:

> Put most simply, any stimulus is significant to the extent that its information can serve a useful, valued function for the observer. Such useful purpose may relate to 'responses' the individual anticipates may be required of him, but may also relate to his curiosity, his fantasies, interests or needs, whether positive or negative, or to any function deemed pertinent by him. (Bernstein, 1979, p. 269.)

O'Gorman (1979), however, expressed doubts whether the traditional OR concept (i.e., the OR is a detector of stimulus-induced novelty) would indeed be in need of including subjectively-based stimulus evaluations such as its significance instead of referring only to objectively defined stimulus properties. Similarly, Stephenson and Siddle (1983) conclude:

> In summary, the significance hypothesis asserts that 'significant' stimuli, or those aspects of a stimulus which provide information about other stimuli or response requirements ... are more effective in eliciting ORs than 'non-significant' stimuli. As already noted, there is a substantial body of evidence to support this contention, and clearly, any comprehensive theory of the OR must be able to account for these data ... More important, however, is the assertion that the relationship between stimulus change and stimulus significance in [sic!] multiplicative such that significance is a *necessary* factor for OR elicitation. The evidence does not appear to provide whole-hearted support for this assertion unless the tautology that a change stimulus is significant if it evokes a response is accepted. (Stephenson & Siddle, 1983, p. 212; authors' italics.)

This statement clearly shows the reluctance of many investigators to embrace the concept of a functional situation primarily because of the obvious problems of its operationalization. Self-reports of stimulus significance often do not seem to correspond to the magnitude of physiological responses, nor does a theory exist that would specify a mechanism relating the two domains. To employ physiological responses that are used to signify both the construct under study (e.g., electrodermal activity signifying the OR) and stimulus significance is clearly circular. However, it should be noted that it is not the concept of stimulus significance, or more generally, of the functional situation per se which fuels the aforementioned concerns, but how to assess this concept independently.

One way to cope with this problem is to rely on the plausibility that experimental procedures can produce variations in stimulus significance. But this approach only allows looking for response mean differences among treatment groups. Another solution is to use the previously stated conclusion (see Equation 13) that individual differences in the functional situation contribute to the person x situation (experimental condition) interaction effect. But as has been emphasized in the previous section, other sources of individual differences (e.g., differential sensory and efferent channel sensitivities) may also contribute to the interaction effect. Thus, the confound Lacey mentioned still persists. Adhering to an experimental approach to disentangle such confounds, Obrist underscored the scientific advantage of having no a priori preferable measure of one or the other neurophysiological process that is hypothesized to effect specific changes in observed physiological responses:

> But I shall only be convinced by research which moves away from demonstrations that our stimulus manipulations can influence cardiovascular processes, to work which demonstrates that cardiovascular activity provides unique information about

> the behavioral state of the organism. By unique, I don't mean that the magnitude of cardiovascular changes differentiates the intensity of an auditory stimulus. My ears can so inform me. What I mean by unique is information about the organism I can't obtain by asking it or observing it. (Obrist, 1976, p. 98.)

Besides the aspect of unique information carried by physiological measures, physiological responses may convey in certain experimental procedures psychologically relevant information - whether unique or not - in a less confounded way than, for example, a verbal report. Thus Lang, on the basis of his theory of emotion as an action set and his view that even the subovert processing of response information can generate efferent outflow, argues

> ... our research suggests that verbal report of arousal following an imagined emotional experience could be, depending on the context, an appraisal of the meaning of the content (e.g., 'If that happened to me, I'd be frightened') or, alternatively, it could be a pertinent comment on the emotional processing that preceded the report. It is obvious that our method of deciding between these possibilities depends on data obtained from bioelectric recording of the somatic muscles and the viscera ... Physiological recording provides a real-time analysis of emotional processing that does not require the subject to perform the confounding second task of observer. From our perspective, it is the most practical method currently available for assessing cognition in emotion. (Lang, 1984, p. 215.)

Radical behaviorist approaches to psychophysiology (see, e.g., Phillips, 1987a, b), it seems, are not in the danger of being trapped in the problem what physiological responses might "mean" and how inner states, such as the attribution of "significance", might mediate, moderate, or cause physiological responses. Radical behaviorism regards (internal) psychological states unnecessary for the prediction and control of behavior; also, radical behaviorism would not substitute hypothetical constructs for as yet unidentified physiological mechanisms (it will be recalled that such a substitution has been proposed earlier). Rather, physiological activity is seen as behavior and, as in the experimental analysis of overt somato-motor behavior, one would search for predictors or contingencies of its occurrence. As such, radical behaviorism rejects, as has also been proposed earlier, the notion that physiological activity be explained by the psychological domain. However, if the contingencies of observed physiological behavior are most conveniently summarized with reference to psychological terms (e.g., when different experimental procedures designed to increase the "significance" of a stimulus lead to the same physiological behavior) without giving the psychological term a reifying or causal status, the use of such terms as summary statements or labels for constructs would be justified. These psychological terms would gain their meaning from the experimental procedures used but certainly not from their connotations and surplus meanings. The empirical basis for the usage of these terms would broaden in the course of an inductive-deductive research program leading to convergences and discriminations as has been described in Chapter 1.4 on constructs.

The behavioristic approach to the issue of stimulus-response mediation has been well articulated by Engel (1986) in his essay on the circulation as behavior and his response to the open peer commentary. Engel argues that "the responses of the circulation in awake vertebrates are conditional and integral components of the behavior of the animal" (p. 285). By behavior, Engel means "the sum total of the organism's interactions with its environment" (p. 285). As somato-motor, so are also circulatory responses behavior because they

- can be reflexly elicited by adequate stimuli,
- will vary as a function of the associative characteristics of environmental cues (i.e., they can be classically conditioned),
- can vary as a function of their ability to modify the environment (i.e., they can be instrumentally conditioned).

These three propositions guarantee the plasticity of circulatory activity in response to varying environmental demands. First, if different reflexes are invoked by their respective adequate stimuli, they interact to produce that circulatory response which has the largest functional utility for the organism's survival. For example, baroreceptor reflexes that usually dampen cardiovascular activation following excitation are inhibited upon stimulation of the hypothalamic defense center. Responses of the circulation are thus modifiable by the environmental condition under which they are elicited. The responses are integrated and regulated in the central nervous system. It will be recalled that in the S-R mediation model the adequate stimulus for such reflex-like physiological behavior has been termed the physico-biological situation.

Second, stimuli that elicit circulatory reflexes "acquire secondary significance as a result of experience ... this significance determines the behavior the animal will emit" (Engel, 1986; p. 287). Thus, stimuli can acquire meanings as a result of experience. Consequently, with different individuals having had different experiences with and therefore different stimulus meanings "attached" to one and the same stimulus, physiological responses will accordingly vary interindividually. In the S-R mediation model, such response differences have been attributed to differences in "meaning analysis" giving rise to the functional situation.

Third, circulatory responses are not necessarily reactive: Sometimes they are not linked to concomitant somato-motor behaviors but can "be said to have a role in *purposive* behavior" (Engel, 1986; p. 289, italics mine). As, for example, in an anticipatory response, circulatory behavior can be emitted proactively. Within the behavioristic framework, proactive behavior is also elicited by, in this case, discriminative, stimuli; in this approach, there is, needless to say, no internal agency which would determine purpose.

Engel describes his behavioristic S-R model as follows. Behavior is initiated by genetically determined motor plans or programs. These plans can be modified in two ways:

- Inputs to the neural motor program centers are determined either genetically or by experience, that is, some inputs exist and some develop.

- Outputs from the neural motor program centers impinge on effectors and on other motor programs. These efferent projections also evolve through genetical predisposition and experience. The probability of occurrence of various motor plans is influenced by (1) antecedent events (contextual stimuli), (2) physiological states, and (3) stimuli that occur as a consequence of certain behaviors.

Such a deterministic notion of behavior is likely to provoke protest. One of the commentators of Engel's essay writes:

> Apart from urgent priorities of cardiovascular responses when survival is at stake ... what Engel calls contextual factors become dominant in determining what response pattern emerges. In man these factors consist of a complex of circumstances, timing, preconceptions, beliefs, social pressures, emotionally significant past experiences, self-doubts, aspirations, and personal values. These and other intangible but powerful forces, acting through the central neural circuitry, shape the response pattern and thereby provide a severe challenge to the investigator who would pose behavioral questions to man. (Wolf, 1986, p. 304.)

As noted already several times in this section, investigators do not seem to disagree upon the empirical fact (1) that individuals differ in their responses to the same situation or (2) that these differences are not explainable alone by error fluctuations. They disagree, however, whether these differences are at least in part a function of the individual-specific perceptions, learning histories, cognitions, attributions of significance, and so forth. Employing a different vocabulary obviously does not preclude describing the same experimental outcomes. Actually, adopting the stance proposed earlier (i.e., the psychological should not try to explain the physiological domain, but conversely, the physiological might accrue information about the psychological domain) would render the vocabulary used less important than when it is thought to reflect efficient causes.

In sum, there is clear evidence in the psychophysiological literature that peripheral physiological responses constitute one portion of the organism's efferent systems. There is a broad concensus among investigators that different input systems impinge upon the efferent structures. Distinctions among input systems almost always include

- a reflex-like, automatic processing input circuit, which should function relatively similarly within different individuals,
- an input circuit responsible for the generation of consistent group or individual differences in responses after different learning histories, manipulations of stimulus significance, or individual evaluations (although this latter point may easily run into a circular argument),
- an input circuit representing diverse influences on the efferent system that are not contingent upon external or internal stimuli but that arise from physiological, motivational, and cognitive states and from traits.

The S-R mediation model proposed above incorporates these distinctions among input systems and with this can contribute to a conceptual differentiation of different definitions of "the situation". The issue in dispute among investigators is the nature of the second input circuit mentioned above that gives rise to the functional situation. I have argued that this controversy at present cannot be rationally or empirically decided, given, on the one hand, potentially fallible non-physiological indicators of "individual meaning" such as verbal reports and, on the other hand, difficult, if at all obtainable accounts on individual histories of S-R contingencies. I propose instead that what cannot be unambiguously measured should be treated as a construct and studied with the methods appropriate to such a conceptualization (see Chapter 1.4). The constructs in question should be tentatively linked in a nomological network. The S-R mediation model proposed in the previous section is an explicit attempt in this direction. I have also proposed to "work backwards" from what we know, that is, from the profiles of physiological behavior, to what we are uncertain of, that is, to the factors determining this observable behavior. This clearly is description and not explanation. But even description within an inductive framework inevitably rests upon theoretical assumptions (see Chapter 1.5 on assessment). Therefore, on the basis of the assessment models and the S-R mediation model proposed earlier, in Chapter 9.2 I will present examples for such a description of the physiological response surface which will be called *physiological maps*.

4 Activation

4.1 Activation and Psychological Constructs

The short history of the construct of activation[7] can be traced back to the work of Cannon on the generalized response of the sympathetic nervous system to threatening events (Cannon, 1929). This generalized response should prepare the organism for fight or flight. The behavior energetics group around Duffy elaborated on the activation construct and commented upon its psychological significance (Duffy, 1957; see below; see also Malmo, 1959). The concept of generalized drive from Hull's behavior theory (Hull, 1943) was a second important tradition. Finally, the early work on the reticular activating system appeared to offer an anatomical substrate for nonspecific activation (Moruzzi & Magoun, 1949).

Until recently, activation as a psychological construct was based on the unitary and nonspecific notion mentioned above. Duffy (1957, 1962), in particular, pointed out that behavior could be described as variations in either the *direction* or the *intensity* of behavior. Since, according to Duffy, the intensity of behavioral responses can vary independent of its direction, the intensity aspect can be measured independently as excitation, activation, or energy mobilization. One psychologically important consequence of Duffy's conceptualization was the breakdown of the distinction between "drives" or "motivation" and "emotion". She contended that the same kinds of effects upon behavior could be observed under these variously designated conditions. In addition, physiological measurements could be used to directly measure "the 'motivating' value of a given situation" (Duffy, 1957, p. 267).

The concept of activation was further believed to be psychologically significant because the speed, intensity, and coordination of overt responses should vary with the degree of activation. This assertion linked the concept of

[7] "Activation" is often also called "arousal"; it will be noted where a distinction between activation and arousal is necessary, otherwise the term activation will be used.

activation with the quality of performance; an optimal performance should be obtained at medium levels of activation and performance decrements at low or high activation levels (i.e., an inverted-U relationship as postulated much earlier by Yerkes & Dodson, 1908). Another principle incorporating activation as a mediating variable in performance is the "narrowed attention hypothesis" (Callaway & Dembo, 1958). This hypothesis states that as activation increases the range of cues attended to decreases, that is, attention narrows. It should be noted that this hypothesis specifically deals with the effect of activation on sensory input processes, whereas the previously mentioned inverted-U hypothesis sensu Duffy referred to activation effects on efferent output processes. Selective attention as an element of the cognitive system has more recently been studied in an attempt to understand the interrelationship between energetic and computational concepts (Posner & Rothbart, 1986).

According to Duffy, the concept of activation could also be used to assess individual differences in responsiveness, "the response of highly integrated systems of reaction described as 'personality traits'" (Duffy, 1957, p. 271). However, a persistently followed line of research has not evolved from her proposal. To a large extent, the study of individual variations followed a lead that equated anxiety with activation. Whereas this identification has proved useful in clinical work, for example, with neurotic patients (Lader & Wing, 1966), it has been less statisfactory in normal samples, where an over-activation has not consistently been shown for individuals scoring high on self-reported anxiety in contrast to low scorers (Fahrenberg, 1987b; Myrtek, 1984). States of chronic under-activation have also been seen as being important biological determinants of behavior and of individual differences. Berlyne (1960) and Fiske and Maddi (1961) have both argued that there is a spontaneous tendency for persons to seek their optimal level of activation. Individuals characterized by chronic under-activation have been extensively studied by Zuckerman (1983, 1987; Zuckerman & Como, 1983) and typified as "sensation-seekers".

The major influence, however, to explain the biological basis of personality dimensions with reference to the construct of activation has been put forward by Eysenck (1957, 1967, 1981). Referring in his earlier theorizing to the notion of "excitation" and "types of nervous system" originating in Pavlov's work (cf. Mangan, 1982), Eysenck (1967) reformulated his biological personality theory in terms of the Western concept of "arousal" and "activation". Eysenck's proposal was that the dimension of extraversion-introversion is linked to differences in the threshold of the reticular activating system (giving rise to differences in "arousal" and "arousability"), and neuroticism, to threshold differences of the limbic system (giving rise to differences in "activation"). Thus, introverts are more arousable and therefore have a "weaker nervous system" than extraverts; persons scoring high on Eysenck's second personality dimension, neuroticism, are more activated in their limbic functions (the "visceral brain" regulating the excitation of the autonomic nervous system) than persons scoring low on neuroticism. A more detailed discussion of Eysenck's biological personality theory will be deferred until Chapter 11.

Psychological constructs that refer to activation as a unitary phenomenon have not fared particularly well in the last 20 years. This is also true for the inverted-U hypothesis of performance efficiency which has seldom received convincing support (see Neiss, 1988; note also Anderson's critique and Neiss's reply "Ending arousal's reign of error ..."; Anderson, 1990; Neiss, 1990). Theories that have predicted general activation and arousal differences between personality types have been partly reformulated in order to meet the challenges (see Chapter 4.3) levelled against the unitary activation construct (Eysenck & Eysenck, 1985). It appears that only a reconceptualization of activation as a multidimensional construct (Fahrenberg, 1987a, b) or as a manifestation of discrete psychobiological states (Neiss, 1988) will advance beyond the early energetics theory of intensity and directionality. However, the appeal of a unitary activation construct is still strong:

> ... I have often felt that as an explanatory concept in psychology 'arousal' has many of the qualities of a difficult but persuasive lover, whom reason tells one to abandon yet who continues to satisfy an inescapable need. (Claridge, 1987, p. 134.)

4.2 Activation as a Physiological Descriptor

Beginning with the work of Hess (1928, 1948), topical electrical stimulation of subcortical, in particular, hypothalamic, brain areas established the observation of fairly specific subsequent autonomic response patterns and behavioral adjustments. For example, Folkow and Rubinstein (1965) considered it "unlikely that some of the observed autonomic adjustments should merely be expressions of a current spread to some common excitable region" (p. 299). Thus, the notion of an undifferentiated general activation process, on which much of the work referred to in the preceding section was based, likely was a questionable overgeneralization. Although this changed notion of activation processes has had some effects on psychophysiological theorizing (namely on a multicomponential view of activation), consequences for empirical research have not been very pervasive.

The diversity of target organs and the wide range of their responses during in vivo regulations require a complex organization of activation processes in the central, autonomic and somato-motor system. In this section, I will briefly review notions of "activation", understood as a descriptive term for distinct physiological processes within particular parts of the central and peripheral nervous system.

One often cited distinction between molar neural systems is that of Pribram and McGuinness' (1975) "arousal", "activation", and "effort" systems. "Arousal" is said to occur when phasic physiological (central and autonomic) or behavioral responses following sudden and unexpected changes of sensory stimuli have taken place. Berlyne's (1968) collative variables referred to earlier constitute an example for conditions that elicit "arousal", as does Sokolov's orienting response paradigm. Neural circuits hypothesized to constitute the "arousal system" extend from the spinal cord through the brainstem reticular function, including hypothalamic sites. Forebrain control over this core-brain "arousal system" is exerted by reciprocal facilitation and inhibition by amygdaloid centers. The "activation system" prepares the organism to respond; it is hypothesized to be located in the basal ganglia. The "effort system" comprises the hippocampal circuit; it is involved in uncoupling stimulus and response. Without such a mechanism "behaving organisms would be constantly aroused by their movements and moved by arousing inputs" (Pribram & McGuinness, 1975, p. 439). The coordination of "arousal" and "activation" effected by the "effort system" demands resistance to or the initiation of rapid shifts in cerebral metabolism and is experienced as effort.

Pribram and McGuinness's (1975) model of three kinds of central activation systems, grossly relating to input, central organization, and output processes, has the merit of providing some overall distinctions within the once-thought unitary activation construct. As to its conceptual merit for psychophysiology, the model points to the possibility that different sources of activation can each project onto one physiological variable, making, on the one hand, their distinct contributions perhaps difficult to disentangle but offering, on the other hand, at least a post hoc "explanation" for results that are difficult to interpret.

A considerably more focused discussion by Vanderwolf and Robinson (1981) presents a new conceptual synthesis of the reticular activating system once at the core of unitary activation theory. The authors accumulate evidence that contrary to unitary activation theory, the projections from the brainstem reticular formation to the cerebral cortex do not play an essential role in sleep and waking behavior, nor in psychological phenomena of vigilance, awareness, alertness, or attention. Studies with decorticate or decerebrate preparations show only little impairment of the sleep-wakefulness cycle. However, descending reticular projections appear to be of considerable importance. What then is the function of the ascending reticular system?

The ascending reticular system is comprised of at least two functional components with quite different relations to behavior. One component is probably dependent on cholinergic transmission (studied often by cholinergic atropine blockade). Activity in this component occurs during behavioral immobility, simple reflexive or consummatory behavior, during anesthetic states and the quiescent intervals of an active sleep episode. The fact that atropine-sensitive, low-amplitude, and fast-frequency neocortical activity can be readily elicited by sensory stimulation without concurrent elicitation of phasic motor activity suggests the activity of mechanisms involved in the stimulus control of behavior. The second component of the ascending reticular activation system is noncholinergic and its activity is unmasked only after atropine. This component produces low-amplitude and fast-frequency neocortical activity if voluntary behaviors such as locomotion or head turning are being performed.

The theme of unitary activation has also been prominent in accounts on the central nervous control of the circulation, where a medullary cardiovascular center had long been described. As Hilton (1975) has pointed out, empirical and theoretical arguments have made this notion questionable. The old view had assumed that each cardiovascular variable must have its own brainstem center, all of which would be integrated in a special medullary center. This center was thought to interact with the depressor area of the ventromedial medulla. Recent pharmacological and neuroanatomical evidence seems to indicate (Reis, Ruggiero, & Granata, 1986) instead that there indeed exists a neuron pool in the rostral ventrolateral medulla that exerts an excitatory background tone to preganglionic sympathetic neurons and functions as the tonic vasomotor center. Still, Hilton's argument is well corroborated,

> that the central nervous system is organised to produce not single, isolated variables but integrated patterns of response. Any variable which can be described or measured independently is actually a component of several such patterns. (Hilton, 1975, p. 215.)

Hilton's argument actually goes beyond medullary centers regulating, or better, integrating afferent and efferent influences on the circulation. His main claim is to view cardiovascular control as being longitudinally organized, with hypothalamic regions initiating a limited number of patterns of cardiovascular responses (Hilton, 1979). More so, these hypothalamic sites receive information from the old protoreptilian brain (important for the more stereotyped, species-typical behaviors), the later developed paleomammalian brain or the limbic system (involved in more complex self- and species-preserving behavior such as instincts and emotions), and the neocortex (allowing for individualized behavior). The hypothalamus then triggers the final coordinated circulatory responses that are but one part of the total somato-motor, neuroendocrine, and visceral behavior emitted. Patterns of responses that can be evoked by hypothalamic topical stimulation include the defense pattern, the pressor pattern, the depressor pattern, and the dive pattern (Folkow, 1979; Lisander, 1979).

The defense reaction (cardiovascular component only) consists of increased heart rate, elevated systolic and diastolic blood pressures, cholinergic vasodilatation in the active muscles (shown at least in cats and dogs), and an increase in cardiac output. Under conditions of cardiovascular regulation that do not involve the defense reaction, pressor responses would lead to an activation of the baroreceptor feedback loop (e.g., Brooks, Fox, Lopez, & Sleight, 1978, elicited the pressor response by an injection of phenylephrine, an alpha-adrenergic agonist). Baroreceptor activation leads to an increase of vagal cardiac tone which effectively lowers heart rate in order to dampen the pressor effect (see Spyer & Jordan, 1980, for details of the neural pathways of the baroreflex). Another action of the baroreflex dampens the sympathetic vasoconstrictor tonus of the vascular bed (this action is most prominent in muscle, and less so in skin, vasoconstrictors; cf. Jänig, 1979). However, stimulation of the hypothalamic defense center abolishes part of the baroreflex action (Coote, Hilton, & Perez-Gonzalez, 1979; Hilton, 1980): Vagal bradycardia does not occur. That part of the baroreflex which acts on the vasoconstrictor tonus is not suppressed; this mechanism enables the arterial system to buffer more blood where it is needed most in an emergency situation , namely in the skeletal working muscles (Lisander, 1970). Taken together, the defense reaction prepares and supports an organism for an emergency situation which demands special cardiovascular adjustments.

The pressor response has already been mentioned; it consists of an increased sympathetic nervous system outflow which leads to elevations of systolic and possibly also diastolic blood pressure, enhanced cardiac chronotropic and inotropic function, and vasoconstriction. The baroreflex, however, is not suppressed as during the defense reaction, nor does an active vasodilatation occur. Therefore, the excitatory effects of the pressor response on cardiovascular variables are likely to be modified by the homeostatic action of the baroreflex.

The depressor response consists of an overall sympathetic inhibition and vagal activation which leads to decreases in heart rate and blood pressure, and a drop of the total peripheral resistance. If very intense, this centrally induced depressor response may not be compensated for by the homeostatic cardiovascular reflexes which might lead to a vasovagal syncope. The depressor response has been linked to the "playing dead" reaction seen in animals and with "emotional fainting" in humans. Finally, the diving response is another specialized type of sympatho-excitatory response. Submersion in water leads to a pattern of vasoconstriction and increases in diastolic blood pressure, bradycardia and a marked drop in cardiac output.

Another instance for a hypothalamically regulated vegetative function is hyperpnea, or increased ventilation. This response has been studied by Eldridge, Millhorn, and Waldrop (1981) under conditions of exercise in order to clarify the origin of ventilatory adjustments. These adjustments closely parallel the increased metabolic rate during moderate exercise and keep therefore arterial CO_2, O_2, and pH relatively constant. The authors conclude from their study on cats that the hyperpnea is not regulated by brainstem reflexes but by hypothalamic command signals that are primarily responsible for this effect.

In sum, there is considerable evidence (1) that cardio-respiratory-vascular responses can be elicited by hypothalamic neuron pools and (2) that patterns of responses and not just single physiological variables are initiated by these hypothalamic sites. It may well be the case that in conditions other than those represented by the laboratory studies on animals, on which most of the work referred to above is based, that is, in naturally occurring human behavior, the number of centrally induced visceral response patterns is larger and more complex.

After briefly reviewing hypotheses regarding general central nervous activation systems (Pribram & McGuinness), more specific activation systems in the ascending reticular system (Vanderwolf & Robinson), and hypothalamic response programs influencing cardiovascular response patterns (Hilton, Folkow, Lisander), I will finally turn to the longitudinal organization of the sympathetic nervous system innervating specific visceral target organs. Recently,

Jänig (1988) gave a lucid account of this longitudinal sympathetic organization, in which he compared the old concepts of undifferentiated sympathetic efferent mass action proposed by Cannon and Hess with the wealth of new data indicating highly differentiated sympathetic excitation of visceral target organs. Despite the "atomization" of traditionally more undifferentiated views of efferent sympathetic actions that results from the synthesis of new data, Jänig nevertheless emphasizes "the function of the autonomic system as interface between body and environment" (as Jänig's, 1988, essay is titled).

The starting point for Jänig's discussion is a comparison of somato-motor and autonomic integrative programs of the brain, the former having been investigated much more thoroughly than the latter. Simple motor programs such as spinal motor reflexes are organized at the level of the spinal cord. These programs have both agonistic and antagonistic connections to final common motor pathways as well as synaptic connections with spinal afferents and with spinal descending command systems. Activation of these motor programs produces coordinated changes of the skeletal muscles. The neuronal motor programs in the brain are "representations of the environment which is biologically relevant for the organism" (Jänig, 1988, pp. 143-144). Similarly, central autonomic neuronal programs can also be conceived of as "central representations of the environmental challenges which are encountered by the organism" (Jänig, 1988, p. 144).

Anatomically, the peripheral autonomic nervous system is divided into three parts, the thoraco-lumbar or sympathetic system, the cranio-sacral or parasympathetic system, and the enteric nervous system. In which way are these nervous systems centrally integrated? The hypothalamus plays an essential role in this integration. The hypothalamus and, in particular, its perifornical-lateral region obtains afferent inputs from rostral brain structures and from various regions of the brainstem. The rostral afferents include those from limbic system structures such as the amygdala, septum, and the preoptic area (all of which are likely involved in the organization of emotional behavior). The afferents from the amygdala are important insofar as inputs from the higher order sensory cortices (i.e., the visual, auditory, somato-sensory, gustatory, and olfactory sensory cortices) converge on the amygdala. Efferent projections of the perifornical region of the hypothalamus run via regions of the brainstem to the intermediate zone of the thoracolumbar spinal cord where the sympathetic preganglionic nuclei are located. Another region of the hypothalamus, the paraventricular nuclei, are probably highly important for the integration of autonomic, endocrine, and somato-motor systems during complex adaptive processes.

The sympathetic outflow from the thoraco-lumbar spinal cord innervates various autonomic target organs. Because information is integrated from supraspinal brain structures at the level of the preganglionic neurons, as described above, and from visceral afferents, these neurons constitute the final common sympathetic motor pathway. However, other possible sites of integration include the paravertebral and prevertebral ganglia, where preganglionic axons diverge and converge synaptically on postganglionic neurons, and the effector organs, where hormonal (e.g., circulating catecholamines), local metabolic, mechanical, and environmental (e.g., temperature) information may converge.

Until recently, the action of the sympathetic autonomic nervous system on its target organs had been described to be undifferentiated. However, considering the variety of functionally different autonomic target organs, the complex organization of the sympathetic nervous system indicated above, and the multitude of different environmental demands necessitating selective cardiovascular adaptations, this notion does not seem to be adequate. Indeed, experimental physiological work has identified functionally separate pre-postganglionic sympathetic channels which might also have their characteristic central organization. Jänig (1988) reviews some of his work where neurons of the lumbar sympathetic outflow supplying skeletal muscle, skin, pelvic organs, and colon have been studied in the cat. He could show that these neurons supply at least nine sympathetic channels; directed at the skeletal muscle are vasoconstrictor and vasodilatatory fibers; at the skin, vasoconstrictor, vasodilatatory, sudomotor, and pilomotor fibers; at the viscera, vasoconstrictor and two different types of motility regulating fibers.

Moreover, Jänig could in a semi-quantitative manner describe the possible sources of excitatory and inhibitory influences on the activity of each of these nine sympathetic channels. For example, skeletal muscle vasoconstrictor tonus is increased by the excitation of arterial chemoreceptors, cutaneous nociceptors, and visceral afferents; skeletal muscle vasoconstrictor tonus is inhibited, however, by afferents from arterial baroreceptors. In contrast, skeletal muscle vasodilatatory tonus and pilomotor activity seem to be solely influenced by hypothalamic commands.

That these nine sympathetic channels of lumbar outflow in the cat produce organized response patterns has also been demonstrated. Jänig (1979) has shown that the skeletal muscle vasoconstrictor and the sudomotor activity act synergistically, whereas both sudomotor activity and muscle vasoconstriction act antagonistically with respect to cutaneous vasoconstrictor tonus. Jänig concludes:

> Summarizing, it can be assumed that there is a high differentiation in sympathetic systems supplying different target organs, this reflecting a high degree of differentiation in the neuraxis and hypothalamus. On the other hand, we are aware - last but not least from Cannon and Hess - that the sympathetic systems function as a unity in the freely acting organism, this being an expression of the organization in the hypothalamus and suprahypothalamic structures. Both points of view are not exclusive, but only complement one another. (Jänig, 1988, p. 169.)

The conceptual and methodological conclusions that can be drawn for psychophysiology from the work reviewed in this section is a reiteration of points made previously: In order to investigate integrated behavioral responses we need to study physiological profiles and not just single variables. We must be aware that concepts of undifferentiated activation are grossly misleading and hinder progress in psychophysiology. However, where to look for such physiological profiles (i.e., according to which assessment model) and how to organize them has not been proposed in the literature reviewed. But the literature encourages the view that by studying physiological profiles we might open a window to a better understanding of the initiation and regulation of behavior by the central nervous system.

4.3 The Covariation Problem in Psychophysiology

One of the most often noted challenges of the unitary notion of activation are the ubiquitous low intercorrelations among putative indicators of activation. The history of this "covariation problem" in psychophysiology dates back to the turn of this century. Darrow (1929) reviewed early work on differences in the physiological reactions to sensory and ideational stimuli which had already shown that upon stimulation physiological response did not always follow a common course. These were early examples of what Lacey (1962) later called "directional fractionation", by which he meant a "qualitative" difference of response patterns under different experimental conditions. For example, on the basis of the hypothesis of differential excretions of epinephrine and norepinephrine under different emotional conditions, Ax (1953), Funkenstein (1956), and Schachter (1957) described distinct physiological patterns of "anger-in" and "anger-out" or "fear" and "anger". Davis et al. (1955) established differential modal physiological response patterns under warmth and cold, while viewing at affectively toned pictures, tapping, and during listening to auditory stimuli. The observation that these response profiles not only varied in their levels but also in their patterning clearly showed that the intensity aspect of (physiological) behavior was not overwhelmingly large as compared to the directional aspect of behavior, as had been postulated by the energetics group (see Chapter 4.1). It is intuitively clear that directional fractionation of physiological variables inevitably leads to low intercorrelations among variables if calculated across subject means or across an array of subjects x conditions scores. But there are several other candidate "explanations" for the covariation problem (see below).

The chapter of Lacey (1967) is the seminal work for anyone who wants to refer to the untenability of a unitary activation concept. Lacey accrued evidence that

> there are many experimental results that sharply contradict activation theory .... I think the experiments show electroencephalographic, autonomic, motor, and other behavioral systems are imperfectly coupled, complex interacting systems. (Lacey, 1967, p. 15.)

From this evidence Lacey suggested that "electrocortical arousal, autonomic arousal and behavioral arousal may be considered to be *different forms* of arousal, each complex in itself (Lacey, 1967, p. 15; author's italics). However important Lacey's blow against unitary activation theory was, the tentative suggestion to consider three different forms of arousal partitioned according to physiological systems was not very progressive, since it left the low intercorrelations among variables within each system unexplained (for a critique on Lacey's argumentation, see Corcoran, 1981).

Possible "explanations" for the covariation problem can be grouped around three general topics:

- Explanations from a system analytic point of view,
- explanations related to the assessment model of the construct of "activation",
- explanations pertaining to "irrelevant sources of variance".

An overview of the "explanations" offered to account for the covariation problem is given in Table 3. In the following, I will briefly comment on these "explanations"; more detailed treatments of particular tropics appear in later chapters.

Explanations from a system analytic point of view. From a system analytic point of view, activation is conceptually on a higher system-level than somatomotor, autonomic, or hormonal responses. This difference in levels might give rise to several complications that would tend to reduce the correlations among response variables. These complications include:

(1) Some physiological variables might be involved in maintaining homeostasis whereas others could reflect activation more directly. Venables (1984) called the former type of variable the "controlling" and the latter the "controlled" aspects of the system.

(2) The autonomic nervous system contains feedback loops, that is, visceral afferents that may change the activity of higher system levels (e.g., baroreceptor afferents reducing sympathetic and increasing vagal tone). Variables that cause changes in higher-level activations may be called "cause-indicators". Variables that are under the direct influence of higher-level activations may be termed "effect-indicators". Feedback loops usually contain both types of variables constituting "mixed models". Bollen (1984) investigated which type of correlation (negative, zero, or positive) could be expected among several cause-indicators, several effect-indicators and a mixture of cause- and effect-indicators. Correlations among cause-indicators underly no constraints; they may be positive, zero, or even negative. Correlations among effect-indicators should be positive if they measure the same concept. Correlations among three or more cause- and effect-indicators in a mixed model may again be positive, zero, or negative. Thus, correlations among variables influenced by and acting back on higher levels of a controlled system, as is the case with the autonomic nervous system, can be expected to be low and even negative. Bollen concludes:

> In sum, the advice of Blalock seems particularly appropriate: 'One should be especially on guard against procedures that supposedly permit one to appraise the 'validity' of an indicator on the basis of magnitudes of correlation coefficients,

> without the benefit of a specific theoretical model' (Namboodiri et al., 1975, p. 600). (Bollen, 1984, pp. 383-384.)

(3) Several distinct sources of activation project onto one single variable leading to a difficult to disentangle confound of influences from diverse activation processes. If the amount of such influences varies among variables, their intercorrelations are bound to be low. One example for such a confound is heart rate which reflects both bodily maintenance as well as the impact of activation processes related to specific task or psychological influences (Gale, 1987, Venables, 1984). Given the linear relationship between heart rate and oxygen uptake under normal conditions of maintaining the metabolic demands of somatic activity, one way to disentangle the metabolic from additional "psychological" influences on heart rate is by the method of "additional heart rate" (Blix, Stromme, & Ursin, 1974). Further discussion of confounded effects of different sources of activation will be given in Chapter 6.3, where the effects of the context of emotion induction and emotion effects proper are treated.

(4) Another "explanation" for the covariation problem from a system point of view emerges from the consideration of unique transfer functions (see Chapter 6.1) between higher system levels and different variables at lower levels. If one and the same activation process relates differently (i.e., by different transfer functions) to various variables, all of which purportedly are effect-indicators of that process, intercorrelations among the variables are deemed to be low (Lader, 1975b). The related problem of different time courses upon stimulation has also been long recognized:

> A model of arousal which is more in accord with physiological facts recognizes that as stress mounts, it triggers reactions at different points in time in different systems. Up to a point, one system may rise in activity and then be partially or fully inhibited while another continues to rise. (Taylor & Epstein, 1967, pp. 522-523.)

Table 3. "Explanations" for the Covariation Problem in Psychophysiology

Explanations from a System Analytic Point of View
1) Physiological variables refer to different system levels
2) Physiological variables are cause- or effect-indicators
3) Several activation systems project onto single physiological variables
4) Physiological variables are linked to activation via unique transfer functions
Explanations Related to the Assessment Model of the Construct of "Activation"
5) The individual-differences versus the process perspective on activation
6) Response measures imply different assessment models
Explanations Pertaining to "Irrelevant Sources of Variance"
7) Unreliability of measurements
8) Individual response specificities

Explanations related to the assessment model of the construct of activation. In the discussion of assessment models (see Chapter 1.5) it has been argued that assumptions about the locus of a construct are critically important for the construction and validation stages of constructs. The construct of activation is a prime example for the foundation of a construct within two different assessment models rendering the usage of one and the same descriptor, namely "activation", questionable for both assessment model choices. There are at least two points that can be subsumed under this issue:

(1) Activation can be understood from an *individual differences perspective*, much as personality traits or intelligence have been. Here, the locus of the construct is between subjects: Persons differ with respect to the levels of physiological variables because individuals represent different instantiations of the activation construct (Assessment Model 1). To the extent that physiological variables correlate "significantly" high within between- subjects variance, an activation construct could be constructed. However, studies have repeatedly shown that the between-subjects correlations are disappointingly low. For example, Fahrenberg and Foerster (1982) calculated between-subjects correlations among 21 physiological variables (from the cardiovascular, somatomotor, electrodermal, and respiratory systems as well as from electroencephalography) across N = 125 male subjects for the first resting period of their experiment. The authors concluded that the correlations reflected "low consistency" (p. 159).

On the other hand, activation can be understood from a *process-oriented perspective*. Here, the locus of the construct is between conditions: Conditions differ with respect to the levels of physiological variables because of different instantiations of the activation construct across different situations (Assessment Model 2 analyzing between-conditions variance). The *process-oriented perspective can also be formulated from an individual-differences point of view*, if individual differences in processes are hypothesized (Assessment Model 7 analyzing person x condition interaction variance, or the combination of Assessment Models 2 and 7 analyzing within-subjects variance). A process rather than a trait approach to activation has often been claimed to be a more adequate perspective, because activation is in the first place an organismic process preparing and supporting an individual's behavior (see Chapter 4.2). Actually, correlations among physiological variables computed within subjects have revealed higher relationships compared to between-subjects correlation (e.g., Fahrenberg & Foerster, 1982; Gale & Edwards, 1983; Lazarus, Speisman, & Mordkoff, 1964; Schnore, 1959; Taylor & Epstein, 1967). The issue of correlation within different sources of variance and covariance will be further pursued in Chapters 6.2 and 6.3.

(2) Different response measures implicitly give more or less weight to a trait or a process conceptualization of activation. Unless this characteristic of response measures is fully recognized, the application of an assessment model may be inconsistent. Chapter 6.1 further elaborates on this issue.

Explanations pertaining to "irrelevant sources of variance". Test theory and psychometrics (e.g., Lord & Novick, 1968; Nunnally, 1978) distinguish between observed, true, and error scores. As is well-known, the correlation between two observed variables cannot exceed the square root of the product of the variables' reliabilities. Thus, in the presence of error variance, or more generally, of irrelevant sources of variance, the correlation between observed as compared to the correlation between true-score variables is attenuated. This attenuation might also contribute to the covariation problem. Two sources of irrelevant variance may be distinguished:

(1) Measurement imprecision or unreliability obviously is a threat to all statistical operations. Reliability of physiological variables is often estimated by their stability or retest correlation. It should be noted, however, that stability coefficients are a function of measurement precision only if no true change occurred between the first and the second measurement occasion. Although stability coefficients from different investigations are not easily compared (since parameter definitions, response scalings, experimental conditions, subject samples, length of sampling intervals, and length of retest-intervals often differ), the stability coefficients reported fare fairly well (see Arena, Blanchard, Andrasik, Cotch, & Myers, 1983; Faulstich, Williamson, McKenzie, Duchmann, & Hutchinson, 1986; Foerster, 1985; Foerster, Schneider, & Walschburger, 1983a; Manuck & Garland, 1980; Myrtek, 1984, 1985; Robinson, Whitsett, & Kaplan, 1987; Seraganian, Hanley, Hollander, Roskies, Smilga, Martin, Collu, & Oseasohn, 1985). A comparison of stability coefficients for a broad spectrum of physiological measures within and over replications of an experiment at intervals of three weeks, three months, and one year was obtained by Fahrenberg, Foerster, Schneider, Müller, & Myrtek, 1986; Fahrenberg, Schneider, & Safian, 1987). These authors reported that (1) short-term stability (electrodes not removed) exceeded 0.70 for most physiological measures, (2) heart rate, pulse wave velocity, and respiration attained higher stabilities than blood pressure, parameters from impedance cardiography, eye blinks, and electrodermal activity, (3) raw scores yielded relatively higher stability coefficients than change scores, and (4) comparing three-week and one-year retest intervals, from a total of 30 stability coefficients the numerical values of 22 coefficients declined (8 increased), but 19 coefficients remained significant. These results suggest that, exceptions notwithstanding, imprecise measurement is unlikely to be a major source for the covariation problem.

(2) Under the perspective of individual-differences notions of activation, individual response specificity (ISR) constitutes a threat for high between-subjects correlations, because ISR increases the between-subjects variance unsystematically. The trait approach to activation is influenced by all three sources of ISR variance described (see Chapter 3.1), namely the individual average effective stimuli, response channel sensitivities, and response channel constants. Turning to the process-oriented individual differences perspective on

activation, two sources of ISR variance still remain; individual average effective stimuli and response channel sensitivities influence individual reactivities in a way that is unrelated to the substantial issues at hand. Lykken (1968) has forcefully argued that irrelevant sources in between-subjects variance should be excluded. He proposed a range-corrected response measure that aims at excluding individual differences in the range of physiological responses. More on this issue will be found in Chapter 6.1.

Consequences of the covariation problem for the measurement of activation. The preceding discussion suggests several ways to cope with the covariation problem. Apart from the general recommendation to increase the reliability of physiological measurements, the suggestions put forth in the literature are conceptually oriented. They include (1) the quest for a multicomponent conceptualization of activation, (2) the application of an "appropriate" assessment model of activation, and (3) a physiologically instead of a statistically based derivation of activation processes.

First, with the rejection of a unitary notion of activation, most authors have demanded a multicomponent conceptualization of activation. Lacey's (1967) proposal to differentiate between electrocortical, autonomic, and behavioral forms of activation has already been noted. While Lacey's proposal does not give any indication about how these forms of activation should be operationalized, Fahrenberg has urged the psychophysiological community to proceed in the actual implementation of a multivariate theory of activation:

> The relevance of the psychophysiological approach to theoretical development in psychology, psychosomatics, psychiatry and other settings will greatly depend on progress in overcoming basic difficulties in the traditional psychophysiological theories of activation (arousal), emotionality, anxiety, stress and related phenomena through more precisely defined theoretical constructs and mechanisms and eventually through a multicomponent model of psychophysiological activation processes and synergisms. (Fahrenberg, 1987a, p. 9.)

Fahrenberg and his associates have laid the groundwork for such a multicomponent conceptualization of activation by demonstrating through large-scale multivariate investigations and appropriate multivariate analyses the substantial proportion of variance in activation processes accountable by stimulus-specific, individual-specific, and motivation-specific physiological response patterns (for reviews see Fahrenberg, 1986, 1987b, 1988). In Chapter 9.1 I shall review some of my own work on the delineation of activation components within physiological maps of stimulus-specific physiological response profiles. Although adhering at the time to a unidimensional theory of activation, Corcoran (1981) envisioned where a multidimensional theory of activation might start from. His description essentially anticipated the procedure of locating physiological maps within the state-space of situational physiological profiles:

> It is my view that 'arousal' should be used as a psychological construct for the present, at least, until much more is known about bodily reaction to stress. Such effects are bound to be complex and partially idiosyncratic, and the eventual model

> may be approximated .... by a 'multi-dimensional' theory, which is some description of the total state of the organism. More formally, one might assume an origin in a multidimensional space representing a hypothetical state of zero arousal. Obviously there are many points within such a space which are *equidistant* from the origin, but which represent *qualitatively* different states of the organism. Such points are by virtue of their distance from the origin *equal* to each other in arousal level (i.e. *quantitatively* equal), but are nevertheless different. (Corcoran, 1981, p. 115; author's italics.)

Some qualifications of Corcoran's statements about qualitative and quantitative differences among physiological profiles in a state-space need to be made, but this is deferred until Chapter 7.

Second, the choice among assessment models for the construct of will probably continue to be a matter of controversy because substantive questions, which reflect the interests of an investigator in the construct of activation, will determine the "appropriateness" of one or the other assessment model. However, the empirical evidence suggests that a pure trait approach to activation (Assessment Model 1) will not, or not alone, provide a solution to the covariation problem. There is much that recommends, instead, the process orientation for a definition of the construct of activation. It should be noted that individual-differences questions can be part of a process approach to activation. For example, similar to the discussion within personality psychology (see Chapter 2.2), individual differences in the situation-specific physiological responses (which, provided they are replicable, have been termed individual situational response specificities; see Chapter 3.1) might reveal important aspects of differential behavior regulation. An application of such a differential perspective within the psychophysiology of personality will be presented in Chapter 11.

Third, Taylor and Epstein (1967), in discussing ways to deal with the covariation problem, recommended basing the concept of activation on explicitly physiological considerations. Although this suggestion was not new, it was contrasted by Taylor and Epstein with the many attempts at that time to find a solution to the general measurement of activation "by transforming single measures, by innovations in data reduction, or by combining measures" (p. 514). Even if it seems odd in the light of the importance of assessment model definitions (of which response measures, data reduction procedures, and variable combinations are a part) to contrast physiologically based approaches to activation with psychometrically based ones, this contrast nevertheless fairly accurately describes the separation of investigators into a more psychometrically-oriented and a more physiologically-oriented camp. Clearly, a rapprochement of these camps would be highly desirable because neither of these orientations alone is capable of successfully advancing the study of multiple activation processes.

Several investigators have proposed physiologically based activation systems. For example, Wenger attempted to define a factor of "Autonomic Balance" representing different degrees of balance or imbalance between the sympathetic and the parasympathetic nervous systems (Wenger, 1966; Wenger & Cullen,

1972). Wenger's work was based on the concept of a functional antagonism of the sympathetic and the parasympathetic systems proposed by Eppinger and Hess (1915). Ursin (1978), in reviewing his work on parachutists, identified several endocrinologically defined "activation mechanisms":

> Our data point to several different types of activation mechanisms. The cortisol axis was related to defense mechanisms, the free fatty acids were related to performance, and testosterone was related to role identification. The catecholamines, in particular epinephrine, were also related to performance, and it may be that free fatty acid measurement simply is a better way of estimating adrenergic activity. (Ursin, 1978, p. 212.)

An example for a neuroendocrine-cardiovascular definition of activation systems is the proposal set forth by Williams (1986). He starts with the basic assumption that "broad classes of environmental events may produce a relatively small number of integrated patterns of response" (p. 112). Williams proposes two broad environmental conditions that tend to elicit two different patterns of physiological response. Effective eliciting stimuli for Pattern 1 are defense and emergency situations, fear, anxiety, active effortful coping, mental work, and uncontrollable aversive stimuly. Pattern 1 is described as increased motor activity; muscle vasodilatation and increased cardiac output; increased epinephrine, cortisol, and prolactin. Effective eliciting stimuli for Pattern 2 are vigilance, sensory intake, passive coping, and perhaps controllable aversive stimuli. Pattern 2 is described as decreased (but alert) motor activity; muscle vasoconstriction; increased testosterone. Although these patterns may describe broad classes of physiological behavior, they are still only very cursorily defined.

Other attempts at defining physiologically based concepts of activation have made use of the pharmacologically characterized receptors transmitting hormonal and nervous excitations to autonomic nervous system target organs. Following this approach, a wealth of physiological investigations has referred to patterns of alpha-adenergic, beta-adrenergic, and cholinergic activation in order to characterize the effects of particular tasks, the autonomic influences upon cardiovascular variables, and also groups of individuals (see Krantz & Manuck, 1984). In the following chapter, I shall introduce this concept and present a model that relates these components to both the measured cardiovascular variables and the protocol of autonomic blockade studies.

5 Autonomic Cardiovascular Activation Components

5.1 Foundations for a Conceptualization of Autonomic Cardiovascular Activation Components

5.1.1 Autonomic receptors

Both the nervous system and the endocrine system perform the task of controlling and integrating autonomic body functions. As pointed out in Chapter 4.2, these systems are coordinated at the hypothalamic brain level. The major difference between these systems is in the mode of transmission of information; it is chemical in the endocrine system and electrical in the nervous system. However, between preganglionic nerve cells, postganglionic nerve cells, and the target organs signals are carried by chemical rather than electrical signals. This chemical transmission across the synaptic cleft is accommodated through the release of transmitter substances from nerve terminals that activate or inhibit the postsynaptic cell by binding to a specialized receptor cell (Mayer, 1980).

Autonomic nerve cells can be classified according to the transmitter substances released from their terminal boutons. A large number of peripheral autonomic nervous system neurons synthesize and release acetylcholine; they are *cholinergic* fibers. These include all preganglionic efferent autonomic fibers and the (nonautonomic) somatic motor fibers. In addition, all parasympathetic and some sympathetic postganglionic fibers are cholinergic. In contrast, most postganglionic sympathetic fibers release norepinephrine; they are *adrenergic* fibers. Some peripheral sympathetic fibers release dopamine. Adrenal medullary cells, which are embryologically analogous to postganglionic sympathetic neurons, release a mixture of epinephrine and norepinephrine.

The terminals of cholinergic neurons contain large numbers of small membrane-bound vesicles that contain acetylcholine. Most of the acetylcholine is synthesized in the cytoplasm from choline and acetyl-CoA through the catalytic action of the enzyme choline acetyltransferase. Acetyl-CoA is synthesized in

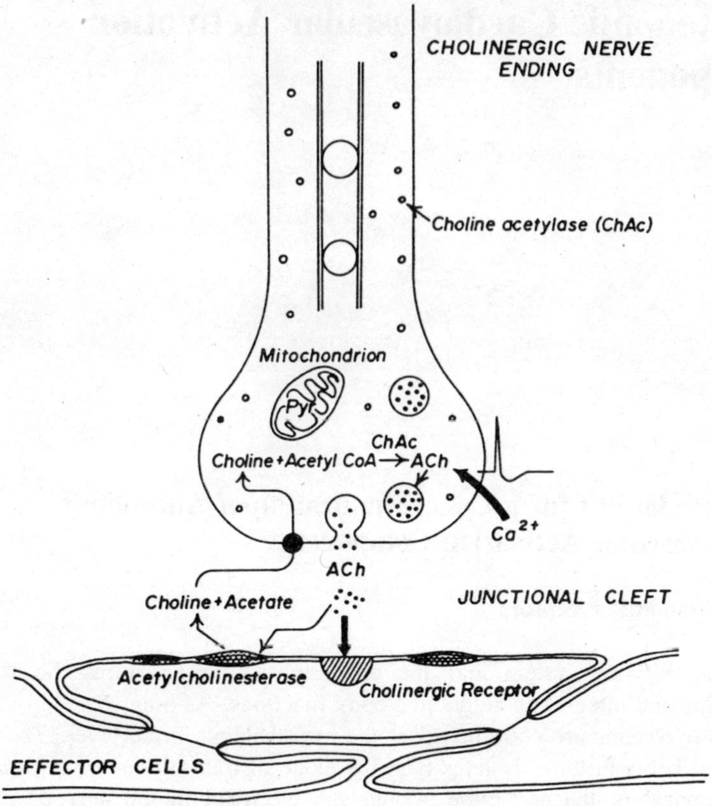

Figure 2. Formation and release of acetylcholine at the parasympathetic nerve endings, and its action and breakdown at the effector cells. Acetyl CoA = acetyl coenzyme A. ChAc = choline acetylase. ACh = acetylcholine. From "The human cardiovascular system" by J.T. Shepherd and P.M. Vanhoutte, 1979, p. 125. Copyright 1979 by Raven Press. Reproduced by permission.

mitochondria, which are present in large numbers in the nerve ending. Choline is transported by a membrane carrier mechanism from the extracellular fluid into the neuronal terminal. Release of transmitter occurs when an action potential reaches the terminal and triggers sufficient influx of calcium ions to "destabilize" the storage vesicles. After release from the presynaptic terminal, acetylcholine molecules may bind to and activate an acetylcholine receptor. Acetylcholinesterase very efficiently splits acetylcholine into choline and acetate and thereby inactivates the transmitter (see Figure 2).

Adrenergic neurons too store their transmitter substances in membrane-bound vesicles. Release of the vesicular content from adrenergic nerve terminals is similar to the calcium-dependent process described above for cholinergic nerve endings (see Figure 3). As a consequence of the increased intraneuronal calcium

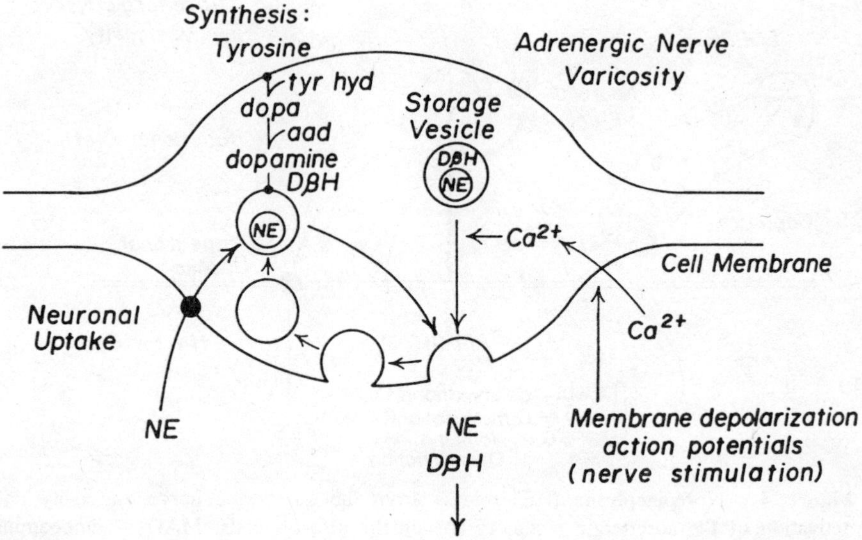

Figure 3. Synthesis and exocytotic release of norepinephrine and recycling of the storage vesicles at the sympathetic (adrenergic) nerve varicosities. NE = norepinephrine. tyr hyd = tyrosine hydroxylase. aaa = aromatic L-amino decarboxylase. DßH = dopamine-ß-hydroxylase. · = active carrier. From "The human cardiovascular system" by J.T. Shepherd and P.M. Vanhoutte, 1979, p. 113. Copyright 1979 by Raven Press. Reproduced by permission.

ion concentration, the vesicles migrate toward and fuse with the neuronal cell membrane, and empty their content of norepinephrine and dopamine-ß-hydroxylase into the junctional cleft (exocytotic release). Norepinephrine and epinephrine can be metabolized by several enzymes (e.g., monoamine oxidase). However,metabolism is not the primary mechanism for termination of noradrenergic action. Termination of noradrenergic transmission results from several processes including simple diffusion away from the receptor site and reuptake into the nerve terminal or into perisynaptic glia or smooth muscle cells (see Figure 4).

The cholinergic and adrenergic transmitters act upon the postsynaptic cell membrane. The cell membrane not only recognizes the chemical structure of the transmitter but can transduce it across the membrane to initiate an intracellular signal, which alters the activity of the cell. Sites at the cell membrane, that upon binding of a transmitter molecule cause a change of cellular activity, are called

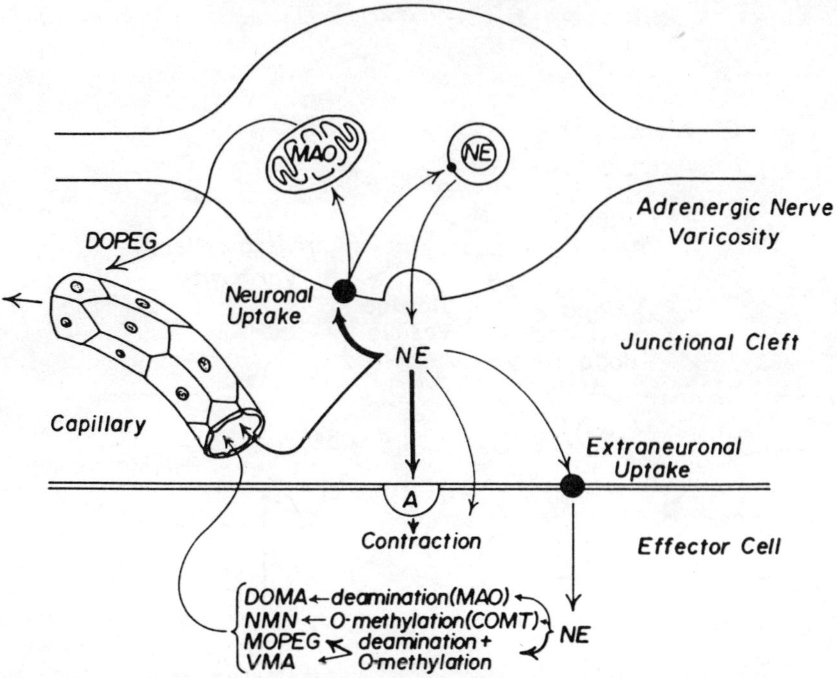

Figure 4. Norepinephrine (NE) release from the adrenergic nerve varicosity and activation of the adrenergic receptors (A) on the effector cells. MAO = monoamine oxidase. DOPEG = 3,4-dihydroxyphenylglycol. COMT = catechol-O-methyltransferase. DOMA = 3,4-dihydroxymandelic acid. NMN = normetanephrine. MOPEG = 3-methoxy-4-dihydroxyphenylglycol. VMA = 3-methoxy, 4-hydroxymandelic acid. · = active carrier. From "The human cardiovascular system" by J.T. Shepherd and P.M. Vanhoutte, 1979, p. 114. Copyright 1979 by Raven Press. Reproduced by permission.

"receptors" and the action-initiating molecules, "agonists". Generally, when a low concentration of a drug initiates a strong response, it is said to act as an agonist with "high intrinsic activity". Other drugs may also easily bind to a receptor site but have only weak or no intrinsic activity and thus elicit little or no response. Such drugs are called "antagonists". One type of antagonists (the noncompetitive antogonist) binds strongly to the receptor and cannot be displaced by the true agonist. The second type of antagonists (the competitive antagonist) can, however, be replaced by an agonist, provided a high agonist concentration is present.

Historically, Ahlquist (1948) created the receptor theory in order to explain the autonomic effects of sympathetic nerve excitation and exogeneous sympathetico-mimetic amines. Today, at least seven autonomic receptor sites are distinguished (Kenakin, 1984):

- Muscarinic cholinoceptors, located at parasympathetic effector cells, smooth muscle, cardiac muscle, exocrine glands, brain;
- Nicotinic cholinoceptors, located at autonomic ganglia, skeletal muscle neuromuscular end-plate, spinal cord;
- Alpha1 adrenoceptors, located at postsynaptic effector cells, especially smooth muscle;
- Alpha2 adrenoceptors, located at presynaptic adrenergic nerve terminals, platelets, lipocytes, smooth muscle;
- Beta1 adrenoceptors, located at postsynaptic effector cells, especially heart; lipocytes, brain, presynaptic noradrenergic nerve terminals;
- Beta2 adrenoceptors, located at postsynaptic effector cells, especially smooth muscle;
- Dopaminergic receptors, located at brain and postsynaptic effectors, especially vascular smooth muscle of the splanchnic and renal vascular beds; presynaptic receptors on nerve terminals, especially in the heart, vessels, and gastrointestinal system.

There are two important presynaptic mechanisms which include presynaptic receptors that deserve mentioning. First, an alpha2 adrenoceptor located on the presynaptic nerve terminal is activated by norepinephrine. Activation of this receptor diminishes further release of norepinephrine from the nerve terminal. This mechanism prevents an excessive liberation of the adrenergic transmitter. Second, in the heart and the blood vessels, acetylcholine released in the vicinity of adrenergic nerve endings binds to muscarinic receptors of the adrenergic neuronal cell membrane and inhibits the release of norepinephrine. This presynaptic effect of the cholinergic transmitter greatly reinforces its direct inhibitory effect on cardiac and vascular effector cells.

With the aid of the receptor theory, the effects of autonomic nerve impulses on target organs can be described much more succinctly than with a consideration of the anatomy of the autonomic nervous system alone. Table 4 (modified from Mayer, 1980) gives an overview of effector organ responses to adrenergic and cholinergic impulses (note that these are not necessarily sympathetic or parasympathetic actions!) and the mediation of these responses according to receptor type.

Table 5 provides a detailed overview of alpha-adrenergic, beta-adrenergic, and cholinergic contributions to the activation of noninvasively registered cardiovascular variables and their parameters. The table is an adaptation of Fahrenberg and Foerster's (1989) compilation of information extracted from Jänig (1987), Witzleb (1987), Antoni (1987), Levy and Martin (1979), Gilman, Goodman, and Gilman (1980), and Braunwald and Ross (1979).

Table 4. Cardiovascular Responses to Autonomic Nerve Impulses

Effector Organ	Adrenergic Impulses Receptor Type	Responses[a]	Cholinergic Impulses Receptor Type	Responses[a]
Heart				
Sinoatrial node	ß1	Acc++	M	Dece+++
Atria (contract.)	ß1	Inc++	M	Decr++
A-V node (cond.vel.)	ß1	Inc++	M	Decr+++
Ventricles (contract.)	ß1	Inc+++	M	Decr?
Arterioles				
Coronary	α,ß2	Con+ Dil[b]++	M	Dil±
Skin, mucosa	α	Con+++	M	Dil[c]
Skeletal muscle	α,ß2	Con++ Dil[b,d]++	M	Dil[e]+
Cerebral	α	Con	M	Dil[c]
Pulmonary	α,ß2	Con+ Dil[b]	M	Dil[c]
Abdominal viscera	α,ß2	Con+++ Dil[d]+	-	
Renal	α,ß2	Con+++ Dil[d]+	-	
Salivary glands	α	Con+++	M	Dil++
Skin				
Pilomotor muscles	α	Con++	-	
Sweat glands	α	Loc sec[f]	M	Gen sec+++
Adrenal Medulla				
Catecholamine excretion	-		M	Sec ep & norep

Note. Table adapted and modified from Mayer (1980). Contract. = Contractility. Cond. vel. = Conduction velocity. Acc = Acceleration. Dece = Deceleration. Inc = Increase. Decr = Decrease. Con = Constriction. Dil = Dilatation. Loc sec = Local secretion. Gen sec = General secretion. Sec ep & norep = Epinephrine and norepinephrine secretion. [a] Responses are designated + to +++ to provide an approximate indication of the importance of adrenergic and cholinergic nerve activity in the control of the various organs and functions listed. [b] Dilatation predominates *in situ* due to metabolic autoregulatory phenomena. [c] Cholinergic vasodilatation at these sites is of questionable physiological significance. (Most blood vessels have uninnervated muscarinic receptors.) [d] Over the usual concentration range of physiologically released, circulating epinephrine, ß-receptor response (vasodilatation) predominates in blood vessels of skeletal muscle and liver; α-receptor response (vasoconstriction), in blood vessels of other abdominal viscera. [e] Sympathetic cholinergic system causes vasodilatation in skeletal muscle, but this is not involved in most physiological responses. [f] Palms of hands and some other sites ("adrenergic sweating").

5.1.2 Autonomic receptor agonists and antagonists

In order to define and understand the action of the various receptor types, physiological and pharmacological investigations have applied naturally occurring agonists (like dopamine, epinephrine, and norepinephrine), their synthetic analogs (like isoproterenol and phenylephrine), and antagonists to tissue preparations and to intact organisms. *Alpha-adrenoceptors* are very sensitive to norepinephrine and phenylephrine, less sensitive to epinephrine and relatively insensitive to isoproterenol. Alpha1-adrenoceptors are selectively antagonized by indoramin and prazosin, and alpha2-adrenoceptors, by yohimbine. Unselective alpha-blockade is performed by phentolamine which has intrinsic cardiostimulatory effects. *Beta1-adrenoceptors* are sensitive to isoproterenol, epinephrine, and norepinephrine but insensitive to phenylephrine. They can be selectively blocked by, for example, metoprolol and atenolol. *Beta2-adrenoceptors* are sensitive to terbutaline, isoproterenol, and epinephrine, but insensitive to norepinephrine and phenylephrine. Selective blockade of beta2-adrenoceptors is pharmacologically possible (Stiles, Caron, & Lefkowitz,

Table 5. Effects of Sympathetic (Alpha-Adrenergic and Beta-Adrenergic) and Parasympathetic Activation on Noninvasive Cardiovascular Parameters (Without Regard to Compensatory Regulations)

Variable	Parameter	SNS α	SNS β	PNS
Heart Rate			Inc	Dec
Respiratory Sinus Arrhythmia				Inc
Electrocardiogram	P-Q Time		Dec	Inc
	P-Amplitude		Inc	Dec
	Relative Q-T Time		Inc	Dec?
	T-Amplitude		Dec	Inc?
	ST-Elevation		Dec?	
Systolic Time Intervals	PEP		Dec	Inc?
	LVET		Dec	Inc?
Cardiac Output (Stroke Volume)			Inc	Dec?
Contractility	Heather Index		Inc	Inc?
Arterial Blood Pressure	Systolic	Inc	Inc	
	Mean	Inc?	Inc?	
Total Peripheral Resistance		Inc		
Pulse Wave Velocity		Inc	Inc	
Skin Blood Flow (Hand)	PVA	Dec		
	BV	Dec		
Skin Temperature (Hand)		Dec		
Skeletal Muscle Blood Flow			Inc	

Note. Adapted from Fahrenberg and Foerster (1989). Inc = Increase. Dec = Decrease. SNS = Sympathetic nervous system. PNS = Parasympathetic nervous system.

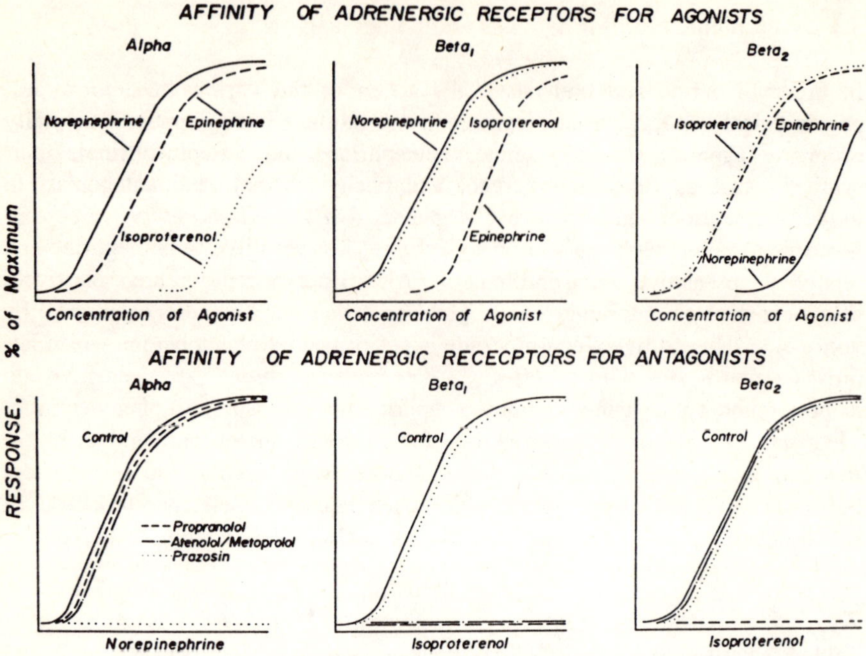

Figure 5. The adrenergic receptors have varying affinities for the agonists epinephrine, isoproterenol, and norepinephrine, as indicated by the concentrations of these compounds needed to elicit their activation *(upper)*. In addition, the response of these receptors to their preferred agonist can be antagonized using the appropriate adrenergic blocking agent *(lower)*. For example, in the bottom left panel the response to alpha-adrenergic activation by norepinephrine (control) is abolished by the alpha-adrenergic blocking drug prazosin but is unaffected by the beta-adrenergic blocking drugs atenolol, metoprolol, and propranolol. From "The human cardiovascular system" by J.T. Shepherd and P.M. Vanhoutte, 1979, p. 187. Copyright 1979 by Raven Press. Reproduced by permission.

1984) but is not yet marketed. Unselective beta-adrenergic blockade, for example by propranolol, has been one of the first pharmacological treatments of hypertension.[8] Figure 5 gives a summary of findings concerning the affinity of adrenergic receptors for agonists and some antagonists. *Muscarinic cholinoceptors* have a high affinity to acetylcholine and muscarine; they are competitively blocked by atropine. *Nicotinic cholinoceptors* are sensitive to acetylcholine and nicotine; they are competitively blocked by muscle relaxant drugs or drugs blocking transmission at the autonomic ganglia.

---

[8] Today, antihypertensive medication that acts upon autonomic receptors includes substances exerting dual unselective alpha-adrenergic and beta-adrenergic blockade (labetolol), selective beta1- and alpha2-adrenergic blockade plus beta2-adrenergic stimulation (celiprolol), or unselective beta-adrenergic plus alpha1-adrenergic blockade plus direct vasodilatation (carvedilol).

Applying naturally occurring or synthetic agonists to the intact organism allows to study the cardiovascular system's response including the compensatory adjustments by which homeostasis is attempted to be retained. After norepinephrine, the blood pressure increases as a result of an elevated blood flow resistance. Heart rate drops because of the baroreceptor negative feedback loop. Applied to the isolated heart, norepinephrine raises heart rate. Since epinephrine also stimulates beta-adrenoceptors, its cardiovascular effects are complex: Epinephrine increases the systolic and decreases the diastolic blood pressure; heart rate raises because of the beta-adrenoceptors at the sinoatrial node; blood flow in the skeletal muscles increases. Isoproterenol stimulates beta-adrenoceptors and leads to increases in heart rate and systolic blood pressure; the diastolic blood pressure decreases, however, because skeletal muscle blood flow increases and total peripheral resistance drops.

Endogeneous excretion of epinephrine and norepinephrine leads to specific cardiovascular effects which are dependent on the particular ratio of these catecholamines' excretion. Excretion from the adrenal medulla leads to an approximate ratio of 80% epinephrine and 20% norepinephrine; the amount of norepinephrine may be greatly increased by its release from adrenergic nerve terminals. For example, a lower baroreceptor activity leads to a selective rise of norepinephrine; a drop in blood sugar levels caused by insuline, to a selective rise of epinephrine. Recently, psychophysiologists' interest in the effects of agonists has extended from their action on the activity of target organs to their action at the receptor sites themselves (Mills & Dimsdale, 1988). Receptor binding techniques provide a direct measure of the functional link between neurohormonal signals and the responses they stimulate. Factors that may influence the effects of both agonists and antagonists include individual variations in receptor sensitivity, number of receptors, and of course the bioavailability of the drug. For example, McDevitt, Frisk-Holmberg, Hollifield, and Shand (1976) showed that the effects of propranolol on isoproterenol tachycardia was only poorly correlated with total plasma concentrations of propranolol but highly predictable from free drug concentration. In addition, individual variations in receptor sensitivity were minor compared to variations in propranolol bioavailability.

In general, the effects of autonomic receptor antagonists are opposite to those of the respective agonists. *Unselective alpha-adrenoceptor blockade* lowers the diastolic blood pressure whereas heart rate and cardiac output increase (Taylor, 1982). Because of the higher sympathetic tonus, these effects are more pronounced during standing than in the supine position. The increase in heart rate is produced by the activated baroreceptor reflex following the lowered diastolic blood pressure; this increase can be reduced by a beta-adrenergic blocker. Another mechanism leading to the heart rate increase under a nonselective alpha-adrenergic blockade involves the presynaptic alpha2-adrenoceptors. The blockade of these alpha2-adrenoceptors results in an enrichment with norepinephrine at the synaptic cleft which leads to the stimulation of cardiac beta1-adrenoceptors and the ensuing chronotropic effects.

The increase in cardiac output can be explained with these chronotropic effects. *Selective alpha1-adrenoceptor blockade* results in a drop of total peripheral resistance and diastolic blood pressure. Because of the unrestricted action of presynaptic alpha2-adrenoceptors, positive chronotropic and inotropic effects are not seen.

Unselective beta-adrenoceptor blockade leads to reductions in heart rate, cardiac output, and systolic blood pressure, whereas the total peripheral resistance and the diastolic blood pressure are elevated. The latter effect results from the blockade of vasodilatatory beta2-adrenoceptors. Since these beta2-adrenoceptors are not innervated by the sympathetic nervous system, the vasoconstrictive effect after unselective beta-blockade can be expected to occur only after a larger sympathetic excitation and the excretion of epinephrine from the adrenal medulla into the blood. Another potential explanation of the vasoconstrictive effect is the stimulation of alpha1-adrenoceptors in the vasculature (Shanks, 1984). *Selective beta1-adrenoceptor blockade* results in specific chronotropic and inotropic cardioinhibitory effects but no changes in diastolic blood pressure. Recent evidence indicates that in the healthy human heart beta2-adrenoceptors also exhibit functional chronotropic as well as inotropic effects (Levine & Leenen, 1989).

Muscarinic cholinoceptor blockade increases heart rate, except that low atropine doses by central vagus stimulation lead to a bradycardia. Atropine accelerates atrioventricular conduction time (Das, Talmers, & Weissler, 1975). Furthermore, cardiac output is increased and stroke volume decreased (Berry, Thompson, Miller, & McIntosh, 1959); salivary secretion and palmar sweating are depressed (Herxheimer, 1958). Atropine prevents the peripheral vasodilatation and the drop of the diastolic blood pressure following cholinergic agonists; for itself it has no consistent circulatory effects.

The question of central nervous system effects of autonomic receptor antagonists is an important consideration in experiments with human subjects. Indeed, autonomic receptor antagonists, such as atropine and lipophilic beta-adrenoceptor blockers, particularly propranolol (Peart, 1985), have mostly sedative, central nervous system effects (Gilman, Goodman, & Gilman, 1980). Following Koella (1978), a discussion of central effects has to take into account three alternative or simultaneously applicable explanations of these effects:

- The drug produces a specific effect within the brain;
- the drug has unspecific effects on the brain, that is, effects that are independent of its properties as an antagonist;
- the drug's peripheral effects are signalled to the brain.

Turner (1978) questioned the problematic interpretation of studies using beta-adrenergic blockers that attempt to index central nervous system properties, such as "attention", through the measurement of reaction times. He pointed out that beta-adrenergic blockers could delay motor reactions solely by peripheral mechanisms, namely by a decrease of the contraction speed of slow muscle fibers. Tyrer (1980), discussing the anxiolytic effects of propranolol, came to the conclusion that these effects probably are of a peripheral origin provided the usual therapeutic doses are given.

Studies using autonomic receptor blockades face a difficult problem: With the blockade of single autonomic receptor types various homeostatic interactions of the unblocked parts of the autonomic nervous system may occur. These unblocked influences on cardiovascular variables make it sometimes difficult to attribute the change from placebo to blockade measurements to the pure effect of the blocked receptor. Using more than one blockade at a time could offer a solution to this interpretational problem (for a detailed discussion, see Chapter 5.2).

With a *dual blockade of muscarinic cholinoceptors and beta-adrenoceptors*, heart rate increases, however less than under atropine alone (Flessas & Ryan, 1983). Seiler, Mehmel, and Krayenbühl (1974) found an increase of arterial mean blood pressure. Additional isometric exercise led to considerable further elevation of mean blood pressure (obviously of an alpha-adrenergic origin) but no further heart rate increase. This stabilization of the heart rate nicely demonstrates the expected pharmacological "denervation" of the heart under this dual blockade. The reflex tachycardia produced by vasodilatatory drugs (e.g., nitroprussid) in the unblocked state is also completely blunted by this dual cholinergic and beta-adrenergic blockade (Arnold & McDevitt, 1983; Brown, McLeod, & Shand, 1983).

The *dual alpha-adrenergic and beta-adrenergic blockade* leads to a marked anti-hypertensive reaction with a drop of plasma norepinephrine levels (Agabiti-Rosei, Alicandri, Beschi, Castellano, Corea, Beggi, Motolese, & Muiesan, 1983) and an inhibition of the vasoconstriction observed under unselective beta-adrenergic blockade alone (Nelson, Silke, Hussain, Verma, & Taylor, 1984). Nelson et al. (1984) found with patients under antihypertensive chronic treatment with an alpha1-adrenoceptor blocker that an additional application of propranolol further decreased the systolic blood pressure and raised the total peripheral resistance to the unmedicated basal level. These results exemplify the theoretically expected effects of a dual alpha-adrenergic and beta-adrenergic blockade.

Under a *dual muscarinic cholinoceptor and alpha-adrenoceptor blockade* only the beta-adrenergic autonomic receptors are left free. Empirical investigations using this dual blockade protocol are extremely infrequent. Theoretically, one would expect an increase of heart rate, cardiac inotropic functions, and systolic blood pressure, as well as vasodilatation and a drop in diastolic blood pressure.

Table 6 gives a summary account of the effects on selected cardiovascular variables of single and dual autonomic receptor blockades during rest. Needless to say, the studies incorporated in the table form a sample from a much larger number of investigations that can be found in the literature (at least for single autonomic receptor blockades). The table reports the levels of cardiovascular variables under unblocked resting (control) conditions and the changes observed under blockade. With this and the additional information about drug dosages and subjects, the effect size of autonomic receptor blockades can be judged.

Table 6. Adrenergic and Cholinergic Blockade Effects During Rest

Score	HR	SBP	DBP	MBP	CO	SV	TPR	other	other
Alpha-Adrenergic Blockade									
Nelson et al. (1984). Trimazosin, 2mg/kg i.v. N=10 m. Patients with essential hypertension.									
C[a]	81	163	98		3.3i[c]	42i	2950i		
D[b]	ns	-16	-14		ns	ns	-460i		
Sheridan et al. (1986). Indoramin, 0.2 mg/kg i.v. N=11 m. Patients with stable angina were on chronic beta-blockade. Data from "resting sinus rhythm" condition.									
C	?			99	5.5		1428		
D	ns			-7	ns		-171		
Weiss et al. (1980). Trinitroglycerine, infusion until MBP dropped by 10 mmHg. N=6 ?.								PTT	
C	65			81				219	
D	14			-11				16	
Beta-Adrenergic Blockade									
Arnold & McDevitt (1983). Propranolol, infusion until a drug plasma level of 110 ng/ml. N=6 m, f.									
C	59			87					
D	-9			-7					
Brown et al. (1983). Propranolol, 40 mg p.o. N=6 m.									
C	85								
D	-20								
Guazzi et al. (1975). Propranolol, 10 mg i.v. N=12 m. Patients with hyperkinetic syndrome.									
C	91	154	75		5.5i		799		
D	-12	-10	ns		-1.3i		271		
Hurwitz et al. (1988). Propranolol, 10 mg i.v. N=6 m.									
								T-Ampl	
C	76							0%	
D	-18							31%	
Katona et al. (1982). Propranolol, 0.2 mg/kg i.v. N=10 m. Data from non-athlete sample.									
C	61			91					
D	*-10*			*1*					
Martin et al. (1974). Propranolol, 0.15 mg/kg i.v. N=7 m.									
								PEP	LVET
C	62	127	67	88	5.8	96	1228	101	311
D	-6	-4	ns	ns	-0.8	ns	209	ns	ns
Nelson et al. (1984). Propranolol, 0.2 mg/kg i.v. N=10 m. Patients with essential hypertension. D=incremental effect of propranolol over trimazosin.									
C	81	163	98		3.3i	42i	2950i		
D	*-12*	*-11*	*-1*		*-0.7i*	*-3i*	*535i*		

(Table continues)

Table 6. Adrenergic and Cholinergic Blockade Effects During Rest *(continued)*

Score	HR	SBP	DBP	MBP	CO	SV	TPR	other	other
Pollak & Obrist (1988). Propranolol, 4 mg i.v. N=15 ?.									
C	69								
D	-4								
Seiler et al. (1974). Propranolol, 0.2 mg/kg i.v. N=6 m, f. Patients with normal left-ventricular functioning.									
C	70			91	3.6i	51i	1950i		
D	*-11*			*1*	*-0.7*i	*-3*i	*468*i		
Silke et al. (1983). Propranolol, Patients with coronary heart disease.									
C	72	141	83	104	3.5i		2440i		
2 mg i.v. N=20 m.									
D	-4	ns	ns	ns	-0.3i		207i		
4 mg i.v. N=20 m.									
D	-6	ns	ns	ns	-0.4i		308i		
8 mg i.v. N=20 m.									
D	-7	ns	ns	ns	-0.5i		386i		
16 mg i.v. N=20 m.									
D	-8	ns	ns	ns	-0.6i		483i		
v.Eiff et al. (1969). Propranolol, 80 mg p.o. N=24 m.									
C	72	114	69						
D	-8	-8	-3						
Weiss et al. (1980). Propranolol, 0.2 mg/kg i.v. N=6 ?.								PTT	
C	68			81				220	
D	-12			-3				16	
Cholinergic Blockade									
Arnold & McDevitt (1983). Atropine, 0.04 mg/kg i.v. N=6 m, f. D=incremental effect of atropine over propranolol.									
C	59			87					
D	51			12					
Berry et al. (1959). Atropine 2 mg i.v. N=22 m, f. Twenty healthy Ss, 2 patients (1 essential hypertension, 1 peptic ulcer).									
C	69	124	63	81	6.1	91	1084		
D	48	ns	ns	5	1.7	-23	-173		
Das et al. (1975). Atropine. Healthy Ss and patients undergoing diagnostic atrial pacing.									
0.1 mg i.v. N=11 ?.								P-Q	
C	71							158	
D	-6							-7	
0.2 mg i.v. N=14 ?.									
C	68							157	
D	-6							-16	
0.3 mg i.v. N=9 ?.									
C	72							163	
D	ns							-21	

(Table continues)

Table 6. Adrenergic and Cholinergic Blockade Effects During Rest *(continued)*

Score	HR	SBP	DBP	MBP	CO	SV	TPR	other	other
0.4 mg i.v. N=16 ?.								P-Q	
C	66							161	
D	ns							-18	
0.8 mg i.v. N=12 ?.									
C	70							149	
D	21							-12	
Flessas & Ryan (1983). Atropine, 1.2 mg i.v. N=11 ?. Patients prior to coronary angiography. Patients received chronic propranolol and acutely 10 mg diazepam.									
C	57				2.2i	41i	1968		
D	15				0.3i	ns	ns		
Goldstein & Keiser (1984). Atropine, 0.0286 mg/kg i.v. N=12 m, f.								NE	
C	74			82				182	
D	34			7				-73	
Hurwitz et al. (1988). Atropine, 0.04 mg/kg i.v. N=6 m.									T-Ampl
C	71								0%
D	45								-43%
Katona et al. (1982). Atropine, 0.04 mg/kg i.v. N=10 m. Data from nonathlete sample.									
C	63			89					
D	54			14					
Knoebel et al. (1974). Atropine, 1 mg i.v. N=10 ?. Patients without coronary artery disease.									
C	74		70	97	4.2				
D	40		5	ns	0.6				
Levine & Leenen (1989). Atropine, 0.02 mg/kg i.v. N=6 m. TPRi calculated by current author (G.S.).									
C	55	113	67		2.7i	95	2430i		
D	34	8	10		1.8i	ns	*-795*i		
Martin et al. (1974). Atropine 2 mg i.v. N=12 m.								PEP	LVET
C	66	151	75	96	6.2	94	1289	104	299
D	*49*	*1*	*15*	*12*	*1.4*	-28	*-107*	*3*	-64
Pollak & Obrist (1988). Atropine, 0.02 mg/kg i.v. N=15 ?.									
C	62								
D	*39*								
Seiler et al. (1974). Atropine, 0.04 mg/kg i.v. N=6 m, f. Patients with normal left-ventricular functioning.									
C	70			91	3.6i	51i	1950i		
D	*43*			*8*	*1.3*i	*-7*i	*-568*i		
Stratton et al. (1987). Atropine, 2 mg i.v. N=5 m. Values registered during infusion of NE (125 mg/kg/min) and E (50 mg/kg/min). Percentages refer to no-drug baseline.									
C	67	140		93	54%	41%	-31%		
D	60	39		19	208%	17%	-32%		

(Table continues)

Table 6. Adrenergic and Cholinergic Blockade Effects During Rest *(continued)*

Score	HR	SBP	DBP	MBP	CO	SV	TPR	other	other
Weiss et al. (1980). Atropine, 0.04 mg/kg i.v. N=6 ?.								PTT	
C	72			90				200	
D	57			ns				-8	
Alpha-Adrenergic and Beta-Adrenergic Blockade									
Nelson et al. (1984). Trimazosin, 2 mg/kg, and propranolol, 0.2 mg/kg i.v. N=10 m. Patients with essential hypertension.									
C	81	163	98		3.3i	42i	2950i		
D	-9	-27	-15		-0.6i	ns	ns		
Beta-Adrenergic and Cholinergic Blockade									
Arnold & McDevitt (1983). Propranolol, infusion until a drug plasma level of 110 ng/ml and atropine, 0.04 mg/kg i.v. N=6 m, f.									
C	59			87					
D	46			8					
Hurwitz et al. (1988). Propranolol, 10 mg, and atropine, 0.04 mg/kg i.v. N=6 m.								T-Ampl	
C	74							0%	
D	16							ns	
Katona et al. (1982). Propranolol, 0.2 mg/kg, and atropine, 0.04 mg/kg i.v. N=10 m. Data from nonathlete sample. Values are averages from both drug application sequences.									
C	62			90					
D	*39*			*15*					
Martin et al. (1974). Propranolol, 0.15 mg/kg, and atropine, 2 mg i.v. N=7 m.								PEP	LVET
C	66	151	75	96	6.2	94	1289	104	299
D	*23*	*2*	*14*	*12*	*0.8*	*-18*	*-20*	*14*	*-22*
Seiler et al. (1974). Propranolol, 0.2 mg/kg, and atropine, 0.04 mg/kg i.v. N=6 m, f. Patients with normal left-ventricular functioning.									
C	70			91	3.6i	51i	1950i		
D	*32*			*9*	*0.6i*	*-10i*	*-100i*		

Note. All studies cited used a within-subjects design to determine blockade effects and acute drug administrations. Subjects were healthy volunteers if not otherwise indicated. HR = Heart rate in bpm. SBP, DBP, MBP = Systolic, diastolic, and mean blood pressure, respectively, in mmHg. CO = Cardiac output in l/min. SV = stroke volume in ml. TPR = Total peripheral resistance in dynes*sec/cm^5. PTT = pulse transit time in msec. T-Ampl = T-wave amplitude. PEP = Preejection period in msec. LVET = Left-ventricular ejection time in msec. P-Q = P-wave to Q-wave onset time in msec. E = Epinephrine. NE = Norepinephrine. [a]Control score without blocker (e.g., baseline or placebo). [b]Difference score drug - control condition. Given are significant difference scores. An "ns" indicates a nonsignificant difference. Italics indicate that statistical tests were not reported. [c]Index of CO, SV, or TPR, that is, values relative to body surface in m^2.

5.1.3 Cardiovascular activation components

As has been described in the previous section, descriptive units for the major contributions to the regulation of the cardiovascular system include the division of the autonomic nervous system into its sympathetic and parasympathetic branches and the corresponding differentiation among the various types of autonomic receptors that are involved in the transmission of information within the cardiovascular system. To speak of cardiovascular activation *components* means that these distinct autonomic influences vary quantitatively and are functionally organized in partial independence from and in partial interaction with each other (Levy & Martin, 1979).

The use of a notion as broad as that of cardiovascular activation components may be criticized for not being consistent with recent neurophysiological evidence that shows highly specific and independent sympathetic efferent regulation of different effector organs (see Chapter 4.2). It has already been argued, however, that broad and narrow approaches to autonomic influences are compatible with each other when considering the "longitudinal" organization of the control of the cardiovascular system: Adopting the perspective of cardiovascular response integration at the hypothalamical level (e.g., ergotropic versus trophotropic activation; Hess, 1948), it seems appropriate to base a Model of Cardiovascular Activation Components on broadly defined components. Empirical evidence for broad cardiovascular activation components can be found in many physiological and psychophysiological studies, particularly in those that use agonists and antagonists of adrenergic and cholinergic receptors. In fact, even a cursory review of the cardiovascular physiological literature reveals the voluminous empirical support for such attributions (e.g., Shepherd & Vanhoutte, 1979).

Three examples from the literature are presented here to concretely illustrate the notion of cardiovascular activation components. Data from these example studies are presented as three-dimensional plots, because such geometrical representation, better than two-dimensional plots, reveals the impact of different autonomic influences on cardiovascular functioning, as well as the relationships between autonomic components. Points in these plots represent profiles of physiological levels or responses (see Chapter 7) during specified tasks or conditions. The orientation of the axes has been chosen for each single graph such that the critical features to be demonstrated are best visualized. The examples serve to demonstrate different aspects of cardiovascular activation components. Employing pharmacological interventions during rest, the first example nicely illustrates the notion that cardiovascular activation *components* imply a quantitative variation along linearly independent directions within the geometric space of cardiovascular variables. The second example substantiates this claim with data showing the effects of different experimental tasks. The third example introduces and illustrates the idea of a decomposition of task effects into the contributions of cardiovascular autonomic activation components.

Example 1. The study by Weiss, Del Bo, Reichek, and Engelman (1980) is particularly interesting because intravenous administrations of alpha-adrenergic, beta-adrenergic, and cholinergic agonists (phenylephrine, isoproterenol, and edrophonium, respectively) and corresponding antagonists[9] (trinitroglycerin until a 10 mmHg fall in mean arterial blood pressure occurred, propranolol 0.2 mg/kg, and atropine 0.04 mg/kg, respectively) were carried out on the same subjects on different occasions. Response profiles consisted of three variables, pulse transit time, heart rate, and mean arterial blood pressure. The data reported in the authors' Table 1 are presented here (see Figure 6) as control-drug differences (in both occasions registered under resting conditions).

Figure 6 illustrates (1) that the response profiles of agonists and antagonists of the same receptor type are positioned roughly on a line through the origin (i.e., the resting drug-free control condition R) and (2) that the lines of different receptors' agonists and antagonists are linearly independent. These characteristics are consistent with the notion of cardiovascular activation components in that they imply quantitative variation in partial independence. The location of these components suggests the following main characteristics (see Weiss et al., 1980, for a detailed presentation of these characterizations):

- Alpha-adrenergic activation is reflected by increasing mean arterial blood pressure and decreasing heart rate,
- beta-adrenergic activation, by elevations in heart rate and shortening of pulse transit time,
- cholinergiccholinergic activation, solely by heart rate lowering.

Example 2. In a study by Guazzi, Fiorentini, Polese, Magrini, and Olivari (1975), cardiovascular variables were recorded during rest, head-up tilting, mental arithmetic, and cold pressor under both placebo and beta-blocking propranolol (10 mg i.v.). Of the results reported in the authors' Table 2, condition means (across hyperkinetic patients) of heart rate, total peripheral resistance, and mean arterial blood pressure are shown in Figure 7 (these variables were selected for graphical presentation in order to provide comparability between examples).

Figure 7 illustrates that the changes from rest and task profiles under placebo to the respective profiles under propranolol follow approximately the same direction: heart rate decreases and total peripheral resistance increases, whereas mean arterial blood pressure remains nearly unchanged. This roughly parallel change across conditions again confirms the notion that cardiovascular activation components (in this case, propranolol-induced changes in beta-adrenergic activation) can be conceived of as dimensions, or linear combinations in the statistical sense. This largely parallel change also suggests that the beta-adrenergic component did not strongly interact with other autonomic

---

[9] Dosages of antagonists are given to facilitate comparisons across examples. It should be noted that trinitroglycerin is not strictly an alpha-adrenergic antagonist, even though it has comparable effects.

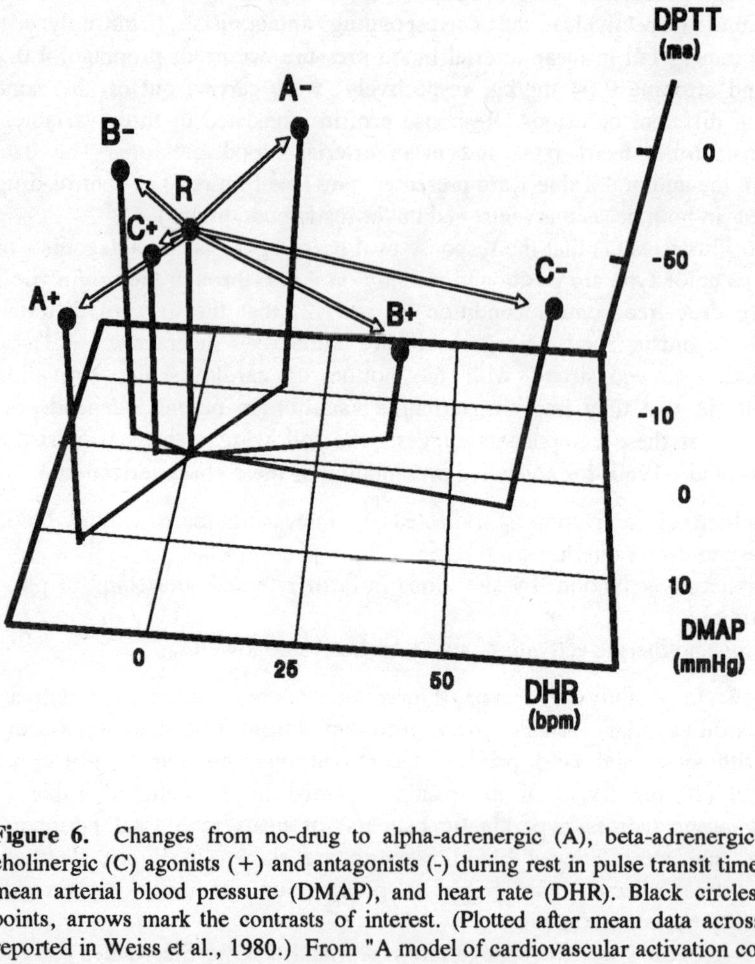

Figure 6. Changes from no-drug to alpha-adrenergic (A), beta-adrenergic (B), and cholinergic (C) agonists (+) and antagonists (-) during rest in pulse transit time (DPTT), mean arterial blood pressure (DMAP), and heart rate (DHR). Black circles are data points, arrows mark the contrasts of interest. (Plotted after mean data across subjects reported in Weiss et al., 1980.) From "A model of cardiovascular activation components for studies using autonomic receptor antagonists" by G. Stemmler, P. Grossman, H. Schmid, & F. Foerster, 1991, *28*, 367-382. Copyright by The Society for Psychophysiological Research. Reproduced by permission.

components. This conclusion seems likely because the tasks used can be expected to differ markedly in one or both of the remaining activation components, an expectation that is corroborated by the task profiles' widely spread locations on the bottom plane of the cube in Figure 7.

Example 3. The study by Seiler, Mehmel, and Krayenbühl (1974) used a within-subjects design to investigate autonomic influences upon handgrip

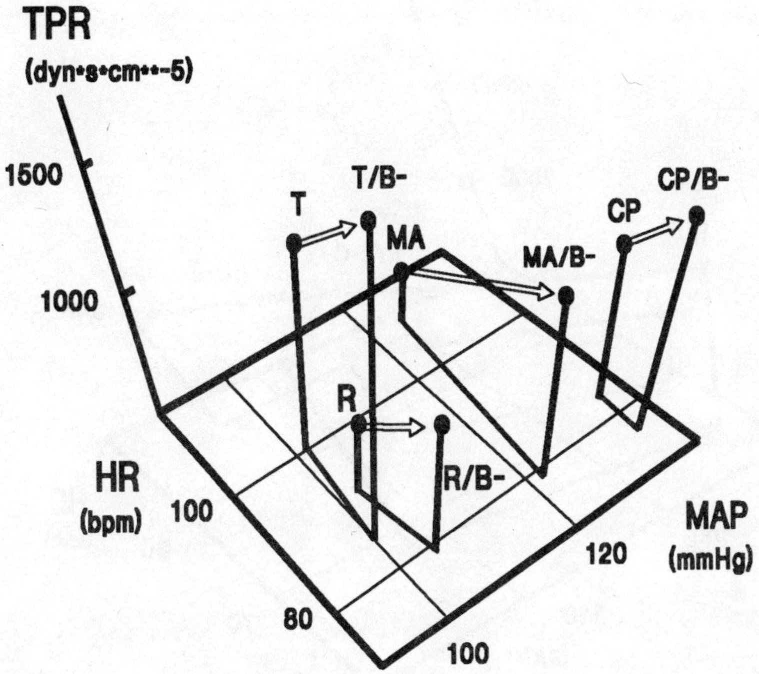

Figure 7. Rest (R), tilting (T), mental arithmetic (MA), and cold pressor (CP) under no-drug and beta-blocked (B-) conditions in total peripheral resistance (TPR), heart rate (HR), and mean arterial blood pressure (MAP). Black circles are data points, arrows mark the contrasts of interest. (Plotted after mean data across subjects reported in Guazzi et al., 1975.) From "A model of cardiovascular activation components for studies using autonomic receptor antagonists" by G. Stemmler, P. Grossman, H. Schmid, & F. Foerster, 1991, *28*, 367-382. Copyright by The Society for Psychophysiological Research. Reproduced by permission.

isometric exercise. Handgrip exercise was performed before and after administration of single and dual blockades by propranolol (0.2 mg/kg i.v.) and propranolol plus atropine (0.04 mg/kg i.v.). Of the hemodynamic variables registered, only heart rate, mean arterial blood pressure, and total peripheral resistance are depicted in Figure 8 (data are from the authors' Table 1).

Figure 8 discloses that irrespective of the particular drug condition, the handgrip task increased both the index of total peripheral resistance and mean

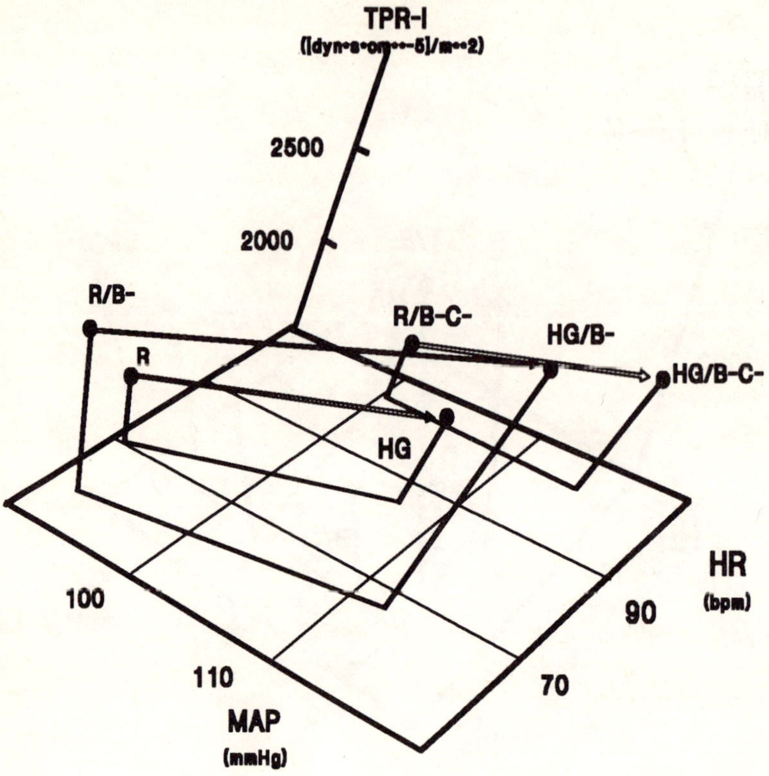

Figure 8. Rest (R) and handgrip (HG) under no-drug, beta-blocker, and beta- plus cholinergic blocker (B-C-) conditions in the index of total peripheral resistance (TPR-I), heart rate (HR), and mean arterial blood pressure (MAP). Black circles are data points, arrows mark the contrasts of interest. (Plotted after mean data across subjects reported in Seiler et al., 1974.) From "A model of cardiovascular activation components for studies using autonomic receptor antagonists" by G. Stemmler, P. Grossman, H. Schmid, & F. Foerster, 1991, *28*, 367-382. Copyright by The Society for Psychophysiological Research. Reproduced by permission.

arterial blood pressure. The heart rate increase seen during handgrip in the no-drug condition was successively blocked by propranolol and atropine. Because the blockades were nearly complete, the response under beta-adrenergic plus cholinergic blockade should have been mediated by the alpha-adrenergic component of the handgrip task and by residual influences,[10] the response solely

[10] All other influences on cardiovascular variables than those produced by the three kinds of autonomic receptors, for example, the action of neuropeptides or the metabolic

under beta-adrenergic blockade by the alpha-adrenergic plus cholinergic drug components, as well as by residual influences, and the response under the no-condition by all three activation components and by residual influences.

It should be intuitively clear that the successive blockades can be used to disentangle the contributions of the three cardiovascular activation components on the variables. The difference of rest-task responses between the no-drug and the beta-adrenergic blockade condition should reflect changes in the beta-adrenergic component during handgrip. Similarly, differences of rest-task responses between beta-adrenergic and the combined beta-adrenergic plus cholinergic blockades should disclose changes in the cholinergic component. Finally, the rest-task response under dual beta-adrenergic plus cholinergic blockade should reflect changes in the alpha-adrenergic component during handgrip.

Figure 8 also demonstrates the "unmasking" of alpha-adrenergic effects through propranolol (which also blocks vasodilatory beta-2 receptors; Bonelli, 1982) which is indicated by the high levels of total peripheral resistance under this blockade. However, Figure 8 also reveals that under additional cholinergic blockade this alpha-adrenergic unmasking is completely blunted.

In sum, these examples strongly suggest that the notion of cardiovascular autonomic activation components is a promising one to be explored. In particular, the quantitative decomposition of observed cardiovascular responses into contributions from cardiovascular activation components, as has been geometrically demonstrated in the third example, is the major idea that will be more rigorously treated in the next sections.

5.2 A Model of Autonomic Cardiovascular Activation Components

5.2.1 The unrestricted model of cardiovascular activation components

Statistical models explaining changes in single cardiovascular variables as a function of autonomic activation components are well-known in the literature. Rosenblueth and Simeone (1934) and later Katona, McLean, Dighton, and Guz (1982) modeled heart rate levels as a function of indices of sympathetic and parasympathetic tone, and of the intrinsic heart rate freed of all neural influences (Jose & Taylor, 1969). The experimental protocol needed for the estimate of the unknown parameters consists of successive single and dual autonomic blockades. Levy and Zieske (1969; see also Levy & Martin, 1979) modeled changes in heart rate and in atrioventricular conduction time as a function of vagal and sympathetic nerve stimulation frequency. In a regression analysis, vagal and

---

autoregulation of the peripheral circulation, remain for the present purposes unspecified and will be collectively termed "residual influences".

sympathetic stimulation frequency were additively combined in linear, quadratic, and linear-interactive terms.

The model to be proposed here (which is a refined version of the model proposed by Stemmler, Grossman, Schmid, & Foerster, 1991) is an elaboration of the one Levy and Zieske suggested. It is distinct from the latter insofar as it more comprehensively contains three (alpha-adrenergic, beta-adrenergic, and cholinergic), rather than two (sympathetic and vagal) autonomic activation components and also includes indices for subjects (i), situations (j), and variables (m). However, in contrast to the Levy and Zieske model, quadratic or other nonlinear terms are not specified (see Chapter 5.2.5 for a discussion of model limitations including the number of components specified). According to this model, the measurement x_{ijm} of a cardiovascular variable is decomposable into

- the intrinsic activity a_{m0i} that obtains when the effector organ is (pharmacologically or surgically) completely isolated from all autonomic influences,
- the magnitude of pure[11] alpha-adrenergic (α_{ij}), pure beta-adrenergic (β_{ij}), and pure cholinergic (τ_{ij}) activations elicited by situation j, where these activations are quantitatively "distributed" to the target organs as indicated by the coefficients a_m and affect the activity of variable x_m by the amounts of $a_{m1}\alpha_{ij}$, $a_{m2}\beta_{ij}$, and $a_{m3}\tau_{ij}$,
- interactive effects of activation components ($a_{m4}\alpha\beta_{ij}$, $a_{m5}\alpha\tau_{ij}$, $a_{m6}\beta\tau_{ij}$, and $a_{m7}\alpha\beta\tau_{ij}$) on variable x_m,
- residual influences ($a_{m8}\Gamma_{ij}$) (e.g., local metabolic influences on variable x_m), and
- an error component ϵ_{ijm} which incorporates systematic (e.g., deviations from the model) and measurement error effects.

Because in this section the emphasis lies on the structural model and not on questions of estimation, the error term will be omitted. Therefore the structural model for the true-score variable X_m (observed variables are written in small, true score variables, in capital letters) reads:

$$X_{ijm} = a_{m0i} + a_{m1}\alpha_{ij} + a_{m2}\beta_{ij} + a_{m3}\tau_{ij} + a_{m4}\alpha\beta_{ij} + a_{m5}\alpha\tau_{ij} + a_{m6}\beta\tau_{ij} + a_{m7}\alpha\beta\tau_{ij} + a_{m8}\Gamma_{ij} \,. \tag{14}$$

In order to focus the discussion of the model to the issue of task characterizations, the next equation expresses the model in terms of situation means across subjects:

$$X_{jm} = a_{m0} + a_{m1}\alpha_j + a_{m2}\beta_j + a_{m3}\tau_j + a_{m4}\alpha\beta_j + a_{m5}\alpha\tau_j + a_{m6}\beta\tau_j + a_{m7}\alpha\beta\tau_j + a_{m8}\Gamma_j \,. \tag{15}$$

[11] I shall call the activation of a component "pure", if it is not influenced by the activations of the other components. Pure activation obtains, for example, when there are no interactions among the components, or if so, when the other components are completely blocked, that is, have zero activity.

In general, both the coefficients a_m and the magnitude of activity in the activation components (α_j, β_j, τ_j) are unknown, unless an experimental variation of the activation components is performed, as, for example, through nerve stimulation (see Levy and Zieske, 1969). Furthermore, information about the unknown coefficients and components can also be obtained from experiments presenting tasks under certain forms of pharmacological blockades. The next section will consider such blockade experiments in light of some simplifying assumptions about the unrestricted model of Equation 15.

5.2.2 Two restricted models of cardiovascular activation components

The unrestricted model of cardiovascular activation components is difficult to identify with the experimental tool of autonomic receptor blockades. This will become obvious when I first consider a slight restriction of the general model (with the omission of the term representing residual influences, i.e., an "r-restricted model") which still requires a complicated blockade protocol for its complete identification. A considerably more restricted model will then be introduced (with an additional omission of all interaction terms, i.e., an "ir-restricted model") which demonstrably is the implicit basis for the logic, the experimental protocol, and the interpretation of nearly all physiological, cardiological, and psychophysiological investigations using autonomic receptor blockades.

The r-restricted model. The structural equation of the r-restricted model that dispenses with residual influences reads

$$ {}^{r}X_{jm} = a_{m0} + a_{m1}\alpha_j + a_{m2}\beta_j + a_{m3}\tau_j + a_{m4}\alpha\beta_j + a_{m5}\alpha\tau_j + a_{m6}\beta\tau_j + a_{m7}\alpha\beta\tau_j \,. \tag{16} $$

Under the assumption that this model is actually true and that complete blockades have been administered, the following equations describe the separate effects of autonomic activation components on variables. It should be noted that under incomplete blockades the identification of the effects of cardiovascular activation components on variables is not as straightforward as described below (see Chapter 5.3.2 for a treatment of incomplete blockades). The following notation is used below: "R" stands for rest period, "A-" for alpha-adrenoceptor blockade, "B-" for beta-adrenoceptor blockade, and "C-" for cholinoceptor blockade; expressions of the type "(*j*/A-)" stand for 'task *j* under alpha-adrenergic blockade'. The following expressions show that a complete identification of the r-restricted model of Equation 16 requires all of the three single (A-, B-, and C-) and all of the three dual blockades (A-B-, A-C-, and B-C-) as well as the triple blockade (A-B-C-):

$$ a_{m0} = {}^{r}X_{(j/\text{A-B-C-})m} \,, \tag{17a} $$

$$a_{m1}\alpha_j = {}^{r}X_{(j/\text{B-C-})m} - {}^{r}X_{(j/\text{A-B-C-})m}\,, \tag{17b}$$

$$a_{m2}\beta_j = {}^{r}X_{(j/\text{A-C-})m} - {}^{r}X_{(j/\text{A-B-C-})m}\,, \tag{17c}$$

$$a_{m3}\tau_j = {}^{r}X_{(j/\text{A-B-})m} - {}^{r}X_{(j/\text{A-B-C-})m}\,, \tag{17d}$$

$$a_{m4}\alpha\beta_j = {}^{r}X_{(j/\text{C-})}\text{m} - {}^{r}X_{(j/\text{B-C-})m} - {}^{r}X_{(j/\text{A-C-})m} + {}^{r}X_{(j/\text{A-B-C-})m}\,, \tag{17e}$$

$$a_{m5}\alpha\tau_j = {}^{r}X_{(j/\text{B-})m} - {}^{r}X_{(j/\text{B-C-})m} - {}^{r}X_{(j/\text{A-B-})m} + {}^{r}X_{(j/\text{A-B-C-})m}\,, \tag{17f}$$

$$a_{m6}\beta\tau_j = {}^{r}X_{(j/\text{A-})m} - {}^{r}X_{(j/\text{A-C-})m} - {}^{r}X_{(j/\text{A-B-})m} + {}^{r}X_{(j/\text{A-B-C-})m}\,, \tag{17g}$$

$$a_{m7}\alpha\beta\tau_j = {}^{r}X_{jm} - {}^{r}X_{(j/\text{A-})m} - {}^{r}X_{(j/\text{B-})m} - {}^{r}X_{(j/\text{C-})}\text{m} + {}^{r}X_{(j/\text{B-C-})m} + {}^{r}X_{(j/\text{A-C-})m} + {}^{r}X_{(j/\text{A-B-})m} - {}^{r}X_{(j/\text{A-B-C-})m}\,. \tag{17h}$$

The ir-restricted model. A blockade protocol necessary to determine the effects of cardiovascular activation components in the r-restricted model of Equation 16 will be most often practically impossible to realize. Therefore, another restriction that can be imposed upon the unrestricted model in Equation 15 that omits both the interaction terms and the term for the residual influence is particularly relevant for applied work. For practical purposes, this ir-restricted model will be stated in either of two forms, one that explains task levels and one that explains differences between two tasks (often task-rest differences):

$${}^{ir}X_{jm} = a_{m0} + a_{m1}\alpha_j + a_{m2}\beta_j + a_{m3}\tau_j\,, \tag{18a}$$

(Task Level Form)

$${}^{ir}X_{jm} - {}^{ir}X_{\text{R}m} = a_{m1}(\alpha_j - \alpha_\text{R}) + a_{m2}(\beta_j - \beta_\text{R}) + a_{m3}(\tau_j - \tau_\text{R})\,. \tag{18b}$$

(Task-Rest Response Form)

In the following, I will describe how under the assumption of the restricted form of the Activation Components Model the influence of autonomic activation components on cardiovascular variables can be disentangled with the use of blockade data. (Demonstrations of the formalism will be given in Chapters 5.2.4 and 5.3.1.) Again I shall assume that complete blockades have been administered. Terms in the ir-restricted model can be determined from blockade protocols that use either single, or dual, or mixed single and dual pharmacological blockades. These three types of blockade protocol will now be separately described.

The ir-restricted model: Single pharmacological blockades. Given complete single autonomic blockades with alpha-adrenergic, beta-adrenergic, and cholinergic antagonists, the structural model of Equation 18a simplifies (by dropping terms including the activation components α, β, and τ, respectively) to:

$$^{ir}X_{(j/\text{A-})m} = a_{m0} + a_{m2}\beta_j + a_{m3}\tau_j \,, \tag{19a}$$

$$^{ir}X_{(j/\text{B-})m} = a_{m0} + a_{m1}\alpha_j + a_{m3}\tau_j \,, \tag{19b}$$

$$^{ir}X_{(j/\text{C-})m} = a_{m0} + a_{m1}\alpha_j + a_{m2}\beta_j \,. \tag{19c}$$

Task *level* effects of activation components on variables can then be obtained by forming the difference between the means of the unblocked and the appropriately blocked task conditions (e.g., use of a beta-blocker to obtain the beta-adrenergic level effect on a variable):

$$a_{m0} = {}^{ir}X_{(j/\text{A-})m} + {}^{ir}X_{(j/\text{B-})m} + {}^{ir}X_{(j/\text{C-})m} - 2\,{}^{ir}X_{jm} \,, \tag{20a}$$

$$a_{m1}\alpha_j = {}^{ir}X_{jm} - {}^{ir}X_{(j/\text{A-})m} \,, \tag{20b}$$

$$a_{m2}\beta_j = {}^{ir}X_{jm} - {}^{ir}X_{(j/\text{B-})m} \,, \tag{20c}$$

$$a_{m3}\tau_j = {}^{ir}X_{jm} - {}^{ir}X_{(j/\text{C-})m} \,. \tag{20d}$$

In order to evaluate *response* effects in single blockade studies, it is critically important which terms are subtracted (if the "response" is measured by a difference score) from one another. Differences between tasks (or task and rest) within one blockade condition (e.g., between task and rest means, both from beta-blockade data) do not provide information concerning the differential beta-adrenergic effects of one condition over the other. On the other hand, the tetrad difference between two tasks (or task and rest) under blocked and unblocked conditions does give valid information about these response effects:

$$a_{m1}(\alpha_j - \alpha_\text{R}) = ({}^{ir}X_{jm} - {}^{ir}X_{\text{R}m}) - ({}^{ir}X_{(j/\text{A-})m} - {}^{ir}X_{(\text{R/A-})m}) \,, \tag{21a}$$

$$a_{m2}(\beta_j - \beta_\text{R}) = ({}^{ir}X_{jm} - {}^{ir}X_{\text{R}m}) - ({}^{ir}X_{(j/\text{B-})m} - {}^{ir}X_{(\text{R/B-})m}) \,, \tag{21b}$$

$$a_{m3}(\tau_j - \tau_\text{R}) = ({}^{ir}X_{jm} - {}^{ir}X_{\text{R}m}) - ({}^{ir}X_{(j/\text{C-})m} - {}^{ir}X_{(\text{R/C-})m}) \,. \tag{21c}$$

It should be noted that most authors, when evaluating the results of their blockade studies, form - either explicitly or indirectly by calculating analysis of variance effects - exactly the kinds of differences that have just been described to reflect levels or responses of activation components (e.g., Langer, McCubbin, Stoney, Hutcheson, Charlton, & Obrist, 1985; Light, 1985; Maciel, Gallo, Neto, & Martins, 1987; McAllister, 1979; Netter, 1986; Pollak & Obrist, 1988; Weiss et al., 1980). Given that interactive effects are not taken into account in this approach, the ir-restricted form of the Activation Components Model appears to be the implicit basis for most of the empirical work in cardiovascular blockade studies and for the theoretical integration of results.

The ir-restricted model: Dual pharmacological blockades. Given complete dual autonomic blockades, the ir-restricted model simplifies (by dropping terms that include the blocked activation components) to:

$$^{ir}X_{(j/\text{A-B-})m} = a_{m0} + a_{m3}\tau_j\,, \tag{22a}$$

$$^{ir}X_{(j/\text{A-C-})m} = a_{m0} + a_{m2}\beta_j\,, \tag{22b}$$

$$^{ir}X_{(j/\text{B-C-})m} = a_{m0} + a_{m1}\alpha_j\,. \tag{22c}$$

Thus, task means under dual blockade correspond directly to task *level* effects:

$$a_{m0} = ({}^{ir}X_{(j/\text{A-B-})m} + {}^{ir}X_{(j/\text{A-C-})m} + {}^{ir}X_{(j/\text{B-C-})m} - {}^{ir}X_{jm})/2\,, \tag{23a}$$

$$a_{m1}\alpha_j = {}^{ir}X_{(j/\text{B-C-})m} - a_{m0} = ({}^{ir}X_{jm} + {}^{ir}X_{(j/\text{B-C-})m} - {}^{ir}X_{(j/\text{A-B-})m} - {}^{ir}X_{(j/\text{A-C-})m})/2\,, \tag{23b}$$

$$a_{m2}\beta_j = {}^{ir}X_{(j/\text{A-C-})m} - a_{m0} = ({}^{ir}X_{jm} + {}^{ir}X_{(j/\text{A-C-})m} - {}^{ir}X_{(j/\text{A-B-})m} - {}^{ir}X_{(j/\text{B-C-})m})/2\,, \tag{23c}$$

$$a_{m3}\tau_j = {}^{ir}X_{(j/\text{A-B-})m} - a_{m0} = ({}^{ir}X_{jm} + {}^{ir}X_{(j/\text{A-B-})m} - {}^{ir}X_{(j/\text{A-C-})m} - {}^{ir}X_{(j/\text{B-C-})m})/2\,. \tag{23d}$$

In contrast to single blockades, the differences between two task means (or task and rest), both under the same dual blockade, permit valid conclusions to be drawn regarding task *response* effects for each of the activation components:

$$a_{m1}(\alpha_j - \alpha_R) = {}^{ir}X_{(j/\text{B-C-})m} - {}^{ir}X_{(R/\text{B-C-})m}\,, \tag{24a}$$

$$a_{m2}(\beta_j - \beta_R) = {}^{ir}X_{(j/\text{A-C-})m} - {}^{ir}X_{(R/\text{A-C-})m}\,, \tag{24b}$$

$$a_{m3}(\tau_j - \tau_R) = {}^{ir}X_{(j/\text{A-B-})m} - {}^{ir}X_{(R/\text{A-B-})m}\,. \tag{24c}$$

The ir-restricted model: Single and dual blockades. The effects on *task* levels of single and dual blockades administered in one experiment can be obtained in several alternative ways:

$$a_{m0} = {}^{ir}X_{jm} - 2*({}^{ir}X_{(j/u)m} - {}^{ir}X_{(j/uv)m}) - {}^{ir}X_{(j/v)m} + {}^{ir}X_{(j/uw)m}\,, \tag{25a}$$

(for $\{u, v, w\} = \{\text{A-, B-, or C-}\}$)

$$a_{m1}\alpha_j = {}^{ir}X_{(j/\text{B-})m} - {}^{ir}X_{(j/\text{A-B-})m} = {}^{ir}X_{(j/\text{C-})m} - {}^{ir}X_{(j/\text{A-C-})m}\,, \tag{25b}$$

$$a_{m2}\beta_j = {}^{ir}X_{(j/\text{A-})m} - {}^{ir}X_{(j/\text{A-B-})m} = {}^{ir}X_{(j/\text{C-})m} - {}^{ir}X_{(j/\text{B-C-})m}\,, \tag{25c}$$

$$a_{m3}\tau_j = {}^{ir}X_{(j/\text{B-})m} - {}^{ir}X_{(j/\text{B-C-})m} = {}^{ir}X_{(j/\text{A-})m} - {}^{ir}X_{(j/\text{A-C-})m}\,. \tag{25d}$$

Finally, *response* effects under single and dual blockades are obtained by:

$$a_{m1}(\alpha_j - \alpha_R) = ({}^{ir}X_{(j/\text{B-})m} - {}^{ir}X_{(R/\text{B-})m}) - ({}^{ir}X_{(j/\text{A-B-})m} - {}^{ir}X_{(R/\text{A-B-})m}) = ({}^{ir}X_{(j/\text{C-})m} - {}^{ir}X_{(R/\text{C-})m}) - ({}^{ir}X_{(j/\text{A-C-})m} - {}^{ir}X_{(R/\text{A-C-})m})\,, \tag{26a}$$

$$a_{m2}(\beta_j - \beta_R) =$$
$$({}^{ir}X_{(j/A-)m} - {}^{ir}X_{(R/A-)m}) - ({}^{ir}X_{(j/A-B-)m} - {}^{ir}X_{(R/A-B-)m}) =$$
$$({}^{ir}X_{(j/C-)m} - {}^{ir}X_{(R/C-)m}) - ({}^{ir}X_{(j/B-C-)m} - {}^{ir}X_{(R/B-C-)m})\,, \qquad (26b)$$

$$a_{m3}(\tau_j - \tau_R) =$$
$$({}^{ir}X_{(j/B-)m} - {}^{ir}X_{(R/B-)m}) - ({}^{ir}X_{(j/B-C-)m} - {}^{ir}X_{(R/B-C-)m}) =$$
$$({}^{ir}X_{(j/A-)m} - {}^{ir}X_{(R/A-)m}) - ({}^{ir}X_{(j/A-C-)m} - {}^{ir}X_{(R/A-C-)m})\,. \qquad (26c)$$

5.2.3 Consequences of model misspecifications

It has been noted in the preceding section that the ir-restricted form of the Activation Components Model, which neither considers interactions between different autonomic branches nor residual nonautonomic influences upon cardiovascular functioning, is the implicit basis for most of the work on the effects of autonomic blockades in physiology and psychophysiology. However, given the demonstrated fact that at least some cardiovascular variables are generally or occasionally influenced by interactions between activation components or by residual factors (see Levy & Martin, 1979), the ir-restricted form of the model is not always valid. What are the consequences of such restricted model assumptions when they are erroneous?

Violation of the "no interaction components" assumption. Here the case is considered that, instead of the ir-restricted (Equation 18a), the r-restricted model (Equation 16) holds (accounting for autonomic interactions but not residual nonautonomic influences). The consequence of this violation can be revealed if activation component effects as described by ${}^{ir}X_{jm}$ (representing the falsely assumed model) are expressed in terms of ${}^{r}X_{jm}$ (representing the true model). This is demonstrated below, without loss of generality, only for the task level effects of the alpha-adrenergic component (see Equations 20b, 23b, and 25b). The bias of erroneously assuming the ir-restricted model shows up in differences (apart from replacing ${}^{ir}X_{jm}$ by ${}^{r}X_{jm}$) between the middle and the right-hand expressions of the following equations:

$$a_{m1}\alpha_j = {}^{ir}X_{jm} - {}^{ir}X_{(j/A-)m} = {}^{r}X_{jm} - {}^{r}X_{(j/A-)m} - a_{m4}\alpha\beta_j - a_{m5}\alpha\tau_j - a_{m7}\alpha\beta\tau_j\,, \qquad \text{(single blockade)} \quad (27a)$$

$$a_{m1}\alpha_j = {}^{ir}X_{(j/B-C-)m} - a_{m0} = {}^{r}X_{(j/B-C-)m} - a_{m0}\,, \qquad \text{(dual blockade)} \quad (27b)$$

$$a_{m1}\alpha_j = {}^{ir}X_{(j/B-)m} - {}^{ir}X_{(j/A-B-)m} = {}^{r}X_{(j/B-)m} - {}^{r}X_{(j/A-B-)m} - a_{m5}\alpha\tau_j, \qquad (27c)$$

$$a_{m1}\alpha_j = {}^{ir}X_{(j/C-)m} - {}^{ir}X_{(j/A-C-)m} = {}^{r}X_{(j/C-)m} - {}^{r}X_{(j/A-C-)m} - a_{m4}\alpha\beta_j. \qquad (27d)$$

(single and dual blockades)

As can be seen from Equation 27b, a violation of the "no interaction components" assumption of the ir-restricted model *introduces no bias under a dual blockade protocol*. However, *bias is introduced both under a single and a combined single and dual blockade protocol* (see Equations 27a, 27c, and 27d): simple differences (for task level effects) and tetrad differences between means (task-rest response effects) not only include the respective contribution from one activation component but additionally one (combined blockade) or all (single blockade) of the contributions from interactions of that component with the other autonomic influences.

The usefulness of autonomic blockades as a means for disentangling the effects of autonomic cardiovascular activation components on particular cardiovascular variables has been questioned, because "blocking one system can lead to compensatory adjustments which augment the other system" (Heslegrave & Furedy, 1980, p. 489). Indeed, as is shown in Equation 27a, the usual way of determining - within a single blockade protocol - the effect upon a cardiovascular variable of one particular autonomic activation component (i.e., by forming the difference between unblocked and single blockade levels or responses of a cardiovascular variable) can lead one astray, if profound compensatory adjustments, or more generally, interactions exist. But these possible errors are not a principal weakness of the technique of autonomic blockades; instead, these errors result from the erroneous invocation of both a blockade protocol and a set of calculations which are tied, for example, to the ir-restricted model, but are biased, if an interactive model actually applies. The blockade protocols and the calculations needed to determine effects on variables of cardiovascular autonomic activation components under the interactive model of Equation 16 have been shown in Equations 17a to 17h. These equations can, however, be simplified if a variable is known to receive net effects (i.e., both direct and indirect influences) from just two (or even one) autonomic activation components: Terms including activation components that can be neglected are simply dropped from the equations.

Violation of the "no residual influences" assumption. Here the case is considered that, instead of the ir-restricted (Equation 18a), the following *i-restricted model* holds (accounting for nonautonomic residual influences but not autonomic interactions):

$$^{i}X_{jm} = a_{m0} + a_{m1}\alpha_j + a_{m2}\beta_j + a_{m3}\tau_j + a_{m8}\Gamma_j \,. \qquad (28)$$

If, as above, $^{ir}X_{jm}$ in Equations 20b, 23b, and 25b is replaced by $^{i}X_{jm}$ (again this is demonstrated only for the task level effects of the alpha-adrenergic component) and the resulting expressions solved for the effect of the alpha-adrenergic component on variable m, $a_{m1}\alpha_j$, the bias of erroneously assuming the ir-restricted model is demonstrated in differences (apart from replacing $^{ir}X_{jm}$ by $^{i}X_{jm}$) between the middle and the right-hand expressions of the following equations:

$$a_{m1}\alpha_j = {}^{ir}X_{jm} - {}^{ir}X_{(j/A-)m} = {}^{i}X_{jm} - {}^{i}X_{(j/A-)m}\,, \qquad \text{(single blockade)} \quad (29a)$$

$$a_{m1}\alpha_j = {}^{ir}X_{(j/B-C-)m} - a_{m0} = {}^{i}X_{(j/B-C-)m} - a_{m0} - a_{m8}\Gamma_j\,, \quad \text{(dual blockade)} \quad (29b)$$

$$a_{m1}\alpha_j = {}^{ir}X_{(j/B-)m} - {}^{ir}X_{(j/A-B-)m} = {}^{i}X_{(j/B-)m} - {}^{i}X_{(j/A-B-)m}\,, \qquad (29c)$$

$$a_{m1}\alpha_j = {}^{ir}X_{(j/C-)m} - {}^{ir}X_{(j/A-C-)m} = {}^{i}X_{(j/C-)m} - {}^{i}X_{(j/A-C-)m}\,. \qquad (29d)$$

(single and dual blockades)

Exactly opposite to the previously discussed case, the inclusion of residual nonautonomic influences over and above the pure effects of activation components does not *introduce a bias under either a single or a combined single and dual blockade protocol* (see Equations 29a, 29c, and 29d), so that task level and task-rest response effects can still be determined. However, *bias is introduced under a dual blockade protocol* (see Equation 29b): both task level and task-rest response effects include over and above the wanted contribution from one activation component also that of the residual influence.

It thus appears that on the one hand, both single and combined single and dual blockade protocols, and, on the other hand, dual blockade protocols may be for different reasons vulnerable to violations of the assumptions of the most often used ir-restricted model. Whether or not such violations occur, depends (1) on the variables considered (e.g., interactive effects are likely to operate in the regulation of heart rate, but probably to a much lesser extent in measures of respiratory sinus arrhythmia) and (2) on the type and amount of activation induced by the tasks (e.g., with the exception of strenuous exercise, many of the laboratory tasks used in psychophysiological investigations do not provoke potent nonautonomic residual effects on the customarily employed autonomic variables). In the case of interactive effects, such violations could be experimentally assessed by using both single and dual blockade protocols for determining the size of interaction effects. The statistical analysis for a "componential intertask comparison" can also give some indication whether such violations are operating, as will be demonstrated in Chapter 5.3.1.

5.2.4 Uses of the cardiovascular activation component model: Towards a quantitative evaluation of task effects

In cardiovascular pharmacology, physiology, and psychophysiology, physiological responses are often analyzed in three steps:

- Reactivity scores are formed to gauge the physiological changes from rest to task. These scores are often difference or percentage scores (the validity of the latter depends on whether quite strong implicit assumptions are met or not; cf. Stemmler, 1987a).

- The differential reactivity of subject (e.g., medication) groups or tasks is compared with univariate statistical tests.
- The characterization of tasks in terms of their effects on alpha-adrenergic, beta-adrenergic, and cholinergic activation components is assessed nonquantitatively, that is, in the absence of an explicitly formalized comparison of the profiles of obtained reactivities with those which would be expected under varying degrees of alpha-adrenergic, beta-adrenergic or vagal activation.

This analytical procedure may sometimes suffice when the experimentally varied effects are large compared to measurement error and individual differences in response, as, for example, in much physiological or pharmacological research. However, in domains utilizing comparatively weak stimuli and mainly noninvasive measurements, and where large individual differences are typically encountered (as is often the case in cardiovascular psychophysiology), an analysis strategy that is not formally stated adds another source of disturbance and thereby potentially weakens the validity of the related research. Furthermore, if it is conceded that the cardiovascular system produces finely tuned adjustments to internal and external demands, then a *statement about the particular quantitative composition of activation components* during tasks (i.e., specifying the degree of contribution of individual activation components) would seem more appropriate than the *typical simply binary statement* that one component either characterizes a task or not.

A "componential task description" is a first step in an application of the formalism developed in the previous sections in order to achieve a more succinct description of tasks in terms of autonomic components of elicited cardiovascular responses (further steps are discussed in Chapter 5.3). It will be recalled that this formalism produces a decomposition of cardiovascular responses into the contributions stemming from the different cardiovascular autonomic activation components. It is suggested that these decomposed autonomic responses should constitute the units for a quantitatively pursued task description. To this end, the same procedure as outlined above for determining the effects that cardiovascular autonomic activation components exert on single physiological variables can also be applied to studying detailed multiple cardiovascular effects of task activation.

I will illustrate this approach with the data of Example 3 from Chapter 5.1.3, where the administration of single and dual blockades permit the autonomic decomposition of handgrip-induced changes in a number of cardiovascular variables. The calculations were performed under the assumption of the true-score ir-restricted form of the Activation Components Model (see Equation 18a), which neither accounts for nonautonomic residual influences nor for autonomic interactions.

As is shown in Table 7, heart rate increases of 8 bpm were effected by vagal withdrawal and increases of 6 bpm by beta-adrenergic activation. These two contributions sum up to the observed response of 14 bpm under placebo, because there is no direct alpha-adrenergic contribution to the heart rate response. Mean blood pressure responses (16 mmHg increase under placebo) were achieved by a large alpha-adrenergic contribution (14 mmHg) and by vagal withdrawal (6 mmHg). Both of these effects were counteracted by the well-known beta-adrenergic lowering of mean blood pressure (via vasodilatatory beta-2 adrenoceptor activation; -4 mmHg). This beta-adrenergic vasodilatatory effect is most clearly seen in the drop of the index of total peripheral resistance, which was approximately of the same magnitude as the alpha-adrenergically mediated increase. Vagal withdrawal also increased the peripheral resistance. Based on the data in the bottom part of Table 7, Figure 9 shows the decomposition of the rest-to-handgrip changes into the contributions from the alpha-adrenergic, beta-adrenergic, and cholinergic activation components.

This analysis suggests that the handgrip task brought about cardiovascular responses that were mediated by all three activation components. Most importantly, the analysis revealed synergistic (see the vagal withdrawal and beta-adrenergic activation effects on heart rate acting in the same direction) and antagonistic effects (see the alpha-adrenergic and vagal activation effects on peripheral resistance and on mean blood pressure acting in opposite direction to the beta-adrenergic effect) of activation components on single physiological variables. These conclusions should, however, be regarded as tentative only, because Seiler et al. (1974) used a blockade protocol in accordance with the ir-restricted model that does not permit an evaluation of interaction effects between autonomic components.

Table 7. Componential Task Description for Example 3 of Chapter 5.1.3

Scores	Mean Blood Pressure (mmHg)	Index Total Peripheral Resistance (dyn*s*cm^{-5}/m^2)	Heart Rate (bpm)
Experimental Data			
${}^{ir}X_{HGm}$	107	2043	84
${}^{ir}X_{Rm}$	91	1950	70
${}^{ir}X_{(HG/B-)m}$	112	2792	67
${}^{ir}X_{(R/B-)m}$	92	2418	59
${}^{ir}X_{(HG/B-C-)m}$	114	2125	102
${}^{ir}X_{(R/B-C-)m}$	100	1850	102
Contributions from Cardiovascular Activation Components to Handgrip Responses			
Alpha-adrenergic component[a]	14	275	0
Beta-adrenergic component[b]	-4	-281	6
Cholinergic component[c]	6	99	8

Note. Data from Seiler et al. (1974). HG = Handgrip. R = Rest. B- = Beta-adrenergic blockade. C- = Cholinergic blockade. *m* = Index for variables. [a]Calculated by Equation 24a. [b]Calculated by Equation 21b. [c]Calculated by Equation 26c.

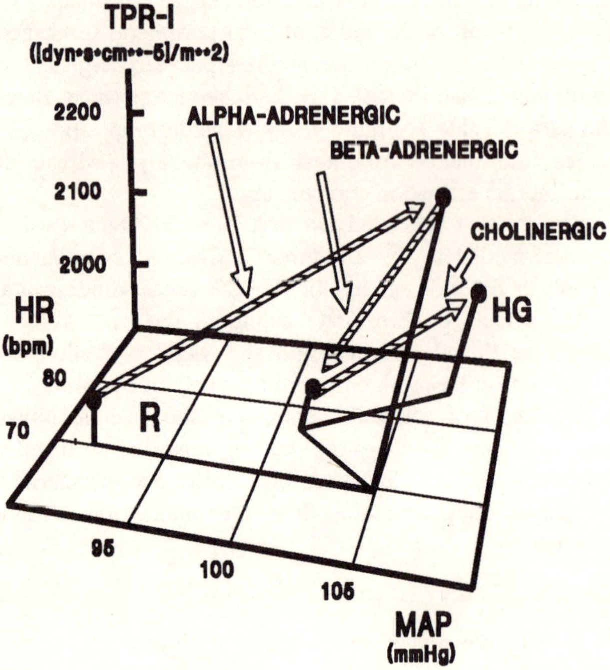

Figure 9. Decomposition of changes from rest (R) to handgrip (HG) into alpha-adrenergic, beta-adrenergic, and cholinergic contributions (shaded vectors), as reflected in the index of total peripheral resistance (TPR-I), heart rate (HR), and mean arterial blood pressure (MAP). The ir-restricted form of the Cardiovascular Activation Model is assumed to hold. Black circles are data points or the intermediate results of successive additions of alpha-adrenergic, beta-adrenergic, and cholinergic effects. (Based on the data of Table 7.)

5.2.5 Limitations of the unrestricted model of cardiovascular activation components

Some general limitations of the Model of Cardiovascular Activation Components and ways of relaxing them, when appropriate, should be finally discussed. These limitations concern

- the number of cardiovascular activation components specified,
- a system-general instead of an organ-specific designation of cardiovascular activation components,
- the linearity of the model in the coefficients a_m.

First, the number of cardiovascular activation components included in the model is not restricted to the three employed in the preceding sections. In general, other components can be included by adding the respective single and interactive effects to the terms of Equation 14, provided that specific pharmacological blockades inhibiting the actions of the respective receptor type can be applied. A likely candidate for such a model revision is the beta-adrenergic activation component which might be replaced by beta1- and beta2-adrenergic components. Given their separate effects on the heart and the vasculature, respectively, and the availability of selective antagonists (see Chapter 5.1.2), such a model revision would be highly recommended. Two separate beta-adrenergic components have not been specified in order to keep the formal development of our argument easier to communicate. Furthermore, many investigators have used nonselective beta-adrenergic blockades (e.g., by propranolol) for which the model as specified above applies.

Regarding the second point, I have argued earlier that despite some evidence for organ-specific manifestations of both vagal and sympathetic activity, it is preferable to state the Model of Cardiovascular Activation Components in terms of broad, or molar, system-general mechanisms. The voluminous empirical support for such molar conceptions is one argument for that position, parsimony of the model is another. The issue of parsimony may be better understood if the model revisions are considered that would be necessary to incorporate organ-specific effects of cardiovascular autonomic activation components. To this end, the problem may be reformulated: The occurrence of organ-specific effects means that a particular activation component activates specific target organs in some situations but different target organs in other situations. This is the description of a variable x situation interaction which could be incorporated into the model by specifying M (number of variables) * J (number of situations) coefficients a_{mj} instead of $M * 3$ a_m's (for the ir-restricted model with three components). Clearly, such an inflation of model parameters would not be desirable, not to mention the estimation problems that could arise. It has to be realized, however, that organ-specific effects, if they occur, increase the error variance. Analyzing only very few variables or very few situations at a time might give an indication of the severity of such adverse effects.

Concerning the third point mentioned above, nonlinearities between cardiovascular activation components and single target organs would indeed not be captured by the model as formulated above. However, linear relationships usually account for a large portion of variance. If the evidence suggests to account for nonlinearities, the model could be changed either by logarithmic, exponential or other functions in the a_m's or by polynomial expansions. The latter solution, however, would again add terms to the equation and its merits with respect to accuracy might not outweigh its costs with regard to loss of parsimony.

In conclusion, the Model of Cardiovascular Activation Components as proposed in Chapter 5.2.1 is open to revisions, but the most likely one will probably only concern the differentiation of beta1- and beta2-adrenergic components.

5.3 Estimation of the Parameters in the Model of Cardiovascular Activation Components

5.3.1 Estimation of parameters given complete autonomic receptor blockades

The formalism developed in Chapter 5.2 for the determination of effects that autonomic cardiovascular activation components exert on cardiovascular variables presupposed a true-score model (see Equation 14) that omitted errors arising from factors such as systematic deviations from the model or measurement error. It is obvious that the usage of one of the several forms of model restrictions discussed in Chapters 5.2.2 and 5.2.3 (the r-restricted, the i-restricted, and the ir-restricted forms) in a concrete application might lead to larger model errors than the use of the unrestricted model. However, given the practically difficult implementation of autonomic receptor blockade protocols that would be needed for the application of a model including interactive terms, the ir-restricted form will often be the model of choice. But especially with this choice it should be recognized that errors in the determination of model parameters are likely to occur. In other words, in practice the model parameters have to be *estimated* instead of simply *determined* according to the equations given in the previous sections.

The general procedure for the estimation of model parameters includes two steps. In the first step, the experimental data are used to calculate preliminary effects ($a_{m1}\alpha_j$, $a_{m2}\beta_j$, $a_{m3}\tau_j$) for each of the cardiovascular components on the registered variables (as demonstrated in the bottom part of Table 7). For this calculation, the equations given above are employed. In the second step, parameter estimates are obtained (mostly by using a least-squares criterion) by applying an adequate statistical procedure in turn to each of the three preliminary component effect matrices (where the preliminary effects for all variables, subjects, and situations are collected). The choice of the statistical technique used to obtain parameter estimates depends upon the assessment model (see Table 1) on which the particular investigation is based:

- If a trait conceptualization of activation is followed (i.e., Assessment Model 1) is followed, the experimental design will call for the registration of multiple cardiovascular variables in one or a few "typical" situations. A dimension reduction technique, such as principal components analysis, would be calculated according to the R-technique, that is, by reducing the dimensionality of the variable-space with the use of between-subjects variance.

- If a process conceptualization of activation (i.e., Assessment Model 2) is followed, the experimental design will call for the registration of multiple cardiovascular variables in multiple situations. A dimension reduction technique would be calculated according to the P-technique (with data from a single subject or with situation means across a sample of subjects), that is, reducing the dimensionality of the variable-space with the use of between-situations variance.
- If a mixed trait-state conceptualization of activation (i.e., a combination of Assessment Models 1 and 7) is followed, the experimental design will call for the registration of multiple variables and multiple situations. One application of such a mixed trait-state conceptualization of activation is concerned with the determination of cardiovascular activation components underlying individual response specificity. A dimension reduction technique that simultaneously maximizes the trait (between-subjects) and minimizes the differential state (subjects x situations interaction) variance, such as discriminant analysis, with subjects defined as "groups" and situations as "cases", would be appropriate.
- If a mixed process-state conceptualization of activation (i.e., a combination of Assessment Models 2 and 7; previously called an individual-differences process perspective), the experimental design will again call for the registration of multiple variables and multiple situations. One application of such a mixed process-state conceptualization of activation is concerned with the determination of cardiovascular activation components underlying situational response specificity. Again, discriminant analysis, which simultaneously maximizes process (between-situations) and minimizes the differential state (subjects x situations interaction) variance, with situations defined as "groups" and subjects as "cases", would be appropriate.

These statistical procedures are preferably applied to the task-rest response form of the cardiovascular activation components model, because estimation of the coefficients of intrinsic activity, a_{mo}, can be set aside. Estimates of the variable-coefficients a_{m1}, a_{m2}, and a_{m3} are given by factor estimation coefficients or by discriminant function coefficients; estimates of scores α_j, β_j, and τ_j on cardiovascular activation components by factor scores or by discriminant scores. A principal components analysis should be performed on the variance-covariance matrix of variables so that the original variable units are retained (this is automatically done in standard discriminant analysis).

The estimation of model parameters with the aid of discriminant analysis, on the basis of an individual-differences process conceptualization of activation, will be illustrated next. The following demonstration is at the same time an example for the comparison of experimental tasks with respect to single cardiovascular activation components. Such a *componential intertask comparison* allows a much more detailed characterization and, finally, systematization, of tasks than is usually accomplished by the nonquantitative classification of tasks as "alpha-adrenergic", "beta-adrenergic", or "cholinergic" (more on this in Chapter 10).

The following illustration uses data reported by Robinson, Epstein, Beiser, and Braunwald (1966) which were reanalyzed. These authors investigated the control of heart rate by the autonomic nervous system in conscious human subjects. Among their experimental conditions were the injection of phenylephrine (which is an alpha-adrenergic agonist; data from the 0.05 mg/min infusion are used here) and nitroglycerin (which acts as an alpha-adrenergic antagonist; 0.4 mg sublingually) both during rest and treadmill exercise; this protocol was performed on a no-drug control day, a beta-adrenergic blockade (0.25 mg/kg i.v. propranolol), a cholinergic blockade (2 mg i.v. atropine), and a combined beta-adrenergic plus cholinergic blockade day. For these conditions, the individual scores of four subjects in heart rate and mean arterial blood pressure are reported by Robinson et al. (1966).

As shown in Table 8, the experimental conditions on the no-drug control day effectively altered the levels of heart rate and mean blood pressure. The effects that the activation components exerted on these two variables were determined for the task-rest response form of the ir-restricted Activation Components Model (Equation 18b) with the use of Equations 21b (beta-adrenergic component), 21c (cholinergic component), and 24a (alpha-adrenergic component). It should be recalled from the previous discussion concerning the effects of model misspecification in Chapter 5.2.3 that the alpha-adrenergic effect could be confounded with residual nonautonomic influences, should they be operating (because this alpha-adrenergic component has to be determined from the dual blockade data; see Equation 29b), and that beta-adrenergic and cholinergic effects could be confounded with interactions among activation components (because these autonomic effects must be determined from the single blockade data; see Equation 27a).

I also performed intertask profile comparisons in turn for each activation component, following the repeated-measurements model. The profiles of responses to the five conditions had, for all three components, significantly different elevations, $F(4/12)$ = 21.82, 20.07, and 9.16 ($p < .01$), for the alpha-adrenergic, beta-adrenergic, and cholinergic component, respectively. The null hypothesis of profile parallelism (which states that the profiles of autonomic responses to experimental conditions are equal, if differences in profile elevations are disregarded), however, was rejected only for the alpha-adrenergic component, Roy's $\Theta(1/1/5) = 0.935$, $p < .01$. These initial statistics indicated that the experimental conditions had substantial effects on the response profile of each of the activation components. These effects were delineated further by multivariate discriminant analyses, which were aimed at estimating, in turn for each activation component, the variable coefficients and activation component scores of the underlying ir-restricted form of the Cardiovascular Activation Components Model. These analyses revealed a significant first discriminant function for each of the components, Roy's Θ(2/0.5/4.5) = 0.95, 0.88 (both $p < .01$), and 0.77 ($p < .05$), in the above order, and a significant second function for the alpha-adrenergic component, Roy's Θ(1/0/4) = 0.88, $p < .01$. Centroids (i.e., average responses during conditions) on the significant discriminant functions were tested against zero (functions were scaled such that zero indicates a "zero response", with the mean square error as the function's unit). In addition, six comparisons between centroids were specified a priori (see Table 8) and tested with Bonferroni-adjusted significance levels. All of these statistical tests used the critical *F*-value for a priori contrasts on post hoc determined discriminant functions (see Table 12, Chapter 7).

Table 8 also shows the estimates of the responses to the experimental conditions on the activation components and contrasts between them as well as

Table 8. Illustration of Estimation of Model Parameters by Discriminant Analysis and of Componential Intertask Comparison

Condition/ Contrast	Mean Heart Rate	Blood Pressure	Discriminant Function Alpha1	Alpha2	Beta	Tau
Response Means on Original Variables and Estimates of Activation Components [a,b]						
P	-8.00	8.50	-1.42	**2.81**	-0.37	-0.27
N	19.75	-14.75	0.45	**-2.63**	**2.07**	**-2.31**
E	49.50	2.25	**4.90**	**1.64**	**2.46**	**-3.43**
EP	46.00	5.50	**3.05**	**3.14**	**2.31**	**-3.55**
EN	80.00	-13.25	**8.02**	0.49	**6.08**	**-4.34**
Contrasts between Response Means [c]						
P versus N	-27.75	23.25	-1.87	**5.44**	-2.44	-2.04
P versus EP	-54.00	3.00	**-4.47**	-0.33	-2.68	**-3.28**
N versus EN	-60.25	-1.50	**-7.57**	**-3.12**	**-4.01**	-2.03
EP versus E	-3.50	3.25	-1.85	1.50	-0.15	0.12
EN versus E	30.50	-15.50	**3.12**	-1.15	**3.62**	0.91
EP versus EN	-34.00	18.75	**-4.97**	2.65	**-3.77**	-0.79
Estimates of Variable Coefficients						
Heart Rate			.276	.148	.158	-.092
Mean Blood Pressure			-.082	.122	.125	-.056

Note. P = Phenylephrine. N = Nitroglycerin. E = Exercise. EP = Exercise and phenylephrine. EN = Exercise and nitroglycerin. [a]For heart rate (baseline level = 62.50 bpm) and mean blood pressure (baseline level = 84 mmHg) the response means on the drug-free control day are given. [b]Tests of centroids (on post hoc discriminant functions) against zero, based on a critical *F*-value with $df = (2,11)$, bold = $p < .05$. [c]Tests of a priori contrasts (on post hoc discriminant functions) between centroids, based on the Bonferroni-adjusted .05/6 alpha level and a critical *F*-value with $df = (2,11)$, boldface numbers: $p < .05$.

estimates of variable coefficients. The variable coefficients of the *first "alpha function"*[12] (alpha1 = 0.276 * "alpha plus residual contributions to heart rate response" - 0.082 * "alpha plus residual contributions to mean blood pressure response") describe a reciprocal relationship between the two variables which reminds one of the effects of the baroreceptor-mediated negative feedback loop (increases in mean blood pressure lead to decreases in heart rate, given constant set-points and sensitivities of this reflex; Robinson et al., 1966). The contrasts show (1) that the exercise compared to the nonexercise conditions produced a significantly larger reciprocal response in the two variables and (2) that nitroglycerin during exercise compared to the other exercise conditions led to an extraordinarily large reciprocal effect. It seems likely that residual influences established the variation that brought about this function. (During exercise, local metabolites, heat, and acidosis are profound contributors to such residual influences with regard to blood pressure but not heart rate; see references in Buell, Alpert, & McCrory, 1986.) The *second "alpha function"* contrasts the action of phenylephrine with that of nitroglycerin which exactly is the definition of an alpha-adrenergic activation component (see the data of Example 1 in Chapter 5.1.3). Interestingly, exercise - in the exercise plus nitroglycerin condition - completely restored the alpha-adrenergic tone which was greatly diminished in the response to nitroglycerin alone. The *"beta function"* corresponds to the increases in beta-adrenergic reactivity during the exercise conditions and especially during exercise with nitroglycerin; phenylephrine, however, as expected, did not affect this component. The centroids on the *"tau function"* were in nearly inverse order of that on the "beta function". This inverse variation is in agreement with the interpretation of the "tau function" as the vagal response component. On the basis of this interpretation, nitroglycerin and all of the exercise conditions, but not phenylephrine, led to a significant vagal withdrawal.

This example not only illustrates the methods (1) of obtaining parameter estimates for the employed Model of Cardiovascular Activation Components and (2) of componential intertask comparisons. It also demonstrates the plausibility of the estimated cardiovascular autonomic activation components. However, more cardiovascular variables, a greater variety of experimental tasks, and a blockade protocol that permits the determination of interactions, would be needed to properly substantiate the tentative interpretations given.

---

[12] Names of discriminant functions are put in quotation in order to underscore that they still need substantial interpretation (e.g., in order to differentiate them from contributions of interactions or residual influences).

5.3.2 Estimation of parameters given incomplete autonomic receptor blockades

In psychophysiological, in contrast to pharmacological or physiological, investigations it is often inappropriate to administer complete autonomic receptor blockades:

- In order to be complete, blockades have to be administered intravenously which constitutes a clear example of obtrusiveness of measurement conditions (see Chapter 1.1).
- With dosages as high as those required for complete blockades, central nervous system side-effects often occur, such as blurred vision, marked dryness of the mouth, or photophobia (with atropine; not to mention atropine's peripheral effect of heart rate increases of up to 60 bpm in the studies listed in Table 6!) and tiredness, dizziness, and hallucinations (with propranolol; see Gilman, Goodman, & Gilman, 1980). Such side-effects will inevitably compromise psychological research questions.
- With increasing dosages, the danger of complications increases. This heightened risk for subjects has to be carefully weighted against the strength of blockade achieved. In any case, the intravenous drug application requires that the investigation is carried through in a medical department under the surveillance of a cardiologist. This will not always be possible or desirable in psychophysiological studies.

These points render it often impossible to employ complete autonomic receptor blockades in psychophysiological investigations. Incomplete blockades, however, particularly when drugs are given orally,[13] present a challenge to the evaluation of activation component effects on cardiovascular variables. If, for example, the procedures for the estimation of model parameters recommended in the previous section are applied to data obtained from an incomplete blockade protocol, the estimates may become imprecise. This problem will become apparent if the Model of Cardiovascular Activation Components is expanded to incorporate different blockade strengths. If the strength of a blockade is denoted by π_1, π_2, and π_3 for an alpha-adrenoceptor, beta-adrenoceptor, and cholinoceptor antagonist, respectively, the general true-score model of Equation 14 reads

$$X_{ijm} = a_{m0i} + \pi_1 a_{m1}\alpha_{ij} + \pi_2 a_{m2}\beta_{ij} + \pi_3 a_{m3}\tau_{ij} + \pi_1\pi_2 a_{m4}\alpha\beta_{ij} + \pi_1\pi_3 a_{m5}\alpha\tau_{ij} + \pi_2\pi_3 a_{m6}\beta\tau_{ij} + \pi_1\pi_2\pi_3 a_{m7}\alpha\beta\tau_{ij} + a_{m8}\Gamma_{ij}\,, \tag{30}$$

where the π's can assume values between 0 (complete blockade) and 1 (no blockade).

---

[13] The oral, compared to the intravenous, administration is, on the positive side, less obtrusive but, on the more negative side, less standardized, because the absorption of an orally given drug can be unreliable and highly variable from subject to subject.

For demonstration purposes, I will present a brief exposition of incomplete blockade effects. The demonstration is confined to a consideration of the ir-restricted model (which neither considers interactions among autonomic components nor nonautonomic residual influences) and, in particular, to its task level form under single and dual blockade protocols. The task level form of the ir-restricted model under *incomplete single blockades* reads

$$^{ir}X_{jm} = a_{m0} + a_{m1}\alpha_j + a_{m2}\beta_j + a_{m3}\tau_j\,, \qquad (31a)$$

$$^{ir}X_{(j/A\text{-})m} = a_{m0} + \pi_1 a_{m1}\alpha_j + a_{m2}\beta_j + a_{m3}\tau_j\,, \qquad (31b)$$

$$^{ir}X_{(j/B\text{-})m} = a_{m0} + a_{m1}\alpha_j + \pi_2 a_{m2}\beta_j + a_{m3}\tau_j\,, \qquad (31c)$$

$$^{ir}X_{(j/C\text{-})m} = a_{m0} + a_{m1}\alpha_j + a_{m2}\beta_j + \pi_3 a_{m3}\tau_j. \qquad (31d)$$

These equations describe the activity of variable m during task j without drugs (Equations 31a) and under alpha-adrenergic, beta-adrenergic, and cholinergic blockades (Equations 31b to 31d) in terms of the parameters of the ir-restricted model. Task level effects can then be obtained by

$$a_{m0} = f_1{}^{ir}X_{(j/A\text{-})m} + f_2{}^{ir}X_{(j/B\text{-})m} + f_3{}^{ir}X_{(j/C\text{-})m} + {}^{ir}X_{jm}*(1 - f_1 - f_2 - f_3)\,, \qquad (32a)$$

$$a_{m1}\alpha_j = f_1*({}^{ir}X_{jm} - {}^{ir}X_{(j/A\text{-})m})\,, \qquad (32b)$$

$$a_{m2}\beta_j = f_2*({}^{ir}X_{jm} - {}^{ir}X_{(j/B\text{-})m})\,, \qquad (32c)$$

$$a_{m3}\tau_j = f_3*({}^{ir}X_{jm} - {}^{ir}X_{(j/C\text{-})m})\,; \qquad (32d)$$

with $f_1 = 1/(1 - \pi_1), f_2 = 1/(1 - \pi_2)$, and $f_3 = 1/(1 - \pi_3)$.

These equations show that with nearly incomplete blockades the activation component effects in the limiting case (i.e., $\pi \rightarrow 1$) become more and more error-prone. For example, the alpha-adrenergic activation component effect (Equation 32b) in the limiting case is determined

- in the nominator, by the difference between no-drug ($^{ir}X_{jm}$) and "almost no-drug" ($^{ir}X_{(j/A\text{-})m}$) true-scores which approaches zero;
- in the denominator, $(1 - \pi)$, by a value approaching zero, which means that the more and more error-prone nominator will become increasingly inflated.

The ir-restricted model under *incomplete dual blockades* reads

$$^{ir}X_{jm} = a_{m0} + a_{m1}\alpha_j + a_{m2}\beta_j + a_{m3}\tau_j\,, \qquad (33a)$$

$$^{ir}X_{(j/A\text{-}B\text{-})m} = a_{m0} + \pi_1 a_{m1}\alpha_j + \pi_2 a_{m2}\beta_j + a_{m3}\tau_j\,, \qquad (33b)$$

$$^{ir}X_{(j/A\text{-}C\text{-})m} = a_{m0} + \pi_1 a_{m1}\alpha_j + a_{m2}\beta_j + \pi_3 a_{m3}\tau_j\,, \qquad (33c)$$

$$^{ir}X_{(j/B\text{-}C\text{-})m} = a_{m0} + a_{m1}\alpha_j + \pi_2 a_{m2}\beta_j + \pi_3 a_{m3}\tau_j\,. \qquad (33d)$$

Task level effects can be obtained by

$$a_{m0} = [{}^{ir}X_{(j/A\text{-}B\text{-})m}{}^*(f_1 + f_2 - f_3) + {}^{ir}X_{(j/A\text{-}C\text{-})m}{}^*(f_1 - f_2 + f_3) + {}^{ir}X_{(j/B\text{-}C\text{-})m}{}^*(-f_1 + f_2 + f_3) - {}^{ir}X_{jm}{}^*(f_1 + f_2 + f_3 - 2)]/2 \,, \tag{34a}$$

$$a_{m1}\alpha_j = f_1{}^*({}^{ir}X_{jm} + {}^{ir}X_{(j/B\text{-}C\text{-})m} - {}^{ir}X_{(j/A\text{-}B\text{-})m} - {}^{ir}X_{(j/A\text{-}C\text{-})m})/2 \,, \tag{34b}$$

$$a_{m2}\beta_j = f_2{}^*({}^{ir}X_{jm} + {}^{ir}X_{(j/A\text{-}C\text{-})m} - {}^{ir}X_{(j/A\text{-}B\text{-})m} - {}^{ir}X_{(j/B\text{-}C\text{-})m})/2 \,, \tag{34c}$$

$$a_{m3}\tau_j = f_3{}^*({}^{ir}X_{jm} + {}^{ir}X_{(j/A\text{-}B\text{-})m} - {}^{ir}X_{(j/A\text{-}C\text{-})m} - {}^{ir}X_{(j/B\text{-}C\text{-})m})/2 \,. \tag{34d}$$

The same consequences as described above for single blockades also apply for dual blockades: In the nominator, the activation component effects tend towards zero; in the denominator, the expression $(1 - \pi)$ tends toward zero. Both effects lead to an increase of error variance.

How can the parameters of the model with incomplete blockades be estimated? Because the parameters in the general Model of Cardiovascular Activation Components (Equation 30) are connected multiplicatively in more than two terms, other estimation procedures than the standard linear multivariate procedures proposed in the previous section have to be considered, should, apart from variable coefficients a_m and activation components α, β, and τ, blockade strengths π be estimated, too. In the following, I will briefly describe three procedures that, in addition to discriminant analysis, have been used for the analysis of an investigation with dual incomplete autonomic receptor blockades (for a description of the study protocol, see Chapter 8; for results, see Chapters 9 to 10). These procedures are:

- Multistage linear estimation,
- nonlinear estimation,
- estimation based on an analysis of covariance structures.

Multistage linear estimation. This procedure takes as its vantage point the r-restricted model of Equation 16 for incomplete blockades in terms of observed variables, that is, with an added error term:

$${}^{r}x_{ijm} = a_{m0} + \pi_1 a_{m1}\alpha_j + \pi_2 a_{m2}\beta_j + \pi_3 a_{m3}\tau_j + \pi_1\pi_2 a_{m4}\alpha\beta_j + \pi_1\pi_3 a_{m5}\alpha\tau_j + \pi_2\pi_3 a_{m6}\beta\tau_j + \pi_1\pi_2\pi_3 a_{m7}\alpha\beta\tau_j + \epsilon_{ijm} \,. \tag{35}$$

The errors are assumed to be independent, normal random variates with mean 0 and variance $var(\epsilon_{ijm})$ which includes error with regard to systematic model misspecifications ($var[\epsilon_{jm}]$) and between-subjects and subjects x situations interaction variance ($var[\epsilon_{im}] + var[\epsilon_{(ixj)m}]$). Thus, Assessment Model 2 is applied which assumes a process-oriented conceptualization of cardiovascular activation. The procedure of multistage linear estimation consists of seven steps:

Step 1. The estimation of model parameters starts with the task-rest response form of the model in Equation 35, which sets aside (until step 6) the estimation of the coefficients of intrinsic activity, a_{m0}.

Step 2. Linear and quadratic trends over successive resting periods are determined and eliminated from all resting and task period data. This elimination prevents such trends from distorting the parameter estimates.

Step 3. In order to obtain preliminary estimates of situation weights on activation components (α_j, β_j, and τ_j) and of variable coefficients (a_{m1}, a_{m2}, and a_{m3}), by omitting interaction terms the ir-restricted form of the model of Equation 35 is employed in this and the following step (interaction terms are reintroduced in step 5). Each of the three $M*J$ (M = number of variables, J = number of situations) matrices **V** of activation component effects, with elements

$$\mathbf{V}_1 = \{\text{est}(a_{m1}\alpha_j)\},\ \mathbf{V}_2 = \{\text{est}(a_{m2}\beta_j)\},\ \text{and}\ \mathbf{V}_3 = \{\text{est}(a_{m3}\tau_j)\}$$

as determined from Equations 32 (for single blockades) or Equations 34 (for dual blockades) with the preliminary equating of observed with true scores, are subjected to a singular value (Eckart-Young) decomposition (see Mardia, Kent, & Bibby, 1979, p.473):

$$\mathbf{V}_1 = \mathbf{B}_1\mathbf{L}_1\mathbf{G}_1', \tag{36a}$$

$$\mathbf{V}_2 = \mathbf{B}_2\mathbf{L}_2\mathbf{G}_2', \tag{36b}$$

$$\mathbf{V}_3 = \mathbf{B}_3\mathbf{L}_3\mathbf{G}_3', \tag{36c}$$

where $\mathbf{B}_k$ ($M*Q_k$) and $\mathbf{G}_k$ (Q_k*J) are column orthonormal matrices of left- and right-hand eigenvectors of $\mathbf{V}_k\mathbf{V}_k'$ and $\mathbf{V}_k'\mathbf{V}_k$, respectively, and $\mathbf{L}_k$ (Q_k*Q_k) is a diagonal matrix of eigenvalues. Q_k is the rank of $\mathbf{V}_k$. Because the aim of this decomposition is to obtain one component for each effect matrix $\mathbf{V}_k$, only the first eigenvectors are retained. These eigenvectors contain the preliminary estimates of situation weights on activation components and of variable coefficients, preliminary est(α_j) = g_{j11}, preliminary est(β_j) = g_{j12}, preliminary est(τ_j) = g_{j13}; preliminary est(a_{m1}) = $l_{11}b_{m11}$, preliminary est(a_{m2}) = $l_{12}b_{m12}$, preliminary est(a_{m3}) = $l_{13}b_{m13}$, with g_{j1k}, b_{m1k}, and l_{11k} denoting elements in the first column of the matrices $\mathbf{G}_k$, $\mathbf{B}_k$, and $\mathbf{L}_k$, respectively. It should be noted that activation components are scaled to a length of one and variable coefficients to the variance of the first eigenvectors.

Step 4. The singular value decomposition is repeated for blockade strengths π between 0 and 1 in steps of 0.1. The solution with the least model error variance (var[ϵ_{jm}]) is selected and the respective blockade strength retained as a preliminary estimate of π.

Step 5. The preliminary estimates obtained in the two previous steps are improved by successive linear regressions both in the ir-restricted and in the r-restricted model, that is, without and with the inclusion of interaction terms. In each of the three sets of such regression analyses, two of the three parameter groups (situation weights, variable coefficients, and blockade strengths) are held constant while the third one is being estimated.[14]

Step 6. The transition to the task level form of the model is achieved by estimating through regression analyses the coefficients of intrinsic activity, a_{m0}. Means of situation weights on activation components are similarly obtained. It should be noted that this step changes the scaling of activation components and variable coefficients.

Step 7. In the final step, scores of individual subjects on activation components are obtained. A table of regression weights allows the prediction of scores on activation components from no-drug (control, placebo) data.

The validity of the multistage linear estimation procedure was checked with a plasmode study. Inserting parameter values into Equation 35 and adding random variates with standard normal distribution, the multistage linear estimation procedure extracted the model parameters nearly exactly, with a model error of only 0.9%. The stability of the model estimates was studied by inserting arbitrary preliminary parameter estimates in steps 3 and 4 and estimating the parameters in varying sequences of the sets of regression analyses. These different estimates tended to converge on the same values. In sum, the validity and stability of the proposed estimation procedure could be substantiated.

The plasmode data set was also used to study the effect of incomplete blockades on discriminant analysis results following the procedure described in the previous section. Employing the correlation between the true variable coefficients and their estimates (the discriminant function coefficients) as the validity criterion, both the condition with blockade strength $\pi = 0$ (complete blockade) and one with blockade strength $\pi = 0.5$ (incomplete blockade) fared astonishingly well. Under complete blockade, the validity coefficient was 0.92; under incomplete blockade, it still reached 0.80.

Nonlinear estimation. Nonlinear estimation procedures based on a least squares or a maximum likelihood criterion can also be used to obtain model parameter estimates (SAS's *NLIN* procedure is an example for a nonlinear estimation program; SAS Institute Inc., 1988).

Estimation based on an analysis of covariance structures. The class of structural equation models, such as Jöreskog's (1981) LISREL model, may be tailored to obtain estimates for the parameters of the Model of Cardiovascular Activation Components under incomplete blockades. This application is illustrated for the ir-restricted model in the task-rest response form. The *measurement model*, which specifies how the cardiovascular activation component constructs are measured in terms of observed variables reads:

$$^{ir}x_{(dj)m} = a_{m1}\alpha_{(dj)} + a_{m2}\beta_{(dj)} + a_{m3}\tau_{(dj)} + \delta_{(dj)m}\,, \tag{37a}$$

[14] In our data, after three complete runs through these sets of regression analyses, the model error variance could be reduced from 47.6% to 39.3%, but not further in additional complete runs.

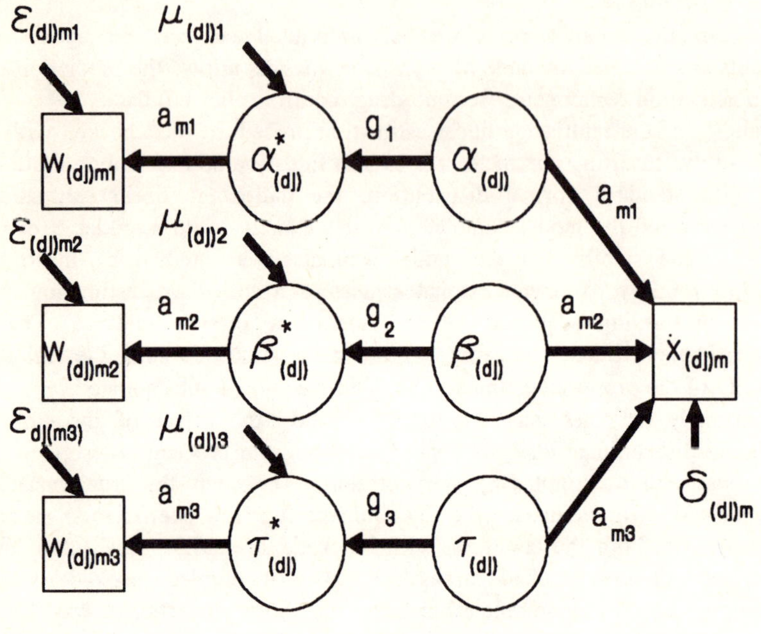

Figure 10. LISREL model of the ir-restricted Model of Cardiovascular Activation Components in the task-rest response form under incomplete blockades.

$$w_{(dj)m1} = {}^{ir}x_{(dj)m} + {}^{ir}x_{(dj/\text{B-C-})m} - {}^{ir}x_{(dj/\text{A-B-})m} - {}^{ir}x_{(dj/\text{A-C-})m}$$
$$= a_{m1}\alpha^*_{(dj)} + \epsilon_{(dj)m1}\,, \qquad (37b)$$

$$w_{(dj)m2} = {}^{ir}x_{(dj)m} + {}^{ir}x_{(dj/\text{A-C-})m} - {}^{ir}x_{(dj/\text{A-B-})m} - {}^{ir}x_{(dj/\text{B-C-})m}$$
$$= a_{m2}\beta^*_{(dj)} + \epsilon_{(dj)m2}\,, \qquad (37c)$$

$$w_{(dj)m3} = {}^{ir}x_{(dj)m} + {}^{ir}x_{(dj/\text{A-B-})m} - {}^{ir}x_{(dj/\text{A-C-})m} - {}^{ir}x_{(dj/\text{B-C-})m}$$
$$= a_{m3}\tau^*_{(dj)} + \epsilon_{(dj)m3}\,, \qquad (37d)$$

where the subscript d denotes a task-rest response, and δ and ϵ represent error variables. The *structural equation model*, which specifies the causal relationships among the constructs reads:

$$\alpha^*_{(dj)} = g_1\alpha_{(dj)} + \mu_{1(dj)}, \tag{38a}$$

$$\beta^*_{(dj)} = g_2\beta_{(dj)} + \mu_{2(dj)}, \tag{38b}$$

$$\tau^*_{(dj)} = g_3\tau_{(dj)} + \mu_{3(dj)}, \tag{38c}$$

where $g_1 = 2^*(1 - \pi_1)$, $g_2 = 2^*(1 - \pi_2)$, and $g_3 = 2^*(1 - \pi_3)$; μ represents an error variable. Figure 10 shows the graphical representation of the above LISREL model.

6 Implications and Interpretations of Psychophysiological Data Treatments

In Chapter 3.1, physiological responses had been "explained" in terms of a theoretical model of stimulus-response (S-R) mediation which specifies a nomological network of various constructs important for a differential psychophysiology. The measurement model part of the S-R mediation model that describes the relationship between the latent efferent activation processes and the observed variable reads (Equation 4):

$$r_{ijm} = h_{im}(SE_{ij(i)m}) .$$

The assessment models (Chapter 1.5) offered a classification of different types of construct definitions and their annotated assessment strategies. One such type of construct definition was used in the derivation of the Model of Autonomic Cardiovascular Activation Components (Chapter 5.2). This particular version of the S-R mediation model postulates a process-oriented conceptualization of activation and disregards (1) individual differences in the effective integration of situation properties, their evaluation, and person variables as well as (2) individual differences in transfer functions h_{im} which mediate between the effective stimulus of response channel m and the observed physiological response. The Model of Autonomic Cardiovascular Activation Components specifies, however, three different activation processes, each with its own set of transfer functions. This brief review might suffice to illustrate the general point that different versions of a general S-R mediation model have to be tailored to particular substantive questions and their related construct definitions. In this chapter, I reverse the question and ask, "What are the implications and interpretations of particular treatments of psychophysiological data in terms of the measurement and the assessment model?", instead of, "What is the nomological network of the constructs of interest?"

6.1 Psychophysiological Response Measures and Measurement Models

One of the first steps of data analysis is the formation of a response measure for scoring physiological activation or reactivity. However, it is often the case that neither an explication of the measurement model underlying a particular investigation nor a theoretical rationale for the use of a specific scoring method is made available. Since it has repeatedly been shown that the scoring method used can considerably affect the theoretical conclusions of a psychophysiological investigation (Edwards & Hill, 1967; Foerster, Schneider, & Walschburger, 1983a; Guski, 1976; Heath & Oken, 1965; Sersen, Clausen, & Lidsky, 1978), it would be desirable to select a scoring method according to the measurement model underlying the research question. The measurement model part of the S-R mediation model recalled above is general enough to discuss the most often used scoring methods as special cases. In particular, it will be shown that the scoring methods each imply their own form of the transfer function h_{im} (for details and a numerical example, see Stemmler, 1987a).

6.1.1 Response measures and their implied transfer functions

Raw score. Using unmodified raw scores amounts to postulating the measurement model

$$r_{ijm} = \mathrm{SE}_{ij(i)m} \, . \tag{39}$$

This means that the transfer function is a straight line with slope one and intercept zero for all variables and persons. All sources of psychological and physiological individual differences enter into the data, as do all differences among the actual, although unknown, transfer functions of the physiological response channels.

Unweighted difference score. The use of simple difference scores (*D*) assumes the measurement model

$$r_{ijm} = a_{im} + \mathrm{SE}_{ij(i)m} \text{, hence} \tag{40a}$$

$$D_{ijm} = r_{ijm} - r_{iRm} = \mathrm{SE}_{ij(i)m} - \mathrm{SE}_{iR(i)m} \, . \tag{40b}$$

Thus it is implied that the transfer function for all variables has a slope of one but may have different intercepts for different persons: The difference score removes individual differences in response channel constants.

The Autonomic Lability Score (ALS). As an example for the class of weighted difference scores, the ALS (Lacey, 1956) will be discussed. According to the Law of Initial Values (Wilder, 1967), interindividually different base values lead to different response magnitudes. The ALS was developed to statistically eliminate the effects of different base or, as is often the case, resting values. The ALS is defined (in terms of standardized scores) as the difference between actual and predicted response magnitudes. The prediction is based on the linear regression (with coefficient b_m) of task on base values. Although its statistical properties have been considered in considerable detail (e.g., Campbell, 1981; Myrtek & Foerster, 1986; Rogosa, Brandt, & Zimowski, 1982; Stemmler & Fahrenberg, 1989), its implicit assumptions with regard to the underlying measurement model are worth delineating:

$$r_{ijm} = \mathrm{SE}_{ij(i)m} - (1 - b_m)^*\mathrm{SE}_{i\mathrm{R}(i)m}\text{ , hence} \tag{41a}$$

$$\mathrm{ALS}_{ij\mathrm{R}m} = r_{ijm} - b_m r_{i\mathrm{R}m} = \mathrm{SE}_{ij(i)m} - \mathrm{SE}_{i\mathrm{R}(i)m}\ . \tag{41b}$$

The measurement model implicit in this interindividual form of the ALS postulates for all variables and persons transfer functions with slope one. However, the intercepts are specific both for variables and for the particular base value R of the individual effective stimulus. Expansion of Equation 41a shows that an observed response is hypothesized to be composed of the individual change in the effective stimulus from base to situation j plus the response magnitude under situation j predicted from knowledge of the individual base effective stimulus.

Percentage score. Of the various definitions of a percentage score (P) I shall comment upon those of the form "change divided by base value". These percentage scores assume the measurement model

$$r_{ijm} = \mathrm{SE}_{i\mathrm{R}(i)m}\mathrm{SE}_{ij(i)m} + \mathrm{SE}_{i\mathrm{R}(i)m}^*(1 - \mathrm{SE}_{i\mathrm{R}(i)m})\text{ , hence} \tag{42a}$$

$$P_{ijm} = (r_{ijm} - r_{i\mathrm{R}m})/r_{i\mathrm{R}m} = \mathrm{SE}_{ij(i)m} - \mathrm{SE}_{i\mathrm{R}(i)m}\ . \tag{42b}$$

The measurement model implicit in the percentage score specifies transfer functions that are linear with a slope equaling the base value of the individual effective stimulus and with an intercept which is a quadratic function of the slope.

Range-corrected score. This is defined as the difference between the response magnitude during situation j and the individual minimum score divided by the individual range of measured scores (Lykken, 1968, 1972; Lykken, Rose, Luther, & Maley, 1966). The measurement model implied by the range-corrected score (R) reads

$$r_{ijm} = a_{im} + b_{im}^*(\mathrm{SE}_{ij(i)m} - \mathrm{SE}_{i\min(i)m})\text{ , hence} \tag{43a}$$

$$R_{ijm} = (r_{ijm} - r_{i\min m})/(r_{i\max m} - r_{i\min m}) = (\mathrm{SE}_{ij(i)m} - \mathrm{SE}_{i\min(i)m})/(\mathrm{SE}_{i\max(i)m} - \mathrm{SE}_{i\min(i)m})\ . \tag{43b}$$

It should be noted that R takes values between 0 and 1; this is the consequence of the score's construction as seen in Equation 43b. The measurement model of the range-corrected score implies linear transfer functions that have specific slopes and intercepts both for variables and persons. Thus, this is the first measurement model described so far to incorporate transfer functions with individual levels and individual slopes that may vary among variables. The range-corrected score is a member of the class of ipsatized scores, which differ in how the slope of a person's transfer function is determined. Whereas the range-corrected score employs the individual observed range for this purpose, Ben-Shakhar (1985) proposed the standard deviation of the individual scores. Stemmler (1987b) argued however against this particular type of slope estimate.

Normalized score. Cattell (1966d) warned against the danger that, given a nonlinear relationship between latent and observed variables, the ranking of individual reactivities might be reversed from latent to observed variables. He proposed to first normalize per variable the sample's total data array and then to perform the response scaling. The measurement model of the normalization transformation (N) is

$$r_{ijm} = \phi_m^{-1}(\mathrm{SE}_{ij(i)m}) \text{ , hence} \tag{44a}$$

$$N_{ijm} = \phi_m(r_{ijm}) = \mathrm{SE}_{ij(i)m} \,. \tag{44b}$$

Thus, the measurement model of normalized scores implies nonlinear transfer functions that are specific for variables but not for persons.

Normalized difference score. This score combines the advantages of the normalized and the difference score in that it allows both for variable-specific nonlinear transfer functions and for person-specific intercepts or response channel constants. The measurement model for normalized differences (ND) reads

$$r_{ijm} = \phi_m^{-1}(a_{im} + \mathrm{SE}_{ij(i)m}) \text{ , hence} \tag{45a}$$

$$ND_{ijm} = \phi_m(r_{ijm} - r_{i\mathrm{R}m}) = \mathrm{SE}_{ij(i)m} - \mathrm{SE}_{i\mathrm{R}(i)m} \,. \tag{45b}$$

It might be noted that the measurement model of normalized difference scores still is not as general as the S-R mediation measurement model of Equation 4: Whereas the latter specifies individual transfer functions, the former accounts only for individual response channel constants.

The diversity of measurement model assumptions, which have become apparent in the preceding brief and selective overview, is striking. Therefore, one straightforward conclusion is that even simple calculations performed on physiological data imply distinct theoretical statements about part of the nomological network of the constructs of interest. Other conclusions concern the relative preference for particular scoring methods within the context (1) of the constructs one is interested in, (2) the type of transfer functions, and (3) experimental designs.

Scoring methods and constructs. If, as in "trait" psychophysiology, an assessment model is employed that defines constructs between-individuals, the choice of a response scoring method may be crucial for one's interpretations. For example, if one is interested in individual differences of the effector systems (which is a structural-physiologically oriented question), one would want to retain all sources of individual differences and use a scoring method that neither allows for transfer functions nor intercepts that are person-specific. Appropriate response scoring methods would be the raw score or the normalized score. However, if one is interested in individual differences of constructs at system levels higher than the efferent system, for example, person variables or the functional situation (see Figure 1 in Chapter 3.1), one would want to exclude all sources of individual differences that arise in the efferent systems and that could blur those higher-level individual differences of interest. With the selection of a scoring method that allows for either person-specific transfer functions or person-specific intercepts, or both, one would exclude the respective sources of between-subjects variance. The unweighted difference score, the ALS and percentage score, as well as the range-corrected and the normalized difference score might be appropriate. It should be noted, however, that the sources of variance excluded by these scoring methods cannot be specified; for example, excluding individual differences in intercepts with the use of the difference score does not mean that these individual differences originated solely in the efferent system, they could as well stem from the higher-level constructs one is actually interested in.

Scoring methods and transfer functions. It has been noted above that the methods for scoring responses implicitly postulate certain forms of transfer functions that mediate between the effective stimulus of a variable's response channel and the observed response. Ideally, the postulated transfer function would exactly correspond to the actual one. If this were the case, the effective stimulus could be estimated by the observed response without distortion of the scale. In contrast, if the postulated and the actual transfer function differ, the effective stimulus will be estimated on a distorted scale (for details, see Stemmler, 1987a). If, for example, the actual transfer function is of a logarithmic (negatively accelerating) form, but the scoring method used assumes a linear one, a ceiling effect will be observed (i.e., with increasing values of the effective stimulus, the increments of the observed responses get smaller and smaller). Linear transfer functions are implied by the raw score, the unweighted difference score, the ALS score and the percentage score (both for a fixed base value), and the range-corrected score; nonlinear transfer functions, by the percentage score (with varying base values), the normalized, and the normalized difference score. If with the latter two scoring methods a McCall-normalization (i.e., normalization of responses converted into ranks; see below) is performed, the implied transfer function may take any form provided it is a monotone increasing function.

Scoring methods and experimental design. Several scoring methods require reference values, for example, base values (the unweighted difference score and the ALS score) or extreme values (the range-corrected score). It is obvious that the decision how reference values are obtained in an investigation is of importance for the interpretation of the response measure (Ben-Shakhar, 1985; Obrist, 1985; Stemmler & Fahrenberg, 1989). In addition, transfer functions of percentage scores depend crucially on the measurement scale's origin, which is often deliberately chosen (e.g., by standardizing physiological data), and on the range of observed data, which of course depends on the experimental conditions used (see Stemmler, 1987a). Some scoring methods depend on the particular sample of subjects (the ALS score, normalized and normalized difference scores; cf. Foerster, Schneider, & Walschburger, 1983a), most depend on the sample of experimental conditions (the difference and normalized difference score; the ALS, the raw and the percentage score). These sample dependencies may limit the generalizability of results to a varying extent.

6.1.2 Estimation of actual transfer functions

From physiological experimentation, particular transfer functions have sometimes been specified. For electrodermal activity, for example, a (linear) relationship between the number of active sweat glands and skin conductance responses has been claimed (Lader, 1970; Lykken & Venables, 1971). Similarly, Lidberg and Wallin (1981) reported a linear transfer function between sympathetic sudomotor nerve impulses and the amplitude of skin resistance responses.

While physiological investigations can determine transfer functions for particular portions of the efferent system in single variables, estimates can be obtained from statistical considerations for all of the registered variables. There are several proposals that are potentially suited for an estimation of transfer functions. Cattell proposed to adopt the "relational simplex theory", which assumes that the constructs to be assessed "are such as will give the greatest mathematical simplicity of relationship over all variables with respect to the universe of scientific laws" (Cattell, 1966b, p. 115). This approach, however, presumes knowledge of how the constructs are to be assessed. Another proposal of Cattell (1966d) does not assume knowledge of the constructs; a normalization of raw scores should be used to obtain scales with equal interval units.

The linearization of a scale by normalization is discussed extensively by Gutjahr (1972). The procedure takes two steps. First, because the metric of the effective stimulus is unknown, the weak assumption of an ordinal or monotone relationship between the effective stimulus and the observed response is adopted and raw scores converted into ranks. Second, the transformation of ranks into normal deviates defines a metric on the scale of the effective stimulus. Gutjahr points out that the metric thus established has to be justified by post hoc evidence of simple relationships between different estimates of the effective stimulus. Stemmler (1984) applied this method to 34 physiological variables, which were scored in terms of differences, and reported estimates of transfer functions in the form of plots of transformed versus original differences. Applying the same technique to raw scores, Foerster, Schneider, and Walschburger (1983b) presented a cross-tabulation of normalized versus original raw scores for seven physiological variables.

Still another proposal for the estimation of transfer functions was advanced by Fahrenberg et al. (1979) who estimated "activation" by the sum of seven standardized physiological variables. Transfer functions were defined as nonlinear best-fitting lines (with certain additional refinements) in the bivariate scatter plots of activation estimate versus raw scores. Although still preliminary, all of the previously mentioned attempts confirmed the notion of clearly different transfer functions among physiological variables.

6.2 Partitioning Psychophysiological Variance

6.2.1 Effect estimates and measurement models

In Chapter 3.1, relationships both among latent variables (the physico-biological situation SP, the functional situation SF, motivational and cognitive person variables PV, and the effective stimuli for the efferent response channels SE) and between the latent variable SE and the obtained response r (Equation 4) have been discussed. Here, I want to change the point of view: Suppose that no independent assessment of these latent variables is available and the only information at hand is the obtained response r. Assume further that data have been collected from a replicated experiment with a Person x Situation design and the corresponding structural equation:

$$r_{ijmk} = \mu_m + \alpha_{jm} + \pi_{im} + \alpha\pi_{ijm} + \epsilon_{ijmk} , \qquad (46)$$

where μ_m is the population grand average, α_{jm} is the effect of situation j, π_{im} is the effect of person i, $\alpha\pi_{ijm}$ is the effect of the person x situation interaction, k is the index for replications, and ϵ_{ijmk} is the error term (comprised of replication variance), all of the above for response channel m. The question to be studied is: Given the usual estimates for the aforementioned effects (see below), to which expressions in terms of the unknown effective stimulus do these estimates correspond? The result of studying this question is apt to elucidate which particular aspect of the effective stimulus contributes to the calculated effects.

Clearly, the critical factor of such an investigation is the assumed measurement model or the particular form of the transfer function mediating between SE and the observed response r. I shall assume a simple linear function h_{im} within the general measurement model (Equation 4) of the stimulus-response mediation model, with response channel constant a_{im}, response channel sensitivity b_{im}, and error term $\epsilon_{ij(i)m}$:

$$r_{ijmk} = a_{im} + b_{im}\mathrm{SE}_{ij(i)m} + \epsilon_{ij(i)mk} \, . \tag{47}$$

Thus, the measurement model assumed in Equation 47 specifies a transfer function similar to the one implied by the range-corrected score (see Equation 43a) with individual intercepts and individual slopes that may vary among variables.

The situation effect. Estimates of situation effects at the level of r are obtained by

$$\mathrm{est}(\alpha_{jm}) = r_{.jm.} - r_{..m.} \, , \tag{48}$$

where, as above, the period denotes the mean across the respective index. Inserting terms yields (n = number of persons)

$$\mathrm{est}(\alpha_{jm}) = (1/n)^{*}\Sigma_i(b_{im}\mathrm{SE}_{i(j\#i)m}) \, . \tag{49}$$

(Measurement model specifying interindividually *unequal* slopes and intercepts)

This equation reveals that under the assumption of the measurement model of Equation 47 *the estimate of the situation effect at the level of r equals the average of the weighted sum of the persons' idiosyncratic effective stimuli under situation j*, that is, of the magnitude of the persons' effective stimuli under situation j over and above the average magnitude each person "produces". The weights in this sum are the individual response channel sensitivities or transfer function slopes. This estimate deviates from the situation effect at the level of SE,

$$\alpha(\mathrm{SE})_{jm} = \mathrm{SE}_{.j(.)m} - \mathrm{SE}_{..(.)m} = \mathrm{SE}_{.(j\#.)m} \, , \tag{50}$$

insofar as portions of the variance of the persons' idiosyncratic effective stimuli under situation j will enter into and consequently bias the situation effect estimate at the level of r. This bias is the larger, the greater the differences are among the persons' transfer function slopes. Only a measurement model that specifies interindividually equal slopes, b_m, will give situation effect estimates at the level of r that are proportional to the situation effect at the level of SE:

$$\mathrm{est}(\alpha_{jm}) = b_m\mathrm{SE}_{.(j\#.)m} \, . \tag{51}$$

(Measurement model specifying interindividually *equal* slopes)

The person effect. Estimates of person effects are given by

$$\mathrm{est}(\pi_{im}) = r_{i.m.} - r_{..m.} \, , \tag{52}$$

which upon insertion of terms from Equation 47 yields

$$\text{est}(\pi_{im}) = (a_{im} + b_{im}\text{SE}_{i.(i)m}) - (a_{.m} + [1/n]*\Sigma_i[b_{im}\text{SE}_{i.(i)m}]) \ . \tag{53a}$$

(Measurement model specifying interindividually *unequal* slopes and intercepts)

Equation 53a shows that under the assumption of the measurement model of Equation 47 *the estimate of the person effect at the level of r equals the deviation of the individual from the average of the linearly transformed habitual magnitudes of effective stimuli "produced" by persons.*

Rewriting Equation 53a,

$$\text{est}(\pi_{im}) = (a_{im} - a_{.m}) + (b_{im}\text{SE}_{i.(i)m} - b_{.m}\text{SE}_{..(.)m}) - (1/n)*\Sigma_i(b_{im}\text{SE}_{i(.*i)m}) \ , \tag{53b}$$

(Measurement model specifying interindividually *unequal* slopes and intercepts)

brings out more clearly the deviation of the person effect estimate at the level of r from that at the level of SE, the latter being

$$\pi(\text{SE})_{im} = \text{SE}_{i.(i)m} - \text{SE}_{..(.)m} = \text{SE}_{i(.*i)m} \ . \tag{54}$$

Comparison of the two previous equations reveals that individual differences in response channel constants and channel sensitivities, as well as a term representing the interaction between response channel sensitivity and the person effect estimate at the level of SE, enter into and consequently bias the person effect estimate at the level of r. As above, this bias is larger, the greater the differences are among the persons' transfer function slopes and intercepts. Only a measurement model that specifies interindividually equal slopes, b_m, and intercepts, a_m, will result in person effect estimates at the level of r that are proportional to the person effects at the level of SE:

$$\text{est}(\pi_{im}) = b_m*(\text{SE}_{i.(i)m} - \text{SE}_{..(.)m}) \ . \tag{55}$$

(Measurement model specifying interindividually *equal* slopes and intercepts)

Equation 53a further shows an important differentiation among sources of between-subjects variance at the level of r:

- Differences between persons in the response channel constants corresponding to individual differences in habitual levels of activation;
- differences between persons in the response channel sensitivities corresponding to individual differences in habitual responsivity;
- differences between persons in the magnitude of the habitual effective stimulus they "produce".

Whereas the first two sources of individual differences are of an anatomical or physiological origin, it is the source of between-subjects variance that arises from differences in the habitual magnitude of effective stimuli which is psychologically interesting. This follows from the reasoning that psychological characteristics of the individual (the functional situation as well as motivational and cognitive person variables, see Equation 3) are likely to determine the effective stimulus but probably not the response channel constants or sensitivities.

The person x situation interaction effect. Estimates of interaction effects at the level of r are given by

$$\mathrm{est}(\alpha\pi_{ijm}) = r_{ijm.} - r_{.jm.} - r_{i.m.} + r_{..m.} \,. \tag{56}$$

Inserting terms yields

$$\mathrm{est}(\alpha\pi_{ijm}) = b_{im}\mathrm{SE}_{i(j\#i)m} - (1/n)^{*}\Sigma_i(b_{im}\mathrm{SE}_{i(j\#i)m}) \,. \tag{57a}$$

(Measurement model specifying interindividually *unequal* slopes and intercepts)

This equation reveals that under the assumption of the measurement model of Equation 47 *the estimate of the person x situation interaction effect at the level of r equals the deviation of a person's idiosyncratic effective stimulus under situation j (weighted with the person's response channel sensitivity) from the average of the weighted sum of persons' idiosyncratic effective stimuli under situation j*. It should be noted that the second term on the right side of Equation 55 is the estimate of the situation effect at the level of r.

Rewriting Equation 57a,

$$\mathrm{est}(\alpha\pi_{ijm}) = b_{im}^{*}(\mathrm{SE}_{ij(i)m} - \mathrm{SE}_{i.(i)m} - \mathrm{SE}_{.j(.)m}) + b_{.m}^{*}(\mathrm{SE}_{..(.)m} + \mathrm{SE}_{.(j\#.)m}) - (1/n)^{*}\Sigma_i(b_{im}\mathrm{SE}_{i(j\#i)m}) \,, \tag{57b}$$

(Measurement model specifying interindividually *unequal* slopes and intercepts)

illuminates the deviation of the interaction effect estimate at the level of r from that at the level of SE, the latter being

$$\alpha\pi(\mathrm{SE})_{ijm} = \mathrm{SE}_{ij(i)m} - \mathrm{SE}_{i.(i)m} - \mathrm{SE}_{.j(.)m} + \mathrm{SE}_{..(.)m} \,. \tag{58}$$

Comparison of the two previous equations shows that individual differences in response channel sensitivities and the interaction between the latter and the idiosyncratic effective stimuli under situation j enter into and consequently bias the interaction effect estimate at the level of r. As above, this bias is larger, the greater the differences are among the persons' transfer function slopes. Only a measurement model that specifies interindividually equal slopes, b_m, will result in interaction effect estimates at the level of r that are proportional to the interaction effects at the level of SE:

$$\mathrm{est}(\alpha\pi_{ijm}) = b_m^{*}(\mathrm{SE}_{ij(i)m} - \mathrm{SE}_{i.(i)m} - \mathrm{SE}_{.j(.)m} + \mathrm{SE}_{..(.)m}) \,. \tag{59}$$

(Measurement model specifying interindividually *equal* slopes)

In sum, the analysis of variance effect estimates at the level of r reflect the corresponding effects at the level of SE only with a certain bias. The magnitude of this bias is a function of the individuals' differing transfer function slopes and/or intercepts. This bias is likely to exist in real data, because a measurement model that allows for interindividually different parameter values, such as the one specified in Equation 47, in this respect is more likely to approximate the reality of physiological effector systems than a measurement model that assumes interindividually equal slopes and intercepts of transfer functions. This consideration underscores the relevance of the discussion about response scoring methods and their implied measurement models in the preceding section.

6.2.2 Specificity of physiological responses

In Chapter 3.1, I have mentioned several notions of specificity which could be distinguished at the level of the effective stimulus. Different portions of the effective stimulus were characterized as the "building blocks" of the respective types of specificity. From a nomothetic point of view, an individual effective stimulus for the response channel m during situation j could be decomposed into

$$\mathrm{SE}_{ij(i)m} = \mathrm{SE}_{.j(.)m} + \mathrm{SE}_{i(j*i)m} \, ,$$

where the first expression on the right side is the average effective stimulus during situation j and the second is the deviation of person i's effective stimulus from that average. From an idiographic point of view, an individual effective stimulus during situation j could be decomposed into

$$\mathrm{SE}_{ij(i)m} = \mathrm{SE}_{i.(i)m} + \mathrm{SE}_{i(j\#i)m} \, ,$$

where the first expression on the right side is the average habitual effective stimulus of person i and the second is the deviation of person i's effective stimulus during situation j from that habitual value.

In order to understand why the different terms on the right side of these equations have been named the "building blocks" of the various types of specificity, I have to give a formal definition of "specificity". Specificity is the interaction between one or more experimental design factors with the "variables" factor. Interaction effects can be used for several purposes:

- The variance of such an interaction can be tested for significance;
- variance components can be calculated in order to judge the effect size of that interaction;
- the interaction variance can be decomposed into linearly independent components.

The first of these purposes will be of interest here only insofar as the construction of the interaction effects is concerned. (The other purposes will be commented upon later on.) These modes of construction directly reveal the "building block" character of the expressions recalled above for the different notions of specificity:

Situational response specificity (SSR), that is, stable differences between situations with respect to their response profiles, is defined as the interaction effect of situations x variables, which at the level of SE is constructed from

$$\alpha \beta(SE)_{jm} = SE_{.j(.)m} - SE_{.j(.).} - SE_{..(.)m} + SE_{..(.).}\,, \tag{60}$$

where α and β are situation amd variable factors, respectively. The term $SE_{.j.(m)}$ is the "building block" of SSR(SE).

Individual situational response specificity (ISSR), that is, stable response profile differences between persons within and also between situations, is defined as the simple interaction effect of subjects x variables for situation j (S_j); at the level of SE, it is constructed from

$$\begin{aligned} \pi\beta(SE)_{im} \text{ for } S_j &= SE_{ij(i)m} - SE_{.j(.)m} - SE_{ij(i).} + SE_{.j(.).} \\ &= SE_{i(j*i)m} - SE_{ij(i).} + SE_{.j(.).}\,, \end{aligned} \tag{61}$$

where π denotes the person factor. The term $SE_{i(j*i)m}$ is the "building block" of ISSR(SE).

Individual response specificity (ISR), that is, stable differences among persons with respect to their response profiles, is defined as the interaction effect of subjects x variables, which at the level of SE is constructed from

$$\pi\beta(SE)_{im} = SE_{i.(i)m} - SE_{i.(i).} - SE_{..(.)m} - SE_{..(.).}\,. \tag{62}$$

The term $SE_{i.(i)m}$ is the "building block" of ISR(SE).

Situational individual response specificity (SISR), that is, stable response profile differences between situations within and also between persons, is defined as the simple interaction effect of situations x variables for person i (P_i); at the level of SE, it is constructed from

$$\begin{aligned} \alpha\beta(SE)_{jm} \text{ for } P_i &= SE_{ij(i)m} - SE_{i.(i)m} - SE_{ij(i).} + SE_{i.(i).} \\ &= SE_{i(j\#i)m} - SE_{ij(i).} + SE_{i.(i).}\,. \end{aligned} \tag{63}$$

The term $SE_{i(j\#i)m}$ is the "building block" of SISR(SE).

Motivational response specificity (MSR), that is, stable response profile differences for each person in each situation, is defined as the triple interaction effect of subjects x situations x variables. It is already included in the simple interaction effects ISSR and SISR:

$$\alpha\pi\beta(SE)_{ijm} = \pi\beta(SE)_{im}\,[\text{for } S_j] - \pi\beta(SE)_{im} = \alpha\beta(SE)_{jm}\,[\text{for } P_i] - \alpha\beta(SE)_{jm} \tag{64}$$

Specificity effects at the level of the observed responses are of course subject to the kinds of biases noted in the preceding section. In the following, I will nevertheless refer to specificity effects at the level of the observed responses, but always with the tacit understanding of the probable presence of these biases.

Under various names, different notions of specificity have been discussed since about 1950 (Lacey, 1950; Malmo & Shagass, 1949). For example, Lacey and Lacey (1958) list the following notions of specificity:

- "Intra-stressor stereotypy refers to reproducible idiosycratic patterns of response to a single form of stressor" (p. 73). This is a constituent part of what has been termed above ISSR.
- "Inter-stressor stereotypy refers to idiosyncratic response-patterns reproduced over different stressors" (p. 73). This definition corresponds to the ISR.
- "Situational stereotypy refers to changes in average response-pattern produced by changes in the stimuli used, or accompanying different affective experiences" (p. 73). This equals the SSR.
- "Symptom-stereotypy refers to constancy of the physiological measure in which maximal activation is induced by stressful experience in patients with psychosomatic disorders, the area of maximal activation being consonant with the somatic complaint" (p. 73). This notion is a special case of the ISR; it results from collapsing the Subject factor into a Group factor.

Ax (1964) described motivational response specificity as the tendency of persons to respond idiosyncratically under specific situations. Dahme and Richter (1980) and Rösler (1983b, 1984) further commented on the various specificity notions. However, to my knowledge a principle of "situational individual response specificity", SISR, has previously not been described although it is the logical counterpart of the ISSR. The SISR represents the idiographic point of view of individual differences (the combination of Assessment Models 4 and 8) as much as the ISSR represents the nomothetic point of view of individual differences (the combination of Assessment Models 5 and 9).

The second of the above mentioned purposes for which interaction effects in the context of specificity analysis can be used (i.e., to provide effect sizes or relative magnitudes of the various specificity effects) has been pursued most extensively by Foerster and associates (Foerster, Schneider, & Walschburger, 1983a,b). Starting with a thorough discussion of various methods for the analysis of specificity,[15] these authors have found for change scores (i.e., excluding individual differences variance with respect to response channel constants; see Chapters 6.1 and 6.2.1) approximately 25% variance attributable to the ISR, 10% to the SSR, and 20% to the MSR in physiological variables. Foerster (1985) has reported approximately 35% variance attributable to the

[15] Apart from analysis-of-variance effect size estimates these methods include (1) comparisons of numbers of extreme responses, (2) the analysis of rank-order concordances, (3) correlations between response-profiles, (4) multivariate analysis of variance effect sizes, and (5) Mahalanobis distances.

ISR, 15% to the SSR, and 15% to the MSR. In addition, about 25% of the subjects showed a stable ISR when retested after two months, and still about 14% after one year (see also Robinson et al., 1987).

Engel (1960) laid the groundwork for the analysis-of-variance conceptualization of specificity which has also been used above (see also Engel, 1972, 1983; Engel & Moos, 1967). Engel has noted that individual and situational response specificity each require for their definition that two conditions hold: uniqueness and consistency. Uniqueness refers to the condition that persons emit or that situations evoke different response patterns. Consistency refers to the condition that persons' response patterns are transsituationally generalizable or that the response pattern elicited by one situation is generalizable across persons.

Interestingly, the methods for the analysis of specificity mentioned above do not provide estimates or tests of specificity effects that simultaneously take into account both the uniqueness and the consistency condition. For example, in the analysis of variance the Person effect estimates and tests the uniqueness condition of the ISR, whereas the simple main effect of the Situation factor for person *i* estimates and tests the consistency condition of the ISR. A simultaneous estimate and test of both uniqueness and consistency can, however, be obtained from discriminant analysis, which also offers a way to pursue the third purpose for which interaction effects can be used in the context of specificity analysis (i.e., to decompose the interaction variance into linearly independent components).

For the study of the ISR with discriminant analysis, one would define subjects as "groups" and situations as "cases within groups". Then, discriminant analysis finds those components that maximize the between-subjects variance (which emphasizes the uniqueness of persons) while at the same time minimizing the situation variance within persons (which emphasizes the consistency of persons). For the study of the SSR with discriminant analysis, one would define situations as "groups" and subjects as "cases within groups". Then discriminant analysis finds those components that maximize the between-situations variance (emphasizing situation uniqueness) while at the same time minimizing the person variance within situations (emphasizing situation consistency).

Discriminant analysis can also be used to decompose the interaction variance into linearly independent components. These components define that subspace of variable space which is the best possible representation of the respective specificity concept in the data set thus analyzed. The construction of such a subspace offers two important advantages over previously used methods for the analysis of specificity effects:

- The discriminant function coefficients allow one to interpret the variable configuration that best represents the respective specificity concept in the data.
- The group centroids (i.e., their mean vectors) in the discriminant subspace permit an evaluation of the similarity among the various groups' physiological profiles (for the formal aspects of such an evaluation, see Chapter 7). This

evaluation offers a further aid in the substantive interpretation of the specificity effects in general and of the characterization of single groups in particular.

In Chapter 10.1, I shall present an application of the discriminant analysis procedure for the elucidation of specificity effects.

6.3 Partitioning Psychophysiological Covariance

In Chapter 4.3, I have discussed the "covariation problem" in psychophysiology. One of the "explanations" for the covariation problem referred to the assessment model of the construct of activation, in particular to the choice between a trait-oriented versus a process-oriented perspective on activation. The covariation among physiological variables differs whether the one or the other perspective is taken. With regard to a Person x Situation design, still other sources of variance have been discussed in the preceding chapter, and such a decomposition of variance is obviously equally valid for the decomposition of sources of covariance between variables. In this chapter I will discuss the interpretation of correlation coefficients between physiological variables that are based on particular sources of covariance.

The choice among the various sources of covariance on which correlation coefficients are based is of course a consequence of the assessment model adopted. It should be recalled that an assessment model links a particular construct definition, that is, a particular theoretical orientation, with a specific orientation of the data analysis. Cronbach, Gleser, Nanda, and Rajaratnam (1972) based their generalizability theory on the same reasoning when they wrote, "to ask which universe is relevant is to ask how the investigator proposes to interpret the measure" (p. 19), as did Wittmann (1988) with his multivariate reliability theory. Grice (1966) gave a highly readable and nontechnical account on some aspects of variance and covariance partitioning. In the abstract, he writes:

> The nature of the relations observed between sets of variables is dependent upon the source of experimental variation employed. Recognition of this principle may lead to the discovery of new and interesting relations or to theoretical clarification. [...] quite different conclusions may be drawn concerning the relation between different response measures when variation is based upon experimental manipulation than when it is based upon individual differences. (Grice, 1966, p. 488.)

Gollob (1968a,b; see also Tucker, 1968) proposed a factor analytic decompensation of the Person x Situation interaction effect if "individual differences in patterns of performance" (Gollob, 1968, p. 357) are of substantive interest. Cleary (1972) advocated the analysis of the between-subjects plus the person x situation interaction variance (i.e., the combination of Assessment Models 1 and 7) in order to study interindividual differences in psychophysiological reactivity. Lader (1975b) explored three sources of covariation (the terms used are Lader's): (1) between-subject covariance, (2) within-subject between-test conditions covariance, and (3) within-subject within-test conditions covariance.

> The appreciable within-individual, between-condition correlates among the measures are indicative that, within the relatively narrow arousal range in an individual at rest and undertaking mental tasks, putative physiological indices of arousal show consistent and reproducible changes [...] The lack of correlation for within-task reading among the measures reflects both spontaneous fluctuations in the measure and the imprecision of the techniques. (Lader, 1975b, p. 364.)

Epstein (1983) mentioned five types of correlation coefficients which can be obtained from a design in which multiple measures are recorded on multiple subjects over multiple situations. The types of correlation coefficients are

- Temporal reliability, or stability, of single variables;
- temporal reliability, or stability, of each subject's profile of response measures;
- between-subjects correlation after collapsing the data over occasions;
- intrasubject relationships between variables over situations in a group of subjects indicating the simultaneous ebb and flow of variables over situations within individuals but common among individuals;
- intrasubject relationships between variables over situations computed separately for each individual.

Epstein noted, as has been the stance taken in Chapters 4.2 and 4.3,

> it is important that future research examine intrasubject relationships to a greater extent than has been the practice in the past and that findings derived from intersubject data not be applied to processes within individuals. (Epstein, 1983, p. 94.)

Wallin, Sundlöf, and Lindblad (1980) reported a striking case of discrepancy between correlation coefficients based on within-subjects (for a single individual over nine occasions) and between-subjects ($n = 29$) sources of covariance. The correlations between muscle nerve sympathetic activity (MSA) and diastolic blood pressure were -0.93 and 0.34 for within-subjects and between-subjects correlations, respectively. Wallin concluded:

> In contrast to this intimate relationship between *dynamic variations* of blood pressure and MSA (present in all individuals), no systemic correlation was found if different subjects were compared with regard to their *mean levels* of diastolic blood pressure and MSA. (Wallin, 1981, p. 474; author's italics.)

Systematic applications in psychophysiology of the method of covariance partitioning (allowing the separation of different sources of covariance) have been presented by Andresen (1987), Fahrenberg and Foerster (1982), Foerster, Schneider, and Walschburger (1983b), Myrtek (1984), and Stemmler (1984).

Covariance partitioning follows the same rules as the decomposition of the total sums of squares (*SS*) according to the sources of variation inherent in a particular experimental design. Consider, for example, a Subjects x Conditions design with repeated measurements on the Conditions factor. The decomposition of the total *SS* reads

$$SS(\mathrm{T}) = SS(\mathrm{BS}) + SS(\mathrm{BC}) + SS(\mathrm{R})\,, \tag{60}$$

where T = total, BS = between subjects, BC = between conditions, and R = residual (composed of the subject x condition interaction and error, separable only if replications are obtained). Composites of these basic sources of variance that are frequently employed are

$$SS(\mathrm{WS}) = SS(\mathrm{BC}) + SS(\mathrm{R}) \tag{61}$$

$$SS(\mathrm{WC}) = SS(\mathrm{BS}) + SS(\mathrm{R})\,, \tag{62}$$

where WS = within subjects and WC = within conditions.

The same relationships hold if, instead of the *SS* of a single variable, the sums of squares and cross-products matrix **S** of several variables is analyzed,

$$\mathbf{S}_{\mathrm{T}} = \mathbf{S}_{\mathrm{BS}} + \mathbf{S}_{\mathrm{BC}} + \mathbf{S}_{\mathrm{R}} \tag{63}$$

$$= \mathbf{S}_{\mathrm{BS}} + \mathbf{S}_{\mathrm{WS}} \tag{64}$$

$$= \mathbf{S}_{\mathrm{BC}} + \mathbf{S}_{\mathrm{WC}}\,. \tag{65}$$

Given the matrices **S**, variance-covariance and correlation matrices can be easily derived (e.g., Morrison, 1976). Following the lead of Fahrenberg and Foerster (1982), the psychophysiological interpretation of correlation coefficients derived from this covariance partitioning is discussed next (see Table 9 for a summary).

Between-subjects correlations (r_{BS}). These correlations indicate the degree of correspondence between two variables across subject means. One such mean is the average over the repeated measures of one subject. If an r_{BS} is large in absolute value, individual differences in mean physiological activity in one variable will be substantially predictable by another variable. The interpretation of between-subjects correlations depends on the size and composition of the sample of conditions used. If the sample is large and in a specifiable way representative of subjects' responsiveness, individual differences in "habitual" physiological responses are depicted. If the sample of conditions is small, individual differences consist of habitual (ISR) and idiosyncratic (MSR) components of physiological activation.

Between-conditions correlations (r_{BC}). These correlations indicate the degree of correspondence between two variables across condition means. One such mean is the average over all subject scores in one experimental condition. If an r_{BC} is large in absolute value, the situation-specific physiological responses in two variables are essentially similar. More specifically, an r_{BC} is a measure of shape similarity of two variables' condition-profiles (conditions are the elements of these profiles). Note that elevations and scatters (i.e., the average responsiveness across all conditions and the response variability respectively; see Chapter 7) of condition-profiles are irrelevant for the magnitude of an r_{BC}. Only when the condition-profile of one variable is absolutely flat (i.e., either no or identical physiological responses were elicited), will the r_{BC} with any other variable be undefined.

Under the assumption that the condition-profile of the "average-subject" is a valid representation of each subject's condition-profile (this assumption is violated in the case of marked idiosyncratic responses), the r_{BC}'s indicate a systemic relationship of variables over conditions. Several factors may lead to systemic relationships:

- Variables may be physiologically or physically closely related. Therefore, they covary irrespective of the type of condition and also within conditions, for

Table 9. Psychophysiological Interpretation of Correlation Coefficients Derived from Covariance Partitioning

Between-Subjects Correlations
Correlation over subject means. Correspondence of variables in predicting individual differences in average physiological reactivity. Average defined over sample of experimental conditions used.

Between-Conditions Correlations
Correlation over condition means, i.e., degree of synchronous increases/decreases over the course of conditions. Correspondence of variables in situation-specific physiological activity due to coupling of response systems but also due to physiological redundancy and technical/algebraical dependencies.

Residual (Subjects x Conditions plus Error) Correlations
Correlation over all data with subject and condition means removed. Subject x condition component (separable from error only with replications): correspondence of variables in predicting individual differences in idiosyncratic activation processes. Error component: remaining systematic and unsystematic sources of covariance.

Within-Subjects Correlations
Correlation over all data with subject means removed. Correspondence of variables in the time domain. Uses situation-specific and idiosyncratic plus error covariance. Contains complete information dealt with in General Psychophysiology.

Within-Conditions Correlations
Correlation over all data with condition means removed. Correspondence of variables in predicting all individual differences in activation processes. Uses individual-specific and idiosyncratic plus error covariance. Contains complete information dealt with in Differential Psychophysiology.

Note. Table adapted from Stemmler and Fahrenberg (1989)

example, finger pulse volume amplitude and finger temperature. Psychophysiological research has repeatedly tried to identify such "redundant" variables to find substitutes for those difficult to measure.

- Variables may be part of a temporarily coordinated, functional mechanism to serve organismic requirements, behavioral goals, situational demands, etc. Variables of quite distinct physiological systems may then be more or less tightly coupled, as, for example, heart rate and muscular activity during certain tasks.
- Variables may be related over conditions because of technical confounds or algebraical dependencies.

Obviously, if the substantive question related to the first or second of these factors (i.e., identification of redundant variables or of functional integrative mechanisms), the remaining factors have to be ruled out as possible rival explanations.

Residual correlations (r_R). Since in a design without replications the S x C and error variances are confounded, residual variance is a mixture of distinct sources.

- The S x C correlation indicates the degree of correspondence between two variables across idiosyncratic processes (see the MSR principle in the previous chapter). The S x C correlation subsumes individual differences of considerable interest, because the idiosyncratic physiological reactivity to particular conditions may be psychologically more relevant than the general level of over- or underactivation (see Chapter 11). If two variables are physiologically or physically closely related (near redundant, see above), or technically or algebraically dependent, these S x C correlations necessarily will be high.
- The error correlation is composed of covariance not accounted for by the previously described sources. The uncorrelated-error model of classical test theory assumes these correlations to vanish.

Within-subjects correlations (r_{WS}). These correlations are established from covariance complementing the between-subjects covariance. Thus, they give a summary account of the correspondence of two variables in the time domain jointly for all subjects. They are based on the information inherent in all individual condition-profiles, stemming from the effects of experimental conditions, from idiosyncratic reactivities, and from systemic or other relationships independent of conditions.

Within-conditions correlations (r_{WC}). These correlations are produced by covariance complementing the between-conditions covariance. They comprise all of the available information on individual differences in activation processes. These are the coefficients of choice when studying, for example, the predictability of individual physiological differences both from other physiological variables and from data of other measurement domains.

It should be noted that the partitioning of covariance is directly related to the specificity principles discussed in the preceding chapter. This is not surprising since both sets of notions are related to the same sources of variance and covariance. Table 10 summarizes the relationships.

The statistical test against zero of some of the correlation coefficients based on covariance partitioning is problematic because the observations, over which the correlations are computed, are not independent. According to Quenouille (1952), approximate tests can be obtained by correcting the degrees of freedom,

$$df_{corr} = df/(1 + 2r_x(1)r_y(1) + 2r_x(2)r_y(2) + \ldots)\,, \tag{66}$$

where df_{corr} = corrected degrees of freedom, df = degrees of freedom for independent observations, $r_x(1)$ and $r_y(1)$ = first-order antocorrelation of the variables x and y; $r_x(2)$ and $r_y(2)$ = second-order autocorrelations. The critical value for a correlation coefficient based on dependent observations is approximately

$$r_{crit} = (F_{(1,dfc)} \,/\, [F_{(1,dfc)} + dfc])^{0.5}\,, \tag{67}$$

where F is the F-value with (1, dfc) degrees of freedom at a specified α-level and $dfc = df_{corr}$.

Similar corrections of the degrees of freedom are in use in the analysis of variance with repeated measurements, where violations of the sphericity assumption can be compensated for by applying the "ϵ-correction" of Greenhouse and Geisser (1959) or Huyhn and Feldt (1976),

$$df_{corr} = df^{*}\text{est}(\epsilon)\,, \text{ ("}\epsilon\text{-correction")} \tag{68}$$

to the degrees of freedom of the repeated measurements factors. The lowest value ϵ can attain equals df so that

Table 10. Relationship between Specificity Principles and the Partitioning of Covariance in a Subjects x Conditions Design with Replications;

Source of Variance/Covariance	Specificity Principle	Correlation Coefficient
Between Subjects	ISR	r_{BS}
Between Conditions	SSR	r_{BC}
Subjects x Conditions	MSR	r_{SxC}
Within Subjects	ISSR	r_{WS}
Within Conditions	SISR	r_{WC}
Error (Replications)	-	r_E

$$df_{\text{corr}} = 1 \text{ , ("worst case")} \tag{69}$$

in the case of maximal violation of the sphericity assumption ("worst case").

These corrections of the degrees of freedom in the context of the analysis of variance suggest themselves as a preliminary way to judge the significance of correlation coefficients based on covariance partitioning. However, the statistical model of the analysis of covariance should actually be used because the latter model specifies the relationship between two variables (the variate and the covariate) in the framework of the analysis of variance. For the Subjects x Conditions design with replications and repeated measurements, Table 11 presents the degrees of freedom under (1) the conventional analysis of covariance, (2) the "ϵ-correction", and (3) the "worst case" assumption. It should be noted that application of the ϵ-correction requires the separate estimation of ϵ for each variable. The correction should use the ϵ (out of each pair of ϵ's) with the lower value.

Table 11. Degrees of Freedom for the Statistical Evaluation of Correlation Coefficients Based on Covariance Partitioning

		Procedure[a]	
Source of Covariance	Conventional ANCOVA	"ϵ-Correction"	"Worst Case"
Total	$nK^*(J-1)+n-3$	$nKJ'+n-3$	$nK+n-3$
Between subjects	$n-2$	$n-2$	$n-2$
Within subjects	$nK^*(J-1)-1$	$nKJ'-1$	$nK-1$
Between conditions	$J-1$	J'	1
Within conditions	$(nK-1)^*(J-1)+n-3$	$(nK-1)^*J'+n-3$	$nK+n-4$
Subjects x conditions	$(J-1)^*(n-1)$	$J'^*(n-1)$	$n-1$
Error	$n^*(K-1)^*(J-1)$	$n^*(K-1)^*J'-1$	$n^*(K-1)-1$

Note. ANCOVA = analysis of covariance. "ϵ-Correction" = Greenhouse-Geisser or Huyhn-Feldt ϵ-correction of degrees of freedom. "Worst case" = assumption of maximal violation of sphericity condition. n, J, K = number of subjects, conditions, and replications, respectively. $J' = (J-1)^*\text{est}(\epsilon)$. [a]Degrees of freedom are based on a Subjects x Conditions design with repeated measurements of the variate and the covariate (Winer, 1971) and replications.

7 The Analysis of Profiles

In Chapter 3.1 it has been proposed that an operationalization of the effective stimulus for the efferent systems might be obtained by the *profile* of observed physiological responses (see Figure 1). Profiles of variables contain important information not accessible through the separate variables. The kind of unique information inherent in profiles and how it can be retrieved from the observed response profiles is the topic of this chapter. Another link between previously discussed issues and the present chapter is (1) the conceptualization of activation as a multicomponent process (see Chapters 4.2 and 4.3) and (2) the analysis of physiological response specificities that simultaneously take into account the *uniqueness* and the *consistency* aspects of specificity (see Chapter 6.2.2). Profile analysis can provide a means to study both of these issues effectively. As has been noted previously, discriminant analysis (DA) provides a tool for the substantive description of specificity effects of physiological profiles; likewise, DA identifies components within specified sources of variance and covariance of an experimental design that might provide a starting point for the definition of activation components. Therefore, in contrast to approaches that analyze profiles in the context of factor analysis (see, e.g., Horn, 1969; Nunnally & Kotsch, 1983; Ross, 1964) or clustering procedures (see, e.g., Overall & Klett, 1972; Skinner, 1978, 1979), the present exposition is directed towards an introduction into the analysis of profiles in the context of DA.

7.1 The Similarity of Profiles

"Similarity" does not constitute a quality by and in itself. Similarity can be assessed only with respect to specified dimensions. The similarity of profiles is usually assessed with respect to the "profile elements" that, in a geometrical sense, span the space within which the profiles are represented as points. This geometrical notion intuitively suggests that the basis for the assessment of profile similarity could as well be a subspace within the complete space (see Chapter 7.3).

After the dimensions for the assessment of similarity have been specified, the question is by which measure similarity should be expressed: Different measures of similarity reflect different aspects of similarity (Butler, 1983; Nunnally, 1962, 1978). Since the Euclidian distance measure D includes all of the information available about the similarity of profiles, the present discussion will be based on D.

Cronbach and Gleser's (1953) main argument in favor of D was that it is a function of the profile parameters elevation (el), scatter (sc) and shape (sh). Profile elevation is defined as the arithmetic mean of scores across profile elements, profile scatter as the scores' standard deviation, and profile shape as the configuration of fully-ipsatized or row-standardized scores (i.e., after elevation and scatter have been accounted for). Denote a fully-ipsatized profile element m of person i by z_{im} and the complete profile by the vector $\mathbf{z}_i$ (of order M). The semi-ipsatized or row-centered profile (i.e., one obtained after elevation has been accounted for) $\mathbf{y}_i$ and the original profile $\mathbf{x}_i$ can then be written as

$$\mathbf{y}_i = sc_i\mathbf{z}_i \tag{70}$$

$$\mathbf{x}_i = sc_i\mathbf{z}_i + el_i \,. \tag{71}$$

Averaged over M variables, the squared distance between two profiles i and i' is

$$\begin{aligned} D^2(x)_{ii'} &= (1/M)*\Sigma_m([sc_i z_{im} + el_i] - [sc_{i'} z_{i'm} + el_{i'}])^2 \\ &= (el_i - el_{i'})^2 + (sc_i - sc_{i'})^2 + 2sc_i sc_{i'}*(1 - r_{ii'}) \end{aligned} \tag{72}$$

$$D^2(y)_{ii'} = (1/M)*\Sigma_m(sc_i z_{im} - sc_{i'} z_{i'm})^2 = (sc_i - sc_{i'})^2 + 2sc_i sc_{i'}*(1 - r_{ii'}) \tag{73}$$

$$D^2(z)_{ii'} = (1/M)*\Sigma_m(z_{im} - z_{i'm})^2 = 2*(1 - r_{ii'}) \,, \tag{74}$$

with $r_{ii'}$ = correlation coefficient between profiles i and i'. The comparison between Equations 72, 73 and 74 shows that profile elevations are both independent of scatter and shape, but that scatter is not independent of shape. The equations also show that with successive stages of ipsatization the distances between profiles get smaller:

$$\begin{aligned} D^2(z)_{ii'} &= (D^2(y)_{ii'} - [sc_i - sc_{i'}]^2/sc_i sc_{i'} \\ &= (D^2(x)_{ii'} - [el_i - el_{i'}]^2 - [sc_i - sc_{i'}]^2)/(sc_i sc_{i'}) \,. \end{aligned} \tag{75}$$

7.2 Dimensional Representation of Profiles

In this section I will give a brief summary account on geometrical properties of profile vectors. (An excellent reference for geometrical concepts in statistics is Green and Carroll [1976].)

Profiles are points in the person-space spanned by the profile elements, which are in the present context the physiological variables. The squared length of the profile vector i (i.e., the vector extending from the origin to the point with coordinates equaling the profile scores) is

$$\| \mathbf{x}_i \|^2 = M{*}sc^2_i + M{*}el^2_i \text{ (raw score profiles)} \quad (76)$$

$$\| \mathbf{y}_i \|^2 = M{*}sc^2_i \text{ (semi-ipsatized profiles)} \quad (77)$$

$$\| \mathbf{z}_i \|^2 = M \text{ (fully-ipsatized profiles).} \quad (78)$$

Thus, raw score profiles have a squared length composed of the sum of two squared distances, one of which is the squared length of its semi-ipsatized profile. Because Equation 76 defines an additive decomposition of squared distances according to the Pythagorean theorem, the two distances on the right-hand side are marked off on perpendicular lines. The length of semi-ipsatized profiles is a function of their profile scatters, whereas fully-ipsatized profiles are located on the surface of a hypersphere with squared radius M.

The coordinates of a raw score profile i equal the elements of $\mathbf{x}_i$. The coordinates of the corresponding semi-ipsatized and fully-ipsatized profiles are

$$\mathbf{y}_i = \mathbf{x}_i - el_i\mathbf{1} \text{ (semi-ipsatized profile)} \quad (79)$$

$$\mathbf{z}_i = \mathbf{y}_i/sc_i \text{ (fully-ipsatized profile)}, \quad (80)$$

with $\mathbf{1}$ = the unit vector of order M. These expressions further clarify the location of the semi-ipsatized and fully-ipsatized profiles in person-space. The expression $el_i\mathbf{1}$ is the perpendicular projection of $\mathbf{x}_i$ onto the main diagonal $\mathbf{1}$. Therefore, the vectors $\mathbf{y}_i$ and $\mathbf{z}_i$ are orthogonal to the main diagonal. With this result, the additive decomposition of the squared length of the raw score profile vector (Equation 76) can be given its proper geometrical interpretation: The vector $\mathbf{x}_i$ projects onto the main diagonal and a line perpendicular to it with squared lengths $M{*}el^2_i$ and $M{*}sc^2_i$, respectively. The fully-ipsatized profile is located on the same line as the semi-ipsatized profile but with coordinates differing by the factor $1/sc_i$. The direction cosinus between the raw score profile and both the semi-ipsatized and the fully-ipsatized profile is

$$\cos\Theta(\mathbf{x}_i,\mathbf{y}_i) = \cos\Theta(\mathbf{x}_i,\mathbf{z}_i) = sc_i{*}(sc^2_i + el^2_i)^{-0.5}, \quad (81)$$

where Θ is the angle between the profile vectors. The direction cosinus between the semi-ipsatized and the fully-ipsatized profile vectors is of course $\cos\Theta(\mathbf{y}_i,\mathbf{z}_i) = 1$.

To sum up thus far, the location of raw score profiles in person-space is a function of the three profile parameters elevation, scatter, and shape. The dissimilarity between two raw score profiles, as measured by their distance, cannot be easily interpreted in terms of their profile parameters. Semi-ipsatization can complexly alter the configuration of raw score profiles if substantial differences in elevations existed. However, the merit of using semi-ipsatization is that the similarity between profiles can be directly interpreted with respect to scatter, as inferred from the vector lengths, and with respect to the similarity of shape, expressed as the angular separation between the profile vectors. Full-ipsatization leads to a configuration that depends only on the similarity of profile shapes. It should be noted that both forms of ipsatization reduce the dimensionality of the person-space by one.

The problem I want to treat next is the search for an "optimal" subspace with generally markedly lower dimensionality than the U-dimensional person-space (U = rank of the n x M matrix $\mathbf{X}$ with row profile vectors $\mathbf{x}_i$). The Eckart-Young theorem provides a solution to this problem: A singular value decomposition of any matrix into its "basic structure" yields for every desired dimensionality of a subspace those dimensions that guarantee the lowest possible sum of squared distances of profile vectors from that subspace. The basic structure of a matrix is

$$\mathbf{X} = \mathbf{PLQ}' , \tag{82}$$

with $\mathbf{X}$ = n x M matrix to be analyzed, $\mathbf{P}$ = n x U orthonormal matrix of left eigenvectors, $\mathbf{L}$ = U x U diagonal matrix of eigenvalues, and $\mathbf{Q}$ = U x M orthonormal matrix of right eigenvectors. The eigenvectors (columns) in $\mathbf{P}$ give the direction cosinus of the axes of the best-fitting subspace within variable-space (variables are the points in space) with respect to the complete variable-space. The coordinates of variable-points on the axes of the subspace are given by $\mathbf{G} = \mathbf{QL}$. In the factor-analytic R-technique $\mathbf{G}$ is called the "factor pattern" of the variables.

The eigenvectors in $\mathbf{Q}$ give the direction cosinus of the axes of the best-fitting subspace within person-space with respect to the complete person-space. The coordinates of person-points or profiles on the axes of the subspace are given by $\mathbf{F} = \mathbf{PL}$. In factor-analytic Q-technique, $\mathbf{F}$ is called the "factor pattern" of the persons. Persons with high loadings on one of the factors in $\mathbf{F}$ have a profile that very much resembles the corresponding basic or "modal" profile (Skinner, 1978) in $\mathbf{Q}$.

7.3 Discriminant Analysis of Profiles

7.3.1 Discriminant functions

Just as the previously discussed singular-value decomposition (and factor analysis) finds an optimal subspace of given dimensionality for n profile vectors, so does discriminant analysis for G groups of each n profiles. The set of axes spanning the discriminant space of dimension V (V = rank of $\mathbf{W}^{-1}\mathbf{B}$, see below) are derived such that the between-groups (*SSB*) relative to the within-groups sums-of-squares (*SSW*) on each successive axis v (discriminant function, *DF*) is a maximum,

$$l_v = SSB_v/SSW_v =! \text{ maximum} \tag{83}$$

$$SSB_v = \mathbf{q}'_v\mathbf{B}\mathbf{q}_v \tag{84}$$

$$SSW_v = \mathbf{q}'_v\mathbf{W}\mathbf{q}_v \,, \tag{85}$$

where l_v and $\mathbf{q}_v$ are eigenvalues and eigenvectors, respectively, of $\mathbf{W}^{-1}\mathbf{B}$, with $\mathbf{B}$ = M x M matrix of between-groups sums-of-squares and cross-products (*SSCP*) and $\mathbf{W}$ = M x M matrix of pooled within-groups *SSCP*. The matrix $\mathbf{W}^{-1}\mathbf{B}$ generally is not symmetrical, hence the eigenvectors are not necessarily orthogonal. The elements q_{mv} of the eigenvector $\mathbf{q}_v$ are the regression coefficients for the prediction of DF_v on the basis of the M original variables. The scaling of the eigenvectors is often changed from $\mathbf{q}'_v\mathbf{q}_v = 1$ to $\mathbf{q}_v'\mathbf{W}\mathbf{q}_v = SSW_v = 1$.

7.3.2 Standard profile tests in discriminant analysis

Standard profile tests (see, e.g., Harris, 1985; Morrison, 1976; Timm, 1975), in contrast to tests on specific *DF*s, are performed in the complete person-space. Thus, for standard profile tests the multivariate general linear model applies:

$$\mathbf{X} = \mathbf{HD} + \mathbf{E} \,, \tag{86}$$

where $\mathbf{X}$ = n x M matrix of raw score profile vectors $\mathbf{x}_i$, $\mathbf{H}$ = n x K design matrix specifying K contrasts (e.g., G - 1 group contrasts), $\mathbf{D}$ = K x M matrix of unknown effect parameters to be estimated, and $\mathbf{E}$ = n x M error matrix. The general form to test any particular combination of parameters from $\mathbf{D}$ is

$$\mathbf{ADC} = \mathbf{S} \,, \tag{87}$$

where $\mathbf{A}$ = k x K matrix specifying contrasts among columns of $\mathbf{D}$, $\mathbf{C}$ = M x m matrix specifying contrasts among columns of $\mathbf{D}$, and $\mathbf{S}$ = k x m matrix specifying the value of the null hypothesis, with k and m equaling the actual number of row and column contrasts needed for the hypothesis. Given this general setup, any test between group-profiles and profile elements (both within a group-profile and between two or more group-profiles) can be constructed within the complete person-space.

Overall differences among group-profiles (overall test). Specifying **A** to be a K-1 x K design matrix contrasting all rows of **D**, **C** to be the M x M identity matrix (a matrix with 1's in the diagonal and 0's elsewhere), and **S** to be the K-1 x M null matrix, provides the null hypothesis of the overall test of no group-profile differences. A special case of the overall test is the contrast between the profiles of two groups (Hotelling's T^2 for two independent samples), where **A** is a 1 x K vector contrasting the selected groups and **S** is a 1 x M null vector.

Overall differences among variable-profiles. This hypothesis asks whether there are differences among the variable-profiles over groups. The null hypothesis of no overall differences among the variable-profiles is constructed by letting **A** be a K x K identity matrix, **C** a M x M-1 design matrix contrasting all columns of **D**, and **S** a K x M-1 null matrix.

Scatter plus shape differences among group-profiles (parallelism test). This hypothesis asks for an interaction between groups and variables. Since differences in profile elevations are irrelevant for this interaction, the hypothesis leads in effect to a simultaneous test of both scatter and shape differences among group-profiles. The parallelism test requires the following specifications: **A** is a K-1 x K design matrix contrasting all rows of **D**, **C** is an M x M-1 matrix contrasting all columns of **D**, and **S** is a K-1 x M-1 null matrix.

Elevation differences among groups-profiles (levels test). The null hypothesis of no differences in the elevations of the group-profiles corresponds to the group main effect in a univariate groups x variables design. In order to specify this hypothesis, let **A** equal a K-1 x K design matrix contrasting all rows of **D**, **C** a M x 1 vector of 1's, and **S** a K-1 x 1 null vector.

Elevation differences among variable-profiles (flatness test). This hypothesis asks whether the grand mean profile (the average of the group-profiles) is essentially flat, that is, whether the M grand means of the variables are equal. In order to construct this null hypothesis, **A** has to be specified a 1 x K vector of 1's, **C** an M x M-1 matrix contrasting all columns of **D**, and **S** a 1 x M-1 null vector.

It should be noted that the preceding constructions of multivariate null hypotheses apply both for independent and dependent (i.e., repeated measures) groups. What differs, of course, is the appropriate error matrix needed to perform the adequate tests. However, as in the univariate analysis of variance, the sphericity assumption may be violated with multivariate repeated measures designs. A correct treatment of this case requires that the G repeated measures be defined as variables yielding a total of M x G variables. As a consequence, the above specifications of the **C** matrix have to be changed. However, in applications where the error degrees of freedom are less than M x G, this solution will not be possible because the inverse of the pooled error $SSCP$ matrix **W** does not exist.

The analysis of semi-ipsatized profiles **Y** instead of raw score profiles **X** (see Equation 86) has some predictable results:[16]

- The overall effect with semi-ipsatized profiles equals the parallelism effect with the same profiles;
- the levels effect of semi-ipsatized profiles is zero;
- the parallelism effect with raw score profiles equals the overall and parallelism effect with semi-ipsatized profiles.

If, instead of raw score profiles X, fully-ipsatized profiles **Z** are analyzed,[17] the overall and parallelism effects are again equal; they exclusively reflect group-profile differences in shape.

The null hypotheses stated above are tested under the usual assumptions of independence, equality of within-group covariance matrices,[18] and the validity of the multinormal law within groups (Timm, 1975; Groff, 1983, gives a practically oriented exposition of available tests). For Hotelling's T^2 stastistic it has been shown (Hakstian, Roed, & Lind, 1979) that T^2 usually is unaffected by heterogeneous covariance matrices, provided that sample sizes are equal and greater than 50. Given even this confidence, one should note that full-ipsatization will alter the within-group covariance matrices of **X** and **Y** (for which they are equal) differentially:

$$\mathbf{W}(z)_g/df_e = sc_g^{-2}\mathbf{W}(x)_g/df_e = sc_g^{-2}\mathbf{W}(y)_g/df_e \,, \tag{88}$$

where $\mathbf{W}_g/df_e$ is the covariance matrix of group g, and sc_g is the scatter of the gth group-profile. Thus, the within-group covariance matrices of **Z** can be estimated only conditionally to the random variable sc, and it is questionable whether the usual test statistics can safely be applied to fully-ipsatized profile tests.

In contrast to the homogeneity of covariance matrices assumption, that of multivariate normality within groups is not crucial. If the method of ipsatization described above is used and if the raw scores conform to multivariate normality, so will semi- and fully-ipsatized scores within groups. This circumstance will become evident when it is recalled that all scores within a particular group (over all variables) are identically linearly transformed. If, however, every single profile i (and not the group-profile g, as proposed) were fully-ipsatized, the

---

[16] Following the proposal of Stemmler (1988), the matrix of semi-ipsatized profiles is obtained from the matrix of raw score profiles by $y_{igm} = x_{igm} - el_g$.

[17] The matrix of fully-ipsatized profiles is obtained from the matrix of semi-ipsatized profiles by $z_{igm} = y_{igm}/sc_g$.

[18] This can be checked with the Box test. Foerster and Stemmler (1990) discuss the sample size required for use of the F-approximation of the Box test.

resulting standardized scores would no longer be normally distributed. Instead, they would be distributed on the surface of an (M-1)-dimensional hypersphere, which is evidently nonnormal. In this case, the Bingham or the Mises-Fisher distribution for directional data could be used (Mardia, Kent, & Bibby, 1979). In cases of nonnormality or heterogeneity of covariance matrices, nonparametric profile analysis could be used (Bhapkar, 1984); however, converting continuous variables into ranks, as required for nonparametric profile analysis, amounts to loosing the shape information inherent in the profiles. Finally, as noted above, ipsatization introduces linear dependence among variables. The number of variables that are entered into the calculation for the degrees of freedom of the multivariate tests with ipsatized profiles should therefore be reduced by one, that is, from M *to* M-1 (see Table 12).

7.3.3 The visual interpretation of profile vectors in discriminant space

It has been noted above that the discriminant analyses with raw score (*DARS*), with semi-ipsatized (*DASI*), and with fully-ipsatized group-profiles (*DAFI*) accentuate the distinctive characteristics of the group-profiles:

- In *DARS*, the profile parameters elevation, scatter, and shape are completely confounded. Neither distances between group-profile vector endpoints (in the following called "centroids"), nor their distances from the origin, nor the angular separations among group-profile vectors can be drawn upon in order to elucidate the sources of the profiles' dissimilarity.
- In *DASI*, distances of centroids from the origin are proportional to their respective profile scatters. The cosine of the angular separation between two group-profile vectors equals the similarity (i.e., correlation) of their shapes: Group-profile vectors with identical shapes are located on the same line; group-profile vectors with opposite shapes (i.e., profiles reflected at zero), on one line but on either side of the origin; uncorrelated group-profile vectors, on perpendicular lines. Thus, the representation through *DASI* allows an unambiguous interpretation of group-profile dissimilarities in terms of profile parameters.[19]
- In *DAFI*, centroids are located on the surface of a hypersphere, that is, with equal distance from the origin (see Footnote 20). The cosines of angular separations among group-profile vectors can be interpreted exactly as pointed out above with regard to the *DASI*.

There are, however, two prerequisites that must hold before the interpretations of the *DASI* and *DAFI* suggested above are valid (Stemmler, 1988):

[19] The characterizations hold for the complete V-dimensional discriminant space. If less than V *DFs* are retained, both distances from the origin and angular separations are likely to be altered and correspond no longer to the actual profile parameters but to those "explained" by the retained *DFs*.

- The origins of the discriminant spaces have to coincide with the origin of person-space. Such a common origin of different discriminant spaces, however, is generally not provided by canned computer programs of multivariate analysis of variance or of discriminant analysis. Usually, the origin of a discriminant space is defined as the overall centroid of all centroids, which will often be different for the *DARS*, *DASI*, and *DAFI* solutions. A change of the origin leads to changes of distances from the origin and to changes in the angular separation between two profile vectors. Therefore it is essential to define a common origin for these discriminant spaces.
- The scaling of the *DF*s both within and between the *DARS*, *DASI*, and *DAFI* solutions should be equal. If they are not equal, distances from the origin of and angular separations among group-profile vectors will inevitably change within each *DA*, and comparisons between the *DA*s will not be possible. The scaling of *DF*s by canned computer programs is usually such that $SSW_v = \mathbf{q}'_v \mathbf{W}\mathbf{q}_v = 1$, which however introduces differences in the units of the *DF*s.

The adjustments both of the origin of a discriminant space (first adjustment) and the scaling of the *DF*s (second adjustment) necessary to avoid the problems of interpretation just mentioned are not difficult to perform. In general, the coordinate h_{gv} of the group-profile vector $\mathbf{x}_g$ in the *DARS* (the following expressions apply equally to $\mathbf{y}_g$ and $\mathbf{z}_g$ in the *DASI* and *DAFI*, respectively) on *DF* v, with the origin defined as the overall centroid as in most computer programs, is

$$h_{gv} = \mathbf{q}'*(\mathbf{x}_g\text{-}\mathbf{x}_.) \,, \tag{89}$$

where, as before, $\mathbf{q}_v$ is the vth (unstandardized) vector of discriminant weights, $\mathbf{x}_g$ is the gth group-profile, and $\mathbf{x}_.$ is the overall mean raw score profile. The adjustment of centroid coordinates to the origin of person-space (first adjustment) is

$$h_{gv(\mathrm{adj1})} = h_{gv} + \mathbf{q}'_v\mathbf{x}_. \,, \tag{90}$$

where $h_{gv(\mathrm{adj1})}$ is the adjusted coordinate as viewed from the origin of person-space. It should be noted that this first adjustment is not necessary if the raw score variables, and with them automatically the variables after semi-ipsatization, had been centered previously (i.e., demeaned), which makes $\mathbf{x}_.$ a zero vector. Full-ipsatization, however, usually changes variable means and hence the adjustment of Equation 90 needs to be performed in the *DAFI*.

The second adjustment concerns the scaling of the *DF*s which should equal exactly the scaling of the variable-axes in person-space. This condition is met if the sum-of-squares of each vector of unstandardized discriminant weights equals 1. Any other scaling of the discriminant weights $\mathbf{q}^*$ can be changed to the desired one by multiplication with a factor f_v ,

$$f_v = (\mathbf{q}^{*\prime}_v\mathbf{q}^*_v)^{-0.5} \tag{91}$$

$$\mathbf{q}_v = f_v \mathbf{q}^*_v \tag{92}$$

which provides the second and final adjustment of centroid coordinates:

$$h_{gv(\text{adj2})} = f_v h_{gv(\text{adj1})} \; . \tag{93}$$

Performing the complete set of standard profile tests and calculating the three discriminant spaces based on the *DARS*, *DASI*, and *DAFI* has previously been termed a *Multistage Discriminant Analysis* (Stemmler, 1988). A Multistage DA includes tests of differences among group-profiles on single *DF*s which may contribute to the interpretation of the configuration of group-profiles in discriminant space. This is particularly true if the *DF*s have been given substantial interpretations, a point stressed by Harris (1985) and already demonstrated in Chapter 5.3.1. Critical values and the degrees of freedom necessary for statistical tests in *DARS* and in *DASI* (tests in *DAFI* are presently not recommended, see above) have been collected in Table 12.

Table 12. Critical Values and Degrees of Freedom for Some Statistics in Discriminant Analyses with Raw Score (DARS) and Semi-Ipsatized (DASI) Group-Profiles

Roy's Θ for the vth Discriminant Function[a]	
Critical Value: $\Theta_{v(\alpha;df1,df2,df3)}$	
DARS	DASI
$df1 = \min(h,M)-v+1$	$df1 = \min(h,M-1)-v+1$
$df2 = (\mid h-M-v+1 \mid -1)/2$	$df2 = (\mid h-M-v+2 \mid -1)/2$
$df3 = (e-M-v)/2$	$df3 = (e-M-v+1)/2$
A priori Contrasts on a posteriori Discriminant Function[b]	
Critical Value: $(we)/(e-w+1)F_{(\alpha;df1,df2)}$	
DARS	DASI
$w = M$	$w = M-1$
$df1 = M$	$df1 = M-1$
$df2 = e-M+1$	$df2 = e-M+2$
A posteriori Contrasts on the vth a posteriori Discriminant Function[b]	
Critical Value: $(e\Theta_{v(\alpha;df1,df2,df3)})/(1-\Theta_{v(\alpha;df1,df2,df3)})$	
DARS	DASI
As in Statistic 1	As in Statistic 1

Note. Critical values at significance level α. Variables h and e are the univariate degrees of freedom for hypothesis and error respectively: M is number of variables. Table adapted from Stemmler (1988). [a] Adjustment of degrees of freedom for discriminant function v following Timm (1975). [b] Critical values for contrasts on a priori discriminant functions are identical for *DARS* and *DASI*. The critical value for an a priori contrast is $F_{(\alpha;1,e)}$ and for an a posteriori (Scheffé) contrast $hF_{(\alpha;h,e)}$.

Part B: Selected Research Areas

8 Overview of Experimental Studies

Part II of this book presents applications and illustrations of the models and tools for a differential psychophysiology that have been described in Part I. Data from four psychophysiological investigations are used in subsequent chapters. Here I want to give a brief overview of these experimental studies. Table 13 summarizes their main characteristics.

8.1 Experiment 1

8.1.1 Subjects

Fifty female medical students voluntarily participated after signing an informed consent. They were paid 80 DM. Eight subjects had to be excluded because of equipment failure and unwanted prior knowledge of the emotion inductions. This left $n = 42$ subjects with an average age of 23 years (standard deviation = 2.5 years).

8.1.2 Setting and apparatus

The experimental room was sound-attenuated and air-conditioned. It had a largely nontechnical appearance. Subjects sat comfortably in a reclined position. Electrophysiological signals were preamplified in an input box behind the subject's seat. Auditory material was presented through loudspeakers. A screen 1.5 m before the subject allowed slide presentation. In an adjacent room were placed amplifiers, couplers, audiovisual equipment, and the polygraph. A laboratory computer was used to store physiological data on magnetic tape, to control the experiment, and to perform the off-line biosignal analyses. With the exception of interviews, subjects stayed alone in the experimental room. Experimenter and subject communicated via intercom, whenever necessary.

8.1.3 Procedure

Subjects appeared three times: during Session 1, they filled out personality

Table 13. Main Characteristics of Experimental Studies

	Experiment			
Characteristic	1	2	3	4
Main theme	Emotion Specificity	Alcohol Withdrawal	Autogenic Training	Task Systematization
Subjects	Female Medical Students	Male Alcoholics	Children (Both Sexes)	Male Medical Students
No. Subjects	42	39	58	48
No. Variables	34	27	24	37
Motor	13	9	3	4
ANS	12	10	11	33
EEG	9	8	10	-
No. Situations	55	26	35	22
No. Replications[a]	-	-	-	4
No. Conditions[b]	55	26	35	88
No. Observations[c]	2310	1014	2030	4224
No. Data[d]	78,540	27,378	48,720	156,288

[a]Replications in Experiment 4 under four different medication schedules. [b]No. Conditions = No. Situations x No. Replications. [c]No. Observations = No. Subjects x No. Conditions. [d]No. Data = No. Observations x No. Variables.

questionnaires; at Session 2, they were shown the laboratory and some procedural details in order to reduce any unwanted apprehension due to the laboratory environment; four weeks later, at Session 3, the experiment was run. It consisted of seven phases, during which physiological data were continuously recorded. Between phases, self-reports of emotion were obtained. Interviews further explored affective experiences. Each phase was composed of several experimental situations. Table 14 gives an overview of the procedure.

The *number tasks* were mild vigilance tasks and in principle already known to the subjects from Session 2. Five-digit numbers delivered auditorily had to be compared with two target digits which remained projected on the screen in front of the subjects (target digits were changed between task repetitions). If the targets were contained in the number, the subject was to press a button. Numbers were delivered at a constant rate (20 numbers in 90 sec).

The *fear induction* consisted of a confusing (so it was hoped) instruction, "Right now you will hear a story, because something will happen to you that is out of your control", followed by a "radio play" with a dramatic recitation of parts from E.A. Poe's "The Fall of the House of Usher", dubbed with sections of Prokofiev's 2nd symphony, which ended with the lights switching off and one minute later on again unexpectedly und without any accompanying instructions.

The *speech tasks* consisted of requests for subjects to recall and speak about either a frightening, an annoying, or an interesting and exciting life episode; these topics were presented in a randomized order. After the instruction the subjects were given a fixed period of 5 min to complete the task. This 5-min period was individually subdivided post hoc into the periods before, during, and after the actual speech. The *imagery tasks* followed the speech tasks; the subjects were asked to imagine their stories vividly.

The *anger induction* was couched in the task of solving 5-letter anagrams, presented as an intelligence test. Anagrams were screened for 5 sec, but the subsequent anagram appeared only after the subject had solved the previous one or admitted that she could not solve it. After 15 solvable anagrams, the subject was asked to speak louder in order to compensate for an alleged breakdown of the intercom. After each of the next two anagrams, the second one unsolvable, the experimenter aggressively insisted that she speak louder. The last eight anagrams were a combination of solvable and unsolvable ones.

The *happiness induction* reassured the subjects of their success and announced an extra monetary bonus (10 DM).

8.1.4 Physiological variables

The following 34 physiological variables, derived from the parameterization of 18 channels, were analyzed.

Table 14. Procedure of Experiment 1

Experimental Situations Number	Name	Duration (min:sec)
Phase 1: Familiarization and Number Task 1		
1	Prestimulus 1	0:30
2- 4	System Check: Instruction, Waiting (1st min, 2nd min)	3:30
5- 7	Number Task 1: Instruction, Task, Poststimulus 1	6:15
	Self-Report of Emotion	8:45
Phase 2: Fear Induction, Speech Task 1, Imagination 1		
8	Prestimulus 2	9:15
9-12	Fear Induction: Instruction, Radio Play, Darkness, Waiting	19:15
13-16	Speech Sample 1: Instruction, Speech (Before, During, After)	24:45
17	Imagination 1: Instruction, Task	26:00
	Self-Report of Emotion and Interview	46:00
Phase 3: Number Task 2		
18	Prestimulus 3	46:30
19-20	Number Task 2: Task, Poststimulus 3	48:15
	Self-Report of Emotion	50:45
Phase 4: Anger Induction, Speech Task 2, Imagination 2		
21	Prestimulus 4	51:15
22-32	Anger Induction: Instruction, Anagrams (Slides 1-15, 1st Interrupt, Slide 16, 2nd Interrupt, Slide 17, 3rd Interrupt, Slides 18-25), Instruction, Waiting (1st min, 2nd min)	58:20
33-36	Speech Sample 2: Instruction, Speech (Before, During, After)	63:50
37	Imagination 2: Instruction, Task	65:05
	Self-Report of Emotion and Interview	85:05
Phase 5: Number Task 3		
38	Prestimulus 5	85:35
39-40	Number Task 3: Task, Poststimulus 5	88:05
	Self-Report of Emotion	90:35
Phase 6: Happiness Induction, Speech Task 3, Imagination 3		
41	Prestimulus 6	91:05
42-44	Happiness Induction: Instruction, Waiting (1st min, 2nd min)	93:50
45-48	Speech Sample 3: Instruction Speech (Before, During, After)	99:20
49	Imagination 3: Instruction, Task	100:35
	Self-Report of Emotion and Interview	120:35
Phase 7: Number Task 4		
50	Prestimulus 7	121:05
51-52	Number Task 4: Task, Poststimulus 7	123:05
	Self-Report of Emotion	125:35
Electrode Displacement, Final Interview		170:35

Electromyograms (EMGs) were obtained from the extensor digitorum, trapezious, orbicularis oculi, and frontalis sites with Ag/AgCl electrodes (surface 0.5 cm^2). Filters were set to 0.53-3000 Hz, amplification was 2 x 10^4. EMG couplers performed low frequency (below 50 Hz) filtering to remove slow artifacts, rectification, and smoothing by a Bessel low-pass filter (20 Hz). After 16 Hz digitization, values were summed to give 0.5-sec scores with the dimension microvolt. These scores were subdivided into a "tonic" (i.e., slowly changing) and a "phasic" (i.e., rapidly changing) component following the procedure of Irrgang and Andresen (1985).

Body movements were recorded at the middle finger of the nondominant hand, at the forehead, and from below the subject's chair, using sensitive accelerometers. Amplification was about 10^5, filters were set to 1.3-5.3 Hz, and the sampling rate was 64 Hz. Digital high-pass filtering which eliminated frequencies below 2 Hz and rectification yielded measures of acceleration in gravitational units.

Electrodermal activity was obtained from the middle and index fingers of the nondominant hand and at the forehead (an unusual site, which nonetheless is suggested by the emotional sweating generally known to occur there). Measurement used the constant voltage principle (0.5 V with Ag/AgCl electrodes, surface 0.5 cm^2). The coupler separated the DC component with a 10-sec time constant and amplified it by about 10^4 (AC: 10^6). The sampling rates were 16 Hz. Skin conductance responses with amplitudes larger than 0.01 μSiemens/cm^2 were automatically detected. Skin conductance level was defined as the average DC level per 0.5 sec in $\mu S/cm^2$. Skin conductance response was defined as the number of fluctuations per second.

Heart period was derived from the electrocardiogram (ECG) of chest leads. Filters were set to 1.6-80 Hz, amplification was at a gain of 500, and the sampling rate was 256 Hz. Self-optimizing digital filters and dynamic criteria were used to obtain a high signal-to-noise ratio for R-wave recognition (Stemmler & Thom, 1979). Output was interbeat intervals in milliseconds.

Peripheral pulses were detected by reflection-photoplethysmography at the middle finger and at the forehead (Irrgang, 1981). A low-pass filter (0.75 Hz) separated the pulse volume amplitude from the low-frequency blood volume component. Pulse volume amplitude (blood volume in parentheses) amplification was about 50 (5) and the sampling rate was 256 Hz (16 Hz). Pulse volume amplitude was automatically determined as the systolic peak's amplitude above the line connecting the neighboring diastolic points. Measures were in arbitrary units. Because of frequent movement artifacts, pulse volume amplitude from the head was excluded from further analyses.

Pulse transit time was calculated as the time difference in milliseconds between the R-wave in the ECG and the systolic peak in the finger plethysmogram.

Respiration period was obtained by an impedance measurement of respiratory activity. Sampling rate was 16 Hz. Automatic parameterization yielded respiratory cycle times in milliseconds.

The *vertical and horizontal electrooculograms* (EOGs) were derived from small Ag/AgCl electrodes (surface 0.125 cm^2). A low-pass filter was set to 100 Hz, digitization rate was 64 Hz, and amplification was at a gain of 200. The vertical EOG was scored as number of blinks per second; the horizontal EOG, as saccadic activities in microvolt/sec.

Skin temperatures were recorded with thermo-elements at the index finger of the nondominant hand and at the forehead.

The *electroencephalogram* (EEG) was recorded from the P3-Cz derivation with 0.5 cm^2-surface electrodes and Grass paste EC2. Time constant was set at 0.3 sec and the low-pass filter at 100 Hz. Digitization rate was 256 Hz and amplification was at a gain of 10^4. The EEG was decomposed by spectral analysis into nine frequency bands (Andresen, Thom, Irrgang, & Stemmler, 1982; Andresen, Stemmler, Thom, & Irrgang, 1984): sub-alpha1 (6-7.5 Hz), sub-alpha2 (7.5-9 Hz), alpha1 (9-10.5 Hz), alpha2 (10.5-12 Hz), sub-beta1 (12-15 Hz), sub-beta2 (15-18 Hz), beta1 (18-21 Hz), beta2 (21-24 Hz), and gamma (24-44.5 Hz). Measures are from the absolute power median spectrum in $microvolt^2$*sec.

For an overview of the variables registered, see Table 17.

8.1.5 Response Scaling

Data were inspected for artifacts and, if possible, corrected. Otherwise artifacts were set as missing data. Raw scores were defined as the arithmetic mean of the data within each experimental situation. Missing values were replaced by estimates which were based on the data of subjects with no missing values in the respective variable (see Stemmler, 1989, for a complete description). Trends over the course of the experiment were controlled for intraindividually by a moving baseline that connected the four poststimulus periods following the number tasks. The differences between raw scores and the moving baseline were individually centered, normalized by the McCall transformation (calculated per variable across all situations and subjects), and again expressed as deviations from the baseline. This procedure yielded normalized difference scores (see Chapter 6.1). Finally, all variables were standardized to a mean of 50 and standard deviation of 10.

8.2 Experiment 2

8.2.1 Subjects

Thirty-nine male patients (Psychiatric Clinic at the Hamburg University Hospital) in alcohol withdrawal therapy with clormethiazole participated voluntarily and after ascertainment of their "testability" by a psychiatrist. Mean age of the subjects was 38.7 years. Mean duration of alcoholism was 11.9 years, mean alcohol consumption before withdrawal therapy was 313 g/day. Delirium tremens had occurred in 12 (31%) patients, pre-delirious states in 27 (69%) patients. At an average of 3.1 days after admission, the patients' condition had improved enough to allow the participation (testability) in the study. Patients were admitted to the study at varying intervals from the day of testability. Patients aged over 50 years, or those with dementia or other severe central nervous system or internal diseases were not included in the study.

8.2.2 Setting and apparatus

Setting and apparatus were the same as in Experiment 1 (however, a screen was not mounted). Throughout the experimental session, the experimenter stayed in the experimental room. He also delivered all of the instructions given to the subject.

8.2.3 Procedure

On ward, patients were instructed that the psychophysiological investigation could help to diagnose their current psychological and bodily state. Table 15 gives an overview of the procedure.

During *relaxation* periods, the light in the experimental room was reduced. Subjects were instructed to close their eyes and to stay in a comfortable and relaxed position.

Anticipation periods were intended to be periods of mental preparation for the ensuing task. Instructions to these periods were formulated to amplify emotional concerns about the results of the forthcoming tests. For example, the instruction of the anticipation period before mental testing mentioned,

> With the following task we want to determine how much the alcohol has impaired your mental performance ...

Digit span was examined with the Subtest 3 of the Hamburg-Wechsler test (Wechsler, 1964). The experimenter read a series of digits with an increasing number of digits in successive series. The subject had to repeat each series of digits aloud. The examination was stopped if the subject could not correctly repeat a series after two trials. In the forward recall condition, the subject repeated the series in the sequence it had been presented. In the backward recall condition, the subject repeated the series in reverse order.

The *mental arithmetic* task required the subject to silently add for one minute the number 17 to the previous sum, beginning with 17.

The *stress interview* lasted 15 minutes. The subject was intensely interrogated about his problems with alcohol, in particular the physical damages and social consequences caused by the alcohol dependence.

The *hyperventilation* period lasted for one minute during which the subject had to breath as deeply as he could at a metronome-paced rate of twelve breaths per minute.

During many periods of this experiment the subject was asked to close his eyes: during relaxation, anticipation, and poststimulus periods as well as during the digit span tasks and the mental arithmetic task.

Table 15. Procedure of Experiment 2

Experimental Situations Number	Name	Duration (min:sec)
Phase 1: Relaxation		
1	Relaxation 1	2:00
	Self-Report of Emotion	6:00
Phase 2: Mental Tests		
2	Prestimulus 2	6:30
3- 4	Anticipation 1: Instruction, Anticipation	7:40
5- 8	Digit Span: Instruction, Forward Recall, Instruction, Backward Recall	10:40
9-10	Mental Arithmetic: Instruction, Task	12:10
11	Result and Poststimulus 2	12:40
	Self-Report of Emotion	16:40
Phase 3: Relaxation		
12	Relaxation 2	18:40
	Self-Report of Emotion	22:40
Phase 4: Stress Interview		
13	Prestimulus 4	23:10
14-15	Anticipation 2: Instruction, Anticipation	24:20
16	Stress Interview	39:20
17	Poststimulus 4	40:20
	Self-Report of Emotion	44:20
Phase 5: Relaxation		
18	Relaxation 3	46:20
	Self-Report of Emotion	50:20
Phase 6: Hyperventilation		
19	Prestimulus 6	50:50
20-21	Anticipation 3: Instruction, Anticipation	52:00
22-23	Hyperventilation: Instruction, Task	53:10
24-25	Instruction, Poststimulus 6	56:10
	Self-Report of Emotion	60:10
Phase 7: Relaxation		
26	Relaxation 4	62:10
	Self-Report of Emotion	66:10

Note. Times are only approximate because of interindividually slightly varying task durations.

8.2.4 Physiological variables

Signal processing and the derivation of parameters were the same as in Experiment 1 if not otherwise indicated. *Electromyograms* were obtained from the extensor digitorum, frontalis, and masseter sites. Hand movements were recorded at the middle finger of the nondominant hand. *Electrodermal activity* was recorded from the middle and index fingers of the nondominant hand. *Heart* and *respiratory period* were obtained from the ECG and impedance measurements, respectively. In distinction to Experiment 1, the respiratory cycle was subdivided into three periods: inspiration, expiration, and the postexpiratory pause. *Inspiration* and *expiration times* were divided by respiratory cycle time yielding their relative durations. *Peripheral pulses* as well as *skin temperature* were detected at the middle finger.

Pulse transit time was derived from the time difference between the R-wave of the ECG and the peripheral pulse. The *vertical* and *horizontal electrooculograms* yielded measures of eyeblink and saccadic activity, respectively. *Electroencephalograms* were obtained from five derivations (F3, F4, P3, P4, Cz, all against linked mastoids), of which only the P3 derivation will be used here. Frequency bands employed were those described for Experiment 1, except that the delta band (1.75 - 3.5 Hz) was included and the beta1 (18 - 21 Hz) and the beta2 (21 - 24 Hz) bands were excluded. For an overview of the variables registered, see Table 17.

8.2.5 Response scaling

Artifact inspection and missing data treatment were performed as in Experiment 1. The response scaling differed from Experiment 1, because the primary aim of Experiment 2 was to detect differences between patient groups, which, however, are not of concern here.[20] In order to retain as much between-subjects (and correspondingly, between-groups) variance as possible, individual trends over the course of the experiment were not removed. Nevertheless, a response scaling on the basis of the normalized difference score was performed: As a first step, the individual data were ipsatized (per variable) and the original individual raw score means and variances saved. Next, the ipsatized data of all subjects were McCall-normalized, separately for each variable. Finally, the normalized data were rescaled to the original individual means and variances. In effect, this scaling retained individual differences in response channel constants and sensitivities (as well as higher-level individual differences of the effective

[20] Groups were defined according to the time elapsed between the day of "testability" (where they were first judged fit enough to take part in the psychophysiological experiment) and the experimental day. In this way, four experimental groups were established: Group 1 was studied at the day of testability; Group 2, at day 5; Group 3, at day 9; Group 4, at day 13 after testability.

stimulus), while at the same time allowing for individual differences in the form of the transfer functions. Finally, variables were standardized to a mean of 50 and standard deviation of 10.

8.3 Experiment 3

8.3.1 Subjects

Fifty-eight pre-adolescent and adolescent former patients (Psychosomatic Department of the Children's Clinic at the Hamburg University Hospital), 21 of which were female and 37 male, with a mean age of 13.9 years (range 10 to 18 years), participated upon individual request in this study. Some of these former patients ($n = 28$) had previously participated in courses on autogenic training (AT) which teach techniques for self-administered relaxation, the other former patients ($n = 30$) had no experience with the AT.[21]

8.3.2 Setting and apparatus

Setting and apparatus were the same as in Experiment 1 (however a screen was not mounted). With the exception of interviews, the subjects stayed alone in the experimental room.

8.3.3 Procedure

Subjects appeared twice: during Session 1, they filled out questionnaires, performed a suggestibility test, and became acquainted with the experimental room; a few weeks later, at Session 2, the experiment was performed. Table 16 gives an overview of the procedure.

The *heartbeat perception* task was included in the experimental protocol in order to obtain a potentially interesting measure of the accuracy of autonomic perception. Subjects had to count their heart beats for 45 sec without any external aid. But psychophysiologically this task was interesting too, because it demanded an inward directed attention. The dimension of inward vs. outward directed attention had been emphasized by the Laceys (e.g., Lacey & Lacey, 1974).

During the 3-min *resting* periods and the 10-min *relaxation* periods subjects closed their eyes. Before relaxation, by mentioning the key expressions

---

[21] The primary aim of this experiment was to evaluate the psychophysiological responses to AT by comparing the AT-experienced subjects with the control group (see Dittmann, 1988; Stemmler, 1987c). This part of the study is not of concern here.

associated with the training (e.g., heavy and warm arms, cool forehead, etc.) experienced subjects were instructed to perform the autogenic training. Subjects from the control group were similarly instructed to relax themselves and to use, for example, mental images of heavy and warm arms, cool foreheads, etc.; however, no reference to the autogenic training was made. During resting periods subjects were simply asked to remain quiet and wait until the next instruction.

The *anticipation* periods before the following three tasks were one minute long and were intended to produce a buildup of apprehension and worry. To approach this goal, the instructions before the anticipation periods articulated putative negative consequences. For example, the instruction of the anticipation period before the noise task said:

> You will soon hear a very loud and unpleasant noise which you can hardly stand. It is forbidden to cover your ears.

The instruction of the anticipation period before the mental arithmetic task explained the task and added, "it is important for you to remember that you do not make one single error". The respective instruction before the sing-a-song

Table 16. Procedure of Experiment 3

Experimental Situations Number	Name	Duration (min:sec)
Phase 1: Heartbeat Perception		
1	Counting Heartbeats	0:45
	Self-Report of Emotion	3:15
Phase 2: Resting and Relaxation		
2- 5	Resting 1: Instruction, Resting (1st min - 3rd min)	6:40
6-16	Relaxation: Instruction, Relaxation (1st min - 10th min)	17:40
17-20	Resting 2: Instruction, Resting (1st min - 3rd min)	21:05
	Self-Report of Emotion and Interview	33:35
Phase 3: Noise Task		
21-22	Anticipation 1: Instruction, Anticipation	35:45
23-25	Noise: Task, Instruction, Poststimulus 3	37:30
	Self-Report of Emotion	40:00
Phase 4: Mental Arithmetic Task		
26-27	Anticipation 2: Instruction, Anticipation	42:15
28-30	Mental Arithmetic: Task, Instruction, Poststimulus 4	43:55
	Self-Report of Emotion	46:25
Phase 5: Sing-a-Song Task		
31-32	Anticipation 3: Instruction, Anticipation	48:10
33-35	Sing-a-Song: Task, Instruction, Poststimulus 5	49:50
	Self-Report of Emotion and Interview	62:20

Note. Times are only approximate because of interindividually slightly varying task durations.

task said:

> Everyone has a favorite song or melody which he or she is well aquainted with. You shall sing us your favorite song in a couple of moments. We are going to tape-record your song, compare it later with other songs, and have it then rated by other children.

The *noise* task consisted of a 1-min, 80 dBA loud mixture of metallic train and heavy machinery sounds. The *mental arithmetic* task demanded adding silently for one minute the number 7 to the previous result. The *sing-a-song* task required the subject to sing a favorite song during a 1-min period.

8.3.4 Physiological variables

With one exception, physiological variables were sampled from those already described in Experiments 1 and 2. Therefore, it may suffice to simply name the variables employed: Extensor digitorum electromyogram subdivided into "tonic" and "phasic" components; body movements recorded by a chair-accelerometer; skin conductance levels and number of reactions at the hand; heart period; pulse-transit time; pulse volume amplitude and blood volume at the finger; respiratory period, relative inspiration and expiration times; skin temperatures at the hand and the forehead. The electroencephalogram was derived from the Cz-Pz sites and yielded in addition to the nine frequency bands as in Experiment 1 a theta (4.5 - 6 Hz) band which was of particular interest for the research question of relaxation. Table 17 gives an overview of the physiological variables employed in Experiments 1 to 3. (Experiment 4 used a largely nonoverlapping sample of variables and is therefore treated separately.)

8.3.5 Response scaling

The artifact and missing data treatments as well as the response scaling were performed exactly as in Experiment 2, that is, a trend correction was not applied and individual differences in means and variances were retained. However, in contrast to Experiments 1 and 2, raw scores were regressed on age before the response scaling with the resulting residuals was performed. This partialling procedure was deemed necessary because physiological levels are likely to change over the age range represented by the subjects. It should be noted, however, that only the individual means of physiological variables can be changed by the partialling procedure.

Table 17. Physiological Variables in Experiments 1, 2, and 3

Variable Name	Experiment 1	2	3
Somato-Motor Variables			
EMG extensor digitorum, tonic and phasic [EMG extt, EMG extp]	x	x	x
EMG trapezious, tonic and phasic [EMG trt, EMG trp]	x		
EMG orbicularis oculi, tonic and phasic [EMG ort, EMG orp]	x		
EMG frontalis, tonic and phasic [EMG frt, EMG frp]	x	x	
EMG masseter, tonic and phasic [EMG mat, EMG map]		x	
Body movements: Accelerometer chair [Body mov]	x		x
Body movements: Accelerometer hand [Hand mov]	x	x	
Body movements: Accelerometer forehead (Head mov]	x		
Electrooculogram vertical: No. eyeblinks [Eyeblinks]	x	x	
Electrooculogram horizontal: Saccadic activity [Sacc]	x	x	
Autonomic Variables			
No. skin conductance responses, hand [SCR-No. hand]	x	x	x
Skin conductance level, hand [SCL hand]	x	x	x
Skin conductance level, forehead [SCL foreh]	x		
Heart period [IBI]	x	x	x
Pulse transit time, finger [PTT fin]	x	x	x
Pulse volume amplitude, finger [PVA fin]	x	x	x
Blood volume, finger [BV fin]	x	x	x
Pulse volume amplitude, forehead [PVA foreh]	x		
Blood volume, forehead [BV foreh]	x		
Respiratory period [Resp per]	x	x	x
Relative inspiratory time [Insp rel]	x	x	
Relative expiratory time [Exp rel]	x	x	
Skin temperature finger [TMP fin]	x	x	x
Skin temperature forehead [TMP foreh]	x		x
Electroencephalographic Variablesa			
Delta (1.75 - 3.5 Hz) [Delta]		x[b]	
Theta (4.5 - 6 Hz) [Theta]			x[c]
Sub-alpha1 (6 - 7.5 Hz) [Salpha1]	x[d]	x	x
Sub-alpha2 (7.5 - 9 Hz) [Salpha2]	x	x	x
Alpha1 (9 - 10.5 Hz) [Alpha1]	x	x	x
Alpha2 (10.5 - 12 Hz) [Alpha2]	x	x	x
Sub-beta1 (12 - 15 Hz) [Sbeta1]	x	x	x
Sub-beta2 (15 - 18 Hz) [Sbeta2]	x	x	x
Beta1 (18 - 21 Hz) [Beta1]	x		x
Beta2 (21 - 24 Hz) [Beta2]	x		x
Gamma (24 - 44.5 Hz) [Gamma]	x	x	x

Note. An "x" means that this variable was used in the respective experiment. [a]Absolute power. [b]P3 versus linked mastoids. [c]Cz versus Pz. [d]P3 versus Cz.

8.4 Experiment 4

8.4.1 Subjects

Fifty-three male medical students voluntarily participated after signing an informed consent (the study had been approved by the Ethics Committee of the Freiburg University) and after it had been established that they fulfilled the inclusion criteria. Inclusion criteria were age between 20 and 40 years, no chronic medication, no cardiovascular diseases or dysregulations (including hypotension and hypertension, no diabetes, no obstructive bronchial diseases or asthma bronchiale, no digestive troubles, no glaucoma. Prospective subjects had also to pass a cardiological check (at the Cardiology Department of the Freiburg University Hospital) to ensure that they could safely be administered autonomic receptor blockades. Five subjects had to be excluded from the sample because of technical difficulties during the experiments, leaving an n = 48 subjects with an average age of 24.6 years (standard deviation = 3 years; range 20 - 37 years). Subjects were paid 170 DM.

8.4.2 Setting and apparatus

The experimental room was sound-attenuated and air-conditioned. Subjects sat comfortably in a reclined position. The laboratory equipment used was a Hellige 16-channel polygraph, an Impedance cardiograph Instrumentation for Medicine Inc. Model 400, an Infraton Tensiomat FIB 4/6 (Boucke) for automatic blood pressure measurements, a pneumograph (Schwarzer, No. 285) and chopper amplifier Hellige 206007, a transmission photoplethymograph at the radialis site (Klenk), a reflection photoplethysmograph (Irrgang), PT100 thermoresistors (Hellige), a Beckman Type 9842 GSR-coupler for constant-voltage measurement of electrodermal activity, a Bruell & Kjaer Type 2206 sound level meter, a Hewlett-Packard HP 1000/65 laboratory computer for the digitalization and storage of data on magnetic tape as well as for the control of the experiment, and two Commodore C64 microcomputers which performed the timing of auditory signals. A screen 2 m in front of the subjects allowed slide presentation. Instructions were delivered through a loudspeaker. Headphones were used during three experimental situations. Sound pressure calibrations were performed with Brüel & Kjaer artificial ear (Type 4153) and Bayer DT48 headphones. The experimenter entered the experimental room only between experimental situations in order to adjust the equipment (see below).

8.4.3 Procedure

Subjects appeared six times: during Session 1, they signed the informed consent and were scheduled for the cardiological examination; at Session 2, they were familiarized with the experimental room and the tasks to be presented later on; Sessions 3 to 6 were the experimental sessions, they were scheduled each one week apart from the previous session. With regard to the procedure, the experimental sessions were exact replications, with two exceptions: (1) Subjects received a different medication each time (in double-blind administration) and (2) at the third experimental session, the last task within each session (a sentence-completion task, see below) was combined with an anger induction.

Because data from Experiment 4 will be used in several of the following chapters, the design of this study will be explained in more detail than the previously discussed experiments. The study employed a placebo-controlled, double-blind cross-over design. Subjects were randomly assigned to an "easy" or "difficult" version of the tasks. Every subject received a different medication at each of the experimental sessions: either placebo, or one of three partial dual autonomic receptor blockades (p.o.), assembled from indoramin (25 mg), a selective alpha1-adrenergic antagonist; propranolol (60 mg), an unselective beta-adrenergic antagonist; and atropine (1 mg), a muscarinic cholinergic antagonist. These combinations resulted in four medication groups:

- Group A (alpha-adrenergic receptors unblocked, "alpha-free"): Subjects received propranolol plus atropine.
- Group B (beta-adrenergic receptors unblocked, "beta-free"): Subjects received indoramin plus atropine.
- Group C (cholinergic receptors unblocked, "chol-free"): Subjects received indoramin plus propranolol.
- Group P: Subjects received placebo.

Across subjects, pharmacological conditions were completely permutated over sessions (which required a multiple of 4! = 24 subjects). The experimental design can be read in either of two ways:

- as a Difficulty (2) x Subjects (24) x Medications (4) x Experimental Situations (22) design with repeated measurements on Medications and Experimental Situations, and with Subjects nested under Difficulty; this design was used to evaluate medication main and interaction effects;
- as a Difficulty (2) x Subjects (24) x Sessions (4) x Experimental Situations (22) design with repeated measurements on Sessions and Experimental Situations, and with Subjects nested under Difficulty; this design was used to evaluate session main and interaction effects.

Upon arrival on the experimental day, subjects received the predetermined medication. The pharmacokinetics of the drugs[22] suggested a waiting period of 1.5 hours between drug application and start of the experiment. During that time, subjects were given a standard breakfast (two rolls with butter and marmelade or cheese, and juice or milk), then they filled out questionnaires. Finally, electrodes and transducers were attached.

Each experimental session consisted of seven phases; each phase began with an announced prestimulus (45 sec) period during which subjects were requested to relax, which was followed by an instruction for the ensuing task, the task period proper, and an announced 45-sec poststimulus period during which subjects were requested to sit quietly. Each phase ended with a self-report of emotion (with regard to the preceding task period). Physiological data were recorded during the prestimulus, task, and poststimulus periods. Subjects kept their eyes open during all recording periods of the experiment. An overview of the procedure is provided by Table 18.

The *speech* task required the subject to count aloud for two minutes from 21 to 99 and to continue counting from 21 onwards. Counting speed was fixed at 63 numbers/min by the beat of a metronome. Subjects had to modulate the loudness of their voice such that the dial of a sound level meter in front of them (1.3 m apart) pointed to 55 dBA in the easy and to 75 dBA in the difficult condition.

In the *handgrip* task, subjects pressed a hand-dynamometer with the dominant hand (which was always the right hand) at 30% (easy condition) or 60% (difficult condition) of their predetermined maximal voluntary force for two minutes.

The *mental arithmetic* task consisted of the consecutive silent addition of one-digit and two-digit numbers that were projected onto the screen in front of the subjects. The numbers were arranged in a 14 x 16 matrix containing a total of 224 numbers. Subjects were instructed to calculate as quickly and accurately as possible, and to announce upon request the sum total as well as the position of the last number processed. During the task, white noise of 70 dBA (easy condition) or 90 dBA (difficult condition) was delivered through headphones. Mental arithmetic was performed for four minutes.

---

22 Indoramin HCl (Wydora[R], Wyeth) attains maximal plasma levels two to three hours after oral administration and it has a half-life of about twelve hours; with only 8%, its bioavailability is low. As the initial dosis, 25 mg twice a day are recommended. Propranolol HCl (Dociton[R], Rhein-Pharma) attains maximal plasma levels about two hours after oral administration; it has a half-life of about four to six hours. Its bioavailability is about 35%. As the initial dose, 40 mg are recommended. Atropine (Compretten Atropinum sulfuricum[R], cascan) attains maximal plasma levels about one hour after oral administration; it has a half-life of about 13 to 38 hours and its therapeutic effects last about three to four hours. Its bioavailability is 10 to 25%. The average adult dose is 0.5 mg.

Table 18. Procedure of Experiment 4

Experimental Situations Number	Name	Duration (min:sec)
Phase 1: Speech Task		
1	Instruction, Prestimulus 1	0:55
2	Instruction, Speech Task	3:40
3	Instruction, Poststimulus 1	4:35
	Self-Report of Emotion	7:05
Phase 2: Handgrip Task		
4	Instruction, Prestimulus 2	8:00
5	Instruction, Handgrip	10:15
6	Instruction, Poststimulus 2	11:15
	Self-Report of Emotion	13:45
Phase 3: Mental Arithmetic		
7	Instruction, Prestimulus 3	14:40
8	Instruction, Mental Arithmetic	19:45
9	Instruction, Poststimulus 3	21:05
	Self-Report of Emotion	23:35
Phase 4: Signal Detection		
10	Instruction, Prestimulus 4	24:30
11	Instruction, Signal Detection	29:35
12	Instruction, Poststimulus 4	30:30
	Self-Report of Emotion	33:00
Phase 5: Loud Noise		
13	Instruction, Prestimulus 5	33:50
14-15	Instruction, Loud Noise (Before, After)	35:50
16	Instruction, Poststimulus 5	36:40
	Self-Report of Emotion	39:10
Phase 6: Cold Pressor		
17	Instruction, Prestimulus 6	40:05
18	Instruction, Cold Pressor[a]	41:25
19	Instruction, Poststimulus 6	42:20
	Self-Report of Emotion	44:50
Phase 7: Sentence Completion		
20	Instruction, Prestimulus 7	45:45
21	Instruction, Anticipation of Task	48:05
22	Task, Instruction, Poststimulus 7	51:05
	Self-Report of Emotion	53:35
Electrode Displacement, Final Interview		83:35

Note. Times are only approximate because of interindividually slightly varying task durations. Physiological data were not recorded during instruction periods. In Phase 7, physiological data were recorded during anticipation of the sentence completion task but not during the task itself. [a]The duration of the cold pressor task differed between the "easy" (1 min) and the "difficult" version (2 min). Durations given in the table are those for the easy cold pressor task.

In the *signal detection* task, subjects were delivered white noise of 48 dBA through headphones in 20 trials of 10 sec duration each, with an interstimulus interval of 2 sec, which amounted to a total task duration of four minutes. Subjects were instructed to detect a short, faint tone, which in some trials, but not in others, would be embedded in the white noise, and to press a button during the interstimulus interval if they believed that the tone had been presented. During interstimulus intervals, subjects did not hear the white noise. A tone (1000 Hz, 0.5 sec duration, 25 msec rise and fall times) of 35.5 dBA (easy condition) or 34 dBA (difficult condition) was quasi-randomly presented in 10 of the 20 trials. Within a trial, tones were delivered at the first or second inspiratory maximum.

Before the *loud noise* task, subjects were told that they would hear a low-level white noise through the headphones and after some time a short additional noise, which could be loud or perhaps very loud. After the loud noise, subjects should wait until the announced end of the task. The total duration of the task was 80 sec. A masking noise of 40 dBA was delivered through the headphones; at the first inspiratory maximum following the first 10 seconds of the task, a 2-sec white noise burst (25 msec rise and fall times) with 90 dBA (easy condition) or 105 dBA (difficult condition) was administered.

In the *cold pressor* task, subjects had to insert their complete dominant hand in a box filled with 4°C-cold water. The task took one minute (easy condition) or two minutes (difficult condition).

The *sentence completion* task requested of the subjects to complete twelve sentences with "neutral", "joyful", or "angry" beginnings, such as "I think that ..." (neutral), "I feel good, when ..." (joyful), or "It drives me mad if ..." (angry). Subjects had to complete the sentences as quickly as possible. After the instruction, subjects had to anticipate the task for 45 sec. Physiological "task" recordings were made during this anticipation period but not during the task itself. It took about two to three minutes to finish the task. As the sentence completion task was primarily designed to offer a context for an anger induction, it was not presented in two difficulty versions. The anger induction took place at the third experimental session. Directly following the task instruction (i.e., before the anticipation period), the experimenter accused the subject in a rude and excited voice of lack of compliance:

> What is going on here! We've had it! The whole registration is totally messed up - we'll have to junk it. Why do you think we keep asking you to sit still?! You'd think we could expect just a little more cooperation from a med-student. Now we have go through the whole procedure again! You'll just have to come back one more time - but you know we can't pay extra for it. - Now let's see if at least the next task will work. - But try to control yourself a little bit this time - sit still and keep your arms as relaxed as possible and don't talk!

The ensuing anticipation period should be able to capture any physiological anger response, if present. If subjects protested against the insinuation expressed in the anger induction, they were given as many successive standard instructions as necessary to appease them (see Schäfer, 1989, for details).

8.4.4 Physiological variables

In Experiment 4, the registration of cardiovascular variables was much more inclusive than in Experiments 1 to 3 because previous research emphasis at the Freiburg Forschungsgruppe Psychophysiologie has been on the cardiovascular system. Computer programs used for biosignal analysis were mostly those described by Foerster (1984) or revisions of them.

Electromyograms were obtained from the extensor digitorum and frontalis lateralis (left) site. Filters were set to 16-1000 Hz, preamplification in the experimental room was 10^3 and again 10^3 in the polygraph. After rectification, EMG signals were integrated (integration constant = 0.1 sec). Whenever necessary, the integrator was reset by the laboratory computer. Measures carried the dimension microvolt x sec.

Body movements were recorded through a micro-switch system beneath the seat of the subjects, measures were in arbitrary units.

The *vertical electrooculogram* was filtered by a time-constant of 3 sec and a low-pass of 35 Hz and yielded the number of eyeblinks/min.

Electrodermal activity (EDA) was recorded with a constant voltage of 0.5 V from the thenar-hypothenar site of the nondominant (left) hand with sintered 0.8 cm^2 Ag/AgCl Hellige electrodes and Hellige electrode jelly No. 21708305. The raw signal was recorded with a time-constant of 10 sec at a sensitivity of 0.04 μSiemens/mm. Phasic EDA responses greater than 0.078 μSiemens (minimal slope of 0.007 μSiemens/sec, maximal half recovery time of 10 sec) counted as skin conductance responses. The analysis yielded skin conductance response amplitude (in μSiemens) and the number of skin conductance responses/min.

Heart rate (in bpm), *P-wave* and *T-wave amplitudes* (in arbitrary units), *P_s-Q_s time* (start of the P-wave to start of the Q-wave in msec), *P_e-Q_s time* (end of the P-wave to start of the Q-wave in msec), relative *Q-T time* (systolic time: start of the Q-wave to end of the T-wave, relativized by Bazett's frequency correction to a heart rate of 60 bpm in $msec^{0.5}$) and *ST-elevation* (in arbitrary units; determined as the amplitude of the ECG-curve at a point 80 msec past the J-point, which was defined as the first point with a null potential after the S-peak) were determined from the ECG. The ECG was taken from the respective impedance cardiograph output. Amplitudes are in arbitrary units because this output could not be calibrated.

Cardiac output (in l/min), the *index of cardiac output* (in l/min/m^2), *ventricular ejection speed* (in Ohm/sec), the *Heather index* (in Ohm/sec^2), *stroke volume* (in cm^3), *left-ventricular ejection time* (in msec), *preejection period* (in msec), and *R-Z time* (in msec) were estimated from impedance cardiography (derived from four band electrodes and using a 4 mA, 100 kHz alternating current), phonocardiogram, and ECG. For details of parameterization, see Fahrenberg and Foerster (1989).

Systolic and *diastolic blood pressure* (in mmHg) were measured intermittently by a non-invasive automatic procedure. The cuff (12 cm x 24 cm) was applied on the right arm. A piezo-electrical microphone, which was placed distal of the cuff in the sulcus bicipitalis medialis, recorded the Korotkov sounds. Together with the cuff pressure, the Korotkov sounds were stored for off-line analysis with a special blood pressure analysis program (for a detailed description, see Schmid, 1990). This program permitted the determination of both *Phase IV* and *Phase V* diastolic blood pressure. *Mean blood pressure* and *total peripheral resistance* (in dyn * sec * cm^{-5}) were estimated from the blood pressure data and from cardiac output, respectively.

Peripheral pulses were detected at the left index finger (by reflection plethysmography as in Experiment 1) and at the sulcus antibrachii radialis (by transmission plethysmography). In order to avoid both external light from interfering with the reflection plethysmography and a cooling of the hand (with concomitant vasoconstriction), the left hand was placed in a mitten. For both pulse measurements, *pulse volume amplitudes* (in arbitrary units) and *pulse wave velocities* (in m/sec; with the R-peak of the ECG as the reference; distances were measured between the transducers and the jugulum) were derived.

Skin temperatures were measured at the left middle finger and at the forehead with PT100 thermoresistors. Together with two reference signals (corresponding to 20°C and 40°C), the voltages derived from a resistor bridge were multiplexed (1 Hz) occupying only one polygraph channel.

Respiration rate (in cycles/min) was recorded using an optoelectronic transducer (Strasburger & Klenk, 1983) which was incorporated in an abdominal belt positioned at the height of the umbilicus. Respiration rate was determined as the frequency with peak amplitude in the power spectrum of 10-sec data windows (with Hanning window) after digitization with 25 Hz. *Respiratory sinus arrhythmia* (RSA) was determined using Grossman's method of taking the difference between the longest interbeat interval during expiration (if on an increasing intervals trend) and the shortest interbeat interval during inspiration (if on a decreasing intervals trend; see, e.g., Grossman, Stemmler, & Meinhardt, 1990). Mainly for the purpose of a methodological comparison, RSA was derived in either of two ways. The first method used a noninteractive, completely automatized procedure and yielded RSA in msec. The second method was in effect a computer-aided hand-scoring analysis which took pains to correctly identify the proper definitions of phases in the respiratory signal. The second method further deviated from the first in taking into account the varying respiratory cycle lengths. Such variations could compromise the alleged interpretation of the RSA as a measure of tonic cardiac vagal activity (Grossman, Karemaker, & Wieling, 1991). Therefore, in an analysis of covariance with subjects as "groups" and experimental situations as "cases", adjusted scores were calculated with RSA as the variate and respiration period as covariate. Thus, based on the pooled within-subjects regression function of RSA on respiration period, adjusted RSA scores were defined. In a last step, these adjusted RSA scores were transformed by the natural logarithm in order to normalize the distribution of scores.

Heart rate variability was assessed by spectral analysis. Two frequency bands were defined, (1) the 0.07-0.14 Hz band purportedly reflecting blood pressure induced variations of the heart rate and (2) the 0.14-0.42 Hz band reflecting variations of the heart rate caused by respiration (see Fahrenberg & Foerster, 1989). The square roots of the average powers in these bands (in bpm) were defined as the heart rate variability measures.

Table 19 gives an overview of the physiological variables employed in Experiment 4.

8.4.5 Response scaling

Autonomic variables were checked for artifacts and, if necessary, set to missing data at three levels of analysis. First, during the parameterization phase, the biosignal analysis program (BIO14, F. Foerster) automatically entered the interactive mode if problems of parameterization were encountered. If the presence of artifacts prevented the determination of a parameter, it was manually set as missing data for the respective heart beat (heart beats were the units of time resolution within recording periods). Second, after parameterization, the time course of physiological data was displayed on a monitor on a beat-by-beat basis (KGB, F. Foerster). Clearly aberrant data points were set as missing data. Third, for experimental situations with more than 30% non-missingdata, period means were calculated, otherwise they were set as missing data. With the help of Box plots and normal probability plots, period means were inspected for outliers, and if so judged, set as missing data. Missing data correction was performed by substituting the mean of the respective medication group x experimental situation cell mean (MDERS, F. Foerster). Because the major aim of this study was to provide estimates of activation components according to the model of Chapter 5.2, the raw scores were not transformed. Thus, depending on the particular research question, the measurement model of raw scores or of unweighted difference scores was used.

Table 19. Physiological Variables in Experiment 4

Somato-Motor Variables
Electromyogram extensor digitorum [EMG ext]
Electromyogram frontalis lateralis [EMG fr]
Body movement chair [Body mov]
Vertical electrooculogram: No. eyeblinks [Eyeblinks]
Autonomic Variables
No. skin conductance responses [SCR-No.]
Skin conductance response amplitude (SCR-Ampl]
Heart rate [HR]
P-wave amplitude [P-Ampl]
T-wave amplitude [T-Ampl]
P_s-Q_s time (P_s-Q_s]
P_e-Q_s time [P_e-Q_s]
Relative Q-T time [Q-T rel]
ST-elevation [ST-elev]
Heart rate variability, 0.07 - 0.14 Hz [HR-SD-BP]
Heart rate variability, 0.14 - 0.35 Hz [HR-SD-Resp]
Respiratory sinus arrhythmia [RSA]
ln adjusted respiratory sinus arrhythmia [RSA adj]
Pulse wave velocity, radialis [PWV rad]
Pulse wave velocity, finger [PWV fin]
Pulse volume amplitude, radialis [PVA rad]
Pulse volume amplitude, finger [PVA fin]
Cardiac output [CO]
Index of cardiac output [CO ind]
Ventricular ejection speed [Ejection sp]
Stroke volume [SV]
Left-ventricular ejection time [LVET]
Preejection period [PEP]
R-Z time [R-Z]
Heather index [Heather ind]
Systolic blood pressure [SBP]
Mean blood pressure [MBP]
Diastolic blood pressure, phase IV [DBP IV]
Diastolic blood pressure, phase V [DBP]
Total peripheral resistance [TPR]
Respiratory rate [Resp rate]
Skin temperature, finger [TMP fin]
Skin temperature, forehead [TMP foreh]

9 The Analysis of Activation

9.1 Variation and Covariation of Physiological Variables

9.1.1 Effect sizes of sources of variation

The assessment models introduced in Chapter 1.5 specified different sources of variance for analyses based on different construct definitions. The specificity and covariance partitioning analyses of Chapter 6 were straightforward applications of the assessment model framework. In this chapter, the effect sizes for different sources of variation will be demonstrated. This demonstration sets into perspective the magnitude of effects that are included or left out of consideration when choosing a particular assessment model for the analysis of the activation construct.

The data of Experiment 4 were selected to demonstrate the effect sizes of sources of variation in physiological responses because, in contrast to Experiments 1 to 3, "replications" (four replications of the same experiment although under different medication schedules) were available that allowed to specify the Subjects x Conditions source of variation separately from the error effect. Two sets of analyses were performed,

- on raw scores, with 48 subjects, 22 experimental situations (conditions), 37 physiological variables, and 4 replications;
- on unweighted difference scores, with the same number of subjects, variables, and replications, but only 7 experimental situations (task-prestimulus differences).

Within each set, seven separate analyses were run (see Table 20), (1) the overall analysis as indicated, (2) the same analysis but separately for n = 24 subjects of the "easy" and (3) n = 24 subjects of the "difficult" task version giving an impression of sampling fluctuations of variance component estimates, (4) - (7) separate analyses (n = 48) for each medication group with the consequence of loosing the distinction between the Subjects x Conditions interaction and the error effect. The estimation of variance components was necessary because the Subject factor and its interactions were random.

Table 20 shows remarkably similar effect sizes within sets of analyses. For raw score analyses, about two-thirds of the total variance estimate is attributable to the Subjects x Variables interaction source of variance and one-fourth to error. Compared to these, the other effects are essentially negligible. The picture changes dramatically, however, if one turns to the difference score analyses. Due to the loss of habitual person variance, the composition of variance estimates across the sources of variation is altered. For the analyses across all medication groups, ISR, SSR, and MSR variance each account for about 25% and error for about 30% of the variance. Interestingly, under Analysis 3 (difficult task versions only) the SSR effect is somewhat larger and the error slightly lower than under Analysis 2 (easy task versions only). Restricting the analysis to one medication group at a time reduces both the ISR and the SSR effect, whereas the relative residual variance increases over the sum of MSR and error effects in Analyses 2 to 3.

By and large, these results are in agreement with previously reported effect size estimates (e.g., Foerster, Schneider, & Walschburger, 2983a), although the number of variables and the kind of experimental situations used were different.

In the discussion about sources of between-subjects variance at the level of the observed response (see Chapter 6.2.2, Equations 53 to 55) three sources of individual differences had been described, two of which are of an anatomical or physiological origin (the third referred to the effective stimulus). These were individual differences in response channel constants and sensitivities, the first of which is excluded as a source of between-subjects variance when forming difference scores (see Equation 40b). As can be judged from the marked drop of relative ISR variance from the raw score to the difference score analyses, this source of between-subjects variance is of an appreciable relative magnitude but, as has often been shown (e.g., Myrtek, 2984; Lykken, 2968), psychologically of questionable value.

I turn, therefore, to the difference score analyses and to the introductory question, how much of the total variance would be excluded upon selection of a particular assessment model. To focus the discussion of this question, two assessment models will be contrasted,

- an individual-differences-oriented assessment model using all sources of variance including the Subjects factor, and
- a process-oriented assessment model using all sources of variance including the Conditions factor.

For the analyses across all medication groups (Analysis 2 to 3), the individual-differences assessment model would be based on 38, 33, and 32 percent of the variance; and the process-oriented assessment model, on 42, 34, and 47 percent. Given the comparable magnitudes of explained variance (with a preponderance of the process-oriented over the individual-differences assessment model in the analysis of the difficult task versions), neither of the two assessment models could claim an a priori priority for the investigation of the activation construct.

Table 20. Relative Effect Sizes of Sources of Variation (Experiment 4)

	Analysis						
Source of Variation	1	2	3	4	5	6	7
Raw Scores							
Subjects	4	3	4	4	4	4	4
Conditions	1	1	2	1	1	1	1
Variables	-[a]	-[a]	-[a]	3	5	3	1
Subjects x Conditions	0	0	0	1	1	2	1
Subjects x Variables (ISR)	65	66	64	68	66	61	66
Conditions x Variables (SSR)	4	3	5	3	2	3	2
Subj x Cond x Var (MSR)	0	0	0	-[b]	-[b]	-[b]	-[b]
Error/Residual[c]	25	27	24	21	21	26	24
Total Mean Squares	4.70	4.87	4.52	4.72	4.62	4.63	4.52
Difference Scores							
Subjects	2	2	2	2	1	2	2
Conditions	5	4	8	4	2	3	3
Variables	9	7	11	5	6	5	5
Subjects x Conditions	4	2	3	3	2	5	3
Subjects x Variables (ISR)	17	18	14	13	13	10	10
Conditions x Variables (SSR)	17	17	22	10	9	9	11
Subj x Cond x Var (MSR)	15	11	13	-[b]	-[b]	-[b]	-[b]
Error/Residual[c]	31	38	27	63	67	66	66
Total Mean Squares	2.11	1.85	2.36	2.01	1.91	2.54	1.98

Note. Numbers are percentages of the sum of variance component estimates. Total mean squares allow the comparison among different analyses. Negative variance component estimates were set to zero. Because of rounding errors, percentages do not necessarily add to 100. Analysis 1 = complete data set (48 subjects; 22 or 7 situations for raw or difference scores, respectively; 4 replications). Analyses 2 to 3 = as analysis 1 but separately with each 24 subjects for the "easy" and "difficult" task version, respectively. Analyses 4 to 7 = as analysis 1 but separately for medication groups placebo, "alpha-free", "beta-free", and "chol-free", in that order, and without replications. All analyses used 37 physiological variables (see Table 19). It should be noted that the magnitude of interaction effects including variables is influenced by the polarity of the variables. In order to achieve a consistent direction of activation, the polarity of the following variables was changed before analysis: RSA, RSA adj, LVET, PEP, TMP fin, HR-SD-BP, HR-SD-Resp, T-Ampl, P_s-Q_s, P_e-Q_s, R-Z, PVA fin. [a] Prior to analysis, variables were standardized across all medication groups. Therefore, for these analyses the main effect for variables vanishes. [b] For analyses without replications, this effect cannot be specified. [c] For Analyses 4 to 7, this source of variation is the residual component.

9.1.2 Situational discriminability

In the preceding section, a relative variance component of between 10% and 20% (see Table 20) had been demonstrated in the difference score analyses of the Conditions x Variables source of variation (i.e., SSR variance). This finding indicates a moderate to substantial degree of dissimilarity among the variable-profiles of the experimental situations. A related question pertains to the amount of between-conditions variance, or situational discriminability of variables. This issue will be pursued in this section. First, from the data of two experiments the situational discriminability of single variables will be illustrated. Second, situational discriminability of two sets of variables (the set of peripheral, i.e., somato-motor and autonomic, and the set of electroencephalographic variables) will be shown. Findings should allow to draw conclusions about (1) the differential situational discriminability by single and by sets of variables and (2) the effect of situation sampling.

In the analyses to be reported first, situational discriminability is captured (1) by the *F*-value of the Conditions effect and (2) by omega-hat square (est [Ω^2]), defined here as the estimate of the variance proportion of the Conditions effect relative to the within-subjects (i.e. total process-related) variance. Table 21 shows these statistics for the data of Experiments 1 and 4. Although in both experiments nearly all variables have significant Condition effects, their magnitudes vary considerably: Within the set of somato-motor variables of Experiment 1, an estimated variance proportion of greater than 30% is obtained for both tonic and phasic EMG orbicularis oculi activity and for head movements. The lowest situational discriminability is provided by the EMG trapezious and hand movements (this latter finding is a compliment to the subjects who obviously conformed to the instructions not to move their hands). With respect to autonomic variables, largest situational discriminabilities are seen for interbeat intervals, number of SCRs at the hand, and skin conductance level at the forehead. The EEG variables generally have lower discriminabilities; with 22%, the gamma band has the best result (see section 9.1.3 for a more detailed analysis of this band).

The corresponding statistics from Experiment 4 are often numerically larger, which might be explained by the different type of conditions included: The analysis of Experiment 1 was performed over all 52 experimental situations which included many prestimulus and instruction periods. The analysis of Experiment 4 was based on 7 experimental situations for each Difficulty level which, in contrast to Experiment 1, included only task-prestimulus differences and neither the prestimulus nor the poststimulus periods themselves. Across all variables, largest situational discriminabilities were obtained for body movements and heart rate (about 66%), followed by SCR amplitude, P-wave amplitude, adjusted respiratory sinus arrhythmia, finger pulse volume amplitude, mean and diastolic (phase IV) blood pressure, and respiration rate with discriminabilities between 40% and 50%. Comparatively low situational

Table 21. Situational Discriminability of Physiological Variables

Experiment 1 Variable	*F*[a]	est(Ω^2)	Experiment 4 Variable	*F*[b]	est(Ω^2)
EMG extt	16.58	0.27	EMG ext	21.24	0.37
EMG extp	9.70	0.17	EMG fr	5.78	0.11
EMG trt	1.61	0.01	Body mov	93.69	0.66
EMG trp	4.00	0.07	Eyeblinks	33.08	0.27
EMG ort	35.87	0.45	SCR-No.	16.82	0.28
EMG orp	21.66	0.33	SCR-Ampl	30.58	0.46
EMG frt	6.58	0.12	HR	66.82	0.67
EMG frp	4.23	0.07	P-Ampl	18.11	0.40
Body mov	14.65	0.24	T-Ampl	7.20	0.17
Hand mov	4.70	0.08	P_s-Q_s	1.68	0.24
Head mov	21.67	0.33	P_e-Q_s	2.51	0.10
Eyeblinks	9.02	0.16	Q-T rel	6.31	0.15
Sacc	11.51	0.20	ST-elev	14.83	0.35
SCR-No. hand	18.18	0.29	HR-SD-BP	12.70	0.22
SCL hand	10.25	0.18	HR-SD-Resp	3.72	0.09
SCL foreh	21.49	0.33	RSA	8.51	0.14
IBI	33.03	0.43	RSA adj	31.94	0.40
PTT fin	4.66	0.08	PWV rad	15.11	0.35
PVA fin	5.96	0.10	PWV fin	14.03	0.30
BV fin	2.06	0.02	PVA rad	2.27	0.28
PVA foreh	12.83	0.22	PVA fin	31.71	0.43
BV foreh	5.85	0.10	CO	12.19	0.30
Resp per	7.81	0.14	CO ind	11.17	0.27
TMP fin	5.29	0.09	Ejection sp	7.61	0.18
TMP foreh	9.13	0.16	SV	4.63	0.11
Salpha1	2.01	0.02	LVET	4.41	0.10
Salpha2	3.56	0.06	PEP	1.61	0.02
Alpha1	6.25	0.11	R-Z	7.39	0.14
Alpha2	8.47	0.15	Heather ind	7.35	0.17
Sbeta1	5.45	0.09	SBP	21.45	0.33
Sbeta2	4.64	0.08	MBP	31.88	0.44
Beta1	4.39	0.07	DBP IV	31.88	0.44
Beta2	3.85	0.06	DBP	21.74	0.33
Gamma	13.16	0.22	TPR	3.73	0.07
			Resp rate	51.64	0.42
			TMP fin	19.15	0.27
			TMP foreh	1.98	0.04

Note. Experiment 1: Univariate *F*-values from a 42 Subjects x 52 Conditions design on normalized difference scores. *Experiment 4:* Univariate *F*-values from a 2 Difficulties x 48 Subjects (nested under Difficulty) x 14 Conditions (nested under Difficulty) design on task-prestimulus difference scores. See Tables 17 and 19 for abbreviations of variable names. [a] Critical *F*-value: $F(12.75, 522.75) = 1.75$ for an est(ϵ) = 0.25 and $\alpha = .05$. [b] Critical *F*-value: $F(6,138) = 2.17$ for an est(ϵ) = 0.50 and $\alpha = .05$.

discriminability (<10%) was obtained for heart rate variability in the respiratory band, preejection period, total peripheral resistance, and forehead skin temperature. Some comparisons between selected variables with respect to situational discriminability might be interesting (data from Experiment 4; numbers are omega-hat squares):

- EMG extensor compared to EMG frontalis (37% versus 11%);
- SCR amplitude compared to number of SCRs (46% versus 28%);
- P-wave compared to T-wave amplitude (40% versus 17%);
- P_s-Q_s compared to P_e-Q_s time (24% versus 10%);
- heart rate variability in the blood pressure compared to the respiratory band (22% versus 9%);
- adjusted compared to unadjusted respiratory sinus arrhythmia (40% versus 14%);
- pulse volume amplitude at the finger compared to the radialis site (43% versus 28%);
- finger compared to forehead skin temperature (27% versus 4%) (However, this difference should not be interpreted substantially, because finger but not forehead skin temperature showed a marked trend over the course of the experiment.)

It should be noted that comparisons between variables such as these do not necessarily indicate the "value" of one particular variable for situational discrimination because a figure of 20% compared to one of 40% is small, if the explained variance overlaps largely, but large, if it contributes unique, nonoverlapping variance.

The comparative magnitude of situational discriminability of peripheral compared to EEG variables can be illustrated with the data of the Experiments 1 to 3 (see Table 22). These data grossly converge in showing a markedly lower situational discriminability of the EEG in comparison to the peripheral variables. Averaged across experiments, the EEG variables explain 53% of the situational variance, whereas the peripheral variables obtain 94.6%. Interestingly, this difference in discriminability holds also for subsets of conditions and irrespective of the eyes-open versus eyes-closed comparison (this context variation has a marked effect on the amplitude and power in the EEG alpha frequency bands). If repeatedly administered conditions with nearly identical physico-biological properties are to be discriminated, such as the three Gottschalk-Gleser speech periods or the three imagination periods in Experiment 1, the total discriminatory power is drastically reduced and fails to reach significance.

In conclusion, the power of physiological variables and, more so, of sets of variables to discriminate between situations is large. This finding empirically substantiates the previous claim that physiological responses are behaviors capable of a high differentiation of eliciting situations or, expressed differently, they are behaviors that sensitively reflect the organismic adaptation to varying situational demands.

9.1.3 Correlations among physiological variables within separate sources of variation

In this chapter I will first present the results of covariance partitioning expressed as Pearson correlations among the physiological variables of Experiment 4

Table 22. Situational Discriminability of Peripheral and EEG Variable Sets

Variable Set	Discriminatory Power[a]	Significance[b]
Experiment 1:		
All Conditions (J = 52) Except Imagination (Eyes Open)		
Peripheral	98.1	*
EEG	55.9	*
Experiment 1:		
Gottschalk-Gleser Speech Sample Conditions (J = 4; Eyes Open)		
Peripheral	98.6	*
EEG	53.7	*
Experiment 1:		
Repetitive Gottschalk-Gleser Speech Tasks (J = 3; Eyes Open)		
Peripheral	30.9	ns
EEG	15.1	ns
Experiment 1:		
Repetitive Imagination Periods (J = 3; Eyes Closed)		
Peripheral	31.2	ns
EEG	18.6	ns
Experiment 2:		
All Conditions (J = 26; Eyes Open and Closed)		
Peripheral	97.7	*
EEG	70.9	*
Experiment 2:		
Conditions with Eyes Open (J = 11) and Eyes Closed (J = 13)		
EEG (Eyes open)	66.6	*
EEG (Eyes closed)	63.6	*
Experiment 3:		
Rest (Eyes Open) and Relaxation (Eyes Closed) Conditions (J = 16)		
Peripheral	89.4	*
EEG	34.4	*
Experiment 3:		
Task Conditions (J = 15)		
Peripheral	93.1	*
EEG	50.9	*

Note. J = number of conditions, ns = not significant. [a] Discriminatory power is defined as (1 - Wilks' lambda) * 100%, where Wilks' lambda was derived from discriminant analyses with J conditions as "groups" and subjects as "cases". It is the percent of the variance in the physiological variable set predictable by group membership. [b] Significance of first discriminant function. $^{*}p < .05$.

(selected because replications allowed the determination of the Subjects x Conditions source of covariation separately from the error effect). Then the question of the correlation between sets of somato-motor, autonomic, and electroencephalographic variables within the Conditions and Residual source of covariation will be pursued. The data from Experiments 1 to 3 are suited for the latter question because variables had been sampled from these three domains.

Table 23 shows the matrix of intercorrelations after covariance partitioning among selected physiological variables of Experiment 4. Of the many potentially interesting relationships that could be highlighted only some examples will be commented upon: (1) The significant correlations of number of SCRs, heart rate, and EMG extensor with all other variables and (2) a selection of variable pairs and their correlations.

Number of SCRs correlates across all sources of covariance only with SCR amplitude. This confirms the intimate relationship of these parameters of electrodermal activity. Number of SCRs has several functional relationships brought forth either by situational demands, systemic or mathematical relatedness, or common errors (the *between-conditions* component BC). Such relationships are seen with heart rate, -left-ventricular ejection time (the minus sign indicates the direction of the relationship), cardiac output, all blood pressure variables, relative Q-T time, pulse wave velocity at the finger, -adjusted respiratory sinus arrhythmia, number of eyeblinks, EMG extensor, and body movements. P-wave amplitude and ST-elevation have with number of SCRs, in addition to the BC component, also a correlation within the *error* component (E). Thus, activation of the electrodermal system covaries with variables of the cardiovascular and somato-motor domain across situations. However, this is not a unitary organismic activation, because only 44% of the variables enter into this relationship, which leaves room for dissociated situationally defined activation processes. There is just one *between-subjects* (BS) correlation of number of SCRs with other variables, namely, with heart rate variability in the blood pressure band. This nicely illustrates the paucity of BS as compared to the BC correlations.

Heart rate has a distinctly different pattern of relationship with other physiological variables. *Correlations within the E component* are mainly seen with other cardiovascular variables: Such systemic relationships are obtained with -respiratory sinus arrhythmia, -preejection period, -left-ventricular ejection time, cardiac output and its index, systolic and diastolic (phase IV) blood pressure, -T-wave and P-wave amplitude, -P_e-Q_s time, relative Q-T time, -total peripheral resistance, heart rate variability in the blood pressure band, -R-T time, the Heather index, ejection speed, ST-elevation, pulse wave velocity at the radialis and finger sites, and body movements. *BC correlations* of heart rate are found with number of SCRs, -left-ventricular ejection time, cardiac output and its index, all of the blood pressure variables, T-wave (reversed sign compared to the E correlation!) and P-wave amplitude, -P_e-Q_s time, relative Q-T time, ST-elevation, pulse wave velocity at the radialis and finger sites, -adjusted

Table 23. Matrix of Intercorrelations Among Selected Physiological Variables After Covariance Partitioning (Experiment 4)

SOC — Variable

1 No. Skin Conductance Responses

	1	2	3	4	5	6	7	8	9	10	11	12	13	14	15	16	17	18	19
T	-	7	8	-6	-3	7	10	7	1	-3	**63**	**16**	11	11	12	6	-3	14	12
BS	-	1	18	-14	5	12	19	-3	-3	-11	**80**	20	10	21	-7	14	-7	**34**	24
BC	-	**80**	-40	**-74**	-17	**70**	**79**	**88**	26	-10	**81**	**80**	**79**	26	**67**	34	-41	61	2
SxC	-	22	-2	-2	-10	9	12	14	2	0	**56**	7	12	-1	12	1	5	2	9
E	-	2	8	2	-5	2	1	2	3	3	**57**	10	3	10	10	2	2	7	11

	20	21	22	23	24	25	26	27	28	29	30	31	32	33	34	35	36	37
T	12	6	**20**	8	10	5	1	3	1	-5	6	12	9	-3	8	-9	9	-4
BS	-14	8	20	8	18	-7	8	10	-4	-7	9	2	4	-15	7	0	2	4
BC	**77**	43	**75**	40	60	**77**	13	-16	18	-9	**69**	**86**	**88**	35	66	-47	**72**	**-70**
SxC	14	9	4	6	0	7	-7	0	5	-3	11	15	17	3	19	-21	15	2
E	**23**	3	**26**	11	9	9	-2	0	2	-4	2	7	2	1	3	-8	7	-3

2 Heart Rate

	1	2	3	4	5	6	7	8	9	10	11	12	13	14	15	16	17	18	19
T	7	-	**-39**	**-58**	**-28**	**31**	**29**	2	**-19**	4	8	7	**15**	-2	**32**	10	8	**17**	10
BS	1	-	**-53**	**-71**	**-34**	15	15	4	-7	16	2	1	7	-17	14	26	13	11	15
BC	**80**	-	-53	**-83**	-15	**81**	**70**	**89**	21	-9	45	**85**	**94**	34	**83**	30	-44	38	-39
SxC	22	-	-28	-28	-12	24	15	23	-4	2	19	17	16	8	**39**	3	-5	8	9
E	2	-	**-29**	**-52**	**-30**	**41**	**38**	14	**-32**	-2	4	0	9	3	**35**	-4	11	**21**	12

	20	21	22	23	24	25	26	27	28	29	30	31	32	33	34	35	36	37
T	**34**	1	**22**	6	**-16**	**45**	**-46**	**-26**	**28**	11	**32**	**23**	13	6	**31**	0	**44**	**-32**
BS	22	13	11	21	6	**40**	**-43**	**-50**	17	5	21	13	8	3	28	8	**43**	**-52**
BC	**95**	**75**	**94**	60	**-69**	**86**	35	-28	3	-25	**81**	**91**	**86**	29	**73**	-40	**75**	**-90**
SxC	**43**	22	**30**	4	-16	**44**	-23	-14	8	-5	22	30	25	4	24	-19	**38**	**-36**
E	**41**	**-20**	**36**	-13	**-42**	**48**	**-55**	-8	**41**	**21**	**40**	**19**	6	8	**31**	2	**42**	-11

5 Preejection Period

	1	2	3	4	5	6	7	8	9	10	11	12	13	14	15	16	17	18	19
T	-3	**-28**	8	**-31**	-	**-56**	**-18**	11	**47**	-4	-1	-1	-4	-5	-8	-6	-5	-8	-9
BS	5	**-34**	24	1	-	**-43**	0	28	**38**	-17	14	-5	7	10	14	-7	-21	3	-10
BC	-17	-15	-9	-12	-	-43	-50	-20	11	15	-4	-27	-12	-10	-13	-24	-5	-17	-22
SxC	-10	-12	2	**-68**	-	**-64**	-12	-4	**53**	-1	-7	-1	-2	-3	-8	-3	-6	-4	-7
E	-5	**-30**	2	**-41**	-	**-60**	**-27**	7	**51**	1	-4	2	-7	-10	**-18**	-6	5	-13	-10

Note. **1** SCR-No. **2** HR **3** RSA **4** LVET **5** PEP **6** CO **7** SBP **8** DBP **9** TPR **10** Resp rate **11** SCR-Ampl **12** Eyeblinks **13** EMG ext **14** EMG fr **15** Body mov **16** TMP foreh **17** TMP fin **18** HR-SD-BP **19** HR-SD-Resp **20** P-Ampl **21** T-Ampl **22** ST-elev **23** P_s-Q_s **24** P_e-Q_s **25** Q-T rel **26** R-Z **27** SV **28** Heather ind **29** Ejection sp **30** CO ind **31** DBP IV **32** MBP **33** PVA rad **34** PWV rad **35** PVA fin **36** PWV fin **37** RSA adj.

(Table continues)

Table 23. Matrix of Intercorrelations Among Selected Physiological Variables After Covariance Partitioning (Experiment 4) *(Continued)*

SOC	Variable																	
	20	21	22	23	24	25	26	27	28	29	30	31	32	33	34	35	36	37
T	-9	**16**	4	8	14	**-21**	**53**	**-42**	**-62**	**15**	**-56**	-4	2	-1	**-30**	-5	**-37**	1
BS	-1	**32**	22	10	4	-27	**73**	-17	**-64**	16	**-47**	8	23	1	**-44**	-25	**-37**	14
BC	-14	-30	-10	28	38	-6	55	-47	-54	-6	-36	-20	-29	-5	-60	6	-57	2
SxC	-10	-4	2	-3	2	-3	27	**-67**	**-57**	**47**	**-65**	-6	-9	-7	-20	3	-21	1
E	-13	9	-13	10	**24**	**-22**	**48**	**-52**	**-63**	**25**	**-59**	-10	-6	-2	**-25**	3	**-40**	-6

7 Systolic Blood Pressure

	1	2	3	4	5	6	7	8	9	10	11	12	13	14	15	16	17	18	19
T	10	**29**	-1	**-19**	**-18**	**17**	-	**27**	12	2	8	3	8	10	14	12	-3	14	10
BS	19	15	13	-27	0	11	-	**38**	14	7	21	2	-3	11	-5	22	-4	26	21
BC	**79**	**70**	-27	-54	-50	**71**	-	**86**	37	-12	50	**71**	**72**	24	59	45	-37	41	-3
SxC	12	15	-4	2	-12	9	-	**35**	22	3	3	4	7	0	15	3	-3	0	3
E	1	**38**	-7	-15	**-27**	**19**	-	14	8	0	-1	-3	5	11	16	6	1	11	8

	20	21	22	23	24	25	26	27	28	29	30	31	32	33	34	35	36	37
T	9	-4	4	5	0	13	**-23**	0	**19**	7	**16**	**51**	**62**	11	**23**	2	**31**	-4
BS	-4	4	-10	19	25	2	-3	1	17	12	13	**61**	**66**	5	16	7	11	2
BC	**68**	53	**68**	19	-62	58	-23	5	37	3	**67**	**85**	**93**	15	**89**	-21	**80**	-55
SxC	4	2	0	5	1	4	-15	3	8	-4	9	**42**	**64**	9	25	-3	28	2
E	15	-15	**18**	-8	**-20**	**21**	**-40**	-1	**22**	5	16	**44**	**57**	14	**23**	2	**39**	-4

8 Diastolic Blood Pressure, Phase V

	1	2	3	4	5	6	7	8	9	10	11	12	13	14	15	16	17	18	19
T	7	2	3	4	11	-11	**27**	-	**47**	-7	7	-3	9	0	6	-7	-12	1	1
BS	-3	4	1	2	28	-23	**38**	-	**59**	-16	10	13	-2	7	5	-26	-12	1	0
BC	**88**	**89**	-45	**-74**	-20	**70**	**86**	-	46	-12	53	**78**	**86**	17	**72**	50	-52	44	-20
SxC	14	23	-5	0	-4	7	**35**	-	**42**	0	8	2	14	-6	14	5	-11	3	6
E	2	14	11	12	7	-12	14	-	**43**	-1	-2	-8	0	-2	-11	3	-7	-3	1

	20	21	22	23	24	25	26	27	28	29	30	31	32	33	34	35	36	37
T	-4	**17**	**15**	2	-1	-3	**25**	-12	**-23**	**-23**	-11	**64**	**92**	7	6	**-18**	8	-10
BS	-9	19	24	-2	-8	-11	28	-22	**-33**	-23	-23	**80**	**94**	7	18	-23	17	-11
BC	**85**	66	**89**	42	**-67**	**73**	17	-26	9	-18	**70**	**96**	**99**	16	**80**	-31	**77**	**-77**
SxC	13	10	4	1	-5	6	11	-2	-5	-14	7	**53**	**91**	0	18	-19	22	-4
E	-9	16	3	5	9	-4	**25**	-6	**-22**	**-25**	-12	**48**	**89**	8	-10	-12	-7	-2

Note. **1** SCR-No. **2** HR **3** RSA **4** LVET **5** PEP **6** CO **7** SBP **8** DBP **9** TPR **10** Resp rate **11** SCR-Ampl **12** Eyeblinks **13** EMG ext **14** EMG fr **15** Body mov **16** TMP foreh **17** TMP fin **18** HR-SD-BP **19** HR-SD-Resp **20** P-Ampl **21** T-Ampl **22** ST-elev **23** P_s-Q_s **24** P_e-Q_s **25** Q-T rel **26** R-Z **27** SV **28** Heather ind **29** Ejection sp **30** CO ind **31** DBP IV **32** MBP **33** PVA rad **34** PWV rad **35** PVA fin **36** PWV fin **37** RSA adj.

(Table continues)

Table 23. Matrix of Intercorrelations Among Selected Physiological Variables After Covariance Partitioning (Experiment 4) *(Continued)*

SOC — Variable

13 Electromyogram extensor digitorum

	1	2	3	4	5	6	7	8	9	10	11	12	13	14	15	16	17	18	19
T	11	**15**	-8	-5	-4	7	8	9	-1	-2	10	11	-	12	**22**	-8	-3	3	-1
BS	10	7	-14	1	7	-11	-3	-2	10	-7	4	9	-	10	28	-26	11	-3	-11
BC	**79**	**94**	-59	**-80**	-12	**80**	**72**	**86**	15	-4	46	**80**	-	37	**76**	29	-46	32	-40
SxC	12	16	1	-2	-2	11	7	14	-1	6	7	4	-	10	**30**	6	-1	7	11
E	3	9	-5	-3	-7	6	5	0	-5	-4	6	3	-	14	3	-6	-4	0	0

	20	21	22	23	24	25	26	27	28	29	30	31	32	33	34	35	36	37
T	9	-1	5	7	2	6	-2	0	10	5	8	11	10	3	7	-6	11	-9
BS	5	-11	-5	27	21	9	-5	-14	14	17	-11	-10	-3	4	6	-10	17	-17
BC	**92**	66	**90**	49	**-73**	**76**	28	-18	10	-14	**81**	**85**	**84**	27	**68**	-22	64	**-91**
SxC	8	12	1	0	-3	3	-3	7	5	2	15	14	14	2	9	0	6	-14
E	5	0	9	-1	-3	0	-3	4	11	4	6	4	3	3	3	-4	5	8

17 Skin Temperature, Finger

	1	2	3	4	5	6	7	8	9	10	11	12	13	14	15	16	17	18	19
T		8	-9	-4	-5	-4	-3	-12	0	6	-4	-4	-3	2	-6	1	-	-3	-2
BS		13	-7	-4	-21	-9	-4	-12	3	12	-12	-3	11	-3	-17	6	-	-2	-1
BC		-44	-12	58	-5	-48	-37	-52	-4	40	-9	-29	-46	40	-30	**-77**	-	-25	-10
SxC		-5	3	6	-6	-3	-3	-11	0	-11	9	-5	-1	8	-7	0	-	2	2
E		11	-13	-11	5	3	1	-7	-3	-1	-2	-1	-4	4	6	-1	-	-3	-3

	20	21	22	23	24	25	26	27	28	29	30	31	32	33	34	35	36	37
T	5	**-16**	5	1	-5	5	-7	-7	1	-2	-3	**-15**	-11	-2	-1	**41**	**-15**	0
BS	12	-21	9	-2	-16	5	-18	-14	10	1	-7	-20	-11	9	3	**67**	-18	-8
BC	-53	-9	-61	11	63	-11	14	-11	-39	-43	-50	-44	-49	43	-46	-14	-29	38
SxC	-4	-4	3	10	11	-9	-4	2	-2	-5	0	-1	-9	11	-5	28	-7	5
E	3	-13	3	4	5	8	4	-3	-2	0	2	-9	-6	-12	0	**28**	-13	1

21 T-Wave Amplitude

	1	2	3	4	5	6	7	8	9	10	11	12	13	14	15	16	17	18	19
T	6	1	0	1	**16**	-3	-4	**17**	5	6	8	2	-1	-5	0	0	**-16**	5	6
BS	8	13	-5	-10	**32**	6	4	19	0	8	15	0	-11	-9	0	1	-21	7	3
BC	43	**75**	-51	-40	-30	52	53	66	38	6	11	**68**	66	29	**71**	18	-9	20	-44
SxC	9	22	1	-3	-4	10	2	10	-5	0	4	8	12	8	10	15	-4	13	18
E	3	**-20**	9	**17**	9	-16	-15	16	11	8	6	1	0	-4	-8	-1	-13	4	8

Note. **1** SCR-No. **2** HR **3** RSA **4** LVET **5** PEP **6** CO **7** SBP **8** DBP **9** TPR **10** Resp rate **11** SCR-Ampl **12** Eyeblinks **13** EMG ext **14** EMG fr **15** Body mov **16** TMP foreh **17** TMP fin **18** HR-SD-BP **19** HR-SD-Resp **20** P-Ampl **21** T-Ampl **22** ST-elev **23** P_s-Q_s **24** P_e-Q_s **25** Q-T rel **26** R-Z **27** SV **28** Heather ind **29** Ejection sp **30** CO ind **31** DBP IV **32** MBP **33** PVA rad **34** PWV rad **35** PVA fin **36** PWV fin **37** RSA adj.

(Table continues)

Table 23. Matrix of Intercorrelations Among Selected Physiological Variables After Covariance Partitioning (Experiment 4) *(Continued)*

SOC	20	21	22	23	24	25	26	27	28	29	30	31	32	33	34	35	36	37
T	**38**	-	**39**	**35**	**18**	**-15**	**31**	-2	**-17**	-11	-3	9	12	11	**-15**	-14	**-18**	**16**
BS	**44**	-	**51**	**37**	14	-11	**35**	-3	-23	-12	1	12	17	12	-28	-23	-21	**43**
BC	**71**	-	66	49	-38	63	37	-35	-21	-54	49	**73**	64	27	**67**	-40	**76**	54
SxC	**42**	-	22	12	-5	2	15	7	4	-2	13	12	9	3	1	-3	3	**30**
E	**29**	-	12	**33**	**27**	**-26**	**28**	-2	-15	-12	-10	2	7	11	-6	-4	**-22**	2

24 P_e-Q_s Time

SOC	1	2	3	4	5	6	7	8	9	10	11	12	13	14	15	16	17	18	19
T	10	**-16**	5	3	14	-5	0	-1	1	2	5	4	2	8	-3	-7	-5	-2	0
BS	18	6	-2	22	4	4	25	-8	-7	6	4	7	21	14	14	-7	-16	11	4
BC	60	**-69**	18	59	38	**-79**	-62	**-67**	14	31	-20	-53	**-73**	-5	-41	-46	63	-32	4
SxC	0	-16	13	4	2	-3	1	-5	5	-4	-1	-4	-3	4	-4	-2	11	1	0
E	9	**-42**	12	**27**	**24**	-12	**-20**	9	9	-2	9	6	-3	6	-15	-8	5	-12	-3

SOC	20	21	22	23	24	25	26	27	28	29	30	31	32	33	34	35	36	37
T	**-18**	**18**	-10	**71**	-	**-22**	**18**	5	-8	1	-2	-7	-1	1	-12	-7	-13	-8
BS	-18	14	-9	**81**	-	-22	3	1	9	14	9	-5	2	4	-8	-14	4	-5
BC	**-72**	-38	**-75**	0	-	-40	13	-23	-47	-18	**-80**	-62	**-67**	11	-64	-13	-51	**-84**
SxC	-12	-5	-2	**37**	-	-5	4	4	-1	0	-2	-8	-5	3	-7	2	-5	-7
E	**-19**	**27**	-12	**59**	-	**-25**	**38**	10	**-26**	-12	-10	-7	-1	-1	-16	0	**-30**	-8

28 Heather Index

SOC	1	2	3	4	5	6	7	8	9	10	11	12	13	14	15	16	17	18	19
T	1	**28**	0	2	**-62**	**60**	**19**	**-23**	**-53**	-4	-3	11	10	4	12	-3	1	**18**	**17**
BS	-4	17	0	-4	**-64**	**48**	17	**-33**	**-50**	-1	-19	28	14	-8	-4	-7	10	20	22
BC	18	3	42	-24	-54	55	37	9	-46	-44	5	8	10	-6	4	42	-39	27	38
SxC	5	8	7	**33**	**-57**	**74**	8	-5	**-58**	6	3	7	5	3	16	3	-2	10	17
E	2	**41**	-4	2	**-63**	**65**	**22**	**-22**	**-54**	-5	2	-1	11	9	**21**	-1	-2	**20**	16

SOC	20	21	22	23	24	25	26	27	28	29	30	31	32	33	34	35	36	37
T	13	**-17**	-12	-7	-8	**20**	**-63**	**43**	-	**57**	**64**	-7	-11	-7	**31**	11	**34**	3
BS	6	-23	**-32**	-2	9	16	**-70**	**30**	-	**80**	**59**	-18	-21	-19	**37**	19	23	2
BC	14	-21	7	-56	-47	-8	**-80**	**84**	-	**83**	55	2	18	-36	39	36	20	-2
SxC	5	4	-7	-3	-1	10	**-39**	**70**	-	**30**	**74**	-9	-2	5	19	3	21	1
E	**20**	-15	10	-14	**-26**	**27**	**-61**	**47**	-	**44**	**66**	1	-8	-2	**29**	5	**44**	4

Note. **1** SCR-No. **2** HR **3** RSA **4** LVET **5** PEP **6** CO **7** SBP **8** DBP **9** TPR **10** Resp rate **11** SCR-Ampl **12** Eyeblinks **13** EMG ext **14** EMG fr **15** Body mov **16** TMP foreh **17** TMP fin **18** HR-SD-BP **19** HR-SD-Resp **20** P-Ampl **21** T-Ampl **22** ST-elev **23** P_s-Q_s **24** P_e-Q_s **25** Q-T rel **26** R-Z **27** SV **28** Heather ind **29** Ejection sp **30** CO ind **31** DBP IV **32** MBP **33** PVA rad **34** PWV rad **35** PVA fin **36** PWV fin **37** RSA adj.

(Table continues)

Table 23. Matrix of Intercorrelations Among Selected Physiological Variables After Covariance Partitioning (Experiment 4) *(Continued)*

SOC — Variable

30 Index of Cardiac Output

SOC	1	2	3	4	5	6	7	8	9	10	11	12	13	14	15	16	17	18	19
T	6	**32**	-3	**16**	**-56**	**92**	**16**	-11	**-76**	-3	2	9	8	-6	**23**	-1	-3	**18**	**15**
BS	9	21	-4	2	**-47**	**90**	13	-23	**-81**	3	-2	3	-11	-5	21	5	-7	24	28
BC	**69**	**81**	-22	**-79**	-36	**99**	**67**	**70**	-26	-34	37	**69**	**81**	24	**73**	36	-50	47	-15
SxC	11	22	-5	**52**	**-65**	**91**	9	7	**-64**	4	7	16	15	8	27	0	0	7	12
E	2	**40**	-2	**21**	**-59**	**93**	16	-12	**-77**	-7	0	7	6	-8	**20**	-6	2	17	13

SOC	20	21	22	23	24	25	26	27	28	29	30	31	32	33	34	35	36	37
T	**17**	-3	1	2	-2	**21**	**-36**	**72**	**64**	**15**	-	4	-2	-2	**15**	-2	**22**	-4
BS	24	1	-1	3	9	7	**-43**	**63**	**59**	**38**	-	-4	-14	-9	23	4	16	2
BC	**85**	49	**78**	24	**-80**	64	-5	32	55	23	-	**68**	**71**	12	**72**	-2	61	**-78**
SxC	13	13	-1	4	-2	15	-12	**78**	**74**	-6	-	3	9	3	14	-4	17	-8
E	10	-10	2	0	-10	**30**	**-36**	**78**	**66**	5	-	2	-3	1	10	-5	**24**	-1

35 Pulse Volume Amplitude, Finger

SOC	1	2	3	4	5	6	7	8	9	10	11	12	13	14	15	16	17	18	19
T	-9	0	3	-3	-5	-2	2	**-18**	-5	-2	-11	-9	-6	-3	**-15**	2	**41**	0	1
BS	0	8	5	-3	-25	3	7	-23	-12	-2	2	-2	-10	-14	-25	2	**67**	11	6
BC	-47	-40	27	22	6	-8	-21	-31	-39	-16	-53	-57	-22	-25	-44	9	-14	-34	-5
SxC	-21	-19	1	4	3	-4	-3	-19	-8	2	-15	-3	0	3	-7	9	28	-3	-7
E	-8	2	-1	-7	3	-4	2	-12	1	1	-8	-9	-4	2	-5	1	**28**	-2	1

SOC	20	21	22	23	24	25	26	27	28	29	30	31	32	33	34	35	36	37
T	1	-14	-5	-6	-7	-3	**-18**	-2	11	**18**	-2	**-18**	-14	-7	0	-	-9	1
BS	8	-23	-8	-13	-14	-2	**-30**	-2	19	20	4	-19	-17	-1	1	-	-7	8
BC	-30	-40	-24	-53	-13	-54	-39	55	36	57	-2	-40	-29	-53	-26	-	-59	16
SxC	-10	-3	-1	3	2	-10	-3	4	3	10	-4	-14	-17	2	-6	-	-17	2
E	-1	-4	1	3	0	2	-8	-7	5	14	-5	-13	-10	-12	3	-	-4	-7

36 Pulse Wave Velocity, Finger

SOC	1	2	3	4	5	6	7	8	9	10	11	12	13	14	15	16	17	18	19
T	9	**44**	-8	**-29**	**-37**	**23**	**31**	8	-11	-3	12	7	11	0	**26**	2	**-15**	13	11
BS	2	**43**	-17	**-37**	**-37**	12	11	17	-3	-11	13	10	17	-5	27	-10	-18	7	16
BC	**72**	**75**	-29	-48	-57	**67**	**80**	**77**	36	-6	43	**80**	64	22	**69**	43	-29	43	-5
SxC	15	**38**	-9	-8	-21	18	28	22	0	5	8	14	6	4	25	-5	-7	4	13
E	7	**42**	-1	**-26**	**-40**	**28**	**39**	-7	**-20**	1	8	-5	5	2	**22**	11	-13	16	11

Note. **1** SCR-No. **2** HR **3** RSA **4** LVET **5** PEP **6** CO **7** SBP **8** DBP **9** TPR **10** Resp rate **11** SCR-Ampl **12** Eyeblinks **13** EMG ext **14** EMG fr **15** Body mov **16** TMP foreh **17** TMP fin **18** HR-SD-BP **19** HR-SD-Resp **20** P-Ampl **21** T-Ampl **22** ST-elev **23** P_s-Q_s **24** P_e-Q_s **25** Q-T rel **26** R-Z **27** SV **28** Heather ind **29** Ejection sp **30** CO ind **31** DBP IV **32** MBP **33** PVA rad **34** PWV rad **35** PVA fin **36** PWV fin **37** RSA adj.

(Table continues)

Table 23. Matrix of Intercorrelations Among Selected Physiological Variables After Covariance Partitioning (Experiment 4) *(Continued)*

SOC	Variable																	
	20	21	22	23	24	25	26	27	28	29	30	31	32	33	34	35	36	37
T	8	**-18**	-1	-4	-13	**32**	**-61**	-3	**34**	**24**	**22**	**23**	**19**	10	**59**	-9	-	-6
BS	-6	-21	-13	1	4	41	**-56**	-17	23	18	16	15	17	12	**82**	-7	-	-19
BC	**70**	**76**	66	28	-51	66	-5	-12	20	-22	61	**82**	**80**	25	**89**	-59	-	-51
SxC	13	3	-1	3	-5	15	**-43**	2	21	8	17	**31**	**29**	6	**40**	-17	-	-3
E	16	**-22**	12	-11	**-30**	**24**	**-72**	7	**44**	**32**	**24**	**21**	12	9	**47**	-4	-	5

37 Adjusted Respiratory Sinus Arrhythmia

	1	2	3	4	5	6	7	8	9	10	11	12	13	14	15	16	17	18	19
T	-4	**-32**	**43**	**19**	1	-1	-4	-10	-6	-11	0	-7	-9	3	-14	4	0	14	**16**
BS	4	**-52**	**84**	**31**	14	13	2	-11	-17	**-31**	12	1	-17	8	-3	9	-8	**36**	**43**
BC	**-70**	**-90**	56	**81**	2	**-76**	-55	**-77**	-6	17	-39	**-71**	**-91**	-35	**-76**	-27	38	-33	54
SxC	2	**-36**	**57**	17	1	-8	2	-4	5	-23	4	-10	-14	-6	-20	-3	5	27	**30**
E	-3	-11	6	7	-6	-2	-4	-2	-1	3	0	-2	8	3	-2	2	1	4	2

	20	21	22	23	24	25	26	27	28	29	30	31	32	33	34	35	36	37
T	-7	1	-8	-2	-3	**-15**	0	**17**	3	5	-4	-8	-10	-7	1	1	-6	-
BS	-12	2	-5	-4	-14	-20	8	**42**	2	13	2	-1	-9	-10	-5	8	-19	-
BC	**-87**	-63	**-84**	-54	**68**	**-76**	-43	19	-2	20	**-78**	**-77**	**-73**	-21	-56	16	-51	-
SxC	-4	-7	-7	14	12	-11	-3	4	1	7	-8	-6	-3	-2	-6	2	-3	-
E	2	4	-8	-3	2	-7	-4	3	4	-2	-1	-1	-4	-6	10	-7	5	-

Note. **1** SCR-No. **2** HR **3** RSA **4** LVET **5** PEP **6** CO **7** SBP **8** DBP **9** TPR **10** Resp rate **11** SCR-Ampl **12** Eyeblinks **13** EMG ext **14** EMG fr **15** Body mov **16** TMP foreh **17** TMP fin **18** HR-SD-BP **19** HR-SD-Resp **20** P-Ampl **21** T-Ampl **22** ST-elev **23** P_s-Q_s **24** P_e-Q_s **25** Q-T rel **26** R-Z **27** SV **28** Heather ind **29** Ejection sp **30** CO ind **31** DBP IV **32** MBP **33** PVA rad **34** PWV rad **35** PVA fin **36** PWV fin **37** RSA adj.

Correlation coefficients multiplied by 100. SOC = Source of Covariance. T = Total. BS = Between Subjects. BC = Between Conditions. SxC = Subjects x Conditions. E = Error. The data set consisted of n = 48 subjects, J = 22 conditions, and K = 4 replications. Significance tests were performed using degrees of freedom of the analysis of covariance model with repeated measures and Greenhouse-Geisser "worst case" correction; for the BC component, the "ϵ-correction" with est (ϵ) = 0.35 was used. Boldface numbers: $p < .05$.

respiratory sinus arrhythmia, as well as with the somato-motor variables number of eyeblinks, EMG extensor, and body movements. *BS correlations* of heart rate are found with -preejection period, -left-ventricular ejection time, relative Q-T time, -stroke volume, -R-Z time, -unadjusted and -adjusted respiratory sinus arrhythmia, and pulse wave velocity at the finger. A correspondence with heart rate across *idiosyncratic processes* (based on the Subjects x Conditions, SxC, source of covariation) is seen with P-wave amplitude, ST-elevation, relative Q-T time, -adjusted respiratory sinus arrhythmia, pulse wave velocity at the finger, and body movements. This sheer enumeration underscores that heart rate enters a variety of different kinds of relationships with other physiological variables: Apart from the total source of covariation, 38% of the significant correlations were within the E component, 36% within the BC component, 15% within the BS component, and 11% within the SxC component.

It may also be interesting to consider the variables, heart rate in all of the sources of covariation is uncorrelated with. Variables uncorrelated with heart rate are SCR amplitude, P_s-Q_s time, heart rate variability in the respiratory band, respiration rate, pulse volume amplitude at the radialis and finger sites, skin temperatures at the forehead and finger sites, as well as EMG frontalis. It is conceivable that under different experimental situations, at least the BC correlations for some of these variables would reach significance.

EMG extensor, as did number of SCRs, shows predominantly BC correlations; there are, however, no significant BS or E correspondences with other physiological variables. BC correlations are found with number of SCRs, heart rate, -left-ventricular ejection time, P-wave amplitude, -P_e-Q_s time, relative Q-T time, cardiac output and its index, all of the blood pressure variables, pulse wave velocity at the radialis, -adjusted respiratory sinus arrhythmia, as well as number of eyeblinks and body movements, the latter of which also shows a correlation within the SxC component. Again it becomes apparent that there is no restriction as to which domain (i.e., electrodermal, cardiovascular, somatomotor) the correlating variables within the BC component belong to.

The following selection of variable pairings is intended to demonstrate that relationships between variables have to be qualified with respect to the source of covariation, otherwise the information will be incomplete or even misleading. The reader might want to compare his or her expectations with the kind of relationship actually found.

Number of SCRs and *SCR amplitude* are positively correlated within all sources of variation. This finding suggests a close systemic relationship under a process-related as well as under an individual differences perspective.

Total peripheral resistance and *cardiac output* are negatively related mainly under the individual differences perspective but not within the BC component, that is, these variables have uncorrelated courses of variation across the experimental situations.

Finger temperature and *finger pulse volume amplitude* refer both to vascular processes; moreover, they are recorded from the same regulatory area. They are indeed positively correlated, but only in the E and the BS component. That is, they share systemic or "method" variance but they do not show correspondent courses of average or idiosyncratic activation over situations. But persons differ jointly in the magnitudes of these variables.

Finger and *forehead temperature* are both representations of the thermoregulatory system, but they are located at different sites. As has been found repeatedly before (Dittmann, 1988; Stemmler, 1984), these temperature measurements have a negative BC correlation. Correlations within other sources of covariation were not found. It is interesting that this opposite temperature regulation at the finger and forehead sites across situations is well-known and used, for example, in the relaxation formulae of the autogenic training (warming of hands and arms, cooling of the forehead).

T-wave and *P-wave amplitude* are both potential indicators of cardiac beta-sympathetic tone. According to Table 5 (in Chapter 5.1.2), one would expect an increase of P-wave but a decrease of T-wave amplitude upon beta-adrenergic activation, that is, a *negative* correlation within either or all of the BC, SxC, and E components. Contrary to this expectation, the correlations within all sources of covariation (including the BS component) are *positive.*

A similar expectation exists with regard to the correlation between *T-wave amplitude* and *preejection period*, which according to Table 5 should be positive (decreases in both variables upon beta-adrenergic cardiac activation). Interestingly, a significant correlation is found only for the BS source of covariation and is indeed positive. That is, subjects differ simultaneously in the levels of the T-wave amplitude and the preejection period, but these variables are not so closely coupled as to give rise to BC or even E component correlations.

Another example for the dissociation of correlations within different sources of covariation is given by the relationship between P_s-Q_s and P_e-Q_s, that is, between atrioventricular conduction time and the duration of complete atrial excitation, respectively. Except for the BC component, these variables are positively correlated within all components.

The correlation between two indices of left-ventricular contractility, *R-Z time* and *Heather index*, should be negative because the Heather index was defined as the ratio of maximal impedance change and R-Z time. This mathematical dependence of both variables is indeed reflected in the negative correlations within all sources of covariation.

Diastolic blood pressure phase IV and *phase V* also show (positive) relationships across all sources of covariation.

Pulse volume amplitudes at the radialis and *finger* sites are completely uncorrelated. This result might have been expected from physiological considerations. Whereas the radialis pulse volume amplitude originates from an arterial pressure pulse which depends on left-ventricular performance, arterial wall elasticity, and the rate of vascular draining, the finger pulse volume amplitude is strongly determined by the vasoconstrictive tonus of the vasculature at the recording site.

Pulse wave velocities at the radialis and *finger* sites, however, are positively related within all sources of covariation.

In order to further summarize the information contained in the covariance partitioned relationships among physiological variables, separate principal components analyses with subsequent Varimax rotation were performed for the intercorrelations within each source of covariation. The method to determine the number of rotated principal components followed the procedure described by Stemmler (1984). Briefly, this method is based on an evaluation of simple structure quality achieved by successive rotations. Criteria for the evaluation of simple structure quality within each rotated factor pattern were

- the hyperplane count, that is, the number of absolute loadings equal to or smaller than 0.20 across all factors;
- the number of "large loadings" per factor, that is, absolute loadings greater than or equal to 0.50;
- the number of marker variables per factor. A variable is a marker variable of a particular factor (1) if it has its largest absolute loading on that factor, (2) if this loading is "large", and (3) if it is at least twice as large as the second largest absolute loading of that variable on any other factor of that solution.

Criteria for the decision about the number of factors to retain were:

- The scree test (Cattell & Vogelmann, 1977) was used to determine the range of probable factor solutions.
- The hyperplane count often shows a steady decline over serial factor rotations. In such cases, the hyperplane count is not very useful as a criterion. Local minima in this downward trend, however, point to solutions with good simple structure.
- A factor solution is acceptable only if the factor with the least number of "large loadings" among the factors of that solution is identified by at least two "large loadings".
- Similarly, even the "weakest" factor within a solution should be identified by at least one marker variable.

Based on these criteria, the following factor solutions were obtained.

Between-subject factors. Factoring the *between-subjects* source of covariation (see Table 24) yielded six factors which explained 59% of the total BS variance. *Factor 1* distinguishes among subjects with high versus low average cardiac activation. High cardiac activation is indicated by elevated contractility (R-Z time, Heather index, ejection speed), increased heart rate and systolic time (relative Q-T time), decreased preejection period, ST-depression, and higher pulse wave velocities. It should be noted that neither stroke volume nor cardiac output, nor blood pressure variables are associated with this factor. *Factor 2* distinguishes among subjects with high versus low average cardio-respiratory coupled activity. Low cardio-respiratory activity is indicated by decreased respiratory and heart rates, large heart rate variability in both the blood pressure and the respiratory bands, and large respiratory sinus arrhythmia (both unadjusted and adjusted). *Factor 3* distinguishes among subjects with high versus low blood pressures. *Factor 4* differentiates subjects with high versus low inotropic activity, as indicated by high cardiac output and stroke volume, as well as decreased total peripheral resistance. P-wave amplitude and the Heather index are elevated, too. *Factor 5* describes differences among subjects across various physiological systems. Subjects with high scores on this factor are characterized by increased heart rate, high heart rate variability, short left-ventricular ejection

Table 24. Rotated Factor Pattern of Intercorrelations Between Physiological Variables After Covariance Partitioning (Between-Subjects)

	Between-Subjects Factor						
Variables	1	2	3	4	5	6	h^2
EMG ext	18	-5	-11	-22	-6	52	38
EMG fr	-10	24	8	-6	0	17	11
Body mov	6	-6	-8	14	-2	53	32
Eyeblinks	22	11	-17	-11	5	28	19
SCR-No.	-7	32	2	0	49	12	37
SCR-Ampl	-8	21	15	-4	44	5	28
HR	43	-52	10	4	60	2	84
P-Ampl	-12	-31	-1	42	23	1	35
T Ampl	52	-16	15	23	38	21	57
P_s-Q_s	-12	-4	-7	3	40	68	65
P_e-Q_s	-2	3	-10	0	22	72	58
Q-T rel	47	-30	-1	-0	13	-5	33
ST-elev	-44	-1	20	7	39	-5	39
HR-SD-BP	13	67	10	14	51	9	77
HR-SD-Resp	22	65	12	18	47	0	74
RSA	-12	93	3	0	3	5	90
RSA adj	-15	75	-6	13	-7	-14	64
PWV rad	74	4	33	5	2	-0	67
PWV fin	71	-12	32	-2	7	19	68
PVA rad	-4	-28	10	-10	0	0	10
PVA fin	23	9	-30	-5	20	-50	45
CO	18	6	-0	93	6	-0	92
CO ind	30	4	-1	88	6	6	88
Ejection sp	58	33	-23	17	-2	22	59
SV	-12	36	-6	78	-32	-2	87
LVET	-30	33	-3	12	-67	-9	68
PEP	-64	17	11	-36	2	23	65
R-Z	-86	1	18	-16	-9	10	83
Heather ind	69	14	-21	41	-6	8	74
SBP	15	13	55	6	32	5	46
MBP	-3	2	92	-16	6	4	89
DBP IV	-6	2	91	-2	8	-4	64
DBP	-10	-1	90	-23	-5	2	88
TPR	-17	-8	40	-84	-2	-3	92
Resp rate	-9	-55	-12	10	2	0	34
TMP fin	14	-9	-29	-16	20	-43	36
TMP foreh	-5	-5	-14	5	45	-34	35

Note. Factor analysis was performed according to the principal components method and varimax rotation. h^2 = Communality. Loadings multiplied by 100.

time, elevated electrodermal activity, and increased forehead temperature. *Factor 6*, too, covers several physiological systems. Subjects with high scores on this factor have increased EMG extensor activity and body movements, prolonged P-Q times, as well as elevated finger vasoconstrictive tonus (as indicated by low finger temperature and decreased finger pulse volume amplitude).

Between-condition factors. Factoring the *between-conditions* source of covariation (see Table 25) yielded five factors which explained 86% of total BC variance. *Factor 1* describes a general activation across several physiological systems. Electrodermal activity increases, as does heart rate and heart rate variability in the blood pressure band. All blood pressure variables are elevated. Left-ventricular ejection time decreases, P-wave and T-wave amplitudes increase, P_s-Q_s time (atrio-ventricular conductance time) increases, whereas P_e-Q_s time (duration of complete atrial excitation) decreases. ST-elevation is heightened and relative Q-T time prolonged. Respiratory sinus arrhythmia decreases as does finger temperature, whereas forehead temperature goes up. Electrodermal activity and pulse wave velocities are increased. Finally, eyeblink and EMG extensor activity rise and body movements are augmented. *Factor 2* describes a more specific cardiac inotropic activation (sign of loadings reversed in this description). Preejection period and the P_s-Q_s time shorten, R-Z time decreases, whereas the Heather index increases. Stroke volume, systolic blood pressure, and pulse wave velocities are elevated. *Factor 3* receives dominant loadings from respiration-related variables (an increase of respiration rate, decreases of heart rate variability in the blood pressure and respiratory band, and a decrease of unadjusted respiratory sinus arrhythmia). Larger loadings also occur for skin conductance amplitude (decrease) and EMG frontalis (increased activity). *Factor 4* describes the balance between cardiac performance and peripheral resistance. The Heather index and ejection speed go up, as does stroke volume and the index of cardiac output. Total peripheral resistance, however, is decreased, which is also indicated by the increases of finger pulse volume amplitude. *Factor 5* is in the first place a vascular factor (decrease of forehead temperature and increase of finger temperature, larger pulse volume amplitude at the radialis but, contrary to the direction of finger temperature, a decrease at the finger site), but the factor also receives loadings from cardiac (prolongations of P_s-Q_s and relative Q-T times, reduction of ejection speed), electrodermal (increase of skin conductance amplitude), and EMG (EMG frontalis activity increases) variables. This factor is somewhat puzzling in its contributions.

Subjects x Conditions factors. Factoring the *Subjects x Conditions* interaction source of covariation (see Table 26) yielded seven factors which explained 53% of the total S x C variance. *Factor 1* describes inotropic cardiac effects on

Table 25. Rotated Factor Pattern of Intercorrelations Between Physiological Variables After Covariance Partitioning (Between-Conditions)

Variables	Between-Conditions Factor 1	2	3	4	5	h^2
EMG ext	94	6	17	0	7	93
EMG fr	27	-6	43	8	58	62
Body mov	84	13	-22	-4	22	83
Eyeblinks	85	-3	-25	-16	26	90
SCR-No.	84	-10	-23	-17	17	83
SCR-Ampl	48	-3	-46	-14	43	66
HR	96	8	9	-10	10	97
P-Ampl	96	9	-5	0	2	94
T-Ampl	67	-4	23	-36	17	68
P_s-Q_s	47	52	4	-25	53	84
P_e-Q_s	-76	20	-5	-25	26	76
Q-T rel	78	7	15	-13	43	85
ST-elev	93	13	0	-9	-10	91
HR-SD-BP	49	0	-81	6	14	92
HR-SD-Resp	-28	-33	-78	6	-7	82
RSA	-41	-15	-68	27	-36	87
RSA adj	-90	-25	-19	-8	-6	93
PWV rad	79	-46	-10	-18	-11	90
PWV fin	74	-44	-9	-35	13	90
PVA rad	19	8	-4	-15	83	77
PVA fin	-26	-3	29	56	-53	76
CO	88	-22	-7	36	3	97
CO ind	88	-16	-2	40	1	98
Ejection sp	-7	-31	-15	62	-49	77
SV	-10	-51	-21	74	-16	91
LVET	-87	-24	14	-16	6	87
PEP	-20	85	3	-6	-12	79
R-Z	19	81	10	-26	34	89
Heather ind	21	-63	-21	61	-29	95
SBP	77	-49	-4	-19	0	88
MBP	89	-20	-2	-28	-6	94
DBP IV	90	-9	4	-34	3	95
DBP	91	-8	-1	-31	-8	94
TPR	14	-2	13	-91	-14	89
Resp rate	-23	-5	66	-34	36	75
TMP fin	-54	-6	18	-6	72	85
TMP foreh	42	-26	-14	-16	-70	80

Note. Factor analysis was performed according to the principal components method and varimax rotation. h^2 = Communality. Loadings multiplied by 100.

idiosyncratic activation processes (sign of loadings reversed in this description). Left-ventricular ejection time increases, preejection period shortens, the Heather index (but not R-Z time!) increases as does stroke volume and cardiac output. The drop of total peripheral resistance is congruent with this picture but its loading could also be explained by its algebraical (inverse) relationship with cardiac output. This interpretation is suggested by the only negligible loadings of variables that are related to vascular processes (finger temperature, pulse volume amplitude, diastolic blood pressure). *Factor 2* closely resembles the blood pressure factor of the BS component. It loads all of the blood pressure variables and total peripheral resistance. *Factor 3* has similarly been found in the BS and BC components. It is a cardio-respiratory coupling factor with loadings from heart rate variability measures (both of the blood pressure and the respiratory band), respiratory sinus arrhythmia (unadjusted and adjusted), and, with opposite sign, respiration rate. *Factor 4* describes reductions in heart rate, P-wave and T-wave amplitudes, ST-depression, as well as reduced body movements. It is not clear whether this factor actually has a physiological-systemic origin. *Factor 5* nicely describes contractility properties of the heart: R-Z time shortens, the Heather index increases as does ejection speed and pulse wave velocity at the radialis and finger sites. *Factor 6* resembles the BS Factor 6. It indicates finger vasodilatation (increases in finger temperature and pulse volume amplitude) and lengthening of P-Q times. *Factor 7* groups together measures of sudomotor and cutaneous vasoconstrictive sympathetic activity (increases of number of SCRs and SCR amplitude as well as a decrease of finger pulse volume amplitude).

Error factors. Factoring the *error* source of covariation (see Table 27) yielded five factors which explained 46% of the total error variance. It should be recalled that replications were confounded with different medications; thus, the "error" source of covariation includes medication variance. *Factor 1* describes a facet of cardiac work load (the sign of the loadings is reversed in this description). Heart rate, systolic time (relative Q-T time), the Heather index, as well as ejection speed increase and left-ventricular ejection time as well as R-Z time and P_e-Q_s time decrease. Systolic blood pressure rises as does the pulse wave velocity at the radialis and finger sites. It should be noted that the facet of cardiac work load that is related to cardiac output is not included here but in the next factor. *Factor 2* is related to cardiac output (signs of loadings are again reversed in this description). Left-ventricular ejection time increases (it should be noted that in the previous factor this variable had a loading with an opposite sign!), preejection period decreases, the Heather index rises (R-Z time is only peripherally loaded) as does stroke volume and cardiac output. Total peripheral resistance falls. *Factor 3* is again a pure blood pressure factor. *Factor 4* loads amplitude measures of the ECG (P-wave and T-wave amplitudes as well as ST-elevation are increased), atrioventricular conductance time (P_s-Q_s time) is

Table 26. Rotated Factor Pattern of Intercorrelations Between Physiological Variables After Covariance Partitioning (Subjects x Conditions)

	Subjects x Conditions Factor							
Variables	1	2	3	4	5	6	7	h^2
EMG ext	-6	16	-4	-28	6	-8	-7	13
EMG fr	-5	-8	6	-25	2	26	-5	14
Body mov	-14	13	2	-45	28	-13	2	34
Eyeblinks	-10	0	8	-30	7	-8	0	12
SCR-No.	-3	12	-5	-12	8	2	74	59
SCR Ampl	-1	1	-12	-10	6	6	75	60
HR	0	19	15	-71	25	-8	25	71
P-Ampl	0	7	-13	-66	-3	10	13	49
T-Ampl	-4	7	-15	-59	-25	4	-10	46
P_s-Q_s	1	4	-14	-21	-5	63	6	47
P_e-Q_s	0	0	-9	13	-1	53	-2	31
Q-T rel	-2	-1	3	-36	21	-11	16	22
ST-elev	11	0	4	-51	-14	25	0	37
HR-SD-BP	-4	0	-80	-19	5	-3	-1	68
HR-SD-Resp	-9	5	-74	-19	8	-8	-1	61
RSA	-1	-5	-84	18	0	5	-3	76
RSA adj	0	1	-62	35	-0	16	3	54
PWV rad	-9	29	5	-12	48	8	19	39
PWV fin	-9	34	2	-17	56	-3	17	51
PVA rad	-1	6	4	1	21	22	3	10
PVA fin	-1	-15	6	9	8	39	-46	41
CO	-89	3	2	-24	12	-6	0	87
CO ind	-87	5	0	-24	10	-4	0	84
Ejection sp	22	-26	-18	-5	60	-17	-27	63
SV	-91	-1	-6	4	-2	-1	-9	85
LVET	-77	8	-6	27	-31	10	5	80
PEP	82	-14	-4	0	0	-14	-18	76
R-Z	13	4	3	-1	-79	-10	-10	67
Heather ind	-74	-8	-9	-8	43	-6	-10	79
SBP	-4	68	1	2	25	10	-4	55
MBP	0	93	0	-8	2	-7	2	89
DBP IV	4	73	4	-16	1	0	8	56
DBP	3	84	-3	-10	7	-14	2	76
TPR	75	44	-5	13	-5	-1	0	78
Resp rate	-5	1	49	-2	7	-9	-12	27
TMP fin	-1	-6	-1	7	2	58	2	34
TMP foreh	-1	8	-4	-8	-7	-1	-17	5

Note. Factor analysis was performed according to the principal components method and varimax rotation. h^2 = Communality. Loadings multiplied by 100.

Table 27. Rotated Factor Pattern of Intercorrelations Between Physiological Variables After Covariance Partitioning (Error)

	Error Factor					
Variables	1	2	3	4	5	h^2
EMG ext	-7	-7	4	13	-6	3
EMG fr	-8	4	5	33	-14	14
Body mov	-37	-15	-1	17	4	19
Eyeblinks	6	-6	-8	22	-4	6
SCR-No.	-2	0	6	61	8	38
SCR-Ampl	-2	0	1	58	4	34
HR	-78	-17	6	17	-15	69
P-Ampl	-38	2	0	58	-1	48
T-Ampl	34	8	9	42	15	33
P_s-Q_s	30	-1	0	54	9	40
P_e-Q_s	58	1	-4	30	9	44
Q-T rel	-43	-23	7	7	-6	26
ST-elev	-29	7	15	60	-16	51
HR-SD-BP	-27	-3	3	8	78	70
HR-SD-Resp	-18	-1	5	12	78	67
RSA	17	0	7	-3	80	68
RSA adj	3	-2	-2	-3	11	1
PWV rad	-53	-4	2	7	8	29
PWV fin	-68	-18	16	-3	9	53
PVA rad	-6	0	19	7	0	4
PVA fin	-9	8	-21	-7	-2	7
CO	-25	-90	1	1	3	87
CO ind	-22	-89	0	4	6	84
Ejection sp	-54	16	-34	-6	15	46
SV	17	-89	-1	-6	16	86
LVET	63	-51	16	0	8	70
PEP	25	74	-20	-4	0	66
R-Z	80	28	1	2	-8	73
Heather ind	-52	-61	-8	1	10	67
SBP	-47	-7	56	-1	-6	55
MBP	-2	8	93	-4	0	88
DBP IV	-16	3	74	2	1	57
DBP	22	14	81	-4	3	74
TPR	18	81	35	-3	-3	82
Resp rate	1	4	0	4	-32	10
TMP fin	-5	2	-16	5	-16	6
TMP foreh	-6	4	10	-13	7	3

Note. Factor analysis was performed according to the principal components method and varimax rotation. h^2 = Communality. Loadings multiplied by 100.

prolonged, and electrodermal activity is augmented. *Factor 5* receives loadings from variables of heart rate variability that are related to respiratory activity (unadjusted respiratory sinus arrhythmia and heart rate variability in the blood pressure and respiratory bands are increased). The adjusted respiratory sinus arrhythmia has only a negligible loading.

In sum, the analysis of physiological covariance demonstrated many substantial correlations which, contrary to frequent commentaries (see Chapter 4.3), described relationships both within and between physiological systems. A prerequisite for an adequate description of physiological relationships is, however, the separation of sources of covariance. The factor analyses showed that activation has to be conceived of as a multicomponent construct. The various factors described do not, however, necessarily conclusively identify such components (although some of the factors could have come close); several of the methodological decisions during the conduct of factor analysis, such as the number of factors to retain or the adequacy of simple structure as a rotation criterion for the analysis of physiological data, remain open to discussion. But caveats such as these are typical for the construct construction stage (see Chapter 1.4), where usually exploratory methods are employed. (In distinction to the exploratory analysis described above, a confirmatory approach on the basis of the Model of Autonomic Cardiovascular Activation Components of Chapter 5.2 will be described in Chapter 9.3.)

An interesting application of covariance partitioning concerns the question of relationships between physiological systems with undoubtedly distinct innervations. The relationships among three systems that are distinctly innervated will be reported, of the somato-motor and autonomic systems, as well as brain activity as reflected by the electroencephalogram (EEG). Clearly, each system is complex and multicomponential in itself. But this within-system complexity does not rule out between-systems relationships, in particular if such relationships can be adequately described. An adequate description of between-systems relationships refers both to the source of covariation considered and to the statistical index employed to capture the relationship.

Whereas the relationship between somato-motor and autonomic variables has received some consideration in psychophysiology (e.g., Obrist, 1976), the covariation between EEG and peripheral variables (meant to include both autonomic and somato-motor variables) has not often been studied explicitly. Do psychophysiologists conceive of them as principally independent? Perhaps the low-voltage and artifact-prone EEG signal with much shorter latencies upon stimulation (Turpin, 1985) or its difficult interpretation (Claridge, 1981) were opposed to its more widespread usage by psychophysiologists.

It should be recalled from Chapter 4.2 that unitary activation theory had postulated a gross correspondence between the EEG and peripheral changes over the continuum of sleep, wakefulness, and excitement. On the basis of data from MacNeilage (1966), Malmo (1966), and Pineo (1961), Malmo and Bélanger (1967) concluded:

> In summary, according to the data we are aware, when the difference between two experimental conditions is sufficiently great, as reflected in reliable mean differences in a number of measures of physiological level, the probability of a reliable mean change in level of EEG amplitude appears high. (Malmo & Bélanger, 1967, p. 319.)

It should be noted that Malmo and Bélanger referred to a between-situations correlation when they argued for the existence of EEG-peripheral relationships. In line with this conclusion are the findings of Luczak, Phillips, and Rohmert (1980), who reported intraindividual multiple correlations between heart rate and the EEG theta (4 - 7 Hz) and beta (15 - 30 Hz) frequency bands. Across five subjects, an average within-subjects $R^2 = 0.58$ was found.

In contrast to the unitary view of activation, a *multi-componential conceptualization with partial independence* among systems (and also among sets of variables within systems) had been postulated (Lacey, 1967). As Simons, Öhman, and Lang (1979) formulated:

> There is no obligatory parallelism between components in the two [cortical and visceral] systems. [....] Activity in one system provides, at least, indirect information about activity in the other, and each system reflects a unique aspect of subject-environment transaction. (Simons, Öhman, & Lang, 1979, pp. 232-233.)

This statement and similar ones by Lacey make it clear that the relationship between systems is not a general but a specific property evolving within subjects over the course of situations. In technical terms, relationships between systems should be expected in the between-conditions and the Subjects x Conditions interaction source of covariance. It will be recalled that Malmo and Bélanger (1967) explicitly referred to the BC component when they accrued evidence for their unitary activation view. Thus, the conceptually disparate positions in the end only tended to cloud the actual empirical correspondences which can be designated with the vocabulary of the assessment models.

In the following paragraphs, between-system correlations from the data of Experiments 1 to 3 are presented. I shall confine the presentation of correlations to the between-conditions and the residual (i.e, SxC plus error) source of covariation, which will be presented first for single variables and then for variable sets (for which also the within-subjects covariance will be reported). Table 28 shows between-conditions correlations between variables of the EEG set and variables of both the somato-motor and autonomic set.

Between-conditions correlations of somato-motor with EEG variables were concentrated within the sub-alpha1, alpha2, and the gamma bands. Many of these correlations can be rather simply explained. Most of the time, subjects kept their eyes open, but during imagination periods, eyes were closed. Such periods are of course described by reduced somato-motor activity, in particular, eyeblink activity, but also by greatly enhanced alpha amplitude in the region of 9 Hz to 15 Hz (alpha1, alpha2, and sub-beta1 bands). Thus it is no surprise to find negative BC correlations in these bands. Similarly, it is well known that high EEG frequencies (gamma band) are prone to muscle potential artifacts, which, with the exception of the EMG trapezious, eyeblink, and tonic EMG frontalis activity, is seen in the positive correlations of the somato-motor variables and the power of the gamma band. The correlations between the sub-alpha1 band and both EMG orbicularis tonic activity and body and head movements are difficult to evaluate.

Table 28. Between-Conditions Correlations Among EEG and Peripheral (Somato-Motor and Autonomic) Variables (Experiment 1)

Peripheral Variables	EEG Variables								
	Sa1	Sa2	A1	A2	Sb1	Sb2	B1	B2	G
Somato-Motor Variables									
EMG extt	41	-12	-41	-40	-39	5	-7	21	**74**
EMG extp	47	-3	-38	-41	-38	11	-1	26	**75**
EMG trt	16	8	-4	-13	-14	7	-4	8	34
EMG trp	16	18	17	19	0	0	-5	-12	-20
EMG ort	**59**	-4	-45	-48	-45	0	-6	28	**89**
EMG orp	48	-16	**-54**	**-52**	-47	-11	-16	24	**87**
EMG frt	19	-31	**-60**	**-61**	**-66**	-11	-26	-21	35
EMG frp	39	-9	-51	**-52**	-44	1	-6	25	**80**
Body mov	**57**	-11	**-52**	**-61**	**-56**	-7	-15	13	**81**
Hand mov	35	-19	-45	**-53**	-41	-2	-8	14	**66**
Head mov	**62**	-8	**-53***	**-62**	-51	7	-2	23	**86**
Eyeblinks	39	-32	**-70**	**-76**	**-70**	-17	-30	-24	46
Sacc	39	20	-13	-20	-8	4	0	28	**63**
Autonomic Variables									
SCR-No. hand	35	-7	-27	-33	-44	-30	-38	-24	24
SCL hand	**53**	-11	-51	**-58**	**-58**	-2	-13	10	**72**
SCL foreh	-7	12	18	18	12	2	-7	7	11
IBI	-48	0	29	43	**55**	32	35	27	-37
PTT	-23	-1	6	20	27	26	30	40	-3
Resp per	29	4	-24	-25	-9	26	21	**53**	**72**
PVA fin	-3	39	42	39	44	50	**55**	44	0
BV fin	43	30	9	3	-9	20	21	33	47
PVA foreh	41	-2	-37	-39	-31	5	2	39	**86**
BV foreh	29	-8	-29	-28	-28	-8	-12	17	**66**
TMP fin	10	33	30	28	26	27	34	16	-13
TMP foreh	15	11	-3	-6	0	45	32	22	28

Note. n = 42 subjects, J = 52 conditions. Decimal points omitted. Sa1 = Salpha1, Sa2 = Salpha2, A1 = Alpha1, A2 = Alpha2, Sb1 = Sbeta1, Sb2 = Sbeta2, B1 = Beta1, B2 = Beta2, G = Gamma. See Table 17 for abbreviations of variable names. Significance of correlations was determined using an estimated Huyhn-Feldt ϵ of 0.25, which gives a critical Pearson r of ± 0.52 (df_{corr} = 12.73). Boldface numbers: $p < .05$.

Between-conditions correlations of autonomic with EEG variables were found to be less frequent but again concentrated in the gamma band, which with respect to the forehead plethysmogram can again be interpreted as common movement-related artifacts. The correlation between respiratory period and the beta1 and the gamma bands can be interpreted similarly since during speech periods (1) respiration cycles become longer and (2) muscular activity increases and with it muscular high-frequency EEG confounds. The correlations between skin conductance level at the hand and several EEG frequency bands, however, are difficult to explain solely by the artifact hypothesis, as is the correlation between interbeat intervals or finger pulse volume amplitude with the sub-beta1 or beta1 band, respectively.

The tentative interpretations of the between-conditions correlations between EEG and peripheral variables were mainly based on rather trivial explanations, such as movement-related artifacts or eyes-open versus eyes-closed conditions. Myrtek (1984) has pointed to this "spurious" aspect of BC correlations. However, this aspect of BC correlations does not rule out other explanations that under a biopsychological perspective are more interesting (see the analyses reported above that dealt with the cardiovascular and the somato-motor system).

Residual correlations between variables of the EEG set and peripheral variables are shown in Table 29. These correlations should further illuminate which of the BC correlations were "trivial" and which were caused by systemic relationships, that is, by a coupling of physiological systems irrespective of situational differences (see Chapter 6.3), since residual correlations can be given the latter but not the former interpretation. An inspection of Table 29 indeed suggests a differentiation of putative explanations for the BC correlations.

Residual correlations of somato-motor with EEG variables are predominantly found within the beta2 and gamma bands and, to a much lesser extent, in the alpha frequencies (alpha1, alpha2, and sub-beta1 bands). For example, whereas both within the BC and the residual component the gamma band correlated significantly with 9 somato-motor variables, within the alpha frequencies there were 15 BC but only 3 significant residual correlations. Thus, it seems safe to conclude that the covariance between the gamma band and somato-motor variables was of a systemic origin, whereas the covariance between the alpha frequencies and somato-motor variables was caused by other incidences, perhaps by the "spurious" eyes-open versus eyes-closed variation between experimental situations.

Residual correlations of autonomic with EEG variables are generally low and will not be substantially interpreted.

As a final summary of between-systems relationships, the squared "set correlations" (Cohen, 1982) between all three variable sets will be reported (see Table 30). Set correlations (R_{set}) are based on the canonical correlations (R_c) between two sets of variables, $R^2_{set} = 1 - (1 - R^2_{c1}) * (1 - R^2_{c2}) * \dots$,

(94) where the number of products on the right side is equal or less than the number of canonical variates in the joint data set.

Interpretation of Table 30 will be restricted to comparisons of the relative magnitude of set correlations within one source of covariation. There is indeed a large between-conditions overlap among all three sets of variables. The degree of overlap of residual covariance, however, is clearly different for the three pairs of variable sets: Electroencephalographic variables have an appreciably lower

Table 29. Residual Correlations Among EEG and Peripheral (Somato-Motor and Autonomic) Variables (Experiment 1)

Peripheral	EEG Variables								
Variables	Sa1	Sa2	A1	A2	Sb1	Sb2	B1	B2	G
Somato-Motor Variables									
EMG extt	-4	-4	-6	-5	-4	-3	0	3	1
EMG extp	3	0	-1	-6	-6	-1	4	1	6
EMG trt	2	-1	-2	-1	6	3	2	0	8
EMG trp	-8	-3	2	5	-3	-5	-3	-4	**-14**
EMG ort	**10**	0	-3	-6	-2	5	5	**13**	**33**
EMG orp	5	1	-3	-5	-1	8	8	**16**	29
EMG frt	3	-5	-6	-3	-3	1	5	**11**	**19**
EMG frp	1	-3	-6	-7	0	4	**10**	**15**	**28**
Body mov	-2	-3	**-10**	-8	0	1	2	8	**17**
Hand mov	1	0	-2	-5	1	3	1	2	**11**
Head mov	0	-1	-8	**-11**	-2	**9**	7	**11**	**20**
Eyeblinks	5	0	**-9**	-8	-1	2	0	1	4
Sacc	**9**	5	-5	-6	2	8	7	**11**	**25**
Autonomic Variables									
SCR-No. hand	3	-3	-6	-6	0	2	2	3	**10**
SCL hand	-4	-4	**-9**	**-11**	-4	0	0	-2	7
SCL foreh	-2	2	7	4	-2	-4	-4	0	-5
IBI	0	-1	6	**11**	2	-1	-2	0	**-13**
PTT	2	-3	2	0	0	-1	-4	-2	-3
Resp per	1	0	-2	0	6	**9**	2	5	**10**
PVA fin	0	4	6	3	-2	-2	-2	-5	-5
BV fin	-2	0	2	0	-2	**-9**	-8	-7	-2
PVA foreh	4	-2	-5	-4	-5	-4	-5	**-9**	3
BV foreh	-1	-3	0	1	1	-6	-3	-2	0
TMP fin	-3	0	-2	-7	-6	-3	-5	-6	-6
TMP foreh	0	0	1	3	2	0	0	-3	-4

Note. n = 42 subjects, J = 52 conditions. Decimal points omitted. Sa1 = Salpha1, Sa2 = Salpha2, A1 = Alpha1, A2 = Alpha2, Sb1 = Sbeta1, Sb2 = Sbeta2, B1 = Beta1, B2 = Beta2, G = Gamma. See Table 17 for abbreviations of variable names. Significance of correlations was determined using an estimated Huyhn-Feldt ϵ of 0.25, which gives a critical Pearson r of ± 0.09 (df_{corr} = 521.75). Boldface numbers $p < .05$.

relationship with the peripheral variables than is seen between somato-motor and autonomic variables. Furthermore, the autonomic variables correlate lower with the EEG than with the somato-motor variables. The squared within-subjects set correlation combines the information of the between-conditions and residual sources of covariance. It demonstrates an increase of between-systems overlap by 20% for the EEG x somato-motor variables over the EEG x autonomic variables combination, and by another 20% for the somato-motor x autonomic variables combination.

These analyses underscore the importance of differentiating between sources of covariation before conclusions concerning the status of the concept of activation can be reached. With respect to process-related sources of covariation, the present data confirm the conclusions of Simons et al. (1979) that "there is no obligatory parallelism between components in the two [cortical and visceral] systems" (p. 232). The degree of correspondence that has been found in the above analyses could at least tentatively be explained by common artifact sources

Table 30. Squared Set Correlations Among Electroencephalographic, Somato-Motor, and Autonomic Variables After Covariance Partitioning (Experiment 1)

	Source of Covariation		
Set Size	BC	R	WS
Electroencephalographic versus Somato-Motor Variables			
1	0.96	0.22	0.42
2	0.99	0.25	0.45
3	1.00	0.27	0.48
All	1.00	0.32	0.52
Somato-Motor versus Autonomic Variables			
1	0.98	0.36	0.52
2	1.00	0.44	0.63
3	1.00	0.50	0.66
All	1.00	0.56	0.72
Electroencephalographic versus Autonomic Variables			
1	0.94	0.08	0.22
2	0.99	0.12	0.27
3	1.00	0.13	0.29
All	1.00	0.18	0.32

Note. BC = Between-Conditions. R = Residual. WS = Within-Subjects. Numbers of electroencephalographic, somato-motor, and autonomic variables were 9, 13, and 12, respectively. Numbers of subjects and conditions were 42 and 52, respectively. [a]Set size denotes the number of canonical variates entering the set correlation.

or by common "trivial", as opposed to biopsychologically more interesting, sources of the covariation between physiological variables or systems.

9.2 Physiological Maps of Situations

In Chapter 3, a case had been made for "working backwards" from what we know, that is, from the physiological response profiles to what we are uncertain of, that is, to the factors determining this observable behavior. It had been pointed out that theoretical assumptions enter into even such a descriptive and inductive framework. The strategy that was suggested by the discussion of the activation construct in Chapter 4 and corroborated by the findings in the preceding chapter (concerning sources of physiological variance and covariance), consisted of defining the locus of the construct of activation across situations, that is, to adopt a process-oriented perspective on activation. This perspective entailed a description of the physiological response surface, or, of physiological maps in a state-space (see also the quotation from Corcoran, 1981, in Chapter 4.3).

Establishing physiological maps in a multidimensional state-space corresponds to a descriptive analysis of situational response specificity (see Chapter 6.2). In order to simultaneously capture both situational uniqueness (i.e., maximizing between-situations variance) and consistency (i.e., minimizing person variance within situations), the discriminant analysis (DA) of physiological profiles, with situations defined as "groups" and persons defined as "cases", had been recommended. Furthermore, the distinction between DAs that analyze raw score (*DARS*), semi-ipsatized (*DASI*), or fully-ipsatized (*DAFI*) group profiles had been advocated (Chapter 7) for a disentangling of the effects of the profile parameters elevation, scatter, and shape. The analyses reported below follow these general recommendations (the data of Experiment 1 are used to illustrate the complete Multistage DA with profile parameter decomposition; the data of Experiments 2 to 4, for *DARS* only).

The nature of the axes of the state-spaces reported below needs a brief comment. These axes, or, in the case of a DA, the discriminant functions (*DF*s), are descriptive units that are specifically "tailored" to the data set analyzed. In a sense, these *DF*s are the components of situational response specificity encountered in a particular investigation. Because of their varying specification with changing subject, situation, and variable samples, these *DF*s do not provide estimates of invariant activation components. They permit, however, a preliminary account of the number of activation components to be considered, and they define the state-space within which such invariant activation components should be located. An attempt at defining invariant cardiovascular activation components will be presented in Chapter 9.3. Clearly, the approaches of this and the following chapter are successive stages of construct identification.

With respect to factor analysis, Royce (1976) made a similar distinction between successive stages of descriptive and confirmatory strategies:

> My experience in the substantive application of the factor model indicates that there are two phases of scientific inference in the typical exploratory factor investigation. The first phase is focused on the identification of *replicable patterns* of observables, and the second phase is concerned with the identification of *latent unknowns* (Royce, 1976, p. 15; author's italics.)

The DAs presented in the next four sections are all based on standardized raw score data. Standardization is a prerequisite for profile analysis, if the variables are measured in different units which are not substantively related to the research question (e.g., indicating the relative "importance" of variables). *DF*s were scaled to unit length (Equation 92), and, in the case of Multistage DA, the origins of discriminant spaces were aligned with the origin of the complete person-space (Equation 90).

9.2.1 Situational maps of Experiment 1

With the data of Experiment 1, a Multistage DA was performed. Although more than three *DF*s were statistically significant, only three will be used for illustration. In the *DARS*, they explained 64% of the total discriminative variance (34%, 18%, and 12% for *DF1* to *DF3*, respectively); in the *DASI*, 61% (31%, 18%, 12%); in the *DAFI*, 59% (28%, 18%, 13%).[23] Both the levels test, F (51, 2091) = 47.61, and the test for profile parallelism, Roy's theta (33, 8.5, 1028.5) = 0.59, were highly significant, $p < .01$.

Physiological maps of the DARS (Figures 11a-c). *DF1* discriminates between phases with speech activity, anger induction (including speech and no-speech periods), and speech preparation on the one hand, and, on the other hand, prestimulus and poststimulus phases, instruction and waiting periods. Thus, *DF1* seems to reflect a dimension of behavioral activity. This interpretation is supported by the between-conditions correlations of physiological variables and *DF*s (see Table 31): Most somato-motor variables have high correlations with *DF1*, as has electrodermal activity, shortened heart period, the forehead pulse volume amplitude and blood volume, as well as alpha frequency reductions in the EEG.

DF2 discriminates phases without from phases with anticipatory threat, such as the instruction periods and the periods before speech in the Gottschalk-Gleser (GG) speech tasks as well as the instruction and ensuing task period of the first number task. It should be noted that with repeated exposure to the same

---

[23] Because profile analyses were planned, some variables were reflected in order to achieve a consistent direction of activation. These were: IBI, PTT fin, PVA fin, Resp per, TMP fin, salpha2, alpha1, alpha2, sbeta1, sbeta2, and beta1. The variables to be reflected were determined from the sign of the between-conditions correlations with the first *DF* of the *DARS* (see Table 31).

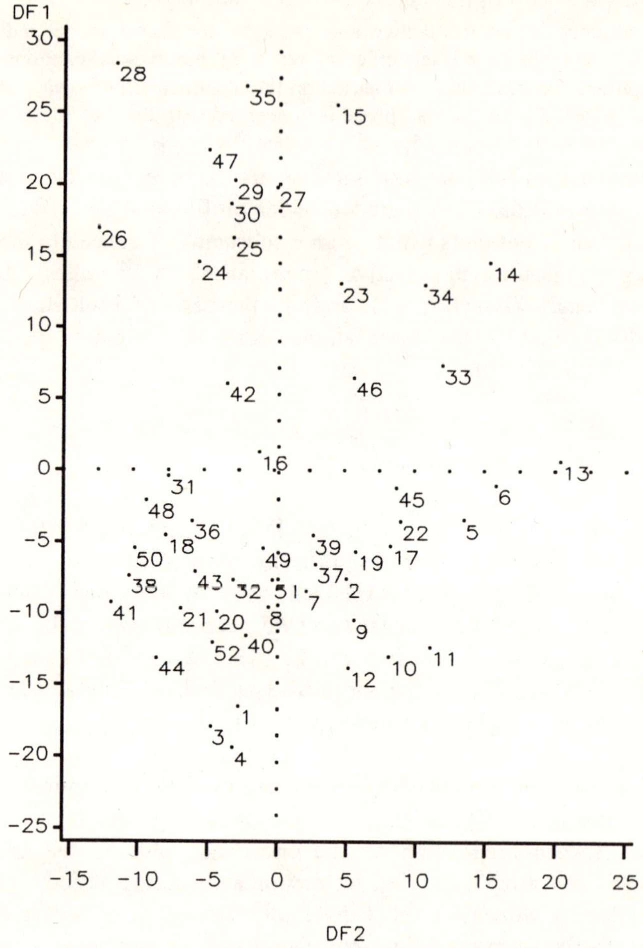

Figure 11 a. Centroids (referred to by condition number) of experimental situations in a three-dimensional subspace of *DARS* (Experiment 1). Plane of *DF1* and *DF2*. For a complete description of periods, see Table 14. Prestimulus periods = 1, 8, 18, 21, 38, 41, 50. Poststimulus periods = 7, 20, 40, 52. Instructions = 2 (system check); 5 (number task); 13, 33, 45 (GG speech task); 17, 37, 49 (imagination); 30 (after anger). GG speech tasks = 14, 34, 46 (before); 15, 35, 47 (during); 16, 36, 48 (after). Number tasks = 6, 19, 39, 51. Waiting periods = 3, 4 (system check); 12 (after fear); 31, 32 (after anger); 43, 44 (after happiness). Emotion inductions = 9-11 (fear); 22-29 (anger); 42 (happiness). *(Figure continues)*

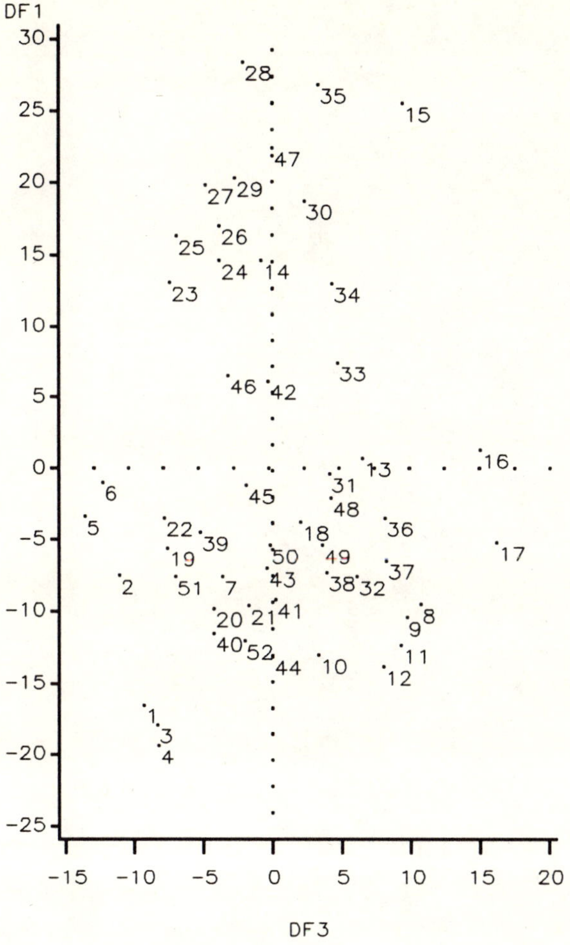

Figure 11 b. Centroids (referred to by condition number) of experimental situations in a three-dimensional subspace of *DARS* (Experiment 1). Plane of *DF1* and *DF3*. *(continued)*

anticipatory experimental situations (e.g., the successive GG instructions), the group profile centroids attain successively lower scores on *DF2*. The between-conditions correlations of variables and *DF2* show that number of SCRs, shortened heart period, reduced pulse transit time, finger vasoconstriction, slower breathing, and reduced beta2 EEG activity are associated with this

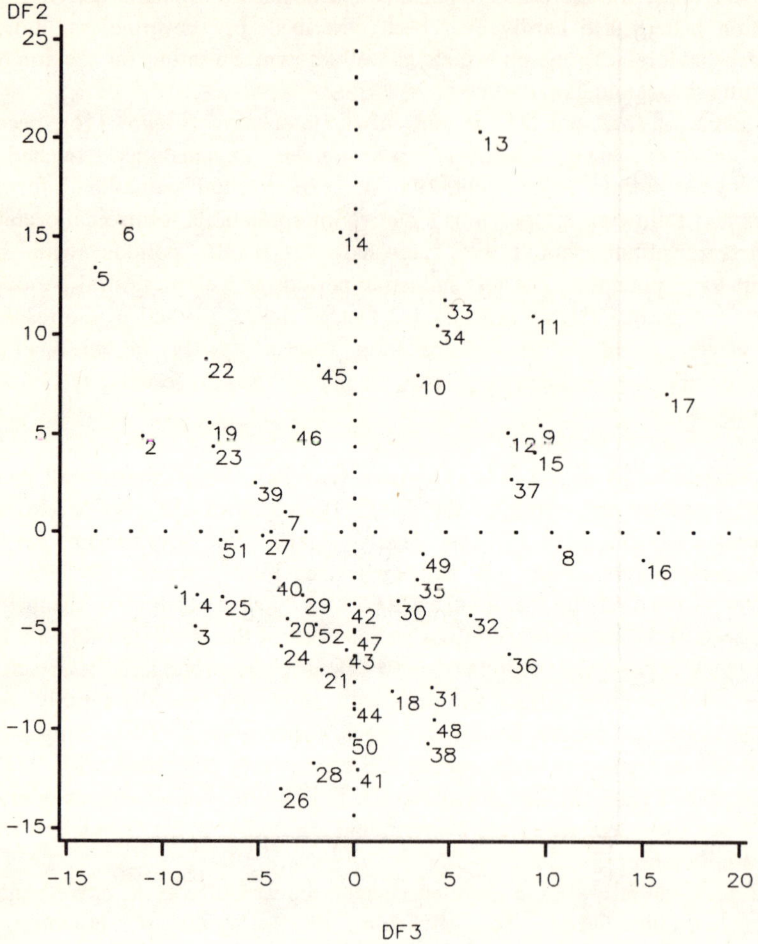

Figure 11 c. Centroids (referred to by condition number) of experimental situations in a three-dimensional subspace of *DARS* (Experiment 1). Plane of *DF2* and *DF3*. *(continued)*

function. The pattern of these correlations suggests a broadly defined autonomic activation represented by *DF2*.

High values on *DF3* are seen with phases that gave subjects the opportunity to become confronted with personally relevant thoughts, such as during and after the first GG speech, when subjects could ruminate about their story for a while, during fear induction or after anger induction. A large between-conditions correlation was found between *DF3* and skin conductance level at the forehead; and lower ones, for increased trapezious and decreased frontalis activity. This activation pattern had hardly ever been described; but nevertheless, it has a related behavioral expression which is well-known: Sweating on the forehead and lifting the shoulders.

The plane of *DF2* and *DF3* is particularly interesting (Figure 11c), because these functions have tentatively been given explanations couched in psychological terms. The centroids of experimental situations form a circumplex; following the previous tentative interpretations, centroids located in the first quadrant should be "personally relevant" periods with high "anticipatory" potential. The fear induction periods as well as several periods of the first and second GG speech task are located there; it is left to the reader to judge whether in his or her opinion (i.e., according to his or her functional situations) these experimental periods might fit the suggested psychological interpretation.

Physiological maps of the DASI (Figures 12a-c). Although the overall picture clearly resembles the maps of the *DARS*, the loss of the profile elevation parameter alters the maps in many details. Again, *DF1* discriminates between experimental periods with low and high behavioral activity. However, the character of the first function of the *DARS* as a "general factor" is changed, as can be seen in the between-conditions correlations of the *DASI* in Table 31. *DF1* of the *DASI* is positively correlated with extensor and orbicularis oculi activity but negatively with trapezious and practically zero with frontalis activity. Body and hand, but no longer head movements correlate with *DF1*. Finger skin temperature and pulse volume amplitude are positively correlated with *DF1*, as is pulse transit time. In comparison to the *DARS*, the alpha frequencies in the EEG lose their negative correlation, but the 15-21 Hz bands correlate substantially with *DF1* of the *DASI*.

DF2 has essentially similar correlations with the variables as the corresponding function of the *DARS*. The advantage of the *DASI* is, however, its interpretational clarity with respect to the configuration of situation profiles. For example, the location of the three periods "before the GG speech" (No. 14, 34, and 46) on one line through the origin but with successively decreasing distance from the origin can now be interpreted that these situations elicited essentially similar profile shapes but with decreasing scatters. What has been said with regard to *DF2* also applies to *DF3*. The location of situation centroids as well as the between-conditions correlations are very similar to the *DARS* analysis; the representation of situation profile similarities in the physiological maps has changed, however, in subtle aspects.

Physiological maps of the DAFI (Figures 13a-c). In the plane of *DF1* and *DF2*, situation centroids of speech periods and the anger induction periods (some of which included speech activity) are located in a cluster in the upper left quadrant. Likewise, the fear induction periods (No. 9-12) are situated in a

Table 31. Between-Conditions Correlations of Discriminant Functions with Physiological Variables (Experiment 1)

	Discriminant Analysis								
	DARS			*DASI*			*DAFI*		
	Function								
Variable	1	2	3	1	2	3	1	2	3
EMG extt	87	-21	20	62	-22	31	58	-29	41
EMG extp	81	-20	26	45	-33	36	29	-38	43
EMG trt	33	2	59	-75	-28	24	-76	-3	30
EMG trp	12	39	-20	-57	19	-22	-32	31	-20
EMG ort	96	-10	8	89	6	25	88	-10	26
EMG orp	88	-17	3	80	-7	12	73	-19	10
EMG frt	56	4	-53	-1	12	-67	2	-2	-57
EMG frp	74	-25	-1	14	-42	-18	-13	-38	-16
Body mov	88	-10	-10	75	2	-12	59	-23	-24
Hand mov	64	-15	12	-7	-33	-1	-36	-35	-2
Head mov	91	-21	-11	86	-9	-10	70	-38	-20
Eyeblinks	59	29	-29	1	42	-40	15	36	-37
Sacc	44	-19	40	-1	-32	39	-25	-16	24
SCR-No. hand	56	72	0	-8	84	14	38	78	7
SCL hand	83	12	-18	45	33	-21	57	10	-14
SCL foreh	16	20	93	-43	-7	85	-28	20	90
IBI	-68	-62	8	-21	-86	-7	-45	-73	17
PTT fin	-29	-66	-20	60	-46	-16	47	-63	0
PVA fin	-26	-70	4	56	-54	10	29	-68	20
BV fin	52	-24	21	-43	-36	1	-47	-26	13
PVA foreh	77	-50	2	60	-57	-1	31	-71	3
BV foreh	72	-14	35	6	-29	40	0	-32	37
Resp per	-54	59	-28	-9	80	-14	27	76	-20
TMP fin	-17	-21	-26	58	2	-6	53	-7	-2
TMP foreh	30	-40	11	-15	-46	-3	-26	-40	14
Salpha1	58	0	-11	-42	-10	-23	-44	-4	-16
Salpha2	-12	-5	22	56	11	39	54	2	34
Alpha1	-53	1	33	6	1	56	6	11	50
Alpha2	-57	-5	36	-9	-11	57	0	6	54
Sbeta1	-58	-25	35	13	-33	53	2	-24	52
Sbeta2	-6	-47	8	62	-24	18	47	-36	30
Beta1	-17	-48	4	61	-27	16	42	-40	28
Beta2	14	-60	24	-39	-61	0	-54	-38	15
Gamma	85	-36	9	72	-43	12	51	-53	22

Note. For abbreviations of variable names, see Table 17. Correlations multiplied by 100. *DARS* = Discriminant analysis (DA) with raw score group profiles. *DASI* = DA with semi-ipsatized group profiles. *DAFI* = DA with fully-ipsatized group profiles.

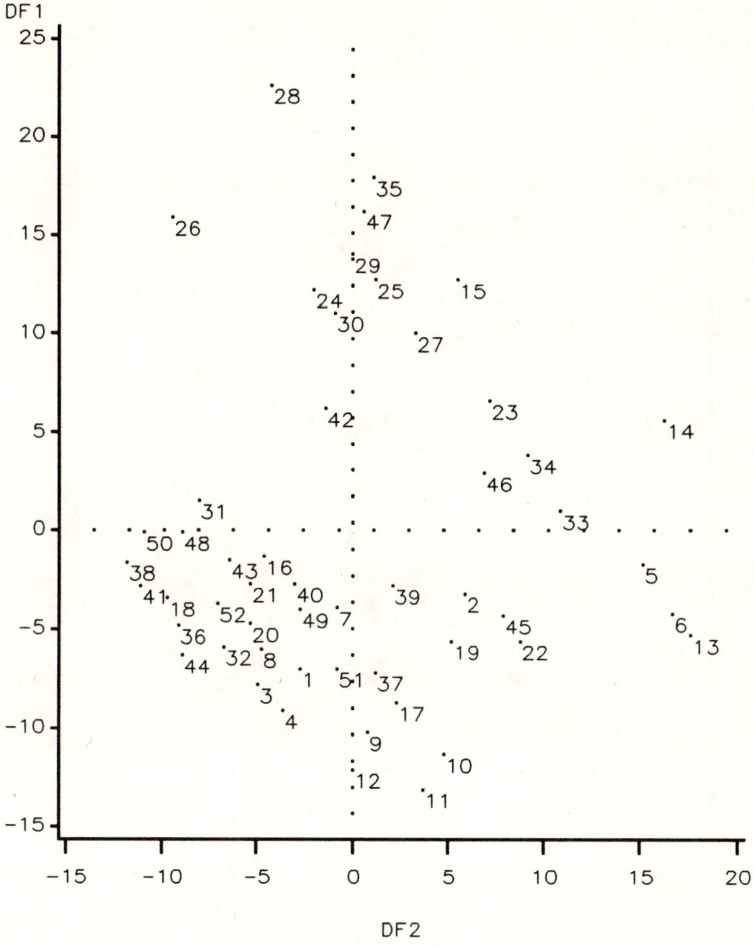

Figure 12 a. Centroids (referred to by condition number) of experimental situations in a three-dimensional subspace of *DASI* (Experiment 1). Plane of *DF1* and *DF2*. See also the legend of Figure 11. *(Figure continues)*

cluster in the lower right quadrant. Most of the prestimulus and poststimulus periods are located in the lower left quadrant. Experimental situations with a high anticipatory potential are distributed in the upper right quadrant. Successive number tasks (No. 6, 19, 39, and 51), which were spread over the course of the experiment and which were invariant with respect to their physical and cognitive

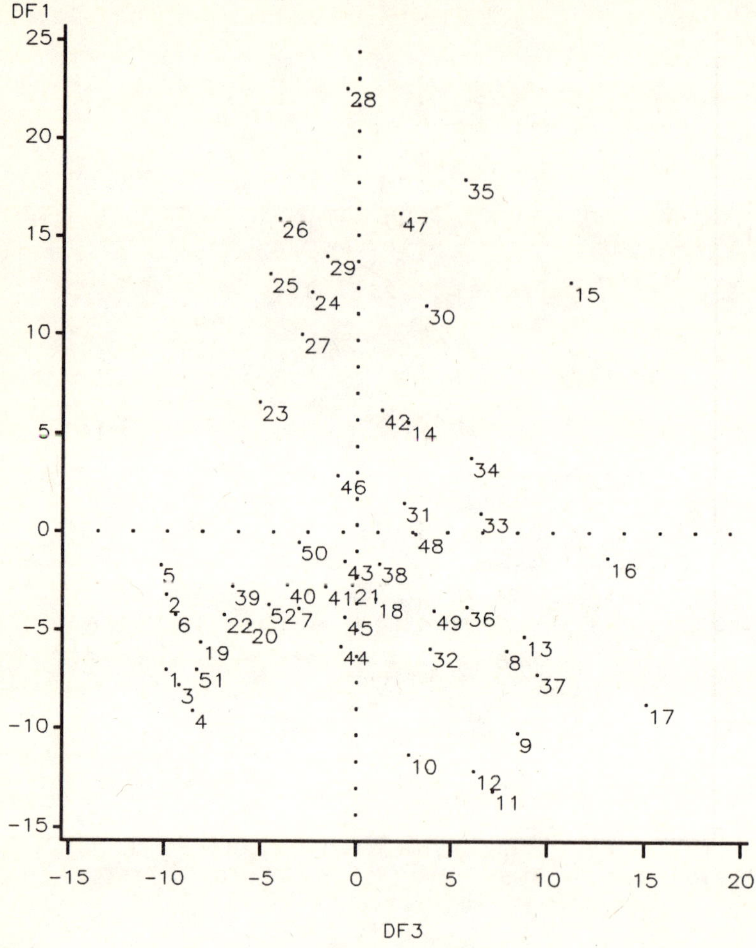

Figure 12 b. Centroids (referred to by condition number) of experimental situations in a three-dimensional subspace of *DASI* (Experiment 1). Plane of *DF1* and *DF3*. See also the legend of Figure 11. *(continued)*

demands, elicited slowly changing modal physiological profiles with decreasing projections on *DF2* and *DF1*. This trend might be interpreted as a sign of a psychological adaptation to the tasks. These examples may suffice to underscore the claim made earlier that physiological behavior may indeed be indicative of some aspects of the organismic transaction and adaptation to the environment. In

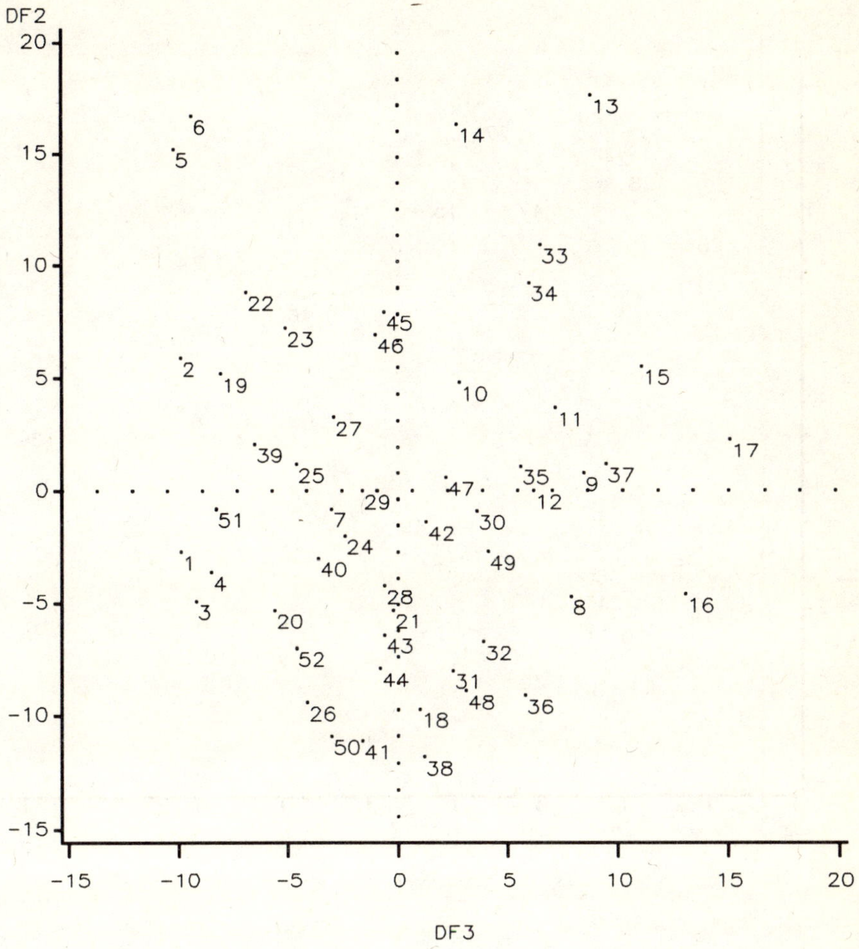

Figure 12 c. Centroids (referred to by condition number) of experimental situations in a three-dimensional subspace of *DASI* (Experiment 1). Plane of *DF2* and *DF3*. See also the legend of Figure 11. *(continued)*

particular, it is evident that not only the physiological concomitants of observable behavior but also aspects which are of particular psychological interest are reflected in the physiological behavior.

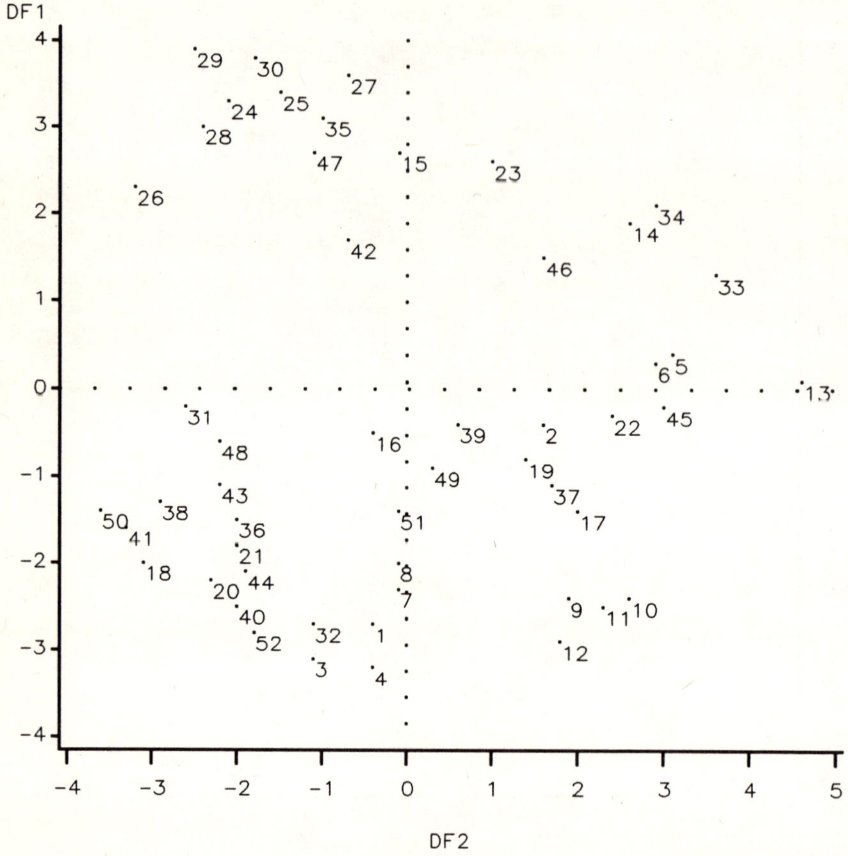

Figure 13 a. Centroids (referred to by condition number) of experimental situations in a three-dimensional subspace of *DAFI* (Experiment 1). Plane *DF1* and *DF2*. See also the legend of Figure 11. *(Figure continues)*

In the plane of *DF2* and *DF3*, the fear induction periods again form a cluster (in the upper right quadrant), joined both by two centroids from instruction-to-imagination periods (No. 17 and 37) and by the instruction period of the second GG speech sample (after the anger induction) and the ensuing period before speech. It is interesting that despite the varying external stimulus properties

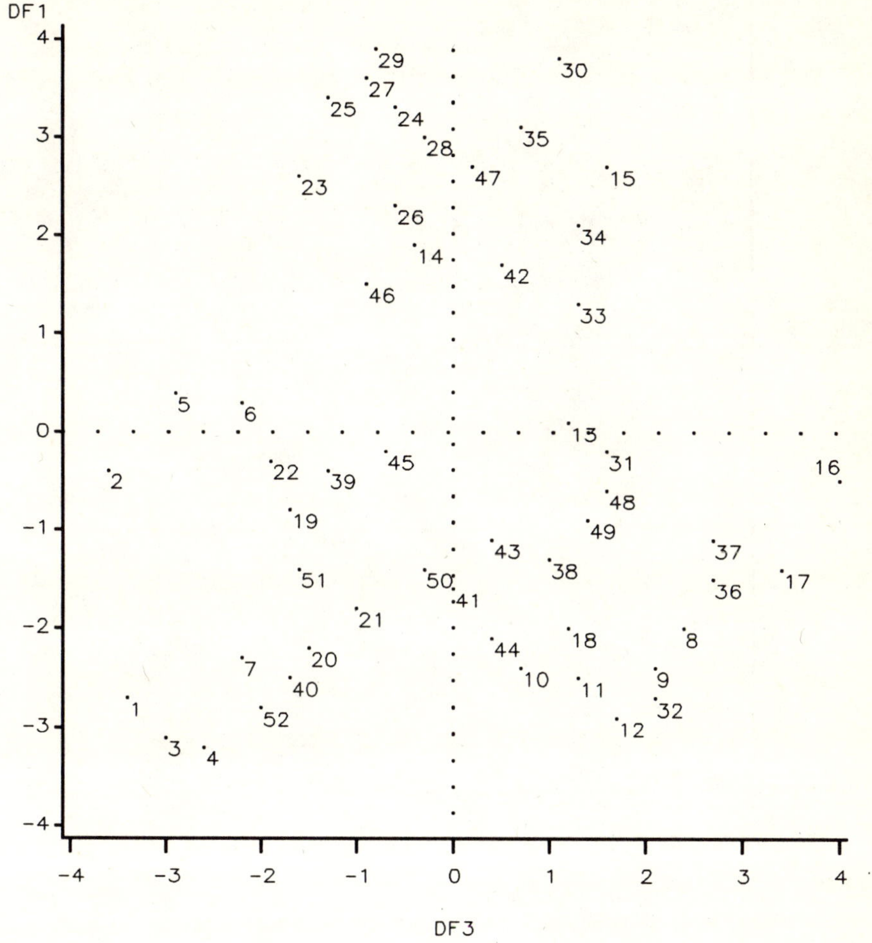

Figure 13 b. Centroids (referred to by condition number) of experimental situations in a three-dimensional subspace of *DAFI* (Experiment 1). Plane *DF1* and *DF3*. See also the legend of Figure 11. *(continued)*

during the fear induction (an instruction, a loud "radio play", sitting in darkness, waiting with lights on), the physiological profiles remained essentially the same. This again illustrates that the physiological responses are not simple reflexes elicited by the physico-biological situation, but that they are the efferent

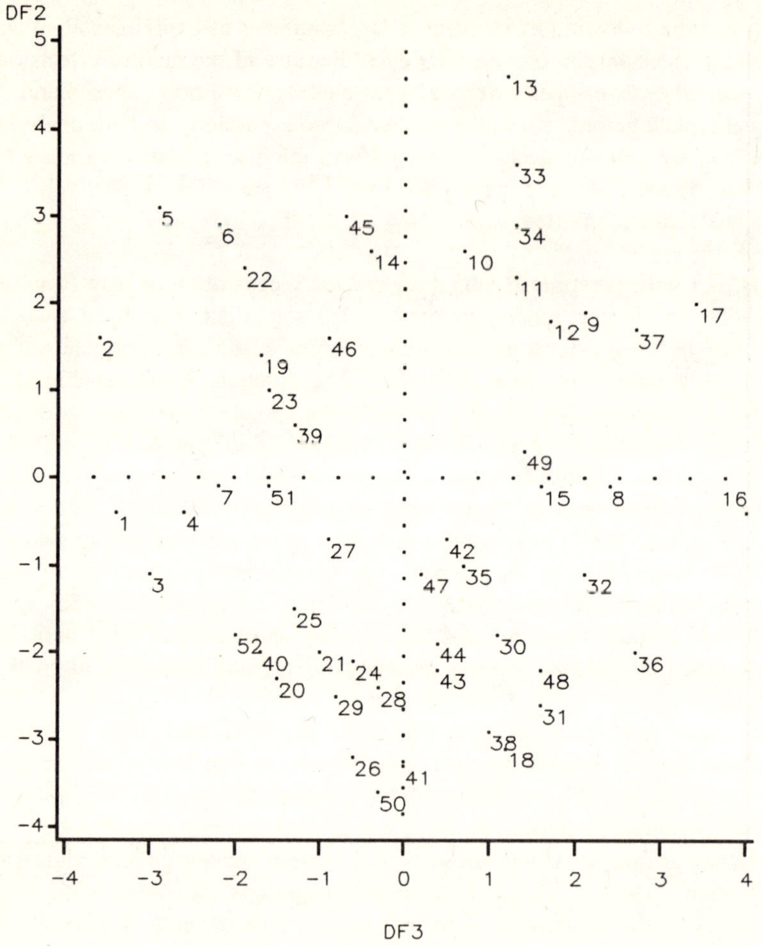

Figure 13 c. Centroids (referred to by condition number) of experimental situations in a three-dimensional subspace of *DAFI* (Experiment 1). Plane *DF2* and *DF3*. See also the legend of Figure 11. *(continued)*

limb of an information integration stage which, according to the situation-response mediation model of Figure 1, integrates a variety of inputs, among them the functional situation, motivational and cognitive person variables, social norms, and the physico-biological situation. Again, this example may suffice to make the general point just mentioned.

9.2.2 Situational maps of Experiment 2

In this and the following experiment, a larger number of experimental situations required of the subjects to close their eyes. Because of the marked effects on the EEG of the eyes-open versus eyes-closed condition, peripheral and electroencephalographic variables were analyzed separately. In both analyses, as few as two *DF*s already accounted for 67% of the discriminative variance (49% and 18%, 56% and 11%, for peripheral and EEG variables, respectively). Only *DARS* analyses are reported.

The DARS with peripheral variables yielded a physiological map (Figure 14) that shows an obvious separation between the conditions with open and closed eyes. The between-conditions correlations of *DF*s and physiological variables confirm this impression (see Table 32): The frontalis EMG, eyeblinks, and saccadic activity nearly perfectly describe the direction (positive correlations with *DF1* and slightly negative ones with *DF2*) in which the two sets of conditions differ. Centroids representing eyes-open situations are located in the upper left quadrant whereas the centroids representing eyes-closed conditions are displaced toward the bottom right corner. Centroids are arranged in two bands from the lower left to the upper right corner. This direction is nearly perpendicular to the aforementioned subdivision of experimental conditions. The correlations indicate that tonic masseter activity, shortening of heart periods and pulse transit time, and an increase of relative expiration time coincide with that direction.

The fine resolution of physiological profiles and their astonishing reproducibility are again demonstrated in Figure 14. The four relaxation periods (No. 1, 12, 18, and 26), together with two poststimulus periods (No. 17 and 25; the third poststimulus period, No. 11, was different; it included the reporting of the mental arithmetic solution) form the bottom cluster of centroids in the deactivation direction. The three anticipation periods (No. 4, 15 and 21) are located above them, with the first anticipation period being displaced toward higher autonomic activation. The largest magnitude of autonomic activation is seen during the three mental tasks (No. 6, 8, and 10). The upper-left band locates at its bottom part the three prestimulus periods (No. 2, 13, and 19), then, with increasing autonomic activation, instruction periods.

The DARS with EEG variables yielded a physiological map (Figure 15) that offered the expected distinction between eyes-open (positive *DF1* scores) and eyes-closed conditions (negative *DF1* scores). The between-conditions correlations of *DF*s and EEG variables (Table 32) show that the alpha frequency band variables are indeed directed downwards, with a rotation to the bottom left corner. Delta, sub-beta2, and gamma activity increase in the direction toward the upper left corner. The stress interview (No. 16) and, to a lesser extent, the instructions before hyperventilation (No. 22) and backward digit recall (No. 7) are displaced in the direction of increased delta activity. Sub-alpha1 and sub-

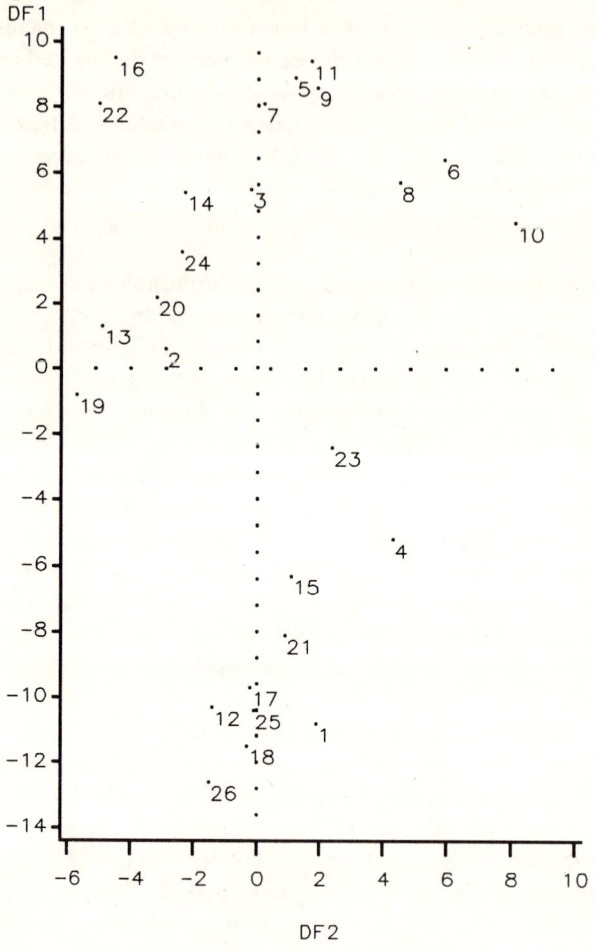

Figure 14. Centroids (referred to by condition number) in a two-dimensional subspace of *DARS* with peripheral variables (Experiment 2). For a complete description of periods, see Table 15. Prestimulus periods = 2, 13, 19. Poststimulus periods = 11, 17, 25. Relaxation = 1, 12, 18, 26. Anticipation = 4, 15, 21. Mental test = 6, 8, 10. Stress interview = 16. Hyperventilation = 23. Instructions = 3, 14, 20 (anticipation); 5, 7, 9 (mental tests); 22 (hyperventilation); 24 (posthyperventilation).

beta1 activity are negatively correlated with *DF2*. The prestimulus periods (No. 2, 13, and 19) form a cluster of centroids with comparatively low sub-alpha1 and sub-beta1 activity, whereas the stress interview and both of the previously

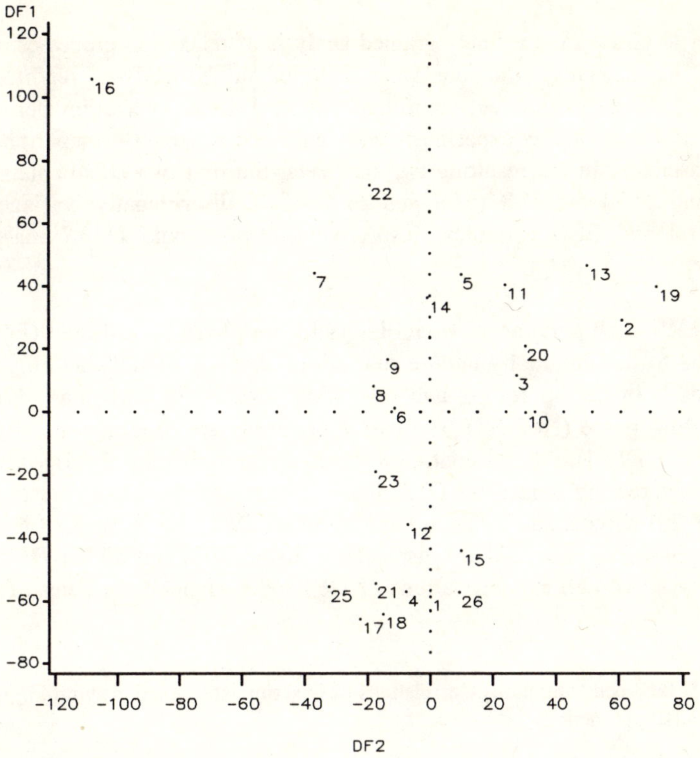

Figure 15. Centroids (referred to by condition number) in a two-dimensional subspace of *DARS* with EEG variables (Experiment 2). See also the legend of Figure 14.

mentioned instructions have relatively high activity in these frequency bands. It should be noted that in the direction of the alpha frequencies, the spread of centroids within the eyes-open and eyes-closed clusters is approximately as large as the between clusters distance. This finding suggests the presence of considerable alpha amplitude variations among experimental situations apart from the eyes-open versus eyes-closed dichotomy. In conclusion, the discrimination of experimental situations and the within-subjects replicability of centroid locations could be established also for EEG variables.

9.2.3 Situational maps of Experiment 3

In order to allow a more finely grained analysis of relaxation processes, only the first 20 experimental situations were included in the analyses reported below (this part of the experiment comprised rest and active relaxation periods). As before, the data of this experiment were analyzed separately for peripheral and EEG variables. In the resulting two data sets, the first two *DF*s explained 81% (54% and 27%) and 78% (54% and 24%) of the discriminative variance in the peripheral and EEG variables, respectively. Again, only *DARS* analyses are reported.

The DARS with peripheral variables yielded a physiological map (Figure 16) that, due to the minute-by-minute resolution, shows a remarkable alignment of centroids both during resting and relaxation periods. In particular, during the first resting phase (No. 3-5), successive centroids are ordered with decreasing values on *DF1*. This trend continues during relaxation (No. 7-16) with a slant towards increasing values on *DF2*. The centroids of the second resting phase (No. 18-20) show a similar decreasing trend on *DF1*, but, compared to the first resting phase, its centroids are displaced to lower *DF1* and higher *DF2* values. The between-conditions correlations of *DF*s and peripheral variables (Table 33)

Table 32. Between-Conditions Correlations of Discriminant Functions with Physiological Variables (Experiment 2)

	Function			Function	
Variable	1	2	Variable	1	2
DA with Peripheral Variables			Resp per	-82	-8
EMG extt	76	31	Insp rel	-33	-7
EMG extp	91	-6	Exp rel	60	58
EMG frt	85	-27	TMP fin	25	51
EMG frp	91	-32			
EMG mat	55	49	**DA with Electroencephalographic Variables**		
EMG map	90	-18			
Hand mov	93	-13	Delta	86	-43
Eyeblinks	90	-32	Salpha1	10	-80
Sacc	81	-48	Salpha2	-75	-56
SCR-No. hand	88	16	Alpha1	-89	-44
SCL hand	63	14	Alpha2	-78	-52
IBI	-81	-56	Sbeta1	20	-90
PTT fin	-84	-49	Sbeta2	51	-75
PVA fin	-30	-14	Gamma	82	-44
BV fin	-48	-3			

Note. For abbreviations of variable names, see Table 17. Correlations multiplied by 100. DA = Discriminant analysis.

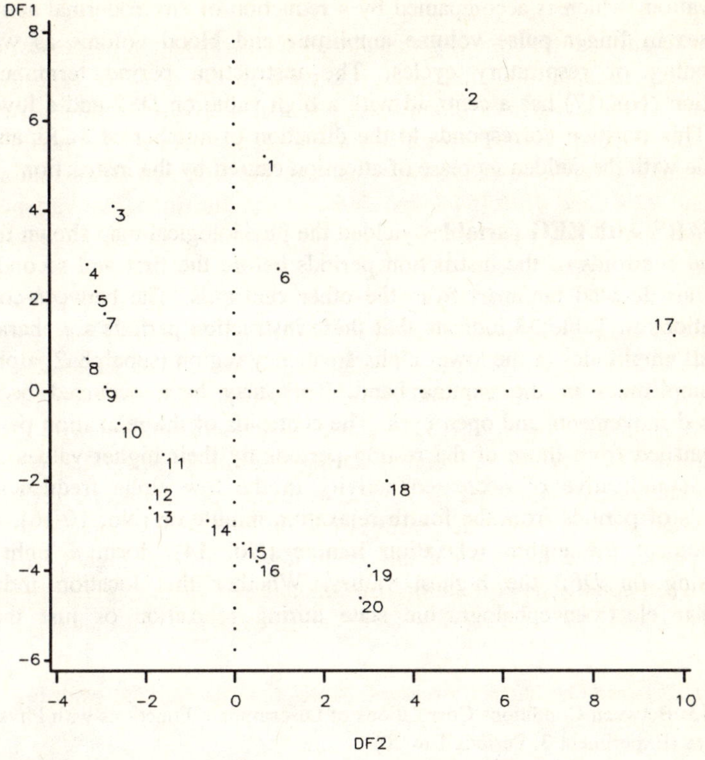

Figure 16. Centroids (referred to by condition number) of experimental periods 1 to 20 in a two-dimensional subspace of *DARS* with peripheral variables (Experiment 3). For a complete description of periods, see Table 16. Heartbeat counting = 1. Instructions = 2, 6, 17. First resting phase = 3 - 5. Relaxation = 7 - 16. Second resting phase = 18 - 20.

reveal that in the first place decreases in pulse transit time and increases in finger skin temperature, but also increases in heart period as well as decreases of relative inspiration and expiration times, and decreases in forehead skin temperature are associated with the trend across successive resting and relaxation periods. Periods where subjects received instructions (No. 2, 6, and 17) are clearly set aside. Whereas the centroid for the instruction to the first resting phase (No. 2) is located quite apart from the centroids of the actual resting periods, the centroid for the relaxation phase instruction (No. 6) is much closer to the centroids of the actual relaxation periods. This difference might be explained by the physiological deactivation produced by the first resting phase. As the between-conditions correlations show, the difference between the centroids of the two instruction periods is related to a somato-motor deactivation, which is accompanied by a reduction of electrodermal activity and increases in finger pulse volume amplitude and blood volume as well as a lengthening of respiratory cycles. The instruction period terminating the relaxation (No. 17) has a centroid with a high value on *DF2* and a low one on *DF1*. This position corresponds to the direction of number of SCRs and might coincide with the sudden increase of attention caused by the instruction.

The DARS with EEG variables yielded the physiological map shown in Figure 17. The centroids of the instruction periods before the first and second resting phases are located far apart from the other centroids. The between-conditions correlations in Table 33 indicate that these instruction periods are characterized by small amplitudes in the lower alpha-frequency region (subalpha2, alpha1) and high amplitudes in the gamma band. This may have occurred because of increased movements and open eyes. The centroids of the relaxation periods are distinguished from those of the resting periods by their higher values on *DF2*, which is indicative of decreased activity in the low alpha frequencies. The centroids of periods from the fourth relaxation minute on (No. 10-16), with the exception of the eighth relaxation minute (No. 14), form a tight cluster possessing on *DF2* the highest values. Whether this location indicates a particular electroencephalographic state during relaxation or just the effect

Table 33. Between-Conditions Correlations of Discriminant Functions with Physiological Variables (Experiment 3, Periods 1 to 20)

Variable	Function 1	Function 2	Variable	Function 1	Function 2
DAs with Peripheral Variables			**DAs with Electroencephalographic Variables**		
EMG extt	70	68	Theta	-9	-2
EMG extp	45	84	Salpha1	39	-20
Body mov	41	76	Salpha2	51	-75
SCR-No. hand	34	85	Alpha1	47	-49
SCL hand	71	63	Alpha2	31	2
IBI	-79	-24	Sbeta1	8	-3
PTT fin	87	-12	Sbeta2	6	-39
PVA fin	-70	-54	Beta1	11	-25
BV fin	-48	-68	Beta2	-6	-28
Resp per	-52	-52	Gamma	-65	-55
Insp rel	59	8			
Exp rel	45	-60			
TMP fin	-95	14			
TMP foreh	79	-54			

Note. For abbreviations of variable names, see Table 17. Correlations multiplied by 100. DA = Discriminant analysis.

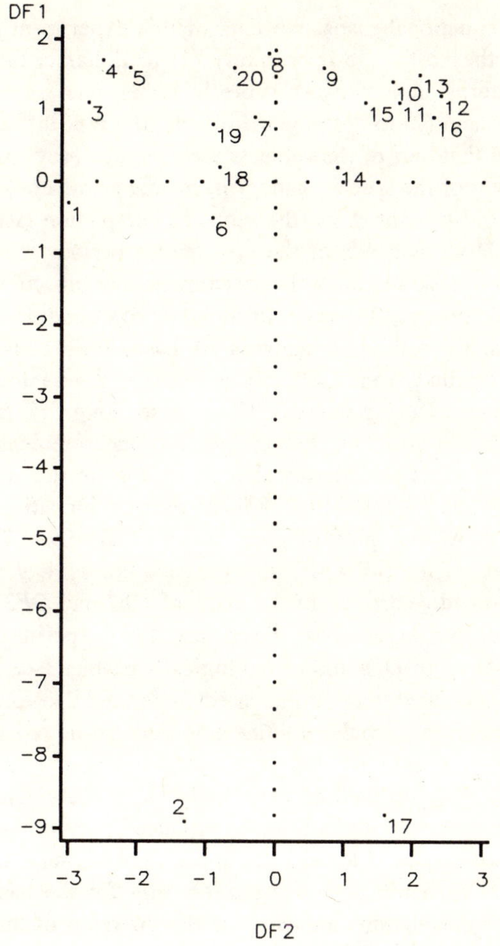

Figure 17. Centroids (referred to by condition number) of experimental periods 1 to 20 in a two-dimensional subspace of *DARS* with EEG variables (Experiment 3). See also the legend of Figure 16.

of prolonged resting cannot be discussed here; the latter alternative seems, however, more probable (see Dittmann, 1988).

9.2.4 Situational maps of Experiment 4

For the issue of situational maps, the data of this experiment are of particular interest, because they offer the opportunity (1) to illustrate the replicability of physiological patterns in a between-subjects rather than in a within-subjects approach as above and (2) to describe the effects of a task difficulty variation. It should be recalled that half of the subjects received an "easy" and the other half a "difficult" version of the speech, handgrip, mental arithmetic, signal detection, loud noise, and cold pressor tasks (the sentence completion task was not varied in difficulty). Ideally, centroids of the prestimulus periods should be identical, whereas centroids of task and possibly poststimulus periods could differ between the two Difficulty groups. In order to avoid a confounding of situation and medication effects, the following analyses are based on placebo data only. The speech task was omitted from the analysis because it was found to markedly influence the solution. During the only 10 to 15 sec long first task period of the loud noise situation (No. 14), blood pressure measurements could not be obtained. Therefore, this period was also omitted from the analysis. The first three *DF*s explained 55% (28%, 19%, 8%) of the discriminative variance.

Figures 18a-c show the physiological maps of the *DARS*. In all planes, prestimulus periods of the two Difficulty groups (No. 1, 4, 7, 10, 13, 17, and 20) had nearby located centroids. In the plane of *DF1* and *DF2*, a marked trend across the centroids can be seen over the course of the experiment. The between-conditions correlations of *DF*s and physiological variables (see Table 34) reveal that this trend is associated with an increased finger and decreased forehead skin temperature, increases in the pulse volume amplitude at the radialis but decreases at the finger site, prolonged left-ventricular ejection and atrioventricular conduction time (P_s-Q_s), as well as more body movements. The handgrip (No. 5) and the mental arithmetic tasks (No. 8) produced physiological profiles with centroids which are displaced toward the upper right corner. A clear separation of the "easy" and "difficult" versions is seen only for the handgrip task. The between-conditions correlations indicate that the direction of these task periods' displacements is associated with increases in blood pressure, heart rate, P-wave and T-wave amplitude, respiration rate, ST-elevation, relative Q-T time, and pulse wave velocity at the finger, with decreases of Heather index, ejection speed, and stroke volume, as well as with increased electrodermal, eyeblink, and extensor activity. Neither the signal detection (No. 11) nor the anticipation of the sentence completion task (No. 21) produced as large a displacement from their prestimulus period's centroid as the two previously described tasks, but these displacements were in the same direction as described above. The cold pressor task (No. 18) changed the profile of activation markedly and, less markedly, the loud noise task (No. 15) in the direction of the trend over the course of the experiment, which among other changes was associated with decreased finger and increased radialis pulse volume amplitude. In sum, in this situational map (1) the between-subjects replicability of prestimulus and also of poststimulus period profiles was high, (2) the tasks produced two different

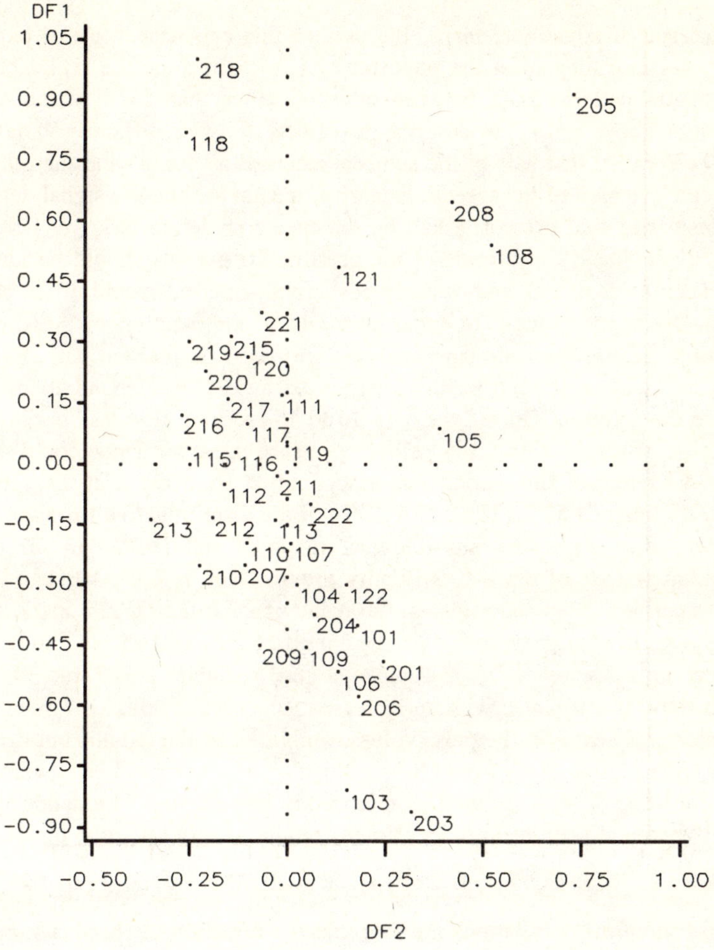

Figure 18 a. Centroids (referred to by condition number) of experimental situations in a three-dimensional subspace of *DARS* (Experiment 4). Plane of *DF1* and *DF2*. For a complete description of periods, see Table 18. Prestimulus periods = 1, 4, 7, 10, 13, 17, 20. Poststimulus periods = 3, 6, 9, 12, 16, 19, 22. Tasks = 5 (handgrip); 8 (mental arithmetic); 11 (signal detection); 15 (loud noise); 18 (cold pressor); 21 (anticipation of sentence completion). The speech task (No. 2) was an outlier and period No. 14 had no blood pressure measurements; both periods were therefore not included in the analysis. A leading "1" indicates the easy, a "2" the difficult task condition. *(Figure continues)*

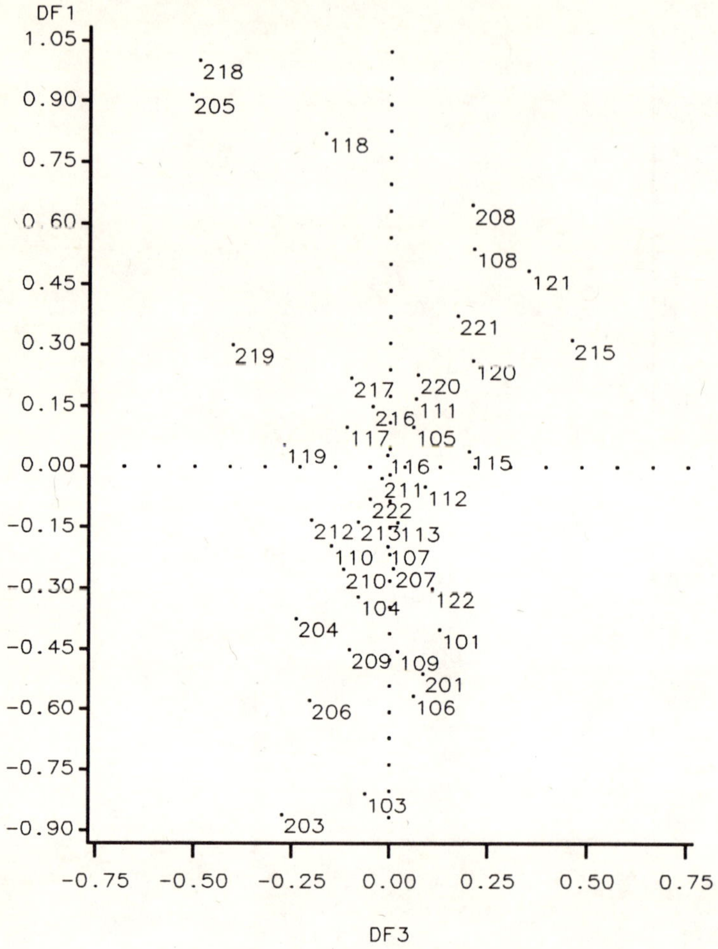

Figure 18 b. Centroids (referred to by condition number) of experimental situations in a three-dimensional subspace of *DARS* (Experiment 4). Plane of *DF1* and *DF3*. *(continued)*

directions of activation, and (3) difficulty variations were seen in the centroids only for the handgrip, loud noise, and cold pressor tasks, the more "difficult" versions being located farther apart from the origin.

In the plane of *DF1* and *DF3*, again two different directions of task-induced changes could be observed. However, compared to the previously described plane, the assembly of tasks with the same direction was different. As before,

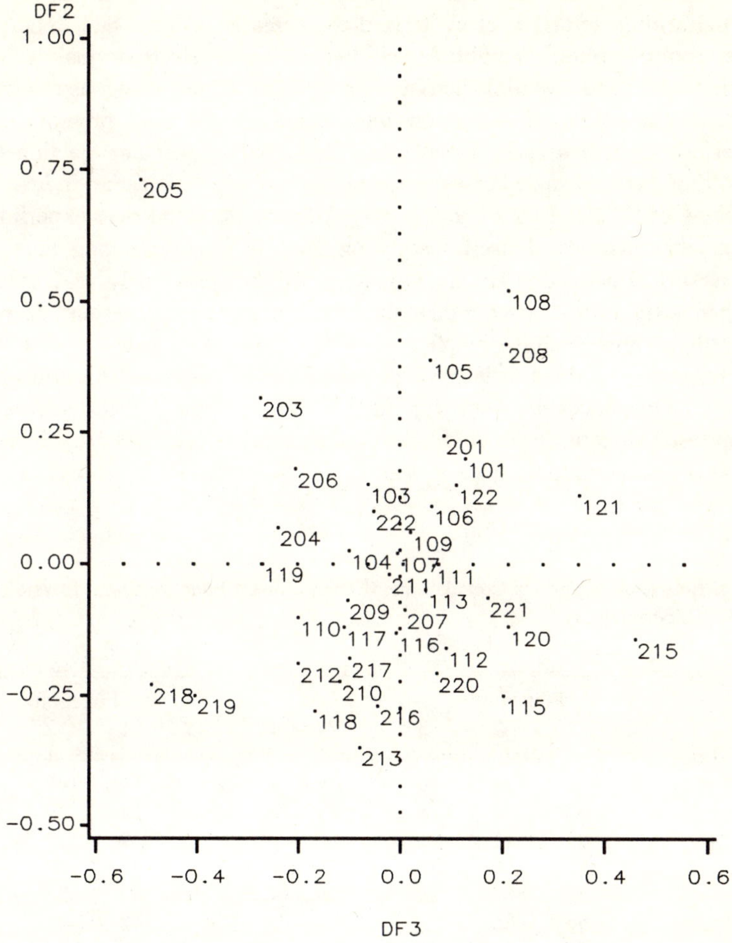

Figure 18 c. Centroids (referred to by condition number) of experimental situations in a three-dimensional subspace of *DARS* (Experiment 4). Plane of *DF2* and *DF3*. *(continued)*

mental arithmetic, signal detection, and the anticipation of the sentence completion task joined one direction of activation from the respective prestimulus periods. However, loud noise also joined the mental arithmetic instead of the cold pressor direction, and handgrip the cold pressor instead of the mental arithmetic direction. As before, there is no marked difference between the "easy" and "difficult" versions of the mental arithmetic task, but a clear differentiation of the loud noise versions has emerged. The between-conditions correlations indicate that the direction of activation represented in this plane by the mental arithmetic task is characterized by increases of heart rate, relative Q-T time, pulse volume amplitude at the radialis, electrodermal activity, respiration rate, and eyeblink activity, as well as finger vasoconstriction. In contrast, the direction of activation represented by the cold pressor task is characterized by increases in T-wave amplitude, left-ventricular ejection time, and R-Z time, as well as decreases in ejection speed and the Heather index.

The plane of *DF2* and *DF3* is interesting, because the trend over experimental situations that manifested itself mainly on *DF1* is largely lacking here. The directions of task activation are much more varied than previously. The handgrip task is primarily associated with diastolic blood pressure increases and decreases of the radialis pulse volume amplitude (which might be a consequence of the greater extension of the arterial wall produced by the increased diastolic blood pressure which reduces its elasticity). In this subspace, the signal detection and (with opposite direction) the cold pressor task are best described by increased (decreased) cardiac output, ejection speed, and SCR amplitude, as well as by a

Table 34. Between-Conditions Correlations of Discriminant Functions with Physiological Variables (Experiment 4)

Variable	Function 1	2	3	Variable	Function 1	2	3
EMG ext	36	74	10	PVA rad	47	-48	20
EMG fr	36	2	38	PVA fin	-84	12	-16
Body mov	80	-11	-26	CO	9	18	23
Eyeblinks	59	20	26	CO ind	8	30	30
SCR-No.	53	63	28	Ejection sp	-67	26	55
SCR-Ampl	56	36	52	SV	-42	-45	-4
HR	61	66	20	LVET	7	-56	-53
P-Ampl	56	49	-3	PEP	-22	17	-2
T-Ampl	65	25	-47	R-Z	28	-12	-65
P_s-Q_s	49	-10	-12	Heather ind	-54	7	55
P_e-Q_s	3	-40	15	SBP	15	55	15
Q-T rel	68	43	30	MBP	34	62	-28
ST-elev	57	47	-6	DBP IV	66	52	-18
HR-SD-BP	-27	-24	-16	DBP	37	55	-42
HR-SD-Resp	-32	-34	-1	TPR	10	37	-40
RSA	-63	-47	-16	Resp rate	66	22	31
RSA adj	-24	-43	18	TMP fin	44	-71	13
PWV rad	16	43	26	TMP foreh	-40	59	-16
PWV fin	56	29	4				

Note. For abbreviations of variable names, see Table 19. Correlations multiplied by 100.

reduced (prolonged) left-ventricular ejection time. Mental arithmetic and the anticipation of the sentence completion task are characterized by increases in heart rate, number of SCRs, radialis pulse wave velocity and a reduction of stroke volume, adjusted respiratory sinus arrhythmia, and finger skin temperature. Loud noise activation is predominantly associated with *DF3* which is correlated with the contractility measures Heather index and, negatively, R-Z time.

In conclusion, apart from the between-subjects replicability of physiological profiles during certain experimental situations, a considerable amount of diverse directions of task activation processes has been observed. These findings underscore the suitability of situational variations for the definition of the construct of activation.

9.3 Cardiovascular Autonomic Activation Components

Through the broad sampling of cardiovascular variables and the placebo-controlled medication design with partial dual autonomic receptor blockades, Experiment 4 was predestined to an application of the Model of Cardiovascular Autonomic Activation Components, which has been described in Chapter 5.2. In contrast to the previous exploratory approach of describing situational physiological maps, in this chapter I shall present the results of a theory-directed, confirmatory approach to the estimation of cardiovascular activation components. To my knowledge, this is the first attempt in this direction. The potential merit of such an approach is that it eventually leads to an invariable frame of reference, for example, for componential intertask comparisons (see Chapters 10 and 12) or the illumination of idiosyncratic activation processes (personality correlates of which are studied in Chapter 11), allowing a comparison of results across different studies. As illustrated in the previous chapter, the exploratory approach led to components (*DF*s in that case) that varied greatly between studies, making direct comparison of results difficult.

As before, process-oriented assessment models (Assessment Models 2 and 7) were used to define the locus of the construct of activation, that is, only between-conditions or within-subjects variance was used in the derivation of the cardiovascular activation components. Four different sets of results will be presented. They differ in the assumptions made:

- The component description rests on the ir-restricted model (Equation 18a in Chapter 5.2.2), that is, a model which omits both interaction terms among cardiovascular autonomic activation components and residual nonautonomic influences.[24] Furthermore, the component description presupposes complete blockades should the results be interpreted as estimates of component coefficients.

- Redundancy analysis (explained below) is based on the assumption of the validity of the ir-restricted model but does not assume complete blockades.
- Separate discriminant analyses for the three activation component effects are based on the same assumptions as the redundancy analysis.
- Multistage linear estimation of activation components assumes only the r-restricted model and allows for the estimation of blockade strengths. However, its results may be influenced by incomplete blockades.

Two other approaches to an analysis of cardiovascular activation components theoretically suited for experiments with incomplete blockades, namely nonlinear estimation procedures and the analysis of covariance structures (see Chapter 5.3.2), each ran into severe computational (convergence) problems. These attempts will therefore not be further commented.

9.3.1 Component description

Prior to the component description, the physiological variables were standardized to a mean of zero and a standard deviation that was obtained from the pooled variance within Session (4) x Medication (4) x Difficulty (2) x Situation (22) subgroups with each six subjects. Original raw score means, standard deviations (the square root of pooled error variances), as well as means and variances within medication groups (in terms of standardized variables) are shown in Table 35.

The component description is the most basic analysis possible to characterize the effects that the cardiovascular activation components exert on the physiological variables. Comparable to a componential task description, which is based on task means (see Equations 23b to 23d for the case of dual blockades), the component description is based on the means of medication groups across all tasks, which reads, for example, for the alpha-adrenergic component

$$a_{m1}\alpha_{.} = {}^{ir}X_{(./B\text{-}C\text{-})m} - a_{m0} \,. \tag{95}$$

Thus, the component description indicates to what extent on the average a particular variable was influenced by an activation component. It might be interesting to apply a similar rationale, instead of to means, to the variances within medication groups. This application would indicate to which degree on the average the variance of a particular variable was influenced by an activation component. It suggests itself to form a ratio of variances, such as

---

24 It should be recalled that under dual blockade a violation of the "no interaction components" assumption of the ir-restricted model introduces no bias (see Equation 27b in Chapter 5.2.3).

$$s^2_{m1} = (s^2_{(X/A\text{-}B\text{-})m} + s^2_{(X/A\text{-}C\text{-})m})/(s^2_{(X)m} + s^2_{(X/B\text{-}C\text{-})m}) \tag{96a}$$

$$s^2_{m2} = (s^2_{(X/A\text{-}B\text{-})m} + s^2_{(X/B\text{-}C\text{-})m})/(s^2_{(X)m} + s^2_{(X/A\text{-}C\text{-})m}) \tag{96b}$$

$$s^2_{m3} = (s^2_{(X/A\text{-}C\text{-})m} + s^2_{(X/B\text{-}C\text{-})m})/(s^2_{(X)m} + s^2_{(X/A\text{-}B\text{-})m}) \, , \tag{96c}$$

with s^2_m = the ratio of variances for variable m in the blocked relative to the unblocked receptor type, $s^2_{(X)m}$ = the sample variance of variable m in the placebo group, and $s^2_{(X/A\text{-}B\text{-})m}$, $s^2_{(X/A\text{-}C\text{-})m}$, $s^2_{(X/B\text{-}C\text{-})m}$ = sample variances of variable m in the chol-free, beta-free, and alpha-free medication group, respectively. Table 36 shows the result of the component description and variance ratio calculations, which employed the medication group means and variances of standardized variables reported in Table 35.

With regard to significant effects of cardiovascular activation components on the grand average of variables, there is a marked difference between components. The alpha component has only 6 significant variables; the beta, 24; and the tau component, 14. It is also the *beta component* that through its effects on the variable means is most unambiguously defined: Heart rate is elevated; P-wave amplitude is increased; atrio-ventricular conductance time and atrial excitation time are shortened; relative Q-T time rises; the ST segment is elevated; T-wave amplitude is diminished; heart rate variability in both frequency bands is increased; the unadjusted respiratory sinus arrhythmia is reduced; pulse wave velocities are elevated, as are cardiac output, left-ventricular contractility (Heather index, -R-Z time), and ejection speed; left-ventricular ejection time and preejection period are reduced; systolic blood pressure rises, as does, interestingly, diastolic phase IV, but not phase V blood pressure, which as expected drops; total peripheral resistance is also reduced; body movements are increased.

The *tau component* is the one next best defined: SCR number and amplitude are elevated, which of course is not a direct cholinergic effect but appears because the receptors at the sweat glands are cholinergic; consequently, electrodermal activity is inhibited under atropine; contrary to expectation, heart rate, P-wave amplitude, pulse wave velocities, the index of cardiac output, and systolic blood pressure are increased, R-Z time is decreased; not unexpected, however, are the prolongation of atrio-ventricular conduction time and atrial excitation, the ST-elevation and the increase in the adjusted respiratory sinus arrhythmia, as well as the skin temperature at the finger.

Finally, according to this descriptive analysis the *alpha component* produces a mixed pattern of activation and deactivation: On the one hand, heart rate is lowered, P-wave amplitude reduced, left-ventricular ejection time prolonged, and T-wave amplitude increased (this picture fits to the nearly significantly elevated adjusted sinus respiratory arrhythmia). On the other hand, preejection period is shortened, stroke volume is increased, pulse volume amplitude at the radialis is elevated, as is pulse wave velocity at the finger site. It appears as if

Table 35. Means and Variances of Physiological Variables (Experiment 4)

			Means[a]				Variances[a]			
			Medication				Medication			
Variable	Mean[b]	SD[c]	P	A	B	C	P	A	B	C
EMG ext	6.43	13.9	52	-44	10	-18	1406	964	1343	866
EMG fr	12.6	21.1	44	53	-111	14	1298	1366	463	1272
Body mov	19.1	7.93	190	-278	155	-68	1228	1392	1321	1508
Eyeblinks	12.7	11.1	-73	83	20	-31	963	1129	1241	1070
SCR-No.	3.47	4.86	226	-165	-237	176	1105	917	797	1333
SCR-Ampl	0.11	0.17	224	-162	-265	201	1348	1169	579	1631
IIR	67.7	9.9	472	-766	588	-293	1055	972	1717	886
P-Ampl	806	341	163	-363	118	82	869	922	1118	1032
T-Ampl	1014	433	-116	241	-288	162	935	1199	1026	961
P_s-Q_s	154	21.8	19	-11	-453	445	836	1354	797	1269
P_e-Q_s	48.6	18.3	-182	297	-575	460	918	1214	749	1344
Q-T rel	12.4	1.47	161	-264	218	-116	1372	981	1332	357
ST-elev	82	422	96	-206	66	44	968	662	827	1342
HR-SD-BP	18.4	623	50	-163	240	-127	834	671	1440	1317
HR SD Resp	16.7	24.9	52	-86	80	-45	708	790	582	2010
RSA	103	64.6	-105	173	-59	-9	786	1534	1008	1094
RSA adj	4.35	0.55	144	-29	-103	-12	1406	817	1225	967
PWV rad	4.67	0.55	416	-427	211	-198	919	845	1364	941
PWV fin	5.07	0.16	616	-466	177	-326	875	740	1498	973
PVA rad	462	342	84	99	-99	-84	820	1361	586	1199
PVA fin	2733	1302	-11	-59	126	-56	1111	1009	1426	1014
CO	6.95	2.01	237	-216	139	-160	696	438	902	496
CO ind	3.62	1.09	296	-252	132	-175	1195	736	1476	813
Ejection sp	39.1	10.6	217	-301	201	-117	1045	925	1160	902
SV	104	30	59	113	-117	-55	1099	882	1249	899
LVET	290	26	-201	508	-402	94	840	1252	1126	933
PEP	69.5	19.5	-381	227	-154	308	934	1106	1064	948
R-Z	128	15.3	-631	603	-319	346	1085	1019	973	1008
Heather ind	17	4.48	386	-330	271	-327	1328	785	1416	701
SBP	118	12.6	411	-388	215	-238	1026	781	947	1415
MBP	84.1	10.9	51	21	-44	-28	1162	916	934	1213
DBP IV	81.2	10.1	167	-102	-15	-50	1225	973	1148	1139
DBP	67.1	13	-130	214	-163	79	1339	876	1004	1058
TPR	1053	318	-228	234	-140	134	1213	949	1161	882
Resp rate	13.1	3.08	32	79	-10	-101	1144	1207	1125	1144
TMP fin	35.9	2.04	63	-155	9	84	971	1563	1018	1092
TMP foreh	34.3	0.53	-54	59	54	-58	1370	833	866	768

Note. SD = Standard Deviation. P = Placebo. A = Alpha-free. B = Beta-free. C = Chol-free. For abbreviations of variable names, see Table 19. [a]Means and variances within medication groups were calculated on standardized variables (using the first two columns) across n = 1056 cases each. Values multiplied by 1000. [b]Raw score mean across the complete sample (n = 4224). [c]Square root of pooled error variances.

Table 36. Description of Activation Components

Variable	Effects on Means[a]			Effects on Variances[b]		
	alpha	beta	tau	alpha	beta	tau
EMG ext	9	62	34	0.93	**0.67**	1.01
EMG fr	97	-67	58	**0.65**	**1.50**	**0.71**
Body mov	-87	**346**	122	1.08	1.14	0.99
Eyeblinks	11	-52	-104	1.10	1.00	1.16
SCR-No.	61	-11	**402**	1.05	1.18	**0.70**
SCR-Ampl	63	-40	**426**	0.88	**1.45**	**0.59**
HR	**-295**	**1060**	**178**	**1.28**	**0.67**	**1.39**
P-Ampl	**-201**	**281**	**245**	**1.20**	0.98	1.07
T-Ampl	**126**	**-403**	47	0.93	1.10	1.17
P_s-Q_s	8	**-434**	**464**	0.94	**1.61**	1.02
P_e-Q_s	114	**-757**	**278**	0.98	**1.53**	0.87
Q-T rel	-103	**380**	45	**0.72**	**0.49**	**1.34**
ST elev	-111	**162**	**140**	**1.33**	1.12	**0.64**
HR-SD-BP	-113	**290**	-78	**1.83**	0.87	0.98
HR-SD-Resp	-35	**132**	6	**1.73**	**2.17**	**0.50**
RSA	68	**-164**	-114	0.91	**1.46**	**1.35**
RSA adj	116	41	**132**	0.99	**0.68**	0.86
PWV rad	-12	**626**	**217**	**1.31**	**0.78**	**1.19**
PWV fin	**149**	**729**	**290**	**1.53**	**0.72**	**1.21**
PVA rad	**183**	-15	-1	**0.82**	**1.82**	0.96
PVA fin	-7	115	-67	1.15	**0.80**	1.15
CO	21	**375**	77	**1.23**	**0.58**	1.12
CO ind	44	**427**	**121**	1.18	**0.58**	1.10
Ejection sp	-84	**418**	99	1.05	**0.83**	1.07
SV	**172**	-58	4	1.08	**0.76**	1.07
LVET	**307**	**-603**	-107	0.98	1.11	**1.34**
PEP	**-154**	**-535**	-73	0.99	1.03	1.15
R-Z	-27	**-950**	**-285**	0.94	0.98	0.95
Heather ind	56	**657**	58	1.00	**0.54**	1.08
SBP	23	**626**	**173**	**1.31**	1.11	**0.71**
MBP	72	7	23	1.03	1.01	**0.78**
DBP IV	65	**153**	117	1.04	0.89	0.90
DBP	84	**-293**	-51	0.93	**0.83**	**0.78**
TPR	6	**-368**	-95	0.94	**0.77**	1.01
Resp rate	111	22	-69	0.96	1.04	1.02
TMP fin	-92	71	**146**	**0.83**	**1.33**	**1.25**
TMP foreh	5	-1	-113	**0.74**	**0.72**	**0.79**

Note. Boldface numbers: $p < .05$. [a]Positive values indicate increases of variable values upon activation. Calculations were based on standardized variables multiplied by 1000. Reported are contrasts against zero. *F*-tests were based on $df = 1, 368$, using an est(ϵ) = 0.35. [b]Values larger than 1 indicate decreases of variance upon activation. Reported are *F*-tests for the comparison of variances, with $df = 369, 369$, using an est(ϵ) = 0.35.

this ambiguous picture reflects the net effect of an alpha-adrenergic activation with an ensuing vagally mediated baroreflex.

Effects of cardiovascular activation components on the variance of variables are even larger than the effect on means. The general comment may suffice that significant variance and mean effects do not necessarily coincide. This finding suggests to regard variance effects in their own right. For example, frontalis activity, finger pulse volume amplitude, mean blood pressure, and skin temperature at the forehead were, on the average, not affected by the cardiovascular activation components with respect to means; they were, however, affected with regard to the variance. In contrast, the mean of R-Z time was greatly influenced by the beta and the tau component, but no effects were seen with regard to its variance.

9.3.2 Redundancy analysis

Similar to canonical correlation analysis, redundancy analysis (Van den Wollenberg, 1977) describes the relationship between two sets of variables and provides statistical tests for the strength of their association. Whereas canonical correlation analysis derives canonical variates within each set of variables subject to the condition that each pair of successive variates is maximally correlated, redundancy analysis derives canonical variates subject to the condition that each variate of the predictor variable set accounts for a maximum of variance in the set of criterion variables. Thus, redundancy analysis is a generalization of multiple regression analysis. It has been shown (Lambert, Wildt, & Durand, 1988) that the canonical variates of canonical as compared to redundancy analysis in terms of variable loadings are often differently defined.

Redundancy analysis seemed to offer the opportunity to obtain in one analysis variable coefficients for components that are able to maximize the prediction of placebo scores from the activation component effects on variables. As before, the cardiovascular activation component effects on variables were defined according to Equations 23b to 23d. It is, of course, not guaranteed that the canonical variates obtained from the redundancy analysis actually correspond to cardiovascular activation components, since the canonical variates are statistically, but not theoretically, defined. With complete blockades, one could at least judge whether it is appropriate to interpret a canonical variate as a cardiovascular activation component, since then only the variables corresponding to one component effect would be expected to load on one canonical variate. Given partial blockades, one would expect loadings of variables of different component effects on each canonical variate. Such a pattern of mixed loadings makes it, of course, difficult to decide whether a certain canonical variate represents an estimate of a cardiovascular activation component. At any rate, the merit of redundancy analysis is that it offers a description of cardiovascular activation patterns.

In order to be consistent with the process-oriented approach advocated in this and in previous chapters, within-subjects variance (i.e., between-conditions plus subjects x conditions plus error variance) was analyzed. The analysis of between-conditions variance alone was impossible because in that case there would have been many more variables than "cases" (22 situations). In order to focus the analysis on cardiovascular variables and to reduce the number of variables in the analysis, a sample of 22 cardiovascular variables was selected on a priori grounds, the main criteria being (1) the availability of the measure in other laboratories and (2) a lack of high systemic dependencies (such as given with CO and CO ind, PWV rad and PWV fin, DBP IV and DBP). Thus, the analysis was based on 22 criterion (placebo scores) and 3 x 22 = 66 predictor variables (alpha, beta, and tau effects on variables). Table 37 presents some basic statistics and Figures 19a-f the correlation of canonical variates and cardiovascular variables.

The first six predictor canonical variates accounted for 53% of the predicted variance. Of this portion, 26% were attributable to alpha effects; 41%, to beta; 33%, to tau effects. Table 37 shows that each of the canonical variates summarizes prediction variance from all of the three component effects, although their relation changes. This finding does not come unexpectedly because in Experiment 4 only partial blockades had been used.

The first canoncial variate (see Figure 19a; signs of correlations are reversed in this description) correlates highly with the contractility measures (-R-Z time, Heather index) and with a shortening of preejection periods. The other correlations confirm that this variate describes an inotropic cardiac activation: Ejection speed, index of cardiac output, and heart rate have positive correlations; diastolic blood pressure, total peripheral resistance, P-wave and T-wave amplitude, and ST-elevation correlate negatively with this canonical variate. Of interest are some peripheral effects, such as the positively correlated skin temperature at the forehead and pulse wave velocity at the finger. The

Table 37. Basic Statistics of Redundancy Analysis

	Placebo Variance Explained By			
	Predictor Canonical Variates[a]	Component Effects[b]		
Variate		Alpha	Beta	Tau
1	15.15	20	46	34
2	9.12	26	46	28
3	9.08	14	42	44
4	6.91	38	39	23
5	6.85	36	23	41
6	6.41	30	44	26

[a]Percentage of total predicted variance. [b]Percentage of variance predicted by the respective canonical variate.

alpha, compared to beta and tau effects, are correlated consistently lower.

The second canonical variate (see Figure 19b; signs of correlations are again reversed in this description) is predominantly characterized by its large negative correlation (with the exception of the alpha effect, which has a near zero correlation) with ST-elevation. The Heather index, ejection speed, and relative Q-T time correlate slightly positively, diastolic blood pressure and total peripheral resistance negatively with this variate. Thus, although sympathetic inotropic cardiac effects are prevalent on this variate, the dominant influence of ST-depression was unexpected. Whether this ST alteration indicates in situ changes of myocardial oxygen supply under conditions of inotropic cardiac activation remains an open question. It is interesting that both beta and tau effects show these high correlations. It is, however, established that ST-depressions can be psychologically induced and that sympathetic cardiac activation augments ST-depression whereas vagal cardiac activation has an inhibitory effect on ST-depression (Jennnings & Follansbee, 1985).

The third canonical variate (see Figure 19c) is characterized by large beta and tau component effects (see Table 37). Heart rate, relative Q-T time, diastolic blood pressure, and total peripheral resistance are positively correlated with this variate, and negatively, left-ventricular ejection time, stroke volume, the index of cardiac output, and the adjusted respiratory sinus arrhythmia. Thus, this variate describes a cardiac chronotropic effect with a reduced ejected blood volume. That vagal cardiac effects contribute to this effect is clearly seen by the high correlations of the tau effects of heart rate and respiratory sinus arrhythmia. The positive correlations of diastolic blood pressure and total peripheral resistance suggest that this pattern of cardiac activity might have been mediated by the baroreceptor reflex.

The fourth canonical variate (see Figure 19d) is characterized by positive correlations with relative Q-T time, left-ventricular ejection time, stroke volume, and the index of cardiac output (the latter three are correlated only for the placebo data and the beta effect), and by negative correlations with R-Z time, systolic blood pressure, and adjusted respiratory sinus arrhythmia. Peripheral variables also show correlations with this variate, in particular within the placebo data and the alpha effect: these correlations are positive for skin temperature at the forehead and pulse wave velocity at the finger site, and negative, for skin temperature at the finger as well as finger pulse volume amplitude. In sum, this canonical variate describes a combination of cardiac (only blood-volume related) beta-sympathetic and peripheral alpha-sympathetic effects. It should be noted that T-wave amplitude and ST-elevation show dissociated component effects: For T-wave amplitude, the beta effect correlates slightly positively and all other groups negatively with this variate; for ST-elevation, the alpha effect has a distinct, negative correlation.

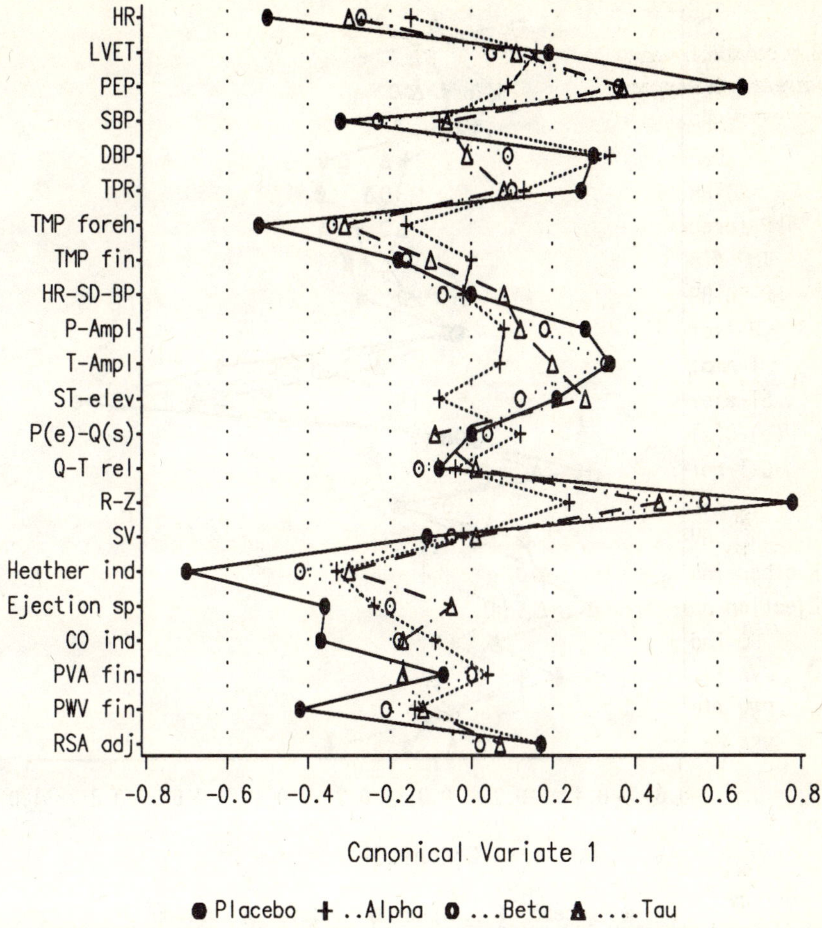

Figure 19 a. Correlations of cardiovascular variables with canonical variates (of the predictor variables) derived by redundancy analysis. Correlations are given separately for the placebo data (criterion variables) and the cardiovascular activation component effects (of alpha, beta, and tau components) on variables (predictor variables). The analysis was conducted with the within-subjects variance of standardized variables (Experiment 4). For abbreviations of variable names, see Table 19. *(Figure continues)*

The fifth canonical variate is associated with relatively large alpha and tau, and with small beta effects (see Table 37). This variate presents a difficult to interpret mixture of activating and deactivating effects. On the one hand, systolic blood pressure and total peripheral resistance are positively correlated. On the other hand, P_e-Q_s time as well as finger pulse volume amplitude are positively, and P-wave amplitude, stroke volume, as well as the index of cardiac output negatively correlated with this variate.

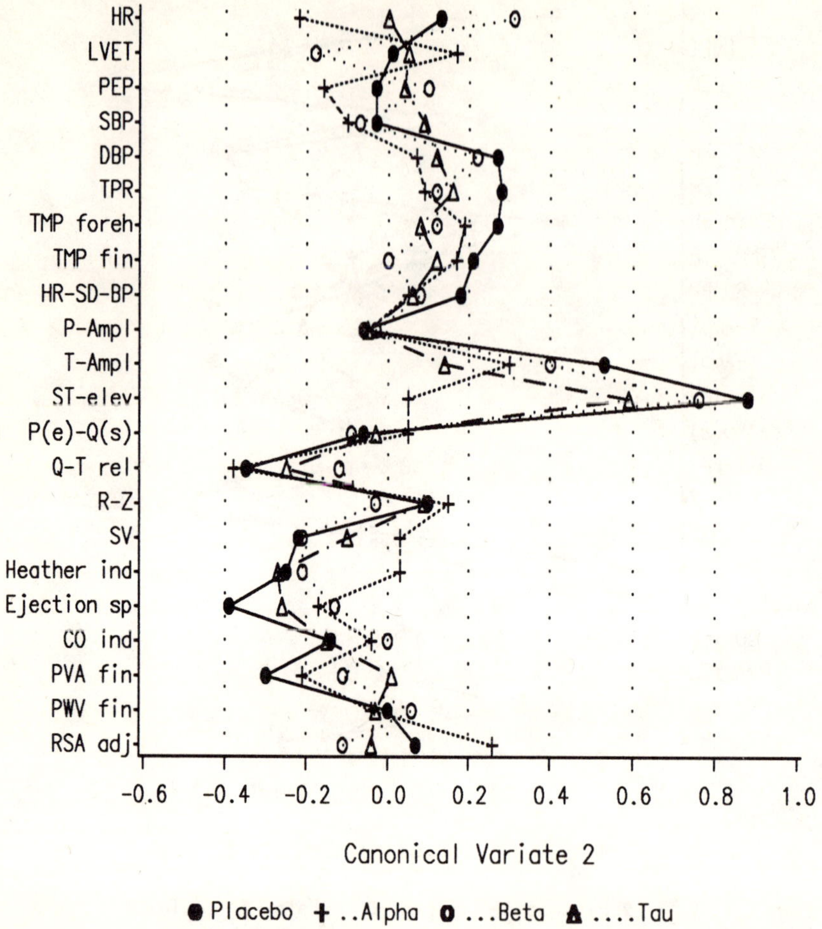

Figure 19 b. *(continued)*

The sixth canonical variate is characterized by positive correlations with P_e-Q_s time, stroke volume, and the index of cardiac output (the latter two only for placebo data and the tau effect), and by negative correlations with adjusted respiratory sinus arrhythmia, relative Q-T time, T-wave as well as P-wave amplitude, and the skin temperature at the finger (beta effect only) as well as at the forehead. Again, this pattern of correlations is difficult to interpret since it suggests an atrial deactivation and a slight ventricular activation effect.

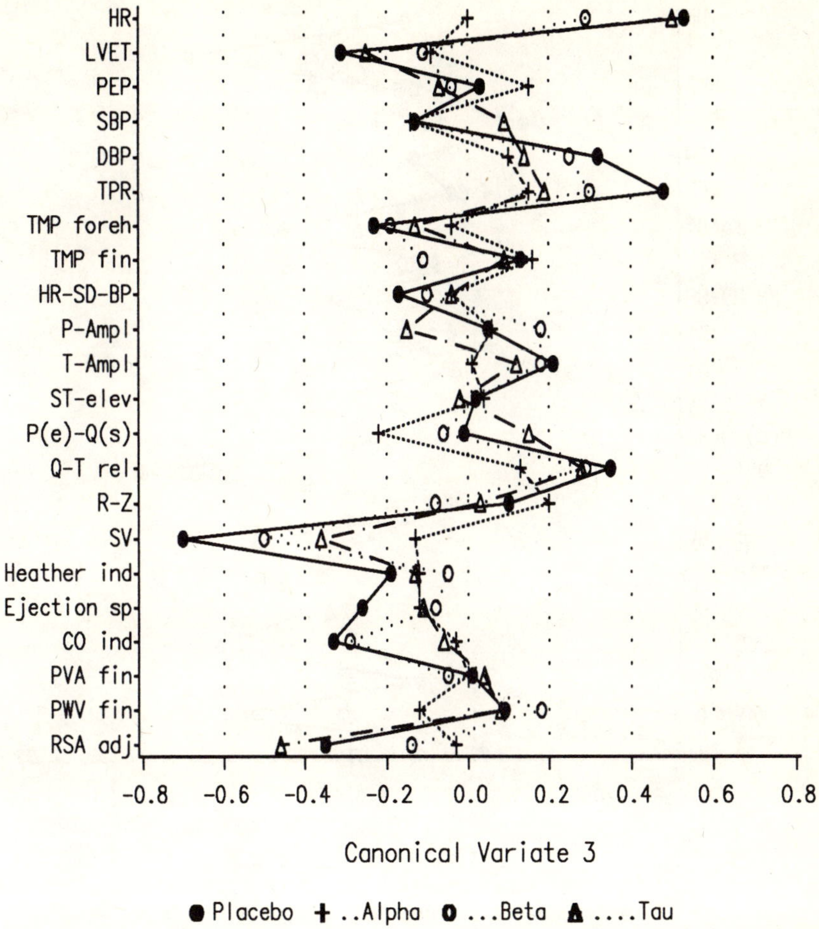

Figure 19 c. *(continued)*

In sum, the redundancy analysis suggested some maximally predictive patterns of cardiovascular activations of the placebo data from the three component effects, some of which could be interpreted as integrated regulatory cardiovascular processes. As noted above, this analysis could not be expected to yield conclusive evidence for the definition of the separate cardiovascular autonomic activation components.

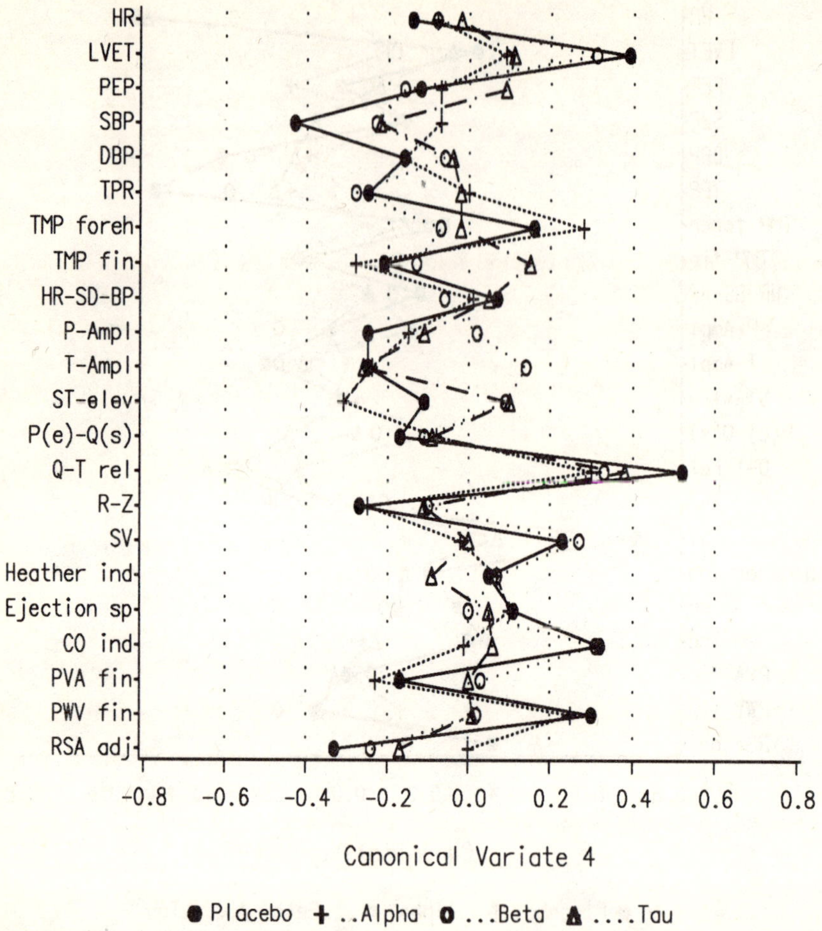

Figure 19 d. *(continued)*

9.3.3 Discriminant analysis

The use of discriminant analysis (DA) has been advocated (see Chapter 5.3) for the estimation of cardiovascular activation components, if a mixed process-state conceptualization of activation (i.e., a combination of Assessment Models 2 and 7) is assumed. In order to derive variable coefficients and activation component estimates, the effects that the three activation components exert on the cardiovascular variables (see Equations 23 or 24) need to be calculated and decomposed in separate DAs, as has been demonstrated in Chapter 5.3.1 with the data of Robinson et al. (1966).

The three DAs were based on the task-rest response form of the ir-restricted Model of Cardiovascular Activation Components (Equations 24 b-d). According to the mixed process-state conceptualization of the construct of activation, only within-subjects variance was analyzed. "Groups" were 14 conditions (2 Difficulty groups x 7 situations) with each 24 subjects. The same 22 cardiovascular variables (standardized according to Table 35) as in the redundancy analysis were entered into the DAs. According to Wilks' lambda, the DA on alpha-adrenergic component effects extracted five discriminant functions (*DF*s) explaining 88% of the discriminative variance before the subsequent *DF*s were insignificant; the DA on beta-adrenergic component effects, four *DF*s explaining 86%; the DA on cholinergic component effects, four *DF*s explaining 84%.

One might ask why four to five *DF*s and not just one *DF* were extracted within each DA, which is what would have been expected for an unambiguous identification of the cardiovascular activation components. At least three factors may have contributed to this finding:

- Given incomplete autonomic receptor blockades, contributions from all three activation components remain in the task-rest difference score instead of just the unblocked component, as would be the case under complete blockades.
- Another consequence of incomplete blockades is that a violation of the "no interaction assumption" of the ir-restricted model under a dual blockade protocol, in distinction to complete blockades (see Equation 27b), introduces a bias into the estimation of component effects on variables. Specifically, interactions among components remain as a source of variance in the DAs.
- Nonautonomic residual influences could also constitute a source of variance in the DAs.

Provided that these factors led to the observed results, one would expect that similar, although not identical, *DF*s were obtained in the three DAs. Across DAs, the *DF*s could not be expected to be identical because (1) the partial blockades and (2) sampling fluctuations between medication groups (in particular, Session x Medication group interactions) might contribute to their dissimilarity. A principal components analysis with the predetermined number of five factors and ensuing promax rotation indeed confirmed the correspondence of *DF*s across the DAs: The first four factors each had one large loading ($> | 0.50 |$) from each of the DAs, the fifth factor was marked only by the fifth "alpha" *DF*.

The allocation of *DF*s to putative cardiovascular activation components was performed on a priori grounds: The alpha-adrenergic component was expected to have marked correlations with diastolic blood pressure and total peripheral resistance. The *DF* from the "alpha" DA was thus identified. The beta-adrenergic component was expected to have marked correlations with cardiac inotropic measures, heart rate, cardiac output, reductions in preejection period, and total peripheral resistance (compare Tables 5 and 6). Three *DF*s from the "beta" DA were identified to conform in one or the other aspect with this expectation. The cholinergic component was expected to have marked correlations with the adjusted respiratory sinus arrhythmia, with lowered heart rate, and a prolonged P_e-Q_s time. One *DF* from the "tau" DA was thus identified. Table 38 gives the standardized discriminant coefficients of the cardiovascular variables for the resulting five component estimates. These coefficients can be used to calculate scores on the five selected *DF*s from data with a mean of zero and variance of one.

The interpretation of the putative cardiovascular activation components will be based on the within-subjects correlations between *DF*s and variables (see Figure 20a-e). Regression coefficients like those in Table 38 are not suited for the derivation of the "importance" of a specific variable; these coefficients are interpretable only in the context of the specified complete regression model. Correlations are not subject to such interpretative restrictions.

Figure 20a shows the correlations between the *putative alpha component* and the effects of the alpha-adrenergic component on the cardiovascular variables (the within-subjects structure of the "alpha" DA). The profile of correlations corresponds quite convincingly to the expected pattern: With growing "alpha" activation, heart rate is slightly decreased, systolic and diastolic blood pressures are elevated, as is total peripheral resistance. The peripheral vasoconstriction, probably initiating the blood pressure increase, is clearly seen in the large negative correlation with finger skin temperature. Left-ventricular contractility is diminished, as are stroke volume and the index of cardiac output. The adjusted respiratory sinus arrhythmia, P_e-Q_s time, and preejection period are slightly reduced.

Figures 20b-d show the within-subjects structures of the "beta" DA. The *putative beta1*[25] *component* (Figure 20b) has positive correlations ($r > 0.20$) with preejection period, R-Z time, finger skin temperature ($r < -0.80$!) and finger pulse volume amplitude. In sum, this component combines a marked cutaneous vasoconstriction with increases in left-ventricular contractility; blood pressure changes, however, are not obtained. The *putative beta2 component* (Figure 20c) has a marked positive correlation with finger pulse volume amplitude and smaller ones with ST-elevation, relative Q-T time, and adjusted respiratory sinus arrhythmia; negative correlations are seen with R-Z time and heart rate variability in the blood pressure band. The *putative beta3 component* (Figure 20d) has again a negative correlation with R-Z time, and positive ones with the Heather index, systolic blood pressure, and heart rate variability in the blood pressure band. Interestingly, this is the only of the beta components that has a marginal negative correlation with T-wave amplitude (discussed to be a putative beta-adrenergic indicator). It should be noted that the T-wave

[25] The designations "beta1", "beta2", and "beta3" components are just names for the successive *DF*s selected from the "beta" DA; they are not intended to suggest an affinity to types of beta-adrenergic receptors.

Table 38. Standardized Discriminant Coefficients for Estimates of Scores on Putative Cardiovascular Activation Components Derived from Discriminant Analysis

	Activation Component				
Variable	alpha?	beta1?	beta2?	beta3?	tau?
HR	-0.307	0.051	0.119	-0.927	-0.323
P-Ampl	-0.153	0.133	-0.004	-0.305	-0.025
T-Ampl	0.092	-0.117	-0.103	0.121	0.065
P_e-Q_s	-0.392	-0.094	-0.193	-0.058	0.016
Q-T rel	-0.156	-0.121	0.249	0.093	-0.117
ST-elev	0.015	0.189	0.321	-0.263	-0.219
HR-SD-BP	0.124	-0.006	-0.694	0.661	0.064
RSA adj	-0.326	0.169	0.558	-0.111	0.511
PWV fin	0.072	0.181	-0.289	-0.283	-0.257
PVA fin	0.052	-0.325	0.900	0.249	-0.422
CO ind	0.186	-0.378	0.464	0.891	-0.537
Ejection sp	0.574	-0.306	0.171	-0.284	0.383
SV	-0.975	0.342	-0.739	-0.222	0.051
LVET	0.466	0.061	0.094	-1.122	0.637
PEP	-1.093	0.357	-0.380	-0.250	-0.287
R-Z	0.269	-0.229	-0.466	-0.385	-0.307
Heather ind	-0.271	0.501	0.005	-0.003	0.113
SBP	0.236	-0.111	-0.123	0.576	-0.402
DBP	0.038	-0.065	0.072	-0.176	-0.184
TPR	0.383	0.066	0.039	-0.029	0.273
TMP fin	-0.544	-0.980	-0.208	-0.038	-0.335
TMP foreh	0.440	0.407	-0.179	-0.119	0.176

Note. The DAs, from which the putative cardiovascular activation components were derived, were based on task-rest changes of cardiovascular variables of the medication groups receiving receptor blockades. Prior to analysis, subject means were subtracted yielding within-subjects variance. Before application of these coefficients to a new data set, variables have to be standardized ($M = 0$, $SD = 1$).

depression in the beta3 component shows up in the context of increased contractility, large systolic blood pressure, but a marginally lowered heart rate. It will be shown later (Chapter 10) that the cold pressor task induced the largest changes on this component.

Figure 20e shows the within-subjects structure of the *putative tau component* from the "tau" DA. The profile of correlations between this component and the cholinergic effects on the cardiovascular variables indicates marked reductions in heart rate, systolic and diastolic blood pressures, P-wave as well as T-wave amplitudes, ST-elevation, relative Q-T time, R-Z time, finger pulse volume amplitude, and pulse wave velocity at the finger. Left-ventricular ejection and P_e-Q_s times are prolonged, and the adjusted respiratory sinus arrhythmia is markedly increased. This pattern of correlations is largely consistent with the

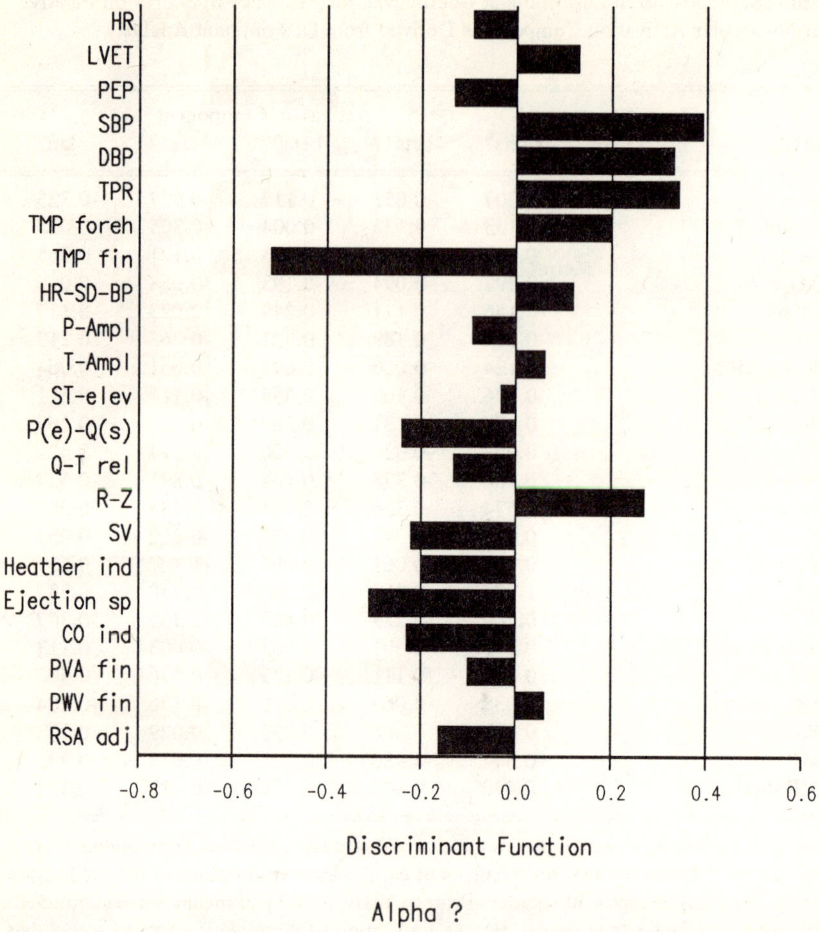

Figure 20 a. Within-subjects correlations between putative cardiovascular activation components derived from the discriminant analysis of experimental situations and task-rest changes of cardiovascular variables (assuming the ir-restricted Model of Cardiovascular Activation Components in the task-rest response form). The correlations are based on 2 Difficulty groups x 7 situations x 24 Subjects = 336 cases of medication group data. (a) Putative alpha component correlated with the scores of the "alpha-free" medication group. (b)-(d) Putative beta components correlated with the scores of the "beta-free" medication group. (e) Putative tau component correlated with the scores of the "chol-free" medication group. *(Figure continues)*

expectation of a cardiac vagal activation. However, the ST-depression and the T-wave reduction do not fit this interpretation (see section 9.3.5 for an evaluation of this finding). With equal right this putative tau component could be interpreted as a cardiac chronotropic component (with reversed sign). Thus, this

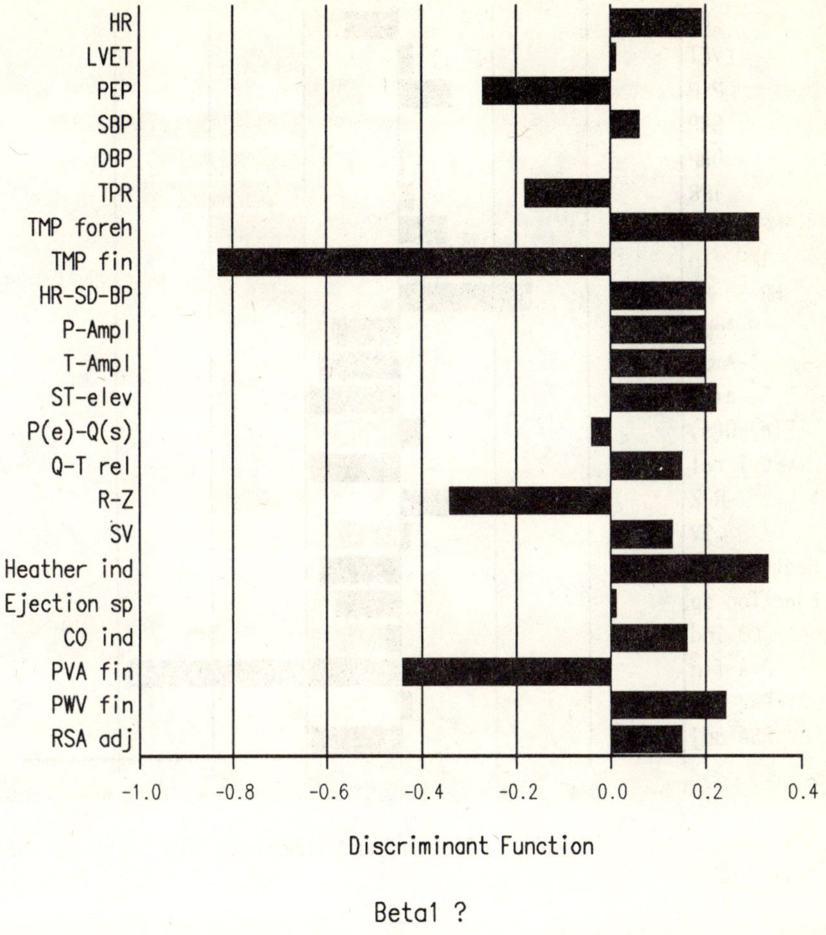

Figure 20 b. *(continued)*

component could also be interpreted as reflecting a cardiac vagal-sympathetic (chronotropic) balance. Table 39 summarizes the results of regression analyses for the prediction of cardiovascular variables *under placebo* from placebo scores on estimated cardiovascular activation components. The standardized regression coefficients are the variable coefficients of the model in Equation 18b.

The data reported in Table 39 are interesting in two respects. First, the standardized regression coefficients for each variable reflect the "influence" that the five putative cardiovascular activation components exert on the variables. Since the five components are only marginally correlated within-subjects ($r < |0.20|$, with the exception of an $r = 0.34$ between the putative beta1 and tau components), the standardized regression coefficients of each variable closely

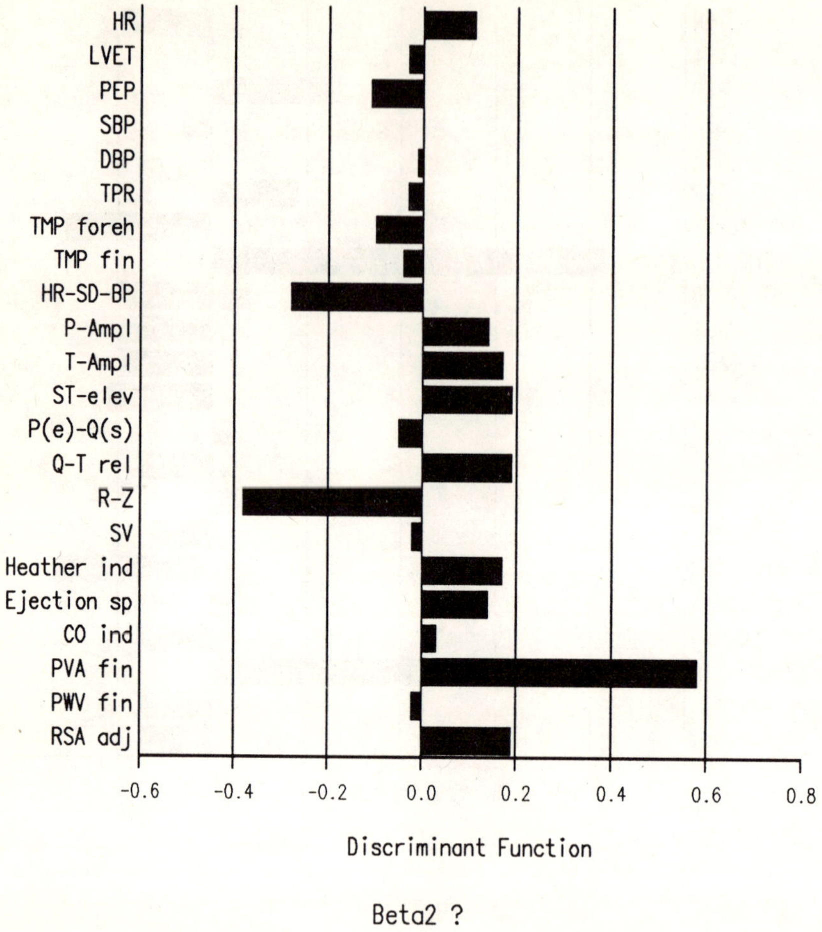

Figure 20 c. *(continued)*

resemble the respective Pearson correlations. Second, the regression analyses were conducted only with the placebo data which constitutes a partial replication of the correlations reported above (Figure 20). It should be noted that these correlations were based only on the data from the three medication groups that had received pharmacological blockades. A comparison between the correlations reported in Figure 20 and the coefficients in Table 39 confirms that the two solutions are essentially similar. This finding attests to the psychometric stability of the derived solutions and makes a separate interpretation of Table 39 unnecessary.

The squared multiple correlations reported in Table 39 indicate that the prediction of within-subjects variance of task-rest changes in cardiovascular

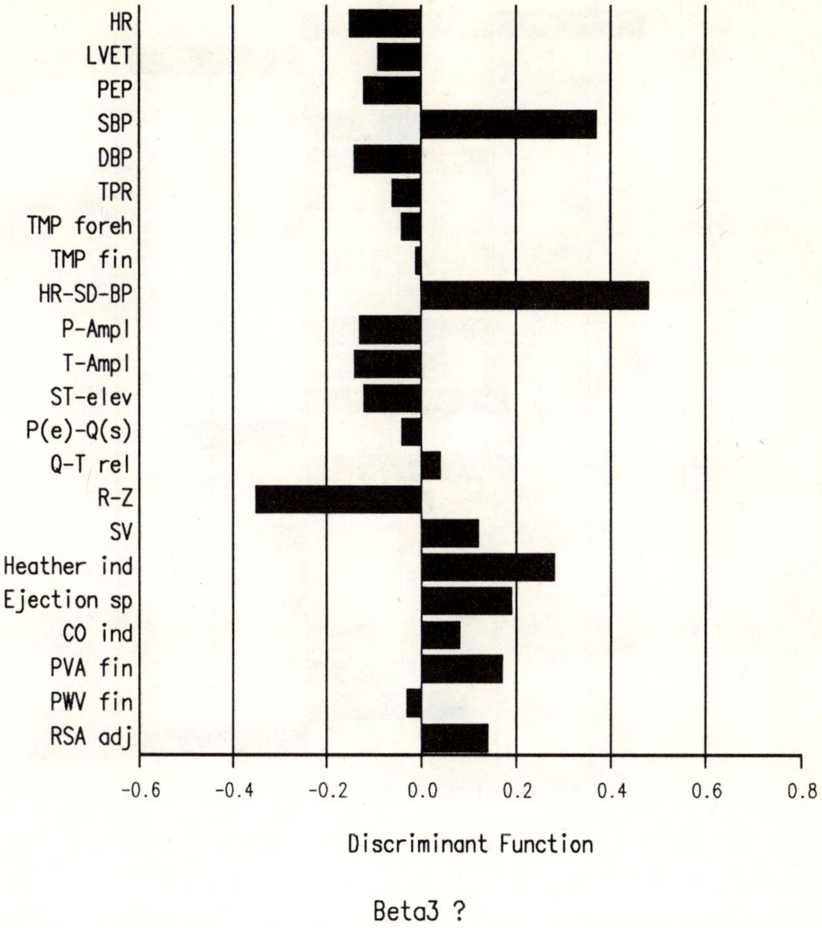

Figure 20 d. *(continued)*

variables based on the five putative activation components varies substantially among variables. In particular, heart rate, adjusted respiratory sinus arrhythmia, finger pulse volume amplitude, and finger skin temperature could be predicted with an $R^2 > 0.50$ from the putative activation components, whereas T-wave amplitude, ejection speed, preejection period, and forehead skin temperature, with R^2's < 0.20, were less predictable.

In sum, the attempt to estimate cardiovascular activation components by separate DAs led, under the caveats necessitated by the incomplete receptor blockades employed, to well defined alpha and tau components and to the proposal of three beta components. It should be kept in mind, however, that the decision which of the *DF*s within the separate DAs should be designated a

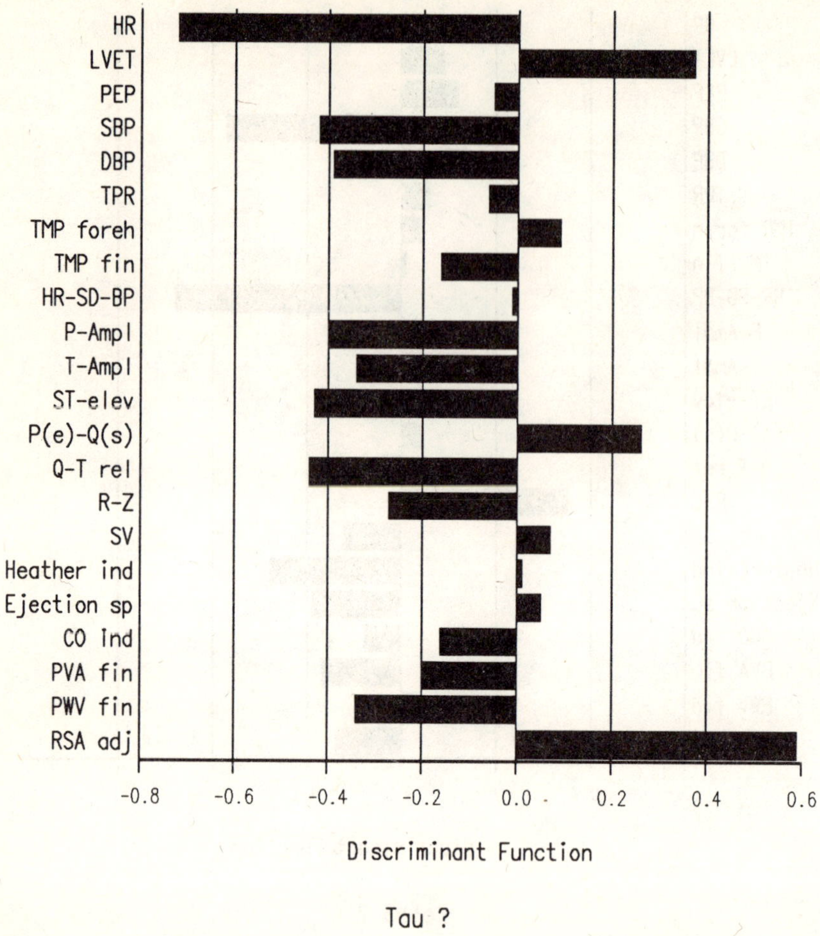

Figure 20 e. *(continued)*

potential cardiovascular activation component was based on a priori expectations about marker variables for each component. In contrast, the multistage linear estimation procedure described in the next section did not refer to such a priori knowledge.

9.3.4 Multistage linear estimation

Among the analyses reported thus far, the procedure of multistage linear estimation (for a formal description, see Chapter 5.3.2) comes closest to the goal

Table 39. Variable Coefficients (Standard Scores) in the ir-Restricted Model (Task-Rest Response Form) of Cardiovascular Activation Components Derived from Discriminant Analysis

		Activation Component				
Variable	R^2	alpha?	beta1?	beta2?	beta3?	tau?
HR	0.72	-0.185	0.332	0.111	-0.137	-0.866
P-Ampl	0.29	-0.179	0.231	-0.005	-0.158	-0.531
T-Ampl	0.07	-0.055	0.061	-0.102	0.023	-0.264
P_e-Q_s	0.21	-0.295	-0.191	-0.254	0.026	0.282
Q-T rel	0.36	-0.252	0.129	0.189	-0.002	-0.502
ST-elev	0.39	-0.049	0.282	0.155	-0.261	-0.609
HR-SD-BP	0.34	-0.081	0.067	-0.409	0.461	-0.008
RSA adj	0.51	-0.246	0.012	0.319	-0.029	0.615
PWV fin	0.37	0.043	0.397	-0.119	-0.171	-0.591
PVA fin	0.63	0.091	-0.375	0.610	0.211	-0.023
Co ind	0.24	-0.195	0.279	-0.033	0.251	-0.349
Ejection sp	0.11	0.025	-0.073	0.191	0.253	0.083
SV	0.21	-0.346	0.236	-0.221	0.188	0.012
LVET	0.24	0.084	-0.056	-0.115	-0.171	0.400
PEP	0.06	0.082	-0.255	0.024	-0.067	0.103
R-Z	0.47	0.205	-0.448	-0.390	-0.319	-0.051
Heather ind	0.34	-0.248	0.334	0.045	0.433	-0.152
SBP	0.45	0.298	0.090	-0.041	0.380	-0.458
DBP	0.28	0.357	0.048	0.050	-0.206	-0.410
TPR	0.22	0.433	-0.197	0.116	-0.102	0.050
TMP fin	0.76	-0.122	-0.870	-0.160	-0.139	0.061
TMP foreh	0.15	0.321	0.165	-0.044	-0.078	-0.037

Note. These variable coefficients were determined by separate regression analyses for predicting task-rest changes of cardiovascular variables (standardized according to Table 35) from scores on putative cardiovascular activation components (*DF*s of separate medication group DAs), using placebo data only. The regression analyses were performed across 2 Difficulty groups x 7 Situations x 24 Subjects = 336 cases after removal of subject means, that is, using within-subjects variance.

of a strictly objective derivation of cardiovascular activation components. In particular, the procedure estimated

- variable coefficients a_m,
- scores of subjects on putative cardiovascular activation components and with it situation means,
- coefficients reflecting blockade strengths, and
- a coefficient reflecting the effect of the task difficulty variation.

Furthermore, the procedure could be tuned (1) to estimate an ir-restricted or an r-restricted model (i.e., a model without or with interactions between cardiovascular activation components) and (2) to estimate a solution according to the task level or the task-rest response form of the model. Some differences to the previously described discriminant analysis should be noted. Whereas the latter procedure directly produced (1) within-subjects regression coefficients for the estimate of components from variables (see Table 38) and (2) within-subjects correlations between components and variables (see Figure 20; variable coefficients, i.e., regression coefficients for the estimation of variables from components, however, had to be calculated separately, see Table 39), multistage linear estimation directly produced variable coefficients (however, the first two items above had to be determined separately). Another important difference concerns the assessment model which underlies the two procedures. Whereas the discriminant analysis procedure was based on a mixed process-state conceptualization of activation (using within-subjects variance), multistage linear estimation was solely process-oriented (using between-conditions variance according to Assessment Model 2). More specifically, the procedure used 22 situations x 2 difficulty versions x 4 medication groups, that is, 176 points of information. Prior to analysis, cardiovascular variables were transformed such that (1) the two difficulty groups had equal means in all prestimulus periods and (2) linear and quadratic trends over prestimulus period means were eliminated. The same 22 variables that have been used in the previous analyses were entered into the present one. I will begin with the direct output of the multistage linear estimation procedure.

The coefficients reflecting blockade strength could vary between zero and one. They denote the relative magnitude of medication effects as derived from the statistical model of cardiovascular activation components. It should be noted that these coefficients do not indicate the degree of actual receptor blockades, since they depend upon the selection of variables and situations. If, for example, the effects of alpha-adrenoceptor mediated activation could not manifest themselves, either because the variables recorded did not respond to this form of activation, or since variations in alpha-adrenergic tone were not elicited, the coefficient of alpha-adrenergic blockade strength would be low (indicating a very low blockade strength), even if physiologically the alpha-adrenoceptors could have been blocked sufficiently. Even under this caveat, the blockade strength coefficients for the three cardiovascular activation components were considerably discrepant: The alpha-adrenoceptor blockade strength obviously was very low ($\pi_1 = 0.062$); the beta-adrenoceptor blockade strength quite high ($\pi_2 = 0.826$); the cholinoceptor blockade strength low ($\pi_3 = 0.270$).

Compared to the "easy" task versions, the "difficult" versions (six of the seven experimental tasks were varied in their difficulty) were estimated to elicit a cardiovascular activation increased by almost 50% (1:1.47). The presence of this difficulty effect had already become visible in the physiological maps of situations in Chapter 9.2; it will be further described in Chapter 10.

Table 40 shows the variable coefficients estimated under the assumption of the ir-restricted Model of Cardiovascular Activation both for physiological levels (task level form of the model) and task-prestimulus difference scores (task-rest response form of the model). It should be noted that these variable coefficients are purely descriptive; statistical tests were not intended at this level of analysis. (Tests will be performed later under the assumption that the putative cardiovascular activation components are "given" variates.) In Table 40 the column labelled "R^2" gives the amount of variance of the complete between-conditions variance in the respective variable predicted from the modelparameters (i.e., blockade strength, difficulty level, variable coefficients, and means of experimental situations, or task-rest changes, on the putative activation components).

The information compiled in Table 40 allows (1) a comparison of the magnitudes of explained variance both among the variables and the two forms of

Table 40. Variable Coefficients (Raw Scores) in the ir-Restricted Model of Cardiovascular Activation Components Derived from Multistage Linear Estimation (Between-Conditions Variance)

Variable	R^2	Activation Component alpha?	beta?	tau?	Intrinsic Activity
Task Level Form of the Model					
HR	0.83	12.78	7.59	-1.99	62.92
P-Ampl	0.50	237.19	70.44	-11.03	779.49
T-Ampl	0.57	171.87	-114.34	66.05	1152.14
P_e-Q_s	0.75	0.42	-9.89	5.75	57.34
Q-T rel	0.73	0.90	0.41	0.01	12.17
ST-elev	0.43	168.30	49.72	-8.28	61.79
HR-SD-BP	0.30	10.79	5.13	-3.99	15.06
RSA adj	0.58	-0.73	0.00	0.11	4.14
PWV fin	0.76	0.25	0.23	0.02	4.88
PVA fin	0.61	-1195.11	128.45	-1093.58	2736.93
Co ind	0.66	0.54	0.37	-0.22	3.42
Ejection sp	0.58	-5.55	3.25	-3.47	35.76
SV	0.04	-4.72	-0.51	-2.80	103.82
LVET	0.57	-12.45	-10.85	7.24	296.63
PEP	0.64	1.99	-7.71	1.92	77.21
R-Z	0.80	8.50	-10.46	4.25	138.64
Heather ind	0.74	-1.50	2.25	-1.60	14.88
SBP	0.69	7.77	5.94	-2.48	114.04
DBP	0.62	15.87	-2.37	0.76	72.54
TPR	0.53	56.13	-86.34	38.33	1145.58
TMP fin	0.04	-0.22	0.07	0.04	35.71
TMP foreh	0.03	-0.02	0.00	-0.04	34.31

(Table continues)

Table 40. Variable Coefficients (Raw Scores) in the ir-Restricted Model of Cardiovascular Activation Components Derived from Multistage Linear Estimation (Between-Conditions Variance) *(continued)*

Variable	R^2	Activation Component alpha?	beta?	tau?	Intrinsic Activity
Task-Rest Response Form of the Model[a]					
HR	0.89	3.69	1.17	-0.31	
P-Ampl	0.73	1.44	0.45	-0.21	
T-Ampl	0.56	1.03	0.36	0.03	
P_e-Q_s	0.28	-0.27	-0.36	0.19	
Q-T rel	0.76	1.74	0.52	0.07	
ST-elev	0.62	1.00	0.40	-0.18	
HR-SD-BP	0.06	0.26	0.07	-0.13	
RSA adj	0.75	-1.48	-0.22	0.30	
PWV fin	0.79	1.48	1.08	0.11	
PVA fin	0.74	-1.55	0.77	-1.77	
Co ind	0.63	0.78	0.75	-0.38	
Ejection sp	0.45	-0.76	0.59	-0.53	
SV	0.33	-0.41	0.45	-0.27	
LVET	0.47	-0.79	-0.17	0.33	
PEP	0.25	-0.02	-0.55	0.07	
R-Z	0.66	1.08	-1.65	0.62	
Heather ind	0.56	-0.48	1.11	-0.54	
SBP	0.71	1.27	1.05	-0.43	
DBP	0.78	1.88	0.27	-0.15	
TPR	0.15	0.33	-0.40	0.16	
TMP fin	0.28	-0.27	-0.36	0.08	
TMP foreh	0.18	0.34	0.34	-0.19	

Note. The variable coefficients are estimates of the model parameters a_{m1}, a_{m2}, a_{m3}, and a_{m0} in Equations 18a and 18b. [a]No coefficient of intrinsic activity in the task-rest response form of the model.

the model, (2) the interpretation of the effects of putative cardiovascular activation components on variables, and (3) a comparison of these effects between the two forms of the model.

First, the comparison of magnitudes of explained variance shows that, with few exceptions, the model was capable of explaining a large amount of between-conditions variance in the cardiovascular variables (on the average, 55% in the task level form and 53% in the task-rest response form of the model). Variables with low explained variance ($R^2 < 0.20$) in either form of the model are heart rate variability in the blood pressure band, stroke volume, total peripheral resistance, and finger as well as forehead skin temperatures. A comparison of the magnitudes of explained variance in the two forms of the model reveals that some variables are better characterized by putative activation component effects on task levels (in particular, P_e-Q_s time, preejection period, and total peripheral resistance), whereas the reverse is true for other variables (in particular, P-wave amplitude, stroke volume, and finger skin temperature).

Second, as noted above, effects of putative cardiovascular activation components on variables are interpreted, separately for each variable, solely by the relative magnitude of variable coefficients. Marked effects of the *putative alpha component* can be seen in elevated heart rate, heightened P-wave and T-wave amplitudes, prolonged relative Q-T time, ST-elevation, larger heart rate variability in the blood pressure band, reduced adjusted respiratory sinus arrhythmia, increased finger pulse wave velocity, decreased finger pulse volume amplitude, increased index of cardiac output, diminished ejection speed and stroke volume, shortened left-ventricular ejection time, reduced contractility (-R-Z time, Heather index), increased systolic and diastolic blood pressures as well as elevated total peripheral resistance, and decreased finger and increased forehead skin temperature. In sum, the pattern is one of chronotropic activation with cardiac vagal withdrawal, inotropic deactivation, and peripheral cutaneous vasoconstriction with increased diastolic blood pressure and peripheral resistance. This pattern suggests that the putative alpha component incorporates both alpha-adrenergic and interactive beta-chronotropic x vagal influences.

According to Table 40, the *putative beta component* influences the activity of the following variables: Heart rate and P-wave amplitude increase, T-wave amplitude decreases in terms of physiological levels but increases in terms of responses (this finding suggests that T-wave amplitude levels are reduced by beta-adrenergic receptor blockade but increased by experimental tasks), P_e-Q_s time is shortened, relative Q-T time is prolonged, ST-elevation increases, levels of heart rate variability in the blood pressure band increase, pulse wave velocity increases, finger pulse volume amplitude goes up, the index of cardiac output is elevated, ejection speed and stroke volume responses are increased, left-ventricular ejection time and preejection period are shortened, the contractility measures (-R-Z time, Heather index) are elevated, systolic blood pressure is increased, whereas diastolic blood pressure (levels only) and total peripheral resistance are reduced, skin temperature responses are directed towards temperature reductions at the finger and increases at the forehead. In sum, this putative beta component almost perfectly describes cardiac and peripheral beta-adrenergic effects: Cardiac chronotropic, inotropic, and dromotropic activities are increased, as is cardiac minute volume; systolic blood pressure, peripheral resistance, and diastolic blood pressure are reduced. These are the effects of physiological doses of epinephrine.

Effects of the *putative tau component* can be seen in slight heart rate reductions, diminished P-wave but increased levels of T-wave amplitude, prolonged P_e-Q_s time, reductions in heart rate variability in the blood pressure band, increased adjusted respiratory sinus arrhythmia, decreases in finger pulse volume amplitude, reduced cardiac output, stroke volume, and ejection speed, increased left-ventricular ejection time, reduced left-ventricular contractility (R-Z time, -Heather index), lowered systolic blood pressure, increased total peripheral resistance, and diminished forehead skin temperature. In sum, the putative tau component describes chronotropic, inotropic, and dromotropic deactivation typical of an increased cardiac vagal tone, and a slight increase of total resistance which might constitute a compensatory alpha-adrenergic response to the cardiac deactivation.

Third, a comparison of the effects of the putative cardiovascular activation components on variables between the level and the response form of the model for most of the variables shows identical directions and comparable relative magnitudes in the variable coefficients. Exceptions of this general correspondence are displayed by T-wave amplitude, P_e-Q_s time, stroke volume, diastolic blood pressure, and finger and forehead skin temperatures. This finding indicates again that the choice between level and reaction information is sometimes crucial for the interpretation of autonomic receptor blockade effects.

The results obtained under the ir-restricted Model of Cardiovascular Activation Components suggest that the putative alpha component represents interactions of alpha, chronotropic beta, and cholinergic (vagal withdrawal) effects; the putative beta component, beta1- and beta2-adrenergic effects similar to those of epinephrine; the putative tau component, cholinergic and alpha effects. From this description one would expect that the putative alpha and tau components are substantially negatively correlated. Indeed, the correlation between the scores of the putative alpha and tau components amounts to r = -0.84 (n = 22 situations x 48 subjects = 1056 cases) which indicates a substantial overlap between these components. The correlation between the putative alpha and beta components is r = -0.56 and that between the putative beta and tau components, r = 0.57. It is interesting to speculate on the latter (positive) correlation, because it could reflect a (beta-) sympathetic-vagal **antagonism**, or balance, where each autonomic branch opposes the effects of the other one. In contrast to this antagonism, the putative alpha component expresses a **synergism** of beta-adrenergic chronotropic and cardiac vagal influences, where each autonomic branch supports the effects of the other one (vagal withdrawal and increase of chronotropic tone). Apart from these interesting speculations, from a psychometric perspective the mere fact of such large correlations among putative components is not welcome.

Explicitly estimating the effects of interactions between cardiovascular activation components, that is, applying the r-restricted model (see Equation 16 in Chapter 5.2.2), could perhaps help to disentangle "pure" from interactive effects. Table 41 shows the variable coefficients (only for the task level form of the model) estimated with the multistage linear estimation procedure.

Comparison of the explained model variances, R^2, between the ir-restricted (Table 40) and the r-restricted (Table 41) forms of the model shows that only four variables had increases in R^2 of 0.05 or larger from the former to the more inclusive latter analysis. These variables are T-wave amplitude (0.05), heart rate variability in the blood pressure band (0.12), stroke volume (0.10), and total peripheral resistance (0.06). Furthermore, comparison of the relative magnitudes of variable coefficients in the putative alpha, beta, and tau components revealed that corresponding components in the two solutions have essentially similar effects on the variables. In other words, the inclusion of interaction terms in the r-restricted form of the model did not substantially change the description and interpretation given above for the ir-restricted components. Component effects were different for only three variables (T-wave amplitude, P_e-Q_s time, and systolic blood pressure). Inspection of variable coefficients of interactive terms for the variables (1) with "substantial" increases in R^2 and (2) with changes in the component effects of the ir-restricted model had the following result. T-wave amplitude receives contributions from all of the interaction effects; this is also true for P_e-Q_s time and systolic blood pressure. Both heart rate variability in the blood pressure band and total peripheral resistance receive large contributions from the putative alpha x tau components interaction and from the interaction

Table 41. Variable Coefficients (Raw Scores) in the r-Restricted Model of Cardiovascular Activation Components Derived from Multistage Linear Estimation (Between-Conditions Variance, Task Level Form of the Model)

		Activation Component						
Variable	R^2	alpha?	beta?	tau?	axb?	axt?	bxt?	axbxt?
HR	0.84	13.2	8.1	0.3	-0.4	3.1	-1.8	-1.3
P-Ampl	0.51	252.2	78.7	5.5	-7.4	-214.8	-21.6	41.5
T-Ampl	0.62	64.1	-142.9	-52.2	90.5	45.5	98.0	-52.1
P_e-Q_s	0.76	-3.8	-10.6	1.8	3.7	-5.2	2.9	-1.6
Q-T rel	0.73	0.8	0.4	0.0	0.1	0.2	0.0	-0.1
ST-elev	0.44	201.2	43.6	-15.8	-28.2	86.6	8.8	-22.4
HR-SD-BP	0.42	9.7	5.2	-4.7	2.6	-31.4	-1.5	-14.2
RSA adj	0.58	-0.8	0.0	0.1	0.0	0.1	0.0	0.0
PWV fin	0.76	0.3	0.2	0.1	-0.1	-0.1	-0.1	0.0
PVA fin	0.63	-1044	165	-907	-164	728	-106	289
CO ind	0.70	0.5	0.4	-0.2	0.1	-0.6	0.0	-0.5
Ejection sp	0.61	-3.0	3.5	-2.9	-1.7	-12.8	-0.9	3.3
SV	0.14	-5.8	-1.6	-7.6	2.2	-22.1	2.5	-9.1
LVET	0.59	-17.5	-12.4	3.0	3.8	27.4	4.1	-11.9
PEP	0.65	-0.4	-7.4	1.5	1.7	-6.1	0.4	8.7
R-Z	0.80	4.0	-10.8	2.3	3.5	4.2	1.7	-1.3
Heather ind	0.77	-0.6	2.2	-1.5	-0.5	-4.5	-0.2	-0.8
SBP	0.70	11.2	6.4	0.0	-2.9	-1.8	-1.9	2.9
DBP	0.64	16.7	-2.9	-0.4	-0.9	9.6	1.3	-1.0
TPR	0.59	40.3	-80.0	63.7	-0.4	223.9	-5.2	104.8
TMP fin	0.08	-0.30	0.14	0.22	0.08	-0.59	-0.17	0.08
TMP foreh	0.04	-0.05	0.01	-0.03	0.02	0.01	0.00	0.05

Note. The variable coefficients are estimates of the model parameters a_{m1} to a_{m7} in Equation 16. The coefficient of intrinsic activity was omitted. axb, axt, bxt, and axbxt are the interaction effects between the putative alpha, beta, and tau components.

among all three putative components. In sum, it appears that the estimate of interaction effects did not contribute much to the understanding of cardiovascular activation component interactions. There are, however, hints in the data presented (see the "axt?" column in Table 41) that point to the marked alpha-adrenergic x cholinergic interaction which is mediated by the baroreceptor reflex.

It has been mentioned before that the multistage linear estimation procedure used between-conditions variance for the derivation of the solutions presented. In contrast, the attempt at characterizing cardiovascular activation components with the aid of discriminant analysis in the previous section used within-subjects variance. In order to allow a comparison of the results of these two procedures, analyses comparable to those reported in the previous section were carried out. These analyses used within-subjects variance of both cardiovascular variables and scores on putative alpha, beta, and tau components of the multistage linear estimation results based on the ir-restricted form of the model. The analyses included:

- a regression analysis for the prediction of the putative cardiovascular activation components from standardized variables (see Table 42, which compares to Table 38). These regressions used the task-rest response data of the "alpha-free" group to predict task-rest responses on the putative alpha component; of the "beta-free" group, for prediction of the putative beta component; and of the "chol-free" group, for prediction of the putative tau component.
- the correlation between the putative cardiovascular activation components and the respective medication group data (see Figure 21, which compares to Figure 20).
- a regression analysis for the prediction of task-rest changes of cardiovascular variables from task-rest changes on the putative activation components using placebo data of the dependent variables (see Table 43, which compares to Table 39).

In contrast to correlations (see Figure 21 and the discussion below), the regression coefficients in Table 42 cannot be interpreted in terms of the importance of single variables for the prediction of putative cardiovascular activation components. It might be noted that for several variables there are quite large differences between the regression and the correlation coefficients. However, the regression coefficients have to be used for the calculation of putative cardiovascular activation component scores from new (standardized) data.

Figure 21 shows the within-subjects correlations between task-rest responses of putative cardiovascular activation components and variables (data from the respective medication groups). The *putative alpha component* (Figure 21a) is associated ($r > |0.20|$) with elevated heart rate, heightened P-wave and T-wave amplitudes, ST-elevation, diastolic blood pressure increases, and reductions in the adjusted respiratory sinus arrhythmia. Similar to the interpretation of variable coefficients in Table 40, this component is best characterized as a combination of chronotropic activation with cardiac vagal withdrawal. In contrast to Table 40, the diastolic blood pressure increase is not combined with cutaneous vasoconstriction; however, the slight increase in cardiac output is still seen.

The *putative beta component* (Figure 21b) is characterized ($r > | 0.20 |$) by increased left-ventricular ejection time, reduced preejection period, decreased total peripheral resistance and T-wave amplitude, and increases in left-ventricular contractility (Heather index), stroke volume, as well as the index of

Table 42. Standardized Regression Coefficients for Estimates of Task-Rest Response Scores on Putative Cardiovascular Activation Components Derived from Multistage Linear Estimation

	Activation Component		
Variable	alpha?	beta?	tau?
HR	0.234	0.103	0.122
P-Ampl	0.277	0.172	-0.175
T-Ampl	0.068	-0.548	-0.088
P_e-Q_s	0.109	0.026	-0.044
Q-T rel	-0.004	0.024	-0.057
ST-elev	0.043	0.151	-0.116
HR-SD-BP	-0.069	-0.095	-0.092
RSA adj	-0.084	0.174	0.030
PWV fin	0.023	-0.026	0.098
PVA fin	0.093	-0.166	-0.357
CO ind	-0.040	0.038	-0.065
Ejection sp	0.003	0.081	0.081
SV	0.143	-0.100	0.010
LVET	-0.096	-0.038	0.323
PEP	0.007	-0.193	0.001
R-Z	0.049	0.009	0.048
Heather ind	-0.090	0.111	0.132
SBP	0.052	-0.069	-0.105
DBP	0.099	-0.085	-0.232
TPR	-0.151	-0.355	0.146
TMP fin	-0.057	-0.112	-0.111
TMP foreh	-0.067	0.088	0.051

Note. The three regression analyses were based on the within-subjects variance of task-rest changes of both cardiovascular variables and putative activation components. The putative alpha component was predicted from "alpha-free" group data; the putative beta component, from "beta-free" group data; the putative tau component, from "chol-free" group data. Before application of these coefficients to a new data set, variables have to be standardized ($M = 0$, $SD = 1$).

cardiac output. This pattern of results is similar to the results reported in Table 40, but it suggests a more focused interpretation: Instead of the full pattern of epinephrinergic effects, the within-subjects correlations describe a pure inotropic effect which lacks the chronotropic and dromotropic aspects.

The *putative tau component* (Figure 21c) is associated ($r > | 0.20 |$) with reduced heart rate, prolonged left-ventricular ejection time, reduced diastolic blood pressure and finger skin temperature, lowered P-wave and T-wave amplitudes, ST-depression, shortened relative Q-T time, and largely reduced finger pulse volume amplitudes. The adjusted respiratory sinus arrhythmia is only slightly increased. In many respects, this pattern is just the reverse of the pattern of correlations reported for the putative alpha component. It will be

Table 43. Variable Coefficients (Standard Scores) in the ir-Restricted Model (Task-Rest Response Form) of Cardiovascular Activation Components Derived from Multistage Linear Estimation (Within-Subjects Variance)

Variable	R^2	Activation Component		
		alpha?	beta?	tau?
HR	0.26	0.578	0.154	0.093
P-Ampl	0.30	0.545	0.203	-0.034
T-Ampl	0.15	0.305	-0.223	0.039
P_e-Q_s	0.05	-0.226	-0.149	-0.009
Q-T rel	0.08	0.224	0.144	-0.093
ST-elev	0.24	0.492	0.178	-0.021
HR-SD-BP	0.02	0.059	0.133	-0.077
RSA adj	0.08	-0.206	0.007	0.093
PWV fin	0.07	0.341	0.037	0.246
PVA fin	0.39	-0.567	0.087	-0.889
CO ind	0.12	0.202	0.338	-0.032
Ejection sp	0.03	-0.198	-0.025	-0.205
SV	0.11	0.030	0.347	-0.025
LVET	0.08	-0.099	0.125	0.139
PEP	0.14	-0.173	-0.376	-0.030
R-Z	0.05	0.038	-0.241	0.078
Heather ind	0.12	0.012	0.398	-0.176
SBP	0.09	0.198	0.012	-0.134
DBP	0.06	0.281	-0.121	0.145
TPR	0.19	-0.059	-0.462	0.058
TMP fin	0.08	-0.194	-0.121	-0.295
TMP foreh	0.03	-0.087	0.165	-0.057

Note. These variable coefficients were determined by separate regression analyses for predicting task-rest changes of cardiovascular variables ($M = 0$, $SD = 1$) from scores on putative cardiovascular activation components, using placebo data only. The regression analyses were performed across 2 Difficulty groups x 7 Situations x 24 Subjects = 336 cases after removal of subject means, that is, using within-subjects variance.

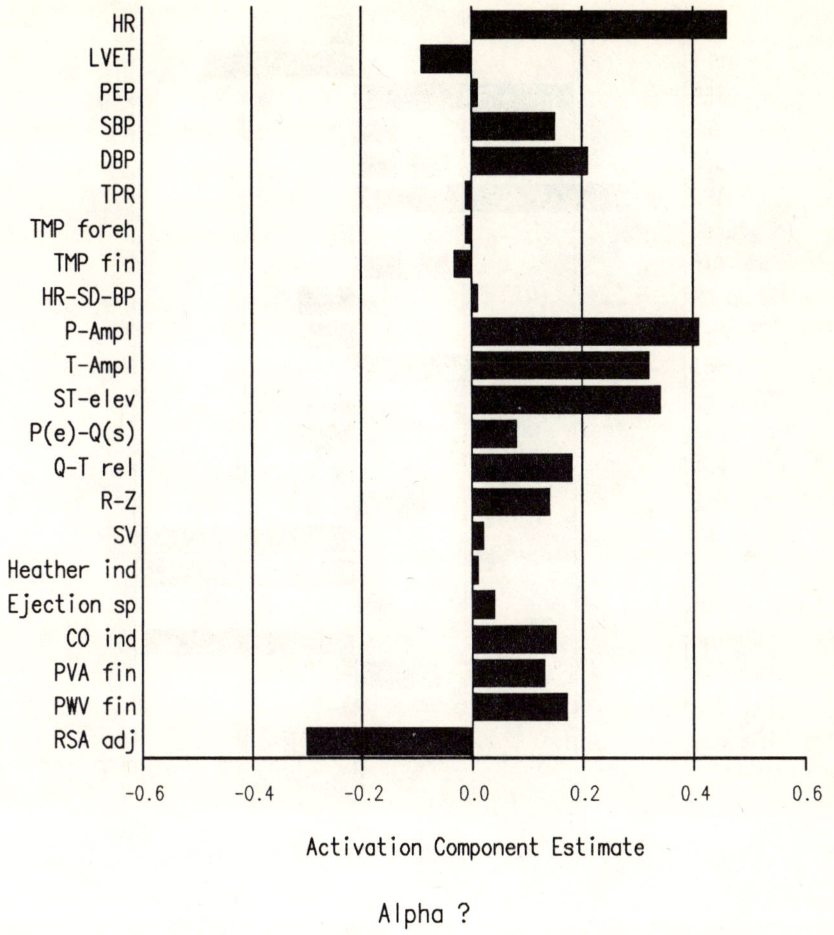

Figure 21 a. Within-subjects correlations between putative cardiovascular activation components derived from multistage linear estimation and task-rest changes of cardiovascular variables (assuming the ir-restricted Model of Cardiovascular Activation Components in the task-rest response form). The correlations are based on 2 Difficulty groups x 7 Situations x 24 Subjects = 336 cases of medication group data. Putative alpha component correlated with the scores of the "alpha-free" medication group. *(Figure continues)*

recalled that the two components correlated highly negatively within the total source of covariation; for the presently employed within-subjects task-rest difference scores, the correlation is still $r = -0.68$.

Perhaps more clearly than the formerly reported results, the present findings suggest caution in the interpretation of the putative alpha and tau components. It might well be that the low-dose receptor blockades employed in Experiment 4,

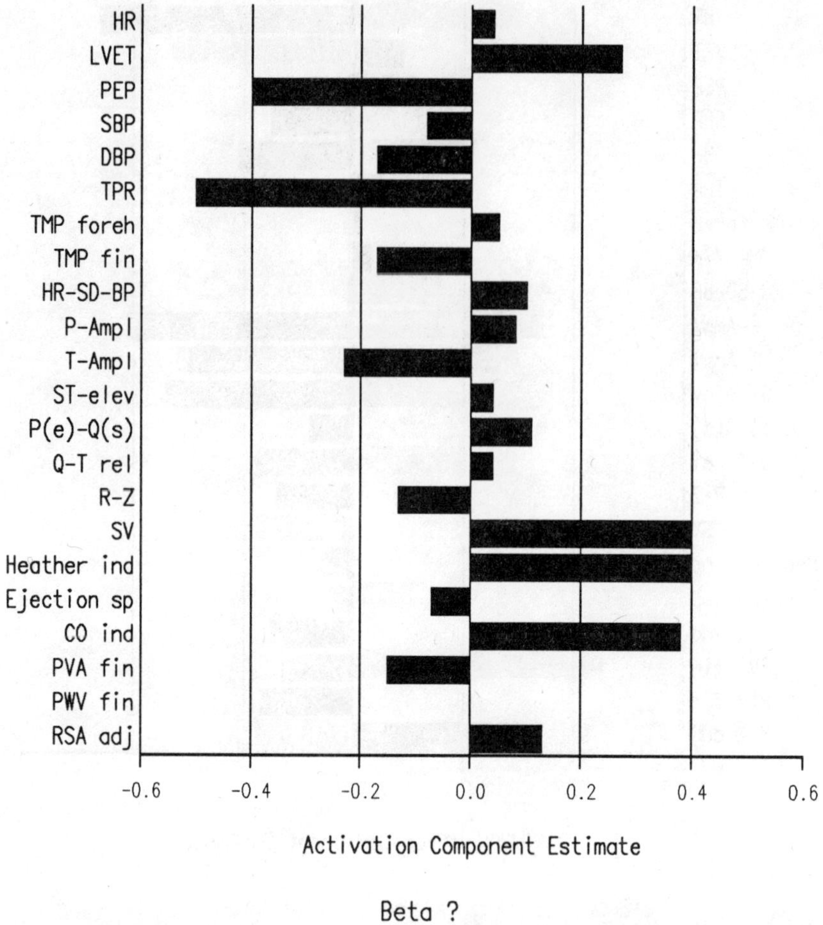

Figure 21 b. Within-subjects correlations between putative cardiovascular activation components derived from multistage linear estimation and task-rest changes of cardiovascular variables Putative beta component correlated with the scores of the "beta-free" medication group. *(continued)*

in particular, the alpha-adrenergic and the cholinergic blocker dosages, were not able to effectively disentangle the strong interactions between alpha-adrenergic and cholinergic activation components.

As does Table 40, Table 43 also reports variable coefficients, that is, estimates of the influence of putative cardiovascular activation components on variables. However, the coefficients reported in the two tables are different in three aspects. First, they refer to between-conditions (Table 40) or within-subjects variance (Table 43). Second, they are raw or standardized coefficients,

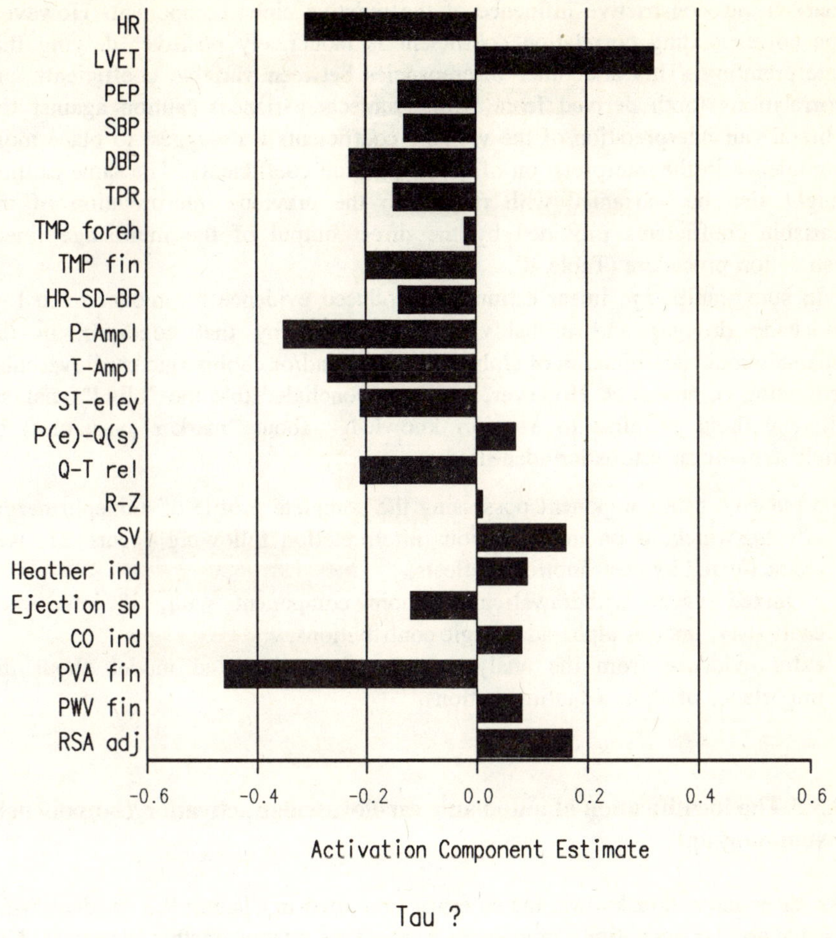

Figure 21 c. Within-subjects correlations between putative cardiovascular activation components derived from multistage linear estimation and task-rest changes of cardiovascular variables. Putative tau component correlated with the scores of the "chol-free" medication group. *(continued)*

respectively. Third, they are derived from the data of all four medication groups or only from placebo data, respectively.

Comparison of the variable coefficients in Table 43 with the correlations reported in Figure 21 shows good overall correspondences. There are, however, some exceptions to this good fit which may highlight the problem of interpreting regression coefficients from a multiple regression analysis with highly correlated predictors. For example, the large negative variable coefficient for finger pulse volume on the putative alpha component would be easily misinterpreted as a marked vasoconstrictive influence of the putative alpha component. However, the corresponding correlation coefficient is moderately positive, defying that interpretation. This and other discrepancies between variable coefficients and correlations (both derived from within-subjects variance) caution against too "literal" an interpretation of the variable coefficients and suggest to place more confidence in the interpretation of the correlation coefficients. The same caution might also be warranted with respect to the previous interpretation of the variable coefficients provided by the direct output of the multistage linear estimation procedure (Table 40).

In sum, multistage linear estimation produced evidence for moderate to low blockade dosages and probably was hampered by that condition in the unambiguous identification of alpha-adrenergic and/or cholinergic cardiovascular activation components. However, it can be concluded that the "blind" analysis (i.e., without recourse to a priori knowledge about "marker" variables) of multistage linear estimation identified

- a putative beta component possessing the complete profile of epinephrinergic effects, which, upon more cautious interpretation following Figure 21, was characterized by clear inotropic effects;
- a mixed vagal withdrawal-chronotropic component with, if interpreted cautiously, unclear alpha-adrenergic contributions;
- extra evidence from the analysis under the r-restricted model about the importance of alpha x tau interactions.

9.3.5 The identification of autonomic cardiovascular activation components: a summing-up

As far as the author knows, the enterprise reported in Chapter 9.3 of identifying cardiovascular activation components is the first attempt in this direction. Not only was it therefore necessary to develop a model of cardiovascular activation (Chapter 5.2) but also to make available or select appropriate statistical tools for its analysis. Furthermore, both the model and the tools had to conform to the general perspective of this book, which calls for the integration of the activation construct into a process-oriented assessment model. As a result, Chapter 9.3 presented various approaches to the description and identification of cardiovascular activation components which need to be integrated in a tentative summing-up.

It should be recalled that under incomplete blockades and with the blockade protocol employed in Experiment 4 (solely dual blockades instead of all combinations of the blockades, see Equations 17), the putative cardiovascular activation components are likely to represent *net effects* of alpha-adrenergic, beta-adrenergic, or cholinergic activation. That is, they describe in vivo regulatory patterns instead of in vitro obtained autonomic organ reactions to isolated receptor stimulations. This characteristic of the present analysis had been particularly noted with respect to the putative components identified by the multistage linear estimation procedure. With this general comment, I can turn to the summary description of the probable effects of cardiovascular activation components on variables.

The effects of an alpha-adrenergic cardiovascular activation probably have been best summarized by the putative alpha component derived by discriminant analysis (DA). The *"alpha-adrenergic" regulatory pattern* (see Table 44) comprises cutaneous vasoconstriction with increases in total peripheral resistance as well as systolic and diastolic blood pressure, reductions in left-ventricular contractility and cardiac output, and slight reductions of chronotropic activity. Signs of cardiac activation are seen in shortened atrial excitation (P_e-Q_s time), slightly reduced preejection periods, and a small withdrawal of cardiac vagal tone. This description is consistent both with the alpha-adrenoceptor blockade effects reported in Table 6 (which also suggested an increased pulse wave velocity, seen only marginally existent in the DA results) and the expectation concerning alpha-adrenergic effects in Table 5. The putative alpha component derived by multistage linear estimation (MSLE) described a more mixed effect of diastolic blood pressure increases and combined chronotropic x vagal withdrawal effects, the latter of which is more consistent with cholinergic deactivation. Indeed, the within-subjects correlations between the putative alpha components derived from MSLE and DA were nearly zero (r = -0.04) but markedly negative (r = -0.46) between the putative MSLE-alpha and the putative DA-tau component.

The effects of a beta-adrenergic cardiovascular activation are likely to be multicomponential. This is suggested by the results of both the redundancy analysis and the DA. Both analyses identified three putative beta components. MSLE was unable to identify more than one putative beta component since the Model of Cardiovascular Activation Components, in accordance with the nonselective beta-blockade used, specified only one beta component. The putative MSLE-beta component yielded perhaps the best description of an inotropic activation (see Table 44). The *"beta-adrenergic" inotropic regulatory pattern* is characterized by increased left-ventricular contractility, augmented stroke volume and cardiac output, increased left-ventricular ejection time, reduced T-wave amplitude, and diminished preejection period. There is also a strong compensatory reduction in total peripheral resistance which is obviously not just produced by the inverse relationship with cardiac output, since finger pulse volume amplitude and finger skin temperature are both reduced.

The multicomponential description of putative beta components derived by DA is also included in Table 44. All three components are characterized by increases in left-ventricular contractility, reduced preejection periods, and slightly increased adjusted respiratory sinus arrhythmia. The first putative beta subcomponent is additionally characterized by increases in ST-elevation and pulse wave velocity, as well as a strong vasoconstriction at the finger, and a temperature increase at the forehead. This first subcomponent might describe a mixed beta-adrenergic x alpha-adrenergic activation. Its variable pattern has some resemblance with the putative MSLE-beta component (within-subjects $r = 0.28$). The second putative beta subcomponent is additionally characterized by a strong finger vasodilatation and a decrease in heart rate variability in the blood pressure band. The third putative beta subcomponent is additionally characterized by increases in heart rate variability in the blood pressure band and a rise of systolic blood pressure. Interestingly, this is the only blood pressure-related putative beta subcomponent.

The effects of a cholinergic cardiovascular activation are similarly captured by the putative MSLE-tau and DA-tau components. The latter description is entered into Table 44 because it represents most clearly the marker variable for tonic cardiac vagal tone, namely respiratory sinus arrhythmia. The *"cholinergic" regulatory pattern* comprises large heart rate reductions, atrial and left-ventricular deactivation but also signs of left-ventricular activation, such as

Table 44. Summary Description of Putative Autonomic Cardiovascular Activation Components

	Activation Component					
Variable	alpha?[a]	beta?[b]	beta1?[a]	beta2?[a]	beta3?[a]	tau?[a]
HR	–	0	+	+	–	–––
P-Ampl	–	0	+	+	–	––
T-Ampl	0	––	+	+	–	––
P_e-Q_s	––	+	0	0	0	++
Q-T rel	–	0	+	+	0	––
ST elev	0	0	++	+	–	––
HR-SD-BP	+	+	+	––	++	0
RSA adj	–	+	+	+	+	+++
PWV fin	0	0	++	0	0	––
PVA fin	–	–	––	+++	+	––
CO ind	––	++	+	0	0	–
Ejection sp	––	0	0	+	+	0
SV	––	++	+	0	+	0
LVET	+	++	0	0	–	++
PEP	–	––	––	–	–	0
R-Z	++	–	––	––	––	––
Heather ind	––	++	++	+	++	0
SBP	++	0	0	0	++	––
DBP	++	–	0	0	–	––
TPR	++	–––	–	0	0	0
TMP fin	–––	–	–––	0	0	–
TMP foreh	++	0	++	–	0	0

Note. Signs in the body of the table indicate the direction and magnitude of the within-subjects correlations reported in Figures 20 and 21. ––– = $r < -0.50$; –– = $r < -0.20$; – = $r < -0.10$; 0 = $r \leq \pm 0.10$; + = $r > 0.10$; ++ = $r > 0.20$; +++ = $r > 0.50$. [a]Derived from discriminant analysis. [b]Derived from multistage linear estimation.

reductions of R-Z time and T-wave amplitude as well as ST-depression, and an indication of cutaneous finger vasoconstriction. Thus, this regulatory pattern represents the picture of a pronounced vagal activation and partial beta-sympathetic withdrawal together with some signs of homeostatic beta-adrenergic and alpha-adrenergic activation. Indications of homeostatic activation upon cholinergic blockade are also revealed by the results of cholinergic blockade studies in Table 6. For example, under atropine Berry et al. (1959) found large heart rate increases as well as decreases in stroke volume and total peripheral resistance (the reverse direction of changes describes the vagal effects). Similarly, under atropine Goldstein and Keiser (1984) found a reduction of plasma norepinephrine.

In conclusion, the attempt at identifying autonomic cardiovascular activation components was successful although it was hampered by low alpha-adrenoceptor and cholinoceptor antagonist dosages. The patterns found in many aspects correspond with the expectations reported in Tables 5 and 6. However, the putative activation components do not reflect the isolated organ reactivity upon specific stimulation but the coordinated systemic cardiovascular behavior including compensatory homeostatic regulations that at first glance might be misunderstood as erroneous representations. The derivation of putative cardiovascular activation components makes it now possible to study some applications of a process-oriented differential psychophysiology on a higher systemic level and in a quantitative fashion.

10 Laboratory Tasks in Cardiovascular Research

The first out of three examples for applied areas of a differential psychophysiology treated in this and the next two chapters deals with the selection and systematization of laboratory tasks in cardiovascular research in the context of behavioral medicine. The motivation behind such an endeavor is the elucidation of the concept of cardiovascular reactivity as a putative risk factor in cardiovascular disease. Krantz and Manuck (1984) discussed this concept and described it as a multifaceted construct covering these main research areas:

- Research on tasks that arouse specific autonomic cardiovascular components. Knowing which tasks are likely to produce specific cardiovascular activations would lead to a more concise development of laboratory analogs of *physico-biological situations* eliciting potentially harmful magnitudes and patterns of cardiovascular reactivity. This line of research would naturally extend into differential-psychophysiological studies focusing on the effects of different *functional situations* varying among persons.
- Research on variables and variable-configurations that are able to measure these cardiovascular activation components. Chapter 9.3 has been devoted to the identification of such variable-configurations. Therefore, the characterization of laboratory tasks will be based on the component operationalizations suggested at the end of Chapter 9.3.
- Research on high-risk compared to low-risk populations or on patients that are already in a medical treatment. This line of inquiry evidently constitutes a necessary complement to research on healthy subjects and could contribute to the validation of the proposed operationalizations of cardiovascular activation components. However, this line of inquiry is beyond the scope of the present treatment.

In the first part of this chapter (Chapter 10.1), empirical studies on the characterization in terms of cardiovascular activation components of laboratory tasks are reviewed. The main conclusion will be that the generally adhered to semi-quantitative, if not even qualitative assessment of reactivity profiles during different tasks constitutes a major weakness that impedes significant progress in the evaluation of cardiovascular task effects. In the second part (Chapter 10.2), the data of Experiment 4 are used to illustrate a quantitative approach to the characterization of task effects on cardiovascular activation components.

10.1 A Review of Task Characterizations: Non-Formalized Approaches

One way to characterize tasks designed to elicit cardiovascular reactivity is by the apparent primary source of the stressor, as suggested by the distinction between physical or psychological (or "mental") stress tasks (Brown, Szabo, & Seraganian, 1988; Buell et al., 1986; Eliot, 1988; Mulder, Mulder, & Veldman, 1985; Rüddel, Langewitz, Schächinger, Schmieder, & Schulte, 1988). Although this distinction quickly leads to principal epistemological problems (see Chapter 2.1), it is widely accepted. Steptoe (1985) discusses several other ways of conceptualizing cardiovascular stress tasks, which might lead to different strategies of task selection in a particular research application. First, laboratory tasks may represent miniature analogs of everyday life; such a view would lead to characterizing tasks in terms of classes of different psychosocial demands. Second, tasks may be grouped according to the diagnostic purpose for which they are validated, for example the ergometer test to determine vital capacity. Third, certain dimensions of task demands may be used to order tasks. Fourth, tasks may be classified according to the elicited response profiles of both psychological and physiological variables.

The characterization of tasks on the basis of average elicited physiological responses (i.e., by the modal situation) has been the preferred line of research in this domain. In the remainder of this section, a brief review of some empirical results will be discussed for some frequently employed laboratory tasks.

10.1.1 Mental arithmetic

Results for the mental arithmetic task are presented in greater detail than for the subsequently discussed tasks. The longer presentation here may suffice to substantiate the general point with regard to systematizing tasks by their response profiles.

Catecholamines. Mental arithmetic produces a substantial excretion of catecholamines from adrenergic nerve terminals and from the adrenal medulla. Compared to other tasks, for example, knee bends, hand dynamometer, venipuncture, cold pressor (Ward et al., 1983), or exercise (Fibiger, Singer, & Miller, 1984), the ratio of excreted epinephrine to norepinephrine and the absolute levels of epinephrine in the plasma during mental arithmetic were especially large. However, Dimsdale (1984) found on the contrary a highly significant increase in norepinephrine but not in epinephrine. The beta-adrenergic antagonist propranolol hardly changes catecholamine levels, and the alpha-adrenergically mediated vasoconstriction is consequently unmasked under propranolol (Bonelli, 1982). The effect on the cardiovascular system of the substantial catecholamine excretion is even amplified by a reduced sensitivity of the baroreceptors (Brooks et al., 1978) in that an elevated cardiac activity is maintained in spite of a large pressor response.

Cardiovascular variables, drug-free conditions. The following cardiovascular effects have been demonstrated under mental arithmetic. Compared to rest, heart rate and both systolic and diastolic blood pressure are elevated (Allwood, Barcroft, Hayes & Hirsjärvi, 1959;, Bonelli, 1982; Corse, Manuck, Cantwell, Giardani & Matthews, 1982; v.Eiff et al., 1969; Jennings & Follansbee, 1985), as is cardiac output (Guazzi et al., 1975; Schulte & v.Eiff, 1985; Ulrych, 1969), and total peripheral resistance is reduced (Guazzi et al., 1975; Schmidt, 1982; Schulte & v.Eiff, 1985). This pattern of reactivity resembles one of a beta-adrenergic activation--with the exception of the elevated diastolic blood pressure. However, this elevation could be explained by an overcompensation for the drop in total peripheral resistance by a large increase in cardiac output (Schulte & v.Eiff, 1985). In particular, Brod (1982) suggests the compensation of renal and cutaneous vasoconstriction by a vasodilatation in skelettal muscle areas, with later additional compensatory changes in cardiac output.

Cardiovascular variables, beta-blockade conditions. With the blockade of beta adrenoceptors it has been shown on several occasions that beta-adrenergic activation is a major component of the cardiovascular response pattern to mental arithmetic, but probably not the only one. While there are common results reported in the literature, there are also notable discrepancies. With regard to *responses* from rest to mental arithmetic tasks, v.Eiff et al. (1969), for example, found that in comparison to placebo heart rate increases were attenuated under propranolol, but not the increases in systolic and diastolic blood pressure. Similarly, Guazzi et al. (1975) observed under propranolol no change in heart rate but large systolic (24 mmHg) and diastolic (16 mmHg) blood pressure increases. Bonelli (1982) reported that increases in heart rate, cardiac output, and systolic, but not diastolic, blood pressure recorded under placebo were significantly reduced by propranolol. Schmidt (1982) as well found persistent cardiovascular effects of mental arithmetic under propranolol: The average blood pressure rose from rest to task by approximately 10 mmHg and the heart rate by approximately 7 bpm, and at the same time the total peripheral resistance increased. Mixed results have also been obtained with respect to physiological *task levels*. During mental arithmetic, Guazzi et al. (1975) found under propranolol in comparison to placebo lowered heart rate and systolic blood pressure, and an elevated total peripheral resistance, while diastolic blood pressure remained constant. V.Eiff et al. (1969), however, reported a significantly reduced heart rate, and attenuated systolic and diastolic blood pressures, whereas Bonelli (1982) noted as well a reduced heart rate but elevated systolic and diastolic blood pressures.

Summary. One group of researchers maintains that cardiovascular reactivity during mental arithmetic is strongly determined by beta-adrenergic activation (Corse et al., 1982; Eliot, 1988; Engel, 1986; Guazzi et al., 1975; Jennings & Follansbee, 1985; Neus & v.Eiff, 1985; Schulte & v.Eiff, 1985). Yet considerable cardiovascular effects persist during mental arithmetic under beta-blockade. These may be explained either by an incomplete beta-blockade or through an "unmasking" of alpha-adrenergically mediated vasoconstriction as seen in increases in peripheral resistance and diastolic blood pressure under beta-blockade. Thus, another group of researchers holds that mental arithmetic produces a mixed beta- and alpha-adrenergic activation (Allwood et al., 1959; Andrén, 1982; Bonelli, 1982; Goldstein & Shapiro, 1988; Krantz & Manuck, 1984; Light, 1985; Schmieder, Rüddel, Neus, Messerli, & v.Eiff, 1987). A third group of researchers assumes participation of the parasympathetic nervous system (reduction of vagal activation) either in combination with beta-adrenergic activation (Grossman et al., 1990; Schmidt, 1982) or as a mixture of all three activation components (Allen, Obrist, Sherwood, & Crowell, 1987; Somsen, 1985).

10.1.2 Cold pressor

Even in the case of this purely "physical stimulus", the physiological reaction may be considerably influenced by perceived threat (Dembroski, MacDougall, Herd, & Shields, 1979), previous experience, anticipation of pain, etc. The stronger such additional factors, the more pronounced the beta-adrenergic reactivity (Buell et al., 1986).

Among the tasks under investigation (mental arithmetic, knee bends, hand dynamometer, venipuncture, cold pressor) Ward et al. (1983) found with cold pressor the most marked concentration of norepinephrine in the plasma; epinephrine, on the other hand, was only slightly increased. The cardiovascular reactivity displayed the following profile: increases in heart rate, systolic and diastolic blood pressures as well as in total peripheral resistance, but only slight changes in cardiac output (Brod, 1982; Buell et al., 1986; Schulte & v.Eiff, 1985).

Beta-blockade does not reduce the blood pressure reaction to cold pressor; this occurs only after an additional alpha-blockade (Prichard, 1984). The cold pressor task is therefore often categorized as predominantly alpha-adrenergic (Buell et al., 1986; Eliot, 1988; Prichard, 1984; Schulte & v.Eiff, 1985).

Guazzi et al. (1975) observed that the reduction in heart rate and cardiac output under cold pressor was blunted after propranolol but not after atropine, which led the authors to conclude that the myocardial sympathetic suppression could not have been elicited by a reflexive vagal activation but by a reduced adrenergic myocardial tonus following the alpha-adrenergic activation. These authors, as well as Allen et al. (1987), classify the cold pressor task as mixed alpha-adrenergic and beta-adrenergic.

10.1.3 Reaction time task

The description of the cardiovascular reactivity during a reaction time task again depends upon the details of the task protocol. Should the imperative stimulus occur at unpredictable timepoints, beta-adrenergic effects will dominate. For example, in a shock-avoidance reaction time task with no warning signal, Langer et al. (1985) observed that the rise in heart rate was blocked completely with propranolol. However, if the imperative stimulus is preceded by a warning signal, the heart decelerates during the anticipatory interval. This phasic response is vagally mediated because it can be blocked by atropine (Obrist et al., 1974). Accordingly, the reaction time task is described as either beta-adrenergic (Neus & v.Eiff, 1985; Pollak & Obrist, 1988), or primarily vagal (Somsen, van der Molen, Boomsma, & Orlebeke, 1985), or mixed beta-adrenergic and vagal (Obrist, 1985). Jennings (1982), too, speaks of the effects of vagal activation that is however supplemented by an alpha-adrenergic activation when the speed the tasks are performed and the effort are high.

10.1.4 Loud noise

The effects of ten-minute 95-100 dB broad-band noise were extensively investigated by Andrén (1982; see also Buell et al., 1986), who found marked increases in the total peripheral resistance and in the diastolic blood pressure. These responses were primarily alpha-adrenergic because after blockade of alpha1 receptors by prazosin the peripheral resistance was lowered, as expected. However, the alpha-blockade produced a shift towards a beta-adrenergic activation as seen in an increased cardiac output. Consequently, the blood pressure did not drop. The combined alpha1- and beta-blockade by labetolol prevented an increase in the systolic blood pressure and the peripheral resistance; it did not, however, prevent an increase in diastolic blood pressure. This effect remains as yet unexplained.

The cardiovascular effects of short tones or bursts of white noise probably permit a temporal separation of different activation components. Turpin and Siddle (1979, 1983) reported that the first presentation of a loud tone (90 or 105 dBA) evoked a tachycardia with a short latency of 5 seconds ("startle response"), a subsequent bradycardia ("orienting response"), and a delayed tachycardia with a latency of about 30 seconds ("defense reaction"). The delayed tachycardia was accompanied by a peripheral vasoconstriction and forearm-vasodilatation (Turpin & Siddle, 1978) and was interpreted to be neurohumorally mediated, whereas the "startle response" was explained as a decline in vagal activation with a concurrent sympathetic activation. These interpretations have not as yet been evinced through experimental receptor blockades.

10.1.5 Speech activity

During some laboratory tasks, for example, in some versions of the mental arithmetic task, speech activity is required of the subjects; or, a "stress interview" should induce certain affects. In these cases, the physiological responses will include the effects of speech activity in addition to the actual effect of interest. For this reason it is pertinent to find the cardiovascular activation components elicited by speech.

Engel (1986) compared a mental arithmetic task requiring continuous report of results with simply counting aloud from 1 to 100. Counting alone led to a heart rate increase of 7 bpm, which was reduced to 4 bpm by the (nonselective) beta-blocker pindolol. The mental and affective load of the combined task led to a heart rate increase of 23 bpm, which was reduced to 10 bpm under the beta-blocker (data derived from Figure 7.6 in Engel, 1986). This result suggests that mental load and speech requirement have distinguishable cardioacceleratory effects. During nonstressful speech, Ulrych (1969) found increases in heart rate, stroke volume, cardiac output, and mean arterial blood pressure, whereas the total peripheral resistance slightly fell. Under the (nonselective) beta-blocker oxprenolol the peripheral resistance increased, while cardiac output was less elevated and stroke volume fell. Blood pressure and heart rate increases were not altered. Ulrych concluded that quiet conversation led partly to beta-adrenergic activation, but he also mentioned the possible release of vagal tone.

10.1.6 Handgrip

At the core of the response to isometric exercise is a rise in blood pressure (Buell et al., 1986; Shanks, 1984; Urbaszek & Modersohn, 1983), which functions in opposition to the reduced effective perfusion pressures in the region of intense muscle contraction. Central and peripheral mechanisms are in play here: vasodilatation in active muscles, increases in heart rate and ventricular contractility, release of norepinephrine, vasoconstriction in the viscera, kidneys, and non-contracting muscles, all of which allows the cardiac output to climb in spite of the augmented total peripheral resistance.

Studies of the handgrip task using pharmacological receptor blockades have shown substantial vagal activation. For example, Flessas and Ryan (1983) compared the chronotropic effects of the handgrip and of infused atropine in patients under chronic propranolol treatment. A significant Pearson correlation ($r = 0.726$; $n = 11$) was obtained between the handgrip and the atropine heart rate changes during rest. It was interpreted to indicate a vagal withdrawal in the chronotropic response to isometric exercise. This interpretation was supported by Seiler, Mehmel, and Krayenbühl (1974; see Figure 8) where the heart rate increase during handgrip could be blocked only after giving atropine in addition to propranolol (cf. Pollak & Obrist, 1988). In addition, a significant beta-adrenergic effect was noted in the blunted response of the cardiac output index to handgrip under propranolol alone in comparison to a drug-free control handgrip. Under atropine plus propranolol, the significant alpha-adrenergic contributions to the handgrip task were revealed by the remaining increases of mean blood pressure and total peripheral resistance from rest to task. McAllister (1979) was able to completely exclude such pressor effects through the combined alpha- and beta-blockade by phentolamin and propranolol. Grossman et al. (1990) report marked reductions of respiratory sinus arrhythmia during handgrip. While these studies indicate fairly clearly that isometric exercise stimulates alpha-adrenergic and beta-adrenergic activity, as well as vagal withdrawal (cf. Buell et al., 1986), the handgrip task is sometimes referred to as predominantly alpha-adrenergic (e.g., Eliot, 1988).

10.1.7 Conclusions

The preceding short review of attempts at categorizing laboratory tasks in terms of cardiovascular activation components does not convey the impression of an already achieved systematization (see Table 45 for a summary). The physiological response characterizations of single tasks vary sometimes across the range of descriptions for all of the tasks discussed. In the same vein, task specificity with respect to cardiovascular activation components appears to be disappointingly low. Several factors conceivably contribute to this inconsistency (cf. Schneiderman, Weiss, & Kaufmann, 1989, pp. x-xi):

- the rudimentary comparison of physiological response profiles from different experimental conditions,
- the lack of task standardization (apparatus, instructions, procedure, experimenter conduct; environments),
- differences in the set of physiological variables and their quantification,
- differences in pharmacological receptor antagonists, their dosage, application, and central effects,
- differences in the subject population, subject motivation, or perception of threat,
- disregard of large individual differences in physiological levels and direction of responding (problematic with small-*n* research).

Table 45. Review of Characterizations of Laboratory Tasks in Terms of Cardiovascular Activation Components

Mental Arithmetic Task
Beta-adrenergic
Corse et al., 1982; Eliot, 1988; Engel, 1986; Guazzi et al., 1975; Jennings & Follansbee, 1985; Neus & v.Eiff, 1985; Schulte & v.Eiff, 1985.
Alpha- and beta-adrenergic
Allwood et al., 1959; Andrén, 1982; Bonelli, 1982; Goldstein & Shapiro, 1988; Krantz & Manuck, 1984; Light, 1985; Schmieder et al., 1987.
Beta-adrenergic, cholinergic
Grossman et al., 1990; Schmidt, 1982.
Alpha- and beta-adrener#gic, cholinergic
Allen et al., 1987; Somsen, 1985.
Cold Pressor
Alpha-adrenergic
Buell et al., 1986; Eliot, 1988; Prichard, 1984; Schulte & v.Eiff, 1985.
Alpha- and beta-adrenergic
Guazzi et al., 1975; Allen et al., 1987.
Reaction Time
Beta-adrenergic
Neus & v.Eiff, 1985; Pollak & Obrist, 1988.
Cholinergic
Somsen, 1985.
Alpha-adrenergic, cholinergic
Jennings, 1982.
Beta-adrenergic, cholinergic
Obrist, 1985.
Loud Noise
(Pattern depends on the particular time sample used)
Alpha- and beta-adrenergic, cholinergic
Andrén, 1982.
Beta-adrenergic, cholinergic
Turpin & Siddle, 1983.
Speech
Beta-adrenergic, cholinergic
Ulrych, 1969.
Handgrip
Alpha-adrenergic
Eliot, 1988.
Alpha- and beta-adrenergic
McAllister, 1979.
Beta-adrenergic, cholinergic
Flessas & Ryan, 1983; Pollak & Obrist, 1988.
Alpha- and beta-adrenergic, cholinergic
Seiler et al., 1974.

The next chapter focuses on the first of these shortcomings and attempts to illustrate a possible solution to the issue of response profile comparisons of laboratory tasks.

10.2 Task Characterization with Putative Cardiovascular Activation Components

Before task characterizations with the aid of putative cardiovascular activation components are reported, results from univariate analyses on the basis of single physiological variables will be presented (Chapter 10.2.1). Then follows the componential description of the tasks (Chapter 10.2.2) and finally the intertask comparison in terms of putative cardiovascular activation components (Chapter 10.2.3).

10.2.1 Analyses by physiological variables

The design of Experiment 4 has been described in Chapter 8.4.3. The overall design was a Difficulty (2) x Subjects (24) x Medications (4) x Experimental Conditions (22) setup with repeated measurements on Medications (permutated over Sessions) and Experimental Conditions. Subjects were randomly assigned to Difficulty groups and one of the 24 possible medication sequences across the four sessions. The sequence of experimental conditions was fixed.

For 16 selected variables, raw data of Session 1 (collapsed over Difficulty groups) are shown in Figure 22. A set of four analyses of variance was conducted on prestimulus, task, poststimulus, and task-prestimulus difference scores with the design factors mentioned above (using, of course, 7 instead of 22 levels on the Experimental Conditions factor, i.e., one of the four scores per task period). The two repeated-measures factors and their interactions were analyzed with multivariate tests (Vasey & Thayer, 1987). Tables 46-49 give the results of these analyses.

The analysis of variance on prestimulus scores (Table 46) yielded, with the exception of one variable, no significant Difficulty effects. This result was expected because the difficulty variation concerned the tasks themselves. This test was therefore a check on the comparability of the two groups of subjects in terms of resting levels. Resting levels of 23 of the 37 variables (62%) were significantly affected by the different medications, with largest *F*-values seen for heart rate, P_e-Q_s time, and pulse wave velocity at the finger. Significant condition effects were obtained for 22 variables (59%) indicating varying resting levels over the course of the experiment, which in some cases (most markedly

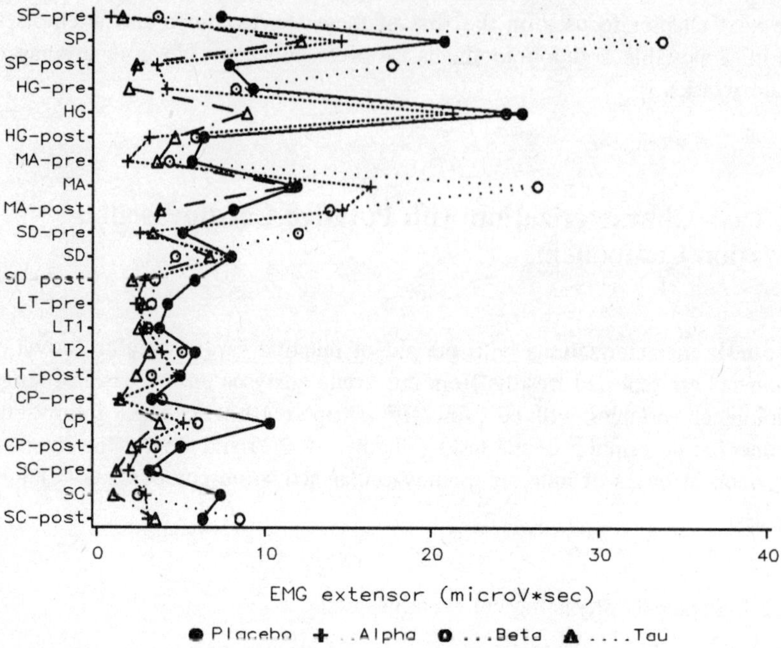

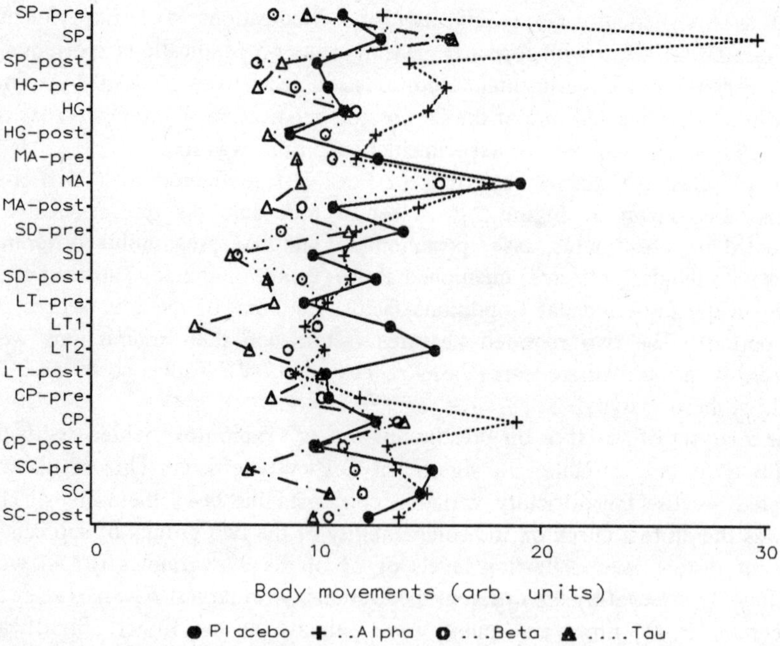

Figure 22. Condition x medication raw data of selected variables during session 1 (placebo group). *(Figure continues)*

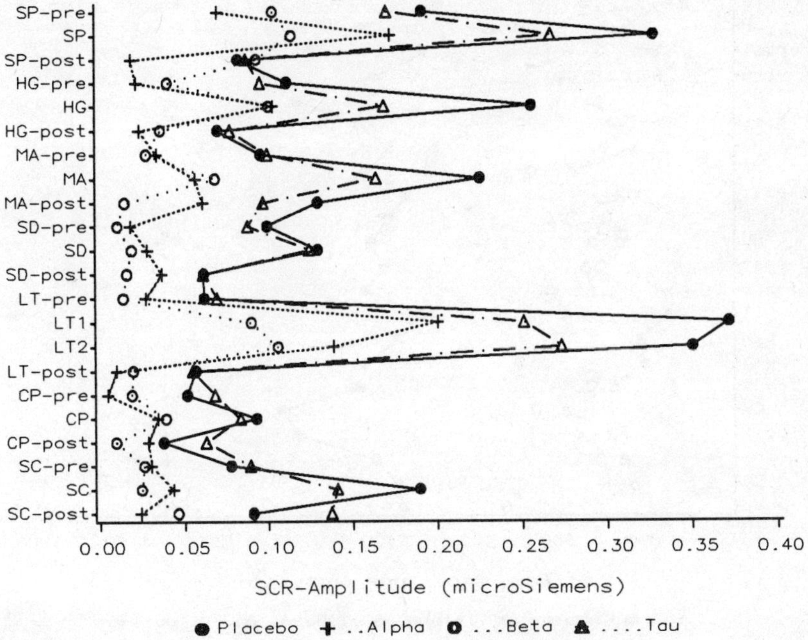

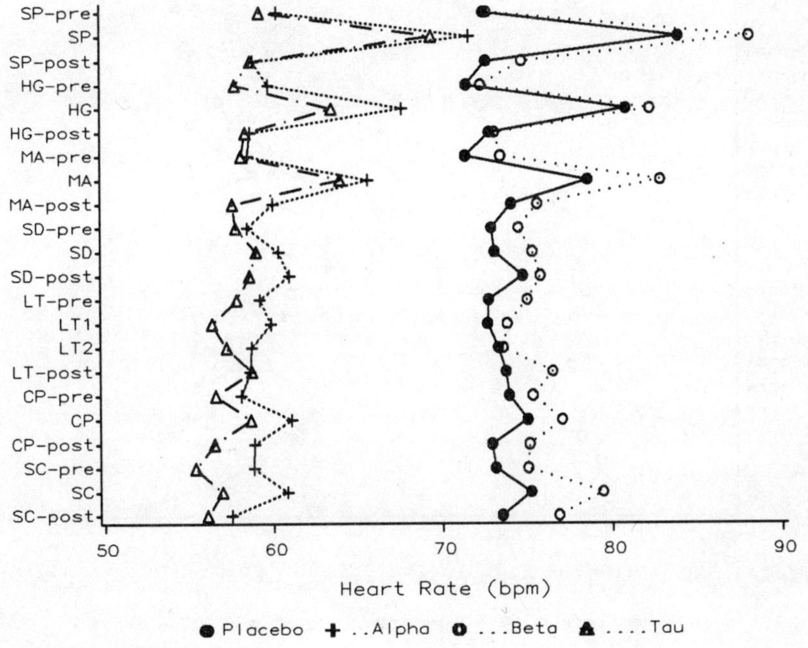

Figure 22 *(continued).*

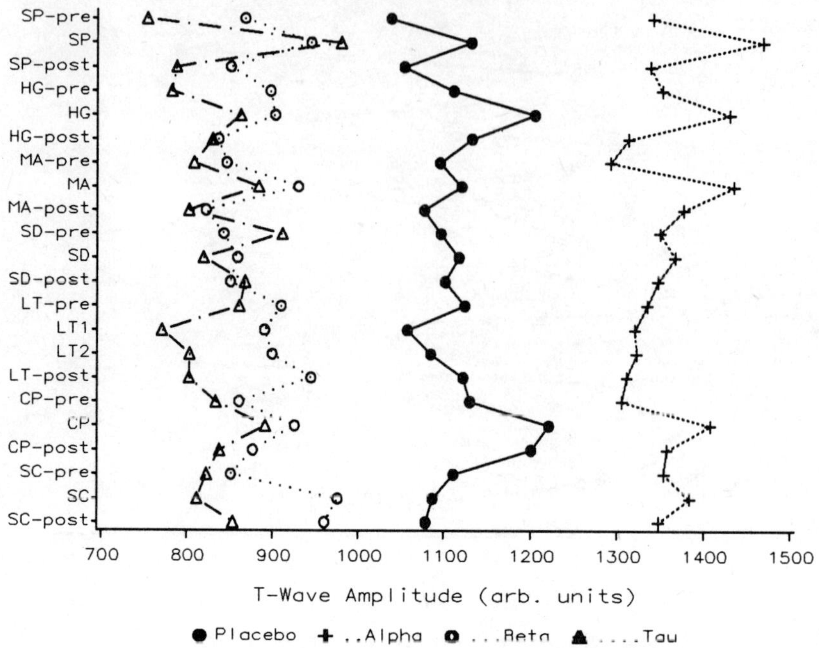

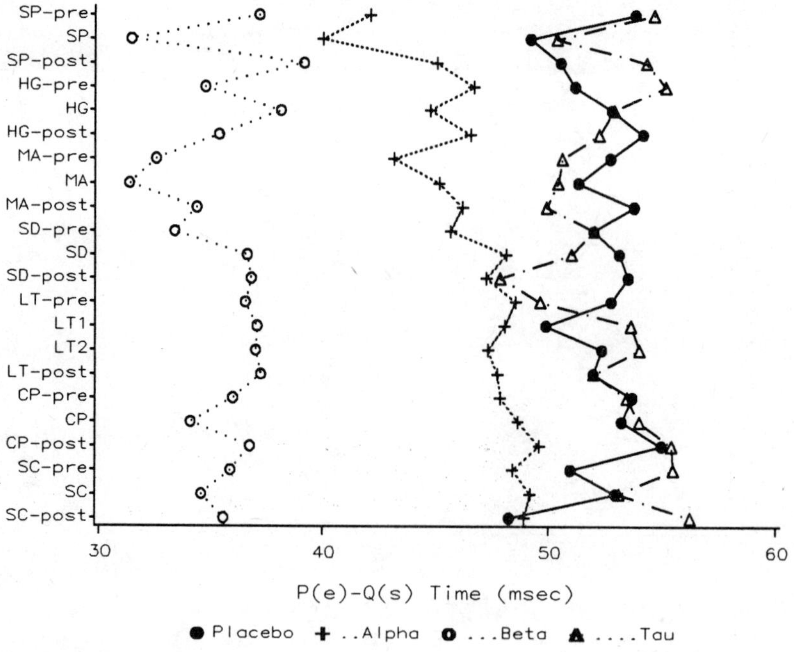

Figure 22 *(continued).*

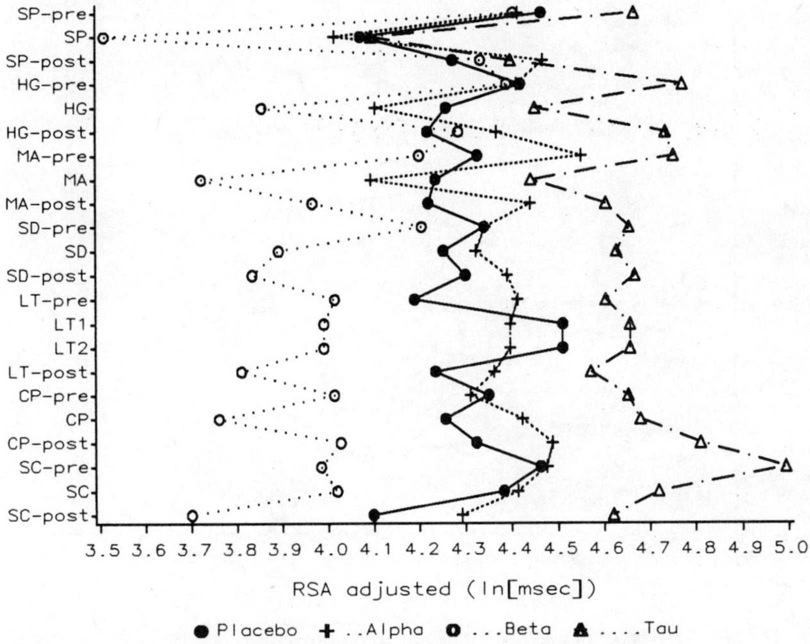

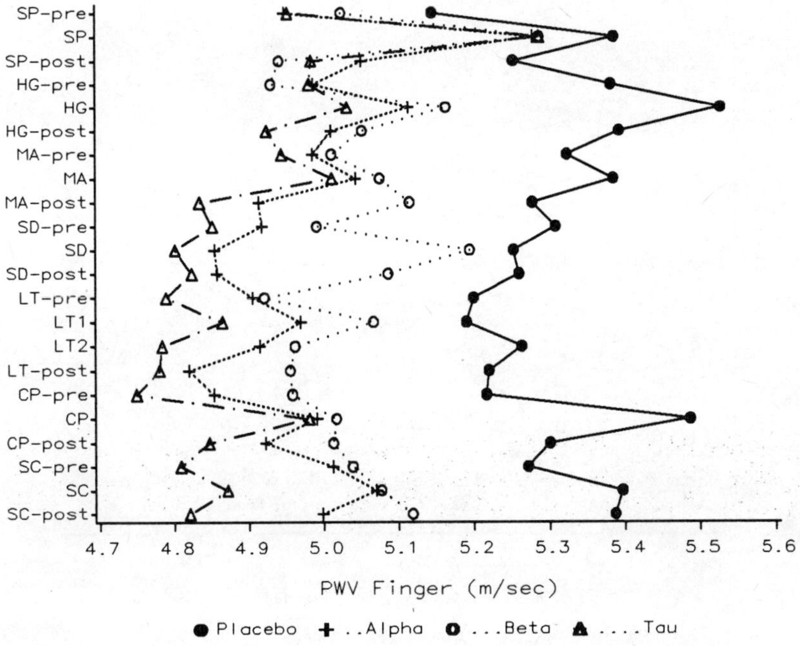

Figure 22 *(continued).*

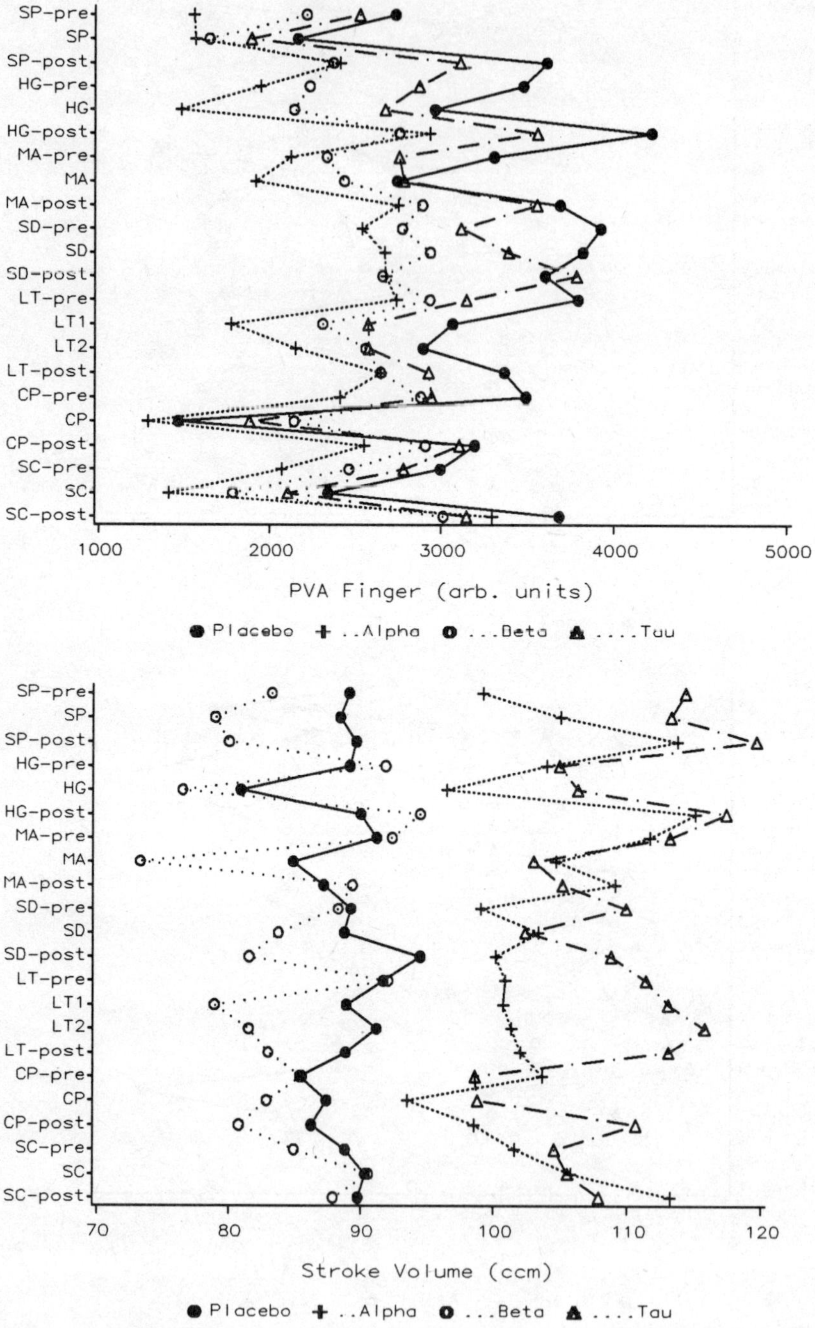

Figure 22 *(continued)*.

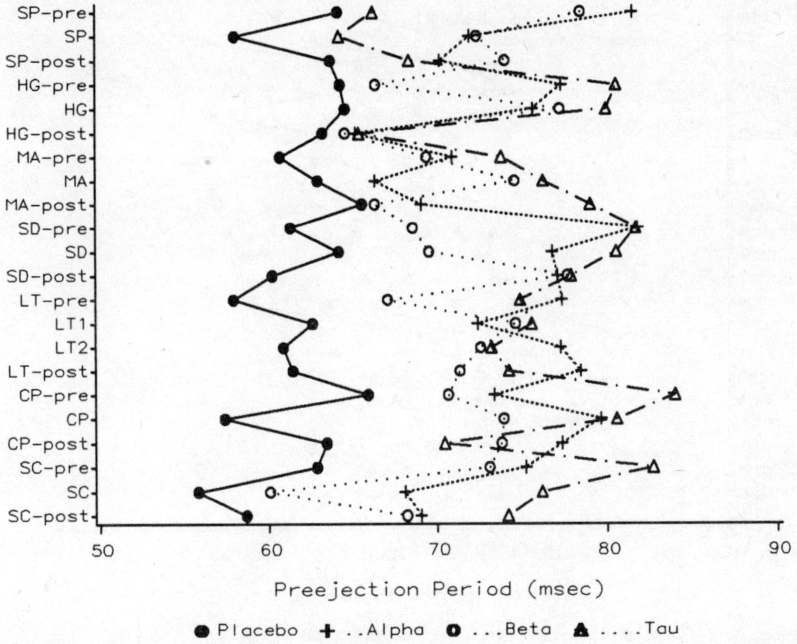

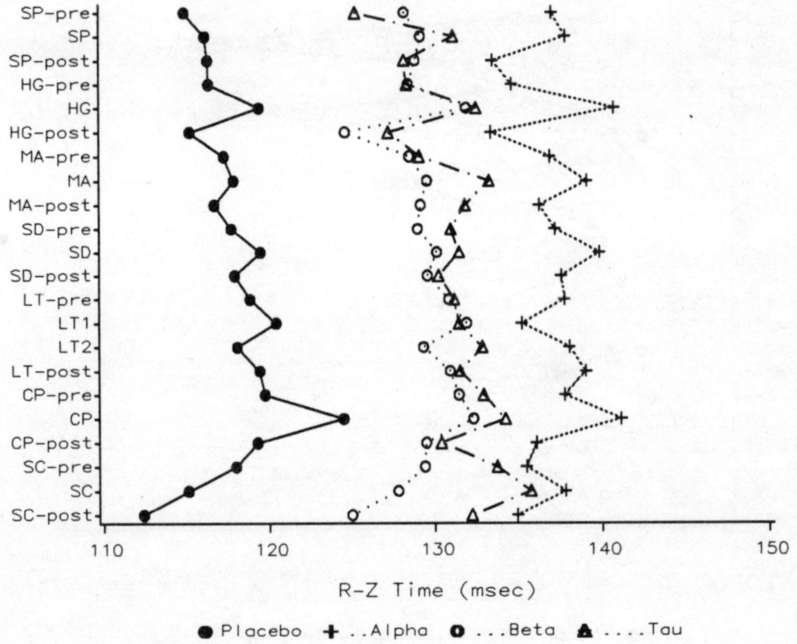

Figure 22 *(continued).*

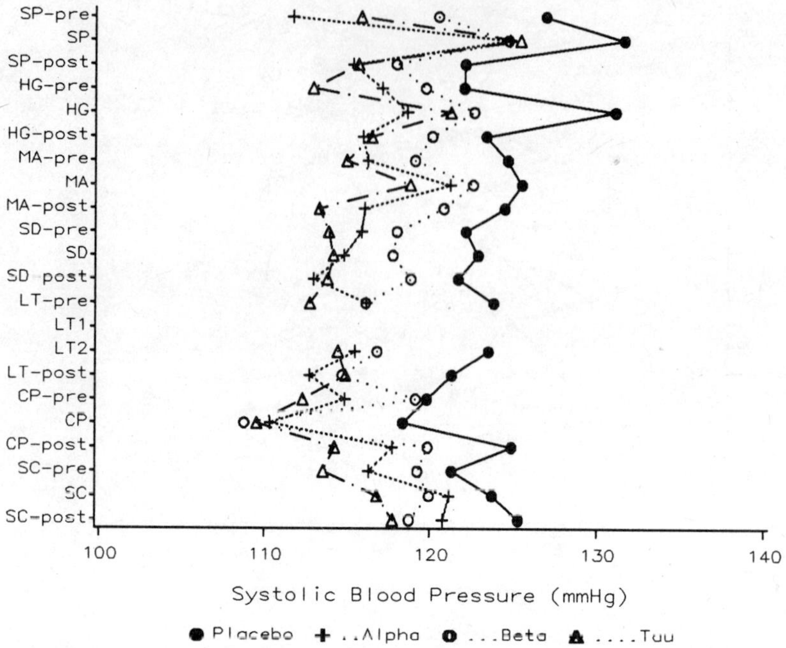

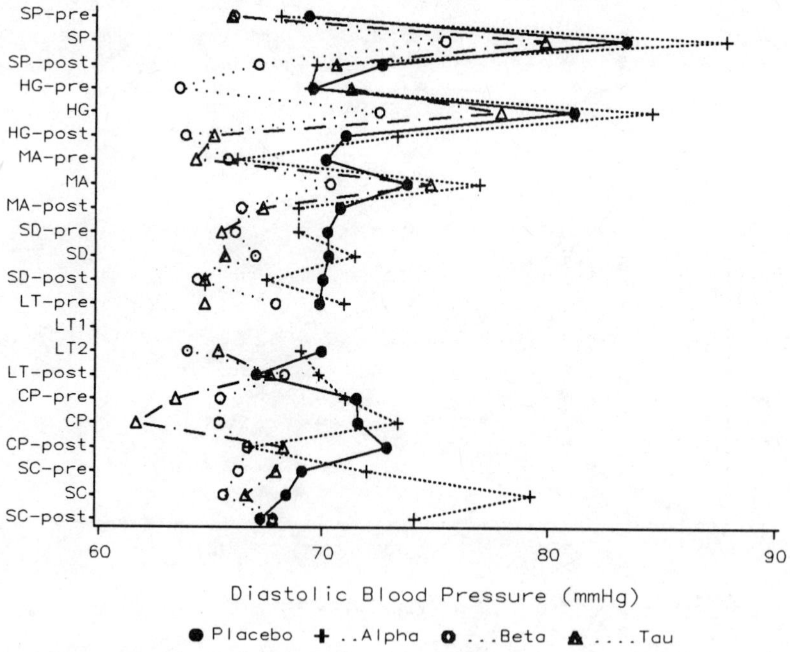

Figure 22 *(continued).*

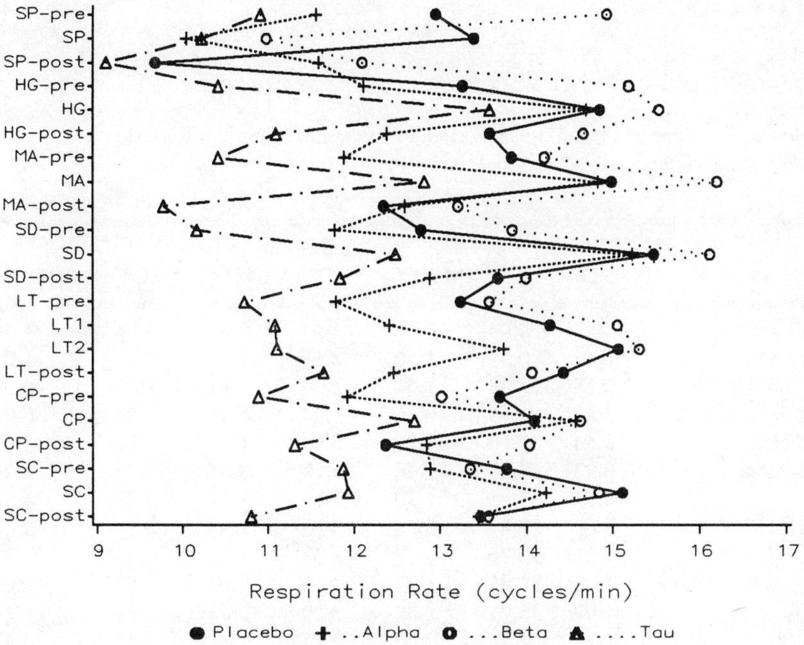

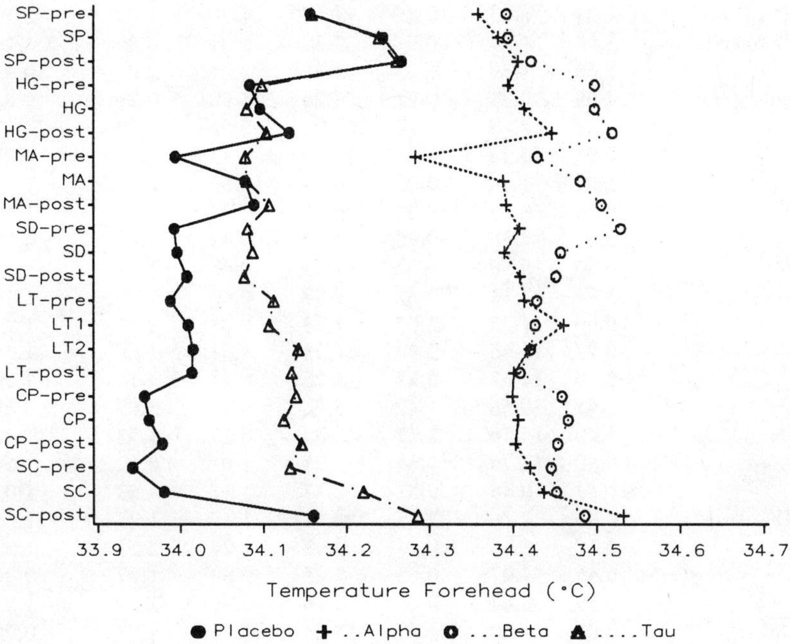

Figure 22 *(continued).*

Table 46. *F*-Values of Physiological Variables in the Difficulty x Medication x Conditions Design (Prestimulus Scores)

	Effect						
Variables	D[a]	M[be]	MxD[be]	C[ce]	CxD[ce]	MxC[de]	MxCxD[de]
EMG ext	0.87	0.94	0.88	**3.05**	0.43	0.64	1.21
EMG fr	0.12	0.39	1.53	**2.59**	1.33	1.56	1.03
Body mov	0.15	**22.38**	1.50	**2.54**	1.81	1.03	0.93
Eyeblinks	2.87	1.05	0.56	**3.24**	0.76	1.94	0.94
SCR-No.	0.54	**4.16**	0.20	**5.93**	1.33	0.62	0.64
SCR-Ampl	0.93	**6.29**	0.70	**6.58**	0.34	1.23	1.21
HR	0.02	**45.63**	1.39	1.88	**2.71**	**4.28**	0.68
P-Ampl	0.00	**11.47**	0.68	0.63	1.92	**2.16**	0.68
T-Ampl	0.11	**10.76**	1.67	**2.37**	1.91	0.89	1.07
P_s-Q_s	1.72	**25.05**	1.27	0.65	0.04	0.60	1.07
P_e-Q_s	1.09	**35.75**	1.32	2.20	2.03	1.71	1.14
Q-T rel	1.92	**7.72**	0.50	2.23	1.19	1.81	0.42
ST-elev	0.04	**6.88**	0.31	1.66	**3.20**	1.56	0.36
HR-SD-BP	1.31	**6.83**	0.21	1.17	1.20	1.00	1.74
HR-SD-Resp	1.98	1.24	0.94	**2.37**	0.97	0.87	1.20
RSA	2.68	1.69	0.45	**2.58**	2.29	0.80	0.95
RSA adj	**4.09**	0.73	0.93	**4.24**	1.90	0.96	0.61
PWV rad	0.21	**14.45**	**4.12**	1.99	0.56	0.97	1.17
PWV fin	0.02	**34.76**	1.45	**10.00**	1.43	**2.53**	1.28
PVA rad	1.07	1.04	0.05	0.54	0.89	**2.14**	1.18
PVA fin	0.04	0.82	2.23	**26.91**	0.51	1.05	1.14
CO	0.01	**7.58**	0.90	1.79	0.44	1.41	0.89
CO ind	0.56	**6.56**	1.22	1.79	0.66	1.31	1.18
Ejection sp	1.74	**7.12**	0.62	**7.87**	0.42	1.76	1.14
SV	0.00	1.22	2.07	**2.53**	0.64	1.17	1.22
LVET	0.77	**15.60**	2.20	2.28	1.31	1.66	1.69
PEP	0.06	**14.32**	**3.21**	1.25	0.58	**2.57**	1.59
R-Z	1.41	**30.66**	1.42	**5.72**	0.76	**3.07**	0.68
Heather ind	1.10	**14.76**	2.67	**3.83**	0.29	1.53	1.40
SBP	0.40	**12.76**	1.84	2.25	1.01	0.82	1.54
MBP	0.14	0.46	0.51	2.17	1.11	1.52	1.02
DBP IV	0.00	2.26	2.15	**4.17**	1.17	1.34	1.15
DBP	0.57	**6.14**	0.14	**3.07**	1.24	**2.57**	1.33
TPR	0.45	**4.27**	0.88	**4.25**	0.89	1.08	0.70
Resp rate	0.09	0.84	0.62	**2.70**	0.48	1.11	1.35
TMP fin	0.07	1.19	1.31	**13.26**	**3.31**	1.02	0.98
TMP foreh	0.00	0.48	0.50	**5.24**	0.52	**2.09**	0.42

Note. D = Difficulty; M = Medication; C = Condition. Boldface numbers: $p < .05$. [a]$df = 1, 46$. [b]$df = 3, 44$. [c]$df = 6, 41$. [d]$df = 18, 29$. [e]F derived from Wilks' lambda.

for finger skin temperature) was caused by linear and quadratic trends. This finding suggested to study task effects with task-prestimulus change scores. The Medication x Condition interaction, which was significant for eight variables (22%), indicated the presence of moderating effects of the medication on changes in resting levels.

The analysis of variance on task level scores (Table 47) showed significant difficulty effects only for few variables. Medication effects were obtained for exactly the same variables as in the analysis on prestimulus scores. Thus, the medications had an outstanding effect on physiological levels. The condition effect was significant for 33 variables, that is, the tasks were accompained by clearly varying levels of activation. However, this result has to be evaluated on the background of the varying resting levels demonstrated above. Therefore, the effect of differential task-elicited activations has to be judged by difference scores (see below). An indication of differential task effects with different difficulty versions of the tasks was suggested by the magnitude of significant Conditions x Difficulty interactions, the number of which found for task level scores (26) clearly exceeded that for prestimulus scores (3). In contrast, the influence of medications on condition task levels was not larger than on prestimulus scores (ten versus eight significant Medication x Conditions interactions, respectively), which again attests to the obviously predominant influence of medications on physiological levels.

Task reactivities of 13 variables (35%) were influenced by task difficulty (Table 48). As expected from the previous results, medication effects were less pertinent for reactivities (eight significant medication effects) than for task or resting levels (23 significant effects). All variables but one exhibited significant condition effects which affirms that the tasks elicited different magnitudes of activation. In terms of reactivity, the difficulty variation was differently effective for the tasks: 21 variables responded differently to the difficulty variations of the seven tasks. Differential reactivities of variables under different medication x condition combinations (i.e., the effect that different medications changed the physiological reacitivities for different taks) was seen for only nine variables (24%).

The pattern of poststimulus score results (Table 49) was very much like that of the prestimulus scores. Only the number of significant condition effects paralleled (and even exceeded) that of task levels. That is, poststimulus periods presumably were strongly influenced by the task periods themselves, which was to be expected since (with the exception of the sentence completion task) these periods were not separated by other conditions.

Of the numerous follow-up tests performed, only a few selected will be reported here. The profile of physiological reactivity elicited by the tasks is further elucidated by Tables 50 and 51, which present t-values of task-prestimulus change scores by tasks. These tables exclusively report the results for the placebo group. Table 50 ("easy" task versions) shows that the speech task elicited increases in somato-motor activity, electrodermal activity, heart rate, heart rate variability in the blood pressure band, blood pressure, cardiac output

Table 47. *F*-Values of Physiological Variables in the Difficulty x Medication x Conditions Design (Task Level Scores)

	Effect						
Variables	D[a]	M[be]	MxD[be]	C[ce]	CxD[ce]	MxC[de]	MxCxD[de]
EMG ext	**4.82**	0.25	0.36	**14.95**	**3.02**	1.41	0.84
EMG fr	0.06	0.53	1.65	**4.27**	1.71	1.01	1.14
Body mov	**8.63**	**7.57**	1.61	**30.46**	**14.63**	1.47	0.96
Eyeblinks	**12.34**	1.86	0.36	**9.77**	**4.05**	0.90	1.27
SCR-No.	0.05	**8.18**	0.21	**15.11**	**6.83**	**2.32**	1.06
SCR-Ampl	0.07	**12.89**	0.47	**16.21**	**7.45**	1.96	0.35
HR	0.30	**54.32**	2.31	**67.41**	**11.42**	**8.75**	1.08
P-Ampl	0.06	**9.47**	1.07	**17.76**	**5.32**	**2.56**	0.98
T-Ampl	0.14	**8.21**	1.06	**5.49**	**3.35**	0.97	0.91
P_s-Q_s	1.66	**27.78**	1.38	1.84	1.65	1.46	0.90
P_e-Q_s	0.45	**36.69**	1.45	**2.68**	0.77	0.70	1.23
Q-T rel	1.36	**10.08**	0.32	**6.46**	**6.59**	**2.37**	0.69
ST-elev	0.01	**6.32**	0.55	**25.43**	**5.80**	**2.33**	1.00
HR-SD-BP	1.17	**14.15**	0.42	**12.89**	**3.11**	**1.99**	1.25
HR-SD-Resp	2.13	1.76	0.66	**4.81**	**2.80**	0.99	0.82
RSA	0.02	2.44	1.32	**8.85**	1.06	**2.30**	1.64
RSA adj	0.00	1.80	1.33	**14.58**	**3.79**	1.61	0.91
PWV rad	0.00	**15.89**	**4.41**	**14.49**	1.19	1.88	0.91
PWV fin	0.60	**55.55**	1.18	**11.30**	**3.98**	1.89	0.95
PVA rad	0.94	1.38	0.11	1.71	1.41	**2.27**	1.30
PVA fin	0.01	0.92	1.93	**50.06**	**5.82**	0.70	0.71
CO	0.48	**7.48**	0.44	**7.96**	**5.98**	1.03	1.32
CO ind	1.89	**5.82**	0.61	**9.02**	**4.50**	0.78	0.81
Ejection sp	1.09	**7.76**	0.76	**10.81**	**3.29**	1.38	1.73
SV	0.01	1.18	1.49	**5.21**	**3.39**	1.25	0.79
LVET	0.87	**18.04**	1.10	**7.03**	1.07	1.40	0.96
PEP	0.42	**16.74**	2.74	1.84	0.24	0.74	0.62
R-Z	1.30	**34.65**	1.76	**13.27**	**3.32**	**3.72**	0.84
Heather ind	1.05	**14.24**	**2.84**	**10.44**	**3.96**	1.56	0.52
SBP	2.07	**16.67**	1.44	**25.63**	**2.84**	0.47	**2.38**
MBP	0.25	0.37	0.15	**34.71**	**3.47**	1.15	0.95
DBP IV	1.50	2.24	1.11	**38.90**	**5.12**	1.27	0.97
DBP	0.00	**6.49**	0.06	**27.11**	**3.14**	1.31	1.53
TPR	0.83	**5.44**	0.67	1.96	**3.37**	0.78	0.77
Resp rate	0.36	1.66	0.27	**15.29**	2.00	0.92	**2.24**
TMP fin	0.11	1.24	1.41	**35.57**	0.61	0.95	0.63
TMP foreh	0.03	0.39	0.41	**3.29**	1.29	**2.77**	1.15

Note. D = Difficulty; M = Medication; C = Condition. Boldface numbers: $p < .05$.
[a] $df = 1, 46$. [b] $df = 3, 44$. [c] $df = 6, 41$. [d] $df = 18, 29$. [e] F derived from Wilks' lambda.

Table 48. *F*-Values of Physiological Variables in the Difficulty x Medication x Conditions Design (Difference Scores)

				Effect			
Variables	D[a]	M[be]	MxD[be]	C[ce]	CxD[ce]	MxC[de]	MxCxD[de]
EMG ext	**5.14**	0.65	0.12	**16.39**	**2.88**	1.58	0.53
EMG fr	0.36	0.79	**3.13**	**5.58**	1.60	1.04	0.92
Body mov	**11.91**	1.40	0.05	**38.62**	**16.10**	1.07	0.84
Eyeblinks	**4.96**	0.49	0.78	**8.75**	**2.70**	1.36	0.56
SCR-No.	3.60	**3.80**	0.95	**12.97**	**4.64**	1.45	0.56
SCR-Ampl	2.63	**12.07**	0.14	**17.69**	**5.67**	**2.26**	0.39
HR	**13.45**	**16.83**	0.43	**69.31**	**8.54**	**6.45**	1.36
P-Ampl	1.13	1.49	0.74	**18.56**	**5.58**	**2.88**	1.37
T-Ampl	0.10	1.12	0.71	**7.67**	1.50	1.11	1.01
P_s-Q_s	0.28	0.79	0.12	1.64	1.13	1.05	1.81
P_e-Q_s	**4.83**	0.35	0.56	**3.66**	1.57	0.50	1.52
Q-T rel	0.25	**4.46**	1.27	**4.81**	**3.67**	**4.37**	0.88
ST-elev	0.84	0.89	0.68	**17.33**	**2.78**	**2.65**	0.82
HR-SD-BP	0.24	**5.18**	0.17	**7.63**	1.52	1.43	1.71
HR-SD-Resp	0.16	2.70	0.30	**3.61**	2.14	1.21	1.05
RSA	**11.98**	0.29	0.36	**8.73**	1.61	1.06	1.45
RSA adj	**10.35**	0.41	0.62	**23.16**	**4.45**	0.65	1.65
PWV rad	3.66	**2.96**	0.32	**16.65**	1.45	1.15	0.99
PWV fin	**9.49**	**2.93**	1.21	**17.35**	**6.17**	1.62	0.59
PVA rad	0.02	1.10	0.31	**3.37**	1.38	0.80	1.06
PVA fin	0.08	2.43	1.33	**29.79**	**4.90**	0.57	0.78
CO	**4.70**	0.24	0.18	**10.48**	**3.86**	**2.10**	1.39
CO ind	2.69	0.13	0.49	**9.85**	**3.43**	1.31	1.30
Ejection sp	1.78	0.20	0.13	**10.70**	**3.97**	1.58	1.62
SV	0.26	0.66	0.31	**5.69**	1.70	1.48	1.25
LVET	0.10	1.41	1.14	**4.85**	0.37	1.44	1.46
PEP	0.83	0.22	0.53	**4.04**	0.44	**2.07**	1.10
R-Z	0.09	**8.49**	0.86	**9.09**	2.31	**2.03**	0.75
Heather ind	0.07	0.37	0.74	**10.26**	**2.92**	1.77	0.68
SBP	**4.37**	0.20	0.76	**24.30**	**2.55**	0.66	0.98
MBP	**6.73**	1.82	1.61	**36.72**	**5.36**	0.43	0.91
DBP IV	**12.14**	1.97	**3.74**	**32.44**	**5.35**	1.85	0.89
DBP	**5.36**	1.78	1.60	**27.35**	**3.92**	0.75	0.88
TPR	0.24	0.58	0.64	**4.46**	1.34	1.41	0.93
Resp rate	1.66	0.41	0.37	**17.75**	1.93	**2.42**	1.64
TMP fin	0.50	1.17	0.16	**31.10**	**3.86**	1.04	0.75
TMP foreh	1.72	0.87	1.79	**3.52**	0.69	1.77	0.75

Note. D = Difficulty; M = Medication; C = Condition. Boldface numbers: $p < .05$.
[a]$df = 1, 46$. [b]$df = 3, 44$. [c]$df = 6, 41$. [d]$df = 18, 29$. [e]F derived from Wilks' lambda.

Table 49. *F*-Values of Physiological Variables in the Difficulty x Medication x Conditions Design (Poststimulus Scores)

Variables	D[a]	M[be]	MxD[be]	Effect C[ce]	CxD[ce]	MxC[de]	MxCxD[de]
EMG ext	2.42	0.26	0.29	**2.74**	1.69	0.56	1.44
EMG fr	0.46	0.42	1.66	**3.38**	1.35	0.89	0.56
Body mov	0.79	**5.74**	1.38	**7.01**	1.91	**2.71**	1.78
Eyeblinks	3.36	2.12	1.07	**7.43**	0.07	1.28	0.81
SCR-No.	0.15	1.88	0.16	**3.25**	**2.88**	1.20	0.88
SCR-Ampl	0.30	**5.24**	0.42	**4.06**	1.63	0.88	0.48
HR	0.00	**47.42**	2.06	**4.23**	**8.79**	**2.20**	0.89
P-Ampl	0.00	**10.01**	0.74	**5.52**	1.34	1.32	1.24
T-Ampl	0.14	**11.52**	1.10	**2.89**	1.21	0.96	0.75
P_s-Q_s	2.24	**23.74**	1.26	**3.71**	0.66	0.77	0.80
P_e-Q_s	1.00	**42.95**	2.24	**5.57**	1.60	0.53	1.00
Q-T rel	2.37	**9.83**	0.70	**6.78**	**3.76**	1.63	1.00
ST-elev	0.02	**6.56**	0.39	**4.46**	**2.81**	0.98	0.41
HR-SD-BP	3.90	**9.17**	0.54	**2.60**	1.06	0.57	0.86
HR-SD-Resp	**4.55**	**4.06**	1.67	**2.59**	0.79	0.95	0.92
RSA	2.80	1.09	1.89	**2.95**	1.10	1.16	1.35
RSA adj	**10.35**	0.41	0.62	**23.16**	**4.45**	0.65	1.65
PWV rad	0.04	**11.84**	2.73	**11.00**	0.66	**2.36**	1.46
PWV fin	0.16	**47.51**	1.64	**23.99**	1.81	**2.04**	0.80
PVA rad	0.91	1.42	0.30	**2.83**	0.60	0.96	1.10
PVA fin	0.48	0.63	2.32	**14.22**	1.62	0.97	1.71
CO	0.00	**7.27**	0.59	**3.84**	0.38	1.74	1.52
CO ind	0.70	**5.55**	0.35	**4.23**	0.31	1.77	1.45
Ejection sp	1.70	**9.17**	**3.00**	**7.88**	0.43	**1.98**	1.12
SV	0.00	1.17	1.88	**3.92**	2.05	1.38	1.24
LVET	0.63	**22.36**	**2.87**	**3.02**	2.17	**2.53**	1.53
PEP	0.27	**14.76**	0.14	**2.86**	0.45	1.46	1.39
R-Z	2.13	**35.40**	1.73	**23.34**	0.88	**4.32**	0.60
Heather ind	1.20	**21.51**	1.74	**10.43**	0.64	1.68	1.38
SBP	0.92	**14.13**	1.49	**14.09**	1.24	0.49	1.00
MBP	0.11	0.19	0.45	**11.11**	0.56	0.97	1.20
DBP IV	0.05	1.70	1.90	**7.84**	**2.89**	1.02	0.72
DBP	0.77	**3.84**	0.07	**7.63**	0.60	1.35	1.39
TPR	0.45	**3.08**	1.30	**5.60**	0.93	1.66	1.53
Resp rate	0.56	1.81	0.36	**22.03**	0.95	0.97	0.61
TMP fin	0.08	1.42	1.53	**33.97**	0.37	1.29	0.64
TMP foreh	0.03	0.33	0.39	**8.44**	1.79	1.87	1.43

Note. D = Difficulty; M = Medication; C = Condition. Boldface numbers: $p < .05$. [a]$df = 1, 46$. [b]$df = 3, 44$. [c]$df = 6, 41$. [d]$df = 18, 29$. [e]F derived from Wilks' lambda.

Table 50. *t*-Values for Changes from Prestimulus to Task Levels ("Easy" Task Version, Placebo data)

	Task						
Variable	SP	HG	MA	SD	LN1	CP	SC
EMG ext	**4.11**	**3.77**	1.82	1.97	0.15	1.41	1.08
EMG fr	0.93	-0.45	**2.32**	1.85	0.28	-0.85	1.81
Body mov	**8.21**	1.04	1.93	0.59	-1.28	**4.15**	0.88
Eyeblinks	1.71	0.91	**2.66**	-1.12	1.05	0.85	-0.70
SCR-No.	**4.53**	**3.23**	**3.66**	1.25	**3.17**	-0.03	1.71
SCR-Ampl	**5.14**	**2.81**	**3.50**	1.11	**4.21**	0.51	1.24
HR	**10.38**	**7.41**	**12.74**	0.04	-1.39	**2.40**	**2.32**
P-Ampl	**4.51**	1.19	**4.16**	**2.14**	-1.24	0.41	1.74
T-Ampl	1.54	1.25	**2.94**	1.28	0.26	**2.11**	**2.18**
P_s-Q_s	0.27	-0.17	0.99	0.30	-0.57	0.02	-0.42
P_e-Q_s	-0.53	-1.23	-0.61	0.55	0.41	-0.27	-0.53
Q-T rel	**2.21**	**2.82**	**5.02**	1.06	0.61	**3.37**	1.90
ST-elev	**4.21**	1.21	**6.08**	-0.59	-1.40	0.02	1.85
HR-SD-BP	**3.61**	-2.06	-0.06	**-2.20**	**2.38**	-0.39	-1.04
HR-SD-Resp	-2.00	**-2.97**	-0.89	-1.87	1.37	0.30	-0.05
RSA	-0.02	**-2.75**	**-3.79**	-1.32	0.58	-1.48	-0.91
RSA adj	-1.45	-1.18	-1.10	-2.02	-0.26	0.79	-0.94
PWV rad	**4.07**	0.35	1.53	-1.42	-0.78	2.03	1.94
PWV fin	**6.10**	-0.90	**3.57**	-1.63	**2.62**	1.42	**2.65**
PVA rad	1.64	-0.98	0.88	0.27	0.97	1.22	0.20
PVA fin	**-2.91**	0.90	**-4.36**	-0.82	**-2.95**	**-6.75**	**-2.56**
CO	**2.90**	0.41	1.64	-1.93	-0.54	0.09	1.14
CO ind	**2.79**	0.30	1.27	-1.98	-0.47	0.04	1.16
Ejection sp	**-2.41**	-0.83	0.52	1.95	-0.80	**-3.62**	0.51
SV	-0.92	-0.60	**-2.61**	-1.88	-0.14	-0.29	0.05
LVET	**-4.54**	-1.46	**-4.07**	-1.43	0.24	1.74	-0.75
PEP	**-3.08**	1.13	0.48	1.70	0.32	-1.14	-1.15
R-Z	-0.76	1.58	-0.08	1.41	2.05	**2.35**	**-2.19**
Heather ind	0.43	-1.61	0.48	**-2.32**	-0.42	-1.59	1.46
SBP	**4.19**	1.30	1.97	-0.09		**-2.21**	1.65
MBP	**4.99**	0.81	**5.39**	-1.18		**-2.48**	1.31
DBP IV	**5.29**	**2.58**	**4.77**	0.84		-0.86	1.46
DBP	**4.16**	0.49	**4.50**	-1.38		-1.92	0.68
TPR	0.08	1.25	1.46	1.47		-0.94	-0.84
Resp rate	**-3.57**	**3.95**	1.14	**5.06**	**2.95**	1.97	1.77
TMP fin	-1.45	1.62	0.07	-0.36	0.25	**-2.67**	**-7.37**
TMP foreh	1.85	-0.38	1.68	-0.54	**3.05**	0.41	1.63

Note. No *t*-values for blood pressure variables and for TPR in LN1. SP = speech task. HG = handgrip. MA = mental arithmetic. SD = signal detection. LN1 = anticipation of loud noise. CP = cold pressor. SC = sentence completion. *t*-tests for correlated samples were based on $df = 23$. Signs indicate direction of change. Boldface numbers: $p < .05$.

(not accompanied by increases in contractility!), pulse wave velocities, and decreases in left-ventricular ejection time, preejection period, finger pulse volume amplitude, and respiration rate.

The isometric handgrip task increased heart rate, relative Q-T time, diastolic blood pressure (phase IV), respiration rate, and electrodermal activity; handgrip decreased both the unadjusted respiratory sinus arrhythmia and heart rate variability in the respiration band.

Mental arithmetic increased somato-motor activity, P-wave and T-wave amplitudes, ST-elevation, relative Q-T time, heart rate, diastolic (phase IV and V) as well as mean blood pressure, finger pulse wave velocity, and electrodermal activity; it decreased left-ventricular ejection time, unadjusted respiratory sinus arrhythmia, and finger pulse volume amplitude.

The signal detection task increased P-wave amplitude and respiration rate; the Heather index and heart rate variability in the blood pressure band were reduced.

Anticipation of loud noise increased electrodermal activity, respiration rate, heart rate variability in the blood pressure band, and forehead skin temperature; it decreased finger pulse volume amplitude.

The cold pressor task increased body movements, T-wave amplitude, relative Q-T time, heart rate, and R-Z time; it decreased finger pulse wave amplitude and systolic blood pressure (an unexpected result, but see Heinecker, 1959, and Lovallo & Zeiner, 1975, for reports of large interindividual differences in the magnitude and even direction of heart rate and blood pressure changes, and on the effect that higher prestimulus skin temperatures are followed by blood volume drops instead of increases during cold pressor).

The sentence completion task increased hart rate, T-wave amplitude, and pulse wave velocity at the finger, and it decreased finger skin temperature and R-Z time.

Many of the responses described above for the "easy" task were amplified under the "difficult" version (Table 51), giving a more accentuated picture of the task effects. Differential effects of the two difficulty versions are described next, if they led to significantly different physiological reactivities.

Table 52 shows the results of a set of analyses of variance performed in order to follow up the difficulty main effect by tasks. These results stem from a Difficulty (2) x Medication (4) design and were calculated from task-prestimulus difference scores. Interpretation of the difficulty main effect tests was not affected by difficulty x medication interactions, because significant interactions were obtained for very few variable-by-task combinations; of these, only two had significant difficulty effects, too.

The difficulty variation of the speech task produced numerous changes in physiological reactivities. Compared to the "easy" speech task, the "difficult" version elicited a three-fold reactivity increase in body movements; in the cardiac output index, from 0.4 to 1.2 $l/min/m^2$; in heart rate, from 9 to 13 bpm; in eyeblinks, from 8 to 19 per minute; in EMG extensor, from 6 to 28 $\mu V*sec$;

Table 51. *t*-Values for Changes from Prestimulus to Task Levels ("Difficult" Task Version, Placebo data)

	Task						
Variable	SP	HG	MA	SD	LN1	CP	SC
EMG ext	**3.38**	**4.48**	**3.34**	1.82	1.13	**3.13**	1.59
EMG fr	-1.00	1.29	**2.22**	-0.34	0.72	0.41	-0.91
Body mov	**9.95**	**2.42**	**3.15**	-0.61	-1.90	**5.47**	-0.86
Eyeblinks	**4.20**	**2.57**	**2.37**	-1.49	1.65	**2.12**	0.15
SCR-No.	**4.56**	**4.03**	**3.55**	-0.66	**3.91**	0.76	1.58
SCR-Ampl	**5.32**	**6.84**	**3.21**	0.33	**6.13**	0.52	1.13
HR	**11.71**	**9.16**	**8.10**	0.48	1.07	**2.29**	1.40
P-Ampl	**5.04**	**2.68**	**2.72**	-0.94	1.32	1.48	-1.18
T-Ampl	**2.86**	2.03	**2.09**	0.28	1.04	**6.65**	-0.85
P_s-Q_s	-0.91	1.35	-0.72	0.26	1.76	0.47	**-2.10**
P_e-Q_s	**-5.51**	-1.15	**-2.50**	2.05	0.77	-0.72	-0.50
Q-T rel	**3.31**	**8.50**	**8.12**	**3.65**	1.35	**2.76**	1.17
ST-elev	**5.20**	**3.10**	**2.90**	-1.36	-0.01	1.28	0.42
HR-SD-BP	1.36	-1.50	-1.82	-1.73	1.93	0.79	-0.92
HR-SD-Resp	0.37	**-2.33**	**-3.29**	**-2.65**	0.59	1.14	-0.64
RSA	**-2.13**	**-5.77**	**-5.22**	**-2.44**	-1.43	-0.02	**-2.63**
RSA adj	**-5.13**	**-3.82**	**-3.79**	**-2.07**	1.67	-0.70	-1.09
PWV rad	**5.78**	**2.39**	**3.49**	0.09	-1.08	-1.00	1.60
PWV fin	**6.53**	**7.53**	**3.43**	**-2.18**	0.60	**2.34**	**2.07**
PVA rad	0.81	**2.60**	1.07	0.22	1.92	1.51	-0.63
PVA fin	**-2.94**	**-2.80**	**-3.28**	0.32	**-4.56**	**-7.04**	**-2.47**
CO	**3.82**	2.00	1.47	-1.60	-1.70	1.14	1.84
CO ind	**4.05**	1.89	1.63	-1.61	-2.03	0.44	1.78
Ejection sp	0.41	**-7.42**	-1.12	**2.31**	-0.53	**-4.13**	-0.31
SV	1.55	**-2.62**	**-3.67**	-1.66	**-2.26**	-0.00	1.38
LVET	**-2.64**	0.32	**-5.65**	-0.79	-1.44	**2.13**	-0.63
PEP	-1.92	-1.62	-0.72	**2.42**	1.23	-1.45	-1.70
R-Z	1.24	**3.75**	-1.67	1.19	-0.11	**4.59**	-1.42
Heather ind	**2.63**	**-5.08**	-0.70	-1.98	**-2.70**	**-2.33**	1.32
SBP	**4.49**	**3.18**	**2.39**	0.22		-0.59	2.00
MBP	**6.91**	**4.43**	**3.82**	-0.13		-0.01	1.85
DBP IV	**8.38**	**7.26**	**4.22**	0.94		**2.82**	1.45
DBP	**6.78**	**3.82**	**3.47**	-0.25		0.21	1.33
TPR	**-2.17**	1.08	0.89	1.43		-0.93	-0.46
Resp rate	-1.28	**4.62**	**5.37**	**4.33**	**2.10**	0.41	1.71
TMP fin	0.27	0.09	-1.72	**2.40**	-1.48	**-5.57**	**-7.57**
TMP foreh	0.95	0.38	-0.43	0.71	**2.58**	0.73	0.25

Note. No *t*-values for blood pressure variables and for TPR in LN1. SP = speech task. HG = handgrip. MA = mental arithmetic. SD = signal detection. LN1 = anticipation of loud noise. CP = cold pressor. SC = sentence completion. *t*-tests for correlated samples were based on $df = 23$. Signs indicate direction of change. Boldface numbers: $p < .05$.

Table 52. *F*-Values for Difficulty Effect in the Difficulty x Medication Design (Difference Scores)

	Task						
Variable	SP	HG	MA	SD	LN1	CP	SC
EMG ext	**10.89**	**8.40**	0.22	0.00	**6.53**	0.22	0.95
EMG fr	0.00	3.50	0.47	2.63	1.04	1.04	1.70
Body mov	**52.09**	**18.16**	0.77	0.00	0.07	0.06	0.02
Eyeblinks	**12.95**	0.02	0.31	0.59	2.20	0.38	0.57
SCR-No.	**5.63**	**8.55**	0.04	**6.77**	2.80	0.11	0.12
SCR-Ampl	1.49	**13.64**	1.51	0.54	**4.71**	1.74	0.87
HR	**15.96**	**40.32**	1.85	2.33	2.52	1.61	0.04
P-Ampl	3.21	3.68	2.40	1.78	**7.17**	1.12	2.35
T-Ampl	0.17	2.72	2.19	0.13	1.28	2.48	1.43
P_s-Q_s	1.58	0.52	0.31	1.25	0.30	0.38	0.07
P_e-Q_s	**6.23**	0.17	0.20	3.37	1.76	**5.15**	0.00
Q-T rel	1.43	**4.27**	1.48	0.45	0.39	0.54	0.01
ST-elev	0.00	**8.53**	0.00	0.28	0.51	3.69	0.41
HR-SD-BP	0.70	3.48	**5.79**	0.11	2.10	0.21	0.15
HR-SD-Resp	0.82	0.00	**7.55**	0.08	3.58	0.29	**4.95**
RSA	**5.18**	**4.89**	**12.81**	**7.06**	0.48	0.24	3.50
RSA adj	**4.51**	**14.99**	**4.81**	2.24	0.02	2.42	2.09
PWV rad	3.99	**7.42**	0.00	0.41	0.01	0.02	0.00
PWV fin	**7.57**	**35.00**	0.03	0.09	0.00	2.22	0.43
PVA rad	0.06	**6.89**	1.32	1.35	1.13	0.14	0.42
PVA fin	0.02	**12.50**	1.14	**4.07**	0.50	0.56	0.00
CO	**15.63**	3.04	1.27	0.18	0.14	0.00	0.40
CO ind	**16.82**	3.64	1.49	0.02	0.17	0.22	0.35
Ejection sp	4.00	**19.50**	1.16	0.55	0.08	1.45	0.24
SV	**8.49**	1.17	0.03	0.81	0.23	0.66	0.22
LVET	0.56	0.64	0.01	0.05	0.28	0.14	0.52
PEP	0.15	3.09	0.00	0.10	0.56	0.09	0.52
R-Z	0.00	**7.68**	1.77	0.29	0.07	0.00	0.05
Heather ind	**8.60**	**5.77**	2.09	0.03	0.00	1.12	0.16
SBP	2.95	**10.92**	0.09	0.01		**5.26**	0.36
MBP	**8.34**	**17.00**	1.55	0.11		0.67	0.00
DBP IV	**6.53**	**28.39**	1.87	0.06		**4.61**	0.02
DBP	**8.15**	**12.86**	1.85	0.37		0.04	0.05
TPR	**8.49**	1.02	0.04	0.27		1.08	0.00
Resp rate	1.59	0.78	**9.63**	0.05	0.00	0.08	0.06
TMP fin	2.81	**10.89**	0.38	0.65	**4.40**	**10.71**	0.37
TMP foreh	0.62	0.20	1.63	0.36	3.51	0.17	0.07

Note. No *F*-values for blood pressure variables and for TPR in LN1. SP = speech task. HG = handgrip. MA = mental arithmetic. SD = signal detection. LN1 = anticipation of loud noise. CP = cold pressor. SC = sentence completion. *F*-test based on $df = 1, 46$. Boldface numbers: $p < .05$.

in total peripheral resistance, from 3 to -110 dyn*sec*cm^{-5}; in the Heather index, from 0.2 to 2.6 Ω/sec²; in diastolic blood pressure, from 8.8 to 10.6 mmHg, to name just a few variables (data from the placebo group).

The difficulty variation of the handgrip task produced even more changes in reactivity (placebo group data): in heart rate, from 4.2 to 9.8 bpm; in pulse wave velocity at the finger, from -0.1 to 0.2 m/sec; in diastolic blood pressure (phase IV), from 5.3 to 13.7 mmHg; in ejection speed, from -1.0 to -7.2 Ω/sec²; in the adjusted respiratory sinus arrhythmia, from -0.1 to -0.6 ln(msec), to name a few variables.

Compared to the previous two tasks, difficulty variations of the mental arithmetic task, signal detection task, anticipation of loud noise task, and the cold pressor task led to markedly less changes in physiological reactivity (the sentence completion task was not varied in its difficulty). Compared to the "easy" task, the "difficult" version of the mental arithmetic task produced larger reductions in respiratory sinus arrhythmia (both unadjusted and adjusted), larger increases in respiration rate, and larger drops in heart rate variability (both frequency bands); of the signal detection task, a smaller instead of a larger number of SCRs in the "easy" version, a larger decrease in unadjusted respiratory sinus arrhythmia, and, instead of a decrease, an increase in finger pulse volume amplitude; of the anticipation period of the loud noise, an increase in the amplitude of the SCR, an increase instead of a decrease in EMG extensor activity and P-wave amplitude; of the cold pressor task, a smaller drop in systolic blood pressure, a larger drop in finger skin temperature, a decrease instead of an increase in P_e-Q_s time, and a larger increase in diastolic blood pressure (phase IV).

Instead of comparing these individual results to the literature, I will immediately turn to the componential task description which hopefully can offer a superior basis for an integrative evaluation of task effects.

10.2.2 Componential task description

In order to be consistent with the derivation of the putative cardiovascular activation components, the componential task description was performed on task-prestimulus change scores of the within-subjects source of variation. Scores on these components of only the placebo group were analyzed; this restriction was intended to make the componential task description independent of the derivation of the components, which had employed the blockade data. Furthermore, the components were standardized by the pooled error standard deviation from an analysis of variance with the 14 experimental conditions (seven from each of the two difficulty groups), because both profile analysis and graphical displays of task effects presuppose a common scaling of the components.

Figure 23 shows the task effects as described by the putative cardiovascular components. Both difficulty versions of the **speech task** were characterized by large-scale reductions in the tau component ($t(23) = 7.30$ and 9.42, $p<.01$, for the "easy" and "difficult" version, respectively) and reductions in the beta2 component ($t(23) = 3.51$ and 4.73, $p<.01$). The "easy" speech task elicited an increase in the beta1 component; $t(23) = 2.63$, $p<.05$. The flatness test (see Chapter 7.3) indicated that both task versions elicited distinct profiles of activation; $F(5/19) = 21.99$ and 57.06, $p<.01$. The test on profile parallelism and profile levels (see Chapter 7.3) indicated that the two task versions elicited nonparallel profiles of activation ($F(5/42) = 2.65$, $p<.05$) which were on different levels ($F(1/46) = 8.80$, $p<.01$). Follow-up tests indicated that, compared to the "easy" task, the "difficult" version led to a still larger drop of tau activation; $F(1/46) = 16.13$, $p<.01$. In sum, the speech task produced a large putative cholinergic withdrawal. The difficulty variation amplified this response pattern.

The **handgrip task** was also characterized by distinct profiles of activation (flatness test: $F(5/19) = 4.58$ and 13.55, $p<.01$, for the "easy" and "difficult" task version, respectively). The "easy" task reduced the beta1 ($t(23) = 2.14$, $p<.05$) and, more pronounced, the tau component ($t(23) = 4.95$, $p<.01$); the "difficult" task led to reductions in the beta, beta2, beta3, and tau component ($t(23) = 2.51$, $p<.05$, and 4.05, 5.96, and 9.83, $p<.01$, respectively). The activation profiles of the two task versions were not parallel ($F(5/42) = 5.72$, $p<.01$) and had different elevations ($F(1/46) = 10.78$, $p<.01$). In particular, compared to the "easy" task, the "difficult" task version had a larger alpha activation ($F(1/46) = 5.43$, $p<.05$) and greater drops in beta2, beta3, and tau activation ($F(1/46) = 10.06$, 12.87, and 15.13, $p<.01$, respectively). In sum, the handgrip task elicited a combination of putative vagal withdrawal and beta2 as well as beta3 reductions. The often described alpha-adrenergic activation under handgrip was seen only in the "difficult" task version (compared to the "easy" task). The difficulty variation ensured the dominant role of vagal withdrawal during handgrip.

The **mental arithmetic task**, too, produced distinct profiles of activation (flatness test: $F(5/19) = 20.60$ and 9.66, $p<.01$, for the "easy" and "difficult" task version, respectively). The only significant effect of the "easy" task was a reduction in the tau component ($t(23) = 6.97$, $p<.01$), which, in addition to a reduced beta3 activation ($t(23) = 2.81$, $p<.01$), was also true for the "difficult" version ($t(3) = 8.38$, $p<.01$). The difficulty variation neither produced differences in profile parallelism nor in profile levels. In sum, mental arithmetic was predominantly characterized by putative vagal withdrawal. The difficulty variation (loudness of a distracting noise) was not able to elicit differential putative cardiovascular activation profiles.

The **signal detection task** did not lead to distinct activation profiles. Only for the "difficult" task version, reduced beta, beta1, and tau components were seen ($t(23) = 2.71$, 2.16, and 2.11, $p<.05$, respectively). There were no differential difficulty effects.

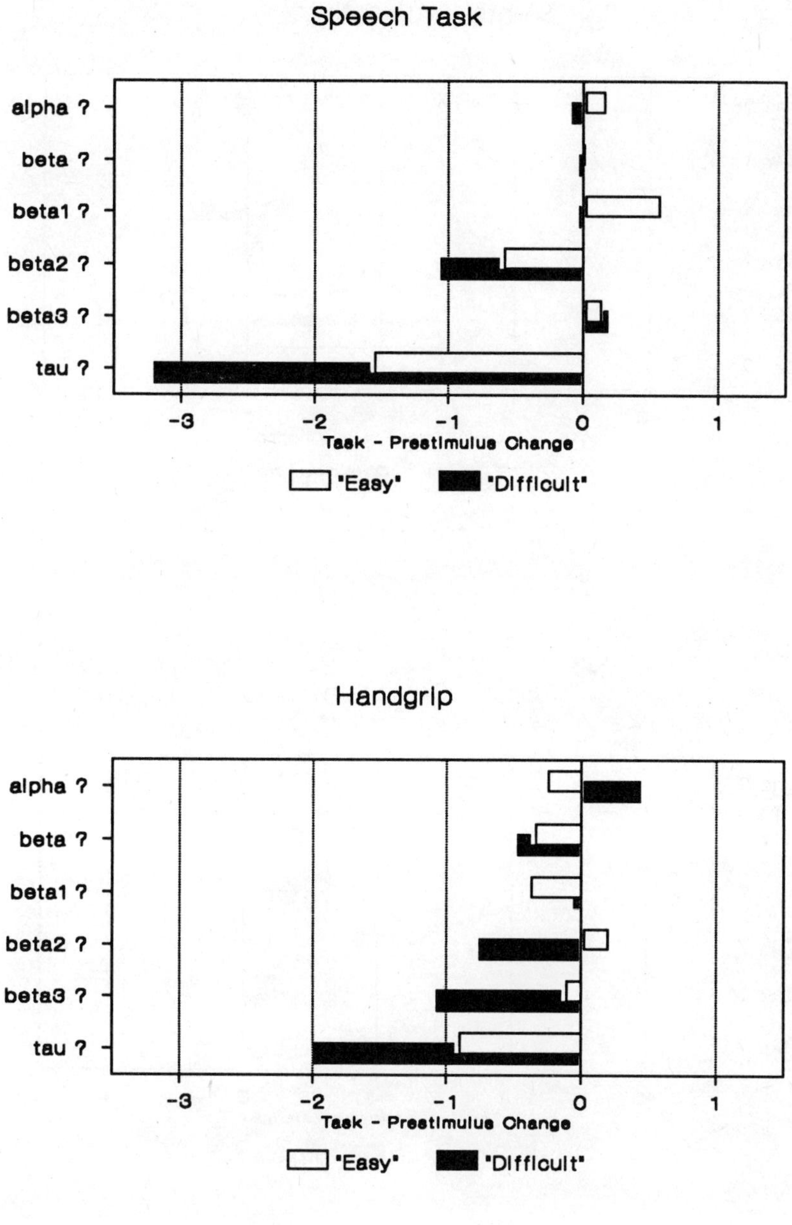

Figure 23. Task effects on putative cardiovascular activation components (within-subjects variance of placebo data); plots of components by tasks. *(Figure continues)*

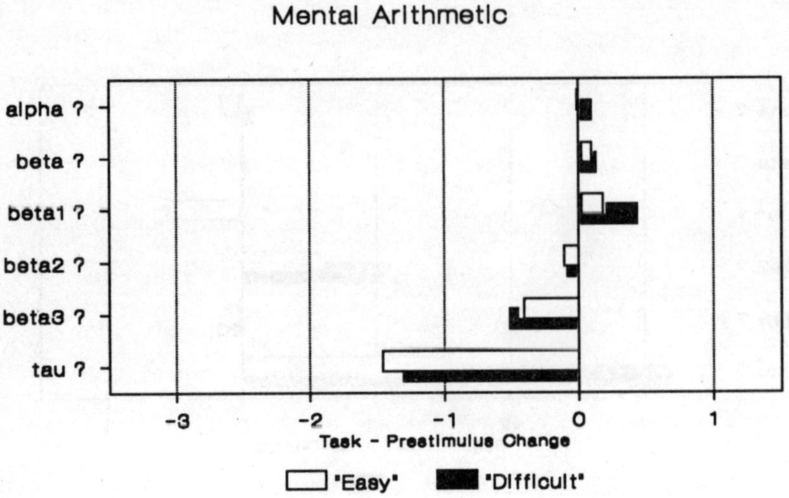

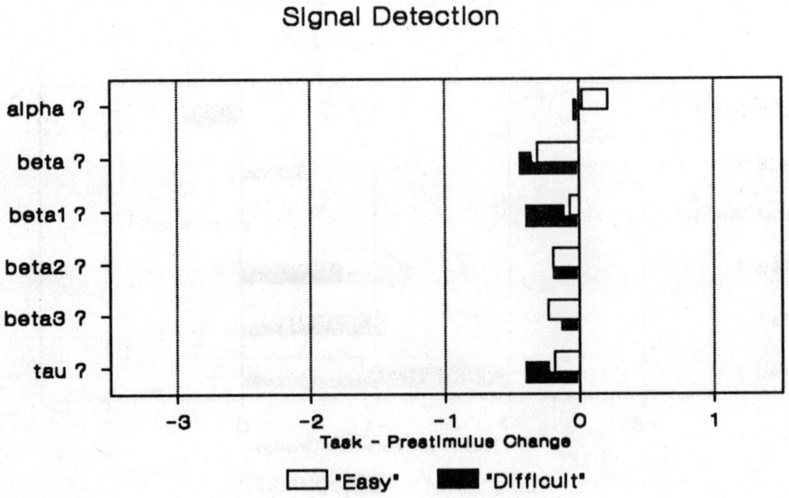

Figure 23. *(continued)*

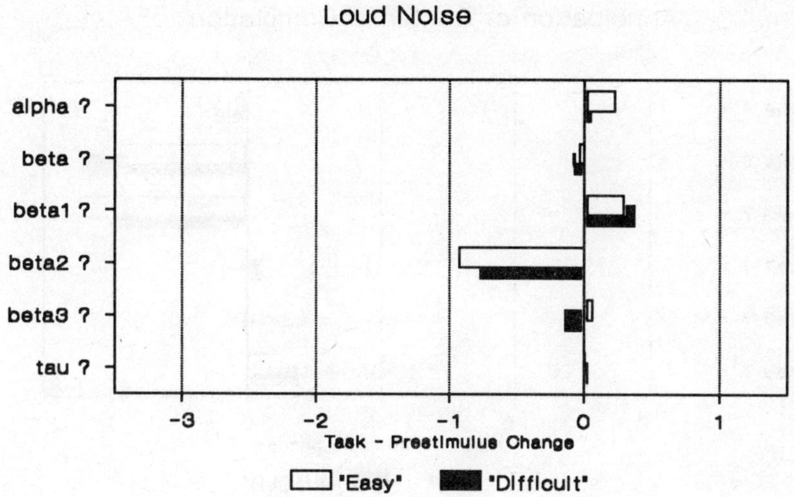

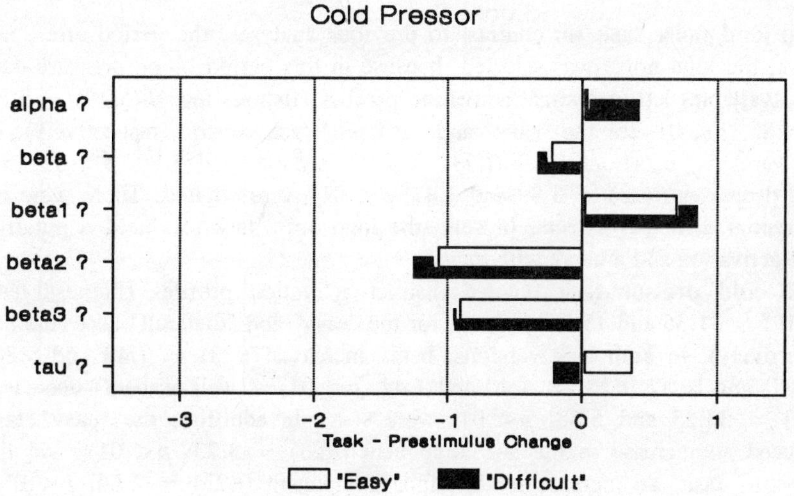

Figure 23. *(continued)*

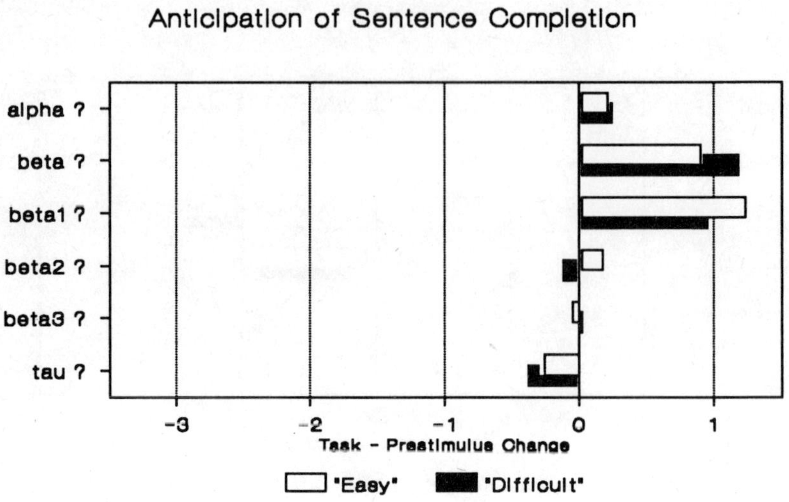

Figure 23. *(continued)*

The **loud noise task** (in contrast to previous analyses, the period after, not before, the loud noise was selected, because in this period blood pressure data were available) led to distinct activation profiles (flatness test: $F(5/19) = 5.89$ and 4.85, $p<.01$, for the "easy" and "difficult" task version, respectively). In both versions, beta1 increases ($t(23) = 2.08$, $p<.05$, and 3.79, $p<.01$) and beta2 decreases ($t(23) = 5.39$ and 3.47, $p<.01$) were elicited. There were no differential difficulty effects. In sum, the loud noise task produced a putative beta1 activation and a beta2 withdrawal.

The **cold pressor task** elicited distinct activation profiles (flatness test: $F(5/19) = 31.36$ and 15.70, $p<.01$, for the "easy" and "difficult" task version, respectively). In both task versions, beta1 increases ($t(23) = 7.48$ and 5.80, $p<.01$) and beta2 ($t(23) = 4.40$ and 7.42, $p<.01$) as well as beta3 decreases ($t(23) = 33.23$ and 5.58, $p<.01$) were seen. In addition, the "easy" task produced an increase in the tau component ($t(23) = 3.23$, $p<.01$); and the "difficult" task, an increase in the alpha component ($t(23) = 2.66$, $p<.05$). Differential effects of the difficulty variation could not be established. In sum, judged by the coincident directions of activation in the two difficulty groups, the cold pressor task was mainly characterized by increases in beta1 and decreases in beta2 and beta3 activation. The lack of a dominant alpha activation was unexpected; however, reports about conflicting directions of activation in several physiological variables (see previous section) suggest (1) the existence of marked individual differences in responses and (2) the impact of the context (specifically, of ambient temperature). With respect to the latter point, the relatively high ambient temperature in the experimental room might have had an effect acting against an alpha-adrenergic activation.

The **anticipation of the sentence completion task** elicited distinct profiles of activation (flatness test: $F(5/19) = 9.10$ and 10.33, $p<.01$, for the "easy" and "difficult" task version, respectively). In both versions, beta ($t(23) = 3.52$ and 4.74, $p<.01$) and beta1 activation ($t(23) = 6.38$ and 5.80, $p<.01$) were increased. The difficulty groups showed no differential effects, which in this case could be expected from the absence of a difficulty variation in this task.

In conclusion, with the exception of the signal detection task, the laboratory tasks used in Experiment 4 were able to elicit specific types of (cardiovascular) activation. When the task profiles described above are compared to the task characterizations in Table 45, similarities (handgrip task) but also marked discrepancies can be noted (cf. mental arithmetic and cold pressor task). Apart from reasons for such discrepancies that refer to the weakness inherent in the labelling of task effects after employing nonformalized approaches, other factors need to be considered, too. One is the difference in experimental procedures used in different studies. Another can be traced back to context differences such as the ambient temperature mentioned above with respect to the cold pressor task. However, more specific for the present investigation is the difference between "pure" cardiovascular activation components (which can be determined after complete blockades) and regulatory patterns (which are likely to be found after partial blockades and which are the net result of the activation of particular cardiovascular components including, e.g. compensatory changes in other components). The reader might recall that in Chapter 9.3.5 it has been concluded that the putative cardiovascular activation components should be considered more broadly defined regulatory patterns instead of "pure" components. For example, in Chapter 9.3.3 it has been noted that with reversed sign the tau component could be equally well interpreted as a chronotropic beta component. Briefly, the tau component seems to express the *synergism* of cardiovascular vagal and chronotropic beta-sympathetic influences in one, instead of two necessarily highly correlated variates. Thus, whereas previous studies on cardiovascular task effects using complete blockades implicitly assumed an ir-restricted Model of Cardiovascular Activation Components and neglected the interaction among components (see Chapter 5.2.3), the present investigation used incomplete blockades and obtained components incorporating such interactions. Undoubtedly, this difference can make a direct comparison of activation component labels difficult. One must await a study employing the complete blockade protocol (see Equations 17a-h) that alone would be able to differentiate between "pure" components and interactions among them.

Another conclusion concerns the effects of the difficulty variation on the profile of activation. For some tasks (speech and handgrip), the difficulty variation amplified the responses in those putative cardiovascular activation components that were already highly responsive under the "easy" task version.

This finding affirms the validity of the respective task characterizations. The finding of no differences between difficulty versions in the other tasks (mental arithmetic, signal detection, loud noise, cold pressor, and anticipation of sentence completion) confirms the validity of the respective task characterizations too, because (a) (with the exception of signal detection) the profiles of activation were found to be distinct and (b) based on independent subject samples. For these tasks, the difficulty variation simply was not effective in terms of the cardiovascular behavior as measured by the putative cardiovascular components. The finding that the difficulty variation was effective and led to different directions of activation was not observed; such a finding would have questioned the internal validity of the derived activation profiles.

Finally, it should be recalled that the componential task description was based only on a subsample of cardiovascular variables. Inclusion of electrodermal and somato-motor variables would have made the characterization of tasks even more succinct. For such a more inclusive characterization (that, however, does not make use of putative cardiovascular activation components), see Chapter 9.2.4 on situational physiological maps of Experiment 4.

10.2.3 Intertask comparisons

The comparison of task effects on putative cardiovascular activation components was performed on the same data set as described in the previous section. Intertask comparisons were performed (1) by tests on the parallelism and levels of the cardiovascular activation profiles of tasks in order to determine their overall cardiovascular uniqueness, (2) upon significance of either of these tests, by analyses of variance with the factors Conditions (7) and Difficulty (2), conducted separately for each component using the multivariate test for the repeated-measures effect Conditions and the interaction Conditions x Difficulty, and (3) upon significance of either of these tests, by pairwise comparisons between condition means with Bonferroni-adjusted alpha significance levels. Figure 24 shows the condition means of Figure 23 but arranged in the order (i.e., tasks per component) appropriate for the issue at hand.

Both the test for task profile parallelism and levels were significant ($F(30/1090) = 11.97$ and $F(6/276) = 22.03$, $p < .01$, respectively). This result points to marked differences among the tasks' putative cardiovascular activation component profiles. Analyses of variance confirmed significantly different task means for all but the alpha component; $F(6/41) = 6.54$, 16.31, 12.58, 7.63, and 40.72, all $p < .01$, for the beta, beta1, beta2, beta3, and tau component, respectively. In particular, for the beta component the sentence completion task attained the largest mean, which was significantly different from all other means (Bonferroni-adjusted pairwise comparison); for the beta1 component, the sentence completion and the cold pressor tasks. For the beta2 component, the

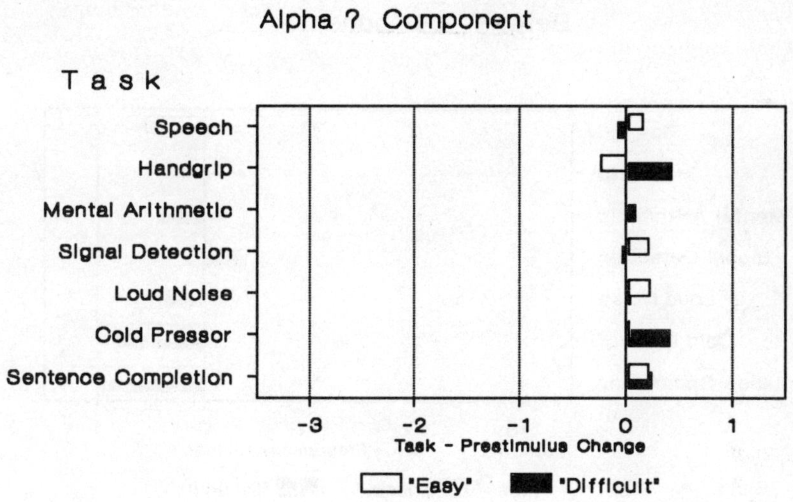

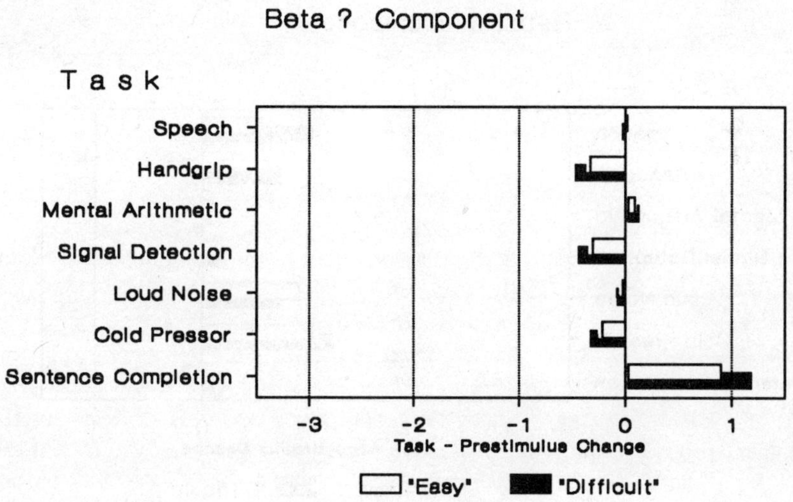

Figure 24. Task effects on putative cardiovascular activation components (within-subjects variance of placebo data); plots of tasks by components. *(Figure continues)*

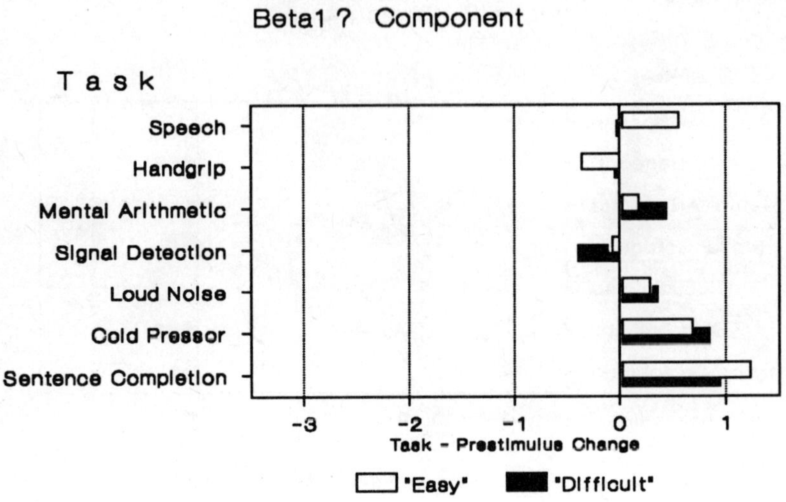

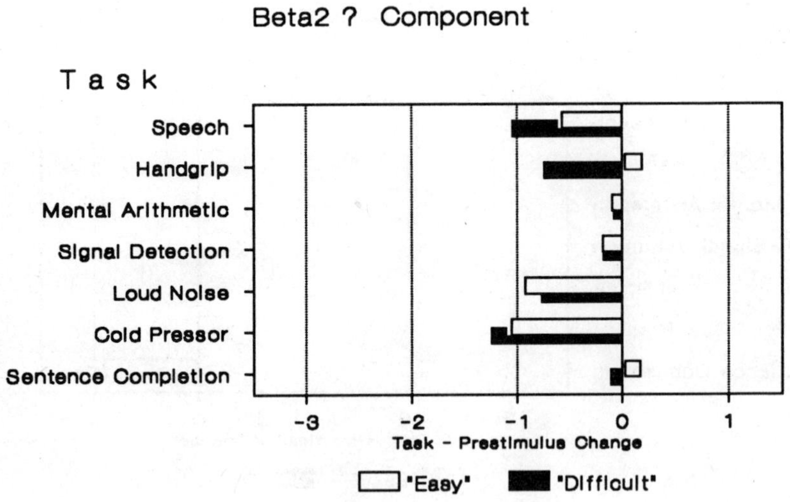

Figure 24. *(continued)*

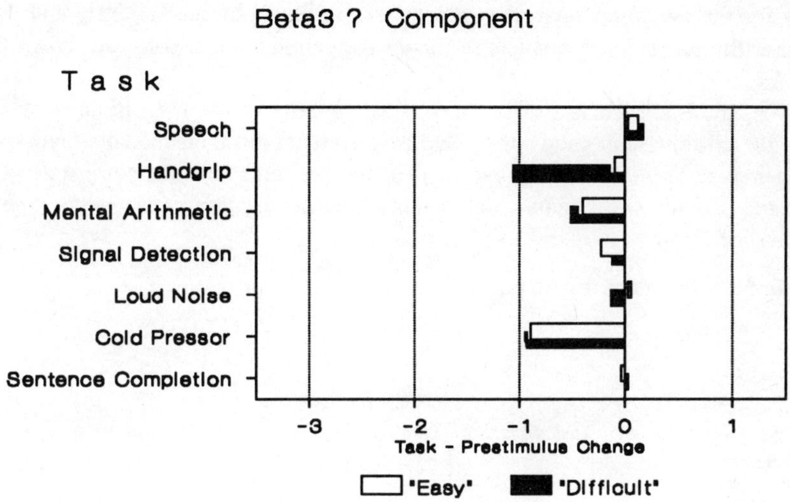

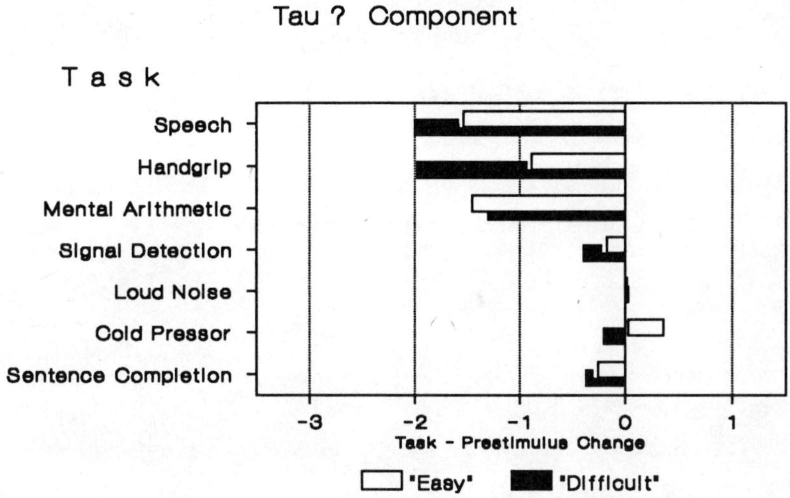

Figure 24. *(continued)*

cold pressor, loud noise, and speech tasks elicited the lowest means; for the beta3 component, the cold pressor, handgrip, and mental arithmetic tasks; finally for the tau component, the speech task, followed by the handgrip and the mental arithmetic tasks. Complete results of the paired comparisons are shown in Table 53.

In sum, there are marked differences between tasks in the magnitude of their effects on cardiovascular activation, that is, differences in their modal situations. Taking into account the results reported in the previous section, comparatively large and significant changes in putative cardiovascular components were obtained for

- the alpha component, by no one task;

Table 53. Comparison of Task Means on Putative Cardiovascular Activation Components

Activation Component	Tasks Ordered by Means						
Alpha ?[a]							
Beta ?	SC	MA	SP	LN	CP	SD	HG
		*	*	*	*	*	*
Beta1 ?	SC	CP	LN	MA	SP	HG	SD
	*	*		+	+	+	+
		x	x	x	x		
			0	0	0	0	
Beta2 ?	SC	MA	SD	HG	SP	LN	CP
	*	*	*	*	+	+	+
				x	x	x	
Beta3 ?	SP	SC	LN	SD	MA	HG	CP
	*	*	*	*	+	+	+
		x	x	x	x	x	
Tau ?	CP	LN	SD	SC	MA	HG	SP
	*	*	*	*	+	+	

Note. Tasks marked by the same symbol are not significantly different (Bonferroni-adjusted pairwise comparisons, $p < .05$). SP = Speech. HG = Handgrip. MA = Mental arithmetic. SD = Signal detection. LN = Loud noise. CP = Cold pressor. SC = Sentence completion. [a]No significant Conditions main effects.

- the beta component (increases), by the anticipation of sentence completion;
- the beta1 component (increases), by the anticipation of sentence completion and cold pressor;
- the beta2 component (decreases), by the cold pressor, loid noise (after the noise), and speech tasks;
- the beta3 component (decreases), by the cold pressor, handgrip, and mental arithmetic tasks;
- the tau component (decreases), by the speech task, handgrip, and mental arithmetic.

These results confirm that laboratory tasks in cardiovascular research indeed may be employed to elicit specific cardiovascular activations. It is the merit of the derivation of putative cardiovascular activation components that on the basis of a quantitative evaluation such conclusions can be drawn. Similarly, in a next step one could describe the effects of both procedural differences and psychological factors (e.g., type of instruction; social or personal threat), such as the difficulty variation in the present experiment.

11 Research on the Psychophysiology of Personality

11.1 Situational Variation and Personality Effects on Activation

Like no other differential psychophysiological approach, H.J. Eysenck's biological theory of personality has stimulated attempts at finding relationships between physiological activation and personality, in particular the questionnaire scales of extraversion and neuroticism (see below). Eysenck (1967, 1981) presents a theory that aims at explaining, instead of describing, these personality traits. Insofar as Eysenck's theory of the relationship between levels of activation and personality has not found unanimous empirical support (Fahrenberg, 1987b; Myrtek, 1984), the more recent expansion of his theory, which emphasizes the role of the stimulus situation (Eysenck & Eysenck, 1985), is of particular interest in the present context of a differential psychophysiology. The shift in emphasis from habitual to situationally varying activation characteristics of personality types implies a shift in the assessment model used, namely from the "pure" trait perspective of Assessment Model 1 to the moderator perspective (situations moderate trait expressions) of Assessment Model 6. Such a shift is one of the recent responses to the inadequacies of a "pure" trait model in personality theory (see Chapter 2.2).

Eysenck's biological personality theory proposes that the broad personality traits of extraversion and neuroticism have their neurophysiological basis in differential thresholds of the Ascending Reticular Activating System and the Limbic System, respectively (Eysenck, 1967).[26] Since introverts as compared to

[26] Eysenck uses the terms "arousal" and "activation" to refer to reticular and limbic activity, respectively. Since the term "activation" is used here as a name for the efferent processes observed in the periphery, the respective cortical activities will be termed "reticular" and "limbic arousal".

extraverts should have higher levels of reticular arousal, a greater arousability, and at the same time lower preferred, or hedonically optimal levels, stimulus intensity is a critical variable in the prediction of differential physiological activation responses: Introverts should be more arousable by and therefore have larger activation responses during low-intensive stimuli, whereas extraverts should be more arousable by and therefore have larger activation responses during high-intensive stimuli. In sum, introverts and extraverts should "differ physiologically in a wide range of situations" (Eysenck & Eysenck, 1985, p. 236). Stimulus intensity is the moderator variable that is supposed to mediate the relationship between personality and activation. This prediction has found some support in psychophysiological studies (for reviews, see Gale, 1983; Stelmack, 1981), although the results were not easily summarized under the posited moderator variable.

Neuroticism is defined as an emotional stability-instability dimension. Individuals scoring high in neuroticism should have a greater limbic arousability and consequently larger autonomic nervous system responses, but only during high-intensive stimulation by emotionally threatening stimuli. According to the Eysencks, the requirement of studying emotionally threatening situations has often been overlooked; consequently, this part of the theory "has not been put to an adequate test" (Eysenck & Eysenck, 1985, p. 232). A corollary of this hypothesis is that since within one and the same situation persons differ in the degree of perceived threat (i.e., their functional situation), the relationship between neuroticism and activation will occur only for subjects with higher levels of perceived threat. Thus, the self-report of emotion will act as a moderator of the relationship between neuroticism and activation.

The empirical study of Eysenck's biological personality theory is beset with problems of operationalization: How should stimulus intensity and stressfulness be assessed, how arousability? As the discussion in Chapter 2.1 showed (see Figure 1), there are several alternative definitions of a "situation" and its properties. Accordingly, *stimulus intensity* could be defined by

- its physical characteristics (physico-biological situation); but this would not assess the intensity of "mental stress" tasks;
- the consensual rating of independent observers, a rating by the experimenter, or the average rating of the subjects with respect to "stimulus intensity" (canonical situation); but both independent raters and subjects would not know whether they should rate a physical property, the mental load, or physical effort they would invest or did actually invest into the experimental task;
- the subject's rating of the impact the stimulus had on them (functional situation); but again, the impact would have to be described in several dimensions;
- the average physiological response (modal situation); but the physiological behavior is the resultant of many factors, for example, of motor requirements or the stressfulness of the task that should not be confounded with stimulus intensity.

The assessment of stimulus stressfulness is more easily accomplished. *Stressfulness* is clearly related to the canonical or functional situation. *Arousability* and its effects on activation again presents a major problem for assessment: Given the "covariation problem" in psychophysiology (see Chapter 4.3), which variable or variable combination is an indicator for limbic arousability? Given individual response specificity (see Chapter 6.2.2), is there a variable or variable combination suited at all for all subjects? How should "arousability" in contrast to "arousal" be assessed (see Chapter 6.3 on covariance partitioning)? In Eysenck's theory, the assessment of *personality* is accomplished by questionnaire scales of extraversion and neuroticism. It is an unsettled question, however, whether extraversion and neuroticism alone or interactively would provide a better predictor of activation responses. Eysenck (1981) assumes that heightened limbic arousal will generate elevations in reticular arousal but not vice versa; it follows from this proposition that introverted neurotics should have the largest and extraverted stables the lowest autonomic responses under stressful stimulation. Stelmack (1981) proposes another facet of an interaction between extraversion and neuroticism: Introverted neurotics should have a predisposition to fear and extraverted neurotics to anger, which implies that fear or anger provoking situations lead to an enhanced autonomic responsivity only within the respective personality subgroup but not for all of the subjects scoring high in neuroticism.

The empirical test of Eysenck's propositions crucially depends on the operationalizations chosen. This is especially true for "stimulus intensity", as can be seen when specific hypotheses are derived from Eysenck's theory:

Hypothesis 1. Introverts respond more strongly than extraverts, if the sample of experimental conditions used consists of predominantly low-intensive stimuli. In this case, the correlation between extraversion and the level of physiological reactivity (i.e., the average magnitude of activation responses) should be negative. In contrast, positive correlations are expected, if the sample of experimental conditions used consists of predominantly high-intensive stimuli, because in this case extraverts respond more strongly than introverts. Correlations around zero are expected for a more balanced sample of stimulus intensities. Thus it turns out that a test of this central hypothesis in Eysenck's theory presupposes either an absolute scaling of "stimulus intensity" or an experimental design using a graded variation of one stimulus (with the risk, however, that high stimulus intensities usually also increase the stimulus' stressfulness). In the absence of both an absolute scaling and a graded variation of stimulus intensity (see Brocke & Liepmann, 1985, for an example of graded variation) this hypothesis is purely exploratory.

Hypothesis 2. Introverts and extraverts differ physiologically in a wide range of situations, high and low scorers on neuroticism, however, only when emotionally threatening stimuli are presented. Thus, compared to neuroticism, one would expect more numerically large correlation coefficients (with a sign depending upon stimulus intensity) between extraversion and activation responses.

Hypothesis 3. With increasing stimulus intensity, extraverts show increasingly larger activation responses. Thus, stimulus intensity is supposed to moderate the regression of activation responses on extraversion. With larger stimulus intensity, the regression slope will become more positive.

Hypothesis 4. With increasing stimulus stressfulness, subjects scoring high in neuroticism show increasingly larger activation responses. Thus, stimulus stressfulness is supposed to moderate the regression of activation responses on neuroticism.

In a primarily exploratory attempt at describing arousability relationships with personality within single experimental situations, it is of interest to study canonical, multiple, and Pearson correlations between autonomic reactivity and personality. Multiple correlations between separate personality scales and a set of physiological variables or components permit determining the predictability of each personality scale by the complete physiological information at hand; thus, multiple correlations can help to get around the problem of selecting the right physiological variable. Canonical correlations between the set of personality scales and a set of physiological variables or components allows one to determine the overall relationship between personality scales and autonomic reactivity; thus, canonical correlation can help to get around the problem of determining which particular combination of personality scales, for example, the combination of introversion and neuroticism, can be predicted best by autonomic reactivity.

The hypotheses and exploratory questions discussed above were investigated with the data of both Experiment 1 and Experiment 4. Experiment 1 was particularly well suited for the study of the arousability concept since it contained a large number of 52 experimental conditions and several "stressful" situations in the context of the emotion inductions of anger and fear (see Chapter 8.1). Its results have been described elsewhere (Stemmler & Meinhardt, 1990, 1991) and will be summarized below. Experiment 4 had a markedly smaller number of experimental conditions, but it offered a distinctive descriptive basis of autonomic cardiovascular activation (see Chapter 9.3).

In both studies, the operationalization of key theoretical terms was very similar. Stimulus intensity was operationalized by the modal situation, that is, by means of experimental conditions on physiological components. Stimulus stressfulness was assessed by self-reports of fear and anger (see Chapter 12) or by the experimenter's judgement (Experiment 1 only). Personality traits were measured by the Freiburger Persönlichkeitsinventar (Experiment 1: Fahrenberg, Selg & Hampel, 1978; Experiment 4: Fahrenberg, Hampel, & Selg, 1984) and the Freiburger Beschwerdenliste (Fahrenberg, 1975) which yielded among others the scales extraversion (FPI-E), neuroticism (FPI-N), aggressivity (FPI-2), and somatic complaints (FBL-11). Arousability was either assessed by physiological discriminant functions (Experiment 1; see Chapter 9.2.1 and Table 31) or by putative cardiovascular activation components derived from discriminant analysis (Experiment 4; see Chapter 9.3.3 and Figure 20; multistage linear estimation components were not appropriate, because they did not give separate scores for sessions, which would have been necessary for the study of the anger induction in session 3). The merit of using components instead of single variables has been discussed at length in Chapters 4 and 5; apart from the theoretical aspects discussed there, components are advantageous since (1) they are aggregates of variables, which reduces method variance, and (2) their usage keeps the number of statistical tests comparatively low. The term arousability clearly points to the subjects x conditions interaction source of variance, which is, on the one hand, independent of the individual arousal level (i.e., the between-subjects source of variance) and, on the other hand, of the situationally elicited arousal level (i.e., the between-conditions source of variance, which has been used for the operationalization of stimulus intensity). Therefore, with the exception of Hypothesis 4 in Experiment 4, in both experiments the subjects x conditions variance was used in the calculations. It might be recalled that this variance had earlier been termed the building block of motivational response specificity (see Chapter 6.2.2).

11.2 Results

11.2.1 Experiment 1

The results of Experiment 1 will be briefly summarized by hypothesis (for a detailed report, see Stemmler & Meinhardt, 1990, 1991). It should be noted that with the exception of the aggressivity scale, subject's personality scores did not deviate from the appropriate norm sample means. With regard to aggressivity, subjects had a significantly lower mean than the norm sample.

- *Hypothesis 1.* Reactivity levels did not correlate with personality scales. Whether stimulus intensity was in a medium range, which should obscure the predicted relationship between extraversion and reactivity levels, or Eysenck's prediction has to be doubted could of course not be determined.
- *Hypothesis 2.* Extraversion did not have higher absolute correlations with activation responses than neuroticism. Instead, aggressivity had higher absolute correlations than the other personality scales.
- *Hypothesis 3.* Stimulus intensity was not a moderator of the relationship between extraversion (or any of the other personality scales) and activation responses.
- *Hypothesis 4.* During selected emotionally stressful situations, neuroticism was not found to correlate positively with activation responses.

Exploratory correlations. Of the twelve experimental conditions (out of 52), for which either the canonical correlation or at least one of the four multiple correlations attained significance, only two belonged to the group of situations classified as stressful. The experimental conditions with significant correlations did not elicit an unusually high stimulus intensity (five were instruction periods, three waiting and prestimulus periods). Only 4.8% of the 768 Pearson correlations were significant (at the 5% level). Therefore it was not their number which was interesting, but their distribution:

- There was a significant trend to more significant correlations in the last third of the experiment (7, 5, and 25 significant correlations).
- Aggressivity had more significant correlations with activation responses than expected by chance (15 versus 9.6). At the beginning of the experiment, subjects scoring high in aggressivity were more responsive than subjects scoring low; at the end of the experiment, they were less responsive.
- Concordant with Eysenck's prediction, extraversion correlated (in four of the eight conditions where the significance level was reached) with a physiological component which was largely defined by EEG alpha reductions.
- Contrary to Eysenck's prediction, neuroticism was not preferentially correlated with the physiological component defined by autonomic reactivity.

In sum, given the operationalizations chosen, the predictions derived from Eysenck's biological personality theory could not be substantiated. However, it has to be kept in mind that theories neither can be verified nor falsified; conflicting empirical evidence can be attributed either to the theory itself or to the theoretical statements subserving the observations.

Although the results obviously did not fall into the range of applicability of Eysenck's theory, there were nonetheless demonstrable interrelations between personality and autonomic reactivity. Three more general conclusions might be drawn from these demonstrated relationships:

- A "tonic factor" (defined over the course of the experiment) influencing activation responses may be distinguished from a condition-specific "phasic factor"; both factors might be differentially related to personality. The "tonic factor" might correspond to the increased tiredness of the subjects or to their lowered levels of self-reported fear (Stemmler, 1984). Even though proposals about the psychological meaning of this "tonic factor" must remain speculative, the existence of a position effect should be considered worthy of further study. The correlation between condition number (1 to 52) and the magnitude of within-conditions correlations between neuroticism and the third component was $r = 0.53$; between aggressivity and the second component, $r = -0.40$. These correlations are descriptive of the linear trend that the "tonic factor" imposed on the relationship between activation responses and personality.
- Aggressivity might play a more important role in personality-arousability relationships than either extraversion or neuroticism.

- The concept of arousability is closely related to the concept of "the situation". Other aspects of situations than stimulus intensity or stressfulness might be important, such as the normative pressure of situations which tend to reduce the individual degrees of freedom of the behavior chosen.

11.2.2 Experiment 4

Experiment 4 differed from Experiment 1 in several respects. First, the number of conditions was smaller (22 versus 52); this difference was even enlarged by the construction of putative cardiovascular activation components, which from the outset were defined by prestimulus-task response scores leaving only seven (combined "easy" and "difficult" task version) change scores. Second, in Experiment 4 the factor Medication introduced an experimental condition that could be able to distort the personality - arousability relationship; therefore, with one exception all analyses reported below were based on the placebo group data only. Third, the selection of physiological variables was markedly different; Experiment 4 sampled largely from cardiovascular variables. Fourth, in Experiment 4 the derivation of physiological components was based on the Model of Cardiovascular Activation Components attempting to measure physiologically and pharmacologically definable quantities. The physiological components of Experiment 1 instead were defined by the given situation sample. Fifth, subjects were female in Experiment 1 and male in Experiment 4. As in Experiment 1, subjects in Experiment 4 were significantly less aggressive but also markedly more introverted than the norm sample (see Table 54).

Table 54. Basic Statistics of Personality Scales (Experiment 4)

Scale	Mean	SD	Skew-ness	Kurt-osis	Correlations A	E	N
A	**3.9** (5.4)[a]	1.76	0.45	0.11	1.00		
E	**4.1** (8.7)	1.66	0.11	-0.44	0.26	1.00	
N	5.3 (5.6)	2.03	0.30	-0.54	**0.29**	0.05	1.00
S	159.8 (155.2)	29.10	0.19	-0.46	0.08	0.00	**0.37**

Note. Means of norm sample in parentheses. A = aggressivity, E = extraversion, N = neuroticism, S = somatic complaints, SD = standard deviation. $n = 48$. Boldface numbers: $p < .05$. [a] Comparison of subject sample and norm sample means.

Hypothesis 1. The four personality scales were in turn correlated (1) with the set of reactivity levels and (2) the set of reactivity variabilities on the five putative cardiovascular activation components. Aggressivity had a significant multiple correlation ($R = 0.48$, $F(5/42) = 2.54$, $p < .05$) with reactivity levels; it could be significantly predicted by the beta1 and the beta3 components. The Pearson correlations between aggressivity and these predictors were $r = 0.25$ and $r = 0.35$ ($p < .05$), respectively. Somatic complaints correlated with the reactivity variability on the beta2 component, $r = 0.32$ ($p < .05$). Thus, rather than with extraversion, reactivity levels correlated with aggressivity; subjects scoring high on the aggressivity scale had larger putative inotropic beta-adrenergic activation responses than low scorers. Subjects scoring high in somatic complaints had a larger variability on the beta2 component compared to low scorers, that is, they responded rather selectively to the experimental conditions.

Hypothesis 2. Since in Experiment 4 the number of experimental conditions was low (see above), this hypothesis could not be evaluated.

Hypothesis 3. Here it was hypothesized that with increasing stimulus intensity, extraverts would show increasingly larger activation responses. The moderator analysis calculations, in turn with each personality scale as the criterion and the activation response and its product with the condition means (separately for each of the five components) as predictors, yielded only one significant effect. Stimulus intensity moderated the relationship between aggressivity and responses on the beta3 component: With larger stimulus intensity, the correlation increased ($t(293) = 2.31$, $p < .05$, after ϵ-correction with est(ϵ) $= 0.88$). Thus, on the beta3 component subjects high in aggressivity not only had larger reactivity levels (Hypothesis 1) but also larger responses in conditions with high stimulus intensity on that component. The speech task, the anticipation of sentence completion, and the loud noise task had a comparatively large beta3 stimulus intensity.

Hypothesis 4. This hypothesis predicted that with increasing stimulus stressfulness, subjects scoring high in neuroticism would show increasingly larger activation responses. In Experiment 1, this hypothesis was studied by comparing the relationship between neuroticism and activation responses across emotionally stressful and nonstressful situations (the *experimental approach*). In contrast, Experiment 4 employed the *differential approach* and studied the influence of individual differences in self-reported emotions (in particular, of fear and anger as indicators of situational stressfulness) on the relationship between neuroticism and activation responses within each experimental condition. Thus, two aspects of the functional situation (fear and anger reports) served as moderator variables in the analyses reported below. In addition, Experiment 4 offered the possibility for an in-depth study of Hypothesis 4 within a particularly stressful situation, the anger induction at Session 3.

Two sets of analyses were conducted. *Analysis 1* tested Hypothesis 4 with the data of all sessions but only within the placebo group (this choice avoids a potential confounding of medication effects on the relationship between neuroticism and activation responses). *Analysis 2* tested Hypothesis 4 within the anger induction of Session 3. The specificity of possible effects was assessed in two ways. First, in both sets of analyses, besides neuroticism the other personality scales were also checked with respect to the posited relationship to activation responses under the moderation of fear or anger. Second, Analysis 2 studied not only the anger induction but also all of the other experimental conditions during Session 3. Finally, in order to explore the differential approach as consistently as possible, activation responses were not freed from the individual reactivity levels (as was done for the analysis of Hypothesis 3 and the exploratory correlations to be reported later on). Thus, differential physiological effects of both the between-subjects and the subjects x conditions sources of variation were included in the activation responses. This variance had earlier been termed the building block of individual situational response specificity (see Chapter 3.1, Equation 8, and Chapter 6.2.2).

Analysis 1 of Hypothesis 4. In order to characterize the stressfulness of the experimental situations, Table 55 gives the placebo group's respective means of self-reported fear and anger calculated from the data of all sessions. The situations differed both in fear and anger (Wilks' lambda $F(6/42) = 10.50$, $p<.01$, and 3.32, $p<.05$). Pairwise comparisons of means (with Bonferroni-adjusted significance levels, $\alpha = 0.05/21 = 0.00238$) established (1) that the anticipation of the sentence completion task (the data included the anger induction on Session 3) elicited larger levels of self-reported anger than the handgrip, mental arithmetic, and the signal detection task; (2) that the loud noise task elicited larger levels of self-reported fear than the other tasks (with the exception of the anticipation of the sentence completion task), whereas the handgrip, signal detection, and cold pressor tasks had the lowest levels of self-reported fear (for details, see Table 55).

The moderator analysis proceeded as follows. For each experimental situation (out of 7), personality scale (out of 4), putative cardiovascular activation component (out of 5), and self-report scale (out of 2) a multiple regression equation, with the personality scale as the criterion and the activation component, the self-report scale, and the component * self-report scale product as predictors, was performed. Those multiple regression equations that had at least a moderate overall model effect (i.e., a joint influence by all predictors) with $p<.10$ *and* a significant ($p<.05$) regression coefficient of either the activation component or the component * self-report product, were further considered. In a first stage of the analysis, the number of significant results found in various combinations of situations, components, personality scales, and self-reports of emotion was compared to the chance expectation. In a second stage, the selected regression equations were simplified by inserting the minimal and, if the product term was significant, also the maximal scale value of the self-report scale (zero and six, respectively). This procedure leads to simple linear equations and helps in the interpretation of the regression equation (Cohen & Cohen, 1983).

Table 55. Means of Self-Reported Fear and Anger (Placebo Group, Across all Sessions) in Experimental Situations and Their Comparison

Variable	Situations Ordered by Means						
Fear	LN	SC	MA	SP	CP	SD	HG
	2.00	1.50	0.81	0.73	0.58	0.37	0.27
	*	*	+	+	+	+	
		x	x	x	0	0	0
Anger	SC	LN	CP	SP	MA	HG	SD
	1.50	1.14	0.75	0.70	0.70	0.62	0.48
	*	*	*	*			
		+	+	+	+	+	+

Note. Situations marked by the same symbol are not significantly different (Bonferroni-adjusted pairwise comparisons, $p < .05$). SP = Speech. HG = Handgrip. MA = Mental arithmetic. SD = Signal detection. LN = Loud noise. CP = Cold pressor. SC = Sentence completion.

The survey of significant results was performed under the assumption of the binomial law with a chance probability of $p = .05$. Although the overall number of significant equations (20) did not markedly exceed the chance level (14), several findings, where significant results were obtained more frequently than expected by chance, are worthy of note. For example, the alpha component contributed to 8 significant regression equations (3.2 by chance); self-reported anger, 13 (7 by chance); the combination alpha component x self-reported anger, 7 (1.4 by chance); the cold pressor task, 5 (2 by chance); the combination of the personality scale somatic complaints x handgrip task, 3 (0.5 by chance); the combination neuroticism x cold pressor task, 3 (0.5 by chance); the combination somatic complaints x alpha component, 3 (0.7 by chance); the combination neuroticism x tau component, 3 (0.7 by chance); the combination somatic complaints x self-reported anger, 5 (1.75 by chance); and finally the combination neuroticism x self-reported anger, 5 (1.75 by chance). It appears that only certain combinations of personality scales, components, situations, and self-report scales contribute to or allow a prediction of personality x arousability relationships: Neuroticism and somatic complaints, alpha component activation, and self-reported anger as a moderator.

Table 56 reports the regression equations selected according to the criteria noted above. I will comment on these equations in turn for each personality scale.

Somatic complaints could be predicted more often (seven times) than the other personality scales. Interestingly, for this scale three significant regression equations occurred in the handgrip task which evoked (together with signal

Table 56. Within-Conditions Prediction of Personality by Putative Cardiovascular Activation Components and Self-Reported Fear or Anger as Moderator Variables (Experiment 4, Placebo Data from all Sessions)

Regression Equations		R^b
Speech Task		
$A = 4.03 + \mathbf{0.44}\beta_3 - 0.28f - 0.10\beta_3 f$		*0.37*
	For Minimum Fear[a]: $A = 4.03 + 0.44\beta_3$	
	For Maximum Fear[a]: -[c]	
$A = 3.64 + \mathbf{0.41}\beta_3 + 0.27a + 0.18\beta_3 a$		*0.39*
	For Minimum Anger[a]: $A = 3.64 + 0.41\beta_3$	
	For Maximum Anger[a]: -[c]	
$E = 3.94 - \mathbf{0.52}\alpha + 0.02a + \mathbf{0.41}\alpha a$		**0.41**
	For Minimum Anger[a]: $E = 3.94 - 0.52\alpha$	
	For Maximum Anger[a]: $E = 4.03 + 1.94\alpha$	
$E = 4.47 - \mathbf{0.52}\beta_3 - 0.34f + 0.48\beta_3 f$		**0.45**
	For Minimum Fear[a]: $E = 4.47 - 0.52\beta_3$	
	For Maximum Fear[a]: -[c]	
Handgrip		
$S = 157.97 - \mathbf{7.80}\alpha + 4.21a - 1.10\alpha a$		*0.39*
	For Minimum Anger[a]: $S = 157.97 - 7.80\alpha$	
	For Maximum Anger[a]: -[c]	
$S = 161.47 + 4.25\beta_1 - 3.63f + \mathbf{18.07}\beta_1 f$		**0.45**
	For Minimum Fear[a]: $S = 161.47 + 4.25\beta_1$	
	For Maximum Fear[a]: $S = 139.69 + 112.67\beta_1$	
$S = 160.97 + \mathbf{5.83}\beta_2 + 5.33f - \mathbf{20.28}\beta_2 f$		*0.37*
	For Minimum Fear[a]: $S = 160.92 + 5.83\beta_2$	
	For Maximum Fear[a]: $S = 192.90 - 115.85\beta_2$	
$N = 4.71 - 0.29\tau + \mathbf{1.00}a + \mathbf{0.52}\tau a$		*0.40*
	For Minimum Anger[a]: $N = 4.71 - 0.29\tau$	
	For Maximum Anger[a]: $N = 10.71 + 2.83\tau$	
Mental Arithmetic		
$S = 157.75 + \mathbf{9.44}\alpha + 2.15a - \mathbf{9.42}\alpha a$		*0.40*
	For Minimum Anger[a]: $S = 157.75 + 9.44\alpha$	
	For Maximum Anger[a]: $S = 170.65 - 47.08\alpha$	
$A = 3.72 + 0.17\alpha + 0.30a + \mathbf{0.59}\alpha a$		**0.42**
	For Minimum Anger[a]: $A = 3.72 + 0.17\alpha$	
	For Maximum Anger[a]: $A = 5.52 + 3.71\alpha$	
$N = 4.97 + \mathbf{0.61}\alpha + 0.40a - 0.51\alpha a$		**0.42**
	For Minimum Anger[a]: $N = 4.97 + 0.61\alpha$	
	For Maximum Anger[a]: -[c]	
$N = 4.92 + 0.25\beta_1 + \mathbf{0.54}a - \mathbf{0.30}\beta_1 a$		**0.41**
	For Minimum Anger[a]: $N = 4.92 + 0.25\beta_1$	
	For Maximum Anger[a]: $N = 8.16 - 1.55\beta_1$	

(Table continues)

Table 56. Within-Conditions Prediction of Personality by Putative Cardiovascular Activation Components and Self-Reported Fear or Anger as Moderator Variables (Experiment 4, Placebo Data from all Sessions) *(continued)*

Regression Equations	R^b
Signal Detection	
$S = 159.33 - \mathbf{13.32}\alpha + 2.48a + 6.75\alpha a$	*0.39*
For Minimum Anger[a]: $S = 159.33 - 13.32\alpha$	
For Maximum Anger[a]: -[c]	
Loud Noise	
$S = 158.38 + \mathbf{10.17}\tau - 1.34a + 1.00\tau a$	*0.36*
For Minimum Anger[a]: $S = 158.38 + 10.17\tau$	
For Maximum Anger[a]: -[c]	
$A = 4.22 + 0.78\alpha - 0.16f - \mathbf{0.28}\alpha f$	*0.39*
For Minimum Fear[a]: $A = 4.22 + 0.78\alpha$	
For Maximum Fear[a]: $A = 3.26 - 0.90\alpha$	
Cold Pressor	
$S = 160.97 - 8.11\beta_1 - 0.39a + \mathbf{7.84}\beta_1 a$	**0.46**
For Minimum Anger[a]: $S = 160.97 - 8.11\beta_1$	
For Maximum Anger[a]: $S = 158.63 + 38.93\beta_1$	
$E = 3.84 + 0.31\tau + \mathbf{0.51}f - \mathbf{0.72}\tau f$	**0.45**
For Minimum Fear[a]: $E = 3.84 + 0.31\tau$	
For Maximum Fear[a]: $E = 6.90 - 4.01\tau$	
$N = 4.87 + \mathbf{0.71}\alpha + \mathbf{0.57}a - \mathbf{0.76}\alpha a$	**0.41**
For Minimum Anger[a]: $N = 4.87 + 0.71\alpha$	
For Maximum Anger[a]: $N = 8.29 - 3.85\alpha$	
$N = 5.35 - 0.48\tau - 0.14f + \mathbf{0.93}\tau f$	*0.39*
For Minimum Fear[a]: $N = 5.35 - 0.48\tau$	
For Maximum Fear[a]: $N = 4.51 + 5.10\tau$	
$N = 5.47 - \mathbf{0.98}\tau + 0.17a + \mathbf{0.62}\tau a$	**0.44**
For Minimum Anger[a]: $N = 5.47 - 0.98\tau$	
For Maximum Anger[a]: $N = 6.49 + 2.74\tau$	
Anticipation of Sentence Completion[d]	

Note. S = Somatic complaints. A = Aggressivity. E = Extraversion. N = Neuroticism. a = Self-reported anger. f = Self-reported fear. The analyses were based on $n = 48$. Boldface numbers: $p < .05$. Italicized numbers: $p < .10$. [a]The minimum value of the emotional self-report scales was 0, the maximum was 6. [b]Multiple R's were tested against zero with $df = 3, 44$. [c]Due to the lack of significant interaction effects in the general regression equation, there are no separate specialized regressions. [d]No significant results found.

detection) the lowest levels of self-reported fear or anger (see Table 55). These equations showed high scorers on this scale to be predictable (1) by small or negative responses on the alpha component, (2) by large responses on the beta1 component if self-reported fear was large, and (3) by large responses on the beta2 component if fear was low, but by small responses if fear was high. During mental arithmetic, scores on the somatic complaints scale were positively related to the alpha component if self-reported anger was low; they were, however, negatively related if anger was high. During signal detection, somatic complaints were predicted by low alpha component scores. During loud noise, somatic complaints covaried with increases in the tau component. Finally, during cold pressor, scores on this scale were predictable by the beta1 component, but only if self-reported anger was high. In sum, putative beta-adrenergic activation responses predicted somatic complaints only in interaction with high fear or anger, whereas putative alpha-adrenergic response decrements covaried with somatic complaints either directly or in combination with high anger. Thus, these results suggest that somatic complaints are predictable by high beta1 and both low beta2 and low alpha component responses provided that emotional involvement was high. One could speculate that a beta-adrenergic - alpha-adrenergic balance is important for this personality dimension.

Neuroticism was significantly predicted on six instances. During handgrip, both the level of self-reported anger and the interaction between anger and the tau component predicted neuroticism. The covariation occurred only if anger was high, in which case increased tau component responses contributed to the prediction. During mental arithmetic, neuroticism was related to large alpha component responses. Only if self-reported anger was high could neuroticism be predicted by decreased beta1 responses. Finally, during cold pressor, (1) an increased alpha component response covaried with neuroticism if anger was low, but a decreased response if anger was high, (2) an elevated tau component response predicted neuroticism, but only if fear was high, and (3) tau component reductions given low anger, and tau increases given high anger were related to neuroticism. The picture which energes from these findings is both unexpected and consistent. Given high levels of self-reported anger, decreased rather than increased cardiovascular responses (larger tau and both smaller beta1 and alpha component) were found to be predictive of neuroticism. Conversely, under low anger, large responses (alpha and tau component responses) covaried with neuroticism. The results also suggest that an alpha-adrenergic - cholinergic balance is important for this personality dimension.

Aggressivity contributed four significant multiple regression equations. During the speech task, aggressivity could be predicted by large beta3 responses. During mental arithmetic, jointly high levels of self-reported anger and large alpha component responses covaried with aggressivity. During loud noise, high levels of self-reported fear and alpha component decrements predicted aggressivity. The increased reactivity levels and the larger response magnitudes with increasing stimulus intensity in the beta3 component of subjects scoring high in aggressivity had already been noted in Hypotheses 1 and 3, respectively.

As expected, this effect reappeared here in the speech task. One should note that the beta3 component is marked by systolic blood pressure increases, as is the alpha component. The latter was involved in the correlations with aggressivity with a positive relationship if anger was high; with a negative relationship, instead, if fear was high.

Extraversion could be significantly predicted only three times. During the speech task, under low self-reported anger, extraversion was predicted by reduced alpha component responses, but under high anger, by increased alpha component responses. During the speech task, also extraversion covaried with beta3 component decrements. During cold pressor, extraversion was predicted by high levels of self-reported fear and, given these high levels, by tau component reductions.

Analysis 2 of Hypothesis 4. Analysis 2 was confined to Session 3 data. It was of particular interest whether the anger induction would lead to a stronger relationship between neuroticism and activation responses than the other less stressful situations. Table 57 shows the means of self-reported fear and anger calculated from Session 3 data across all medication groups. The situations differed with regard to fear and anger (Wilks' lambda $F(6/42) = 12.31$ and 7.11, respectively, $p < .01$). Comparison of situation means (with Bonferroni-adjusted significance levels, $\alpha = 0.05/21$) showed that the anger induction actually led to the largest levels of self-reported anger and that the ordering of tasks according to self-reported fear was essentially the same as in Analysis 1.

The moderator analysis proceeded exactly as in Analysis 1. However, since the analysis used the data from all medication groups which might lead to an interaction of subject selection (the sample of $n = 12$ subjects within each group

Table 57. Means of Self-Reported Fear and Anger (Session 3 Anger Day, Across all Medication Groups) in Experimental Situations and Their Comparison)

Variable	Situations Ordered by Means						
Fear	LN	SC	MA	CP	SP	SD	HG
	1.69	1.52	0.81	0.54	0.42	0.37	0.17
	*	*	+	+	+		
		x	x	0	0	0	0
Anger	SC	LN	CP	MA	HG	SP	SD
	2.71	1.39	1.18	1.00	0.87	0.77	0.66
		*	*	*	*	*	*

Note. Situations marked by the same symbol are not significantly different (Bonferroni-adjusted pairwise comparisons, $p < .05$). SP = Speech. HG = Handgrip. MA = Mental arithmetic. SD = Signal detection. LN = Loud noise. CP = Cold pressor. SC = Sentence completion.

and their particular personality score distribution) and medication effects on activation responses, the following results have to be interpreted with more caution than those of Analysis 1. Caution should be practiced depite the fact that an analysis of variance on personality scores showed no differences between medication groups ($F(3/44) = 0.09$, 0.07, 0.08, and 0.78, $p > 0.50$, for somatic complaints, aggressivity, extraversion, and neuroticism, respectively).

The survey of significant results again revealed a number of significant findings that occurred more frequently than expected by chance. For example, neuroticism was significantly predicted 11 times (3.5 by chance); the tau component contributed to 8 significant regression equations (3.2 by chance); the combination beta1 component x self-reported fear, 4 (1.4 by chance), and likewise tau x fear, 4, as well as tau x anger, 4; the cold pressor task, 5 (2 by chance); the combination of the personality scale neuroticism x handgrip task, 3 (0.5 by chance), and likewise neuroticism x sentence completion plus anger induction, 3; the combination neuroticism x tau component, 6 (0.7 by chance); and finally the combination neuroticism x anger, 6 (1.75 by chance). It appears that more than others, neuroticism and the tau component contributed to or allowed a prediction of personality x arousability relationships. One might also note the common findings of Analyses 1 and 2; both of which showed an emphasis of the cold pressor task, the combination of neuroticism x anger, and the combination of neuroticism x tau component.

Table 58 shows the regression equations selected from Analysis 2. *Somatic complaints* could be significantly predicted by beta1, beta2 and tau component responses almost only if fear or anger ratings were high. *Neuroticism* covaried both during low and high reported fear or anger with beta1, beta2, beta3, and the tau component; however, the direction of correlation changed conditional to the level of emotional self-reports. The expectation that neuroticism should be related to activation responses particularly during the anger induction, was not corroborated by the results (both the low-stressful handgrip task and the high-stressful anger induction each led to three significant predictions). However, neuroticism was the only personality dimension that was predictable during the anger induction. Similar to Analysis 1, low levels of reported fear or anger often allowed a prediction of neuroticism by putative cardiovascular activation response increases, whereas response decrements (in particular, tau component increases) correlated with neuroticism given a high emotional involvement. During speech and loud noise, *aggressivity* showed results similar to Analysis 1. With only one significant prediction, *extraversion* was the personality dimension demonstrating the largest independence of arousability.

In sum, the analysis of Hypothesis 4 unearthed a wealth of findings, the details of which may at present be less important than these general points:

- The prediction of personality dimensions by physiological activation responses seems to be less improbable than suggested by earlier results employing a different research strategy (e.g., an experimental in contrast to a differential

Table 58. Within-Conditions Prediction of Personality by Putative Cardiovascular Activation Components and Self-Reported Fear or Anger as Moderator Variables (Experiment 4, Data from all Medication Groups, Anger Day only)

Regression Equations	R^b
Speech Task	
$A = 3.77 + \mathbf{0.37}\beta_3 + 0.19a - \mathbf{0.22}\beta_3 a$	**0.41**
For Minimum Anger[a]: $A = 3.77 + 0.37\beta_3$	
For Maximum Anger[a]: $A = 4.91 - 0.95\beta_3$	
$A = 3.27 - 0.21\tau + \mathbf{0.91}a + \mathbf{0.23}\tau a$	*0.37*
For Minimum Anger[a]: $A = 3.27 - 0.21\tau$	
For Maximum Anger[a]: $A = 8.73 + 1.17\tau$	
$E = 4.08 - \mathbf{0.54}\beta_1 + 0.29f + \mathbf{0.89}\beta_1 f$	*0.36*
For Minimum Fear[a]: $E = 4.08 - 0.54\beta 1$	
For Maximum Fear[a]: $E = 5.82 + 4.80\beta 1$	
$N = 5.03 + \mathbf{0.74}\beta_1 + 0.42f - \mathbf{0.84}\beta_1 f$	**0.41**
For Minimum Fear[a]: $N = 5.03 + 0.74\beta_1$	
For Maximum Fear[a]: $N = 7.55 - 4.30\beta_1$	
Handgrip	
$N = 4.58 - \mathbf{0.71}\beta_2 + \mathbf{0.66}a + \mathbf{0.51}\beta_2 a$	**0.41**
For Minimum Anger[a]: $N = 4.58 - 0.71\beta_2$	
For Maximum Anger[a]: $N = 8.54 + 2.35\beta_2$	
$N = 4.40 - \mathbf{1.04}\beta_3 + \mathbf{0.80}a + \mathbf{0.64}\beta_3 a$	**0.47**
For Minimum Anger[a]: $N = 4.40 - 1.04\beta_3$	
For Maximum Anger[a]: $N = 9.20 + 2.80\beta_3$	
$N = 4.38 - 0.33\tau + \mathbf{1.37}a + \mathbf{0.53}\tau a$	**0.45**
For Minimum Anger[a]: $N = 4.38 - 0.33\tau$	
For Maximum Anger[a]: $N = 12.60 + 2.85\tau$	
Mental Arithmetic	
$S = 152.16 + 2.01\beta_1 + \mathbf{13.59}f - \mathbf{6.24}\beta_1 f$	**0.43**
For Minimum Fear[a]: $S = 152.16 + 2.01\beta_1$	
For Maximum Fear[a]: $S = 233.70 - 35.43\beta_1$	
$S = 159.94 + 0.44\beta_2 + 1.65a + \mathbf{8.31}\beta_2 a$	*0.36*
For Minimum Anger[a]: $S = 159.94 + 0.44\beta_2$	
For Maximum Anger[a]: $S = 169.84 + 50.30\beta_2$	
$N = 5.05 + 0.21\beta_1 + 0.24a - \mathbf{0.26}\beta_1 a$	*0.37*
For Minimum Anger[a]: $N = 5.05 + 0.21\beta_1$	
For Maximum Anger[a]: $N = 6.49 - 1.35\beta_1$	
Signal Detection	
$N = 5.12 - 0.19\tau + 0.41f + \mathbf{0.65}\tau f$	**0.40**
For Minimum Fear[a]: $N = 5.12 - 0.19\tau$	
For Maximum Fear[a]: $N = 7.58 + 3.71\tau$	

(Table continues)

Table 58. Within-Conditions Prediction of Personality by Putative Cardiovascular Activation Components and Self-Reported Fear or Anger as Moderator Variables (Experiment 4, Data from all Medication Groups, Anger Day only) *(continued)*

Regression Equations	R^b
Loud Noise	
$A = 4.12 + \mathbf{0.90}\alpha - 0.17f - \mathbf{0.29}\alpha f$	*0.38*
For Minimum Fear[a]: $A = 4.12 + 0.90$	
For Maximum Fear[a]: $A = 3.10 - 0.84\alpha$	
$N = 5.43 - 0.47\tau + 0.26a - \mathbf{0.56}\tau a$	**0.42**
For Minimum Anger[a]: $N = 5.43 - 0.47\tau$	
For Maximum Anger[a]: $N = 6.99 - 3.83\tau$	
Cold Pressor	
$S = 143.30 - \mathbf{10.06}\beta_2 + \mathbf{15.45}f + 6.84\beta_2 f$	**0.40**
For Minimum Fear[a]: $S = 143.30 - 10.06\beta_2$	
For Maximum Fear[a]: -[c]	
$S = 154.78 - 4.75\tau + \mathbf{11.25}f + \mathbf{6.97}\tau f$	*0.39*
For Minimum Fear[a]: $S = 154.78 - 4.75\tau$	
For Maximum Fear[a]: $S = 222.28 + 37.07\tau$	
$A = 4.53 - \mathbf{1.09}\beta_1 + 0.36a - 0.22\beta_1 a$	**0.48**
For Minimum Anger[a]: $A = 4.53 - 1.09\beta_1$	
For Maximum Anger[a]: -[c]	
$A = 5.08 - \mathbf{1.55}\beta_1 - 0.44f + 0.51\beta_1 f$	**0.50**
For Minimum Fear[a]: $A = 5.08 - 1.55\beta_1$	
For Maximum Fear[a]: -[c]	
$N = 5.01 - \mathbf{0.54}\tau + 0.61f + 0.36\tau f$	*0.36*
For Minimum Fear[a]: $N = 5.01 - 0.54\tau$	
For Maximum Fear[a]: -[c]	
Sentence Completion	
$N = 4.77 + \mathbf{0.72}\beta_3 + 0.30f - 0.10\beta_3 f$	**0.40**
For Minimum Fear[a]: $N = 4.77 + 0.72\beta_3$	
For Maximum Fear[a]: -[c]	
$N = 4.72 - \mathbf{0.41}\tau + 0.41f + \mathbf{0.19}\tau f$	*0.36*
For Minimum Fear[a]: $N = 4.72 - 0.41\tau$	
For Maximum Fear[a]: $N = 7.18 + 0.73\tau$	
$N = 4.97 - \mathbf{0.63}\tau + 0.10a + \mathbf{0.14}\tau a$	*0.39*
For Minimum Anger[a]: $N = 4.97 - 0.63\tau$	
For Maximum Anger[a]: $N = 5.57 + 0.21\tau$	

Note. S = Somatic complaints. A = Aggressivity. E = Extraversion. N = Neuroticism. a = Self-reported anger. f = Self-reported fear. The analyses were based on $n = 48$. Boldface numbers: $p < .05$. Italicized numbers: $p < .10$. [a]The minimum value of the emotional self-report scales was 0, the maximum was 6. [b]Multiple R's were tested against zero with $df = 3, 44$. [c]Due to the lack of significant interaction effects in the general regression equation, there are no separate specialized regressions. [d]No significant results found.

strategy) and a different "model of personality". The model implied by the moderator analysis views personality dimensions as influencing both the affective involvement and, through it or as part of it, the physiological behavior. Thus, the organizing functions of emotions for behavior, rather than emotions or physiological behavior per se, are related to personality.

- Emotional self-reports capture processes that can obscure, amplify, or reverse the relationship between personality and arousability.
- Compared to extraversion and aggressivity, neuroticism and somatic complaints were more often rather than less often predictable by activation responses (with and without moderation by emotional self-reports).
- The direction of the relationship between personality dimensions and activation responses, at least in the case of neuroticism, turned out to be contrary to common belief: Given high levels of emotional stressfulness, putative cholinergic cardiovascular activation responses increased, that is, cardiac activity was *inhibited*. This observation reminds one of Gray's conceptualization of anxiety as a cortical system governing behavioral inhibition (Gray, 1982). Anxiety sensu Gray is the combination of Eysenck's neuroticism and introversion dimensions, which might have been captured by the present neuroticism effects, since the subject sample was significantly more introverted than the respective population.
- There was preliminary evidence that responses on particular putative cardiovascular activation components could be more characteristic for one than another personality dimension.
- Contrary to Eysenck's prediction, neuroticism was not better predictable during stressful compared to non-stressful situations. Instead, neuroticism was predictable when self-reports primarily of anger were high, irrespective of a situation's average rating of anger. That is, it was not the construal of the canonical but of the functional situation; not the application of the experimental but of the differential perspective of a moderation by stressfulness that led to a manifestation of relationships between neuroticism and arousability.

In comparison to Experiment 1, *exploratory correlations* of personality scales with activation responses within situations did not add new aspects over and above those already discussed. Multiple correlations in turn of each personality scale with the set of five putative cardiovascular activation components yielded three significant (out of 4 personality scales x 7 situations = 28 calculated) predictions, somatic complaints during handgrip ($R = 0.56$, $F(5/42) = 3.94$, $p<.01$) and during loid noise ($R = 0.52$, $F(5/42) = 3.12$, $p<.05$) as well as aggressivity during cold pressor ($R = 0.48$, $F(5/42) = 2.45$, $p<.05$). Neuroticism could not be significantly predicted by activation responses alone, which attests to the superiority of a personality model incorporating emotional responses.

In conclusion, neither Experiment 1 nor Experiment 4 produced evidence in favor of Eysenck's biological personality theory: Extraversion correlated neither with reactivity level nor with activation response magnitudes given increasing levels of stimulus intensity. Neuroticism did not correlate with activation responses during emotionally stressful situations or at least not more frequently than in emotionally non-stressful situations. The experiments did not, however, furnish evidence for a complete lack of relationships between personality and arousability. Both experiments found evidence that the aggressivity dimension of personality was positively related to the magnitude of physiological responses, at least at the beginning of the experiments. The most provocative findings, however, came from the moderator analyses in Experiment 4 (see the summary above), since they point to the need of an integration of personality, emotions, situational evocativeness, and physiological behavior. Although such an integration has only been schematized here in the stimulus-response mediation model of Figure 1, its empirical study is equally possible and should lead to a progress in the biological theory of personality.

12 Research on the Psychophysiology of Anger

12.1 Research Issues

A prominent field of psychophysiological inquiry has been the specificity of physiological emotion profiles (Ax, 1953; Ekman, Levenson, & Friesen, 1983; Fridlund, Schwartz, & Fowler, 1984; Funkenstein, 1956; Levenson, Ekman, & Friesen, 1990; Roberts & Weerts, 1982; Schachter, 1957; Schwartz, Weinberger, & Singer, 1981; Stemmler, 1989). While some authors are convinced that physiological emotion specificity is an already established fact (e.g., Wagner, 1989), other authors are much more skeptical (e.g., Stemmler, 1989). Elsewhere I have suggested that part of the inhomogeneity of the specificity literature can be traced back to different implicit meanings of the notion of physiological emotion specificity that seem to underly different emotion theories (Stemmler, in press). A close inspection of experimental designs that could be employed to test these different notions of specificity revealed that emotion theories are too vaguely formulated as to permit an adequate test. A related difficulty of this research is to disentangle the effects on physiological activation profiles of the situational context within which an emotion induction is embedded from the putative emotion effects themselves (Stemmler, in press).

With respect to physiological emotion specificity, the single most consistent finding has been an elevated diastolic blood pressure during anger (Ax, 1953; Cohen & Silverman, 1959; Erdmann & van Lindern, 1980; Frody, 1978; Funkenstein, King, & Drolette, 1954; Gambaro & Rabin, 1969; Gentry, 1970; Oken, 1966; Roberts & Weerts, 1982; Schachter, 1957; Schwartz et al., 1981). In the sequel of Funkenstein's hypothesis that anger (specifically, "anger-out") leads to the secretion of both norepinephrine and epinephrine, and fear to the predominant secretion of epinephrine, these putative hormonal specificities of anger and fear have been employed to characterize the cardiovascular changes observed (most recently by Wagner, 1989). In particular, the rise in diastolic blood pressure during anger was consistent with the norepinephrine-epinephrine hypothesis of anger.

However, other findings are at variance with this hypothesis. For example, Frankenhaeuser (1975), refering to her vast experience about the effects of situations on the two catecholamines, challenged the view that the ratio of epinephrine to norepinephrine should be specific to emotions. Similarly, Chessick, Bassan, and Shattan (1966) rejected the specificity hypothesis after comparing physiological fear, anger, and pain profiles with profiles of infused catecholamines. Comparing Type A and B subjects under harassment, Glass et al. (1980) found neither differences in diastolic blood pressure nor in norepinephrine.

A second general issue of psychophysiological inquiries into emotions is concerned with the components or referents of emotions and their sequential relationships. For one class of emotion theories, feelings and physiological activation are largely independent outputs of one central nervous system process (W.B. Cannon, R.S. Lazarus, R.W. Levenson). A second class of emotion theories postulates a conditional relationship between feelings and activation (W. James, P. Ekman, C.E. Izard, H. Leventhal, G. Mandler, S. Schachter, S.S. Tomkins, D. Zillmann). The theory of S. Schachter (Schachter & Singer, 1962; Schachter, 1975) stimulated a wave of research which is of particular interest here. According to S. Schachter, unexplained activation (whether or not specifically patterned during particular emotions was deemed irrelevant) is the trigger for a cognitive search for the putative emotional source. Emotional feelings are the result of both the organismic and the cognitive factors: Feeling intensity is determined by the level of activation; the kind of emotion felt, by the cognitive process.

In their classical experiment, Schachter and Singer (1962) varied (1) the level (but, of course, also the pattern) of activation by the injection of epinephrine and (2) the putative cause of activation by context variations (the behavior of a stooge) which in the respective experimental conditions strongly suggested the emotional labels of euphoria and anger. However, the self-reports of anger did not show the expected result according to which, in comparison to the epinephrine-informed or the placebo group, the epinephrine-ignore group would report the highest anger. Referring to the norepinephrine-epinephrine hypothesis of anger, one could speculate that the predominantly beta-adrenergic physiological profile elicited by epinephrine was not "compatible" with the mixed alpha-adrenergic and beta-adrenergic profile supposedly characteristic of anger. Thus, the beta-adrenergic physiological activation under epinephrine might not have been able to trigger the cognitive labelling process.

In a series of studies, Erdmann and associates reached the same conclusion. With respect to the emotion of fear, Erdmann (1983) reported results that were concordant with Schachter's predictions. In a graded speech anxiety (three levels) x medication group (a beta-adrenergic agonist, placebo, and a beta-adrenergic antagonist) design, Erdmann found for the medium level of speech anxiety a significant medication effect on the self-report of fear: the beta-adrenergic agonist elicited the highest levels of reported fear, the beta-adrenergic antagonist the lowest levels. With respect to anger, Erdmann and van Lindern (1980) failed to find support for Schachter's theory. Using the same medications but an anger-inducing and a control condition, the self-report of anger increased significantly only under placebo and not, as expected, under the beta-adrenergic agonist. However, as in the previous study, the agonist was associated with a significant rise in self-reported fear. Following these results, one could question Schachter's notion of unspecific activation and suggest instead that self-reported anger would be elicited or amplified only after an alpha-adrenergically colored activation.

Both the issue of physiological emotion specificity and the question of the relationship between feelings and physiological activation are of concern for a differential psychophysiology. The study of physiological emotion specificity has to deal effectively with the problem of disentangling context from emotion effects, or termed differently, situational from emotional specificity. The study of the relationship between feelings and activation relates the functional (i.e., subjective or psychological) situation to components of physiological behavior.

Physiological emotion specificity has been studied in Experiments 1 and 4. Experiment 1 allowed revisiting the autonomic differentiation of fear, anger, and happiness and has been described elsewhere (see Stemmler, 1984, 1989; Stemmler, Bruhn, & Koch, 1986; Stemmler, Thom, & Koch, 1986). Briefly, using a convergent und discriminant validation approach, physiological emotion profiles from a real-life induction and an imagery context were compared with one another and with a control condition. Self-report data confirmed the generation of affective states in both contexts. Multivariate comparisons between physiological profiles established discriminant validity for fear and anger in the real-life context, whereas under imagery, emotion profiles were indistinguishable. Convergent validity of homologous emotions across contexts could not be substantiated. Neither the notion of "absolute specificity" nor of "nonspecificity" was congruent with the obtained results. Instead, it was concluded that the pattern of results was in large accordance with the "context-deviation" notion of physiological emotion specificity. This notion posits that

> the context [within which an emotion is induced] has a marked influence on the physiological profile, but that an emotion specifically modifies the intensity and/or pattern of this profile. Thus, an emotion is credited with the difference between the profiles representing the context alone and the added emotional stimulus. (Stemmler, 1989, p. 619.)

Experiment 4 allowed revisiting the cardiovascular characterization of anger as a norepinephrinergic-epinephrinergic (i.e., a mixed alpha-adrenergic and beta-adrenergic) pattern of activation. Apart from the single physiological variables (in particular, diastolic blood pressure) and their complete profile, the putative cardiovascular activation components described in Chapter 9.3 were the appropriate units of analysis. Control of context, in contrast to emotion, effects was achieved by the comparison of "neutral days" versus "anger day" data (the anger induction took place at Session 3, the same context without an anger induction was presented at Sessions 1, 2 and 4; see Chapter 8.4.3).

The study of the relationship between feelings and activation in Experiment 4 could be easily followed up by comparing the medication groups both in self-reports of emotion and physiological variables as well as putative cardiovascular components. Complementary to this experimental approach was the correlational investigation of individual differences in feelings and physiological activation.

12.2 Results

12.2.1 Self-reports of emotion

Central to the issue of physiological emotion specificity was the question whether the anger induction elicited an average increase in the feelings of anger over and above those reported on neutral days. For the issue of the relationship between feelings and physiological activation, the comparison of affective self-reports among medication groups on the anger day was important. Both sets of results will be presented in this section, before the specificity and the relationship issues will be addressed in the next two sections.

After each task, an affective self-report was obtained on 20 7-point rating scales. Three items characterized psychological activation/deactivation, "I am active and energetic", "I am tired", and "I am relaxed". Three items referred to anger, "I am angry", "I am bothered", and "I am irritated". The three emotions happiness, fear, and depression each were represented by one item only. Selected emotional effects on cognitive functioning (Epstein, 1984) were assessed by two items, "I am confused" and "I am mentally alert". As a kind of summary statement, subjects rated the amount of "mental" and "physical" stress. Seven more items were about bodily feelings: "Pounding heart", "Rapid heart beat", "Blushing", "Clammy Palms", "Shaky hands", "Tight chest", and "Tense body".

All of the following statistical tests were performed separately for each medication group. On neutral days, for the anticipation period of the sentence completion task nearly all scales (98%) were significantly different from the scale value of zero (i.e., an intensity rating of zero; the feeling was absent). On the anger day, a few less scales, but still 83%, had means larger than zero. Differences within medication groups between neutral and anger days could be tested in a between-subjects analysis of variance on the session effect and an ensuing contrast of the third (anger) to the other (neutral) sessions. With the exception of the "beta-free" group, within medication groups there were only few self-report items differentiating between neutral days and the anger day (see Figure 25 for rating scale means). Differentiating items were

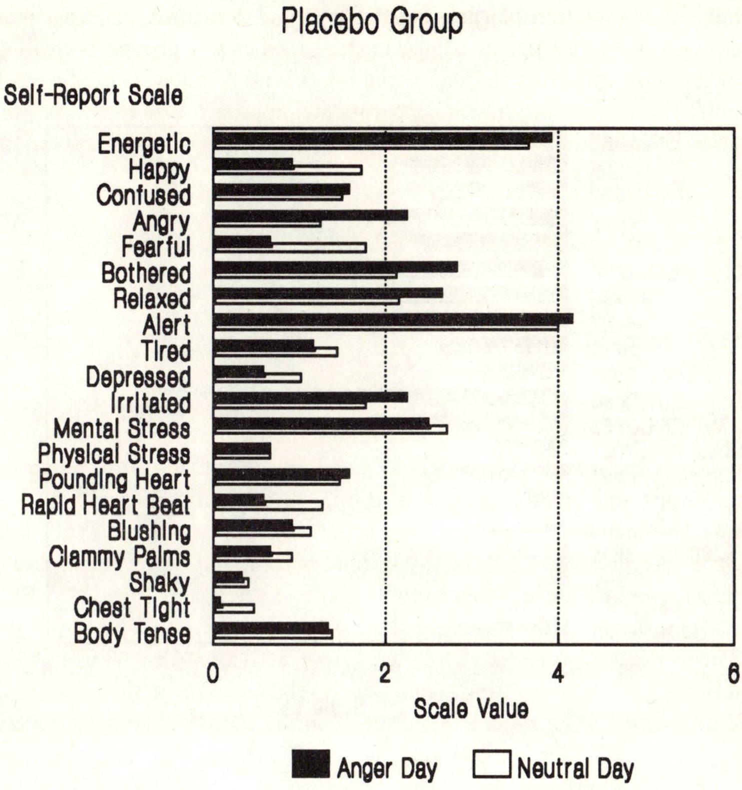

Figure 25. Means by medication groups of self-reports of emotion and bodily symptoms on neutral days ($n = 36$) and the anger day ($n = 12$) *(Figure continues)*.

- for the "alpha-free" group, "alert" and "clammy palms" ($F(1/44) = 9.08$, $p<.01$, and 4.81, $p<.05$, respectively), with lower scores in both items on the anger day;
- for the placebo group, "fearful" ($F(1/44) = 4.10$, $p<.05$), with lower scores on the anger day;
- for the "beta-free" group, "angry", "bothered", "irritated", and "depressed" ($F(1/44) = 20.31$, $p<.01$, 4.50, $p<.05$, 10.27, $p<.01$, and 4.76, $p<.05$), all with increases on the anger day and decreases for "tired" ($F(1/44) = 4.07$, $p<.05$); apart from these changes in the self-report of emotions, bodily feelings were also massively altered: On the anger day, increases were

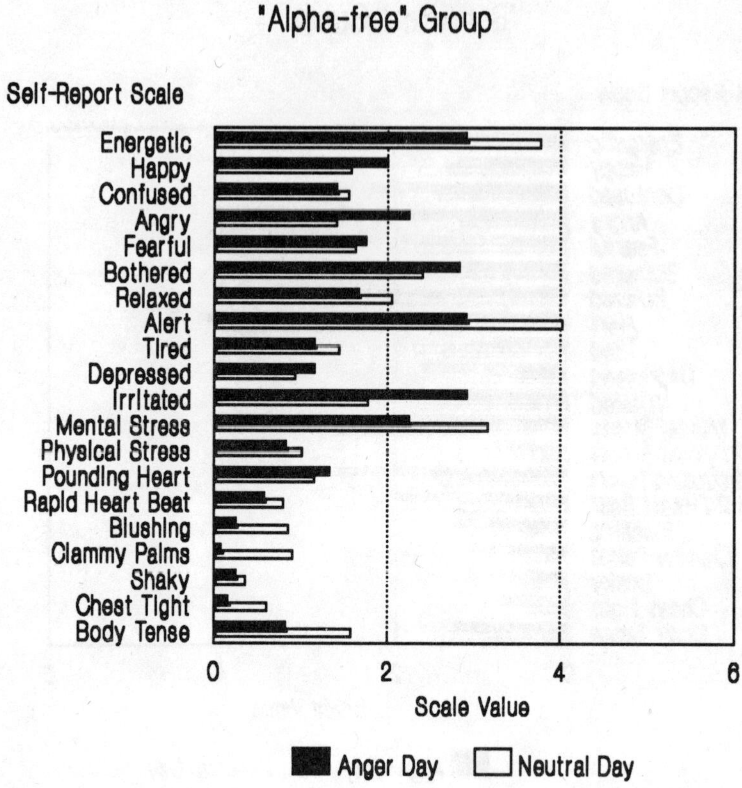

Figure 25 *(continued).*

obtained for the items "pounding heart", "rapid heart beat", "blushing", "clammy palms", "shaky hands", and "tense body" ($F(1/44)$ = 11.29 and 7.62, $p<.01$, 4.44, $p<.05$, 8.06 and 14.16, $p<.01$, and 6.04, $p<.05$, respectively);

- for the "chol-free" group, "angry" and "bothered" ($F(1/44)$ = 5.61, $p<.05$, and 9.30, $p<.01$, respectively), with higher scores in both items on the anger day.

In sum, whereas the "alpha-free" and the placebo groups showed only insignificant increases in the self-report of anger on the anger compared to the neutral days, these increases reached significance in the "beta-free" and the

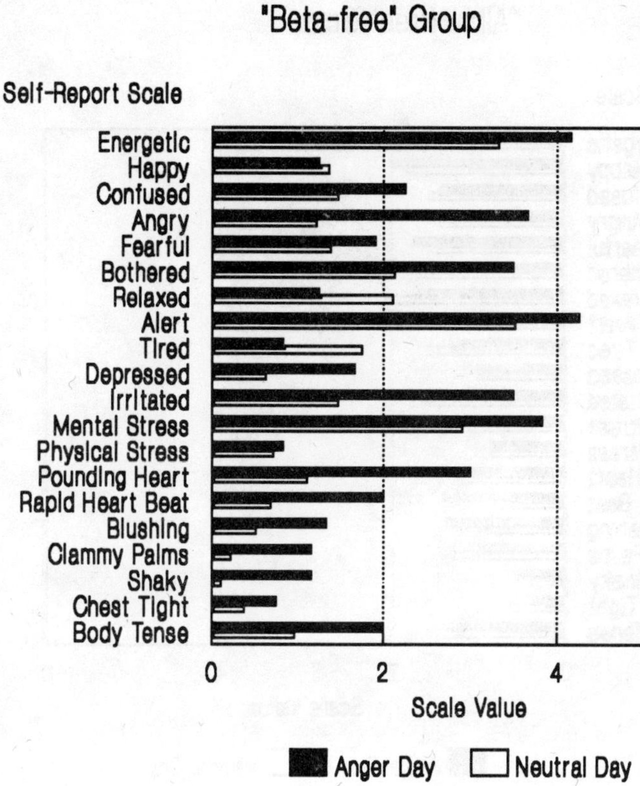

Figure 25 *(continued).*

large increases not only of self-reports of anger but also bodily symptoms covering cardiac, vascular, and somato-motor interoceptions. In contrast, the anger induction neither led to elevations in fear (actually, the placebo group on the anger day reported less fear than the placebo groups on neutral days) nor to changes in happiness. One may therefore conclude that the anger induction raised feelings of anger as intended, with the "beta-free" group reporting the highest anger levels and changes from neutral days.

One should note that ignoring the context (i.e., neutral days) effect would have easily misled an investigator to believe that apart from feelings of anger, the anger induction elicited a whole pattern of "positive" and other "negative" feelings, as indicated by the tests of scale levels during anger against zero.

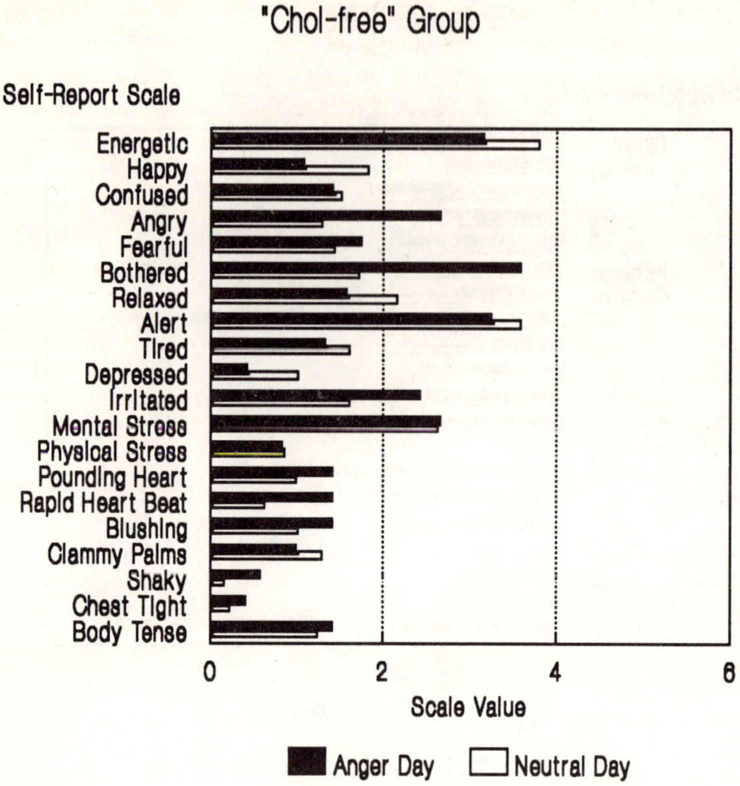

Figure 25 *(continued).*

The next question, which is of particular relevance for the issue of the relationship between feelings and physiological activation, refers to differences in self-reports of emotion among medication groups on the anger day. The average profile (with 20 self-report scales) across medication groups was found to be distinctly shaped (flatness test: $F(19/26) = 20.15$, $p<.01$). The levels of the medication group profiles were not equal, $F(3/44) = 3.34$, $p<.05$. Pairwise comparisons between medication groups clearly showed that highest profile levels were associated with the "beta-free" group, the contrast "alpha-free" versus "beta-free" exceeding the Bonferroni-adjusted significance level of $p = .05/6 = .00833$ ($F(1/44) = 8.47$). The test for profile parallelism only closely missed significance, $F(57/78) = 1.42$, $p = .07$. Pairwise comparisons between medication groups, even if only the unadjusted significance level of $p = .05$ was used, indicated no differences in profile scatters and shapes. Thus the profile tests clearly established a higher elevation but not a specific patterning of the "beta-free" profile of emotional and interoceptive self-reports.

Despite these clear results, follow-up tests were performed comparing medication groups separately on each self-report scale. These comparisons were performed by analyses of variance with the factor Medication (4) followed by pairwise comparisons of means with Bonferroni-adjusted significance levels. These tests showed significant differences among medication groups only for the items "alert" and "rapid heart beat" ($F(3/44) = 3.37$ and 3.79, respectively, $p < .05$). Only for the latter variable the pairwise comparisons between means were able to establish significantly higher scores of the "beta-free" compared to both the "alpha-free" and the placebo groups. These findings corroborate the results of the profile tests that on the anger day, medication groups only incidentally, and not in one of the items related to feelings of anger, showed differences in self-reports of emotion and bodily symptoms.

12.2.2 Physiological specificity of anger

The main interest of this section is on the difference in prestimulus-task responses between neutral days and the anger day. These differences will reflect the effect that the anger induction had in addition to the context. Of course, a test of these differences alone does not constitute a complete evaluation of the specificity hypothesis of anger. A complete evaluation additionally requires (1) comparing the physiological effects of several distinct emotions (2) in more than one context (Stemmler, 1989, in press). Therefore, the present investigation is able to test only a *necessary* condition of physiological emotion specificity, the demonstration of emotion-context differences.

Single physiological variables. First I will describe the physiological effects of the anticipation period of the sentence completion task on neutral days, that is, the context effects (see Figure 26). In the following, significant variables (t-tests against zero, $p < .05$; i.e., tests of no task-prestimulus change) are described. Since these tests were performed separately within each medication group, the letters A ("alpha-free"), B ("beta-free"), C ("chol-free"), and P (placebo) are given in brackets in order to indicate in which group the respective results were obtained. The context raised EMG extensor activity (A), the number of SCRs (C), heart rate (B, C, P), T-wave amplitude (B), P_s-Q_s time (B), relative Q-T time (B, C, P), ST-elevation (B); the context lowered heart rate variability in the respiration band (C, P), unadjusted (C, P) and adjusted respiratory sinus arrhythmia (A, C), pulse wave amplitude at the radialis (B, C) and the finger site (A, B, C, P), and finger skin temperature (A, B, C, P); it increased the pulse wave velocity at the finger (C), R-Z time (A, C), systolic (A), mean (A),

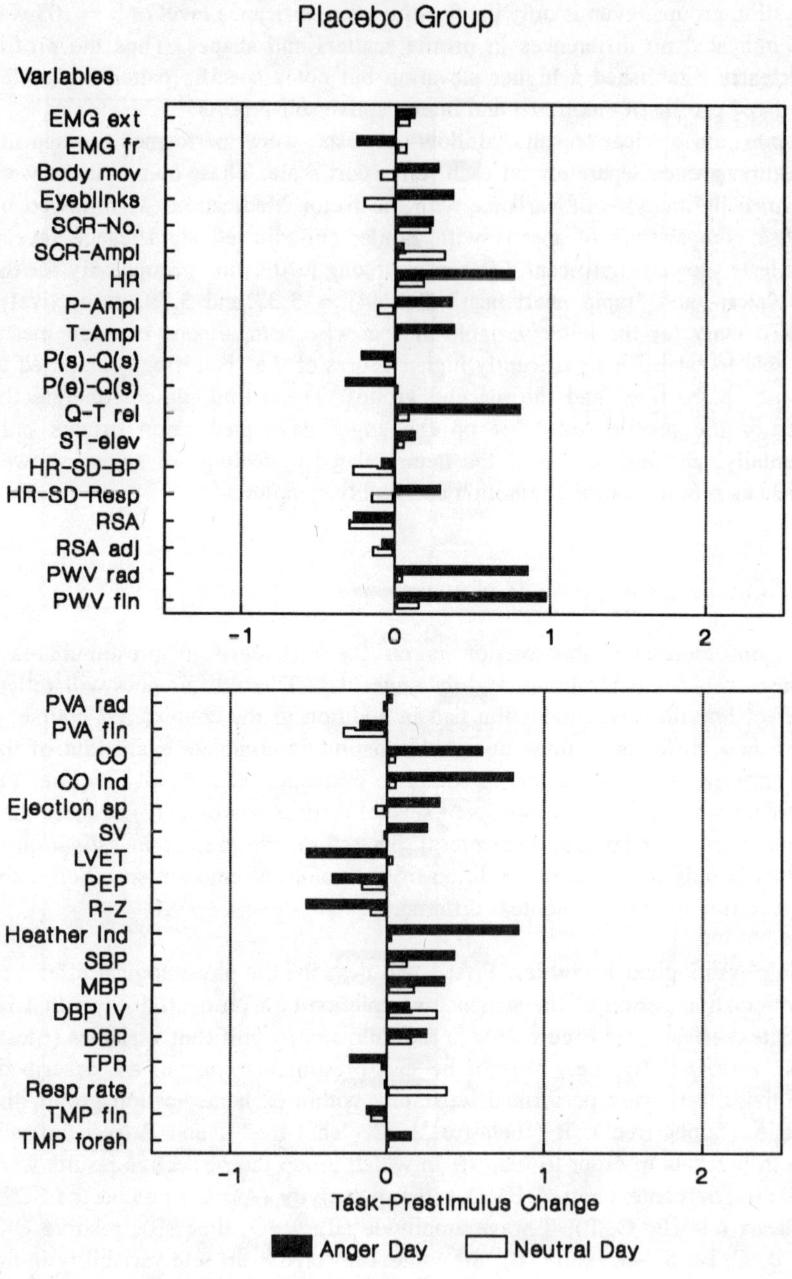

Figure 26. Means by medication groups of physiological variables on neutral days (n = 36) and the anger day (n = 12).

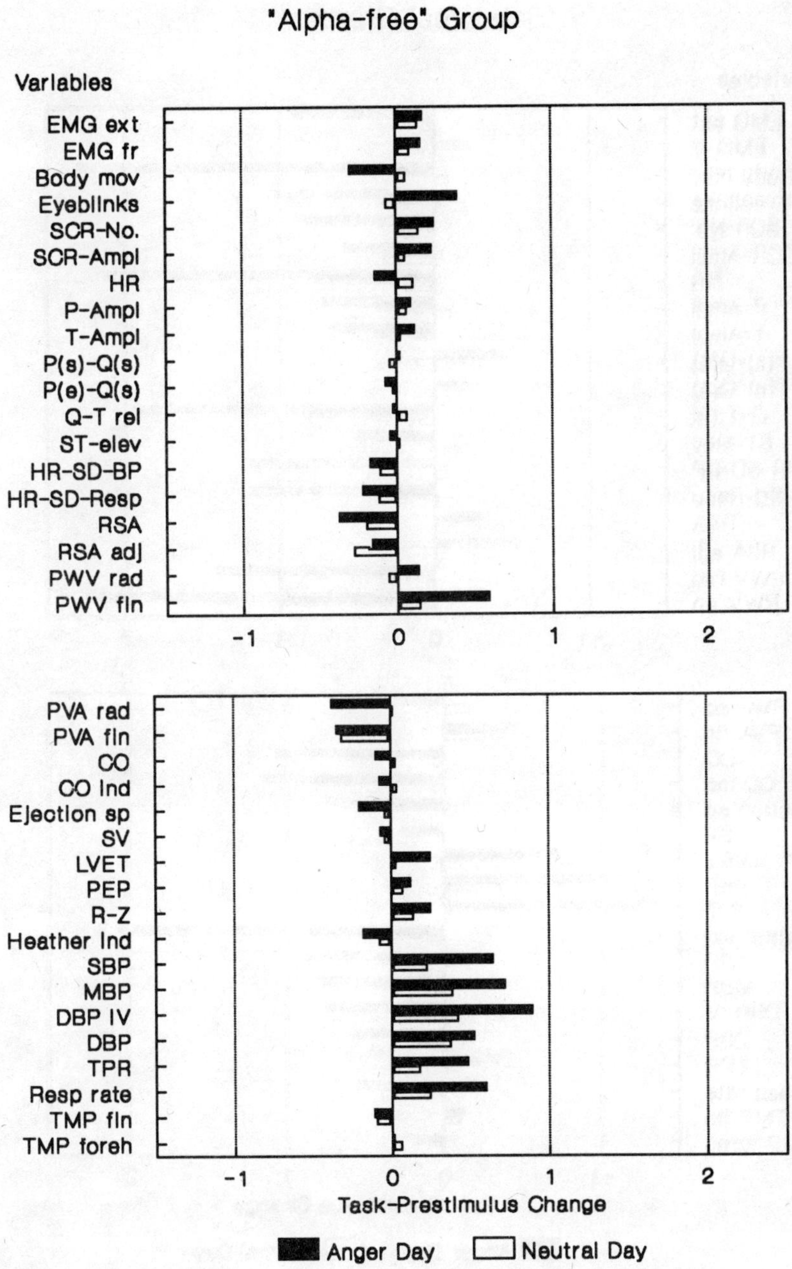

Figure 26 (continued).

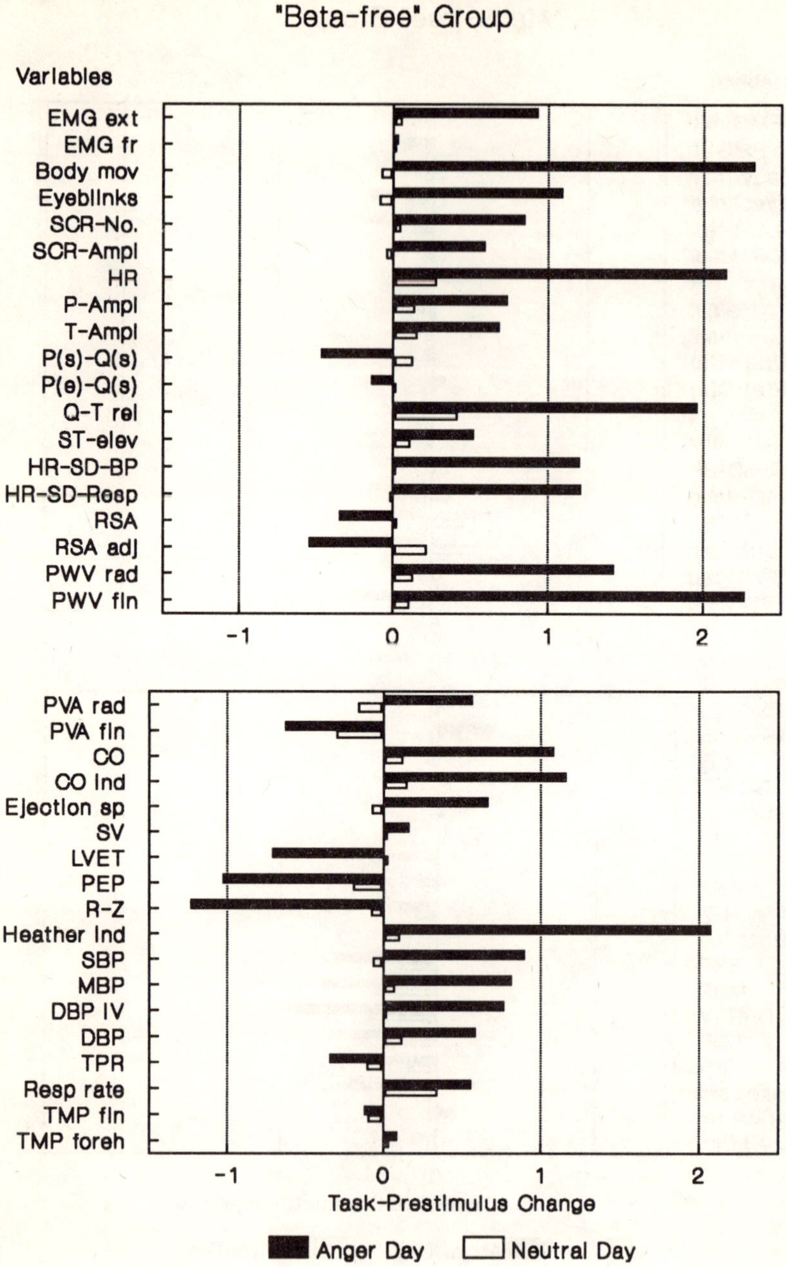

Figure 26 (continued).

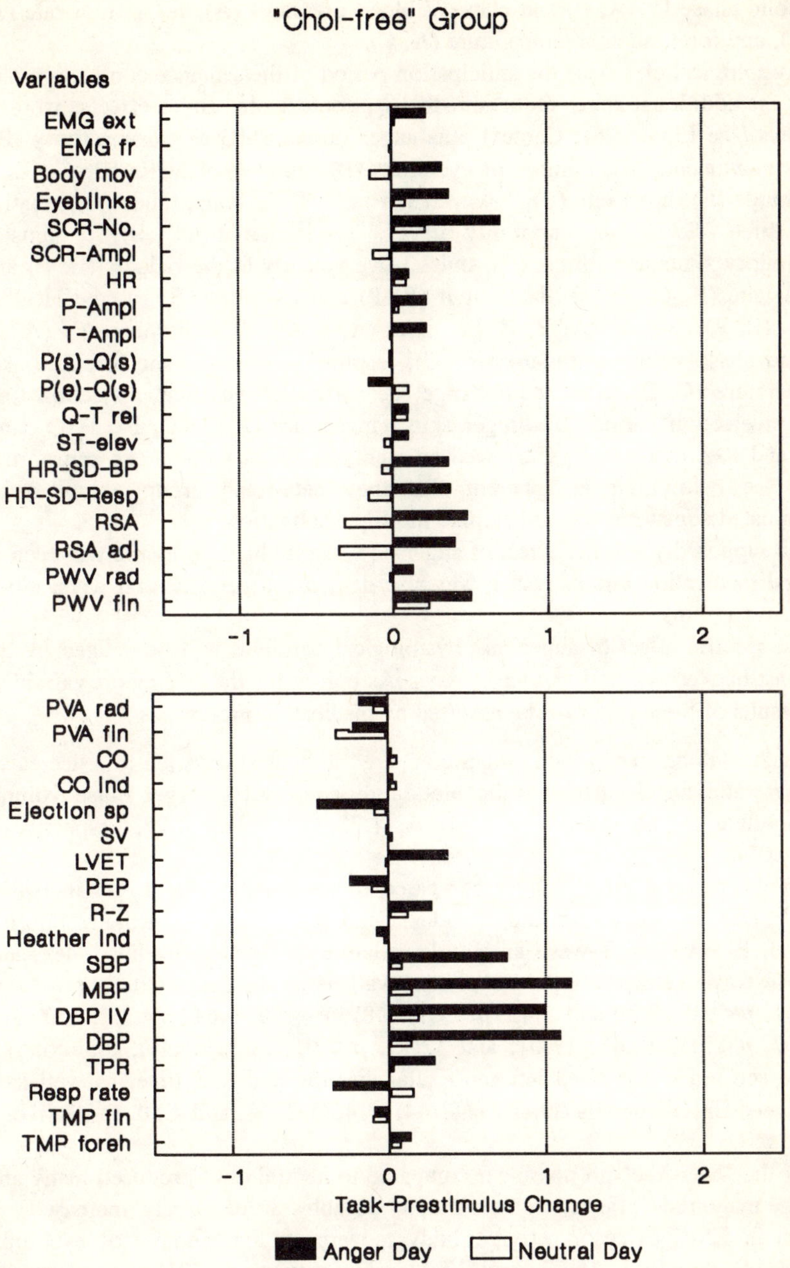

Figure 26 (continued).

diastolic phase IV (A, P) and phase V blood pressures (A), respiration rate (A, B, P), and forehead skin temperature (A, C).

Physiological effects of the anticipation period of the sentence completion task after the additional anger induction, that is, context plus anger effects, were as follows (see Figure 26). Context plus anger raised EMG extensor activity (B), body movements (B), number of eyeblinks (B), number of SCRs (B, C), SCR amplitude (B), heart rate (B), P-wave (B, P) and T-wave amplitude (C), relative Q-T time, heart rate variability in the respiration band (B), unadjusted respiratory sinus arrhythmia (C), pulse wave velocity at the radialis (B, P) and finger site (B, C, P), cardiac output (B, P) and its index (B, P), the Heather index (B, P), systolic (A, B, C, P), mean (A, B, C), diastolic phase IV (A, B, C) and phase V blood pressures (B, C), respiration rate (B), and forehead skin temperature (C, P); context plus anger decreased left-ventricular ejection time (B), preejection period (B), finger skin temperature (A, B, C, P), P_s-Q_s time (B), and R-Z time (B, P; C showed an increase). Even without the appropriate test (see below), it is apparent that the "beta-free" group exhibited an accentuated somato-motor and cardiac inotropic activation.

The supposedly specific effect of anger on diastolic blood pressure was seen in several medication groups, but it was also demonstrated on neutral days, albeit for fewer groups.

The specific effect of anger on physiological variables will be gauged by the contrast between neutral and anger days. As before for the self-report variables, the results of these tests will be reported by medication groups.

- For the "alpha-free" group, anger compared to neutral days led to a decreased heart rate, an elevated systolic blood pressure, and a larger pulse volume amplitude at the radialis ($F(1/44)$ = 4.75, 4.57, and 4.97, respectively, $p<.05$).
- For the placebo group, anger compared to neutral days led to an increased heart rate, cardiac output and its index, heart rate variability in the respiration band, P-wave and T-wave amplitude, relative Q-T time, Heather index, and pulse wave velocity at the radialis as well as at the finger site ($F(1/44)$ = 4.51, $p<.05$, 7.30 and 8.42, $p<.01$, 6.85, $p<.05$, 9.61, $p<.01$, 6.09 and 6.67, $p<.05$, 10.41, 17.01, and 12.99, $p<.01$, respectively); this contrast also showed a decreased left-ventricular ejection and R-Z time, as well as a reduced EMG frontalis activity ($F(1/44)$ = 4.75, 5.68, and 4.50, respectively, $p<.05$).
- For the "beta-free" group, anger compared to neutral days produced many and large-magnitude effects. Somato-motor variables were largely increased, as seen in EMG extensor activity, body movements and number of eyeblinks ($F(1/44)$ = 17.67, 16.72, and 17.33, respectively, $p<.01$). Electrodermal activity was elevated, as shown by number and amplitude of SCRs ($F(1/44)$ = 15.34 and 10.66, respectively, $p<.01$). Cardiac chronotropic and inotropic activation climbed, as demonstrated by increases in heart rate, cardiac output and its index, systolic, mean, diastolic phase IV and phase V blood pressures,

P-wave amplitude, ST-elevation, relative Q-T time, the Heather index, ejection speed, and heart rate variability in the blood pressure and the respiration bands ($F(1/44)$ = 17.86, 15.15, 11.75, 16.54, 10.38, and 9.22, $p<.01$, 4.49, $p<.05$, 8.14, $p<.01$, 6.38, $p<.05$, 8.04 and 17.97, $p<.01$, 4.80 and 7.16, $p<.05$, and 13.29, $p<.01$, respectively) and by decreases in left-ventricular ejection time, preejection period, P_s-Q_s and R-Z time, as well as adjusted respiratory sinus arrhythmia ($F(1/44)$ = 6.41, $p<.05$, 8.03, 16.83 and 21.26, $p<.01$, and 4.43, $p<.05$, respectively). The activity of vascular variables was also elevated, as shown by the pulse volume amplitude at the radialis and the pulse wave velocities at the radialis and the finger sites ($F(1/44)$ = 9.76, 37.80, and 30.43, $p<.01$, respectively). It is worthy of note that peripheral variables that are largely independent of cardiac action, such as skin temperatures and the pulse volume amplitude at the finger, were not specifically affected by the anger induction. This finding suggests that the effects of anger on the diastolic blood pressure were, at least to a considerable extent, not of a peripheral alpha-adrenergic origin but perhaps brought forth by the considerable cardiac and somato-motor activation.

- For the "chol-free" group, anger compared to neutral days led to an increased EMG extensor activity, number of SCRs, unadjusted and adjusted respiratory sinus arrhythmia, heart rate variability in the respiration band, T-wave amplitude, ST-elevation, and systolic, mean, diastolic phase IV and phase V blood pressures ($F(1/44)$ = 6.98, 4.78, 9.57, and 6.93, $p<.05$, 9.55 and 11.18, $p<.01$, 4.70, $p<.05$, and 12.52, 23.29, 14.54, and 19.18, $p<.01$, respectively).

The large differences of activation profiles among medication groups under anger will be of particular interest in the following section. With regard to the specificity issue, the single most important finding was the increase of both systolic and diastolic blood pressures in the "beta-free" and the "chol-free" group, which however was neither accompanied by increases in total peripheral resistance nor by decreases of finger temperature or finger pulse volume amplitude. The latter effects would have been expected under alpha-adrenergic activation postulated by the norepinephrine-epinephrine hypothesis of anger. Another expectation was that alpha-adrenergic effects, if present under anger, would manifest themselves in the first place in the "alpha-free" group. However, this group failed to respond either with diastolic blood pressure or other peripheral indicators of alpha-adrenergic tone.

In sum, the consideration of single physiological variables suggests that (1) there are changes in the physiological activation profile under anger compared to the context of emotion induction; (2) these changes include, but not in all medication groups, rises in diastolic blood pressure; (3) there are arguments suggesting a smaller role of alpha-adrenergic activation under anger then previously posited; (4) as seen in the "alpha-free" group, the context itself exhibited some alpha-adrenergic effects which might have been misinterpreted as a specific anger effect on the anger day, had not the context effect been controlled for.

Putative cardiovascular activation components. A restriction of anger effects to cardiovascular events and their integration into the framework of cardiovascular activation components might further accentuate the question of a physiological specificity of anger. Therefore, the same set of analyses as described for single physiological variables was carried out on the five putative cardiovascular activation components derived by discriminant analysis (components derived by multistage linear estimation were not suited because component scores were not available for different medication groups).

Figure 27 shows means of neutral and anger days on prestimulus-task changes of putative cardiovascular activation components separately for each medication group. The context alone (neutral days) elicited increases in alpha (A, C) and beta1 (A, B, C, P) component activation; it led to decreases in beta2 (A, C) and beta3 (A, B, C) component activation. Under the influence of both context and anger (anger day), effects on the alpha, beta1, and beta2 components were identical to context effects alone. In contrast to neutral days, the anger day did not lead to significant changes on the beta3 component but to a reduction of tau component activation (B). These findings corroborate the hypothesis of context-deviation specificity which states that emotions modify the intensity and/or pattern of situation-specific, context-dependent activation, instead of invoking a specific activation profile of its own (termed "absolute specificity", see Stemmler, 1989, in press).

The anger effect proper was evaluated by contrasts between neutral days and the anger day:

- For the "alpha-free" group, these contrasts remained insignificant.
- For the placebo group, anger compared to neutral days led to increases in the beta1 and beta3 components and to a decrease in tau component activity ($F(1/44) = 7.32$, $p<.01$, 4.94 and 5.35, $p<.05$, respectively).
- For the "beta-free" group, anger compared to neutral days led to a large rise in beta1 and a marked drop in tau component activation ($F(1/44) = 14.45$ and 14.50, $p<.01$, respectively).
- For the "chol-free" group, anger compared to neutral days led to an increase in alpha component activation ($F(1/44) = 4.95$, $p<.05$).

These results reveal that the anger induction elicited a combined putative beta-adrenergic activation and a putative vagal withdrawal. These effects were seen both in the placebo and, amplified, in the "beta-free" group. The groups receiving partial beta-adrenoceptor blockade (the "alpha-free" and "chol-free" groups) did not show this pattern of cardiovascular activation but instead an "unmasking" of putative alpha-adrenergic effects (significantly only in the "chol-free" group). Such an alpha-adrenergic unmasking under beta-adrenergic blockade has been repeatedly noted in the literature (see Chapters 5.1.2, 5.1.3, and 10.1.1).

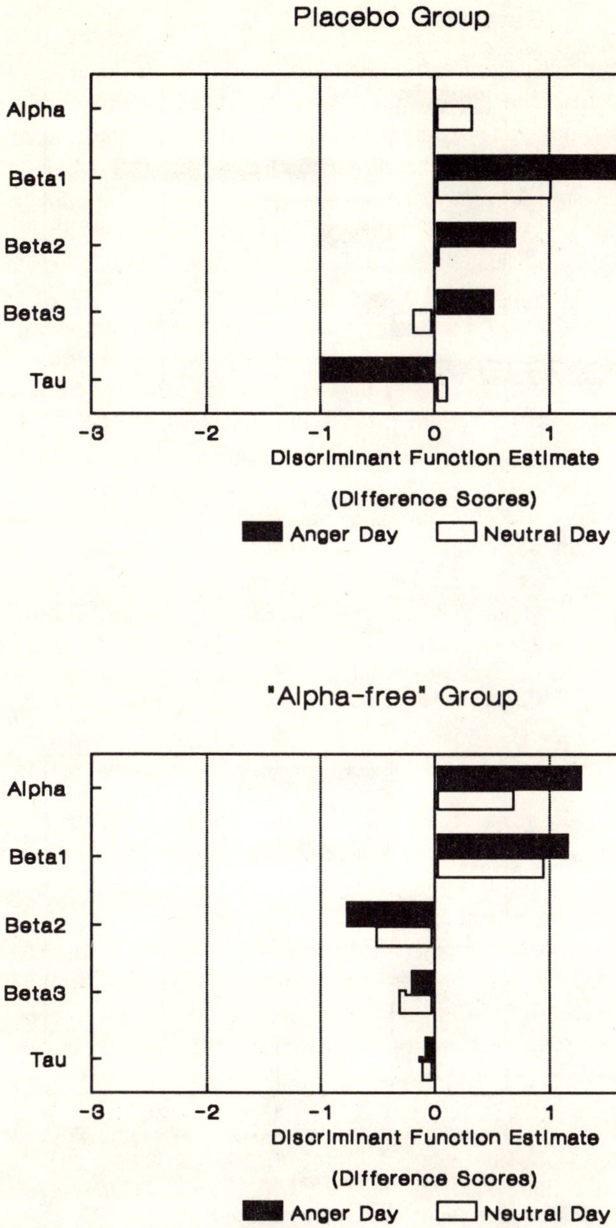

Figure 27. Means by medication groups of putative cardiovascular activation components on neutral days (n = 36) and the anger day (n = 12) *(Figure continues)*.

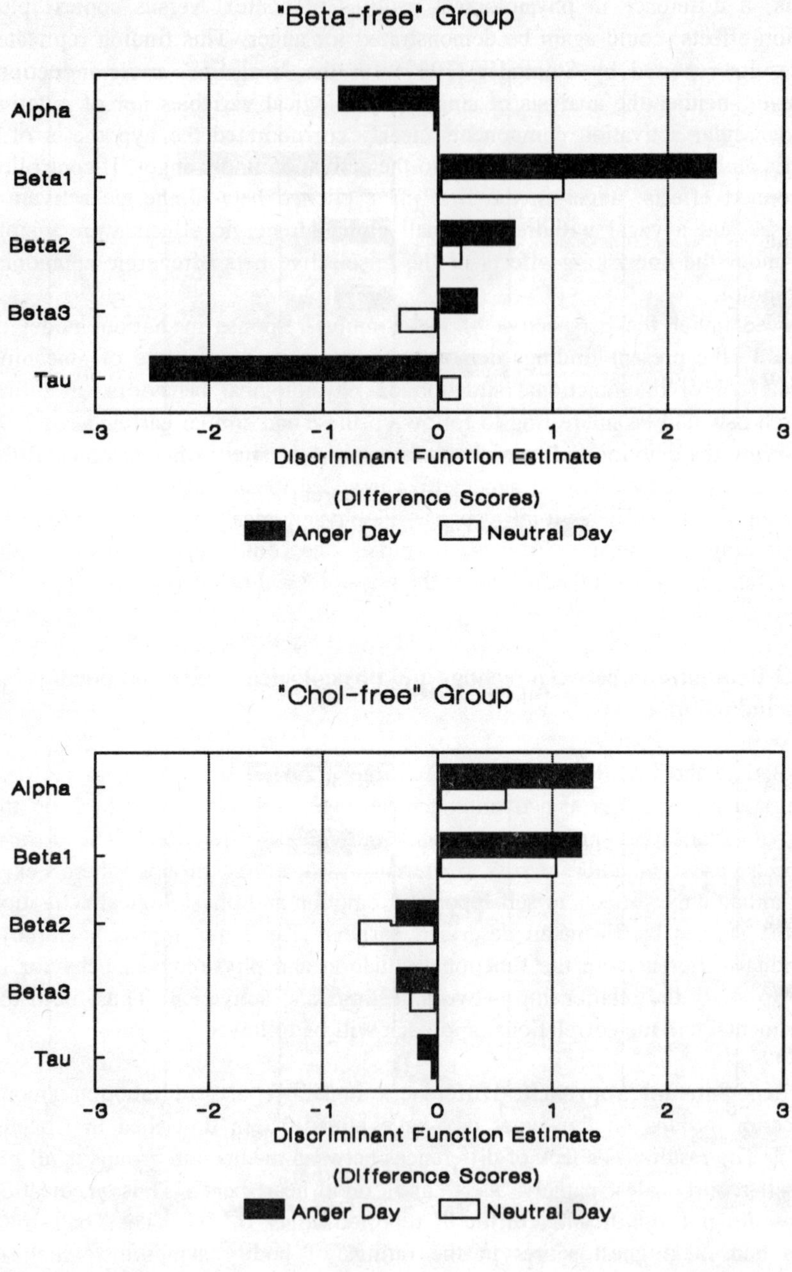

Figure 27. *(continued)*

In conclusion, the *necessary* condition for physiological emotion specificity, that is, a difference in physiological profiles of context versus context plus emotion effects, could again be demonstrated for anger. This finding replicates the results reported by Stemmler (1989) for the "real life" anger induction. However, neither the analysis of single physiological variables nor of putative cardiovascular activation components clearly corroborated the hypothesis of a specific alpha-adrenergic contribution to the activation under anger. If controlled for context effects, anger in the first place elicited beta-adrenergic activation increases and a vagal withdrawal; small alpha-adrenergic effects were visible only under the unmasking effects of the unselective beta-adrenergic antagonist propranolol.

Viewed under the perspective of the stimulus-response mediation model of Figure 1, the present findings demonstrate the marked influence of "meaning analysis" or of the functional situation on physiological behaviors. In future research it would be interesting to follow up these and similar earlier results (1) by varying the emotion induction context in order to study whether one and the same "specific" physiological anger effect is added to the context effect and (2) by asking for which behavioral response the physiological anger effect might be a facilitating prerequisite. From such studies one could hope to elucidate the psychological processes that influence the physiological behavior under anger.

12.2.3 Relationship between feelings and physiological activation during anger induction

As noted in the introductory section (Chapter 12.1), the relationship between feelings and physiological activation during anger will be studied both on the basis of medication group means and individual differences. The former approach asks whether across different medication groups there exist concomitant anger effects in self-reports of emotion and physiological activation (see the studies by Erdmann described earlier). The latter approach employs individual differences in the functional situation and physiological behavior in order to study the relationship between feelings and activation. Thus, both the experimental and the correlational approach will be followed.

The experimental approach. Differences in self-reports of emotion among medication groups on the anger day have already been described in Chapter 12.2.1. The result was a lack of differences between medication groups in all but two self-report scales, namely "alert" and "rapid heart beat". Thus, medication groups did not significantly differ in reported anger or fear. The "beta-free" group had the highest scores in the ratings of bodily symptoms which in comparison to the "alpha-free" and the placebo groups attained significance in the scale "rapid heart beat". Differences in task-prestimulus change scores of physiological variables among medication groups on the anger day will be described next. Due to the large number of physiological variables, a profile analysis could not be calculated. Comparison of medication groups within single physiological variables yielded for 16 of the 37 physiological variables significant *F*-ratios; for 11 variables, multiple comparisons (Bonferroni-adjusted significance levels) also indicated significant differences between pairs of means. The latter eleven variables will be described with results of pairwise comparisons between means given in brackets (a comma separates significantly different medication group means, $p<.05/4 = 0.0125$).

Differences among medication groups were found for body movements ($F(3/44) = 4.75$, $p<.01$; BCP, CPA), heart rate ($F(3/44) = 6.01$, $p<.01$; BP, PCA), relative Q-T time ($F(3/44) = 4.24$, $p<.05$; BP, PCA), ST-elevation ($F(3/44) = 3.09$, $p<.05$; BPC, PCA), heart rate variability in the respiration band ($F(3/44) = 3.77$, $p<.05$; BCP, CPA), cardiac output ($F(3/44) = 4.13$, $p<.05$; BPC, PCA), R-Z time ($F(3/44) = 8.87$, $p<.01$; CAP, PB), the Heather index ($F(3/44) = 6.42$, $p<.01$; BP, PCA), pulse wave velocity at the radialis ($F(3/44) = 8.49$, $p<.01$; BP, PAC) and at the finger site ($F(3/44) = 4.03$, $p<.05$; BP, PAC), and for radialis pulse volume amplitude ($F(3/44) = 3.07$, $p<.05$; BPC, PCA). In sum, an appreciably large number of physiological variables, primarily related to cardiac chronotropic and inotropic activation, differentiated among medication groups. The comparisons among means confirmed that the "beta-free" group, followed by the placebo group, showed the largest degree of activation, and the "alpha-free" and "chol-free" groups, often the lowest.

The comparison of medication groups on the anger day with respect to putative cardiovascular activation components showed significantly nonparallel activation profiles ($F(12/109) = 2.12$, $p<.05$). Pairwise comparisons between medication groups revealed that the "beta-free" group's profile was neither parallel to the profile of the "alpha-free" nor the "chol-free" groups ($F(4/41) = 4.55$ and 5.07, Bonferroni-adjusted $p<.05/4 = 0.0125$). However, profile levels were not different. Follow-up tests on the separate components showed that the alpha component differentiated among the medication groups ($F(3/44) = 5.13$, $p<.01$; CAP, PB), as did the beta2 component albeit without significant pairwise comparisons ($F(3/44) = 3.45$, $p<.05$). The beta1 component just missed statistical significance.

The findings concerning physiological differences of medication groups show that the pharmacological blockades actually led to differential responses under the anger induction. The "beta-free" group exhibited large beta-adrenergic activation, vagal withdrawal, and a tendency toward a decreased alpha-adrenergic tone. The placebo group had less of both beta-adrenergic activation and vagal withdrawal and no change in alpha-adrenergic tone. Both the "alpha-free" and the "chol-free" groups had increases in alpha-adrenergic activation. Thus, as the results in the last paragraph demonstrated, putative alpha-adrenergic activation was significantly different between the "beta-free" and both the "alpha-free" and "chol-free" groups. On the basis of Schachter's theory on the genesis of emotional feelings and the modification suggested by Schachter and Singer's and Erdmann's results (see Chapter 10.1), one would expect that feelings of anger were highest in the "alpha-free" or "chol-free" groups and lowest in the "beta-free" group. Referring to the tendency of the "beta-free" group to express the largest putative beta-adrenergic activation, in accordance with Erdmann one would expect higher levels of self-reported fear in this group. Neither of these results was observed, however. Instead, within the "beta-free" group the level of bodily symptoms climbed.

In conclusion, these results suggest that in the present experiment emotional feelings were not conditional upon the patterning of physiological activation. Subjects were aware, however, of their heightened activation and reported the respective bodily symptoms. It could well be that both in Schachter and Singer's and in Erdmann's experiment subjects were aware of the bodily symptoms of the injected beta-adrenergic agonist which in and by itself could have frightened them, irrespective of any additional opportunity to label their activation with an emotion term. In the present experiment, subjects were medical students who were well informed about the action of drugs, although they did not know which drugs they had received. It should be noted that Schachter's theory also predicted less intense feelings in the "informed" group, but for a different reason than stated here. Whereas Schachter would assert that subjects informed about the source of their physiological activation would not need to enter into a cognitive search for labelling their activation, it is held here that even knowledge of the source of activation does not necessarily prevent one to worry, for instance, about the consequences of this activation, or to be frightened about the strangeness of bodily feelings perhaps never experienced before. Medical students, however, are likely to have experienced such drugs before, and they have larger resources for "short-circuiting" such a threat, for example, through rationalizing explanations.

The differential approach. Whereas the experimental approach studied differences among medication group means, the differential view asks for correlations between the set of physiological variables including putative cardiovascular activation components and self-reports of feelings and bodily symptoms. The correlations calculated were based on the pooled within-medication group variance and covariance. This choice assured that between-medication group variance, which had already been analyzed in the experimental approach, was not included.

Table 59 shows the pooled within-medication correlations between physiological variables and selected self-report variables. This selection was done in order to keep the number of correlations calculated fairly low. In order to focus on the central issue of this chapter, the three anger-related items ("angry", "bothered", and "irritated"), the item "fearful", and items representing bodily symptoms ("pounding heart", "blushing", "clammy palms", "shaky hands") were selected. The bodily symptoms were intended to represent diverse areas of physiological regulation.

The left part of Table 59 contains the original self-report ("Raw Scores") variables. Twelve physiological variables were significantly correlated with at

Table 59. Pooled Within-Medication Group Correlations between Physiological Responses (Task-Prestimulus Change Scores) and Affective Self-Reports during the Anger Induction (Experiment 4)

	Self-Report Scales											
	Raw Scores								Residuals[a]			
Variable	AN	BO	IR	FE	PH	BL	CP	SH	AN	BO	IR	FE
EMG ext	20	5	7	-3	16	-12	6	25	10	-7	-2	-10
EMG fr	3	-7	10	5	1	-17	-16	-6	7	-1	14	11
Body mov	1	6	3	12	**39**	4	10	**45**	-23	-4	-17	-4
Eyeblinks	25	**39**	**31**	18	18	9	12	16	18	**36**	25	11
SCR-No.	20	23	27	5	15	-3	15	15	14	23	21	0
SCR-Ampl	10	-7	16	-9	**31**	-5	7	18	0	-11	6	-18
HR	12	12	18	23	**54**	3	18	**47**	-14	0	-4	6
P-Ampl	13	21	24	**34**	**42**	14	16	**34**	-6	10	7	20
T-Ampl	7	14	10	8	20	-16	-4	28	-5	14	0	2
P_s-Q_s	-8	-10	-7	-2	**-39**	-15	-6	**-38**	13	3	11	15
P_e-Q_s	1	-8	-6	11	-2	24	29	9	-4	-18	-12	5
Q-T rel	-8	-7	-2	7	**37**	4	19	**36**	**-30**	-18	-21	-7
ST-elev	13	13	22	19	**45**	7	1	**38**	-7	4	4	5
HR-SD-BP	-26	-27	-25	-10	-7	-19	-3	-24	-17	-18	-18	0
HR-SD-Resp	-20	**-35**	**-38**	8	2	-13	0	-6	-20	**-33**	**-40**	14
RSA	-26	**-34**	-28	-24	**-37**	-23	-23	**-38**	-5	-21	-11	-7
RSA adj	8	5	-1	-19	-8	10	12	-16	16	5	3	-17
PWV rad	7	4	8	15	**43**	20	25	15	-7	-7	-5	4
PWV fin	15	5	19	21	**36**	10	11	**37**	-4	-6	3	6
PVA rad	9	15	15	20	**30**	20	16	**42**	-12	0	-1	2
PVA fin	-13	-12	-19	2	3	-4	1	-26	-4	-7	-13	11
CO	**43**	**39**	**38**	**30**	**62**	26	**44**	**53**	13	21	12	6
CO ind	**38**	**37**	**33**	24	**54**	28	**32**	**50**	11	19	9	1
Ejection sp	-13	-15	-16	-10	14	-17	1	-10	-12	-10	-17	-6
SV	**39**	**36**	**30**	16	**36**	**32**	**36**	**33**	21	21	14	-1
LVET	23	14	19	1	-20	8	-2	-7	**32**	15	27	4
PEP	**-31**	**-33**	**-31**	-25	**-39**	-23	**-30**	**-42**	-10	-19	-13	-6
R-Z	7	6	7	-21	**-36**	-1	-16	**-29**	27	14	24	-11
Heather ind	13	14	10	10	**51**	3	25	24	-4	7	-7	-1
SBP	**37**	**31**	**38**	24	**47**	27	**44**	**47**	12	13	16	2
MBP	**37**	**36**	**43**	22	**30**	**31**	**37**	**46**	15	20	25	1
DBP IV	**34**	**33**	**47**	4	25	6	19	19	25	**30**	**40**	-5
DBP	29	**34**	**35**	15	17	27	26	**36**	12	21	22	0
TPR	-28	-17	-24	-20	**-45**	-13	-16	**-31**	-10	-6	-8	-6

(Table continues)

Table 59. Pooled Within-Medication Group Correlations between Physiological Responses (Task-Prestimulus Change Scores) and Affective Self-Reports during the Anger Induction (Experiment 4) *(continued)*

	Self-Report Scales											
	Raw Scores								Residuals[a]			
Variable	AN	BO	IR	FE	PH	BL	CP	SH	AN	BO	IR	FE
Resp rate	**30**	16	**29**	24	6	0	-7	4	**31**	17	**31**	25
TMP fin	1	-2	-4	12	15	-17	18	0	0	2	-8	16
TMP foreh	0	11	1	16	-6	20	27	3	-3	5	0	14
Alpha?	-3	3	2	-16	**-54**	-13	**-32**	**-39**	23	18	27	0
Beta1?	2	8	9	1	2	20	-1	11	-3	0	5	-6
Beta2?	0	4	-1	11	**46**	3	9	20	-15	-2	-16	1
Beta3?	-18	-10	-28	-7	7	0	15	-8	-20	-10	**-31**	-6
Tau?	-17	-14	-23	-25	**-55**	-11	-19	**-49**	10	0	0	-6

Note. Correlation coefficients multiplied by 100. Correlations with self-report raw scores had $df = 44$, with residualized scores, $df = 40$. AN = angry, BO = bothered, IR = irritated, FE = fear, PH = pounding heart, BL = blushing, CP = clammy palms, SH = shaky hands. Boldface numbers: $p < .05$. [a]Emotional self-reports after partialling out the four bodily symptom ratings.

least one of the three anger scales ("angry" had eight, or 19%, both "bothered" and "irritated" eleven, or 26%, significant correlations). Subjects reporting high compared to low anger had more eyeblinks, a smaller heart rate variability in the respiration band, less respiratory sinus arrhythmia, a larger cardiac output and a larger index of cardiac output, a higher stroke volume, shorter preejection times, larger systolic, mean, diastolic phase IV and phase V blood pressures, and a higher respiration rate. In contrast, fear was correlated only with P-wave amplitude and cardiac output. It should be emphasized that these correlations signify a marked psycho-physiological relationship.

Bodily symptoms were also numerously and highly correlated with physiological responses. "Pounding heart" and "shaky hands" (23, or 54%, and 20, or 47%, significant correlations, respectively) were correlated with variables indicating an increased cardiac chronotropic and inotropic activation. Numerically largest correlations were found between "pounding heart" and cardiac output ($r = 0.62$), reduced alpha ($r = -0.54$), and tau ($r = -0.55$) component activation. In contrast, "blushing" had only two significant correlations (with stroke volume and mean blood pressure).

These large correlations between physiological responses and bodily symptoms might lead one to question whether the relationship between feelings of anger or fear and physiological activation was primarily mediated by the bodily symptoms. In order to study this argument, the four symptom variables were partialled out of each of the four emotion variables. With the resulting emotion variable residuals, pooled within-medication group correlations were computed with physiological variables (see the right part of Table 59 "Residuals"). Results convey a differentiated picture. Compared to the "Raw Scores" analysis, most correlations dropped, some remained unchanged, and a few newly significant correlations appeared. Correlations that remained unchanged were between "bothered" and number of eyeblinks, and, as was also true for "irritated", between heart rate variability in the respiration band (negative), and diastolic phase IV blood pressure. Unchanged correlations were also found between respiration rate and both "irritated" and "angry". Correlations that newly appeared were between "irritated" and the beta3 component (negative) and between "angry" and both relative Q-T time and left-ventricular ejection time. (It should be noted that these "changes" were not derived by a formal test of differences between correlation coefficients but simply by the inspection of the significance of a correlation.)

These findings suggest that some correlations between physiological activation and the self-report of anger were indeed mediated by bodily symptoms, especially those related to cardiac output and systolic blood pressure; however, other correlations indicated an independent mediation of reported anger with physiological activation, which, interestingly enough, included non-cardiac variables related to respiration, cardiac-respiratory coupling, and diastolic phase IV blood pressure.

Conclusion. We are now in a position to attempt an integration of the results presented. It should be recalled that the investigation reported in this chapter had been put into the context of Schachter's theory about the relationship of emotional feelings and physiological activation. Neither Schachter and Singer's (1962) study nor Erdmann and van Lindern's (1980) was able to demonstrate the theoretically expected result that with an increase of *unspecific* physiological activation (in fact, these studies used beta-adrenergic activation), self-reported anger would rise (given no other putative cause for the activation). Although these negative results could have suggested a dismissal of this theory about the genesis of feelings, a theory postulating a dependency between the intensity of anger and the intensity of physiological activation might be retained with a slight modification: One would postulate that the intensity of self-reported anger is conditional to the intensity of *specific* physiological activation. Contrary both to Schachter's original and the modified version of a theory emphasizing a particular sequence and causal relationship between activation and feelings is the notion that feelings and activation are different output systems of a common underlying neurobiological entity.

What results would the three theoretical positions predict to occur under the experimental and the differential approach?

- Under Schachter's original feedback hypothesis, the experimental approach should show concomitant rises of anger feelings with externally varied physiological activation independent of its specific pattern. Individual differences in activation should bring about correlated individual differences in feelings of anger.

- Under the modified feedback hypothesis, an anger-specific physiological activation would be needed in order to produce the results predicted under Schachter's original hypothesis.
- Under the hypothesis that self-reports of emotion and physiological activation constitute different output systems of one common source, under the experimental approach one would not expect a rise in feeling intensity after changing the level and pattern of activation by external manipulations such as pharmacological agonists or antagonists. The differential approach, however, should yield covariations between the two output systems, because individual differences with regard to the central "emotion structure" would change both output systems.

Comparing these theoretical expectations with the actual results reported in this chapter, Schachter's original and the modified feedback theory seem unlikely, since the experimental approach did not yield the expected findings. The hypothesis that feelings of anger and physiological activation are largely independent output processes found support in the results of both the experimental and the differential approach: Quite substantial differences among medication groups in physiological activity levels and patterns did not lead to marked differences in feelings of anger; however, individual differences in activation correlated with individual differences in feelings of anger, even after the influence of felt bodily symptoms was controlled for. In sum, the results of the investigation into the psychophysiology of anger suggested that

- anger produced a distinct profile of activation characterized in the first place by beta-adrenergic activation and vagal withdrawal, and by a small rise of alpha-adrenergic tone;
- during anger induction, marked psycho-physiological relationships existed between bodily symptoms and feelings of anger on the one hand, and, on the other hand, physiological activation;
- the conceptualization of emotion as a sequence of processes in the sense that physiological activation is a necessary prerequisite of emotional feelings, the intensity of the former determining the strength of the latter, is inconsistent with the data; but that the conceptualization of emotion as a neurobiological process with feelings and activation as output systems that are interrelated but not in a conditional relationship has more explanatory power.

13 Looking back

We have passed a long way from the delineation of psychological explanations, the place of psychophysiology in psychology, notions of situation, personality, and activation, to the empirical demonstrations of research programs that make considerable use of the ideas and methodological characteristics of a differential psychophysiology. Based on the emergentist biopsychological mind-body position and a critical constructivist epistemological view, the stance of this book was that (1) psychological phenomena should be treated as hypothetical constructs and (2) studied by seeking empirical generalizations and law-like structures from knowledge expressable in behavioral terms. It was argued that "behavior" also includes activation processes, that is, the integrated efferent activity initiated and formed by various levels of the organismic system. The concept of "the situation" was found central for such an endeavor, since it enters in various guises (e.g., as the physico-biological and the functional situation) into the formation of activation. The demonstration of subtle and replicable differentiations between profiles of activation during different kinds of experimental situations, that is, of a highly differentiated physiological state-space or map, empirically confirmed this claim.

In order to put a differential psychophysiology into the perspective of psychological construct construction in general, a framework for assessment models was proposed. The assessment models relate theoretical statements about the definition of constructs with empirical and basic data-analytic procedures used in the stage of construct construction. They point to the theoretical assumptions concerning the locus of construct definition that are inevitably embraced in the inductive phase of research.[27] The merit of the assessment model framework could be demonstrated with a digression into the area of personality theory: The different theoretical approaches to personality, which are often discussed as if they were contradictory, could be ordered and shown to be either complementary or asking essentially different questions. The discussion of

[27] Thus, inductive research is never atheoretical; as all other research, it can however be blind to its own assumptions.

the activation construct suggested that a process-oriented conceptualization of activation conforms better to the current physiological and empirical psychophysiological state of discussion than a pure trait conceptualization. This meant that activation should be studied with an assessment model specifying the situation as the locus of the construct. One should note that this choice did not exclude a process-oriented, individual differences point of view as demonstrated in the research on the prediction of personality by arousability.

An area of research cannot get along without explicating its key theoretical terms. Notions from various psychophysiological research programs about the situation, motivational and cognitive person variables, and activation processes were summarized in a necessarily rudimentary stimulus-response mediation model. On the basis of this model, a general and several specialized measurement models relating observed (measurements) to latent variables (constructs) were specified. In addition, on the basis of the stimulus-response mediation model key methodological terms and procedures in psychophysiology were derived and defined, such as specificity analysis and covariance partitioning. As a special case of a measurement model that incorporates the conceptualization of activation as a multicomponent process, the Model of Autonomic Cardiovascular Activation Components was introduced and extensively studied. Its application to an investigation using pharmacological autonomic receptor blockades led to the estimation of alpha-adrenergic, beta-adrenergic, and cholinergic cardiovascular activation components and demonstrated the "bottom-up" strategy proposed for the analysis of constructs, here the physiological construct of activation. Together these various explications and developments constitute elements of a methodology for psychophysiology.

The application of a process-oriented perspective on activation to three substantive research areas proved valuable. The characterization of laboratory tasks in terms of cardiovascular activation components has often been demanded as a necessary prerequisite for studying cardiovascular risk factors in the laboratory. The "componential task description" and "intertask comparison" procedures were clearly superior to the generally adhered to non-formalized approaches. The new procedures allow a much more succinct determination of physically and psychologically describable task effects on the cardiovascular system. If replicable, the results of the present investigation suggest a reevaluation of the cardiovascular effects of certain tasks.

Research motivated by Eysenck's biological personality theory has previously led to conflicting or plainly contradictory results with respect to important predictions of that theory about the relationship between both extraversion and neuroticism and physiological reactivity. Even under the perspective of situational arousability followed up here, Eysenck's predictions could not be substantiated. However, two important results were obtained. First, aggressivity instead of extraversion covaried with the level of reactivity across several experimental situations. Second, in several situations neuroticism and somatic complaints were related to arousability, but only under the moderation of reported emotions. The latter result suggests a reformulation of the theory that should incorporate the organizing functions of emotions for behavior.

The final research area considered was emotion theory, in particular, the physiological specificity of anger and the general question whether the intensity of feelings of emotion depend on the intensity of activation during the emotion induction. Results indicated that the necessary condition for physiological emotion specificity, that is, a difference between context without and with an emotion inducing stimulus in the respective physiological profiles, was true. However, rather than of the hypothesized alpha-adrenergic form, the physiological anger profile exhibited beta-adrenergic activation and vagal withdrawal. The data also suggested a conceptualization of emotion as a neurobiological process with feelings and activation as separate output systems that may be interrelated but not conditional upon one another.

Looking back encourages looking ahead. Psychophysiology will gradually move from mechanistic to functional explanations, from "how" to "why" questions. On its way, psychophysiology can get a good deal of training in the treatment of physiological constructs such as activation and move from construct construction to construct validation stages, from weak to strong theory. One day, with the advancement of biotechnology these physiological constructs will be measurable much more directly than at present. This training with physiological constructs is sorely needed in order to master the neurophysiological constructs hitherto describable only in psychological terms. However, since the characteristics of an organism disclose themselves only in part through its structure and in part - psychologically probably the more interesting part - through its function, a process-oriented differential psychophysiology will have its place in the study of man.

References

Agabiti-Rosei, E., Alicandri, C., Beschi, M., Castellano, M., Corea, L., Beggi, P., Motolese, M., & Muiesan, G. (1983). Relationships between plasma catecholamines, renin, age and blood pressure in essential hypertension. *Cardiology*, *70*, 308-316.

Ahlquist, R.P. (1948). A study of the adrenotropic receptors. *American Journal of Physiology*, *153*, 586-600.

Allen, M.T., Obrist, P.A., Sherwood, A., & Crowell, M.D. (1987). Evaluation of myocardial and peripheral vascular responses during reaction time, mental arithmetic, and cold pressor tasks. *Psychophysiology*, *24*, 648-656, 1987.

Allport, G.W. (1937). *Personality: A psychological interpretation*. New York: Holt.

Allport, G.W. (1961). *Pattern and growth in personality*. New York: Holt, Rinehart, & Winston.

Allport, G.W. (1962). The general and the unique in psychological science. *Journal of Personality*, *30*, 405-422.

Allwood, M.J., Barcroft, H., Hayes, J.P.L.A., & Hirsjärvi, E. (1959). The effect of mental arithmetic on the blood flow through normal, sympathectomized and hyperhydrotic hands. *Journal of Physiology*, *148*, 108-116.

Amelang, M. & Borkenau, P. (1986). The trait concept: Current theoretical considerations, empirical facts, and implications for personality inventory construction. In A. Angleitner & J.S. Wiggins (Eds.), *Personality assessment via questionnaire* (pp. 7-34). Berlin: Springer.

Anderson, K.J. (1990). Arousal and the inverted-U hypothesis: A critique of Neiss's "reconceptualizing arousal". *Psychological Bulletin*, *107*, 96-100.

Andrén, L. (1982). Cardiovascular effects of noise. *Acta Medica Scandinavica*, *657* (Suppl.), 7-45.

Andresen, B. (1987). *Differentielle Psychophysiologie valenzkonträrer Aktivierungsdimensionen.* Frankfurt: Lang.

Andresen, B., Stemmler, G., Thom, E., & Irrgang, E. (1984). Methodological conditions of congruent factors: A comparison of EEG frequency structure between hemispheres. *Multivariate Behavioral Research*, *19*, 3-32.

Andresen, B., Thom, E., Irrgang, E., & Stemmler, G. (1982). An empirically derived 2-systems model of EEG-frequency factors. *Biological Psychology*, *15*, 268-269 (abstract).

Antoni, H. (1987). Funktionen des Herzens. In R.F. Schmidt & G. Thews (Eds.), *Physiologie des Menschen* (23rd ed.; pp. 461-504). Berlin: Springer.

Arena, J.G., Blanchard, E.B., Andrasik, F., Cotch, P.A., & Myers, P.E. (1983). Reliability of psychophysiological assessment. *Behaviour Research and Therapy*, *21*, 447-460.

Arnold, J.M. & McDevitt, D.G. (1983). Heart rate and blood pressure responses to intravenous boluses of isoprenaline in the presence of propranolol, practolol and atropine. *British Journal of Clinical Pharmacology*, *16*, 175-184.

Averill, J.R. & Opton, E.M. (1968). Psychophysiological assessment: Rationale and problems. In P. McReynolds (Ed.), *Advances in psychological assessment* (pp. 265-288). Palo Alto: Science and Behavior Books.

Ax, A.F. (1953). The physiological differentiation between fear and anger in humans. *Psychosomatic Medicine*, *15*, 433-442.

Ax, A.F. (1964). Goals and methods of psychophysiology. *Psychophysiology*, *1*, 8-25.

Bandura, A. (1969). *Principles of behavior modification*. New York: Holt, Rinehart, & Winston.

Bandura, A. (1978). The self system in reciprocal determinism. *American Psychologist*, *33*, 344-358.

Bandura, A. (1989). Human agency in social cognitive theory. *American Psychologist*, *44*, 1175-1184.

Barker, R.G. (1968). *Ecological psychology*. Stanford, CA: Stanford University Press.

Baumeister, R.F. & Tice, D.M. (1988). Metatraits. *Journal of Personality*, *56*, 571-597.

Bechtoldt, H.P. (1959). Construct validity: A critique. *American Psychologist*, *14*, 619-629.

Bem, D.J. (1983). Constructing a theory of the triple typology: Some (second) thoughts on nomothetic and idiographic approaches to personality. *Journal of Personality*, *51*, 566-577.

Bem, D.J. & Allen, A. (1974). On predicting some of the people some of the time. *Psychological Review*, *81*, 506-520.

Ben-Shakhar, G. (1985). Standardization within individuals: A simple method to neutralize individual differences in skin conductance. *Psychophysiology*, *22*, 292-299.

Berlyne, D.E. (1960). *Conflict, arousal and curiosity*. New York: McGraw-Hill.

Berlyne, D.E. (1968). Behavior theory as personality theory. In E.F. Borgatta & W.W. Lambert (Eds.), *Handbook of personality theory and research* (pp. 629-690). Chicago: Rand McNally.

Bernstein, A.S. (1979). The orienting response as novelty and significance detector: Reply to O'Gorman. *Psychophysiology*, *16*, 263-273.

Berry, N.J., Thompson, H.F., Miller, D.E., & McIntosh, H.D. (1959). Changes in cardiac output, stroke volume, and central venous pressure induced by atropine in man. *American Heart Journal*, *58*, 204-213.

Bhapkar, V.P. (1984). On nonparametric profile analysis of several multivariate samples. *Journal of Statistical Planning and Inference*, *9*, 285-296.

Bieri, P. (Ed.) (1981). *Analytische Philosophie des Geistes*. Königstein/Ts., F.R.G.: Hain.

Birbaumer, N. & Schmidt, R.F. (1990). *Biologische Psychologie*. Berlin: Springer.

Blix, A.S., Stromme, G.B., & Ursin, H. (1974). Additional heart rate - an indicator of psychological activation. *Aerospace Medicine*, *45*, 1219-1222.

Block, J. & Block, J.H. (1981). Studying situational dimensions: A grand perspective and some limited empiricism. In D. Magnusson (Ed.), *Toward a psychology of situations. An interactional perspective* (pp. 85-102). Hillsdale, NJ: Erlbaum.

Bollen, K.A. (1984). Multiple indicators: Internal consistency or no necessary relationship? *Quality and Quantity*, *18*, 377-385.

Bonelli, J. (1982). Stress, catecholamines and beta-blockade. *Acta Medica Scandinavica, 660* (Suppl.), 214-218.

Borger, R.T. & Cioffi, F. (Eds.) (1970). *Explanations in the behavioral sciences.* London: Cambridge University Press.

Bowers, K.S. (1973). Situationism in psychology: An analysis and a critique. *Psychological Review, 80,* 307-336.

Bowers, K.S. (1977). There's more to Iago than meets the eye: A clinical account of personal consistency. In D. Magnusson & N.S. Endler (Eds.), *Personality at the crossroads* (pp. 65-81). New York: Wiley.

Braunwald, E. & Ross, J. (1979). Control of cardiac performance. In R.M. Berne, N.Sperelakis, & S.R. Geiger (Eds.), *Handbook of physiology: Sec. 2. The cardiovascular system* (pp. 533-580). Bethesda, MD: American Physiological Society.

Brentano, F. (1874). *Psychologie vom empirischen Standpunkt.* Leipzig.

Bridgman, P.W. (1927). *The logic of modern physics.* New York: Macmillan.

Bridgman, P.W. (1945). Some general principles of operational analysis. *Psychological Review, 52,* 246-249.

Briggs, S.R. (1985). A trait account of social shyness. In P. Shaver (Ed.), *Self, situations, and social behavior - Review of personality and socialpsychology* (Vol. 6, pp. 35-64). Beverly Hills, CA: Sage.

Broadbent, D. (1985). A question of levels: Comments on McClelland and Rumelhart. *Journal of Experimental Psychology: General, 114,* 189-192.

Brocke, B. & Liepmann, D. (1985). Eysencks Theorie der situativen Erregung: Einige Befunde zu einer interaktionistischen Ergänzung der Aktivierungstheorie der Persönlichkeit. *Zeitschrift für Differentielle und Diagnostische Psychologie, 6,* 19-38.

Brod, J. (1982). Emotionelle pressorische Reaktionen und etablierter Hochdruck beim Menschen. In D. Vaitl (Ed.), *Essentielle Hypertonie* (pp. 26-61). Berlin: Springer.

Brooks, D., Fox, P., Lopez, R., & Sleight, P. (1978). The effect of mental arithmetic on blood pressure variability and baroreflex sensitivity in man. *Journal of Physiology, 280,* 75 P-76 P.

Brown, J.E., McLeod, A.A., & Shand, D.G. (1983). Evidence for cardiac beta2-adrenoceptors in man. *Clinical Pharmacology and Therapeutics, 33,* 424-428.

Brown, T.G., Szabo, A., & Seraganian, P. (1988). Physical versus psychological determinants of heart rate reactivity to mental arithmetic. *Psychophysiology, 25,* 532-537.

Brunswik, E. (1956). *Perception and the representative design of psychological experiments.* Berkeley: University of California Press.

Buell, J.C., Alpert, B.S., & McCrory, W.W. (1986). Physical stressors as elicitors of cardiovascular reactivity. In K.A. Matthews, S.M. Weiss, T. Detre, T.M. Dembrowski, B. Falkner, S.B. Manuck, & R.B. Williams (Eds.), *Handbook of stress, reactivity, and cardiovascular disease* (pp. 127-144). New York: Wiley.

Bunge, M. (1980). *The mind-body problem.* Oxford: Pergamon.

Bunge, M. & Ardila, R. (1987). *Philosophy of psychology.* New York: Springer.

Buss, A.H. (1989). Personality as traits. *American Psychologist, 44,* 1378-1388.

Buss, D.M. & Craik, K.M. (1983). The act frequency approach to personality. *Psychological Review, 90,* 105-126.

Butler, J.K. (1983). A vector model for describing and comparing profiles. *Educational and Psychological Measurement, 43,* 747-758.

Cacioppo, J.T. & Petty, R.E. (Eds.) (1983). *Social psychophysiology: A sourcebook.* New York: The Guilford Press.

Cacioppo, J.T., Petty, R.E., & Marschall-Goodell, B. (1985). Physical, social, and inferential elements of psychophysiological measurement. In P. Karoly (Ed.),

Measurement strategies in health psychology (Vol. 1, pp. 263-300). New York: Wiley.

Cacioppo, J.T. & Tassinary, L.G. (1990a). Inferring psychological significance from physiological signals. *American Psychologist, 45*, 16-28.

Cacioppo, J.T. & Tassinary, L.G. (Eds.) (1990b). *Principles of psychophysiology. Physical, social, and inferential elements*. Cambridge: Cambridge University Press.

Callaway, E. III & Dembo, E. (1958). Narrowed attention: A psychological phenomenon that accompanies a certain physiological change. *Archives of Neurology and Psychiatry, 79*, 74-90.

Campbell, D.T. & Fiske, D.W. (1959). Convergent and discriminant validation by the multitrait-multimethod matrix. *Psychological Bulletin, 56*, 81-105.

Campbell, M.E. (1981). Statistical properties with the Law of Initial Values. *The Journal of Psychology, 108*, 85-101.

Cannon, W.B. (1929). *Bodily changes in pain, hunger, fear and rage*. New York: Appleton.

Carver, C.S. & Matthews, K.A. (1989). An overview of issues in psychometric measurement. In N. Schneiderman, S.M. Weiss, & P.G. Kaufmann (Eds.), *Handbook of research methods in cardiovascular behavioral medicine* (pp. 485-494). New York: Plenum.

Cattell, R.B. (1946). *Description and measurement of personality*. Yonkers-on-Hudson, NY: World Book.

Cattell, R.B. (1957). *Personality and motivation structure and measurement*. New York: World Book.

Cattell, R.B. (1966a). Psychological theory and scientific method. In R.B. Cattell (Ed.), *Multivariate experimental psychology* (pp. 1-18). Chicago: Rand McNally.

Cattell, R.B. (1966b). The data box: Its ordering of total resources in terms of possible relational systems. In R.B. Cattell (Ed.), *Handbook of multivariate experimental psychology* (pp. 67-128). Chicago: Rand McNally.

Cattell, R.B. (1966c). The principles of experimental design and analysis in relation to theory building. In R.B. Cattell (Ed.), *Handbook of multivariate experimental psychology* (pp. 19-66). Chicago: Rand McNally.

Cattell, R.B. (1966d). Patterns of change: Measurement in relation to state-dimension, trait change, lability, and process concepts. In R.B. Cattell (Ed.), *Handbook of multivariate experimental psychology* (pp. 354-402). Chicago: Rand McNally.

Cattell, R.B. & Vogelmann, S. (1977). A comprehensive trial of the scree and KG criteria for determining the number of factors. *Multivariate Behavioral Research, 12*, 289-325.

Chalmers, A.F. (1986). *Wege der Wissenschaft*. Berlin: Springer.

Chessick, R.D., Bassan, M., & Shattan, S. (1966). A comparison of the effect of infused catecholamines and certain affect states. *American Journal of Psychiatry, 123*, 156-165.

Claridge, G.S. (1981). Arousal. In G. Underwood & R.G. Stevens (Eds.), *Aspects of consciousness* (pp. 119-147). London: Academic Press.

Claridge, G.S. (1987). Psychoticism and arousal. In J. Strelau & H.J. Eysenck (Eds.), *Personality dimensions and arousal* (pp. 133-150). New York: Plenum.

Clarke, D.D. & Hoyle, R. (1988). A theoretical solution to the problem of personality-situation interaction. *Personality and Individual Differences, 9*, 133-138.

Cleary, P.J. (1974). Description of individual differences in autonomic reactions. *Psychological Bulletin, 81*, 934-944.

Cohen, J. (1982). Set correlation as a general multivariate data-analytic method. *Multivariate Behavioral Research, 17*, 301-341.

Cohen, J. & Cohen, P. (1983). *Applied multiple regression/correlation analysis for the behavioral sciences* (2nd ed.). Hillsdale, NJ: Lawrence Erlbaum.

Cohen, S.I. & Silverman, A.J. (1959). Psychophysiological investigations of vascular response variability. *Journal of Psychosomatic Research*, *3*, 185-210.

Coles, M.G.H., Donchin, E., & Porges, S.W. (Eds.) (1986). *Psychophysiology: Systems, processes and applications*. New York: Guilford.

Coote, J.H., Hilton, S.M., & Perez-Gonzalez, J.F. (1979). Inhibition of the baroreceptor reflex on stimulation in the brain stem defense centre. *Journal of Physiology*, *288*, 549-560.

Corcoran, D.W.J. (1981). Introversion-extraversion, stress, and arousal. In R. Lynn (Ed.), *Dimensions of personality* (pp. 111-127). Oxford: Pergamon.

Corse, C.D., Manuck, S.B., Cantwell, J.D., Giardani, B., & Matthews, K.A. (1982). Coronary-prone behavior pattern and cardiovascular response in persons with and without coronary heart disease. *Psychosomatic Medicine*, *44*, 449-459.

Craik, K.H. (1981). Environmental assessment and situational analysis. In D. Magnusson (Ed.), *Toward a psychology of situations. An interactional perspective* (pp. 37-48). Hillsdale, NJ: Erlbaum.

Cronbach, L.J. (1988). Five perspectives on validity argument. In H. Wainer & H.I. Braun (Eds.), *Test validity* (pp. 3-17). Hillsdale, NJ: Erlbaum.

Cronbach, L.J. (1989). Construct validation after thirty years. In R.L. Linn (Ed.), *Intelligence: measurement, theory, and public policy*. Urbana: University of Illinois Press.

Cronbach, L.J. & Gleser, G.C. (1953). Assessing similarity between profiles. *Psychological Bulletin*, *50*, 456-473.

Cronbach, L.J., Gleser, G.C., Nanda, H., & Rajaratnam, N. (1972). *The dependability of behavioral measurements: Theory of generalizability for scores and profiles*. New York: Wiley.

Cronbach, L.J. & Meehl, P.E. (1955). Construct validity and psychological tests. *Psychological Bulletin*, *52*, 281-302.

Cummins, R. (1983). *The nature of psychological explanation*. Cambridge: MIT Press.

Dahme, B. & Richter, R. (1980). Einige Anforderungen an psychosomatische Aktivierungsdiagnostik. *Medizinische Psychologie*, *6*, 103-122.

Darrow, C.W. (1929). Differences in the physiological reactions to sensory and ideational stimuli. *Psychological Bulletin*, *26*, 185-201.

Das, G., Talmers, F.N., & Weissler, A.M. (1975). New observations on the effects of atropine on the sinoatrial and atrioventricular nodes in man. *American Journal of Cardiology*, *36*, 281-285.

Davis, R.C., Buchwald, A.M., & Frankmann, R.W. (1955). Autonomic and muscular responses, and their relation to simple stimuli. *Psychological Monographs*, *69*, 1-71.

Dembroski, T.M., MacDougall, J.M., Herd, J.A., & Shields, J.L. (1979). Effects of level of challenge on pressor and heart rate responses in Type A and B subjects. *Journal of Applied Social Psychology*, *9*, 209-228.

Descartes, R. (1955). Meditations on first philosophy. In E.S. Haldane & G.R.T. Ross (Eds., Trans.), *Philosophical works* (Vol. 1). New York: Dover. (Original work published 1641).

Dienstbier, R.A. (1989). Arousal and physiological toughness: Implications for mental and physical health. *Psychological Review*, *96*, 84-100.

Dimsdale, J.E. (1984). Generalizing from laboratory studies to field studies of human stress physiology. *Psychosomatic Medicine*, *46*, 463-469.

Dittmann, R. (1988). *Zur Psychophysiologie beim Autogenen Training von Kindern und Jugendlichen*. Frankfurt: Lang.

Donchin, E. (1979). Event-related brain potentials: A tool in the study of human information processing. In H. Begleiter (Ed.), *Evoked brain potentials and behavior* (pp. 13-88). New York: Plenum.

Duffy, E. (1957). The psychological significance of the concept of "arousal" or "activation". *Psychological Review, 64*, 265-275.

Duffy, E. (1962). *Activation and behavior*. New York: Wiley.

Edwards, A.E. & Hill, R.A. (1967). The effect of data characteristics on theoretical conclusions concerning the physiology of emotions. *Psychosomatic Medicine, 29*, 303-311.

Edwards, J.M. & Endler, N.S. (1983). Personality research. In M. Hersen, A.E. Kazdin, & A.S. Bellack (Eds.), *The clinical psychology handbook* (pp. 223-238). New York: Pergamon, 1983.

Ekehammar, B. (1974). Interactionism in personality from a historical perspective. *Psychological Bulletin, 81*, 1026-1048.

Ekman, P., Levenson, R.W., & Friesen, W.V. (1983). Autonomic nervous system activity distinguishes among emotions. *Science, 221*, 1208-1210.

Eldridge, F.L., Millhorn, D.E., & Waldrop, T.G. (1981). Exercise hyperpnea and locomotion: Parallel activation from the hypothalamus. *Science, 211*, 844-846.

Eliot, R.S. (1988). The dynamics of hypertension - An overview: Present practices, new possibilities, and new approaches. *American Heart Journal, 116*, 583-589.

Elliott, R. (1969). Tonic heart rate: Experiments on the effects of collative variables lead to a hypothesis about its motivational significance. *Journal of Personality and Social Psychology*, 12, 211-228.

Endler, N.S. (1981). Situational aspects of interactional psychology. In D. Magnusson (Ed.), *Toward a psychology of situations. An interactional perspective* (pp. 361-373). Hillsdale, NJ: Erlbaum.

Endler, N.S. & Magnusson, D. (1976). Toward an interactional theory of personality. *Psychological Bulletin, 83*, 956-974.

Engel, B.T. (1960). Stimulus-response and individual-response specificity. *Archives of General Psychiatry, 2*, 305-313.

Engel, B.T. (1972). Response specificity. In N.S. Greenfield & R.A. Sternbach (Eds.), *Handbook of Psychophysiology* (pp. 571-576). New York: Holt, Rinehart, & Winston.

Engel, B.T. (1983). Assessment and alteration of physiological reactivity. In T.M. Dembrowski, T.H. Schmidt, & G. Blümchen (Eds.), *Biobehavioral bases of coronary heart disease* (pp. 450-458). Basel: Karger.

Engel, B.T. (1986). An essay on the circulation as behavior. *Behavioral and Brain Sciences, 9*, 285-318.

Engel, B.T. & Moos, R.H. (1967). The generality of specificity. *Archives of General Psychiatry, 16*, 574-581.

Engel, R.R. (1986). *Aktivierung und Emotion*. München: Minerva.

Eppinger, H. & Hess, L. (1915). Vagotonia: A clinical study in vegetative neurology. *The Nervous and Mental Disease Monograph, 20*, 8-13.

Epstein, S. (1979). The stability of behavior: I. On predicting most of the people much of the time. *Journal of Personality and Social Psychology, 37*, 1097-1126.

Epstein, S. (1980). The stability of behavior: II. Implications for psychological research. *American Psychologist, 35*, 790-806.

Epstein, S. (1983). A research paradigm for the study of personality and emotions. In M.M. Page (Ed.), *Nebraska Symposium on motivation* (pp. 91-154). Lincoln, NB: University of Nebraska Press.

Epstein, S. (1984). The stability of behavior across time and situations. In R.A. Zucker, J. Aronoff, & A. Rabin (Eds.), *Personality and the prediction of behavior* (pp. 209-268). New York: Academic Press.

Epstein, S. & Erskine, N. (1983). The development of personal theories of reality. In D. Magnusson & V. Allen (Eds.), *Human development: An interactional perspective* (pp. 133-147). New York: Academic Press.

Epstein, S. & O'Brien, E.J. (1985). The person-situation debate in historical and current perspective. *Psychological Bulletin, 98*, 513-537.

Erdmann, G. (1983). *Zur Beeinflußbarkeit emotionaler Prozesse durch vegetative Variationen*. Weinheim: Beltz.

Erdmann, G. & van Lindern, B. (1980). The effects of beta-adrenergic stimulation and beta-adrenergic blockade on emotional reactions. *Psychophysiology*, *17*, 332-338.

Evans, I.M. (1986). Response structure and the triple-response-mode concept. In R.O. Nelson & S.C. Hayes (Eds.), *Conceptual foundations of behavioral assessment* (pp. 131-155). New York: Guilford.

Eysenck, H.J. (1957). *The dynamics of anxiety and hysteria*. London: Routledge & Kegan Paul.

Eysenck, H.J. (1967). *The biological basis of personality*. Springfield, IL: Charles C. Thomas.

Eysenck, H.J. (1981). General features of the model. In H.J. Eysenck (Ed.), *A model for personality* (pp. 1-37). Berlin: Springer.

Eysenck, H.J. & Eysenck, M.W. (1985). *Personality and individual differences*. New York: Plenum.

Fahrenberg, J. (1967). *Psychophysiologische Persönlichkeitsforschung*. Göttingen: Hogrefe.

Fahrenberg, J. (1975). Die Freiburger Beschwerdenliste FBL. *Zeitschrift für Klinische Psychologie*, *4*, 79-100.

Fahrenberg, J. (1977) Physiological concepts in personality research. In R.B. Cattell & P.M. Dreger (Eds.), *Handbook of modern personality research*. New York: Hasted Pressbook.

Fahrenberg, J. (1983). Psychophysiologische Methodik. In K.-J. Groffmann & L. Michel (Eds.), *Enzyklopädie der Psychologie, Verhaltensdiagnostik. Psychologische Diagnostik* (Vol. 4; pp. 1-192). Göttingen: Hogrefe.

Fahrenberg, J. (1986). Psychophysiological individuality: A pattern analytic approach to personality research and psychosomatic medicine. *Advances in Behaviour Research and Therapy*, *8*, 43-100.

Fahrenberg, J. (1987a). Theory in psychophysiology: The multi-component analysis of psychophysiological reactivity. *Journal of Psychophysiology*, *1*, 9-11.

Fahrenberg, J. (1987b). Concepts of activation and arousal in the theory of emotionality (neuroticism). A multivariate conceptualization. In J. Strelau & H.J. Eysenck (Eds.), *Personality dimensions and arousal* (pp. 99-120). New York: Plenum.

Fahrenberg, J. (1988). Psychophysiological processes. In J.R. Nesselroade & R.B. Cattell (Eds.), *Handbook of multivariate experimental psychology* (2nd ed.; pp. 867-914). New York: Plenum.

Fahrenberg, J. & Foerster, F. (1982). Covariation and consistency of activation parameters. *Biological Psychology*, *15*, 151-169.

Fahrenberg, J. & Foerster, F. (1989). *Nicht-invasive Methodik für die kardiovasculäre Psychophysiologie*. Frankfurt: Lang.

Fahrenberg, J., Foerster, F., Schneider, H.-J., Müller, W., & Myrtek, M. (1986). Predictability of individual differences in activation processes in a field setting based on laboratory measures. *Psychophysiology*, *23*, 323-333.

Fahrenberg, J., Hampel, R., & Selg, H. (1984). *Das Freiburger Persönlichkeitsinventar FPI* (4th ed.). Göttingen: Hogrefe.

Fahrenberg, J., Schneider, H.J., & Safian, P. (1987). Psychophysiological assessment in a repeated-measurement design extending over a one-year interval: Trends and stability. *Biological Psychology*, *24*, 49-66.

Fahrenberg, J., Selg, H., & Hampel, R. (1978). *Das Freiburger Persönlichkeitsinventar FPI* (3rd ed.). Göttingen: Hogrefe.

Fahrenberg, J., Walschburger, P., Foerster, F., Myrtek, M., & Müller, W. (1979). *Psychophysiologische Aktivierungsforschung*. München: Minerva.

Faulstich, M.E., Williamson, D.A., McKenzie, S.J., Duchmann, E.G., Hutchinson, K.M., & Blonin, D.C. (1986). Temporal stability of psychophysiological responding: A comparative analysis of mental and physical stressors. *International Journal of Neuroscience*, *30*, 65-72.

Feuerstein, M., Labbe, E.E., & Kuczmierczyk, A.R. (Eds.) (1986). *Health psychology: A psychobiological perspective*. New York: Plenum.

Fibiger, W., Singer, G., & Miller, A.G. (1984). Relationship between catecholamines in urine and physical and mental effort. *International Journal of Psychophysiology*, *1*, 325-333.

Fiske, D.W. (1983). *Measuring to understand and understanding measuring*. Chicago: University of Chicago Press.

Fiske, D.W. & Maddi, S.R. (1961). *Functions of varied experience*. Homewood, IL: Dorsey.

Flessas, A.P. & Ryan, T.J. (1983). Atropine-induced cardioacceleration in patients on chronic propranolol therapy: Comparison with the positive chronotropic effect of isometric exercise. *American Heart Journal*, *105*, 230-234.

Foa, U.G. & Turner, J.L. (1970). Psychology in the year 2000: Going structural. *American Psychologist*, *25*, 244-247.

Fodor, J. (1968). *Psychological explanations*. New York: Random House.

Foerster, F. (1984). *Computerprogramme zur Biosignalanalyse*. Berlin: Springer.

Foerster, F. (1985). Psychophysiological response specificities: A replication over a 12-month period. *Biological Psychology*, *21*, 169-182.

Foerster, F., Schneider, H.J., & Walschburger, P. (1983a). The differentiation of individual-specific, stimulus-specific, and motivation-specific response patterns in activation processes: An inquiry investigating their stability and possible importance in psychophysiology. *Biological Psychology*, *17*, 1-26.

Foerster, F., Schneider, H.J., & Walschburger, P. (1983b). *Psychophysiologische Reaktionsmuster*. München: Minerva.

Foerster, F. & Stemmler, G. (1991). When can we use the F-approximation of the Box test? *Psychometrika*, *55*, 727-728.

Folkow, B. (1979). Relevance of cardiovascular reflexes. In R. Hainsworth, C. Kidd, & R.J. Linden (Eds.), *Cardiac receptors* (pp. 473-505). London: Cambridge University Press.

Folkow, B. & Rubinstein, E.H. (1965). Behavioural and autonomic patterns evoked by stimulation of the lateral hypothalamic area in the cat. *Acta Physiologica Scandinavica*, *65*, 292-299.

Fowles, D.C. (1980). The three arousal model: Implications of Gray's Two-Factor Learning Theory for heart rate, electrodermal activity, and psychopathy. *Psychophysiology*, *17*, 87-104.

Fowles, D.C., Fisher, A.E., & Tranel, D.T. (1982). The heart beats to reward: The effect of monetary incentive on heart rate. *Psychophysiology*, *19*, 506-513.

Frankenhaeuser, M. (1975). Sympathetic-adrenomedullary activity, behavior and the psychosocial environment. In P.H. Venables & M.J. Christie (Eds.), *Research in psychophysiology* (pp. 71-94). London: Wiley.

Frederiksen, N. (1972). Toward a taxonomy of situations. *American Psychologist, 27,* 114-123.

Frege, G. (1892). Über Sinn und Bedeutung. *Zeitschrift für Philosophie und philosophische Kritik, 100,* 25-56.

Fridlund, A.J., Schwartz, G.E., & Fowler, S.C. (1984). Pattern recognition of self-reported emotional state from multiple-site facial EMG activity during affective imagery. *Psychophysiology, 21,* 622-637.

Frodi, A. (1978). Experiential and physiological responses associated with anger and aggression in women and men. *Journal of Research in Personality, 12,* 335-349.

Funder, D.C. & Ozer, D.J. (1983). Behavior as a function of the situation. *Journal of Personality and Social Psychology, 44,* 107-112.

Funkenstein, D.H. (1956). Nor-epinephrine-like and epinephrine-like substances in relation to human behavior. *Journal of Nervous and Mental Disease, 124,* 58-68.

Funkenstein, D.H., King, S.H., & Drolette, M. (1954). The direction of anger during a laboratory stress-inducing situation. *Psychosomatic Medicine, 16,* 404-413.

Gale, A. (1983). Electroencephalographic studies of extraversion-introversion: A case study in the psychophysiology of individual differences. *Personality and Individual Differences, 4,* 371-380.

Gale, A. (1987). Arousal, control, energetics, and values. In J. Strelau & H.J. Eysenck (Eds.), *Personality dimensions and arousal* (pp. 287-316). New York: Plenum.

Gale, A. & Baker, S. (1981). In vivo or in vitro? Some effects of laboratory environments, with particular reference to the psychophysiology experiment. In M.J. Christie & P. Mellett (Eds.), *Foundations of psychosomatics* (pp. 363-384). Chichester: Wiley.

Gale, A. & Edwards, J.A. (1983). A short critique of the psychophysiology of individual differences. *Personality and Individual Differences, 4,* 429-435.

Gale, A. & Eysenck, M.W. (Eds.) (in press). *Handbook of the psychophysiology of individual differences.* Chichester: Wiley.

Gambaro, S. & Rabin, A.I. (1969). Diastolic blood pressure responses following direct and displaced aggression after anger arousal in high- and low-guilt subjects. *Journal of Personality and Social Psychology, 12,* 87-94.

Gentry, W.D. (1970). Effects of frustration, attack, and prior aggressive training on overt aggression and vascular processes. *Journal of Personality and Social Psychology, 16,* 718-725.

Gibson, J.J. (1960). The concept of the stimulus in psychology. *American Psychologist, 15,* 694-703.

Gilman, A.G., Goodman, L.S., & Gilman, A. (Eds.) (1980). *The pharmacological basis of therapeutics* (6th ed.). New York: Macmillan.

Glass, D.C., Krakoff, L.R., Contrada, R., Hilton, W.F., Kehoe, K., Mannucci, E.G., Collins, C., Snow, B., & Elting, E. (1980). Effect of harassment and competition upon cardiovascular and plasma catecholamine responses in type A and type B individuals. *Psychophysiology, 17,* 453-463.

Goldstein, D.S. & Keiser, H.R. (1984). Pressor and depressor responses after cholinergic blockade in humans. *American Heart Journal, 107,* 974-979.

Goldstein, I.B. & Shapiro, D. (1988). Cardiovascular responses to mental arithmetic and handgrip during different conditions of postural change. *Psychophysiology, 25,* 127-136.

Gollob, H.F. (1968a). Confounding of sources of variation in factor-analytic techniques. *Psychological Bulletin, 70*, 330-344.

Gollob, H.F. (1968b). Rejoinder to Tucker's "Comments on confounding of sources of variation in factor-analytic techniques". *Psychological Bulletin, 70*, 355-360.

Gray, J.A. (1982). *The neuropsychology of anxiety*. New York: Oxford University Press.

Green, P.E. & Carroll, J.D. (1976). *Mathematical tools for applied multivariate analysis*. New York: Academic Press.

Greenfield, N.S. & Sternbach, R.A. (Eds.) (1972). *Handbook of psychophysiology*. New York: Holt, Rinehart, & Winston.

Greenhouse, S.W. & Geisser, S. (1959). On methods in the analysis of profile data. *Psychometrika, 32*, 95-112.

Grice, G.R. (1966). Dependence of empirical laws upon the source of experimental variation. *Psychological Bulletin, 66*, 488-498.

Groeben, N. & Westmeyer, H. (1975). *Kriterien psychologischer Forschung*. München: Juventa.

Groff, M.G. (1983). A scheme for conducting two-sample profile analysis. *Multivariate Behavioral Research, 18*, 169-181.

Grossman, P., Karemaker, J., & Wieling, W. (1991). Prediction of tonic parasympathetic cardiac control using respiratory sinus arrhythmia: The need for respiratory control. *Psychophysiology, 28*, 201-216.

Grossman, P., Stemmler, G., & Meinhardt, E. (1990). Paced respiratory sinus arrhythmia as an index of cardiac parasympathetic tone during varying behavioral tasks. *Psychophysiology, 27*, 404-416.

Guazzi, M., Fiorentini, C., Polese, A., Magrini, F., & Olivari, M.T. (1975). Stress-induced and sympathetically-mediated electrocardiographic and circulatory variations in the primary hyperkinetic heart syndrome. *Cardiovascular Research, 9*, 342-354.

Guski, R. (1976). Sieben Konstruktionsmethoden für psychophysiologische Variablen. *Zeitschrift für experimentelle und angewandte Psychologie, 23*, 413-432.

Gutjahr, W. (1972). *Die Messung psychischer Eigenschaften*. Berlin: VEB Deutscher Verlag der Wissenschaften.

Harris, R.J. (1985). *A primer of multivariate stastistics* (2nd ed.). New York: Academic Press.

Haynes, S.N. (1978). *Principles of behavioral assessment*. New York: Gardner Press.

Heath, H.A. & Oken, D. (1965). The quantification of "response" to experimental stimuli. *Psychosomatic Medicine, 27*, 457-471.

Hebb, D.O. (1955). Drives and the c.n.s. (conceptual nervous system). *Psychological Review, 62*, 243-254.

Heinecker, R. (1959). Individuelle Unterschiede in der Reaktion von Kreislauf und Gasstoffwechsel auf dosierte Belastungen: Cold-Pressor-Test, Flackerlicht, Lärm, körperliche Arbeit. *Archiv für Kreislaufforschung, 30*, 1-103.

Hempel, C.G. & Oppenheim, P. (1948). Studies in the logic of explanation. *Philosophy of Science, 15*, 135-175.

Herrmann, T. (1972). *Lehrbuch der empirischen Persönlichkeitsforschung* (2nd ed.). Göttingen: Verlag für Psychologie.

Herrmann, T. (1982). *Sprechen und Situation*. Berlin: Springer.

Herxheimer, A. (1958). A comparison of some atropine-like drugs in man, with particular reference to their end-organ specificity. *British Journal of Pharmacolgy, 13*, 184-192.

Heslegrave, R.J. & Furedy, J.J. (1980). Carotid dP/dt as a psychophysiological index of sympathetic myocardial effects: some considerations. *Psychophysiology, 17*, 482-494.

Hess, W.R. (1928). Stammganglien - Reizversuche. *Berichte über die gesamte Physiologie und experimentelle Pharmakologie*, *42*, 554-555.

Hess, W.R. (1948). *Die funktionelle Organisation des vegetativen Nervensystems*. Basel: Schwabe.

Hilton, S.M. (1975). Ways of viewing the central nervous control of the circulation - old and new. *Brain Research*, *87*, 213-219.

Hilton, S.M. (1979). The defense reaction as a paradigm for cardiovascular control. In C. McC. Brooks, K. Koizumi, & A. Sato (Eds.), *Integrative functions of the autonomic nervous system* (pp. 443-449). Amsterdam: Elsevier.

Hilton, S.M. (1980). Inhibition of the baroreceptor reflex by the brainstem defense centre. In P. Sleight (Ed.), *Arterial baroreceptors and hypertension* (pp. 318-323). Oxford: Oxford University Press.

Hirschberg, N. (1978). A correct treatment of traits. In H. London (Ed.), *Personality: A new look at metatheories* (pp. 45-68). New York: Wiley-Halsted.

Hobbes, T. (1955). Third set of objections urged by a celebrated English philosopher. In E. Haldane & G.R.T. Ross (Eds., Trans.), *Philosophical works* (Vol. 2, pp. 60-78). New York: Dover. (Original work published 1641).

Hogan, R. & Nicholson, R.A. (1988). The meaning of personality test scores. *American Psychologist*, *43*, 621-626.

Horn, J.L. (1969). Factor analyses with variables of different metric. *Educational and Psychological Measurement*, *29*, 753-762.

Hugdahl, K. (1981). The Three-Systems-Model of fear and emotion - a critical examination. *Behavior Research and Therapy*, *19*, 75-85.

Hull, C.L. (1943). *Principles of behavior: An introduction to behavior theory*. New York: Appleton-Century.

Hume, D. (1886). *A treatise on human nature*. London: Longmans. (Original work published 1739).

Hurwitz, B.E., Ward, M.F., McCabe, P.M., & Schneiderman, N. (1988). Changes in systolic time intervals and T-wave amplitude during sympathetic and parasympathetic pharmacological blockade. Paper presented at the 28th Annual Meeting of the Society for Psychophysiological Research, San Francisco, October 1988.

Huynh, H. & Feldt, L.S. (1976). Estimation of the Box correction for degrees of freedom from sample data in the randomized block and split plot designs. *Journal of Educational Statistics*, *1*, 69-82.

Irrgang, E. (1981). Untersuchungen zum Temperaturproblem physiologischer optischer Meßaufnehmer aus Halbleitern am Beispiel eines Reflektionsfotoplethysmografen. *Biomedizinische Technik*, *26*, 106-109.

Irrgang, E. & Andresen, B. (1985). A method to separate phasic and tonic components of surface EMG in psychophysiological studies. In D. Papakostopoulos, S. Butler, & I. Martin (Eds.), *Clinical and experimental neuropsychophysiology* (pp. 541-557). London: Croom Helm.

Jänig, W. (1979). Reciprocal reaction patterns of sympathetic subsystems with respect to various afferent inputs. In C. McC. Brooks, K. Koizumi, & A. Sato (Eds.), *Integrative functions of the autonomic nervous system* (pp. 263-274). Amsterdam: Elsevier.

Jänig, W. (1987). Vegetatives Nervensystem. In R.F. Schmidt & G. Thews (Eds.), *Physiologie des Menschen* (23rd ed.; pp. 349-389). Berlin: Springer.

Jänig, W. (1988). The function of the autonomic system as interface between body and environment. Old and new concepts: W.B. Cannon and W.R. Hess revisited. In D. Hellhammer, I. Florin, & H. Weiner (Eds.), *Neurobiological approaches to human disease* (pp. 143-173). Toronto: Huber.

Janes, C.L. (1982). Electrodermal recovery and stimulus significance. *Psychophysiology, 19*, 129-135.

Jennings, J.R. (1986). Do cardiovascular changes indicate energetic support of information processing? In G.R.J. Hockey, A.K.W. Gaillard, & M.G.H. Coles (Eds.), *Energetics and human information processing* (pp. 199-216). Amsterdam: Martinus Nijhoff.

Jennings, J.R. & Coles, M.G.H. (Eds.) (in press). *Handbook of cognitive psychophysiology: Central and autonomic nervous system approaches*. Chichester: Wiley.

Jennings, J.R. & Follansbee, W.P. (1985). Task-induced ST segment depression, ectopic beats, and autonomic responses in coronary heart disease patients. *Psychosomatic Medicine, 47*, 415-430.

Jöreskog, K.G. (1981). Analysis of covariance structures. *Scandinavian Journal of Statistics, 8*, 65-92.

Johnson, R., Jr. (1986). A triarchic model of P 300 amplitude. *Psychophysiology, 23*, 367-384.

Jose, A.D. & Taylor, R.R. (1969). Autonomic blockade by propranolol and atropine to study intrinsic myocardial function in man. *Journal of Clinical Investigation, 48*, 2019-2031.

Kahle, L.R. (Ed.) (1979). *Methods for studying person-situation interactions*. San Francisco: Jossey-Bass.

Kahneman, D. (1973). *Attention and effort*. Englewood-Cliffs, NJ: Prentice-Hall.

Kallmann, W. & Feuerstein, M.J. (1977). Psychophysiological procedures. In A.R. Ciminero, K.S. Calhoun, & H.E. Adams (Eds.), *Handbook of behavioral assessment* (pp. 329-364). New York: Wiley.

Kant, I. (1966). *Kritik der reinen Vernunft*. Stuttgart: Reclam. (Original work published 1781).

Kantor, J.R. (1924). *Principles of psychology* (Vol. 1). Bloomington, IN: Principia Press.

Katona, P.G., McLean, M., Dighton, D.H., & Guz, A. (1982). Sympathetic and parasympathetic cardiac control in athletes and nonathletes at rest. *Journal of Applied Physiology, 52*, 1652-1657.

Kelly, G.A. (1955). *The psychology of personal constructs* (Vols. 1 and 2). New York: Norton.

Kenakin, T.P. (1984). The classification of drugs and drug receptors in isolated tissues. *Pharmacological Reviews, 36*, 165-222.

Kenrick, D.T. & Funder, D.C. (1988). Profiting from controversy: Lessons from the person-situation debate. *American Psychologist, 43*, 23-34.

Kline, N.S. (1961). On the relationship between neurophysiology, psychophysiology, psychopharmacology, and other disciplines. *Annals of the New York Academy of Sciences, 92*, 1004-1016.

Knoebel, S.B., McHenry, P.L., Phillips, J.F., & Widlansky, S. (1974). Atropine-induced cardioacceleration and myocardial blood flow in subjects with and without coronary artery disease. *American Journal of Cardiology, 33*, 327-332.

Koella, W.P. (1978). Die zentralen Wirkungen der Betablocker - anatomische, physiologische und pharmakologische Befunde. In P. Kielholz (Ed.), *Betablocker und Zentralnervensystem* (pp. 20-34). Bern: Huber.

Kozak, M.J. & Miller, G.A. (1982). Hypothetical constructs vs intervening variables: A reappraisal of three-system anxiety assessment. *Behavioral Assessment, 4*, 347-358.

Krantz, D.S. & Manuck, S.B. (1984). Acute psychophysiologic reactivity and risk of cardiovascular disease: A review and methodologic critique. *Psychological Bulletin, 96*, 435-464.

Krantz, D.S. & Ratliff-Crain, J. (1989). The social context of stress and behavioral medicine research. Instructions, experimenter effects, and social interactions. In N. Schneiderman, S.M. Weiss, & P.G. Kaufmann (Eds.), *Handbook of research methods in cardiovascular behavioral medicine* (pp. 383-392). New York: Plenum.

Krause, M.S. (1972). The implications of convergent and discriminant validity data for instrument validation. *Psychometrika, 37*, 179-186.

Lacey, B.C. & Lacey, J.I. (1974). Studies of heart rate and other bodily processes in sensorimotor behavior. In P.A. Obrist, A.H. Black, J. Brener, & L.V. DiCara (Eds.), *Cardiovascular psychophysiology* (pp. 538-564). Chicago: Aldine.

Lacey, J.I. (1950). Individual differences in somatic response pattern. *Journal of Comparative and Physiological Psychology, 43*, 338-350.

Lacey, J.I. (1956). The evaluation of autonomic responses: Toward a general solution. *Annals of the New York Academy of Sciences, 67*, 123-164.

Lacey, J.I. (1962). Psychophysiological approaches to the evaluation of psychotherapeutic process and outcome. In E.A. Rubinstein & M.B. Parloff (Eds.), *Research in psychotherapy* (pp. 161-208). Washington: American Psychological Association.

Lacey, J.I. (1967). Somatic response patterning and stress: Some revisions of activation theory. In M.H. Appley & R. Trumbull (Eds.), *Psychological stress* (pp. 14-37). New York: Appleton-Century-Crofts.

Lacey, J.I. & Lacey, B.C. (1958). Verification and extension of the principle of autonomic response-stereotypy. *American Journal of Psychology, 71*, 50-73.

Lader, M.H. (1970). The unit of quantification of the GSR. *Journal of Psychosomatic Research, 14*, 109-110.

Lader, M.H. (1975a). *The psychophysiology of mental illness*. London: Routledge and Kegan Paul.

Lader, M.H. (1975b). Psychophysiological parameters and methods. In L. Levi (Ed.), *Emotions - Their parameters and measurement* (pp. 341-367). New York: Raven.

Lader, M.H. & Wing, L. (1966). *Physiological measures, sedative drugs and morbid anxiety*. London: Oxford University Press.

Lambert, Z.V., Wildt, A.R., & Durand, R.M. (1988). Redundancy analysis: An alternative to canonical correlation and multivariate multiple regression in exploring interset associations. *Psychological Bulletin, 104*, 282-289.

Lang, P.J. (1968). Fear reduction and fear behavior: problems in treating a construct. In J.M. Shilen (Ed.), *Research in psychotherapy* (Vol. 3, pp. 90-102). Washington, DC: American Psychological Association.

Lang, P.J. (1971). The application of psychophysiological methods to the study of psychotherapy and behavior modification. In A.E. Bergin & S.L. Garfield (Eds.), *Handbook of psychotherapy and behavior change: An empirical analysis* (pp. 75-125). New York: Wiley.

Lang, P.J. (1978). Anxiety: Toward a psychophysiological definition. In H.S. Akiskal & W.L. Webb (Eds.), *Psychiatric diagnosis: Exploration of biological predictors* (pp. 265-289). New York: Spectrum Publications.

Lang, P.J. (1984). Cognition in emotion: concept and action. In C.E. Izard, J. Kagan, & R.B. Zajonc (Eds.), *Emotions, cognition, and behavior* (pp. 192-226). Cambridge: Cambridge University Press.

Langer, A.W., McCubbin, J.A., Stoney, C.M., Hutcheson, J.S., Charlton, J.D., & Obrist, P.A. (1985). Cardiopulmonary adjustments during exercise and an aversive reaction time task: Effects of beta-adrenoceptor blockade. *Psychophysiology*, *22*, 59-68.

Lazarus, R.S., Speisman, J.C., & Mordkoff, A.M. (1963). The relationship between autonomic indicators of psychological stress: Heart rate and skin conductance. *Psychosomatic Medicine*, *25*, 19-30.

LeDoux, J.E. (1987). Emotion. In V.B. Mountcastle, R. Plum, S.R. Geiger (Eds.), *Handbook of physiology, Sec. 1. The nervous system (Vol. 5). Higher functions of the brain, Part 1* (pp. 419-459). Bethesda, MD: American Physiological Society.

Levenson, R.W., Ekman, P., & Friesen, W.V. (1990). Voluntary facial action generates emotion-specific autonomic nervous system activity. *Psychophysiology*, *27*, 363-384.

Levey, A.B. & Martin, I. (1987). Theories in psychophysiology: an open forum. Introduction. *Journal of Psychophysiology*, *1*, 3-7.

Levey, A.B. & Martin, I. (1989). Psychophysiology, folk psychology and philosophy. *Journal of Psychophysiology*, *3*, 215-218.

Levine, M.A.H. & Leenen, F.H.H. (1989). Role of β_1-receptors and vagal tone in cardiac inotropic and chronotropic responses to a β_2-agonist in humans. *Circulation*, *79*, 107-115.

Levins, R. & Lewontin, R. (1985). *The dialectical biologist*. Cambridge, MA: Harvard University Press.

Levy, M.H. & Martin, P.J. (1979). Neural control of the heart. In R.M. Berne, N. Sperelakis, & S.R. Geiger (Eds.), *Handbook of physiology, Sec. 2. The cardiovascular system* (pp. 581-620). Bethesda, MD: American Physiological Society.

Levy, M.H. & Zieske, H. (1969). Autonomic control of cardiac pacemaker activity and atrioventricular transmission. *Journal of Applied Physiology*, *27*, 465-470.

Lewin, K.A. (1935). *A dynamic theory of personality*. New York: McGraw-Hill.

Lewin, K.A. (1936). *Principles of topological psychology*. New York: McGraw-Hill.

Lidberg, L. & Wallin, B.G. (1981). Sympathetic skin nerve discharges in relation to amplitude of skin resistance responses. *Psychophysiology*, *18*, 268-270.

Light, K.C. (1985). Cardiovascular and renal responses to competitive mental challenges. In J.F. Orlebeke, G. Mulder, & L.J.P. van Doornen (Eds.), *Psychophysiology of cardiovascular control* (pp. 683-701). New York: Plenum.

Lisander, B. (1970). Factors influencing the autonomic component of the defense reaction. *Acta Physiologica Scandinavica*, *351* (Suppl.), 5-42.

Lisander, B. (1979). Somato-autonomic reactions and their higher control. In C. McC. Brooks, K. Koizumi, & A. Sato (Eds.) *Integrative functions of the autonomic nervous system* (pp. 385-395). Amsterdam: Elsevier.

Lord, F.M. & Novick, M.R. (1968). *Statistical theories of mental test scores*. Reading, MA: Addison-Wesley.

Lovallo, W. & Zeiner, A.R. (1975). Some factors influencing the vasomotor response to cold pressor stimulation. *Psychophysiology*, *12*, 499-505.

Luczak, H., Phillipp, U., & Rohmert, W. (1980). Decomposition of heart-rate variability under the ergonomic aspects of stressor analysis. In R.I. Kitney & O. Rompelman (Eds.), *The study of heart rate variability* (pp. 123-177). Oxford: Oxford Medical Engineering Series.

Lykken, D.T. (1968). Neuropsychology and psychophysiology in personality research. In E.F. Borgatta & W.W. Lambert (Eds.), *Handbook of personality theory and research* (pp. 413-509). Chicago: Rand McNally.

Lykken, D.T. (1972). Range correction applied to heart rate and to GSR data. *Psychophysiology*, *9*, 373-379.

Lykken, D.T., Rose, R., Luther, B., & Maley, M. (1966). Correcting psychophysiological measures for individual differences in range. *Psychological Bulletin*, *66*, 481-484.

Lykken, D.T. & Venables, P.H. (1971). Direct measurement of SC: A proposal for standardization. *Psychophysiology*, *8*, 656-672.

MacCorquodale, K. & Meehl, P.E. (1948). On a distinction between hypothetical constructs and intervening variables. *Psychological Review*, *55*, 95-107.

Maciel, B.C., Gallo, L., Jr., Neto, J.A.M., & Martins, L.E.B. (1987). Autonomic nervous control of the heart rate during isometric exercise in normal man. *Pflügers Archiv*, *408*, 173-177.

MacNeilage, P.F. (1966). Changes in electroencephalogram and other physiological measures during serial mental performance. *Psychophysiology*, *2*, 344-353.

Magnusson, D. (1976). The person and the situation in an interactional model of behavior. *Scandinavian Journal of Psychology*, *17*, 253-271.

Magnusson, D. & Allen, V.L. (1983). An interactional perspective for human development. In D. Magnusson & V.L. Allen (Eds.), *Human development. An interactional perspective* (pp. 3-31). New York: Academic Press.

Magnusson, D. & Ekehammar, B. (1975). Perceptions of and reactions to stressful situations. *Journal of Personality and Social Psychology*, *31*, 1147-1154.

Magnusson, D. & Ekehammar, B. (1978). Similar situations - similar behaviors? *Journal of Research in Personality*, *12*, 41-48.

Malmo, R.B. (1959). Activation: A neurophysiological dimension. *Psychological Review*, *6*, 367-386.

Malmo, R.B. (1966). Cognitive factors in impairment: A neuropsychological study of divided set. *Journal of Experimental Psychology*, *71*, 184-189.

Malmo, R.B. & Bélanger, D. (1967). Related physiological and behavioral changes. What are their determinants? *Proceedings of the Association of Research in Nervous and Mental Disease*, *45*, 288-318.

Malmo, R.B. & Shagass, C. (1949). Physiologic study of symptom mechanisms in psychiatric patients under stress. *Psychosomatic Medicine*, *11*, 25-29.

Maltzman, I. (1979). Orienting reflexes and significance: A reply to O'Gorman. *Psychophysiology*, *16*, 274-282.

Mangan, G. (1982). *The biology of human personality*. Oxford: Pergamon.

Manuck, S.B. & Garland, F.N. (1980). Stability in individual differences in cardiovascular reactivity: A thirteen-month follow-up. *Physiology and Behavior*, *21*, 621-624.

Mardia, K.V., Kent, J.T., & Bibby, J.M. (1979). *Multivariate analysis*. London: Academic Press.

Marr, D. (1982). *Vision*. San Francisco: Freeman.

Martin, C.E., Shaver, J.A., Leon, D.F., Thompson, M.E., Reddy, P.S., & Leonard, J.J. (1974). Autonomic mechanisms in hemodynamic responses to isometric exercise. *Journal of Clinical Investigation*, *54*, 104-115.

Martin, I. (1973a). Somatic reactivity: methodology. In H.J. Eysenck (Ed.), *Handbook of abnormal psychology* (pp 309-332). Belfast: Pitman.

Martin, I. (1973b). Somatic reactivity: interpretation. In H.J. Eysenck (Ed.), *Handbook of abnormal psychology* (pp. 333-361). Belfast: Pitman.

Martin, I. & Venables, P. (1980). *Techniques in psychophysiology*. Chichester: Wiley.

Mason, J.W. (1971). A re-evaluation of the concept of "non-specificity" in stress theory. *Journal of Psychiatric Research*, *8*, 323-333.

Mason, J.W., Maker, J.T., Hartley, L.H., Mongey, E., Perlow, M.J., & Jones, L.G. (1976). Selectivity of cortico steroid and catecholamine response to various natural stimuli. In G. Serban (Ed.), *Psychopathology of human adaptation* (pp. 147-171). New York: Plenum.

Mayer, S.E. (1980). The neurohumoral transmission and the autonomic nervous system. In A.G. Gilman, L.S. Goodman, & A. Gilman (Eds.), *The pharmacological basis of therapeutics* (pp. 56-90). New York: Macmillan.

McAllister, R.G. (1979). Effect of adrenergic receptor blockade on the response to isometric handgrip: Studies in normal and hypertensive subjects. *Journal of Cardiovascular Pharmacology, 1*, 253-263.

McDevitt, D.G., Frisk-Holmberg, M., Hollifield, J.W., & Shand, D.G. (1976). Plasma binding and the affinity of propranolol for a beta receptor in man. *Clinical Pharmacology and Therapeutics, 20*, 152-157.

McFall, R.M. & McDonel, E.C. (1986). The continuing search for units of analysis in psychology: Beyond persons, situations, and their interactions. In R.O. Nelson & S.C. Hayes (Eds.), *Conceptual foundations of behavioral assessment* (pp. 201-241). New York: Guilford.

McGuigan, F.J. (1978). *Cognitive psychophysiology*. Englewood Cliffs, NJ: Prentice-Hall.

Messick, S. (1981). Constructs and their vicissitudes in educational and psychological measurement. *Psychological Bulletin, 89*, 575-588.

Metzinger, T. (1985). *Neuere Beiträge zur Diskussion des Leib-Seele-Problems*. Frankfurt: Lang.

Miller, G.A., Galanter, E., & Pribram, K.H. (1960). *Plans and the structure of behavior*. New York: Holt, Rinehart, & Winston.

Mills, P.J. & Dimsdale, J.E. (1988). The promise of receptor studies in psychophysiologic research. *Psychosomatic Medicine, 50*, 555-566.

Mischel, T. (1976). Psychological explanations and their vicissitudes. In W.J. Arnold (Ed.), *Nebraska Symposium on the conceptual foundations of theory and method in psychology* (Vol. 23; pp. 133-204). Lincoln, NA: University of Nebraska Press.

Mischel, W. (1968). *Personality and assessment*. New York: Wiley.

Mischel, W. (1973). Toward a cognitive social learning reconceptualization of personality. *Psychological Review, 80*, 252-283.

Mischel, W. (1976). *Introduction to personality* (2nd ed.). New York: Holt, Rinehart, & Winston.

Mischel, W. (1984). Convergences and challenges in the search for consistency. *American Psychologist, 39*, 351-364.

Morrison, D.F. (1976). *Multivariate statistical methods* (2nd ed.). New York: McGraw-Hill

Moruzzi, G. & Magoun, H.W. (1949). Brain stem reticular formation and activation of the EEG. *Electroencephalography and Clinical Neurophysiology, 1*, 455-473.

Mulder, G., Mulder, L.J.M., & Veldeman, J.B.P. (1985). Mental tasks as stressors. In A. Steptoe, H. Rüddel, & H. Neus (Eds.), *Clinical and methodological issues in cardiovascular psychophysiology* (pp. 30-44). Berlin: Springer.

Murray, H.A. (1938). *Explorations in personality*. New York: Oxford University Press.

Myrtek, M. (1984). *Constitutional psychophysiology*. New York: Academic Press.

Myrtek, M. (1985). Adaptation effects and the stability of physiological responses to repeated testing. In A. Steptoe, H. Rüddel, & H. Neus (Eds.), *Clinical and methodological issues in cardiovascular psychophysiology* (pp. 93-106). Berlin: Springer.

Myrtek, M. & Foerster, F. (1986). The law of initial value: A rare exception. *Biological Psychology*, *22*, 227-237.

Nagel, E. (1961). *The structure of science. Problems in the logic of scientific explanation*. New York: Harcourt, Brace & World.

Namboodiri, N.K., Carter, L.F., & Blalock, H.M. (1975). *Applied multivariate analysis and experimental designs*. New York: McGraw-Hill.

Neiss, R. (1988). Reconceptualizing arousal: Psychobiological states in motor performance. *Psychological Bulletin*, *103*, 345-366.

Neiss, R. (1990). Ending arousal's reign of error: A reply to Anderson. *Psychological Bulletin*, *107*, 101-105.

Nelson, G.I., Silke, B., Hussain, M., Verma, S.P., & Taylor, S.H. (1984). Rest and exercise hemodynamic effects of sequential alpha-1-adrenoceptor (trimazosin) and beta-adrenoceptor (propranolol) antagonism in essential hypertension. *American Heart Journal*, *108*, 124-131.

Netter, P. (1986). Einflußfaktoren auf die zentral-nervöse Wirkung von Beta-Rezeptorenblockern. In W. Janke & P. Netter (Eds.), *Angst und Psychopharmaka* (pp. 169-204). Stuttgart: Kohlhammer.

Neus, H. & von Eiff, A.W. (1985). Selected topics in the methodology of stress testing: Time course, gender and adaptation. In A. Steptoe, H. Rüddel, & H. Neus (Eds.), *Clinical and methodological issues in cardiovascular psychophysiology* (pp. 78-92). Berlin: Springer.

Ney, T. & Gale, A. (1988). A critique of laboratory studies of emotion with particular reference to psychophysiological aspects. In H.L. Wagner (Ed.), *Social psychophysiology and emotion: theory and clinical applications* (pp. 65-83). Chichester: Wiley.

Nunnally, J.C. (1962). The analysis of profile data. *Psychological Bulletin*, *59*, 311-319.

Nunnally, J.C. (1978). *Psychometric theory* (2nd ed.). New York: McGraw-Hill.

Nunnally, J.C. & Kotsch, W.E. (1983). A reciprocity principle that permits profile-factoring with very large numbers of people. *Educational and Psychological Measurement*, *43*, 693-703.

Obrist, P.A. (1976). The cardiovascular-behavioral interaction - As it appears today. *Psychophysiology*, *13*, 95-107.

Obrist, P.A. (1985). Beta-adrenergic hyperresponsivity to behavioral challenges: A possible hypertensive risk factor. In: J.F. Orlebeke, G. Mulder, & L.J.P. van Doornen (Eds.), *Psychophysiology of cardiovascular control* (pp. 667-682). New York: Plenum.

Obrist, P.A., Lawler, J.E., Howard, J.L., Smithson, K.W., Martin, P.L., & Manning, J. (1974). Sympathetic influences on cardiac rate and contractility during acute stress in humans. *Psychophysiology*, *11*, 405-427.

O'Connor, K.P. (1981). The intentional paradigm and cognitive psychophysiology. *Psychophysiology*, *18*, 121-128.

Öhman, A. (1979). The orienting response, attention, and learning: an information-processing perspective. In H.D. Kimmel, E.H. van Olst, & J.E. Orlebeke (Eds.), *The orienting reflex in humans* (pp. 443-472). Hillsdale, NJ: Erlbaum.

O'Gorman, J.G. (1979). The orienting reflex: novelty or significance detector? *Psychophysiology*, *16*, 253-262.

Oken, D. (1960). An experimental study of suppressed anger and blood pressure. *Archives of General Psychiatry*, *2*, 105-120.

Olweus, D. (1977). A critical analysis of the "modern" interactionist position. In D. Magnusson & N.S. Endler (Eds.), *Personality at the crossroads* (pp. 221-233). New York: Wiley.

Osgood, C.E. (1953). *Method and theory in experimental psychology*. New York: Oxford University Press.

Overall, J.E. & Klett, C.J. (1972). *Applied multivariate analysis*. New York: McGraw-Hill.

Ozer, D.J. (1986). *Consistency in personality*. Berlin: Springer.

Peart, S. (1985). Role of drugs modifying sympathetic nervous system activity in the treatment of hypertension. *Journal of Hypertension*, *3* (Suppl. 4), 51-55.

Pervin, L.A. (1978). Definitions, measurements, and classifications of stimuli, situations, and environments. *Human Ecology*, *6*, 71-105.

Peterson, D.R. (1968). *The clinical study of social behavior*. New York: Appleton-Century-Crofts.

Phillips, D.C. & Orton, R. (1983). The new causal principle of cognitive learning theory: Perspectives on Bandura's "Reciprocal Determinism". *Psychological Review*, *90*, 158-165.

Phillips, K. (1987a). Psychophysiology: a discipline in search of a paradigm? *Journal of Psychophysiology*, *1*, 101-104.

Phillips, K. (1987b). Behaviour, science, and a science of behaviour. A reply to Howard. *Journal of Psychophysiology*, *1*, 345-348.

Pinneo, L.R. (1961). The effects of induced muscle tension during tracking on level of activation and on performance. *Journal of Experimental Psychology*, *62*, 523-531.

Pollak, M.H. & Obrist, P.A. (1988). Effects of autonomic blockade on heart rate responses to reaction time and sustained handgrip tasks. *Psychophysiology*, *25*, 689-695.

Popper, K.R. (1959). *The logic of scientific discovery*. New York: Basic Books.

Popper, K.R. & Eccles, J.C. (1977). *The self and its brain - An argument for interactionism*. Heidelberg: Springer.

Porges, S.W., Ackles, P.A., & Truax, S.R. (1983). Psychophysiological measurement: Methodological constraints. In A. Gale & J.A. Edwards (Eds.), *Physiological correlates of human behaviour, Vol. 1. Basic Issues* (pp. 219-240). London: Academic Press.

Posner, M.I. & Rothbart, M.K. (1986). The concept of energy in psychological theory. In G.R.J. Hockey, A.W.K. Gaillard, & M.G.H. Coles (Eds.), *Energetics and human information processing* (pp. 23-40). Amsterdam: Martinus Nijhoff.

Powell, A. & Royce, J.R. (1981). An overview of a multifactor-system theory of personality and individual differences: I. The factor and system models and the hierarchical factor structure of individuality. *Journal of Personality and Social Psychology*, *41*, 818-829.

Pribram, K.H. & McGuinness, D. (1975). Arousal, activation and effort: Separate neural systems. In D.H. Ingvar & N.A. Lassen (Eds.), *Brain work* (pp. 428-451). Copenhagen: Munksgaard.

Prichard, B.N.C. (1984). Beta-adrenoceptor blocking agents in hypertension. In W. Kobinger & R.P. Ahlquist (Eds.), *Alpha and beta adrenoceptors and the cardiovascular system*. Princeton: Excerpta Medica.

Quenouille, M.H. (1952). *Associated measurements*. London: Butterworth.

Rachman, S. (1978). Human fears: A three systems analysis. *Scandinavian Journal of Behavior Therapy*, *7*, 237-245.

Raush, H.L. (1979). Epistemology, metaphysics, and person-situation methodology: conclusions. In L.R. Kahle (Ed.), *Methods for studying person-situation interactions* (pp. 93-106). San Francisco: Jossey-Bass.

Ray, R.L. & Kimmel, H.D. (1979). Utilization of psychophysiological indices in behavior assessment: Some methodological issues. *Journal of Behavioral Assessment*, *1*, 107-122.

Ray, W.J., Cole, H.W., & Raczynski, J.M. (1983). Psychophysiological assessment. In M. Hersen, A.E. Kazdin, & A.S. Bellack (Eds.), *The clinical psychology handbook* (pp. 427-453). New York: Pergamon.

Reis, D.J., Ruggiero, D.A., & Granata, A. (1986). Brainstem mechanisms governing the tonic and reflex control of the circulation. In T. Stober, K. Schimrigk, D. Ganten, & D.G. Sherman (Eds.), *Central nervous system control of the heart* (pp. 19-36). Boston: Martinus Nijhoff.

Roberts, R.J. & Weerts, T.C. (1982). Cardiovascular responding during anger and fear imagery. *Psychological Reports*, *50*, 219-230.

Robinson, B.F., Epstein, S.E., Beiser, G.D., & Braunwald, E. (1966). Control of heart rate by the autonomic nervous system. *Circulation Research*, *19*, 400-411.

Robinson, J.W., Whitsett, S.F., & Kaplan, B.J. (1987). The stability of physiological reactivity over multiple sessions. *Biological Psychology*, *24*, 129-139.

Rösler, F. (1983a). Endogenous ERPs and cognition: Probes, prospects, and pitfalls in matching pieces of the mind-body puzzle. In A.W.K. Gaillard & W. Ritter (Eds.), *Tutorials in ERP research: Endogenous components* (pp. 9-35). Amsterdam: North-Holland.

Rösler, F. (1983b). Physiologisch orientierte Forschungsstrategien in der Differentiellen und Diagnostischen Psychologie: I. Zur Konzeption des psychophysiologischen Untersuchungsansatzes. *Zeitschrift für Differentielle und Diagnostische Psychologie*, *4*, 283-299.

Rösler, F. (1984). Physiologisch orientierte Forschungsstrategien in der Differentiellen und Diagnostischen Psychologie: II. Zur Systematisierung psychophysiologischer Untersuchungen. *Zeitschrift für Differentielle und Diagnostische Psychologie*, *5*, 7-36.

Rogosa, D., Brandt, D., & Zimowski, M. (1982). A growth curve approach to the measurement of change. *Psychological Bulletin*, *92*, 726-748.

Rosenblueth, A. & Simeone, F.A. (1934). The interrelations of vagal and accelerator effects on the cardiac rate. *American Journal of Physiology*, *110*, 42-45.

Ross, J. (1963). The relation between test and person factors. *Psychological Review*, *70*, 432-443.

Rotter, J.B. (1975). Some problems and misconceptions related to the construct of internal versus external control of reinforcement. *Journal of Consulting and Clinical Psychology*, *43*, 56-67.

Rotter, J.B. (1981). The psychological situation in social-learning theory. In D. Magnusson (Ed.), *Toward a psychology of situations. An interactional perspective* (pp. 169-178). Hillsdale, NJ: Erlbaum.

Royce, J.R. (1976). Psychology is Multi-: Methodological, variate, epistemic, world view, systemic, paradigmatic, theoretic, and disciplinary. In W.J. Arnold (Ed.), *Nebraska Symposium on the conceptual foundations of theory and methods in psychology* (Vol. 23, pp. 1-63). Lincoln, NA: University of Nebraska Press.

Royce, J.R. & Buss, A.R. (1976). The role of general systems and information theory in multi-factor individuality theory. *Canadian Psychological Review*, *17*, 1-21.

Rüddel, H., Langewitz, W., Schächinger, H., Schmieder, R., & Schulte, W. (1988). Hemodynamic response patterns to mental stress: Diagnostic and therapeutic implications. *American Heart Journal*, *116*, 617-627.

SAS Institute Inc. (1988). *SAS/STAT. User's guide, release 6.03 edition*. Cary, NC: Author.

Schachter, J. (1957). Pain, fear, and anger in hypertensives and normotensives. *Psychosomatic Medicine, 19*, 17-29.

Schachter, S. (1975). Cognition and peripheralist-centralist controversies in motivation and emotion. In M.S. Gazzaniga & C. Blakemore (Eds.), *Handbook of psychobiology* (pp. 529-564). New York: Academic Press.

Schachter, S. & Singer, J.E. (1962). Cognitive, social, and physiological determinants of emotional state. *Psychological Review, 69*, 379-399.

Schäfer, H. (1989). *Der Einfluss spezifischer Rezeptorenblocker auf die Emotion Ärger* (Diplomarbeit in Psychologie). Unpublished manuscript, University of Freiburg.

Schandry, R. (1989). *Lehrbuch Psychophysiologie* (2nd ed.). München: Psychologie Verlags Union.

Schmid, H. (1990). *Musteranalyse kardiovaskulärer Aktivierungskomponenten: Modellierung und Validierung* (Diplomarbeit in Psychologie). Unpublished manuscript, University of Freiburg.

Schmidt, T.H. (1982). Die Situationshypertonie als Risikofaktor. In D. Vaitl (Ed.) *Essentielle Hypertonie* (pp. 77-111). Berlin: Springer.

Schmieder, R.E., Rüddel, H., Neus, H., Messerli, F.H., & von Eiff, A.W. (1987). Disparate hemodynamic responses to mental challenge after antihypertensive therapy with beta blockers and calcium entry blockers. *American Journal of Medicine, 82*, 11-16.

Schmitt, N. & Stults, D.M. (1986). Methodology review: Analysis of multitrait-multimethod matrices. *Applied Psychological Measurement, 10*, 1-22.

Schneiderman, N., Weiss, S.M., & Kaufmann, P.G. (Eds.) (1989). *Handbook of research methods in cardiovascular behavioral medicine*. New York: Plenum.

Schnore, M.M. (1959). Individual patterns of physiological activity as a function of task differences and degree of arousal. *Journal of Experimental Psychology, 58*, 117-128.

Schulte, W. & von Eiff, A.W. (1985). The importance of cardiovascular reactivities to different types of stress for the development of hypertension. In A. Steptoe, H. Rüddel, & H. Neus (Eds.), *Clinical and methodological issues in cardiovascular psychophysiology* (pp. 53-65). Berlin: Springer.

Schwartz, G.E., Weinberger, D.A., & Singer, S.A. (1981). Cardiovascular differentiation of happiness, sadness, anger, and fear following imagery and exercise. *Psychosomatic Medicine, 43*, 343-364.

Seiler, G., Mehmel, H.C., & Krayenbühl, H.P. (1974). Isometrische Belastung vor und nach autonom-venöser Blockade mit Propranolol und Atropin. *Schweizer Medizinische Wochenschrift, 104*, 1564-1566.

Seraganian, P., Hanley, J.A., Hollander, B.J., Roskies, E., Smilga, C., Martin, N.D., Collu, R., & Oseasohn, R. (1985). Exaggerated psychophysiological reactivity: Issues in quantification and reliability. *Journal of Psychosomatic Research, 29*, 393-405.

Sersen, E.A., Clausen, J., & Lidsky, A. (1978). Autonomic specificity and stereotypy revisited. *Psychophysiology, 15*, 60-67.

Shanks, R.G. (1984). The physiological role of alpha- and beta-adrenoceptors in the regional circulation. In W. Kubinger & R.P. Ahlquist (Eds.), *Alpha and beta adrenoceptors and the cardiovascular system* (pp. 109-123). Princeton: Excerpta Medica.

Shepherd, J.T. & Vanhoutte, P.M. (1979). *The human cardiovascular system*. New York: Raven.

Sheridan, D.J., Thomas, P., Culling, W., & Collins, P. (1986). Antianginal and haemodynamic effects of alpha1-adrenoceptor blockade. *Journal of Cardiovascular Pharmacology*, *8* (Suppl. 2), 144-150.

Shiffrin, R.M. & Schneider, W. (1977). Controlled and automatic human information: II. Perceptual learning, automatic attending, and a general theory. *Psychological Review*, *84*, 127-190.

Silke, B., Nelson, G.I., Almja, R.C., Okoli, R.C., & Taylor, S.H. (1983). Comparative haemodynamic dose-response effects of intravenous propranolol and pindolol in patients with coronary heart disease. *European Journal of Clinical Pharmacology*, *25*, 157-165.

Simons, R.F., Öhman, A., & Lang, P.J. (1979). Anticipation and response set: Cortical, cardiac, and electrodermal correlates. *Psychophysiology*, *16*, 222-233.

Skinner, B.F. (1953). *Science and human behavior*. New York: Macmillan.

Skinner, B.F. (1960). Pigeons in a pelican. *American Psychologist*, *15*, 28-37.

Skinner, B.F. (1974). *About behaviorism*. New York: Alfred A. Knopf.

Skinner, B.F. (1989). The origins of cognitive thought. *American Psychologist*, *44*, 13-18.

Skinner, H.A. (1978). Differentiating the contribution of elevation, scatter and shape in profile similarities. *Educational and Psychological Measurement*, *38*, 297-308.

Skinner, H.A. (1979). Dimensions and clusters: a hybrid approach to classification. *Applied Psychological Measurement*, *3*, 327-341.

Smith, L.D. (1986). *Behaviorism and logical positivism*. Stanford: Stanford University Press.

Snyder, M. (1983). The influence of individuals on situations: Implications for understanding the links between personality and social behavior. *Journal of Personality*, *51*, 497-516.

Sokolov, E.N. (1960). Neuronal models and the orienting reflex. In M.A.B. Brazier (Ed.), *The central nervous system and behavior* (pp. 187-276). New York: Josiah Macy, Jr. Foundation.

Sokolov, E.N. (1963). *Perception and the conditioned reflex*. Oxford: Pergamon.

Sokolov, E.N. (1966). Orienting reflex as information regulator. In A. Leontiev, A. Luria, & S. Smirnov (Eds.), *Psychological research in the USSR* (pp. 334-360). Moscow: Progress Publishers.

Somsen, R.J.M. (1985). Phasic heart rate and vagal reactivity: Methods and interpretations. In A. Steptoe, H. Rüddel, & H. Neus (Eds.), *Clinical and methodological issues in cardiovascular psychophysiology* (pp. 144-158). Berlin: Springer.

Somsen, R.J.M., van der Molen, M.W., Boomsma, D.I., & Orlebeke, J.F. (1985). Phasic cardiac responses in reaction time and mental arithmetic tasks: The dominant influence of mental task performance on heart rate in adolescents. In J.F. Orlebeke, G. Mulder, & L.J.P. van Doornen (Eds.), *Psychophysiology of cardiovascular control* (pp. 583-597). New York: Plenum.

Spyer, K.M. & Jordan, D. (1980). The baroreceptor input to vagal pre-ganglionic neurons: The neural pathway and physiological control. In P. Sleight (Ed.), *Arterial baroreceptors and hypertension* (pp. 238-243). Oxford: Oxford University Press.

Stegmüller, W. (1969). *Probleme und Resultate der Wissenschaftstheorie und Analytischen Philosophie, Bd. 1. Erklärung und Begründung*. Berlin: Springer.

Stelmack, R.M. (1981). The psychophysiology of extraversion and neuroticism. In H.J. Eysenck (Ed.), *A model for personality* (pp. 38-64). Berlin: Springer.

Stemmler, G. (1984). *Psychophysiologische Emotionsmuster*. Frankfurt: Lang.

Stemmler, G. (1987a). Implicit measurement models in methods for scoring physiological reactivity. *Journal of Psychophysiology*, *1*, 113-125.

Stemmler, G. (1987b). Standardization within subjects: A critique of Ben-Shakhar's conclusion. *Psychophysiology*, *24*, 243-246.

Stemmler, G. (1987c). Entspannungsübungen - Mythos und Realität. *Der Informierte Arzt - Gazette médicale*, *8*, 14-19.

Stemmler, G. (1988). Effects of profile elevation, scatter, and shape on discriminant analysis results. *Educational and Psychological Measurement*, *48*, 853-871.

Stemmler, G. (1989). The autonomic differentiation of emotions revisited: Convergent and discriminant validation. *Psychophysiology*, *26*, 617-632.

Stemmler, G. (in press). The vagueness of specificity: Models of physiological emotion specificity in emotion theories and their experimental discriminability. *Journal of Psychophysiology*.

Stemmler, G., Bruhn, M., & Koch, U. (1986). Eine psychophysiologische Validierungsstudie zum Gottschalk-Gleser-Verfahren: Einführung. In U. Koch & G. Schöfer (Eds.), *Sprachinhaltsanalyse in der psychosomatischen und psychiatrischen Forschung* (pp. 104-116). Weinheim: Beltz.

Stemmler, G. & Fahrenberg, J. (1989). Psychophysiological assessment: Conceptual, psychometric, and statistical issues. In G. Turpin (Ed.), *Handbook of clinical psychophysiology* (pp. 71-104). Chichester: Wiley.

Stemmler, G., Grossman, P., Schmid, H., & Foerster, F. (1991). A model of cardiovascular activation components for studies using autonomic receptor antagonists. *Psychophysiology*, *28*, 367-382.

Stemmler, G. & Meinhardt, E. (1990). Personality, situation and physiological arousability. *Personality and Individual Differences*, *11*, 293-308.

Stemmler, G. & Meinhardt, E. (1991). Personality, situation and physiological arousability: A reply to Zuckerman. *Personality and Individual Differences*, *12*, 507-509.

Stemmler, G. & Thom, E. (1979). Ein Programm für die interaktive Auswertung des Herzschlagabstands aus stark artefaktbehafteten EKG-Aufzeichnungen. *EDV in Medizin und Biologie*, *10*, 122-127.

Stemmler, G., Thom, E., & Koch, U. (1986). Zur Psychophysiologie von Gottschalk-Gleser-Sprachproben: Ein Beitrag zur Validierung des Gottschalk-Gleser-Verfahrens? In U. Koch & G. Schöfer (Eds.), *Sprachinhaltsanalyse in der psychosomatischen und psychiatrischen Forschung* (pp. 143-165). Weinheim: Beltz.

Stephenson, D. & Siddle, D. (1983). Theories of habituation. In D. Siddle (Ed.), *Orienting and habituation: Perspectives in human research* (pp. 183-236). Chichester: Wiley.

Steptoe, A. (1985). The theoretical bases for task selection in cardiovascular psychophysiology. In A. Steptoe, H. Rüddel, & H. Neus (Eds.), *Clinical and methodological issues in cardiovascular psychophysiology* (pp. 6-15). Berlin: Springer.

Stern, R.M., Ray, W.J., & Davis, C.M. (1980). *Psychophysiological recording*. New York: Oxford University Press.

Stiles, G.L., Caron, M.C., & Lefkowitz, R.J. (1984). ß-Adrenergic receptors: Biochemical mechanisms, physiological regulation. *Physiological Reviews*, *64*, 661-743.

Strasburger, H. & Klenk, D. (1983). Opto-electronic belts for recording respiration in psychophysiological experimentation and therapy. *Psychophysiology*, *20*, 230-238.

Stratton, J.R., Pfeifer, M.A., & Halter, J.B. (1987). The hemodynamic effects of sympathetic stimulation combined with parasympathetic blockade in man. *Circulation, 75*, 922-929.

Strelau, J. & Eysenck, H.J. (Eds.) (1987). *Personality dimensions and arousal.* New York: Plenum.

Strosahl, K.D. & Linehan, M.M. (1986). Basic issues in behavioral assessment. In A.R. Ciminero, K.S. Calhoun, & H.E. Adams (Eds.), *Handbook of behavioral assessment* (2nd ed.; pp. 12-46). New York: Wiley.

Strübe, M.J. (1989). Assessing subjects' construal of the laboratory situation. In N. Schneiderman, S.M. Weiss, & P.G. Kaufmann (Eds.), *Handbook of research methods in cardiovascular behavioral medicine* (pp. 527-542). New York. Plenum.

Suppe, F. (1977). The search for philosophic understanding of scientific theories. In F. Suppe (Ed.), *The structure of scientific theories* (2nd ed., pp. 3-232). Urbana: University of Illinois Press.

Taylor, S.H. (1982). Alpha-adrenoceptor antagonists in hypertension. In A. Amery (Ed.), *Hypertensive cardiovascular disease: Pathophysiology and treatment* (pp. 755-782). The Hague: Martinus Nijhoff.

Taylor, S.P. & Epstein, S. (1967). The measurement of autonomic arousal. *Psychosomatic Medicine, 29*, 514-525.

Timm, N.H. (1975). *Multivariate Analysis*. Monterey, CA: Brooks/Cole.

Tolman, E.C. (1932). *Purposive behavior in animals and men*. New York: Century.

Tucker, L.R. (1968). Comments on "Confounding of sources of variation in factor-analytic techniques". *Psychological Bulletin, 70*, 345-354.

Turner, P. (1978). Die zentralen Wirkungen der Betablocker - Klinische und experimentelle Untersuchungen beim Menschen. In P. Kielholz (Ed.), *Betablocker und Zentralnervensystem* (pp. 35-44). Bern: Huber.

Turpin, G. (1985). Quantification, analysis and interpretation of phasic cardiac responses. In D. Papakostopoulos, S. Butler, & I. Martin (Eds.), *Clinical and experimental neuropsychophysiology* (pp. 500-530). London: Croom Helm.

Turpin, G. (1986). Effects of stimulus intensity on autonomic responding: The problem of differentiating orienting and defense reflexes. *Psychophysiology, 23*, 1-14.

Turpin, G. & Siddle, D.A.T. (1978). Cardiac and forearm plethysmographic responses to high intensity auditory stimulation. *Biological Psychology, 6*, 267-281.

Turpin, G. & Siddle, D.A.T. (1979). Effects of stimulus intensity on electrodermal activity. *Psychophysiology, 16*, 582-591.

Turpin, G. & Siddle, D.A.T. (1983). Effects of stimulus intensity on cardiovascular activity. *Psychophysiology, 20*, 611-624.

Tyrer, P.J. (1980). Use of beta-blocking drugs in psychiatry and neurology. *Drugs, 20*, 300-308.

Ulrych, M. (1969). Changes in general haemodynamics during stressful mental arithmetic and non-stress quiet conversation and modification of the latter by beta-adrenergic blockade. *Clinical Science, 36*, 453-461.

Urbaszek, W. & Modersohn, D. (1983). *Funktionsdiagnostik des Herzens*. Stuttgart: Enke.

Ursin, H. (1978). Activation, coping, and psychosomatics. In H. Ursin, E. Baade, & S. Levine (Eds.), *Psychobiology of stress* (pp. 201-228). New York: Academic Press.

Van den Wollenberg, A.L. (1977). Redundancy analysis - An alternative to canonical correlation analysis. *Psychometrika, 42*, 207-219.

Vasey, M.W. & Thayer, J.F. (1987). The continuing problem of false positives in repeated measures ANOVA in psychophysiology: A multivariate solution. *Psychophysiology, 24*, 479-486.

Velden, M. (1978). Some necessary revisions of the neuronal model concept of the orienting response. *Psychophysiology, 15*, 181-185.

Venables, P.H. (1984). Arousal: An examination of its status as a concept. In M.G.H. Coles, J.R. Jennings, & J.R. Stern (Eds.), *Psychophysiological perspectives* (pp. 134-142). New York: Van Norstrand.

von Eiff, A.W., Czernik, A., & Zanders, H. (1969). Zur medikamentösen Beeinflussung der Sympathikus-Hyperaktivität. Parasympathomimetikum und Beta-Rezeptorenblocker im kurzdauernden pharmakologischen Experiment am Menschen. *Klinische Wochenschrift, 47*, 701-708.

Wagner, H. (1989). The peripheral physiological differentiation of emotions. In H. Wagner & A. Manstead (Eds.), *Handbook of social psychophysiology* (pp. 73-98). Chichester: Wiley.

Wagner, H. & Manstead, A. (Eds.) (1989). *Handbook of social psychophysiology*. Chichester: Wiley.

Wakefield, J.C. (1989). Levels of explanation in personality theory. In D.M. Buss & N. Cantor (Eds.), *Personality Psychology* (pp. 333-346). New York: Springer.

Wakenhut, R. (1978). *Über die Einarbeitung von Situationen in psychologische Messungen*. Frankfurt: Lang.

Wallin, G.B. (1981). Sympathetic nerve activity underlying electrodermal and cardiovascular reactions in man. *Psychophysiology, 18*, 470-476.

Wallin, G.B., Sundlöf, G., & Lindblad, L.E. (1980). Baroreflex mechanisms controlling sympathetic outflow to the muscles in man. In P. Sleight (Ed.), *Arterial baroreceptors and hypertension*. (pp. 101-108). Oxford: Oxford University Press.

Walsh, W.B. & Betz, N.E. (1985). *Tests and assessment*. Englewood Cliffs, NJ: Prentice-Hall.

Ward, M.M., Mefford, I.N., Parker, S.D., Chesney, M.A., Taylor, C.B., Keegan, D.L., & Barchas, J.D. (1983). Epinephrine and norepinephrine responses in continuously collected human plasma to a series of stressors. *Psychosomatic Medicine, 45*, 471-486.

Watson, J.B. (1913). Psychology as the behaviorist views it. *Psychological Review, 20*, 158-177.

Wechsler, D. (1964). *Die Messung der Intelligenz Erwachsener* (3rd ed.; Trans. A. Hardesty & H. Lauber). Bern: Huber.

Weiner, H. (1989). The dynamics of the organism: Implications of recent biological thought for psychosomatic theory and research. *Psychosomatic Medicine, 51*, 608-635.

Weiss, T., Del Bo, A., Reichek, N., & Engelman, K. (1980). Pulse transit time in the analysis of autonomic nervous system effects on the cardiovascular system. *Psychophysiology, 17*, 202-207.

Wenger, M.A. (1966). Studies of autonomic balance: a summary. *Psychophysiology 2*, 173-186.

Wenger, M.A. & Cullen, T.D. (1972). Studies of autonomic balance in children and adults. In N.S. Greenfield & R.A. Sternbach (Eds.), *Handbook of psychophysiology* (pp. 535-576). New York: Holt, Rinehart, & Winston.

Widaman, K.F. (1985). Hierarchically nested covariance structure models for multitrait-multimethod data. *Applied Psychological Measurement, 9*, 1-26.

Wilder, J. (1967). *Stimulus and response: The Law of Initial Value*. Bristol: Wright.

Williamson, D.A., Waters, W.F., & Hawkins, M.F. (1986). Physiologic variables. In R.O. Nelson & S.C. Hayes (Eds.), *Conceptual foundations of behavioral assessment* (pp. 297-327). New York: Guilford.

Winer, B.J. (1971). *Statistical principles in experimental design* (2nd ed.). New York: McGraw-Hill.

Wittmann, W.W. (1988). Multivariate reliability theory: Principles of symmetry and successful validation strategies. In J.R. Nesselroade & R.B. Cattell (Eds.), *Handbook of multivariate experimental psychology* (2nd ed.; pp. 505-560). New York: Plenum.

Witzleb, E. (1987). Funktionen des Gefäßsystems. In R.F. Schmidt & G. Thews (Eds.), *Physiologie des Menschen* (23rd ed.; pp. 505-572). Berlin: Springer.

Wolf, S. (1986). Circulatory behavior: Historical perspective and projections for the future. *The Behavioral and Brain Sciences*, *9*, 304-305.

Yerkes, R.M. & Dodson, J.D. (1908). The relation of strength of stimulus to rapidity of habit formation. *Journal of Comparative Neurology and Psychology*, *18*, 459-482.

Zuckerman, M. (1983). A summing up with special sensitivity to the signals of reward in future research. In M. Zuckerman (Ed.), *Biological bases of sensation seeking, impulsivity, and anxiety* (pp. 249-260). Hillsdale, NJ: Erlbaum.

Zuckerman, M. (1987). A critical look at three arousal constructs in personality theories: Optimal levels of arousal, strength of the nervous system, and sensitivity to signals of reward and punishment. In J. Strelau & H.J. Eysenck (Eds.), *Personality dimensions and arousal* (pp. 217-231). New York: Plenum.

Zuckerman, M. & Como, P. (1983). Sensation seeking and arousal systems. *Personality and Individual Differences*, *4*, 381-386.

Zuroff, D.C. (1986). Was Gordon Allport a trait theorist? *Journal of Personality and Social Psychology*, *51*, 993-1000.

Subject Index